# Arnisdale and Loch Hourn

## - the clachans, people, memories and the future

### Peter R. English

*Peter R. English*
*Glenelg*
*December 10, 2000.*

*Dedicated to the lives and spirit of the people, past and present, of the Arnisdale and Loch Hourn Community.*

*"Fond memory brings the light of other days" (Thomas Moore)*

*"Memory is a painter" (Grandma Moses)*

Published in 2000

by the Arnisdale and Loch Hourn Community Association

© Peter R. English

ISBN 0 9539696 0 6

Printed and bound by

Polestar Scientifica Aberdeen Ltd.

# Acknowledgements

Some four years ago, the idea of this book was conceived and an appeal was made to Arnisdale and Loch Hourn friends at home and away to help by "jotting down personal memories and stories heard from the old folk, and looking out old photographs of people and places". Every one of the many friends contacted have responded magnificently, with the result that the original concept of 'a little book' has grown substantially!

The considerable number of Arnisdale people who provided memories, writings, articles, photographs, and also generous hospitality, are too numerous to mention, Their identities will be clear from their contributions to the many chapters. A great deal of typing and computer scanning was involved in the production of the book and the author is particularly indebted to Mrs Isobel James for her dedicated and meticulous contributions. Thanks are also due to Blair Anderson, Martin Guppy, Ruurd and Mieke Groot, Donald Fisher, Victor Corbett, Murray Webster, Joey Parker, Julian and Stuart Richmond-Watson who provided valued help in a variety of ways. The author is most grateful to colleagues in the University of Aberdeen for their general support of this initiative.

The author gratefully acknowledges the contributions of Hugh Barron. M.Univ. (Abdn), the recently retired Secretary of the Gaelic Society of Inverness, who took time to read the entire draft. In addition to meticulous checking of Gaelic place names, Hugh also contributed useful snippets from his vast memory store of relevant history.

Since this venture was speculative, involving high printing costs per copy and uncertainty regarding sales, sponsors had to be sought to ensure that the Printers could be paid. The author and the local Community Association are very indebted to the following for providing financial support in the form of sponsorship or loans: The Highland Fund Ltd, Skye and Lochalsh Enterprise, The Russell Trust, The Gaelic Society of Inverness and several private individuals who wish to remain anonymous. The staff of the Aberdeen University Library (George Washington Wilson Collection) and the Royal Commission on the Ancient and Historical Monuments of Scotland (RCAHMS) were also very helpful.

My wife Anne, through her continuous positive support in very many ways and by her extreme patience and good humour in the face of much provocation, helped greatly to lighten the load.

Finally, I must thank all those whose assistance I have inadvertently omitted to mention and apologise to all those to whom full justice has not been done in the text of this book. Collectively, all those who assisted contributed immensely to the production of this book. To all of them must go any credit for any praiseworthy parts of the production while the author is due all the brickbats for its many faults.

Peter R English
Arnisdale, 13 Fintray Road, Aberdeen, AB15 8HL
November 2000

Iomairt An Eilein
Sgitheanaich & Loch Aillse
**Skye & Lochalsh**
ENTERPRISE

# Foreword

It is a great pleasure to welcome and commend to the public this book by Professor Peter English.

In this vivid and well balanced account we derive a measure of the close bonding the author has with this delectable west Inverness-shire district and its people, to many of whom we are introduced as we read. This is indeed a splendid and sympathetic portrayal of the locality in which he passed, soon after the Second World War, a memorable part of his boyhood and made many lasting friendships. At the time, the old crofting system was still intact, albeit in its twilight, while Gaelic was still the working language of the day. In the interim period, the old ways have changed but the memories of the folk are still vibrant and Peter English has recorded and moulded these into this very interesting book.

The work records the history of now uninhabited places on Loch Hourn, as well as the memories of a fine people, who had a simple lifestyle and made the most of nature's bounties in a very balanced, sustainable way, while deriving joy and satisfaction from their way of living together and caring for each other and nature.

While making a major contribution to preserving the history, folklore and culture of the people, the author emphasises the potential for exploiting these valuable assets, along with the scenic splendour and rich flora and fauna of the district, as a basis for regenerating and invorating these communities, particularly in tourist orientated activities.

The author has fanned the embers of fading memories and recorded much of the spirit and culture of the Arnisdale and Loch Hourn people and their ways of living and working together, for the interest of others.

This labour of love, so assiduously compiled from documents and folk memory, will greatly benefit present and future generations as, with the passing of time and the many changes which have taken place in the last half century, a way of life which was common throughout the Highlands is now almost forgotten.

Professor English is to be congratulated on preparing this very readable social history of an honourable, interesting, industrious and mutually caring people.

Hugh Barron
Inverness

**Previous literary works by the Author**

Glen Urquhart: its places, people, neighbours and its shinty in the last 100 years and more. pp255. 1985.

Founder and first editor of 'The Shinty Yearbook'. Editions 1 to 5 (1971 - 1976).

Technical Books. Various.

**Reading Guide**

This book has a somewhat unconventional layout and some guidance may be helpful to the reader.

Photographs of people and places relevant to a section are grouped together at the end of each chapter. A colour section providing an impression of the unique landscape and seascapes of the Arnisdale and Loch Hourn areas is to be found at the end of the book. These placements of photographs have been in the interest of achieving economies in the production of the book and will undoubtedly inconvenience readers relative to having photographs interspersed appropriately through the text. Perhaps most readers will find it useful to scan the colour section first of all to obtain a general impression of the landscape and then, before reading a chapter, refer to the section of black and white photographs at the end of each. The author apologies for the poor quality of many of the black and white photographs. This is due either to the fact that many were already old and faded or because they were converted from coloured versions. The justification for including poor quality photographs is as a 'conservation measure' since so many interesting photographs, which depict life in the past, are lost forever. Now, at least, many of the Arnisdale and Loch Hourn pictures are preserved between these covers - warts and all! It is hoped that the small size and variable quality of photographs will not cause undue frustration to readers.

The author's aim in compiling this book was to provide a basic foundation on the Arnisdale and Loch Hourn areas, of their people and their ways of living and working together through the ages. In the future, others with greater literary ability and artistic gifts will have the opportunity to build on this foundation.

# ARNISDALE AND LOCH HOURN
## - the clachans, people, memories and the future.
### Contents

| | | |
|---|---|---|
| Preface | The village of Arnisdale on Loch Hourn | 1 |
| Chapter 1. | That first long summer holiday | 5 |
| Chapter 2. | Schooldays in Arnisdale | 24 |
| Chapter 3. | Arnisdale revisited | 37 |
| Chapter 4. | The Glenelg era for Roddy Mor and Lizzie | 51 |
| Chapter 5. | The MacLeod family and their arrival in Arnisdale | 69 |
| Chapter 6. | Ian MacKenzie and the Arnisdale Estate | 77 |
| Chapter 7. | The Camusban Crofting Township and Charlie MacTavish | 96 |
| Chapter 8. | The Corran Crofting Township and Willie MacKenzie | 106 |
| Chapter 9. | Schooldays as recalled by Morag, Flora and Sheena | 119 |
| Chapter 10. | The memories of Nellie Leitch and her history searches | 131 |
| Chapter 11. | War Time and the Welcomes Home | 144 |
| Chapter 12. | Some recollections and experiences of visitors to Arnisdale over the years | 159 |
| Chapter 13. | The MacDonald Family – memories of Jessie, Mary and Johan | 171 |
| Chapter 14. | Chrissie MacCuaig and the Corran of her youth | 187 |
| Chapter 15. | Donald MacCuaig, Glasgow. Arnisdale holidays and ceilidh stories | 194 |
| Chapter 16. | The Murchison family – their achievements and memories | 209 |
| Chapter 17. | Childhood holidays in Corran – Mary Murchison | 227 |
| Chapter 18. | The Fletcher Family – their links and their contributions | 235 |
| Chapter 19. | Mabel's special memories | 256 |
| Chapter 20. | Sandaig and its people | 262 |
| Chapter 21. | The Mialairidh Forest | 280 |
| Chapter 22. | Rarsaidh and its mysteries | 287 |
| Chapter 23. | Caolasmor and the Paterson Family | 291 |
| Chapter 24. | Kinloch Hourn, Torr a'choit and Glen Quoich – memories of Peter and Roddy MacRae | 296 |
| Chapter 25. | Runival and Skiary – The MacMillans and their visitors | 316 |
| Chapter 26. | Barrisdale and its people | 328 |
| Chapter 27. | Lea and Maggie's memories | 338 |
| Chapter 28. | Crowlick, Willie Campbell, the Stoddarts and MacKays | 353 |
| Chapter 29. | Archie, his unique video record and his stories | 359 |
| Chapter 30. | The MacLeans – the Arnisdale Merchants. Peggy Ann and Mary | 375 |
| Chapter 31. | Suil Air Ais: Looking back – An Ulsterman's reflections | 385 |
| Chapter 32. | Duncan MacTavish's memories of the 1880s and 1890s | 396 |
| Chapter 33. | The herring fishing and the 'Sgadan Beag Loch Hourn' | 408 |
| Chapter 34. | Sightings of 'sea monsters' of uncertain origin in Loch Hourn | 419 |
| Chapter 35. | Knoydart – a brief potted history | 431 |
| Chapter 36. | The future of the Arnisdale and Loch Hourn Community - hopes and possibilities | 441 |
| Colour Section | | 452 |

# Preface

## The Village of Arnisdale on Loch Hourn

As the long and glorious summer holidays approached in 1946 there was the usual wonderful excitement for a nine year old to escape from the rigours of school to the freedom, fun and adventure which characterised the holidays in Glenurquhart. Yet this summer held even more exciting prospects for a vigorous, happy and healthy boy - that of embarking on his very first holiday along with an older sister. The destination was Arnisdale on Loch Hourn where my Aunt Lizzie had gone from Glenurquhart as a teacher in 1917. Fate decreed that she would spend the rest of her life there as, when Roddy 'Mòr' MacLeod, a son of the home farm, survived his service in the Lovat Scouts throughout the Great War and got home to Arnisdale, a romance blossomed, Roddy and Lizzie were married and Roddy later took over the tenancy of the farm from his father. To travel from Glenurquhart to Arnisdale in those days was a never to be forgotten experience. To put matters into perspective, a hurl for a mere two miles down the Glenurquhart road on the back of the roadman's lorry to a smallholder's field for the annual Sunday School Picnic for fifty cheering, excited children was a thrilling experience. To get a twenty mile trip on the Glen bus into the great city of Inverness, perhaps once a year, was the ultimate in anticipation and excitement. But now the thrill of my young life was in store - the bus to Inverness, the great train journey from Inverness to Kyle of Lochalsh with so many stops at those great names such as Lochluichart, Achnasheen, Achnashellach and Stromeferry, the mail boat from Kyle to Glenelg and Uncle Roddy's car from Glenelg to Arnisdale. I can relive every minute of the adventure and still savour the hissing and puffing of the great train, the nostalgic smell of the soot and combustion of coal in the great steam engines in the stations, the aroma in the newly cleaned and polished carriage compartments, the tidiness and floral beauty of the station gardens en route, the wonderful scenery of mountain, water, moor and scattered dwellings - and the anticipation of all that lay ahead.

I well remember as we boarded Calum Garde's mailboat in Kyle for the journey via the Narrows of Kylerhea to Glenelg, meeting up with two girls from Arnisdale whom my sister Betty recognised from a previous holiday. They were Nellie and Flora MacKenzie from Arnisdale. They had come to Kyle for a rare day out - to do some essential shopping for the family and, as they put it - 'to buy a little present for our little brother, Iain' whose tenth birthday was fast approaching. That was the first I had heard of the existence of Iain MacKenzie but I was to get to know him very well in later ploys and adventures together - which still continue!

As the high, slippery, seaweed infested vertical ladder was negotiated with trepidation at low tide at the Glenelg pier, among the usual crowd congregated at the pier to collect goods and welcome friends were Uncle Roddy and Aunt Lizzie - and soon we were on the circuitous humpback of a gravel road to our final destination. As we progressed on our journey, while the great feeling of excitement and anticipation continued, perhaps I was now becoming a little impatient to see the 'promised land'. From time to time, I would quietly ask my sister a perennial question of children on any unknown journey - 'have we far to go?' As the old Austin Seven chugged its way up yet another of these forty five degree hills on the Arnisdale road - to bring into view one more majestic peak (Druim Fada) in the far distance - I was told rather mischievously (as it turned out) by Betty, that Arnisdale lay just beyond the said distant peak. My heart sank momentarily until that particular incline of the road had been negotiated and, as we levelled out and began to descend down the other side - there it lay - with the village of Camusban hugging the crescent shaped bay, with the Lodge and the home farm beyond. We had arrived at the end of a great adventure - but another was just about to begin.

The village has changed, the old folk have gone, the vibrant crofting system of the time has all but disappeared, the Loch Hourn herring fishing is no more - but the memories are still vibrant. For me,

Arnisdale was a wonderful community and I was fortunate enough to experience life in the village at the crucial stage of early transition from the tried and tested ways of history to the modern era.

This book sets out to provide an impression of Arnisdale as it was, its people, and its everyday life. It is based partly on my own memories and impressions but mainly on additional information gleaned from many friends, some still in the old family homes, and other Arnisdale exiles now resident in other parts - but with a large part of their soul still very much resting in the homes and community which were very dear to them in their earlier years.

**Top Left.** The route from Kyle to Glenelg to Arnisdale.   **Right.**   Calum Garde and Johnny MacLean at the controls of Calum's boat the 'Grace' which carried the mails and passengers on the Glenelg to Kyle route for many years.
**Middle Left.**   The high slippery, seaweed infested vertical ladder at Glenelg pier which had to be negotiated from Calum Garde's boat at low tide.   **Right.**   The busy Glenelg pier with the late afternoon arrival of passengers and the mails from Kyle.
**Bottom Left.**   Flora and Nellie MacKenzie who had been to Kyle for the day to do some special shopping.
**Right.**   The recipient of part of his sisters' shopping – young Iain MacKenzie.

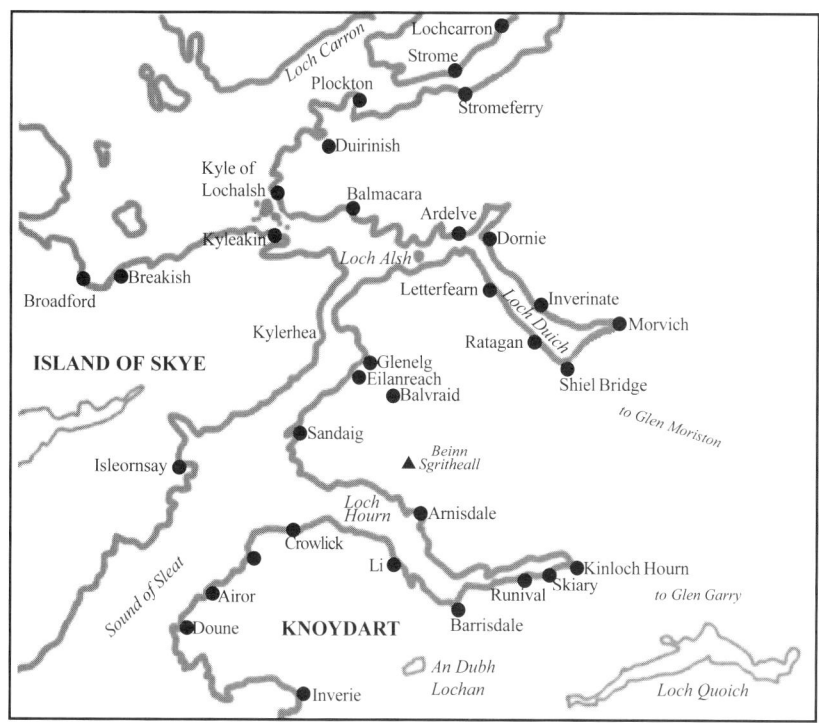

**Top Left.** Part of the circuitous humpback of the gravel road from Glenelg to Arnisdale. **Right.** As yet another of those majestic peaks came into view on the Arnisdale road, I would ask 'Have we got far to go?'

**Middle Left.** As we reached another of these summits on the Arnisdale road – there it lay - with the village of Camus Ban hugging the crescent shaped bay with the Lodge, the farm and Corran beyond. **Right.** The author with Uncle Roddy - 'Roddy Mor' and the fine old collie Whisky after a sheep gathering.

**Bottom Left.** The author with Aunt Lizzie and older sister Betty. Towards the end of the long summer holiday came the totally unexpected question from Aunt Lizzie: 'Would you like to stay with us and go to school here?'
**Right.** In the interim, the vibrant crofting system of the time has all but disappeared, the old folk have gone but the memories are still vibrant.

# Chapter 1

**That first long summer holiday**

Although I remember clearly the events of the day following my arrival in Arnisdale, my memories of that first evening are more hazy. Without doubt, the first introduction would have been a sumptuous tea of sandwiches and home baking, after which it would have been a case of being outside exploring and absorbing the new atmosphere - the village of Camusban to the right of the farmhouse and in full view - with the little pier in between - and the lodge tucked in behind the trees. Then the magnificent Beinn Sgritheall and the nearer Beinn na h-eaglaise towering above with their very steep slopes plunging to the very edge of Loch Hourn. The gaze directly in front of the farmhouse was to the mouth of Loch Hourn, between the dry island (Eilean Tioram) on the right and the hills of Knoydart to the left and then out to the Sound of Sleat, Isleornsay and its lighthouse - and beyond the Island of Skye and the mighty Cuillins.

To the left of the house was the 'milk house' and the 'wash house' and then the tidy U shaped corrugated iron clad steading - with its back to the Sound of Sleat and the frequent gales which funnelled up Loch Hourn. Beside the steading was the sheep fank and then onwards the road went past the sentinel holly tree at the 'cross-roads' to Glenfield, Achadh a'Ghlinne, Glen Arnisdale and Kinlochourn. A little further on after the Crudh Ard on the right, the little village of Corran at the mouth of the River Arnisdale came into view, flanked by the inbye little parcels of arable crofting land to each side, with the heights of Druim Fada protecting the cosy village from behind. And when the eye moved from Corran slightly to the right and spanned the loch, there were the tiny habitations of Barrisdale and Lea tucked in on the Knoydart shore - with the majestic Ladhar Bheinn and the other great hills of Knoydart towering above.

This was the wonderful vista which lay before the wide-eyed youngster on that first night. There is little doubt that when first introduced to his tiny bedroom upstairs, tucked under the eaves and beside the landing, with little more space than that for the camp bed which was tucked in there, that sleep was very sound, and that there was excitement at dawn for anticipated new experiences and explorations. And the little bedroom did not know then that it was to have its new occupant for somewhat longer than either had anticipated.

After a hasty mini breakfast (for the main breakfast always followed after the regular early morning chores had been completed), it 'was outside' with Uncle Roddy to release the dogs Whisky and Maddy for their morning exercise and then to proceed up the Corran road a little bit before Uncle Roddy bellowed 'Trobhad' to what appeared to be nothing but the wide open peat flats with the rising rough ground beyond. His call soon got a bellowed response. The cows were now located, so off we set to guide them home for the morning milking. On reaching the steading, and the byre, in they went, each one automatically to her own stall in the 6 stalled byre - in the order from left to right of Skye, Rosy, Gandhi, Noel, Maggie and Greyack. After fastening the neck chain to each, then the milking began, but before that, the youngster had to be initiated in the hand milking technique - for there was no space for spectators, nor was there a wish to be one. I was 'sat down' on a little stool beside Noel, told to stroke each teat to remove any dirt, then put the milking pail in place, milk some milk into a hand to wet the teats so as to both lubricate the teat and facilitate the milking. So off I set very slowly at first, but surely, to eventually milk out the very patient and tolerant Noel. They were all lovely cows (with one exception) but Noel was always my special favourite. Apart from her patient nature, she had a good yield and had good milk flow - so one got a lot of satisfaction from milking her. She got her name, of course, from being a Christmas baby.

After milking was completed, the milk was taken to the milk house and sieved into large earthenware bowls and the milk allowed to settle before the cream was skimmed off with a scallop shell for churning into the fine fresh butter which was a feature of every tea-time. On reflection, present day Health Inspectors would not have been impressed with hygiene standards at milking. Milking pails were always clean but the milking technique would be frowned upon. It was the same hand milking technique which had been used from time immemorial and everybody remained in excellent health. Food poisoning and stomach upsets were conspicuous by their absence.

After a fine breakfast, the next job was in the 'slaughterhouse' where a sheep carcass was suspended from the rafters. This was July 1946 and, throughout the war, Uncle Roddy had been designated to supply butcher meat to the Arnisdale community because of the difficulty of ensuring regular supplies from places such as Glenelg, Kyle of Lochalsh or Inverness. This was to be the very last day of Uncle Roddy's role as the local butcher so I was very fortunate to 'get in' on this experience. The carcass was put on the slab and with deft strokes of his cleaver, the carcass was soon divided into the 50 or so pieces to supply each Arnisdale household. Almost certainly the carcass would have been that of a 2 to 3 year old Blackface or South Country Cheviot wether, perhaps weighing between 45 and 50 pounds (21 to 23 kilograms), so the ration of each household (for, of course, meat was rationed up to this time) would have been close to 1 pound. While each piece was labelled according to the recipient, I remember only the allocation for one person - that of Granny MacKenzie. Iain, Flora, Nellie and Willie's Granny had a standing order for the sheep's head. Undoubtedly the head made a fine pot of broth and there would also be good pickings of meat with which Granny (Mairi Bhan) was very satisfied, while purchase would have been possible within the constraints of her meagre old age pension.

In retrospect, another comment is appropriate regarding the hygienic standards of the 'butcher's shop'. There were cobwebs in the roof space, the butcher's slab was wiped down after the weekly operations with a clean cloth steeped in hot water, but, despite this, the slab was serrated with the regular strokes of the cleaver in cutting up the carcass, these serrations were etched with the suet from previous butchering - but nobody appeared to suffer from what today would be classified as very poor hygiene standards. The main reasons for this were, almost certainly, that people's immune systems were regularly challenged, strong immunity was developed and meat was properly cooked.

After being an interested on-looker at the procedures of the very last day of the Arnisdale 'butchery', the next errand of Uncle Roddy was to go to Glenelg to collect Peter MacRae of Kinlochourn from the Glenelg Hotel. On the previous day there had been a big wedding in Glenelg - that of Bobby MacLean of Lower Sandaig and Ann MacRae of Immergradden in Glenelg, who was also the Arnisdale school teacher. Peter had been a guest and was also the main piper at the wedding and at the dance which followed in the hotel. To travel on the gravel road from Arnisdale to Glenelg in those days was always an exciting adventure in itself with its very steep inclines, the multiplicity of Z bends and the precipitous cliffs which threatened on the seaward side if the driver failed to pay full and skilled attention on the extremely narrow road. However, perhaps the magnificence of the scenery looking across Loch Hourn and the Sound of Sleat to Knoydart, Skye, the Cuillins and further down the Sound to the 'upturned boat' which was Eigg and the heights of Rhum, diverted the attention of the traveller from the possible dangers to the surrounding splendour of the vista.

In any case, on arrival in Glenelg, Peter was soon located within the splendid Glenelg Hotel with its fine setting looking across the Sound to Kylerhea and Skye. The conversation on the way back to Arnisdale between Peter and Uncle Roddy was very interesting, I am quite sure of that, because it would have been about the wedding, the young couple, all the folk and the 'goings on' at the reception and dance, but it was all in the Gaelic so I understood not a word. However, my ear was receiving its first initiation in being attuned to a language which was the predominant one in the district at that time.

As we descended the formidable Arnisdale brae and approached Peter's reunion with his little boat with outboard engine - which would take him back up the loch to Kinlochourn, the Gaelic conversation suddenly became more excited as a car was confronted at the bottom of the hill. The occupants were none other than the newly weds Ann and Bobby who had started off their married life in the Arnisdale Schoolhouse and were now venturing forth on their life's journey together.

The summer holidays proceeded from this very interesting start to the usual round of daily chores which included the morning and evening milkings, the bucket feeding of young calves on skim milk with added oilcake, the feeding of the lone pig with household scraps, skim milk and buttermilk, and throwing a token few handfuls of oats to the twenty or so laying hens, whose territory was around the farm steading; the oats provided only a small supplement to the varied diet they obtained for themselves by foraging around and harvesting nature's bounty of worms, insects, seeds and small pebbles to keep their gizzards in good working order to process their feed. On these provisions of nature they were thriving and laying well.

The big summer jobs on the farm included gathering the sheep from the high hills for the shearing, the cutting, making and the winning of the hay and later, of the oats. When the peats had dried they had also to be barrowed home and stored in the peat shed. And there was always excited anticipation as to when the new tatties would be ready. As the great day approached, the same question was repeated from neighbour to neighbour a hundred times and more - 'Did you try your tatties yet?' When the big day duly came, the questions turned to those involving numbers per shaw, size and quality. Of course, the quality was always wonderful, especially in terms of flavour - but also of texture. So much so, in fact, that everybody over-indulged and the overflowing large bowl at the start of the meal would be cleared completely by the end of it. It was a veritable feast and the excitement and appetite for the new tatties would last for 2 weeks and more. On the farm -and all the crofts there was a succession of varieties from early to main crop. The popular earlies were Duke of Yorks and Sharpes Express with the most prized maincrop varieties being Home Guard, Edzell Blues, Kerrs Pink and Golden Wonders. These last three varieties, and Golden Wonder in particular, were great companions of the salt herring which formed a large component of the winter diet, washed down with plentiful supplies of milk which also helped to dilute the high salt content of the herring. 'A feast fit for the king'!

One very notable difference in Arnisdale from Glenurquhart was the very high rainfall and the many days on which mist shrouded the mountains. There were few days without rain, and even although it was only a slight drizzle, it would greatly curtail activities such as the sheep gatherings for the clipping (the shearing) and the haymaking. Although this dampness was disconcerting on first experience, at least it was warm rain and, in between the showers, the sea breezes would blow and soon dry off dampened clothes. Perhaps the rain and the mugginess were not so bad as those other pestilences which warm dampness encouraged - and the midges (meanbh-chuileag) were the greatest pest of all. They were always a fearsome foe to have surrounding and annoying you in uncertain weather - while working at the hay or in the handling of the sheep - and even at otherwise very pleasurable pursuits such as fishing for cuddies off the pier. And yet, when the fine days came, or even the fine weather periods within the day, they were much more memorable, because they made such a contrast with the more usual weather.

In planning the sheep gatherings for the clipping there had to be shrewd weather forecasting based on local knowledge and long experience of signs and portents. There would be considerable debate in the Gaelic between the shepherds for the day such as Roddy Mor, Ludovic Fraser, Kenny Fletcher and Donald MacLaren before the decision was made that the weather looked fairly settled, the visibility in the high tops was good and that they should take the chance to gather. It was miserable work taking to the high hills trying to gather on wet days and, in any case, when it was wet, the mist was down, especially on the high tops - and in these conditions trying to outfox the wily hill ewes was a losing battle. Weather and visibility had to be perfect to allow the gatherers and their great collie dogs to achieve a good gather. The telescope or 'glass' was a vital part of the armoury to spot the little families of sheep on their high hefts in the rock and boulder strewn hills and then to alert and direct the dogs at heel to spot one's vision of the sheep from the glass. There is always tremendous empathy, communication and teamwork between shepherd and dog in the spotting of the 'quarry' before the dog is allowed to set off on the gather. Hill sheep in mid to late July are reaching a peak of fitness and dogs have to be even fitter and wilier to outpace and outwit them. It is a great experience to see collie dogs such as old Whisky drifting up a mountainside, skirting the rocks, becoming an increasingly smaller dot as the tops are approached - with just their movement helping the eye to spot them from time to time - and then perhaps losing sight of them altogether. As the glass is trained on the target group of sheep, gradually their heads are seen to turn backwards to something which has stirred them from behind. Then gradually they begin to move towards the shepherd, their early slow canter quickening into a faster pace as they come trickling as a group down the mountainside to the hill pass below - followed and guided by these clever, gentle collies. There follows a succession of such small streams of sheep from the tops until the whole area to be gathered is covered. Then it is a case of pulling together the small groups of sheep which have been 'sprung' from their high hefts into the glens between the high tops. The flock then grows from its little group of five to its twenties and gradually to its fifties and then to its many hundreds. It is always exciting to see the tiny stream grow into ever bigger ones and then eventually into a great river of a white moving mass as they move down the steep hillsides followed by the fit, skilled shepherds and clever dogs who, together, have achieved a fine gather of the flock from all the far corners and crannies of the hill and mountain grazings.

There is relief for man and beast as the valley floor on the homeward journey is reached on the way to the fank. There is great bleating of ewe and lamb pairs which have lost contact with eachother as the mass scrambled down the slope - in their attempts to regain contact now that they have reached plenty of flat space on the Achadh a'Ghlinne and are moving at a more leisurely pace. The communication between mother and young is highly effective and usually full bonding and pairing has been restored before the last mile from the hill to the fank is covered. And relative silence now prevails within the panting flock. These are some of my memories from the sheep gatherings.

The sheep stock on Arnisdale Farm numbered around 800. The 400 or so South Country Cheviots belonged to Roddy Mor while the 400 Blackface ewes were a 'Club' stock, being a shared enterprise between Roddy Mor and the Estate which was in the ownership of Captain Kitson at the time. Once at the fank, the sheep would be given plenty of time to settle and for lambs to suckle. Meanwhile the gatherers would also get their breath back over lunch or 'brunch' or whatever was going. There was always a good spread - but often the cup of reviving tea was the top priority.

Preparation for the clipping would begin by shedding off the lambs and separating the farm ewes from the 'club' stock; the hoggs (last year's lambs) were also separated, since at that time a higher price was on offer for hogg wool because of its finer staple. In that era all the shearers clipped on the clipping stool. Each was sitting comfortably at the back of the long stool as the next sheep was caught by the crogger (catcher) and delivered to the shearer. The ewe was then 'upended' and the two fore legs bound with one hind leg using a piece of thick cord to help with the control of the animal during the shearing process. This method, while laborious, was probably easier on the back of the shearer than the modern method and it helped to keep the wool very clean; wool was a much more valuable commodity at that time in relation to the total annual value of output from the hill sheep flock than at the present time. At the completion of shearing of each ewe, there would be a triumphant shout of 'buest' and after the fleece was carefully removed, the buester (the author's usual job) would appear with the 'paint pot' and buesting iron for the appropriate colour mark to be applied to the correct part of the anatomy of the ewe for delineating ownership. Then the fleece would be spread out by the ladies on a clean platform and folded with care and skill after any dirty taggs were removed. The fleeces were folded according to breed - with the folded Cheviot fleece having the inside 'out' while the Blackface fleece had the outside 'out'. The hogg fleeces were also kept separate. All the folded fleeces would then be removed to the barn where they would be stacked on a clean floor in their different categories. They were now ready for bagging which was a good wet weather job.

The author remembers the clipping as almost a leisurely and certainly very sociable job. The click-click-click of several sets of hand shears were relatively quiet and certainly rhythmic, there was constant conversation between all involved, most of it in the Gaelic, with plenty of leg pulling and playful teasing of the children present. There were frequent breaks as each shearer would regularly stop to process pieces of 'Black Twist' or 'Bogie Roll', fill the pipe and have a smoke before calling for the next ewe. The pipe smoke also helped to keep the midges at bay! There were also the regular breaks for tea and the copious supplies of sandwiches and home baking. Although a considerable amount of hard graft was involved, the way the whole operation was orchestrated - with the team, comprising all age groups and sexes, working very harmoniously together, really made it a great social occasion. The banter and the chat were always very entertaining. It was a veritable ceilidh. These folk knew how to transform hard work into a pleasurable experience. We could certainly do with more of that spirit in many workplaces at the present day.

There is always great satisfaction in the harvesting of nature's bounty - and wool was a treasured commodity from the hill farms at that time.

The only dampener on these occasions was the threat of drizzle or rain coming in, for fleeces had to be perfectly dry to prevent moulding and ensure top quality wool. When the weather broke, the ewes would have to be returned to Achadh a'Ghlinne for the job to be completed on the next fine day.

Hay making, of course, was equally dependent on fine weather. Hay making would start in Arnisdale with the retrieval of the scythe from its winter storage - and sharpening it with the stone to achieve a fine cutting edge. The farm had a horse drawn mower which had to be oiled and the cutting blades sharpened. When the weather looked promising, Dick, the russet garron, would have to be retrieved from his summer retreat on the Achadh while his working companion 'Major' would be collected from the Lodge field. They would be yolked to the mower and the hay cutting would start, usually in early August. Cutting was never uneventful, with frequent breakages of drive shafts or other essential working parts. Since spare parts took perhaps a week or more to arrive from Inverness or Dingwall, home repairs had to be made or at least attempted. If these were impossible - because no welding equipment or blacksmith was available locally - it was a case of resorting to the scythe. This was a formidable job for Roddy Mor - with a five acre field in front of him.

However, he was in good company whether the farm hay-cutting was taking place in the fields close to the Camusban crofts or across the river at Glenfield from the Corran Crofts. Memories are very vibrant still of beautiful summer days in the fields beside the Arnisdale River with the scything in progress on each river bank, with Roddy Mor on one side getting into his rhythmic stride as he swathed away and with the Corran crofters moving in harmony on the other bank. The Corran Crofters included the families of MacKenzies, the Murchisons, the MacAskills, the MacCuaigs and the Stewarts.

The ripple of the river, the swishing of the scythe as the meadow grasses were swathed and the regular strokes of stone against metal as the sharp cutting edges of scythes were restored, the humming of the bumble bees and the fluttering of the butterflies provided a splendour in terms of sight and sound which was a veritable joy to the senses. And that is why the whole atmosphere remains so vibrant in the memory. The only pity is that modern technology for recording the music, the rhythm, the movement, the life and the whole atmosphere was not available at the time to record that wonderful synergy of man with nature for the benefit of current and future generations. However, it was not always so beautiful. The sky would begin to cloud over, the humidity would drift in from the sea or from the mountain tops, the midges would emerge, the drizzle would start and the 'monsoon' would be with us once again. The hay would have to be abandoned for another day and we would have to resort to the barn to start packing the wool. The big wool bags would be strung up with rope from the barn rafters, a few fleeces would be loaded into the bag and then the packer (the author's usual job) would have to lower himself into the seven feet high bag. Fleece after fleece was supplied by Roddy Mor to be arranged in a symmetrical order within the bag, layer by layer, so as to maintain the integrity of each valuable fleece. Each successive layer brought the packer nearer the 'surface' of the bag and - when the mouth and nostrils attained a height beyond the bag top - this always provided relief from the claustrophobia and airlessness of the lower confines of the bag, and deep breaths could be inhaled once again without being polluted by wool fibres sucked into the mouth and nostrils. Achieving a good tight and tidy pack for each of the twenty or so bags of wool was always the objective and then the tops would be sewn by Roddy Mor, using the bag needle and special binding string provided along with the bags by the wool merchant.

But, if the weather cleared, the wool packing was abandoned meanwhile, and it was back to the hay. After a week of wet weather, the mower part awaited from Inverness may have arrived so the horse drawn mower would again be operational to perform its clickety-click around the hay meadow. There was one potentially horrendous occasion when only great alertness and expert horsemanship prevented a very serious injury to Aunt Lizzie. She had wandered suddenly for some reason into the uncut hay, out of the path of the horses and mower, but directly in the path of the unseen mower blade working its way stealthily along near ground level. Rena MacDonald was in control of the horses while seated on the mower. She spotted the danger immediately and - with great spontaneity of action and expert horsemanship - she brought the machine to a complete halt at the instant the mower fingers had penetrated the leg of Aunt Lizzie. There was consternation, of course, a serious injury had occurred which demanded instant medical treatment from the resident district nurse in Camusban. However, the consequences would have been much more dire were it not for the magnificent spontaneous alertness and reactions of Rena. Rena was a wonderful lady who helped on the farm at that time and had a great range of skills, as well as a beautiful demeanour and personality. It is one of the heartfelt disappointments of the author that the wonderful Rena did not live to help with the compilation of this book and to savour the end product. Rena would have been invaluable and she - and the author - would have treasured the experience - but it was not to be. Maggie 'Lea' was another who worked on the farm at times. Maggie was a great pal of Rena's and they were of the same mould - friendly and full of fun, hard working and skilful in all that they did.

Hay making in Arnisdale and in all high rainfall parts of the West Coast was a laborious, frustrating job. After the hay was cut, it would lie in the swath undisturbed for a few days until it had wilted or dried out a bit. On the first dry day which followed it would be turned by the hand rake to allow access of breeze and sun (when visible) to the underside. If the rain kept away and the breeze continued to dry out the turned swath, a start would be made to the next stage in the process - that of making 'prappags' This involved picking up about two pounds (one kilogram) of semi dried hay, shaking it vigorously into a small heap; then flattening this heap lightly between the hands and turning the flat mass into a circle and placing this circle of hay on the ground with the 'ends' of the flat mass or circle underneath with the 'middle' above - so as to shed the rain which would undoubtedly come before the next step in the process could be taken. Making prappags in a five acre or even a one acre field, was a backbreaking slow process (and the tedious nature of the job was often compounded by the fiendish midges!) - but it was an essential step in the winning of the hay for the winter feeding of the cattle.

The next stage in the process when there was a drying day, and the prappags had dried above and below, was to make little coles, which involved much shaking of the hay to maximise the shedding of any moisture and also to maximise the drying effects of any breeze and sunshine before the shaken mass was incorporated into the cole. The cole was carefully finished with a good roof, with the outward wisps of hay at the top and sides carefully combed with the hay fork so as to provide a good hat and perimeter coat which would be effective in shedding the rain. After the hay cured and dried further in the small coles, several small coles would be combined to form bigger coles - often built around a tripod of wooden stakes to aid the further drying and curing process. This would involve considerable further shaking of each wisp of hay in the construction of the large cole. Much attention would again be given to the finish so as to ensure good waterproofing of the outer coat. The final step was to make the cole secure against the wind by roping it down, usually using binder-twine or even ropes made out of twisted hay. There was a great sigh of relief and a feeling of ultimate achievement by all concerned when this stage of the battle against the elements was reached. But there was still one further step before ultimate victory was achieved. The hay had to be transported to the barn once the final stages of drying and curing had been completed - and again a fine dry day or part of a day was eagerly awaited for this final step on the path to ultimate triumph to be achieved.

Often the first such suitable day to arrive would be a Sunday. However, the Fourth Commandment was never broken, as the normal Sabbath activities of attendance at morning and evening worship and only works of necessity such as the feeding of the stock and milking of the cows, received their due attention.

If the day and evening of the Sunday continued to be good, thoughts then turned to midnight and, with the rain at bay and the drying breeze still blowing in from the sea, the stroke of midnight would see a ferment of activity - with all hands and energies being directed to transporting the hay from the coles in the field to the barn. The transport mechanisms included the hay fork, roped bundles on the back. - or the cole, in whole or part, being sledged along the dry ground by two or more folk with hay forks as the pulling mechanisms. Roddy Mor, with a much larger quantity to get into the barn than the crofters, would use his little lorry, converted ingeniously into a 'truck' from an old Austin car. After an all night session of excited activity, there would be great satisfaction by dawn as fields were cleared and the barns were stuffed full to ensure that wintering cattle would have something to fill their bellies and engage their rumens each day - so as to ensure that they would still be around when the time of plenty came round again in the following May and June; then the new tasty and digestible shoots of a new Spring would provide a welcome relief from relative winter hardship and also help restore their depleted body condition.

The extreme difficulty of winning the hay for the winter feeding of cattle, horses and sheep probably did as much damage as any other factor to destroy the spirit of the crofters in the western seaboard of Scotland and contributed greatly to the drift of young people from these areas to easier ways of living beyond.

Haymaking would start in August because, by that time, the grass would be stemmier and would be easier to dry and win. However, by this stage it had lost considerable feeding value and loss of digestibility. Further considerable losses in feeding value occurred in all the handling and shaking of the hay in the successive stages of turning, making the prappags, the small coles and the larger coles - up to the final carting to the storage barn. At each of these stages there was considerable loss of the nutritious seeds of the herbage and of the finer leaf materials - so that the final product fed to the stock was a good 'belly filler' but had low digestibility and feeding value.

Some of the folk tried very hard to make the hay making job easier in Arnisdale. One such was Archie MacLean. When the author was first thinking of preparing this 'little book' late in 1996, one of the first folk that he planned to visit was his old friend Archie, because Archie was around Arnisdale from the very early part of the century, he had a great memory and he was a fine teller of stories and a communicator of his experiences. Alas, as so often happens, Archie passed away in the very early part of 1997 and with Archie's departure from this world went many priceless memories of Arnisdale and its people.

Archie was a great character and he was always thinking of easier ways to do difficult jobs. Archie, like Roddy Mor, had also converted an old Austin car into a little truck and he used it for taking in the hay from the coles in the field to the barn. The author remembers also Archie's attempts to automate the cutting of the hay, to save him having to use the scythe as in the past. Archie got an old horse drawn mower and also converted this, attaching a single shaft to be hitched to the back of the lorry. It was a brave and ingenious invention but it never seemed to work. It seemed that the lowest gear of the lorry was still too high for the working mechanisms of the mower to keep pace. As a result, there were very frequent breakages, from the outset of Archie's brave new world, of one working part of the mower after another. Perhaps Archie ended up having even more frustrations with his brave experiment than he would have had by tackling the hay with the old scythe in the first place. But at least Archie tried his very best to change the old order of things for the better. And despite the failure of his master plan to work, Archie's activities and their consequences generated great discussion and leg pulling, which Archie himself enjoyed as much as everybody else! Archie was a wonderful character.

In the author's visits to his old haunts in Glenelg and Arnisdale now, while conventional hay making, often using 'on the fence' drying, is still being practiced, there has been almost a complete switch to conserving the plentiful supply of summer forage in the form of 'in bag' silage. This is a tremendous development for high rainfall areas - because it is much easier to take advantage of brief spells of fine drying weather to win cut grass in bagged silage form than in the making of hay. Not only is the product easier to win but the feeding value will be considerably higher because of earlier cutting at a more digestible stage and the preservation of high quality leaf and seed head materials. If only the bagged silage technique had been in existence from the period following the new Crofting Acts which followed the Napier Commission Report over a century ago now, then more of the good young people from crofting areas would have stayed around and the crofting system would have been much stronger and vibrant than it is today. It is also relevant in this context to comment on the so-called 'West Coast temperament' which implies an 'easy going' and often laziness element. While the easy going aspect of the nature is a very attractive asset, the laziness accusation is not justified. Visitors to West Coast districts are often surprised to see the folk not rising too early in the morning and then enjoying long discussions with family and neighbours or even ceilidhs, sitting around the house often late into the morning. The author would suggest that this behaviour indicates good adaptation to the prevailing conditions. Very often in the summer and autumn in particular, the mornings are wet and overcast while the weather often clears in the afternoon and ends up fine well into the evening. Thus, for 'good weather' dependent jobs such as hay making, sheep gathering, shearing, and sea fishing, the weather might not be suitable to allow work to start until after mid-day and, with the weather becoming progressively better into the late evening, a long working day of ten hours or more is possible. The easy going part of the nature helps the folk to accept the bad weather while it lasts and enjoy themselves at ceilidhing, but at the first opportunity provided by an improvement in the weather, the people are as industrious as any other folk. They have learned to be highly adaptable to fit into the varying moods of the weather, for they can do nothing to influence the sun and the rain, the mist, the breeze and the gales and they know that all too well.

hay, the peats also had to be won from the bog and the weather. They were usually cut ...ss, which was very close to the farm, in May and then set up on their ends in 'stooks' on ...o allow all available sunshine and sea breezes to dry them out gradually. Three to four ...'ting and stooking - in late August or September - they were perfectly dry and on a good ...ed from the moss to the peat shed attached to the farm house. The peats, along with ...e main fuel sources, for very little timber was available except for some driftwood ...shore.

...raft working with the sheep, milking the cows, making hay and carting peats, there ...f time for leisure activities. One of the author's favourite pastimes at any spare ...down to the little pier to fish for cuddies (small saithe). They were very plentiful ..., other fish species made their appearance and were duly captured to keep the farm ...anner to which they had become accustomed! There were also full blooded games ...de football as the local boys were supplemented with others who came to holiday ...or other relatives. These games took place at various locations - on the moor behind ...ouse at Corran, on one of the fields in front of the farm-house and sometimes in the ...le 'Dry Island' at Camusban. Among the 'combatants' would be Iain and Willie ...ie MacTavish, Ian MacGillivray, Ian Sinclair, Willie Wilson, the Sandaig boys - ...d Willie MacLeod, Angus Murchison, the author and his brothers, Sandy and Bob.

...climbing, while Beinn Sgritheall provided too formidable a challenge for a youngster to skip up and down within an odd spare hour or two's freedom from the chores, the adjacent Beinn na h-eaglaise, the author remembers, was conquered along with sister Betty in an hour or so on one fine summer's evening.

Another most enjoyable pastime was taking off on Roddy Mor's old army bike to obtain essential supplies at the two shops in Camusban, Johnnie MacGillivray's in the middle of Camusban village and Peggy Ann's at the far end. Johnnie's shop was not always open as he doubled up as the local roadman, maintaining the gravel road by barrowing road metal from the shore or from the regular little quarries on the Arnisdale brae and beyond on the route to Glenelg. Peggy Ann ran the Post Office and had a great range of goods in her shop - all essential household food supplies. At the time of the author's first visit to Arnisdale, most goods were still rationed after the war so that coupons as well as money had to be handed over to obtain goods. Rationed materials included sugar, butter, cheese, tinned meat and sweets. Both Peggy Ann and her sister Mary were very pleasant elderly ladies and they gave a great welcome to all callers at the shop, and especially to the children. After the shopping and transactions had been completed, there was always a handful of sweets pressed into the hand on leaving the shop. The author remembers on one occasion when all the sweets had obviously been sold out, a hunk of fine red cheese was cut off the block and gifted to the young shopper. One always got the impression that Peggy Ann ran the shop more as a 'calling' than as a business. Journeys between the farm and the shop on the 'old boneshaker' were always interspersed with hearty greetings from all the folk in Camusban who were walking along the road, working on their boats on the foreshore or beavering away in their garden. News items were exchanged and everybody knew most of everybody else's business - good news and bad news - in the fine community spirit which pervaded the whole of Arnisdale.

The shops obtained their supplies on MacLennan's boat from Mallaig every Tuesday. This boat also carried passengers and the particular orders from the lodge, the farm and all the crofts and households. It may have been cans of paraffin or sheep dip or creosote, spare parts for outboard motors, drums of petrol, empty wool bags or any other commodity which had been ordered from the Stores in Maillaig or beyond. There was always great anticipation on a Tuesday awaiting the boat. Eyes would be fixed on the left hand point at the junction between the Sound of Sleat and the mouth of Loch Hourn to spot the very small dot in the distance. This would be the signal for everybody to make for the pier with their barrows, dogs and children. Goods would be off loaded at the pier and then the boat would make its way round the bay, first to stop in front of Johnnie MacGillivray's shop, and then Peggy Ann's. Bread, buns and all other grocery orders would be transferred to the rowing boat which came out to rendezvous, after which the rowing boat would make for the shore to the many willing hands waiting there to transport all goods to the shops. Tuesday afternoon would see a bit of a 'shopping spree' to get supplies of fresh bread, the quantities of other rationed goods due and other supplies which may have been sold out before the arrival of the Tuesday boat.

MacLennan's boat had been such a lifeline to Arnisdale and other clachans around Loch Hourn for a very long time and this service continued into the 1960s. Passengers were also carried to and from Arnisdale and the other clachans and bags of wool and other outgoing produce would fill the boat on return journeys to Mallaig. The boat would return on other days as required with special consignments of goods for the lodge. The author remembers one such occasion when three beautiful but fiery little Icelandic ponies were delivered for the use of the Estate in transporting shot stags and hinds from the hill.

If Tuesday was a special day in Arnisdale, so also was the Sabbath. Preparation was made for the Sabbath on the Saturday with the potatoes being peeled and the main Sunday meal prepared, all the week's washing and ironing would be completed - so that only works of necessity - such as the feeding of the stock and the milking would have to be done on the Sabbath. There was a fairly long morning service and the evening service was equally long. Roddy Mor and his old First World War army pal, Willie (MacKenzie) the Post, were the precentors. Aunt Lizzie and all thirty or so present at each service would join heartily in the singing of the Psalms and Paraphrases. The sermons were long and the concentration of children in particular was severely tested. The author remembers well the intriguing round window above the pulpit in the Free Church. With its spars going from the centre to the circumference it was like a cart wheel and the mind and vision often strayed from the sermon and the minister to conjure up alternative designs in the mind, of this attractive part of the architecture. The other thing recalled about the sermons was that Mr MacDonald, the Free Church Missionary who was based at Glenelg, would start his sermon in normal tones but as he got into it, his preaching would become very musical and the remainder would be delivered in an attractive, almost chanting, form. Although probably many of the important spiritual messages missed their mark somewhat because of drifting concentration, the tone of most of the sermon certainly was 'music to the ears'.

Often Sunday lunch was followed by a walk up Glen Arnisdale as far as Achadh a'Ghlinne to view the scenery and at the same time to check the sheep, Dick the horse and the yearling stirks; the latter were usually to be found on the flat moor beyond the Achadh (Blar nan each) but before the famous Zig Zag path which raised the Glen path very quickly to a much higher level on its continuing route to the little lochs (the Dubh Lochain) and thence to Kinloch Hourn. These leisurely walks were enjoyable and usually uneventful. There was always the prospect of finding one of the regular 'men of the road' or tramps who plied the Invergarry - Kinlochourn - Arnisdale - Glenelg route regularly, asleep on a bed of dry bracken in the now unused house in the Achadh. A careful eye also had to be kept open for any sheep with maggots. The dirty rear end, the swishing of the tail, and attempts to turn the head round to reach the tail head, were always tell-tale signs that the blowfly eggs had hatched and that the maggots were beginning to eat their way into flesh. Since the dogs Whisky and Maddy were constant companions on these walks, such a sheep was soon cornered, caught and examined. If in fact the dreaded maggots were present, the unfortunate beast had its affected part cleaned thoroughly and strong dip was administered, a supply of which was always kept in the old house for such contingencies.

The old army bike was used for general leisure activities and for exploring all over the place in addition to the shopping errands. On one occasion, Iain MacKenzie and the author decided to have a race on our old bikes, both of which were far too big for us, but we improvised very effectively and we could handle them quite well. The chosen course for the race was from the farm down to the pier. This, however, involved going down a fair incline and the negotiation of two Z bends on the gravel road. The second of the Z bends was situated just as the shore was reached after which the road skirted the shoreline on its way to Camusban.

The order to 'Go' was given and off we sped, accelerating quickly as we raced neck and neck. After the first Z bend was negotiated miraculously, the pace quickened even more down the steepest part of the incline and soon the second Z bend was right there in front of us. Both handlebars turned in the correct direction but the bikes carried on regardless straight ahead. Down the foreshore both of us hurtled over the rocks and boulders and suddenly the bikes with riders were horizontal as they slithered over the rough foreshore before grinding to a halt - thanks to the braking forces of the friction of bikes, clothes and bare flesh with the stony surface. Both boys had very little skin intact on those parts of their anatomy which had lost the battle with the grinding stones and gravel over which they had slithered. Foreheads, chins, hands, arms and knees had suffered most. However, both fools were soon on their feet brushing themselves down and pulling pieces of gravel out of affected body parts. We were both sorry sights and we never sought any sympathy for, quite rightly, none would have been forthcoming! Amazingly, both bikes also survived but that experience ended the races on the Ceann a' Gharaidh race track! The only permanent evidence which remains of that infamous race are the permanent scars on wrists, elbows and knees of two erstwhile small boys now more than half a century on from the foolhardy encounter.

These then, were some of the experiences of the author in that first holiday in Arnisdale. It had been a great learning experience and had been hugely enjoyable and, at times, highly exciting.

However, the longer and more exciting the holiday, the more thoughts turn - towards the end - to less exciting things, such as the return to school. Nevertheless, as indicated earlier, a totally unexpected offer was to be made to the youngster within only a few days of the completion of a superb summer's experience. When Aunt Lizzie uttered the words - 'would you like to stay and go to school here?', for a moment there was a feeling of incredulity and in the next the spontaneous excited response of 'Oh - yes'! That response was no reflection of the lovely home environment the author had in Glenurquhart but just the selfish spontaneity of a child who wants a great holiday to continue. Now there was only a day or two left to anticipate the exciting prospect of going to the little school in the village along with fellow youngsters, all of whom the author had already got to know very well in the preceding few weeks.

**Top Left.**  The Arnisdale Farmhouse with the peat shed annex on the left and the milk house/wash house on the right.  The slopes of Beinn Bhuidhe and the mass of Beinn Chlachach provide the background.  **Right**.  The farm steading on the right with Glen Arnisdale beyond and Druim Fada on the right.

**Middle Left.**  Arnisdale Lodge tucked round behind the trees to the right of the farmhouse.  **Right**.  The view from the farm of the village of Camusban with the little pier in between.

**Bottom Left**.  The magnificent Beinn Sgritheall and adjacent Beinn na h-eaglaise rising steeply from the seashore and dominating the village of Camusban and the croftlands below.  **Right**.  The vista down to the mouth of Loch Hourn with Eilean Tioram (the dry island) on the right and the hills of Knoydart on the left.  The Sound of Sleat, Isleornsay, the Island of Skye and the mighty Cuillin are beyond.

**Row 1 Left.** The U-shaped steading with its back to the Sound of Sleat and the strong winds which 'tunnel' down from the mouth of Loch Hourn. The steading components from the left were the slaughterhouse, the hen house, the barn, the byre, the stable and bull shed, the haybarn, the calf house, the pig shed, and the garages for the farm 'lorry' and the car. **Right**. The view to the left of the farmhouse beyond the steading to the sheep fank, the shoreline fields, the Crudh Ard, the road to Corran branching left to Glenfield and Glen Arnisdale at the sentinel holly tree at the 'cross-roads', with Ladhar Bheinn and Knoydart's other magnificent mountains beyond across Loch Hourn. **Row 2 Left.** The village of Corran at the mouth of the River Arnisdale, flanked by the inbye little parcels of arable crofting land to each side, with the mass of protective Druim Fada behind. **Right**. The now tiny habitations of Barrisdale (far left) and Li (centre) tucked in on the Knoydart shore with Ladhar Bheinn and its sister peaks towering above. **Row 3 Left.** The view up Glen Arnisdale. The small arable fields at Glenfield are to the left of the tree lined river with the Corran crofting parcels of arable land on the right. Further up the Glen is Achadh a' Ghlinne and thereafter the hill track winds its way to Kinloch Hourn. **Right**. The call of 'Trobhad' to the cows on the rough grazings received a bellowed response. **Row 4**. The local shopkeepers. **Left**. Peggy Ann with her sister Mary and a summer visitor. **Right**. Johnny MacGillivray with John MacCuaig (left) and Maggie MacTavish.

**Top Left**. Granny MacKenzie (Mairi Bhan) in front of the row of Corran byres. Mairi Bhan had a standing order for the sheep's head as Roddy Mor butchered the fat wedder for the Arnisdale community each week. **Right**. Peter MacRae (left) of Kinloch Hourn with his great friend Donald MacKillop. Peter had to be collected from the Glenelg Hotel where he had been the piper at the wedding of Arnisdale teacher Ann MacRae to Bobby MacLean of Lower Sandaig.

**Middle Left**. The old Glenelg Hotel photographed from the boat sheds near the village of Quarry. **Right**. The wedding photograph of Ann MacRae, the Arnisdale teacher, and Bobby MacLean of Lower Sandaig with Sandy MacDiarmid as best man and Bessie MacDonald as bridesmaid.

**Bottom Left**. Magnificent views from the Arnisdale to Glenelg road from the high ground above Sandaig at the Gorstan looking down the Sound of Sleat to Knoydart on the left, the Islands of Eigg and Rhum, and the south east corner of Skye on the right. **Right**. Peter MacRae's seven mile route in his little boat with its outboard motor from Arnisdale up the loch to Kinloch Hourn.

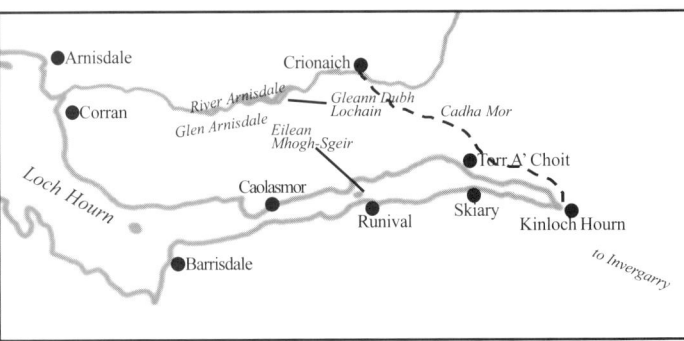

**Top Left.**  In planning the sheep gatherings there had to be shrewd weather forecasting to try to make sure that the day would remain dry and that mist would not close in on the high tops to make the gathering impossible.  Debating weather prospects are (LtoR.) Angus Beaton, Roddy Mor, Ludovic Fraser and Willie MacKenzie Jun.  **Right.**  The telescope or 'glass' – a key part of the armoury in the hill sheep gatherings from the high tops.

**Middle Left.**  The clever work of the collies in being more cunning and fleet of foot in outfoxing the fit and wily hill ewes in the sheep gatherings.  **Right.**  The small trickles of ewes from their high hefts gradually grow into bigger streams and rivers of ewes as the fine teamwork of shepherds and dogs coax them down the mountainsides.

**Bottom Left.**  The culmination of the gather approaches as the hill gate is reached.  **Right**.  Now the fank is reached and before the sorting starts the first priority is a big mug of tea – usually with plenty of sugar.

**Top Left.** Angus Beaton (left) and Roddy Mor at the clipping with Aunt Lizzie doing the buesting and folding the fleeces. Almost all the shearers used the clipping stool. **Right**. The 'crogging' – delivering each sheep to the shearer.

**Middle Left**. The cleaning and careful rolling of the fleeces. **Right**. The clipping, although hard work for all members of the team, was a fine social occasion – constant chatter and banter, brief stops to process the Black Twist tobacco, fill the pipe and have a good puff to keep the midges at bay, and regular stops for tea, sandwiches and home baking.

**Bottom Left.** The culmination of a good day – the weather kept fine, the entire gathering of ewes have been shorn, returned with their lambs to Achadh a' Ghlinne and out the hill gate to make their way back gradually to their favourite hefts – much cooler than when they came in with the gather and their full fleece. (LtoR.) Angus Beaton, Roddy Mor, Aunt Lizzie, Willie MacKenzie Jun, Ludovic Fraser, the author's younger brother Bob and the author (the 'buester'). **Right**. Packing the wool. At the farm, the fleeces were stored safely in the shelter of the clean barn and the packing awaited a wet day when no outside work at sheep gathering, hay and peats was possible.

**Top Left.** On good hay making days, lower Glen Arnisdale was a hive of activity with the MacLaren family, Roddy Mor, Aunt Lizzie and their helpers busy on one side of the river and the Corran crofters – the MacKenzies, Murchisons, MacAskills, MacCuaigs and the Stewarts – beavering away on the other side. This view from the base of Druim Fada with the Murchison family busy at their hay looks across the Corran crofts, the River Arnisdale to the Glenfield and farm fields on the other side. **Right**. Roddy Mor, Aunt Lizzie and Maggie Lea (now Mrs MacDonald, Caol) winning the battle to secure the hay in the fields along the riverside in lower Glen Arnisdale.

**Middle Left.** A view from the hayfield up Glen Arnisdale. **Right**. The culmination of what was a long drawn out process in winning the hay. A dry day has arrived and the hay is loaded on to the little lorry (converted from an Austin car) for transport to the safety of the hay barn. Ina Stewart is building the load with Aunt Lizzie and Roddy Mor doing the forking.

**Bottom Left.** Left to right. Maggie 'Lea', the author's sister Lally and Rena MacDonald. Rena and Maggie worked on the farm from time to time. They were of the same mould – friendly and full of fun, hard working and skilful in all that they did. **Right**. A break from the hard graft to 'draw a breath' and a cup of reviving tea. LtoR. Nora MacDonald, Cathie Finlayson, Roddy Mor and Aunt Lizzie. (Early 1930s)

**Top Left.** Archie MacLean in his young days. Archie did his very best in his early years to 'automate' the hay making on his croft at Camusban but as he hitched his converted horse drawn mower on to his old converted Austin car, the working mechanisms of the mower experienced great difficulty in keeping pace with the lowest gear of the old Austin. Very frequent breakages resulted and then Archie would have to resort to the scythe like the rest of his fellow crofters. But Archie had at least made a very determined attempt to create a brave new world! **Right**. Archie, in his later years, along with his wife Betty gets a cap on a fine cole of newly won hay and secures the ropes to protect it from the Loch Hourn 'monsoon' and the frequent gales.

**Middle Left**. 'In bag' silage which has revolutionised the conservation of winter forage for cattle and sheep in high rainfall areas such as the West Coast of Scotland. It is much easier to take advantage of brief spells of fine drying weather to win cut grass in bagged silage form than in the making of hay. **Right**. As well as the hay, peats had to be won from the bog and the weather. The peat moss was on the left hand side of the road to Corran – very close to the farm. Druim Fada dominates the scene

**Bottom Left.** Taking home the cows from the rough grazings for the evening milking. **Centre**. The author and younger brother Bob with Maddy and one of her new pups. **Right**. The pier below Arnisdale Lodge. This was a hive of activity every Tuesday when MacLennan's boat came in from Mallaig with the weekly supply of provisions for the shops and other materials. When all was quiet and between jobs on the farm it was also a favourite haunt of the author in fishing for cuddies (small saithe) and an intriguing variety of other fish.

**Top Left**. Peggy Ann's shop and Post Office at the start of the Camusban village just at the base of the Arnisdale brae. **Right**. Johnny MacGillivray's shop midway along the Camusban village with Rena MacDonald about to open it up for the day.

**Middle Left**. Willie MacKenzie (Willie the Post) returns to Arnisdale with his new bride, Christina (late 1920s). Giving them a big welcome home are Mary Ann MacCuaig and Roddy Mor with his bagpipes. Roddy Mor and Willie were lifelong friends through their schooldays and served together in the Lovat Scouts throughout the Great War (1914-18). Later they were the precentors (leaders of praise) in the Arnisdale Free Church. **Right**. Only works of necessity were performed on the Sabbath. Cows had to be milked and fed morning and evening and between the church services a walk up Glen Arnisdale to check the wellbeing of the sheep and lambs in Achadh a' Ghlinne was permissible, as well as taking the cows home for the evening milking. LtoR. Roddy Mor, Aunt Lizzie, Jessie MacDonald and Johnnie Murchison beside the Arnisdale River in Achadh a' Ghlinne.

**Bottom Left**. The double Z bends on the Ceann a'Gharaidh race track. The nine year old contestants in the great race, Iain MacKenzie (centre) and the author (right) whose knees and wrists still bear the scars of the ignominious climax on the seashore to the foolhardy challenge over half a century later!

## Chapter 2.

**Schooldays in Arnisdale**

I have no memory of my first day in the Arnisdale School so it must have been very uneventful. That could certainly not be said about many other days in the school. When our children, Anthony, Martin and Susan were toddlers and it came to demands for storytelling, high on their list of priorities was to hear yet again some of the escapades in Arnisdale school. Some of these can not be retold here because the hundred year 'confidentiality agreement' has not yet expired!

The start of the 1946-47 session saw two new recruits to the school - yours truly and the new teacher, Miss Lexy Campbell from Skye. This was Lexy's first posting as a teacher. The school roll consisted, in declining order of age, of Willie Wilson, Morag MacIntyre, Flora MacKenzie, Iain MacKenzie (brother of Flora), the new pupil, Betty Wilson (sister of Willie), Ruaridh MacLeod (Sandaig), Ian MacGillivray (Gingee), the twins Calum and Willie MacLeod (brothers of Ruaridh) and Sheena Stewart. Thus, there were eleven of us and we probably ranged in age from about 6 to 12 years.

Lexy took her job very seriously, her discipline was very firm and she soon got us down to very serious work. Our day always started off with a Bible reading followed by a prayer by the teacher. We had homework to do, which mainly consisted of reading and spelling. The author remembers very little of writing and arithmetic so these may have been manageable. The reading and the spelling were tough and the author is quite sure, in retrospect, that the reading in which Betty, Iain and he were involved was far above the standard appropriate to our tender nine years of age.

As always with children, it is the events which occurred outwith the schoolroom which remain in the memory. There was a tiny strip of land over the school wall between the school and the 'school burn' (Allt an sgoile) where we used to play football at each playtime. At the start of the school in late August we were almost covered by the very rank grass which grew there but, as the seven boys got going each playtime at their football, it was quickly tamed by the trampling and kicking of many little feet to a surface of putting green standards, quite ideal to demonstrate the fine skills of the game, which none of us unfortunately possessed. However, we always had great fun, interspersed with frequent arguments about the legitimacy of some of the play and the goals claimed by each team. The confines at the sides of the pitch were the school dyke and the school burn which usually carried a fair spate of water down from Beinn na h-eaglaise, towering directly above. The ball would often end up in the burn as a result of severely off-target shots for goal or as a result of desperate defending. However, we never lost our little ball to the darting waters of the burn, although this was often achieved at the expense of very wet boots and stockings. Perhaps it was during our forays into the burn to retrieve our ball that we discovered its wealth of aquatic life of darting trout, elvers and other interesting fish and molluscs. Sometimes even our beloved football was abandoned as we diverted our attention to the burn and our 'teach yourself biology' lessons. The fun was always at its height when the whistle would sound and it was back to the hard graft imposed by Lexy in the classroom.

Apart from weekends, there was often the temptation to miss the chores of school for a day or two. Illness only extremely rarely afforded such an opportunity to get a day away from the grind of school, since all the children kept tremendously healthy and absences through illness were extremely rare. With no illness to afford an excuse for a day off, truancy was often given very careful consideration, but our lack of real courage and the fear of tough retribution for such delinquency usually won the day and reason prevailed. Iain MacKenzie and the author almost achieved notoriety one day when Sandy 'Mor' MacLean from Mallaig, and his little white fishing boat, were berthed at the pier one morning as we went to school.

Sandy was always ready for a blether as he puffed away on his Black Twist filled pipe. The two 'scholars' made their way down the pier to have a crack with him and his yarns were as interesting as ever. Then he made us a fine offer: 'I'm just leaving for Mallaig for the day and will be coming back tonight. What about coming with me for the trip?' What a chance to dodge the school for the day! We were on the point of accepting Sandy's great offer and were about to set off with him for what would have been a fine day's jaunt - when reason finally prevailed. So the two of us just 'trudged unwillingly to school' as Shakespeare himself had done a century or two previously.

We would have certainly fallen foul of Lexy if we had taken off with Sandy Mor for the day and the retribution would have been severe and perfectly just. There were other occasions when retribution was not quite so just. On one such occasion, Lexy came to school in a very smart outfit which seemed very new to us. When playtime came we did not rush off to our football or our biology lessons in the burn but stood around for a while discussing the new outfit. It was suggested that Lexy should be told how very smart we all thought she looked. This suggestion won immediate and unanimous approval. The next big decision to be made was who the spokesperson should be who would convey this unanimous compliment to the teacher. The seniority rule was applied but one after another - from Willie Wilson downwards - declined to express the 'scholars' feelings to the teacher. When the Iain MacKenzie stratum in the rank order was reached, he was all but persuaded to be the spokesman when, at the very last moment, he proposed very strongly that the next in rank should convey the group's sentiments. This sudden about-turn received immediate strong support from the gang assembled at the foot of the school steps just as Lexy appeared - to make her way out of the school to go to the schoolhouse for her cup of tea. She was visibly taken aback as she saw the 'deputation' which awaited her but it was 'now or never', so, as she looked at us all enquiringly, the author addressed her with as much coolness and politeness as he could bring to bear" Please Miss" - "Yes, Peter?" - "Please Miss, we think you are a toff today". She looked at the spokesman, asked him to follow her back into the school and he was administered with four harsh strokes of the cane, no explanation being offered for such a response to what was a totally genuine compliment. The recipient of the punishment has been very wary ever since in offering genuine compliments to ladies! It is very probable that Lexy was totally taken aback by her sudden and unexpected confrontation with all her pupils at the school steps, she was further nonplussed by the comment made, felt that she had to respond in some way, and chose a response which was spontaneous, but which she probably very much regretted on further reflection.

On frequent return visits to Arnisdale the author would always visit her, he would get a great welcome and they were great pals. Lexy was a fine lady who later married Iain MacCuaig from Corran and both Lexy and Iain passed away a few years ago.

There was another occasion when the rank order in the school was also applied. One day there was a bit of a crisis because the water supply to the school and schoolhouse was non-existent. The supply was from a dam well up Beinn na h-eaglaise behind the school. Willie Wilson, being the senior boy pupil, was asked to go up to investigate lest some dead sheep or deer or other obstacle was blocking the outlet pipe from the dam. However, after an excessively long interval, Willie had not returned, so Iain, being next in line, was despatched up the mountain to investigate what had happened to Willie and what was blocking the pipe. Lexy possibly pondered to herself that perhaps the dead sheep or boulder or whatever was causing the blockage was too big for Willie to remove on his own. When, after another reasonable interval, Iain had not returned, yours truly was sent off on a further investigatory and rescue mission. When the dam and the steep hillside which sloped into the dam was reached, there were Willie and Iain having the time of their lives, rolling big boulders down the mountainside which gathered tremendous momentum, causing wonderful effects and great explosions of water as they hit the dam . This was wonderful fun and not to be avoided at any price so the 'dam busters', boosted by extra recruits, started to dislodge increasingly bigger boulders which produced even more spectacular effects on hitting the dam. When 'next in rank' Gingee appeared on the scene he immediately joined in the great fun.

But - all good times come to an end and four small boys froze, with mouths agape just for a very brief moment, when Lexy herself came into view over the rim of the bowl of the dam! The 'frozen' boys were then transformed immediately into four 'bundles' hurtling down Beinn na h-eaglaise and back into the school - almost as fast as the boulders on their lightning path into the dam a few moments before. Amazingly, I recall no further reprimand when Lexy caught up with us in the classroom. She was probably so relieved to find that we were all OK. On reflection, our irresponsibility had conjured up in Lexy's mind all sorts of dire fates having befallen her pupils as, one by one, they failed to reappear. We had caused Lexy severe worry and placed her in a very difficult situation, with her divided responsibilities between the well behaved pupils remaining in the school and the four about whose fate she probably grew increasingly uncertain as time progressed. We were vagabonds — but boys will be boys!

Despite our misdemeanours, Lexy worked extremely hard on our behalf. I remember that she encouraged each of us as Christmas approached to think up a little piece, such as a song or a poem or a little sketch which we would present at a ceilidh for all the Arnisdale folk. We duly dreamed up a contribution and the subsequent ceilidh featured the school pupils' pieces. Although there were certainly no potential Oscar winners among us, the good folk at the ceilidh, as always, were very complimentary about our very moderate presentations. Although I was in the school for only nine months (August to April), Lexy very kindly presented me with a new Bible on my departure. I very much enjoyed visiting Lexy subsequently whenever possible. Although Lexy and her husband, Iain, had lived for a large number of intervening years in the Lothians, it was good to see them return to Arnisdale for their retirement.

Apart from school, there were many other interesting activities during that continuous period of about ten months which I spent in Arnisdale. I learned many new tricks and skills, there were very many positive experiences and very few negative ones and the latter were very minor. One such related to a feeling of loneliness when I went to bed at night. My self-imposed bedtime was 8.30 p.m. and this, on reflection, was far too early even although I was always up in the morning before 7 a.m. to help with the chores before I went to school. There was a chiming clock in the living room of the house which heralded the arrival of each quarter hour period with a tuneful but noisy acclaim. At home in Glenurquhart, while sharing a bedroom with my older brother (Sandy) and younger one (Bob), I never had any problem in going to sleep and would soon banish any worrying thoughts from my mind. I took some considerable time to adapt to being alone at night. I would try very hard to get to sleep before the next chiming of the bally clock. Because I tried too consciously to sleep - I was less likely to succeed. Then all sorts of thoughts would be conjured up in my mind about my family at home in Glenurquhart, about death and other sombre possibilities. But sleep would eventually intervene and all was well in the morning.

I spent my tenth birthday in Arnisdale and I remember feeling rather worried that I was getting so old, having gone from single to double figures in terms of my age! I have never been worried about advancing years ever since! My only disappointment was that I did not pick up more of the Gaelic language. Since the language was used almost universally in Arnisdale at that time, I got plenty of opportunity to develop an ear for the language and I was understanding more and more of the conversations as time progressed. But I never developed the confidence and facility to speak the language. One issue in this respect is that Aunt Lizzie, while having a very good understanding of the language, never spoke it herself. Her mother and father in Glenurquhart were native speakers, Roddy Mor, of course, was fluent but Aunt Lizzie found herself in a dilemma situation during her teaching days. The conversation, and even the writing in school, of children from Gaelic speaking areas such as Arnsdale, may have been partly in English and partly in Gaelic. Like many other teachers, she may have discouraged use of the Gaelic so that the ability of the pupils in the English language would improve. Aunt Lizzie was an excellent teacher and she would undoubtedly have been very patient and adept at coaching the author in the Gaelic language and in Gaelic conversation. Of course, it is only in retrospect that I regret not picking up conversational abilities, at least, in the Gaelic language and Aunt Lizzie had no way of knowing what aspirations a nine year old boy might have later in life.

If Aunt Lizzie did not help to develop my abilities in Gaelic conversation, she certainly taught me many other skills and things about life in general. But one venture in which she tried and failed was in teaching me how to play the organ. While I like music very much, I have no ear for it - so I was a 'lost cause' from the start. However, I did learn (by rote) to play with one finger of my right hand the tune to the Gaelic song 'Failte Rudha Bhatairnis' (Salute to Waternish), a song which Roddy Mor was sure to sing at the ceilidhs. If I was challenged, even now, the index finger might still find the piano keys to dirl out the tune!

Before going to school in the morning there were the usual chores of feeding the stock, mucking out the byre and stable, and milking the cows to be done. It was a fine routine which was interesting rather than onerous. There was always a welcome from the cows, the dogs, the bull, Dick the horse, the calves, the pig and the cackling of the hens as they anticipated their morning feed. There was further interest too as cows would approach calving, and even more so when there was a shiny wet new arrival, tottering around on spindly uncertain legs, trying instinctively to reach the udder to get their first vital suckle of colostrum. Was it a bull or heifer calf? And there was always great interest in the colour pattern which might provide the first suggestion of a name such as Spotty, White Nose or Rosy, for all the calves were accorded a name very soon after birth. Another responsibility which I was given after the wether lambs had been sold was to go up to the fields adjacent to Achadh a'Ghlinne each morning to check the ewe hoggs. These were home-wintered on the hay fields and they had to survive the winter on what they could glean themselves from what was left over in the field from the summer period of plenty. Only very rarely did snow lie in the area so what was left of the grass was always visible and available to the hoggs. However, round the perimeter of the fields beside the dykes and the fences were plenty of bramble bushes with tasty bites for the hoggs lurking below. As winter progressed and the pickings left on the fields dwindled, the hoggs would seek out the 'goodies' under the bramble bushes and often got stuck - and the more they struggled, the more they got caught up in adjacent bramble shoots. So quite often on the regular morning check, a hogg would be found totally trapped in the prickly web of bramble bushes. One had first to control the hogg so as to stop it struggling even more and then set out to remove the bramble shoots from the wool - one by one. Both hogg and rescuer were very relieved when the last prickly shoot was extricated from the wool, the beast was freed from its prickly trap and the rescuer could return to get ready for school. If the regular morning visit to the hoggs was incident-free, there would often be time before school to nip down to the goodly crop of tall whin (gorse) bushes just below the steading with the bushman saw to cut a supply of firewood blocks from dead bushes. This tidied up the whins, creating space for grazing cows and sheep and helped to fill the remaining space in the peat shed with a good supply of whin firewood to complement the usual coal and peat fuels for the fire.

On the first dry Saturday in October, the remaining potatoes would be lifted by graip and the Golden Wonders, Kerrs Pinks and Edzell Blues would be carefully separated in the tattie pit which would be established in the driest area of the field. The tatties would be protected from winter frosts by being given a thick coat of dry bracken covered over with a good depth of soil. Then a drainage channel would be constructed round the perimeter of the pit to divert winter rains away from the pit to ensure that the potatoes remained dry, as well as being protected from the frost. The pit would be opened at intervals over the winter for supplies as required for household use. Potatoes were a hugely important and treasured component of the daily diet, the universal liking being for dry (high dry matter) varieties and the Kerrs Pinks, Golden Wonders and Edzell Blues met that requirement admirably.

Without warning, on returning from school one day, the pig was no more. Instead, there were various vats in the wash- house with pieces of meat steeped in pickle. The cured meat formed a regular component of the winter diet. The poor pig had been put to sleep humanely using a captive bolt. A new young pig would soon be acquired and be accommodated in comfort to dine regularly on a fine diet of household scraps, skim milk and butter milk, totally unaware of its impending fate when it grew big enough. The lone pig was not only a unique pig on the farm but also very often within the entire Parish of Glenelg. In a Statistical Account of the Parish around that time , the livestock inventory itemises very large numbers of poultry, sheep and cattle, a few horses but just one pig! The pig was totally unaware that it received such a unique mention in such an auspicious publication!

On going outside to start the chores early one morning in October, the activity and noise level in the bay indicated that another regular component of the winter diet was about to materialise. The seagulls were there in huge numbers, they were swooping down to the surface of the sea in a frenzy of activity and were creating a great din in their apparent excitement. The author surveyed the scene from the front of the house in wondrous disbelief at such behaviour and clamour when he was joined by the emerging Roddy Mor. The youngster's question "What on earth is going on there?" brought the immediate excited response from Roddy Mor - "Oh - the sgadan, boy, the sgadan!" So the herring had arrived on their annual visit to Loch Hourn as their forebears had done for hundred of years before. On going down to the shore of the bay, the first three to four feet of water was a seething mass of herring sprats which were being gobbled up in great quantities by marauding mackerel and dogfish.

Very soon there was great excitement throughout Arnisdale - for a huge component of the winter diet of the folk had arrived. The little rowing boats were soon out to harvest their share, for cleaning and then salting away in the barrel, to be drawn on regularly for almost every meal throughout the winter and into the spring.

It was not long after mid-day when the first herring drifters began to arrive in the bay from places such as Mallaig, Kyle of Lochalsh and Lochcarron. News travels fast. By evening there was a great mass of boats in the bay. Those which were first to arrive were getting lower and lower in the water as the holds were filled with the 'silver darlings' - and one by one they would set off laden for their nearest port and market. The departing boats were replaced very quickly by more incoming boats. It was not long before all the Arnisdale villagers had their barrels full and a large component of their winter diet secured. Salt herring in most households would be served at every lunchtime throughout the winter (with perhaps the exception of Sundays when a piece of boiled mutton might be on offer). The boiled herring would be accompanied by good supplies of Golden Wonders or Kerrs Pinks and cupfuls of milk when available. Even for a child, the meal was always eagerly awaited and it was a diet of which one never tired.

There was also excitement one Saturday morning when John Angus MacRae from Beolary in Glenelg came over to the Lodge stables to shoe the horses. The needs of the placid Major from the Lodge and equally manageable Dick from the farm were attended to first. Hooves were pared with the rasp as required and the horses were re-shod in preparing them for the spring ploughing and other cultivations. With John Angus's skill in handling the horses and in the shoeing process, that early part of the job was straightforward. The next in line for attention were the three Icelandic ponies which had been delivered by MacLennan's boat from Mallaig a few months previously. Thus they had been around the

Lodge fields for some time during which they had been fed with daily supplements of hay and got used to the folk who tended them and to their new environment. Perhaps, like old Major and Dick, they too would now be fairly placid and the shoeing could be completed reasonably quickly. Each pony in turn was bridled and held fast by Ludovic Fraser or Ian MacCuaig or Kenny Fletcher while John Angus got to work. Despite John Angus going about his work in a cool, calm and collected manner, and much gentle vocal encouragement to each pony in turn to 'take it easy' and 'settle down', there followed great displays of bucking and kicking by the ponies and other violent objections to the attempts to get them shod. However, John Angus, Ludovic, Ian and Kenny stuck to the task valiantly with great patience, resolution and skill and eventually the farrier and the handlers won the day - and the fiery ponies were duly shod. They were now ready for their treks over hill tracks and rough hill terrain to bring home the shot stags and hinds to the Lodge.

A livestock handling challenge of a different kind cropped up one evening in late August when one of the cows over the Loch at Lea, in aspiring to harvest the tasty grasses in the far reaches of a peat bog, just took a few steps too many and got herself thoroughly stuck. Donald MacKenzie, being the sole crofter in Lea along with his wife Lisa, had to call for extra help. He came speeding across the loch on his outboard motor driven little boat and sounded the alarm in Corran. As always, neighbours immediately responded to such a call for help and soon two or three boats were prepared to make the crossing. The author and Iain MacKenzie were never too far away from any excitement and although their nine year old physiques rendered them useless in terms of providing any help, they had got to be in on this rescue attempt, so off they sped across the water with the men for Lea. The poor old cow seemed doomed to its fate in the dreadful bog. There was animated discussion in the Gaelic and a frenzied collecting of planks and ropes, while the midges were becoming unbearable in the warm humid atmosphere of a late August evening with little or no wind. The useless boys spent the time surveying the scene at the bog, running back to report to Lisa at the croft house of the sombre 'state of play', consuming the fine 'pieces' of home made scones and blackcurrant jam she was preparing and then running back up the hill to check on progress - or the lack of it. Donald had about four cows so the loss of one was very serious. That was one great incentive to extricate the poor cow. Another was the inherent determination of all the able-bodied men not to see any animal succumb to such a fate. They were very dependent on their livestock, there was a great empathy between man and beast and they would do all in their power to prevent suffering. There was also the challenge involved. They refused to concede defeat in extremely difficult situations. With careful planning, ingenuity and power, gradually more of the cow appeared above the surface of the bog and eventually the cow was extricated. The men - and the cow - were equally exhausted - but all was well and the mercy mission was accomplished. There has always been great neighbourliness in these communities.

On returning across the loch, there were concerns about the whereabouts of two lost boys for there had been no seeking of leave of absence or even reporting of intentions. Most folk were on their way to the ceilidh dance in the school that evening so while there was undoubtedly anger on the part of the guardians on the irresponsibility of the two lost boys, this was thankfully demonstrated as relief that both the boys and the Lea cow were all OK. Soon everybody was at the dance and the triumph of the extrication of the Lea cow from the bog formed a major part of the news exchanges in the early stages of the proceedings.

The ceilidh - dances in Arnisdale were great affairs that seemed to start properly around 11 p.m. and they would go on until 4 or 5 o'clock in the morning. All in the district would attend from the oldest to the youngest. Local musicians such as Donald and Peter Fletcher, Peter MacRae and 'Do' MacKillop from up the loch, along with the MacLaren family (Donald, Jessie, Effie and Betty), would provide the music on the 'box', fiddle, the pipes and the organ. There was dancing, singing, much foot tapping and clapping by the old folk who were no longer able to dance, and regular breaks for sumptuous teas, sandwiches and home baking. They were great community affairs and the 'goings on' would remain talking points in the village for days and weeks after the event.

There were also many other regular social occasions. These included Whist Drives and Bridge Drives in the School and much informal ceilidhing, with visits to eachother's houses in the winter evenings for a good blether and the enjoyment of the great teas and 'goodies' which would be provided at an appropriate stage of the evening. There was great togetherness, awareness of and the sharing of problems, and genuine joy and pleasure at the successes of neighbours. There was great collective sadness during illness and when deaths occurred. The folk in Arnisdale were just like one big family and every case of illness and death was felt very personally by all. It was the essence of 'mutual care in the community'.

While Arnisdale was a fairly independent community, there was always awareness of events and problems in neighbouring places such as Kinlochourn and the clachans around the shore of Loch Hourn such as Skiary, Runival, Barrisdale, Lea, Crowlick, Caolasmor, Rarsaidh, Port Luinge, Mialairidh and Sandaig. Likewise there was a very close affinity with Glenelg. The local Doctor was based in Glenelg, the Arnisdale Mails which came in Calum Garde's boat from Kyle of Lochalsh were sorted in Donald and Charlotte Chisholm's Post Office there and, of course, the only hotel in the area was in Glenelg. The author remembers as a nine year old, attending Whist Drives and a fine Christmas Party hosted by the proprietors, the kindly Weir family, in the old Glenelg Hotel in 1946. There was great sadness in the whole community when the news came through of the terrible fire which destroyed the old hotel early in 1947.

Homework from school could not have been that onerous because the author has little memory of doing any apart from going over spellings and reading for the next day. The reading was tough going and probably much advanced in relation to our tender years. I was probably encouraged to get my homework done soon after getting home from school and the evening feeding of stock and milking was done before tea-time. After that, there was time for leisure. Willie the Post might arrive around 6 p.m. with the mails which would include the daily newspaper ('The Bulletin') and perhaps the regular weekly letter from my mother and father in Glenurquhart. Aunt Lizzie would send return letters weekly and I enjoyed writing a weekly epistle to my family in which, apparently, I went into intricate detail about all the happenings at school, on the farm and in Arnisdale in general. Later in the evening before bed-time, the author and Rory Mor would have their nightly game of cribbage. It was a great game, both of us were very fond of it and it kept us on our toes regarding our strategies and mental arithmetic. We were great pals, he had a superb way with children and I used to accompany him everywhere he went whenever I got the chance. Folk used to say that I was like a dog at his heel. He was a wonderful man, he was patient, he had a great sense of humour, he was great at teaching me new tricks and skills and was always very encouraging. He had a great range of talents and was a true Highland gentleman. Only on one occasion did I refuse to do what he asked me. We went over to Eilanreach near Gleneig one evening with John Donald MacLeod from Sandaig for three fearsome and fit looking Blackface tups on the old Austin which
Roddy Mor had converted into a lorry. There was little space on the platform of the truck and the containing sides were fairly low. Each tup in turn had its two forelegs and one rear leg bound together with strong cord and all the tups were then lifted into the back of the lorry. The three, lying on their sides, occupied almost the whole space. Roddy Mor asked me to go in the back with the tups to keep an eye on them just in case any one escaped from its leg binding. With the prospect of the very steep inclines and Z bends on the Arnisdale gravel road in front of us, the low sides of the lorry and three big, very fit, struggling tups for company, I refused as politely as I could to go on the back with them. I was terrified of the prospect. Roddy Mor did not question my response - he obviously read my innermost feelings and nervousness very sensitively. I duly went in the front of the Austin with Roddy Mor while

the unlucky John Donald had to accompany the tups in the back. John Donald was dropped off at Sandaig - and the tups were still on board with leg bindings intact when we got to Arnisdale!

So my continuous ten months period in Arnisdale was fairly eventful and very memorable. Of my school friends, many have stayed on or returned to the old homes. Iain MacKenzie is at the time of writing, resident in the Farm House as the estate manager, Flora and Morag are near neighbours in Camusban, Gingee still returns from time to time on holiday, Willie Sandaig has his grandmother's house in the village and returns on frequent holidays, while Sheena is back in the old family home in Corran where she runs her tea-hut in the summer months. It is always great to see them all again and to reminisce on very happy, and sometimes eventful, days in the Arnisdale school.

A decision was obviously made between Aunt Lizzie and my mother and father that I should return to Glenurquhart during the Easter holiday. The news was broken to me by Aunt Lizzie who explained that I could come back to Arnisdale as often as I wished. That message was reassuring and consoling. I loved Arnisdale and its people and my feelings were exactly the same for my family and friends in Glenurquhart. So again it was a matter of going back to home from home.

On the last day in Arnisdale School I was presented with a fine new Bible by Lexy and assured them all that I would be back among them at the next summer's holiday, so there was no grief in our parting.

The way back to Glenurquhart was not to be by the same route as we took ten months before - via Inverness, the train to Kyle, boat to Glenelg and the car to Arnisdale. A man from Glasgow had come to buy Roddy Mor's old Wolseley car, which had stayed tucked up in the garage for all the time I had been there, and arrangements were made for Aunt Lizzie and I to get a lift with him as far as Invergarry. So off we set after farewells to Roddy Mor and all the good folk of Arnisdale. I remember some comment being made about the steering on the Wolseley and there were some anxious moments as it veered dangerously from side to side on the treacherous Arnisdale road, with great precipices awaiting in parts any faulty turn of the wheel! However, the Arnisdale road was negotiated safely, although somewhat unsurely, and then it was on to Glenelg, over Mam Ratagan, to Shiel Bridge, on to Cluanie and there turning right onto the old road over to Tomdoun. On that road (now disused because of the Loch Loyne Hydro Electric dam) to Tomdoun and Invergarry in early April, I remember seeing the most massive herds of red deer (mainly stags but also hinds) which I have ever seen. They were loafing around close to the roadside trying obviously to keep going as best they could on the meagre poor quality hill forage available until the new shoots of Spring would start to restore their magnificence of the previous Autumn. We parted company with the old Wolseley at Invergarry and then awaited MacBraynes' bus to take us to Drumnadrochit - and there caught the bus to take us up the Glen to Balnain. Our arrival was to be a surprise. As we walked the final half mile from Balnain to my home in Lochletter, my pace quickened excitedly. I did not want to be spotted prematurely and, luckily, nobody was visible outside my home. I passed the living room window quickly and moved in from the front door without knocking, through the porch and lobby into the living room. Mouths were agape for a moment and then there were the joyous reunions. It was great to be home again from the other great home which I had left behind.

Soon I was outside investigating what changes may have occurred in the interim and checking up on all my favourite haunts. There were many exchanges of experiences with my mother, father, brothers and sisters and soon I was meeting up with all my old Lochletter and Balnain pals again. I sensed some amusement on occasions when my friends greeted me and it did not take very long to determine its source. My accent had changed during the ten months I had been in Arnisdale. I had developed a West Coast twang. The 'ducks' had become 'tooks' but soon, I suppose, I reverted quickly back to my native Glenurquhart accent, as children do so very quickly.

**Top Left**   The pupils in Arnisdale School in the session before the author's enrolment.  L to R  Iain (Ruaridh) MacLeod, Calum MacLeod, Morag MacIntyre, Iain MacGillivray, Willie MacLeod, Nellie MacKenzie, Sheena Stewart, Iain MacKenzie and Flora MacKenzie.   **Right.**   Some of the Arnisdale School pupils after the author's period in the school with their teacher Lexy Campbell (later Mrs Iain MacCuaig).  L to R. at rear – Iain MacGillivray and Iain MacKenzie.  Front – Sheena Stewart, Jimmy Dickie and Mary Beaton.

**Middle Left.**   Anthony, Susan and Martin  as toddlers.  When it came to bedtime stories, high on their list of priorities was to hear again about some of the escapades of their father and his friends in Arnisdale School.   **Right.**   The tiny strip of land between the school playground (bottom right hand corner) and Allt an Sgoil (the school burn) which was converted into the football pitch by the flailing of the tall lush foliage by many little feet.  The Lodge and farm are beyond.

**Bottom Left.**   The old dam which at one time provided the water for the school can just be seen in the bottom left hand corner of the picture.   The school lies just to the right of the burn (Allt an Sgoil) as it joins the sea.   **Right.**  The precipitous slope from the dam to the school down which four wayward small boys hurtled at great speed in 1946, pursued by a legitimately furious teacher.

**Top Left.**   The fields beyond Glenfield near Achadh a' Ghlinne in the Arnisdale Glen where the hoggs had to be checked each morning and often extricated from the bramble bushes before going to school.   **Right.**   A brief stop for a photograph at the lifting by graip of the precious potato crop in October.   L to R.   Ina Kennedy, Morag and Rena MacDonald, Aunt Lizzie with Roddy Mor and the ever present collie Whisky in front.

**Middle Left.**   On going outside one morning in October to start the morning chores with the cows and other stock, there was frenzied activity of the seagulls in the bay.  Roddy Mor's immediate analysis of the situation was 'Oh – the sgadan boy, the sgadan'.  The herring had arrived for their annual sojourn in Loch Hourn.   **Right.**   Soon after mid-day, the first of the herring drifters had arrived in the Bay.

**Bottom Left.**   The Lodge stables in the middle foreground where John Angus MacRae from Beolary in Glenelg stuck manfully to his task in fitting shoes to the fiery Icelandic ponies.   **Right.**   Kenny Fletcher (left) and Ludovic Fraser who along with Iain MacCuaig succeeded in holding on to the ponies until they were fully shod.

**Top Left.** Lea (centre of picture) on the Knoydart shore of Loch Hourn opposite Arnisdale where one of Donald Lea's cows got herself almost totally immersed in a peat bog with only her nostrils, upper head and ears showing above the surface. Boatloads of able bodied Arnisdale men sped across the loch in a rescue mission. **Right.** Donald MacKenzie, Lea, his wife Liza, daughter Mary and the grandchildren.

**Middle Left.** The story of the rescue of the Lea cow from its grimy grave formed a major topic of conservation at the Arnisdale ceilidh dance later in the evening. The picture is one of a more recent dance in progress with Charlie MacTavish and Len Morrison to the fore. **Right.** Donald MacLaren, Arnisdale Estate head stalker (right) with daughters Effie (Fay) and Betty. They along with mother Jessie were regular music makers at the Arnisdale dances. Others in the picture are Back Row (L to R) Archie MacLean and Sandy MacAskill. Front Left. Angus Campbell.

**Bottom Left.** Johnny Sinclair (left) who ran the 'mail car' between Arnisdale and Glenelg to connect with Calum Garde's boat on the main run from Glenelg to Kyle. With him is Archie MacLean (centre) and Willie Campbell. **Centre.** Donald and Charlotte Chisholm who sorted the Arnisdale incoming mail at their Glenelg Post Office. **Right.** Donald and Charlotte with the children Janet, Ishbel and baby Alice.

**Top Left.**   The old Glenelg Hotel.  There was great shock and sadness in the whole community in January 1947 when the news came through that the hotel was completely destroyed by fire.  **Right.**  The first 'Willie the Post' (Willie MacKenzie) with Roddy Mackay in Lea.  Willie sorted the Arnisdale Mail along with Peggy Ann after Johnny Sinclair arrived with it from Glenelg each evening and then proceeded to do his Arnisdale deliveries.  Willie also delivered the mail up the loch to Caolasmor and across the water to Barrisdale and Lea three times each week.

**Middle Left.**   Roddy Mor and the author would have a few games of cribbage each evening.   Behind is Maggie 'Lea' and Aunt Lizzie.  **Right.**  John Donald MacLeod from Upper Sandaig who rode on the back of the little lorry along with the three Blackface tups collected from Eilanreach on the gravel surfaced Arnisdale road with its precipitous braes and Z bends.

**Bottom Left.**   The start of the old road from Cluanie to Tomdoun with Cluanie Hotel in the foreground.   Part of this road was submerged under the extended Loch Loyne following the construction of the Loch Loyne Dam in the 1950s.  **Right.**  The old road and some of the old bridges emerge from the depths of Loch Loyne in 1997 when the water level was lowered temporarily.   Mieke Groot from the Netherlands proves that the old structure is still quite sound (photographed by Mieke's husband Ruurd).

**Top Left.** Another portion of the old Cluanie-Tomdoun road which 'emerged from the deep' in 1997 with the lowering of Loch Loyne. It is running westwards here on the north bank of Loch Loyne towards Cluanie. **Right.** Tomdoun Hotel around the 1930 period.

**Middle Left.** There were great herds of deer close to the roadside doing their best to survive until the new shoots of spring arrived to lead into the summer period of plenty. **Right.** MacBraynes' bus was the transport link from Invergarry to Drumnadrochit with a further MacBraynes' link from Drum up Glenurquhart. The MacDonald brothers from Glenurquhart with their families. Sandac (left) and Jock (Seanair) were well known 'worthies' who served MacBraynes as bus drivers throughout their working lives on the Fort William to Inverness and Glenurquhart to Inverness routes.

**Bottom Left.** Lochletter bridge in GlenUrquhart (L to R.) Brothers Bob and Sandy, and sister Christine. **Right.** Back among old pals in the Glen.

# Chapter 3

**Arnisdale revisited**

Following the end of schooldays in Arnisdale, the author spent every long summer holiday at the farm for as long as Roddy Mor and Lizzie remained as the tenants - up to May 1952. And after they retired to Glenelg - a visit there was not complete without a run over to Arnisdale to meet up with old friends and to inspect the old haunts. This re-visiting has continued over the years and has been intensified in recent months in the search for history, old tales and to collect photographs - of people and places - and of the flora and fauna.

As a child, it was always exciting to return and to renew regularly all the old acquaintances. One exciting additional opportunity on the farm from around the age of ten, was that of accompanying the men and their dogs to the sheep gatherings on the high tops of Beinn nan Caorach, Beinn Chlachach, Druim na firean and the other hirsels. There was the day in the middle of July when a newly born lamb was found on the very top of Beinn nan Caorach. A rogue tup must have been on the loose to achieve such a late conception (late February) for the tups were removed from the ewes in mid-January after being out with the ewes for about seven weeks. A very clear memory is that of feeling the effects of summer heat in mid-July as one climbed up the slopes but then, on reaching the high tops, the chilliness similar to a winter's day was felt - with the combination of a much lower temperature and the strong biting wind.

There was another occasion as the bridle path on Beinn Chlachach was being scaled, Roddy Mor stopped for a spy on the blar east of Achadh a'Ghlinne (Blar nan Each) - to check on the sheep and cattle (the fifteen month old stirks) grazing in that area. He seemed to focus long and hard on a particular location and then, handing the glass to his young 'assistant' said "See what you make of that, Peter" pointing to a particular spot. As the author trained the glass on the object, he noticed that it was black and was moving - flapping about a bit. It seemed almost like a crow flapping its wings and that was the response of the author to Roddy Mor - "I think it is a crow!" "No", Roddy Mor said, "I think it is one of the stirks in a peat bog". So off the two of us set with all speed. When we reached the spot - sure enough - it was one of the stirks, weighing close on 3 hundredweights (336 pounds or 150 Kg) - totally immersed in the bog except for the mouth, nostrils, the crown of the head and the ears - and the poor beast was still flapping them and doing its best to keep the pestering flies away.

Roddy Mor sunk his cromag into the peat bank, took off his bonnet and jacket, rolled up his sleeves and got one hand under the lower jaw of the beast, with the other hand taking a good grip of one of the ears. He tried to lift its head and moved it sideways, this way and that, hoping that the beast might get a firmer footing for either its front or hind legs and help to propel itself out of the saturated bog - as Roddy Mor, and his ten year old companion, did their very best to pull.

Roddy Mor, never one to give up a battle without giving his all, appeared despondent - although not openly admitting it. The beast was being held by tremendous surface tension forces and, as it did its best to struggle, it just kept sinking lower and lower into the morass. Help for the poor beast had not arrived a moment too soon and efforts to save it might still prove to be futile. Only Roddy Mor's firm grip of its lower jaw was preventing the only remaining part of the beast which was still above the surface - the mouth, the nostrils and its ears - from sinking below the peaty porridge to its doom.

The author suggested that he should run the three or so miles to Arnisdale and get reinforcements while Roddy Mor did his very best to keep the mouth and nostrils above the surface of its imminent watery grave.

Roddy Mor agreed immediately - so off the youngster sped. As the first few hundred yards were being covered, the able bodied men who would be sought were going through the author's mind - Ludovic Fraser, Donald MacLaren, Kenny Fletcher, Willie the Post, Alan MacAskill etc. etc. Their likely whereabouts was being worked out in the speeding youngster's mind, as well as the most direct route to locate them. The distance from the drowning beast was increasing rapidly and that from the would-be rescuers was dwindling with every passing second. There was no point in diverting energy to ask oneself questions such as - is there any chance that help will reach the spot in time? There was a need only for totally positive thinking! But then there was a great yell from behind - "Peter!!". The youngster stopped in his tracks, turned round for the first time since he had left Roddy Mor. He could not believe his eyes! There was Roddy Mor waving in exhausted triumph - for the bedraggled, filthy beast was standing beside him with arched back - a miserable looking, wet, exhausted thing on four tottering legs.

By the time the unbelieving youngster got back to man and beast, Roddy Mor had cleaned himself up a bit with lumps of sphagnum moss and, with the same material, he was now clearing the worst of the thin peaty porridge off the head, neck, shoulders, back and loin of the exhausted beast.

How did Roddy Mor succeed in such a Herculean task? Not even he could fully explain the outcome. Roddy was in his mid-50s at the time, he was still a very strong, fit man. He was also very determined - with a great will to win. And he had a great love for his beasts and a great way with them - an empathy which helped him to get the best out of them - whether it was the cattle - or working horses - or the sheep. The drowning beast knew him well, he had reared it on the bucket from the day of its birth, it had no fear of him, it trusted him - and perhaps as he made his last great effort, he encouraged the beast to work with him - to get all four legs working together in the depths of the bog - and with man and beast working desperately together - together they succeeded - with the pulling, the swimming and the driving - out of the dreadful bog.

Sin thu bhalaich, Ruaridh Mor! (Good for you, Roddy Mor!)

That was a diversion from the sheep gathering on Beinn Chlachach - but soon that objective was also under way again.

Getting a good gather off the hill was not easy - with all the rocks and hiding places for cunning hill sheep, along with the risk of misty conditions on the tops. In addition, some sheep would stray over the march into Eilanreach, Glen Shiel and Kinlochourn territory. So some sheep from these estates would often come in with an Arnisdale gather as well as some sheep with two or more fleeces - because they had managed to escape the gatherings for the clipping in previous years. Sometimes the Shiel shepherd would comb the march areas and take his gather of Glenshiel ewes which strayed out of their territory down to Arnisdale and shepherd his strays by road to Glenelg and then over Mam Ratagan to Shiel Bridge. The Glenshiel Highland garrons which were used to carry stags and hinds off the hill during the shooting season would also often be seen in Arnisdale hill territory in high summer. The considerable distances between localities across the hills meant nothing to fit ponies, hill sheep and good shepherds in these areas.

Between the sheep gatherings and the clippings, work continued down on the farm according to weather conditions - at hay making in particular. It was a job that seemed to span two and sometimes three of the summer months - being prolonged by wet weather and poor drying conditions. Roddy Mor decided to become less dependent on the horses by purchasing a little BMB tractor which was hand driven. It had two large spade lug wheels and two hand held shafts containing all the controls. There were various attachments for it such as an ordinary plough, a drill plough (for the potatoes), a mower and also a simple fan-shaped shovel device for lifting the potatoes.

Both Rena MacDonald and Maggie Cameron (Maggie Lea) continued to provide considerable help on the farm and also in the farm house when conditions were unsuitable for weather-dependent farm jobs. Rena and Maggie were extremely competent in all that they did and were great fun. There were few dull moments around the farm. The author almost looked forward to wet days when there could be no hay making or sheep shearing. On such days, Rena might do a big baking of doughnuts, pancakes, scones and other goodies. Rena had few equals in these arts. These were some of the treasured bonuses of the wet days. Maggie also recalls one incident when the author returned from collecting some household requirements from Peggy Ann's shop. She was fully aware of Peggy Ann's generosity in providing a copious handful of sweets to most children who called at her shop. When the author returned from his errand, Maggie requested a sweet. The youngster indicated that he did not receive any sweets from Peggy Ann, but Maggie quite correctly disbelieved this and gave chase. Fit and fast though the youngster was, Maggie must have been even faster, overtook him, captured him and plunged her hand into a pocket to find the expected sweets. Alas, she went into the wrong pocket - and instead of finding a sweet - her finger found a fish hook - for that was the pocket which housed the spare hooks for fishing down at the pier. The unfortunate Maggie was well and truly hooked! The barb was well embedded into the flesh and all attempts at the farm to release the 'catch' from the hook failed. When Mrs MacIver, the district nurse, who lived about 400 yards away from the farm, also failed in a valiant bid to separate Maggie and the fish hook, Dr Devon had to be summoned urgently from Glenelg. However, the nurse's call to Glenelg got the response that Dr Devon was not at home - she was over in Glenshiel doing some salmon fishing. With Maggie in increasing agony, Dr Devon was summoned from her salmon fishing. She responded to the call, sped back home to Glenelg, collected her medical bag and rushed over to Arnisdale to attend to the emergency. When she saw the nature of Maggie's predicament and had established the cause, she was certainly not amused! She yanked the hook out without ceremony and returned forthwith to her fishing! Maggie, despite the pain, saw the funny side of it all, as she always did - and still does!

Around 1948, the MacLaren family left Arnisdale when father Donald retired and they moved to Inverness. This family with a wide range of musical talents had been a great asset in Arnisdale and they were a key part of providing the music at the ceilidh dances. They were a ceilidh band in themselves with father Donald on the pipes or fiddle, mother Jessie on the organ, Betty on the box and Effie on the fiddle. Such families and their talents are not easy to replace in Highland communities.

However, Arnisdale was fortunate with the replacement gamekeeper - he was Angus Beaton - a fine piper and he also enjoyed the ceilidhs. Angus and his wife Margaret had a young family - Jimmy, Mary, Anne and Iain. Margaret's sister, Ina, also made her home with them - so one vibrant and interesting family was replaced by another.

As well as the resident folk, the Arnisdale population was always greatly boosted in the summer when the many natives who worked in other parts returned home for their summer holiday period. There was always great excitement and a big influx of holiday-makers at the time of the Glasgow Fair - because the majority of the Arnisdale exiles appeared to work in Glasgow or in the adjoining areas.

Although at that time few people had cars, Arnisdale still had passing traffic in the summer time - mainly of hikers on foot or on their bicycles and tandems. Many would walk or cycle down the Glen from Kinlochourn and they would be independent in terms of accommodation requirements - because they carried their tents and camping equipment in their big rucksacks. When some of these first came to Arnisdale, they fell for the place and returned annually over very many years. One such was John

Thomson who set up a little semi-permanent home in Arnisdale in his little hut which was situated in the field between the boathouse and the school. John was a very keen photographer who built up a big library of photographs of people and places in Arnisdale.

Another hiker who returned to Arnisdale on a regular basis after his first 'baptism' was Victor Corbett from Belfast (See Chapter 31). Victor was also very adept with his camera and many of the pictures which Victor took of Arnisdale folk at work and play are interspersed through these pages.

The author recalls Victor's first arrival in Arnisdale along with his brother, Harold and another friend, Brendan Hogan - who hailed from Dublin. It was in the summer of 1949 that the author and Aunt Lizzie were on their way up to Achadh a'Ghlinne to check on some sheep in the late afternoon of one of the very worst of Arnisdale summer days - when the 'monsoon' poured down from the heavens all day long. At the gate of the Achadh they met three badly bedraggled hikers who had obviously walked down from Kinlochourn through the day - talk about the joys of summer! Greetings were exchanged as the parties met and there were comments about the dreadful weather on which all were of the same opinion! Then one of the hikers asked if they could get into a barn or byre for the night as their tents were waterlogged. Agreement was soon reached that the hay barn at the farm which was half-filled with the new hay crop would be a suitable place for the night. When the author and his aunt returned from the Achadh, having checked their sheep, the three Irish lads looked quite different -having doffed their oilskins and they were now drying out a bit.

An invitation was extended to come into the farmhouse later in the evening. The invitation was gratefully accepted and a fine ceilidh resulted. Victor and Harold were accompanied by their tin whistles, Roddy Mor took down the chanter from the shelf, Lizzie played the organ to accompany her singing, there was comparisons of Irish and Scots Gaelic - and of course, there was the supper - tea, sandwiches and home baking. Lasting friendships were formed. Victor also forged strong friendships with Angus Beaton and his family, with the Campbells in Galder, Glenelg and with Archie and Barbara MacLellan in Mallaig. Victor returned regularly to enjoy these associations and was accompanied after his first visit by his wife Margaret and later by their son Garry. These lasting bonds were very important to Victor and his family and were greatly appreciated by Roddy Mor, Lizzie, Angus Beaton and his family and by their many other friends in the area. It is intriguing to know the little things which remain in the memory from the first encounters in these long friendships. On a visit to Victor and Margaret in Belfast in 1993, Victor was reminiscing about that first very dreich introduction to Arnisdale - and then the memories of the fine ceilidh and hospitality in the farmhouse later in the evening. "I remember how much the three of us enjoyed the tea - and I remember how good Lizzie's sardine sandwiches, scones and pancakes tasted". On visiting Aunt Lizzie soon afterwards, the author gave her a full report of his visit to Belfast and on Victor, Margaret and Garry and mentioned that Victor had been reminiscing about that first ceilidh in the Arnisdale farmhouse and how much he and his friends had enjoyed the spread that she had prepared for them. She smiled and then said "Oh yes, I remember it so well - and I think I gave them sardine sandwiches". How proud the sardine sandwiches would have felt if they had known that, 44 years on, they were still equally well remembered by the now not so young Victor in Belfast and the ninety-six year old hostess of that ceilidh-supper so long ago in Arnisdale.

One of the great joys of Arnisdale so fondly remembered by the author is the great variety of activities and sources of amusement and recreation both in the work situation and outwith the daily chores.

On a dry evening of an Arnisdale summer, a fair number of boys and youths would get together for a game of football on one of three locations - on the field beside the Dry Island (Eilean Tioram) in Camusban, in one of Roddy Mor's fields along the shoreline, or on the blar just behind Alan MacAskill's house in Corran (the venue for the shinty matches of old - involving both girls and boys which Johan (nee MacDonald) describes in her own memories in Chapter 13).

Among the contestants in these games would be the Camusban contingent - Charlie MacTavish, Iain Sinclair, Willie Wilson, Iain MacGillivray and the MacLeod boys - Ruaridh, Calum and Willie, the holidaymakers at the farm, the author, his older brother Sandy and younger brother Bob, and the Coulags from Corran - Willie MacKenzie, Iain MacKenzie and Angus Murchison. With jackets or jumpers as goal posts - full blooded encounters raged into the darkness on many an evening. A challenge was never issued to the old rivals, Glenelg - which is a pity - for, without doubt, that would have made another good story!

In that era too, perhaps Arnisdale's last shinty match to date was staged - but it could never compare with the great battle staged between Arnisdale and Glenelg in the early 1930s which is recorded elsewhere in these pages (See Chapter 18). On his first return from Arnisdale to his home in Glenurquhart in the spring of 1947, the author was surprised to find all his old school friends playing shinty with their home made camans. It had not been played by these boys previously but the returning ex-servicemen in the Glen and a few other enthusiasts had got the old game going again in the district - and boys very quickly follow the lead of their elders in sporting pursuits. The author soon cut and shaped his own caman and great enthusiasm for the old game developed very quickly. On subsequent vacations in Arnisdale, the author soon enthused his old class-mate, Iain MacKenzie, and they were soon scouring the sparse Arnisdale woods for branches of the appropriate shape. Their most productive 'woodland' was the row of elderberry trees which grew along the edge of the roadside field opposite the farmhouse. One-a-side games followed on regular occasions when these two enthusiastic young fellows were looking for outlets for their not inconsiderable energies.

Fishing for little cuddies and a wide range of other fish off the pier was a very regular recreation when even a few minutes became available between jobs on the farm. It only took about one minute to get to the pier and another to get back to work again - it was like having private fishing on one's doorstep. On one occasion, when fishing with young Alasdair MacIver, the son of the then District Nurse, a strange fish head was seen appearing from a hole in the concrete foundations of the pier. Alasdair's father was quickly summoned and he extricated a conger eel of over one yard in length. The next day, a sumptuous high tea with fresh conger eel as the main dish, was enjoyed by all the 'fishermen' in the Nurse's cottage. On other occasions, the author would go out in the boat with Iain and Willie MacKenzie to the good fishing banks which were well known to them - close to Sgeir Leathann - just south of Corran on the route to Barrisdale. There, with the darrow, plentiful supplies of a wide range of fish would be caught - including saithe, cod and mackerel. The catch, as always, would be shared with the neighbours on the return to Arnisdale.

Although the author was never a participant in the fishing, there was one occasion each year when he would enter the 'wash-house' next to the farmhouse first thing in the morning - to be confronted with a good catch of salmon and sea trout occupying the big sink. This booty was also surreptitiously shared with neighbours and friends. No questions were asked about the origins - of who the successful fishers were, where and how the fish had been caught - because it was understood that no answers to such questions would be given! When first eye to eye contact was made with Roddy Mor on such mornings, the mischievous boyish grin which creased his fine features was the only response that would be forthcoming.

When the author first went to Arnisdale in 1946, he was surprised by the apparently complete absence of rabbits because his home area of Glenurquhart teemed with the beasts. While they were a pest to the farmers and crofters in the Glen - consuming vast quantities of grass, oats and turnips - hunting them provided good sport and most of the folk in the Glen ate more rabbit meat - in the form of excellent stew - than they did any other meat. It was fresh - it was free- and it was before the dreadful days of myxomatosis.

Before Roddy Mor gave up his tenancy in Arnisdale, the rabbits started to appear and he and the author had some good sport hunting the rabbits with a .22 rifle and other means. The quality of the Arnisdale rabbit stew was every bit as good as the Glenurquhart variety!

The cows on the farm and on the crofts were a great hotchpotch of colours, shapes and sizes. Retrospective analysis of their genealogy would suggest that they probably contained components of breeds such as the Aberdeen Angus, Dairy Shorthorn, Highland, Galloway, Beef Shorthorn, Ayrshire, Red Poll, White Shorthorn and even Guernsey and Dexter. The Hereford had no apparent influence at that time - nor had the Friesian. Perhaps the predominant type was the Blue Grey cow - a cross between the White Shorthorn bull and the Galloway cow. The only bull in Arnisdale was Roddy Mor's Aberdeen Angus at the farm. In the summer, there was a regular succession of cows in heat from Corran and Camusban being lead on the halter to the bull at the farm for service. Between the twenty or so cows on the Corran crofts, another twenty at Camusban, seven on the farm and about three on the keeper's croft at Glenfield, the bull had a very busy summer - but perhaps rather than work - he looked upon it all as recreation! Conception in the summer meant Spring calving and hopefully the new season's grass would be starting to grow by then and soon the great flush of late spring and summer grass would ensure plenty of milk - with surplus to be made into butter, crowdie and cheese. Of course, the calves also had to get their share - but they would get skimmed milk - after the cream was harvested from the surface of the settling earthenware bowls for churning into the highly prized and savoured fresh butter. Oilcake would be added to the skim milk in the bucket feeding of the calves to compensate them from being deprived of the butterfat in their mother's milk. On the crofts and on the farm, the cows were not only providers of a very important part of the daily diet - milk, crowdie, butter, cheese, skim milk and butter milk - but they provided much else besides. The cows provided income from the sale of the calf. They provided dung which was particularly vital in producing a good crop of potatoes. In the old days, within living memory, they provided blood. In winter in hard times for the many hard pressed crofting families - the cows would be bled at intervals through the winter, the blood would be collected and mixed with oatmeal to produce black puddings which would form an important part of the diet - particularly for the young children - where higher requirement for protein for their health and growth would be partly met by such ingredients in their daily diet. The cows also made one other contribution to enhancing the life and living of the crofters - they provided company and solace. By this time, of course, they did not live within the same air space as the crofters - as they did of old. They had their separate byre. But the cow was always there, she was always in the same mood - or if she was not - you knew it and would be wondering what might be wrong - was she coming into season, was she about to calve or was she ill?

In the not infrequent trials and tribulations - and deprivations - in crofting households, it was probably often a great relief for the milker to escape to the byre to 'talk' to the cow, to unload burdens and to find solace from a trusty friend who never answered back, was almost always in the same constant mood and perhaps often seemed to understand the problems - and then to sympathise and empathise with the milker. Of course also, all the empathy which flowed in each direction during the milking would make the milking easier - the milk flow would be faster and the milking more complete.

Then, of course, there would be further relief and pleasure in walking the cows to their grazings after milking - along with the neighbours and their cows. This provided further opportunity to put domestic problems and hardships in proper perspective and to relieve burdens and worries. Perhaps by the time they were on their way home again from the grazings, they would start to think of how relatively fortunate they were, of their 'blessings' relative to other folk, such as those in the cities on in foreign parts whose needs and problems were considerably greater than theirs. As they went to fetch the cows home for the evening milkings with their calls of 'Trobhad' to locate their 'friends' and call them home - this gave them another chance to 'count their blessings', as they would put it, in their simple but very telling phrases.

The relationships of the crofters with their other animals - their sheepdogs, the cats, the hens and the sheep were just as important to them - and to the animals.

The children of the croft too, benefitted from the daily 'lessons in natural biology' as they worked and interacted with their animals through the seasons. They would also be taught very important lessons in conservation of resources. If the children went out fishing and caught fish for the sake of catching them and ended up with too many for all the neighbours to use to meet their needs, they would be severely reprimanded by their elders. They had to think of tomorrow - and next year - and about the needs of future generations. The people in crofting communities were, and still are, knowledgeable and dedicated conservationists of nature's bounties - a fact which appears not to be fully appreciated by many of the modern era of so-called conservationists. Another aspect of conservation, rarely raised at the present time in discussions on the subject, are the many treasures of the crofting people and of Highland communities in general - their language, their music, their faith, their history, their attitude to life, their ability to derive great pleasures and satisfaction from simple and basic lifestyles and, perhaps above all, their great sense of community - of loving and caring for their neighbours.

Many modern conservationists appear to be mainly concerned about the flora and the fauna - and too little concerned about the native people of the Highlands and Western seaboard of Scotland. In the opinion of the author, the first priority in these parts is to preserve the native people, who have a proud history of conserving all that is important to people and to nature - and then to provide much needed support and guidance - so that all with a really genuine, knowledgeable and well-balanced interest in these parts can move forward together with common objectives. With such clearly thought out and well balanced objectives on the whole package of conservation of native 'treasures', there will be no sector more dedicated, more enthusiastic and more vigorous in the attainment of these objectives than the native folk, whose ancestors have, for decades and centuries, been the foundation of these communities and their unique culture and traditions.

While the crofting system in west coast communities such as Arnisdale was a tough existence because of the vagaries of the weather and the not infrequent hardships, it had many compensations. The children could find relief from tedious work on the croft such as at the hay, by making the most of their wonderful natural playground along the seashore, on the croftlands and the adjoining hill areas. Many of the jobs to be done, such as taking home the cows from the grazings, the sheep gatherings, the dipping and the clipping, were communal affairs and the work done was perceived more as recreation than as toil. Children had great opportunities for self learning, of communicating with each other and their elders, of adventure, of contributing to the care of the folk in their village and of developing a good sense of values which would stand them in good stead throughout their lives. They had no chance whatsoever of feeling bored - they had every opportunity for making their own entertainment and organising their own recreation - and they all did it very well.

The adult folk, while experiencing their full range of deprivations, sadnesses and other worries, and a standard of living close to subsistence level - and 'worked to live and lived to work', nevertheless derived considerable satisfaction from working their croft and working with their animals. There was also a strong community spirit developed by the way they worked together on many of the daily and seasonal jobs to be done and by their sharing of nature's bounties, such as a good catch of fish. It was often a hard struggle - but the winning of the struggle together provided considerable satisfaction and a keen sense of achievement.

These are the impressions gained by the author in his boyhood and in the light of subsequent more mature analysis of a proud people. It was a privilege to have been in Arnisdale at a time when the old crofting system was still intact, albeit in its twilight - for most of the crofters were close to or in excess of retiring age. Very few of their progeny and successors have maintained the old ways. For example, at the present time, not one Arnisdale crofter keeps a cow, very few have hens and only the sheep remain - and they are also much reduced in number.

Up to the end of Roddy Mor's tenancy of Arnisdale Home Farm, the author returned for his summer and sometimes also for his Easter holidays. Although considerable work was undoubtedly done, only the recreations and the pleasures stand out in the memory - even all the rain, the mist and the midges are long forgotten. With each arrival on holiday, it was always a great pleasure for the author to have that first run down the village to Peggy Ann's shop on Roddy Mor's old bike. That journey would take a considerable time, as all friends - young and old - were greeted and news exchanged. It was not so pleasurable at the end of the great holidays as the 'cheerios' were carried out on the last run down the village. Many would say - 'just wait a minute' as they would disappear into the house and emerge again - proffering a clutched hand to yours and slipping half-a-crown or a two shilling piece into the palm of the recipient. The attempts at 'no, thank you' were summarily dismissed. They had so little themselves but their generosity -materially and spiritually - was enormous. Before the farewells at the farm, a new suit would appear each summer. A few weeks previously there would be surreptitious and unexplained use of the measuring tape to measure waist, hips, height, etc, and - a few days before departure, Willie the Post would deliver a COD (Cash on Delivery) package from J D Williams. Then there would be the great surprise - the 'unveiling' of the new suit and perhaps also a raincoat - a great reward for a wonderful summer's recreation and total enjoyment - with first class board and lodgings thrown in for a bonus!

In some summers, the annual visit of the coal boat would be made. It would come into the Camusban beach at high tide - just below Archie MacLean's house. Ropes and chains would secure the boat to trees and boulders and, as the tide ebbed, the boat would be beached. Meanwhile, props would be inserted along each side to keep the boat on the level. As the tide was ebbing, there would be a ferment of activity on the road and the foreshore. Iain 'Garbh' Cameron (Garbh - 'broad' or 'thick set') would be there from Glenelg, as he was the 'agent' who arranged the visit of the boat for the annual delivery of the year's coal supply to the Arnisdale and Glenelg communities. Afterwards he would collect the payments due from all the households and then organise the total payment to the suppliers.

Willie Campbell would be there from Letterfearn with his little lorry and perhaps also a horse and cart might be at the ready, the cart being pulled in turn by Dick from the farm and Major from the Lodge. As soon as the tide receded beyond the beached vessel, some of the fit youngsters, such as Donald Fletcher, Willie MacKenzie and Charlie MacTavish - with other able bodied men taking their turn - would get into the hold of the ship and start filling the grab. When full, the grab would be raised, swung over the side, lowered close to the waiting lorry or cart and the contents emptied. When full, Willie Campbell with his lorry and Ludovic, Kenny or Roddy Mor with the horse and cart, would set off to dump the required quantity of coal as close as possible to each house - usually at the roadside. This process would continue at each low tide for the two or three days it took to supply all the households. Although the coal would be lying in heaps at the roadside below each household, completely unguarded, there was never any incident of pilfering of the material. A little bit of poaching of the deer or of the salmon was legitimate in the unwritten laws of the community, but petty theft of coal or other belongings did not occur.

In 1951, the year before Roddy Mor gave up his tenancy, preparations were being made for fuel of a different kind to be delivered to Arnisdale - electricity.  Over the winter and spring months, the big wooden hydro poles had been carted in big trucks along the narrow Arnisdale road from Glenelg and off-loaded as required along the way.  In the summer holiday of 1951, a squad of about eight able bodied men would arrive in Arnisdale each morning to shoulder carry the big poles to their 'planting' locations.  The author watched this operation and accompanied the line of men on their carry as often as his chores on the farm allowed.  The men were organised from 'tallest at the front to shortest at the back'.  They would position themselves along the length of the pole and then, in unison, lift the heavy pole on to their shoulders.  They would then set off to their target area without having a rest on the way.  Often the route was up steep slopes and precipitous, rocky territory, but the men were fit, well organised and they soon had all the poles in their appointed places.  The author remembers only one of that squad, although he became friendly with all of them at the time.  The lead man - the tallest - was Donald Lamont, brother of Calum Iain, Teenie and Ronnie from Glenelg.  Donnie was on holiday from University for the summer.  He was training for the Free Church Ministry at the time and later he was to become Free Church Minister in Kilmallie and Edinburgh.  Like Roddy Mor at the farm, he also found his life's partner in Glenurquhart - Rena Matheson - the eldest of the three daughters of the Rev. Farquhar Matheson and Mrs Matheson of the Glenurquhart Free Church.  Sadly, Donnie passed away only recently (1997), after a long illness which he endured with great grace and fortitude.

The hydro line to Arnisdale from Glenelg and the power source beyond was completed in the autumn of 1951, and a great thrill was experienced in Arnisdale when such fine lighting and other 'mod cons' could be achieved by the simple pressing of a switch.  However, the old tilly lamps, the aladdins and the candles were not thrown away.  They had been faithful friends for a very long time - and they still might be needed if and when there were cuts in the hydro power supply.

There was a 'summons' to the author to come to spend the Easter holidays of 1952 at the farm to help with the preparations for the May Valuation.  As it turned out, there was not as much work to do as usual since Roddy Mor did not have much in the way of machinery or equipment which could be cleaned up and prepared for the valuation.  The sheep would have to be gathered and the cattle prepared much nearer the date of the valuation on 28 May.  Also, there was no potato ground to be prepared for planting or the seed to get ready, because Roddy Mor and Aunt Lizzie would not be around for the harvesting.  Roddy Mor's behaviour seemed to be less lively and jovial than usual - and perhaps the author's was likewise.  They both had a great attachment to Arnisdale and the farm and that association was about to be severed.

Although the author was back at school in Glenurquhart by the time of the valuation, sister Lally went to help Aunt Lizzie with all that had to be done before the big final day and to prepare for the flitting to the 'retirement' home for Lizzie and Roddy Mor in Cosaig Road in Glenelg.

So the author expressed his goodbyes to the Arnisdale Farmhouse and Farm at the end of that Easter holiday in 1952.  Little did he know then that, some three decades later, his old school pal, Iain MacKenzie, would become the occupant of the Farmhouse and the Manager of the 'Estate' and he would have the opportunity to return to check up on all his old haunts and to savour the atmosphere, once again, of what was always a very happy home.

**Top Left.** The Arnisdale Mountains from the top of Ladhar Bheinn in Knoydart with the villages of Camus Ban and Corran dwarfed below. From Left to right are Beinn Sgritheall, Beinn na h-Eaglaise, Beinn Bhuidhe, Beinn nan Caorach, Beinn Clachach and Druim Fada. **Right.** A view of Arnisdale's high tops looking southwards from Gleann Mor in Glenelg. From left to right are Beinn nan Caorach, Beinn na h-Eaglaise, Beinn Sgritheall and Beinn a' Chapuill. Gleann Mor leads into Gleann Beag, they merge into Gleann Aoidhdailean and the main drove route from Kylerhea to Gleann Beag to Crionaich and onwards to Spean Bridge and the south.

**Middle Left.** A spy with the glass from well up the bridle path on Beinn Clachach detected a crisis situation far below on Blar an Each – a stirk up to its neck in a peat bog. **Right.** With subtle and skilful technique, tremendous determination and great 'will to win', Roddy Mor succeeded in extricating the beast from the depths of the bog.

**Bottom Left.** Rena MacDonald and Maggie 'Lea' with the author's young brother Bob cradling one of Maddy's collie pups. Rena and Maggie were a great pair who tackled the great range of jobs on the farm and the farmhouse with great enthusiasm, light-heartedness and skill. **Right.** Angus Beaton (second left) who replaced Donald MacLaren as head stalker on the Arnisdale Estate around 1949. Others in the picture are Margaret Corbett, Aunt Lizzie and Roddy Mor.

**Top Left.** The hill track from Kinloch Hourn to Arnisdale down the Arnisdale Glen – a busy thoroughfare with hikers on foot and on their bicycles in the summer months and (right) once on the route of the Scottish Six Day Motor Cycle Trials. **Middle Left.** One of the hikers who first visited Arnisdale in 1949 was Victor Corbett (left) from Northern Ireland, accompanied here by Angus Beaton, Aunt Lizzie and Roddy Mor. Victor and his wife Margaret have been regular visitors ever since. (See Chapter 31).

**Right.** The impromptu Arnisdale football pitches included the green sward adjacent to Eilean Tioram (bottom right), one of the farm fields along the shoreline and on the Blar before reaching MacAskill's house in Corran.

**Bottom Left.** Alasdair MacIver, young son of the District Nurse and her husband with Lally and Whisky on the Arnisdale Pier – the site of the conger eel catch. **Right.** Sgeir Leathann – the island just offshore from Corran - a favourite fishing haunt on boat trips with Willie and Iain MacKenzie. Good catches of saithe, cod and mackerel were always made on the adjacent banks.

47

**Top Left.**   Around autumn time, on the way to the early morning farm chores, a check in the wash-house would reveal a good catch of salmon and sea trout.  No explanations were sought or offered.  When first eye to eye contact with Roddy Mor, a mischievous boyish grin creasing his fine features was the only response that would be forthcoming!   **Right.**   The cows on the farm and the crofts were a great hotch potch of attractive colours, shapes and sizes.

**Middle Left.**   The faithful cow – a provider of many good things to the crofters – milk, butter, crowdie, cheese, butter milk, skim milk, dung to 'fertilise' the land, calves and income, a fine companion and a faithful friend.  Ina Semple at the milking of the MacLean family cow in Camus Ban.   **Right.**   The children of the crofts benefitted from their daily 'lessons in natural biology'; as they worked and interacted with their animals through the seasons.  Maggie MacTavish and the children in Camus Ban have a 'chat' with their friend and provider, the cow.

**Bottom Left.**   The children were always trained to be good conservationists – when they went out fishing they were told not to catch more than met the needs of the folk in the village.  They were also taught by example to derive great pleasure and satisfaction from simple and basic lifestyles and from caring for neighbours.   Corran children in the early 1930s L to R. Angus Stewart, Morag and Jessie MacDonald, Chrissie MacCuaig, Johnnie Murchison, Mary MacDonald, Iain MacCuaig and Rena MacDonald.   **Right.**   The regular daily chores on the crofts and the big seasonal jobs such as hay making and the sheep gathering and shearing were a case of 'all hands on deck' as all age groups had a common purpose – to get the job done well and to have fun and fellowship in doing it together.   Here the Corran folk take a break for a photograph from the work at the clipping.   L to R. Flora and Nellie MacKenzie, their grandmother Mairi Bhan, Mary and Johan MacDonald, Ina Stewart, Christina MacKenzie, Chrissie MacCuaig and Rena MacDonald.

**Top Left.** There was a hive of activity with the annual arrival of the coalboat as it beached at Camusban. **Right.** Ian 'Garbh' Cameron from Glenelg, the Agent who organised the annual coal delivery.

**Middle Left** Willie Campbell from Letterfearn (right) with Johnny Sinclair (left) and Archie MacLean in Camusban. Willie with his little truck played a key role in driving on to the Camusban beach beside the coalboat when at low tide to collect and deliver the allocation of coal to each household in Arnisdale. **Right.** Donnie Lamont from Glenelg during his University holiday while studying for his Divinity Degree was a member of the squad who carried the hydro poles to their locations in preparation for electricity coming to Arnisdale in 1951.

**Bottom Left.** The electricians who 'wired' the Arnisdale houses for the coming of electricity. Kenny MacRaild (far left) and ?? MacPhee (second from right) stop for a breather when wiring the farmhouse and a bit of fun by donning a range of headgear with (L to R) Gwennie Stoddart, Aunt Lizzie, the author's sister, Betty and Roddy Mor in his bowler. **Right.** The 'power house' beside Allt an Sgoil which had provided hydro electricity to Arnisdale Lodge from the 1930s.

49

**Top Left**  The valuation of the sheep in progress at the Arnisdale fank in May 1952 as Roddy Mor was about to relinquish the tenancy of Arnisdale Home Farm.  The farm reverted to the estate and a Farm Manager, Jimmy Mitchell from Aberdeenshire was appointed to the post.  **Right.**  The Valuation proceeds under the direction of (L to R.) Mr Fraser (Valuer) along with Roddy Mor, Jimmy Mitchell, Robert Kitson, Aunt Lizzie and Mrs Fraser.

**Middle Left**  L to R.  Roddy Mor, Mr Fraser, Jimmy Mitchell and Robert Kitson on top of the circular platform adjacent to the barn which once housed the horse powered mechanism for driving the threshing mill for the oats.  **Right.**  Robert Kitson (left) the owner of the Arnisdale Estate and Roddy Mor enjoy a 'screw-top' of beer at the end of a momentous day.

**Bottom Left**  A line-up of all the folk who helped on Valuation Day and for many days beforehand.  (Photograph by Lally English – another Valuation helper).  L to R.  Standing:  Daniel MacDonald, Robert Kitson, Steve 'Lea', Ian Neil MacInnes (Glenelg), Willie MacKenzie, Mr Fraser, Kenny Fletcher, Alan MacAskill, Mrs Fraser, Peter MacRae (Kinloch Hourn), Jimmy Mitchell, Ludovic Fraser.  Seated:  L to R.  Roddy Mor, Donald MacKenzie (Lea) and Aunt Lizzie.  **Right.**  Iain MacKenzie, the author's great school pal, who later became Farm Manager on the Arnisdale Estate and made his home in the Farmhouse, with sister Flora (left) and Morag MacIntyre on top of Beinn Sgritheall.

## Chapter 4

**The Glenelg era for Roddy Mor and Lizzie**

One thing which probably made it slightly easier for Roddy Mor to sever his own very long association with Arnisdale Farm was the fact that, although he was giving up the tenancy of the farm, he was by no means retiring from all activities. He had just taken over the mail delivery contract between Arnisdale and Glenelg from Johnnie Sinclair, so he would be visiting his beloved Arnisdale twice daily for six days of the week - to collect the Arnisdale mail in the morning for its onward journey and for further processing at Glenelg Post Office. From there the on-going mail was taken in Calum Garde's boat to Kyle via the narrows of Kylerhea. And then in the evening, when Calum Garde would return from Kyle with the incoming mail, it would be sorted by Donald and Charlotte Chisholm in the Glenelg Post Office and the Arnisdale bag would be prepared for Roddy Mor to transport over to Peggy Ann's. There it would be sorted further before Willie the Post would make his house to house evening calls in Camusban, the lodge, the farm, Glenfield and Corran.

In between the morning and evening mail runs to Arnisdale, Roddy Mor, having been released from the many regular daily chores on the farm, would now have more time to please himself - to go over to Kylerhea Pier to do some fishing with his spinning rod, to have a blether with the tourists, to go up to Corrary in Glen Beag to give Duncan and Maggie MacKenzie a hand with the hay or do anything else which took his fancy. Aunt Lizzie too could enjoy more freedom and was to become thoroughly involved in the wider spectrum of activities on the go in Glenelg - social events in the Reading Room and in the School, the WRI weekly meetings and much more besides. She also had more freedom to travel to visit her relatives in Glenurquhart and elsewhere. Aunt Lizzie had a great yen for travelling and visiting other places of interest and beauty, while Roddy Mor was very contented with his Arnisdale and Glenelg environs and with all his cronies there. So now each had more freedom to do their own things - at least for some of the time.

Despite the wrench with the farm in Arnisdale, the author headed back to the west at the start of the 1952 Summer holiday, and Roddy Mor had arranged with Mr MacLeod, Manager of the Eilanreach Estate, for 'yours truly' to work there for the seven weeks of the summer vacation. So instead of Roddy Mor's old army bike hurtling through the village of Camusban or over the blar to Corran, it was now speeding each morning to cover the two miles to Eilanreach to arrive there by the 7 a.m. starting time. Those seven weeks at Eilanreach provided further rich experiences.

The large estate, owned by Lord and Lady Dulverton of the Wills' Tobacco family, was vibrant at that time with many exciting developments in progress. Apart from the large number of stags and hinds in the deer forest, there was a big sheep stock and the breeding herd of suckler cows was being expanded fairly rapidly. The forestry activities on the estate were also being developed. But the author was almost entirely involved with the squad on the farm, with the manager's son, young Y. MacLeod as the foreman, his younger brother Hamish and a fellow fifteen year old - Tosh (Norman) Elder from Glenelg.

The estate was just in the process of changing over from conserving surplus summer grass as hay to silage making and there were fairly major reclamation activities in progress on the hill pastures - particularly in the Lower Sandaig areas. The more fertile and drier areas of the hill had been ploughed in the spring time using the crawler tractor and mashlum (a mixture of oats, peas and vetches) had been sown for making into silage. Among the activities of the 'pioneers' during the summer of 1952 was the building of silage pits. First, two parallel trenches were dug. Then pre-stressed concrete slabs were lowered into the trenches and bolted together to form the two sides of the silage pit. Earth was then moved and built up against the outside of these concrete walls to bolster them. All four of the squad would build these silos, then Y would get going on cutting the grass or the mashlum. Hamish would set off with his tractor and buckrake and carry the cut material to the pit. There, Tosh and the author had to spread out the carted material and build up the silage in the prescribed way, removing the many clods of earth brought in by the buckrake as it collected the cut material from fairly rough, uneven ground. Hamish would also consolidate the built up material with his tractor, while in the late afternoon, Y would appear with his crawler to further consolidate the mass. The two young fellows who were spreading out the material in the pit did not have the most difficult of jobs and had plenty 'breathers' between the loads brought in by the buckrake. Sometimes that fine old gentleman, Duncan Cameron, from Cul an Dun who was still one of the shepherds on the estate - would come round for a little blether and to see what was going on. As the season progressed, the peas in the mashlum were coming to their peak in terms of fullness of pod and sweetness. There was one unforgettable day when the buckrake loads were coming from a far distance away - so there was very liberal time for leisure at the pit. This time was used experimenting with smoking cigarettes and consuming vast quantities of the delightful peas. It proved to be a dire combination for both fifteen year olds. That night, the author recalls being as ill as he ever has been in all his days. Eilanreach was visited at the appointed time the next morning but when Y saw the greenish-yellow pallor of his two silage spreaders, he very wisely advised them to return home to their beds - for they were fit for nothing! A day's rest - away from peas and cigarettes - worked wonders - and very few peas were consumed thereafter, while the smoking was also kept in greater moderation.

Y and Hamish were key members of the Glenelg football team which played in the Wester Ross Summer League against teams from Kyle, Plockton, Balmacara, Kyleakin and Portree. The games took place on Saturday evenings and attracted a fairly substantial, enthusiastic crowd of supporters who gave strong vocal support to their own team and also tried to advise the referee on the many errors of his ways and his decisions! While still in Arnisdale, Roddy Mor and Lizzie would never miss a Saturday night football match in Glenelg so the author was already familiar with all the local heroes. Roddy Mor had donated a Challenge Cup for a knock-out competition between the teams in the area and the MacLeod Cup is still played for. Glenelg were the proud winners on one occasion, much to the delight of Roddy Mor and all the other supporters. In addition to Y and Hamish, the author remembers such as Calum Garde, the Kyle-Glenelg Ferryman, Willie Gordon - who ran the Glenelg shop, Jocky O'Kane, Bobby MacLean, Ewan Cameron, Hugh Iain MacLure, Tommy Moffat, Alan MacAskill and that great goalkeeper - Kenny MacRae.

While, naturally, all the Glenelg supporters considered that their team was the greatest, victories were relatively few - but all the sweeter when they occurred. The team management was always on the lookout for more talent - and the hikers who were resident at the Kylerhea Youth Hostel were thoroughly screened each Saturday to find out if any of them could play football. Sometimes, great stars were unearthed and - on such occasions - Glenelg would defeat the top teams in the league. However, on other occasions they would be scraping the barrel for players - and later in the 1952 summer - the two fifteen year old chain smoking, pea-eating silage spreaders had to be roped in for a few games.

There was a sensation in the village on the Saturday night of one of the big home games, when Willie Gordon's shop was broken into and the massive sum of £300 was stolen. Since every inhabitant was at the football, nobody was around in the village to notice anybody suspicious in the precincts of the shop. However, the ever meticulous Rena MacDonald had earlier noted the numbers of the bank notes spent in Willie Gordon's shop in Arnisdale, which was run by Rena. The local shops and pubs were alerted to keep a lookout for these notes whose numbers were known. When the culprit passed over one of these in exchange for goods in the Post Office - he was 'nabbed' and duly admitted to his crime.

Roddy Mor continued doing the Arnisdale mail run in his landrover for many years. He had a narrow squeak on one winter's morning as he set off in the darkness after a night of incessant rain. When he took the right angle bend to cross the Eilanreach Bridge - he found that the bridge had disappeared overnight. He stopped with only a few feet to spare as the torrent raged in front of him. Gradually, he saw the Arnisdale road improving over time, first of all with two lanes of tarmacadam on the wheelways. This was a big advance from the loose gravel road, but perhaps more treacherous when frosty winter weather came in after heavy rain. Later the whole road surface was tarmacadamed and, later still, there was major work of realignment and the steepness of the worst inclines was reduced. The road still has great character and provides some wonderful views of mountain, sea and distant islands - but the old route - with its numerous Z bends and precipitous hills was quite unique. It had provided road access for foot traffic, riding and pack horses since time immemorial, before being improved for the horses and carts and the pony and trap (the machine) and, later still, for the car and small lorries. It appears that the major improvements to the road were financed partly by the County Council and partly by the Forestry Commission. The Commission required good access for the huge trucks required to bring out the mature timber from the Mialairidh Forest planted in the 1930s by Bill Stoddart as Head Forester, Foresters Tony Mackay and Jimmy MacLean and the young lads - and not so young folk - from Arnisdale, Sandaig and Glenelg.

Arnisdale was revisited by the author over the years as often as was possible, first on his own or along with Roddy Mor and Aunt Lizzie, but through time, along with Anne, daughter of Tony Mackay, and then afterwards with their children Anthony, Martin and Susan. The stories which their grandfather told them about his young days in the Mialairidh Forest, and their father's tales of life in Arnisdale School meant much more to them when they saw the places and met all the good folk for themselves. As the children grew, they no longer wanted to admire Beinn Sgritheall - but wanted to climb it. Their father agreed to take them up on the first opportunity which presented itself. One Friday afternoon in summer, when some painting chores in Roddy Mor's and Aunt Lizzie's house in Glenelg were nearing completion, the father decided to set off for Arnisdale with Anthony, Martin and the family Beagle - Shambles - with climbing intentions. Mother was not in favour because of the lateness of the ploy and the risk of mist on the tops.

The party reached Arnisdale, called in briefly to see Lexy MacCuaig, the father's former teacher, and also reported to Kenny Fletcher. Beinn Sgritheall was studied, it was clear to the top, some rain was threatening, but it was worth a chance because the return journey to Aberdeen had to be made the next day. The group left Arnisdale at about 5 p.m. and set off up the east shoulder of the Beinn - heading for Bealach Arnasdail and intending to climb to the top from the north side - over the Bealach. When only half way up - the mist came down - but all were determined to proceed, including the irresponsible father. As the top was approached via the steep scree slope on the north side, Shambles - a strong, determined young beagle - led the way - attached to the senior member of the party by his long lead. The latter was almost being pulled up the slope by the beagle which seemed desperate to reach the top in record time. However, the beagle's enthusiasm was dislodging stones and boulders which were coming hurtling down the mountain towards the followers - including the two little boys - Anthony (aged 11) and Martin (aged 9). Miraculously, the boys managed to avoid the rocks as they sped down the hillside - and the top was reached. Some photographs were hastily taken to record the feat but there was no view to admire - the mist was thick!

The descent soon began with the father's thoughts on the mother who had done her best, with superior wisdom, to discourage the venture. Perhaps the father was in too much of a hurry, or else his route planning was faulty in the misty conditions, as the descent was going wrong. The leader realised this but decided that, in the circumstances, it was probably safer to descend by the north side. Martin was objecting vociferously to the route being taken, stating (quite correctly) that we were going in the wrong direction. Father tried unsuccessfully to reassure him - but to no avail. Fortunately, Anthony was very peaceful and followed the wayward leaders. Shambles was greatly savouring the strong scents he was getting of the deer and was pulling for all he was worth to get off after them. Father decided it was best to follow the course of one of the burns and hoped that it would lead them to the old drove road for the Skye cattle on their way between Glen Beag and Crionaich on their way to Kinlochourn. Martin's objections to the chosen route were only lessened by his gathering exhaustion - developed from a combination of the extreme activity of his vocal chords and his valiant attempts to keep up with the pace.

The father heaved a great silent sigh of relief as the drove road was reached at the valley bottom. Now the party turned westwards - with Fachie MacBeath's house at Balvraid being the first target in the father's mind. Shambles was still pulling him along - and the valiant little boys were following close behind keeping up admirably with the fast pace. Martin was silent - directing all his energies now to covering the miles in the now almost total darkness. Thoughts of a very worried mother were going through the father's mind. Susan would be more worried about her beloved Shambles than about her father and brothers! Kenny and Lexy in Arnisdale would be waiting for the descent of the late evening mountaineers. Balvraid must be getting closer - and there was wonderful relief in the father's mind as the first flicker of Fachie's light was spotted. The now exhausted boys were equally relieved. Shambles was not at all worried - he was enjoying the whole adventure and could have gone on almost for ever!

A knock on Fachie's door at around 11 p.m.! Who on earth could this be at this time of night?, Fachie and Mary his wife must have asked each other. The door opened - there was surprise - then a welcome. A good dram for the father, a cup of tea with plenty of sugar and some biscuits for the boys. The offer of a drink of milk for Shambles which he appreciated greatly and then into Fachie's car and off down Glen Beag and on to Glenelg as quickly as possible - to relieve the worries of a mother about her children and a little girl about her dog. Fachie was thanked for the kindness of Mary and himself.

The boys and Shambles got a great welcome home. Father was reprimanded - correctly so! Having acknowledged his folly, he set off to phone Lexy in Arnisdale. She was greatly relieved. Kenny had been standing out on the road peering through the mist on Beinn Sgritheall since about 7 in the evening - awaiting the return of the climbers. He was reporting to Lexy at regular intervals and was becoming increasingly concerned. Now Lexy would go along to report to him immediately about the safe homecoming of those who lost their way in the mist. The car would be collected somehow from Arnisdale in the morning for the journey back to Aberdeen. It was a great adventure and many lessons were learned - especially by the father!

While the experience proved enjoyable to all - especially in retrospect - none enjoyed it as much as Shambles. When he arrived back to receive a great welcome from Susan and Anne, he garbled away to them excitedly for long enough - obviously trying to get across to them the full story of his great adventure but - perhaps particularly - the great scents of the deer and his wish to get closer to them - and the beasts from which they came!

A few years later, a more orderly pilgrimage was planned of walking up the Arnisdale Glen to Kinlochourn, then down the other side of Loch Hourn to Barrisdale, over to Inverie and back across the hill past the ruins at Fholaich and from there down Mam Li to Li and back across Loch Hourn to Arnisdale. The 'pilgrims' were the author and his brother-in-law, Doey from Glenurquhart, and the youngsters Martin, Ali and Ewan. Before setting off, a visit was made - first to the Ratagan Youth Hostel to meet up with Anthony who was on a cycling tour in the west with his Deeside Thistle Cycling Club - and then to Letterfearn to get the low-down on Knoydart and Inverie from Willie and Nettie Campbell. Willie had spent many months of his boyhood in Knoydart with relatives at Crowlick and

Inverguseran and paid annual visits throughout his retirement to spend a week or more with his cousin Johnny Mackay at Inverie. We were given very clear instructions on where in Inverie to find Johnny Mackay and also Peggy MacRae - a sister of the MacRae family from Kinlochourn - now resident at Invergarry.

Early the following day the journey began at the Arnisdale Farm steading, and then up past Glenfield, via Achadh a'Ghlinne, across the bridge on to the Arnisdale Glen path, up the zigzag, over the bridge below the waterfalls at the Dubh Lochain, past Crionach and then, further east, back to the river. There was a fair spate in the river and, while valiant attempts were made to negotiate a crossing by leaping between large boulders, some of the leaps were unsuccessful - but the crossing to the south side was achieved by all - albeit at the expense of wet feet! Then it was on to Kinlochourn where Peter MacRae was in residence at the Farmhouse. After a welcome cup of tea from Peter and a 'news', the party then set off down the shoreline path, passing Skiary, then Runival and the Barrisdale bothy was reached in good time. Willie MacKenzie (Willie the Post, the second) had arranged a night's stay in the bothy. Soon the effects of a roaring fire helped to dry out wet boots and clothing and the main meal of the day was soon on the table to satisfy the hungry travellers.

The next morning saw the group making its way up Mam Barrisdale and then over the Bealach to start the gradual descent to Inverie. There was a pleasant diversion at the Dubh Lochain on the descent, as the estate boat was about to leave the boat house to go out to the rainbow trout cages to feed the fish. The party was invited to go on the sail and to inspect the fish. On return to the shore, the group set off to complete the last stage of the journey to Inverie with renewed vigour. Johnny Mackay's was the first port of call at Inverie, followed by a visit to Peggy MacRae. Johnny suggested that instead of pitching tents in the damp conditions, we might be able to stay in the village hall overnight. The appropriate permission to do so was sought and granted - so another night was spent in watertight conditions and comparative comfort. After a meal, the kind invitation of Johnny Mackay to ceilidh with him was gladly accepted. There were few, if any, who knew Knoydart as Johnny Mackay and his family knew it. The Stoddarts, on his mother's side, had come up from the south with the sheep at the time of the Clearances and had their first home at the head of Glen Nevis for many years. Since that time of first settling in the district in the middle of last century, the Stoddarts and the Mackays had a major influence in many of the localities and estates on the Knoydart peninsula. The ceilidh in Johnny's house with his great fund of Knoydart stories and history - and his hospitality - was much enjoyed and appreciated by all.

The following morning was fine, and Johnny insisted on convoying the party up to the hill gate to set us on our way across the Knoydart hills to Li. This was a fine walk - only spoiled by the midges on a dry but fairly humid day with not even a hint of a breeze. Young Ewan suffered more from the midges than the rest of the group - or it may have been from the sheep dip! He had armed himself with some sheep dip, carried in a bottle, as his midge repellent and probably did not dilute the stuff sufficiently. So the concentrated material certainly repelled the midges - but at the expense of causing severe irritation to the youngster's delicate skin. It was good to reach the top of Mam Li, sit down and - with the glass take time to absorb the view across the loch to Arnisdale, Rarsaidh, Mialairidh and Sandaig and then eastwards up the Loch to Barrisdale, Caolasmor, Runival and Kinlochourn.

After studying this wonderful landscape, the descent of Mam Li began and Rick Rohde's croft was soon reached. There was time there to study Rick's handiwork - his little electricity generator in one of the hill burns and his other contraptions to achieve the 'mod cons' and home comforts through his own ingenuity and skill which other folk in urban and village communities take for granted.

At a pre-appointed time, the party were to be collected by young Billy MacKenzie. Billy was soon spotted on his way across from Corran in his little boat with outboard engine and the group were soon back in Arnisdale. It was a very edifying and satisfying pilgrimage.

Knowing her previous associations with Barrisdale and Knoydart, the author went to visit Mary Anne MacCuaig, now well into her eighties. Mary Anne was her usual bright and happy self and was delighted to hear about her old haunts - "Oh," she said, "I remember late on a Friday night, when we were young, we would finish our work in the Barrisdale Lodge, set off at about 9 o'clock for the dances in Inverie. We would be up Mam Barrisdale in no time and, running for good stretches down the other side, we would be at the dance by 11 o'clock. They were great dances - going on to 3 o'clock in the morning and sometimes later. At the end of the dance, we would set off walking back to Barrisdale and we would be fully ready for our work at 7 o'clock in the morning. Those were the days!" And there would be a great glint of nostalgia in her beautiful expression.

Mary Anne was a very special lady. Her mother, Lexy, had been one of the survivors from the typhoid epidemic in the village at the end of the last century. Lexy was very short-sighted and this was attributed to the typhoid fever. Theirs was a very popular ceilidh household in Camusban for young and old folk alike. Like her mother, Mary Anne was to lose her sight in her later years but her sense of hearing was all the keener, and her happy disposition was undiminished. The author remembers calling at her - perhaps at intervals of around two years between visits. He would knock at the door and shout "Are you there?" "Come in", she would call and on opening the door and enquiring of her "How are you keeping?" she would have identified the voice with uncanny memory, "Is that you Peter?" she would ask - before her living room door was reached.

The author visited Mary Anne in her final hours in the Royal Northern Infirmary in Inverness. He had been told by Aunt Lizzie that Mary Anne was there and that she was sinking fast. On arrival at Mary Anne's bedside, the author's old teacher, Lexy, was present. Now, together, they spoke to Mary Anne in her apparent deep worldly unconsciousness about the things and folk that were dear to her. In her final few hours in this world, Mary Anne continued to exhibit the essence of peace and grace that she had always shown throughout her life.

Another tour of the Loch Hourn environment was undertaken in 1995, along with Anne, brother Bob and niece Jenny, Tom MacDiarmid, formerly of Sandaig, who has Moffats and Fosters in his ancestry, and three other friends from Glenurquhart. The two Arnisdale boatmen, Charlie MacTavish and Len Morrison, were 'commandeered' to sail the party up the loch to Kinlochourn on a wonderful balmy summer morning with clear skies and good visibility. It was a most enjoyable and interesting sail up the loch past all the clachans and islands en route. The party disembarked at the Kinlochourn pier which was specially erected many decades ago to provide King Edward VII with an attractive, safe and dry landing place on his way by yacht, and pony and trap, to holiday, stalk and shoot on the Glen Quoich Estate.

After tea and scones at the little tea-room at Kinlochourn then operating in the former family home of the MacRaes, the trek up the steep incline on the road back to Arnisdale began. After that, the walk down the Glen was most pleasant and interesting on such a fine, clear summer's day. The river was low and the crossing was negotiated without incurring wet feet. The numerous track-side ruins were noted with adjacent grassy areas containing plentiful white clover. These provided evidence of habitations of old - perhaps where folk lived throughout the year and sustained themselves by their crofting activities. This was a once busy route - not only for the drovers with their big herds of cattle from Skye and the Outer Hebrides on their long trek to southern markets, but of pedlars and other businessmen and travellers. Maybe some of the dwellings served as an inn to provide food and shelter for weary travellers. Then the path led us past the old house at Crionach. This was a nostalgic stop for Tom

MacDiarmid, since his Foster forebears were the last occupants of this cottage. They were shepherds who stayed there with their families throughout the year, tending the very large flocks of sheep with which the Arnisdale Estate was once stocked. Before the Fosters, the Crionach cottage was occupied, according to Iain MacKenzie, by a family of MacRaes from Kintail. John Mor MacRae was the shepherd and the head of the household. Sandy MacAskill at Corran was descended from these MacRaes - again according to Iain.

After Crionach, the route down past the Dubh Lochain, the Zig-Zag and down the Arnisdale Glen to Corran was straightforward and the weather continued to be fine.

On arrival at Corran, the whole party was entertained to a sumptuous tea by that lovely hostess, Rena MacDonald, now sadly no longer with us. Rena was one of the real 'bricks' of the Arnisdale community, and all connected with Arnisdale felt a great sense of personal loss when Rena was taken from our midst.

The fine tribute to Rena by the Rev. Donald Beaton at her funeral service in the Glenelg Church of Scotland was appreciated by all. Rena's life and living was an inspiring example to all who knew her.

Roddy Mor and Aunt Lizzie had a long and happy retirement in Glenelg where both busied themselves in the affairs and social events of the local community. They also had time to engage in their respective leisure pursuits. Both were fine conversationalists and enjoyed meeting new people; so when the summer visitors came and they met up with Roddy Mor or Lizzie when out for their walk or when sitting at the War Memorial ('The Monument') in that beautiful location looking across to Kylerhea, down the Sound of Sleat and in full view of the surrounding mountains, they would exchange pleasantries and then take time to talk. Lizzie would talk to them about their homes and their holidays and the interesting places that they had visited. Roddy Mor would answer their questions about interesting places in Glenelg and neighbouring localities, about places of historical interest, such as the barracks which were in full view from the Monument, the Kylerhea Ferry, the brochs in Glen Beag and many other places further afield. He would relate old stories about people and places. Many would return year after year for their holidays and then there was the excitement of new welcomes, old friendships being renewed and strengthened; and even more stories would be told to satisfy the desires of the visitors to know and understand more of the culture and traditions, the language and the music, of the very fine, generous and cultured folk, and the history and the geography of the beautiful and interesting places.

Roddy Mor died in August 1975 at the age of 82. He had taken a fairly severe stroke some three years before, from which he never fully recovered. Perhaps if he was not such a basically fit, strong man, he would not have survived so long after the stroke. He was often very uncomfortable with prolonged periods of heat stress and associated sweating, but he had his fine comfortable periods also, when he was very much the Roddy Mor of old. The malaria which he contracted in the first world war may have contributed to this problem. He was visited regularly by the many summer visitors who missed him from his usual seat at the monument, and wondered why they were not meeting him in their walks along his favourite routes. His fine old cronies from Glenelg and Arnisdale also visited him regularly and he liked nothing better than to engage with them - in the Gaelic - in the old memories, and in the old stories. They were all very good to him and Roddy Mor greatly valued these regular visits of his old and not so old friends, as did Aunt Lizzie. When Roddy Mor passed on, Aunt Lizzie made her way back home again to her own heft - that of her very happy childhood and adolescence in Glenurquhart - and latterly in Inverness. She died in August 1994 at the ripe old age of 97. She was very comfortable and contented in her latter years - the last of them spent in the Elmgrove Nursing Home in Inverness, surrounded, entertained and tended lovingly by the nurses in that comfortable and happy 'home from home'. Her old friends from Arnisdale and Glenelg did not forget her by any means - Alistair Davidson and many other old and young friends visited her regularly and kept her up to date with the activities and all the news of the folk in Glenelg and Arnisdale. Aunt Lizzie, and her family, greatly appreciated these visits. They were a great source of interest and comfort to her and kept her mentally active to the end of her days. The mortal remains of Roddy Mor and Aunt Lizzie rest in the new Glenelg cemetery, along with those of so many of their great friends.

They had lived through an era of unprecedented changes in this world and in Arnisdale, Loch Hourn and Glenelg. They had their full share of joys and sorrows, of triumphs and failures. They experienced the traumas and worries of two world wars and the joys of peace. They had experienced Arnisdale in some of its finest years and both contributed substantially to the fine community spirit which prevailed. If this book helps to recapture some of the spirit of these times - and the character of the many fine folk who formed a great community, who lived together, who supported each other in tough times, who created their own entertainment and fun in simple, wholesome ways, and who appreciated and conserved nature's bounties for future generations - then it will have served its purpose.

While Arnisdale currently is in serious decline in many ways, this book may help to ensure that the memories of the fine people of an outstanding community live on - along with their history, their culture, their language, their music, their beliefs and their ways of living, and of supporting each other.

And it is possible that when this history and culture is fully understood and appreciated by the current and future generations, that this might provide both a stimulus and a basis for re-invigorating and redeveloping the Arnisdale and Loch Hourn communities, in balanced ways, acceptable to the native folk and to their friends who appreciate the spirit and aspirations of a proud, honourable and generous Celtic people.

**Postscript**

**An Appreciation of the lives of Aunt Lizzie and Uncle Roddy Mòr**

Roddy Mòr died on 8 August 1975 and the following appreciation of his life appeared in the Inverness Courier.

**The late Roderick MacLeod, Glenelg. An Appreciation**

With the recent death of Roddy MacLeod at the age of 82, Western Inverness-shire and Wester Ross have lost a very worthy and widely respected character. One of a family of three brothers and four sisters, Roddy was born in Lochcarron and, at the age of 10, went to Arnisdale on Loch Hourn where his father took over tenancy of the Home Farm. He promptly answered the call of his country at the outbreak of the 1914-18 war and joined the Lovat Scouts. He served throughout the war in Gallipoli, the Dardanelles, Egypt and France. Soon after demobilisation he took over tenancy of the Home Farm, Arnisdale from his father and in 1923 married Elizabeth MacDonald from Glenurquhart who was the teacher in Arnisdale School. Roddy was a fine athletic figure who had a particular love of shinty. He was a successful farmer and his farming knowledge and experience was highly regarded by neighbouring crofters who looked upon him as an adviser and as a faithful friend.

In the Second World War, Roddy was appointed Lieutenant in charge of Arnisdale and Glenelg Home Guard. He later ran the Mail Service from Glenelg to Arnisdale and continued in the role for many years after he and Mrs MacLeod retired to Glenelg in 1952. Roddy was blessed with many admirable qualities. He was a staunch church-goer and acted as precentor in Arnisdale, and later Glenelg, Free

Church. He combined a strong and resolute character with great patience and understanding of people's problems. He was a fluent Gaelic speaker and, in his younger days, he and Mrs MacLeod were much in demand as singers at local ceilidhs. He had a fund of old tales which he had a particular art of relating.

In his trying illness over the past two years he was sustained and comforted by the devoted attention of his life's partner who survives him and he is also survived by a sister, Mrs Flo MacKenzie, Lochcarron and by his brother Murdo in Inverness. Roddy exemplified all that is best in the true Highlander. With his passing goes another link with the past and he will be deeply missed. However, the principles that he maintained and the example which he showed through life live on to influence those of us who had the pleasure of knowing him.

**Aunt Lizzie** died on the 30 August, 1994 in her 98th year. She was born and reared in Bearnock, Glenurquhart where her father Ali 'Ban' MacDonald was gamekeeper / gardener on the local estate. Ali Ban and his wife Jessie (nee Ross) had seven children, Lizzie being the fourth and 'middle' child while Lily, the author's mother, was the youngest of the family. Relevant extracts from an article Aunt Lizzie wrote in 1993 to commemorate the centenary of Drumnadrochit Senior Secondary School in Glenurquhart are as follows:

"My early schooldays were spent at Corriemony which I attended along with my 4 sisters (Annie, Babs, Chrissie and Lily – later Mrs English) and 2 brothers (Alistair and Peter). Very few pupils got the chance of finishing their schooling at the 'Higher Grade' in Drumnadrochit in those days because it was just too expensive for families to finance the lodgings. My father and mother were in this position but Miss Kane, my teacher in Corriemony, persuaded my parents to allow me to proceed to Drum School and to accept a loan from herself to finance my lodgings there. So kindly and trusting Miss Kane gave me my chance and I duly repaid the loan when I started work as a teacher some seven years after my arrival in the 'Higher Grade' School.

I first went to Drum in the Autumn of 1910 at the age of thirteen. I cycled to school on a Monday morning, had good lodgings with kindly people during the week and cycled the eight miles back up the Glen after school on the Friday evening. I was Dux in my final year and I must say that I enjoyed my schooling very much – I had very good friends and fine teachers. After leaving school in 1915, I went to College in Aberdeen to do a two year Teacher Training Course. These were two lovely years. My first teaching job was in 1917 in Arnisdale. I taught for three years there before being appointed to a post near home at Glenconvinth School in the Kiltarlity District in 1920. However, I returned to Arnisdale in 1923 after I changed my name to MacLeod on marrying Roddy, whose people were tenants of the Home Farm there."

So ended Aunt Lizzie's memories for the Centenary Publication of her old school in Glenurquhart. When she first arrived in Arnisdale, Roddy Mor was fighting for his country in foreign fields in the Great War. Apparently she made friends quickly with all the kindly Arnisdale folk, including Roddy Mor's people, and was soon joining in the house ceilidhs. In the 'teasing' which is common on such occasions about possible romances among the young folk, a ceilidh participant in the MacLeod household at the farm was inferring that Aunt Lizzie might 'fancy' a certain eligible young man in the village, but her prompt retort was ' No – I will just wait for this young man to come home from the war' – pointing to the picture of young Roddy Mor which was adorning the wall of the ceilidh room. She duly waited, Roddy Mor was of a like mind and they were married in Inverness in 1923.

They were a devoted and very interesting couple who played a very full part in all the Arnisdale and later, Glenelg, community activities. And they were a wonderful Aunt and Uncle to all their nieces and nephews – always interesting, stimulating, kindly, loving and full of fun.

After Roddy Mor died in 1975, Aunt Lizzie made her way back to the lands of her youth in Glenurquhart and later in Inverness. But she also returned to Glenelg on occasions for holidays with many fine friends. She would sojourn in Lochcarron too with Roddy Mor's youngest sister, Flo and her husband Jeck MacKenzie – and with the families of their sons, Roddy, Kenny and Tommy. These 'ceilidhs' were very special to Aunt Lizzie and also to Flo and Jeck. Flo was a young teenager in Arnisdale when Aunt Lizzie first arrived there in 1917, they had become good friends very quickly and they were great pals for all of their days. They were kindred spirits and greatly enjoyed eachother's company, serious conversation and sense of fun.

Let us now proceed to a conducted tour of the Arnisdale and Loch Hourn communities and to glean something more about the folk who lived and worked there, gave great support to eachother and who enjoyed to ceilidh together – and about their successors – the current residents – who are doing their best in difficult times to guide the community forwards, while at the same time trying to preserve as much as possible of the treasures of the past.

**Top Left.** Roddy Mor on the Arnisdale Mail Run accompanied by Margaret Corbett makes a stop on the Eilanreach brae overlooking Glenelg Bay and the 'Narrows' of Kylerhea – a very familiar view to the Mailman!. **Centre** Lally and Roddy Mor close to the Glenelg Hotel on the look out for the arrival of Calum Garde's boat from Kyle with the mails. **Right.** Roddy Mor makes the most of his release from onerous farm duties and enjoys some evening fishing from the ferryboat anchored off Kylerhea pier.

**Middle Left.** Roddy Mor and Aunt Lizzie give a helping hand to Duncan, Maggie and Catherine MacKenzie with the hay at Corrary in Glen Beag. **Right.** Aunt Lizzie on an 'outing' with the Glenelg WRI to Stromeferry and Inverewe Gardens. L to R. Una MacQueen, Teenie Lamont, Aunt Lizzie, Nan MacPherson, Cathie MacDonald, Isobel Macrae (Tormor, Sandaig) Chrissie MacLeod, Dolly MacDonald, Lizzie MacLeod, Carol MacRae and Peggy MacAskill (Photograph by Beatrice Cameron).

**Bottom Left.** Aunt Lizzie with sister Chrissie on a visit to her old home at Buntait in GlenUrquhart. **Right.** The emancipated pair enjoy a picnic at Kylerhea Ferry – a favourite haunt.

**Top Left** Y and Hamish MacLeod of Eilanreach Farm – regular members of the Glenelg Football Team. This 1950 team won the MacLeod Cup which was donated by Arnisdale's Roddy Mor. Back row (L to R.) Roddy MacPherson, Y MacLeod, Kenny Macrae, Alan MacRae (Ratagan), Roddy MacKenzie and Bobby MacLean. Front: Hamish MacLeod, Neilly Gordon, Jocky O'Kane, Willie Gordon and Malcolm Garde. Glenelg defeated Kyle 1-0 in the final, 16 year old Hamish MacLeod scoring the winning goal. **Right.** A Glenelg Football team immediately before the Second World War (around 1939). Back Row (L to R.) Kenny MacKenzie (Corrary), Ewan Cameron, Jimmy Murchison, Ali 'Beag' MacRae, Roddy MacPherson, John 'Mor' MacDonald, Donnie 'Skibo' MacLeod (Forester). Front (L to R.): Malcolm Garde, Bobby MacLean, Johnnie Murchison and Alick MacPaik

**Middle Left.** Fifteen year olds Tosh (Norman) Elder (right) and the author take delivery of another load of mashlam from Hamish MacLeod in the pioneering silage making operations on Lord Dulverton's estate in the Tormor-Lower Sandaig area. **Centre.** Y. MacLeod on his crawler. **Right.** Duncan Cameron from Cul an Dun (far right) in his early days on Eilanreach Estate. Duncan was a regular visitor to the silage making operations at Eilanreach to have a chat with the silage spreaders on his way round to check the wellbeing of his sheep.

**Bottom Left.** The old inn at Kylerhea which later became a Youth Hostel and is now a private dwelling house. In its Youth Hostel days, the Glenelg Football Team Scouts always checked its occupants thoroughly on a Saturday before an evening match and frequently 'signed on' some stars to boost the performances and results of the team. **Right.** Willie Gordon, shop owner and another regular player in the Glenelg football team. During one Saturday evening's match in 1952, Willie Gordon's shop in the Glenelg village street very close to the football pitch was raided and the vast sum of £300 stolen. This caused consternation in the whole district since crime was unknown in the area.

**Top Left.** Rena MacDonald in the doorway of the Arnisdale shop previously owned by John MacGillivray but sold to Willie Gordon before 1951. Round the corner to the right is Aonghas Dhaidh (MacKintosh). Rena's meticulous recording of the numbers of the pound and ten shilling notes taken in at the Arnisdale shop helped to solve the Glenelg crime in the Glenelg Post Office. **Right.** A 1930s photograph of Donald and Charlotte Chisholm of the Glenelg Post Office with children, Alice, Janet and Ishbel. In the late summer of 1952, a man who was living and working locally spent one of Rena's recorded pound notes in the Glenelg Post Office and this was immediately detected by Donald and Ishbel.

**Middle Left.** Return visits to Glenelg and Arnisdale were made as often as possible. Roddy Mor meets the author off Calum Garde's boat at Glenelg Pier. Later the Glenelg-Kyle mail service was run by Donald John MacLeod. **Right.** Further on in time – in the late 1960s the author's family revisited the old haunts often along with father-in-law, Tony Mackay, who spent many happy years in the 1930s as a young forester in the Mialairidh (Arnisdale) Forest. L to R. Martin, Anthony, Anne, Susan, Anne's brother Charles and Grandpa – Tony Mackay – beside the Glen Beag broch.

**Bottom Left** The author's family in the 1970s. L to R. Susan, Martin, the author, Anne and Anthony. **Right.** The Loch Hourn family web and the four generations. L to R. Mrs Tony Mackay (nee Isabella MacPherson), Tony Mackay, Charles Mackay, 'Granny' MacPherson (nee Isabella MacRae) with baby Anthony and Anne. Isabella MacRae was born and reared in Kinloch Hourn and married Donald MacPherson of Glenelg.

**Top.** The Beinn Sgritheall adventure.   **Left**. The author's former teacher, Lexy MacCuaig (second from right) and **Right**. Kenny Fletcher (on the left) were visited beforehand.
**Middle Left.** The route of the adventure which went wrong.   **Right.** Fachie and Mary MacBeath of Balvraid Farm in Glen Beag were disturbed very late at night, provided welcome sustenance and transported the mountaineers to their destination.
**Bottom Left.** Susan was delighted to be reunited with her beloved Shambles.   **Right.** Anne was very relieved to see her boys. The father was reprimanded – and rightly so!

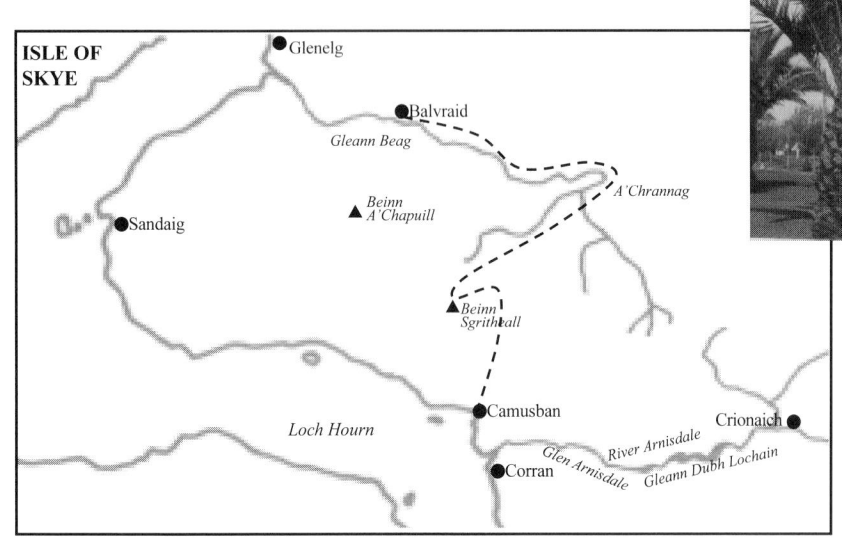

**Top Left.** The start of the Glen Arnisdale, Kinloch Hourn, Barrisdale and trans-Knoydart trek. Advice from Willie Campbell (left) at Letterfearn who knew Knoydart and its people so well. **Right.** Wet feet crossing the Arnisdale River above Crionaich were difficult to avoid.

**Middle Left.** Meeting up with Peter MacRae at Kinloch Hourn. **Right.** Setting off over Mam Barrisdale

**Bottom Left.** Descending the path towards An Dubh Lochain en route to Inverie. **Right.** The welcome from Johnny MacKay at Inverie.

**Top Left.** Farewell from Johnny MacKay at the hill gate on the route across Knoydart to Li. **Right.** Overlooking Loch Hourn from Mam Li

**Middle Left.** Li under the care of the Rohde family was in good heart. **Right.** Billy MacKenzie sailed the party back across Loch Hourn to Arnisdale.

**Bottom Left** The author reports to Mary Anne and the wonderful lady recalls her own youthful experiences working in Barrisdale Lodge, walking the seven miles over to the dances in Inverie after finishing the evening chores on a Friday night and walking back again after the dance in time to start the duties at 7 a.m. on Saturday morning. **Right.** Mary Ann and her mother Lexy (a sister of Mairi Bhan MacKenzie in Corran and Ann MacLure of Riverfoot, Glenelg. Their mother and father died in the typhoid epidemic in Arnisdale around 1890).

**Top.** A sail up Loch Hourn and a walk back from Kinloch Hourn to Arnisdale for a group of GlenUrquhart folk. A fine round trip doing it the easy way. **Left.** Len Morrison sails some of the GlenUrquhart party up Loch Hourn. **Right.** Alighting from the boats of Charlie MacTavish and Len Morrison at the Landing Place at Kinloch Hourn which was built to help King Edward VII to make his way ashore on his way to Glen Quoich Lodge for a few days stalking.

**Middle.** The walk from the Landing Place to the old Farmhouse. A welcome cup of tea in the Farmhouse. Emerging from the very steep climb through the wooded policies surrounding Kinloch Hourn Lodge. **Right**. A halt to admire the view at the junction of the tracks to Glen Shiel and Arnisdale.

**Bottom Left.** En route down the hill path from towards Crionaich. L to R. Neil and Margaret MacLeod, Tom MacDiarmid, Anne, John (Mando) MacLeod, Bob and Jenny English. **Right.** Crossing a much more peaceful River Arnisdale above Crionaich than others have experienced over the years and centuries.

**Top Left.**  The old house at Crionaich at the junction of the hill track from Kinloch Hourn, with the right hand fork (the old drove route from Skye and Kylerhea) making for Glen Beag, Glenmore and Glenelg, the left hand branch winding its way to Arnisdale.  The Fosters were the last family of shepherds to stay in the Crionaich house and tend their large hirsel of sheep in this area.  **Right**.  Tom MacDiarmid of Lower Sandaig, whose Moffat and Foster forebears lived and worked in these parts, examines the old home of the Foster family at Crionaich.

**Middle Left.**  Tom welcomes the group to the old family home.  **Right.**  Tom MacDiarmid at the top of the zig-zag in full view of Achadh a' Ghlinne and the easy walk home down alongside the River to Corran and Arnisdale.

**Bottom Left.**  The fine War Memorial at Quarry in Glenelg.  The 'Monument' was a favourite location for Roddy Mor and Aunt Lizzie in their latter years.  They enjoyed a walk down to that spot on a fine day with a wonderful view across the bay to Kylerhea and Skye.  Both greatly enjoyed meeting and talking to the many summer visitors to these parts.  **Right.**  A surprise meeting in Quarry, Glenelg in the 1960s with old Arnisdale friends who had moved to Lochaber many years previously.   L to R. Mark and Jean Allett (Bessie Logan's niece and her husband), Sandy Campbell, Roddy Mor, Mary Campbell, Aunt Lizzie, Bessie Logan and David Campbell (son of Sandy and Mary).  Bessie Logan had been the teacher in Arnisdale in the late 1920s while Mrs Mary Campbell had lived at Glenfield as a young girl when her father Alick Campbell was the Head Gamekeeper on the Arnisdale Estate (from about 1915 to the 1920s).

# Chapter 5

**The MacLeod family and their arrival in Arnisdale**

Roddy Mor's father, Kenneth, or 'Coinneach' as he was popularly known, took over the tenancy of Arnisdale Home Farm in 1902 and his first temporary home there was in Corran. Kenny had been a shepherd with the Lochcarron Estate at Reraig, a little community on a sea inlet between Loch Kishorn and Lochcarron. He and his wife Annie MacKenzie married in 1883 and they had a family of seven - from Christina (Tina or Teenie) who was born in 1884 to Flora (Flo) (born in 1899), with Donald (1886), Bella (1889), Murdo (1891), Roddy (1893) and Ella (1895) arriving in between. Part of the conditions of the job as shepherd with the Lochcarron estate was that Coinneach had tenancy of the small croft at Reraig so they kept one or two cows and followers and had around twenty sheep and, of course, hens to provide their eggs in season and a rare meal of chicken as the old hens were culled. It is likely that the meagre shepherding wages and the produce of the croft could not sustain the large young family and Kenny had confidence that, with the help of his growing sons and daughters, he could make a success of farming on a bigger scale.

While Tina and Donald had left school before the family moved to Arnisdale, Bella, Murdo, Roddy and Ella were enrolled in Arnisdale School on 8 June 1903. Little Flora (Flo) did not start school until 3 April 1905.

The young children lost their mother, (and Kenny his wife, Annie), on 23 December 1905, when she was only 44 years of age, so life was tough for the family in their early years in Arnisdale. But the already closely-knit family bonded together even more and together they built up their stock of sheep and cattle on the home farm. There was always plenty of work to do in running the home and the farm and each and every member of the family played their part with energy and enthusiasm. Kenny eventually left Arnisdale to take over the tenancy of the Lochcarron Hotel and the adjoining farm in 1920. He died in 1936 at the age of 75. Despite their sadnesses in Arnisdale and Kenny's comparatively short stay before returning to Lochcarron, the MacLeod family left their mark in Arnisdale and the surrounding localities.

Daughter Tina married Ally Fletcher from Camusban and the resulting families had a major impact on Arnisdale which is still there today. Donald married the local Arnisdale teacher, Mary MacKinnon, who belonged to Tiree. Donald and his wife later took over the tenancy of Erracht Farm near Fort William and then went to farm in Essex where their family of Alistair and Anne were raised. In 1917, Mary was succeeded as teacher in the Arnisdale School by a young girl from Glenurquhart, Lizzie MacDonald. When Roddy returned from the First World War in 1918, another alliance was soon forged between one of the MacLeod sons and the Arnisdale teacher of the time - and Roddy and Lizzie were married in 1923. If that liaison had not materialised, this book would not have been written and the very many providers of the information which the book contains would have been saved a great deal of intensive interrogation, time and effort! When father Kenny moved back to Lochcarron, Roddy took over the tenancy of Arnisdale Home Farm.

So Tina, Donald and Roddy each met their life's partner in Arnisdale. What about the other members of the MacLeod family?

Murdo married Bella Finlayson from Lochcarron and he and his wife had their first home there before emigrating to Montana in the USA where Murdo worked along with other exiles from Lochcarron, Arnisdale and other neighbouring localities on the big sheep and cattle ranches in that area of the USA. Murdo and Bella had three children, Kenny being born in Lochcaron, Nan in Montana while the young est, Rhoda, was born in Lochcarron when the family moved back after things went wrong on the Montana ranches with prolonged droughts undermining the cattle and sheep stock and rendering the enterprise unprofitable. Most of the other exiles from Lochcarron and Arnisdale, such as Murdo's brother Donald and Willie MacKenzie (Willie the Post) from Arnisdale, returned home at the same time.

The second oldest daughter of the MacLeod family, Bella, married Donald Forbes from Immer on the south side of Lochcarron. Donald's father had been a 'watcher' on the Inverness to Stromeferry railway line before the railway was extended to Kyle. His job was to check the line regularly for fallen rock or other obstacles before the trains were due. Donald Forbes succeeded his father under the same employer, working for British Railways at Stromeferry on the Inverness to Kyle line for many years. Donald and Bella had one son, James. James is now resident in Inverness with his wife Peggy (from North Uist). He is an expert fiddler and is still in great demand in the Highland Capital and further afield to play his 'fine tunes' to delighted audiences. He has made regular pilgrimages to his mother's old home in Arnisdale over the years to visit his cousins, Lachie, Peter, Kenny and Donald Fletcher and his other great friend there, Iain MacKenzie, a real craftsman in the making of fiddles. They had many fine ceilidhs together in the past and these visits still continue. If time permits, James will also fit in a bit of fishing in Arnisdale - another of his favourite addictions.

Ella married Dan Mackay from Lochcaron and their only son Neil, an expert weaver in the Lochcarron Tweed Mill, died at a comparatively young age in 1996. The youngest member of the family, Flora (Flo), followed her sisters' partiality for Lochcarrron and Stromeferry men and married Jeck MacKenzie from Lochcarron, an expert joiner and a great player in the fine Lochcarron shinty teams of his day. Jeck and his cousin, 'Big Donnie' MacKenzie, were regular visitors to Glenelg, Arnisdale and clachans around Loch Hourn where they carried out fine building and renovation work. They told, and heard, many couthy stories at the same time. Their work, and their company, were greatly appreciated and enjoyed by the folk for whom they worked. Jeck and Donnie also enjoyed the 'crack' of the Arnisdale and Loch Hourn folk. Jeck and Flo had three sons, Roddy, Kenny and Tommy, who are all current stalwarts of the Lochcaron community in their individual ways and contributions. Kenny and Tommy were key members of the Lochcarron shinty team of the 1960s and 1970s which was one of the best in the land. Roddy, the local undertaker, is a fine Gaelic singer. Roddy's wife Janet, is the daughter of the late Kenneth MacKenzie of Ardneaskan who was one of the many Lochcarron folk (the Carrannachs) who frequented Loch Hourn at the time of the herring fishing. Kenneth and his brothers, Donald and Ewan, owned and ran the herring drifter, the 'Caberfeidh'.

To return to Kenny MacLeod's generation around 1900, Kenny's sister Helen married Finlay MacKenzie who was one of the Strome Ferry rioters who objected vehemently to the Highland Railway sending fish off from Strome on the Sabbath, six of them ending up in jail. Kenneth's brother, Murdo, had the ferry at Strome which was operated by oars in the early days. Stromeferry was the end point of the railway line from Inverness at that time. It was a busy place and in the autumn even busier as drovers took their sheep there from such places as Kintail, Glenelg and Arnisdale for loading on to the train at Stromeferry and transporting to Dingwall for the big autumn lamb sales. The sheep from Glenelg and Arnisdale were shipped across Loch Duich on the ferry at Totaig before being shepherded to Stromeferry. Another brother of Kenneth, Finlay, took the tenancy of Balnabeen Farm in the Black Isle and his descendants are still farming there today. Kenny's brother Willie went to America and was never heard of again by his relatives at home. Kenny's wife, Annie MacKenzie, had an uncle (Murdo MacKenzie) who was inducted as the Free Church Minister of the old North Church in Inverness in 1887, succeeding Dr George Mackay who died in the previous year. The Rev. Murdo inspired the congregation to build a much larger church to accommodate their expanding numbers and this leadership culminated in the building of the new Free North Church and its opening in 1893.

When Kenny MacLeod took over the Lochcarron Hotel around 1920 he was much more interested in the Hotel Farm than in the Hotel itself. One man who drove Kenny's first car said of him "He was the most honest man I ever met" and went on to tell the story of the cattle beast Kenny bought from a crofter and later sold at the Dingwall sales. The beast made much more than expected at the sale so Kenny went back to the crofter and gave him half of his profit. The new daughter-in-law whom Kenny left in Arnisdale after Lizzie MacDonald, the young Arnisdale teacher, got married to Kenny's third son, Roddy, always spoke very highly and lovingly of her father-in-law. Kenny was a very couthy, kindly man with very high principles.

Iain MacKenzie who now occupies the farm house in Arnisdale, once occupied by Kenny and his family successors, often claims that Coinneach's fine character and spirit still pervades the old home. Coinneach was a fine fiddler and Iain MacKenzie has in his possession a fiddle which Coinneach bought from one of the Travelling People in Lochcarron around 1920. Coinneach was also a very competent piper and often was referred to as Coinneach a'Piòbaire (Kenneth the Piper).

James Forbes, of Inverness, a grandson of Kenny, remembers being told that his grandfather's first home in Arnisdale when he went to take up the tenancy of the Home Farm there in 1902 was at Rarsaidh before he moved temporarily to Corran, after which he moved to the Farmhouse when his family joined him in the summer of 1903. That Kenneth found a temporary home and a big welcome in Rarsaidh is very likely because old Mrs Cameron who occupied the house at Rarsaidh at that time, along with her husband and family, belonged to Kishorn and it is very likely that the Camerons knew the MacLeods from across the hill at Reraig very well from their days together in that community.

Mabel Fletcher, a grand-daughter of Kenneth is convinced that the MacLeods and Camerons were great friends before the MacLeods ever came to Arnisdale. She heard stories how Roddy Cameron from Rarsaidh would walk the three miles or so to visit Kenny at the Arnisdale farm. When they had finished their fireside ceilidh, Kenny would convoy Roddy back to Rarsaidh and when they reached Rarsaidh, Roddy would in turn accompany Kenny back to Arnisdale after which Kenneth would back-track towards Rarsaidh with his friend. Mabel claims that the two of them would continue this 'Scotch convoy' backwards and forwards between Rarsaidh and the Arnisdale Farm House many times over. They were obviously very fine friends and greatly enjoyed each other's company and 'crack'.

The MacLeods and their progeny had a great impact on the life and soul of Arnisdale and, according to Iain MacKenzie, that influence remains there today.

**Top Left.**  Kenneth MacLeod or Coinneach a'Piobaire (Kenneth the Piper) who along with his wife Annie took over the tenancy of the Arnisdale Home Farm in 1902.   **Right.**  The Arnisdale Farm House as it was when Kenneth took over the tenancy.  The hump of Cnoc Or is in the background and the Arnisdale Lodge policies had not been planted.   .

**Middle Left.**   Kenneth MacLeod with two of his sons – Donald (left) and Roddy (Roddy Mor).   **Right.**  Kenneth with his 3 daughters (L to R) Bella, Flo and Ella.

**Bottom Left.**   A Lochcarron group with Kenneth's sons Donald (rear on left) and Murdo (front left).
**Right.**  Kenneth's grandson Kenny MacKenzie (Kenny 'Jeck') of Lochcarron within sight of the old family croft home at Reraig which the family left to come to Arnisdale.

**Top Left.**  A closer view of the location of the former croft home of the MacLeod family at Reraig before their move to Arnisdale.
**Right.**  The oldest member of the MacLeod family, Christina, and her husband Ally Fletcher from Arnisdale with the eldest six of their nine children.  L to R.  Roddy, Lachie, Kenny, Annie, Peter and baby Mabel.

**Middle Left.**  The marriage of eldest son Donald to the Arnisdale teacher of the time, Mary MacKinnon who belonged to Tiree, with Roddy Mor as best man.   **Right.**   Donald and Mary MacLeod, who later farmed in Norfolk with son Alistair and daughter Anne.

**Bottom Left.**  The marriage of Murdo MacLeod to Bella Finlayson from Lochcarron.  Murdo and Bella had 3 children – Kenny, Nan and Rhoda.   **Right.**  The marriage of Bella MacLeod to Donald Forbes from Lochcarron with Bella's sister Flo as bridesmaid.

**Top Left.** A group at the Norfolk farm of Donald and Mary MacLeod includes daughter Anne and son Alistair and on the far right Bella (nee MacLeod) and her husband Donald Forbes.  **Centre.**  Young James Forbes, son of Bella and Donald in his naval uniform.  James is now resident in the Highland Capital with his wife Peggy and is widely known as an expert fiddler.  **Right**.  James Forbes playing some fine tunes.

**Middle Left**.  James Forbes and his young grandson Laith Ezzet from Vancouver, Canada play some tunes together.  **Centre**.  Ella (left) and Flo MacLeod.  Flo married Jeck MacKenzie of Lochcarron, a noted Lochcarron shinty player in the 1920-1930 era.  **Right.**  seated:  Flo and Bella MacLeod with Jeck MacKenzie (left) and Dan Mackay.

**Bottom Left**.  Neil Mackay (right), son of Dan and Ella, as a young lad with his Dance Band mates, Arthur Harper and Charlie Wilson.  **Right.**  Jeck MacKenzie (left foreground) with his Lochcarron team-mates after winning the Conchra Cup Final in 1932.

**Top Left.** Another victorious Lochcarron team, winners of the 1972 Dewar Shield, containing Kenny 'Jeck' and Tommy 'Jeck', two of Jeck and Flo's sons. The team members are Front (L to R.) Murdo MacLean (Monty), Lachie MacKenzie, Tommy MacKenzie (Jeck), Kenny Cameron, Alasdair MacKenzie (Ham), Jimmy Cushnie (and son Gregor). Back (L to R.) Roddy MacLennan, Hugh Matheson, David Ross, Calum MacKenzie (Cappy), Kenny MacKenzie (Jeck), Willie MacKenzie (Dula), Kenny John Stewart, Norrie Matheson, Ronnie Ross. **Right.** The new teacher in Arnisdale School in 1917, Lizzie MacDonald from GlenUrquhart (seated) with her youngest sister, Lily (the mother of the author).
**Middle Left.** Roddy Mor during his First World War Service in the Lovat Scouts. **Right.** Roddy Mor is the middle member of this trio.
**Bottom Left.** A group of Lovat Scouts in World War 1 with Willie MacKenzie (Willie the Post) far right in the back row and Roddy Mor far right in the second row. When Roddy Mor returned to Arnisdale when War ended in 1918 a romance blossomed with the new Arnisdale teacher. **Right.** The marriage of Roddy Mor and Aunt Lizzie in 1923 with Roddy's brother Murdo as best man and Aunt Lizzie's youngest sister, Lily (the author's mother) as bridesmaid.

**Top Left.** Kenneth MacLeod transferred the tenancy of Arnisdale Home Farm to his youngest son Roddy Mor soon after the latter returned from the War in 1918. Kenneth then took the tenancy of the Lochcarron Hotel and the adjoining farm. **Right**. Kenneth at the doorway of the Lochcarron Hotel.

**Middle Left**. Totaig Ferry on Loch Duich. In the old days, drovers took sheep and cattle from Arnisdale and Glenelg to Totaig, crossed on the ferry and took the beasts onwards to Stromeferry where they were loaded on to the train for sale at the Dingwall Market. **Right.** The house at Rarsaidh which was occupied by the Cameron family at the time of Kenneth MacLeod's tenancy of the Arnisdale Home Farm. Old Mrs Cameron had originated from Reraig across the hill from Kishorn and the families were great friends.

**Bottom Left.** Although 'monsoons' occur frequently in Arnisdale, on sunny days many flock to the beach like this handsome trio in the 1930s. L to R. Alistair Fletcher, Charlie MacTavish and Roddy 'Jeck' MacKenzie. **Right.** Roddy 'Jeck' MacKenzie, eldest son of Jeck MacKenzie and Flo (nee MacLeod) beside the grave of his maternal grandfather and grandmother, Kenneth and Annie MacLeod, in Lochcarron Churchyard.

# Chapter 6

**Iain MacKenzie and the Arnisdale Estate**

Iain has been the Arnisdale Estate's resident manager for many years. The Lodge and Estate is now owned by the Richmond Watson family who have their base in Northants. At the time of writing, Iain is the Estate's sole remaining employee.

Apart from his Army Service, Iain has been an ever present resident in Arnisdale. Iain was born in Corran, received all his schooling in Arnisdale and, on leaving school at 14 years of age, his first job was as a ghillie/handyman on the Arnisdale Estate, when it was owned by the Kitson family. At that time, between the Lodge staff, the gardeners, boatmen and ghillies/stalkers/gamekeepers/shepherds, the estate employed almost twenty folk in the season and four or five for the remainder of the year. The part-time seasonal work was very important to many of the crofters and, between what the croft provided and their income from estate work, they kept themselves above the subsistence level. Therefore, the estate was an extremely important part of the Arnisdale economy, providing employment for the parents of young families and helping to preserve a viable population and services in the village such as the shops (Peggy Ann's and Johnny MacGillivray's, the School and the District Nurse, while also maintaining reasonable congregations for both the Free Church and Church of Scotland communities.

Later in Iain's first summer of working for the estate in 1951, Roddy Mor at the farm approached Robert Kitson with a view to employing Iain for a few weeks to help with the hay as Roddy's previous 'assistant' (the author) had returned to school after the long summer holiday. Robert Kitson kindly agreed to Iain's temporary transfer to the farm.

Having reached agreement in principle for the transfer, Roddy Mor then had to agree a wage with his new employee. "How much were you getting a week at the Lodge?" queried Roddy Mor. "One Pound and Ten Shillings (£1.50)" replied Iain. "I'll give you £3", said Roddy. "OK, that's fine" Iain enthused - and the deal was done. The hay was won and all safely stored in the barn within the next two weeks, so Iain returned to his employment at the Lodge.

"How much was Roddy paying you?", Robert Kitson asked. "£3", replied Iain. "I'll give you Three Pounds Ten Shillings (£3.50)", said Robert. "OK, that's fine, thank you very much", the surprised Iain responded. Iain reminisced recently - "that was a man's wage I was getting at the age of 14 - it's a pity that Roddy did not have another job for me for a few weeks later on!" And Iain did not even ask for a rise - he only answered the questions asked of him - and Roddy and Robert did the rest!

That was Roddy Mor's last hay crop in Arnisdale, for arrangements were already under way for Roddy and Lizzie to give up the tenancy of the Arnisdale Home Farm at the 1952 May Term and to 'retire' to Glenelg.

In the following year, Iain was offered a job as ghillie/handyman on the Barrisdale Estate on the Knoydart side of Loch Hourn. His friend Charlie MacTavish was already working there and living in the bothy which he would now share with Iain.

When the mystery of the fabled beast of Barrisdale is mentioned to Iain he emphasises that he has seen nothing unusual, but one night while sitting in the bothy alone, he heard one of the most grotesque noises of his life. When he went outside to investigate further, he heard the same gruesome noise coming from across the river and up the Glen. Later Tom Swanney, his wife Ivy and Tom's brother-in-law, Gordon Waters, all of whom came from the Orkney Islands, all heard similar frightening sounds to those heard earlier by Iain.

Folk such as George MacDougall from Camusban, who worked in Barrisdale as a shepherd while in his 70s, used to suggest that the noises might be associated with the loss of life of a man who resided in the bothy when a big squad of men (reportedly 28) were based there while building and maintaining the fine footpaths along the southern shore of Loch Hourn, up Mam Barrisdale and down the other side to Inverie, as well as the other footpaths up traditional stalking routes.   The mystery remains.

When he was eighteen years old, Iain left to do his National Service in the Seaforth Highlanders.  After training at Fort George, Iain then saw service in Gibraltar, Egypt and Aden.  On his demob, he got a job on the Eilanreach Estate of Lord Dulverton.  'Y' MacLeod was the Manager but Iain spent a lot of his time planting conifers in the new forest which was being established under the direction of forester Angus Campbell.   However, Iain got a change of work during the stag shooting season when he was deployed as a stalker.  After three years at Eileanreach, Iain's next three year stint was as assistant to his cousin, Murdo MacKenzie, running the ferry at Kylerhea to and from Skye.

But then the time came for him to get back to Arnisdale in the mid 1960s - for Lachie Fletcher, as Estate Manager, had been building up the sheep stock since he took over in 1959 and he wanted a good young shepherd/ghillie/ stalker - so Lachie did not have to look too far for his man.

But, let us back track a little to the completion of Roddy Mor's tenancy of the Arnisdale Home Farm.

The MacLeod tenancy of the farm had lasted since 1902 when Roddy Mor's father, Kenny (Coinneach) was awarded the tenancy, Roddy taking over soon after he returned from serving in the Lovat Scouts throughout the Great War - in the Dardanelles, Gallipoli, Egypt and France - along with Iain's father - the first 'Willie the Post', Willie's brother, Norman and Glenelg lads including Rory MacPherson from Moyle.

During Roddy Mor's tenancy of the Home Farm, he kept six or seven cows which were all hand milked, with the calves being reared on skim milk along with some oil cake.  Calving took place mainly in the early spring and, after the calves had been separated from the cows for the first four or so weeks of their lives, they then joined the cows between milkings on the rough inbye grazings to the south (towards Corran and the Crudh Ard) and the east of the farm steading.  The calves (later stirks) were then sold as store cattle in the following Autumn sales as 18 month old beasts.  However, Roddy's main enterprise was the sheep.  He had approximately 400 Cheviots (South Country) of his own and a further 400 Blackfaces which were a 'Club' stock, shared equally between himself, Donald MacLaren (the head gamekeeper/ stalker/ghillie/shepherd) and the Kitsons.   The 800 ewes on the 9500 acres of the Arnisdale hill grazings was considerably lower than the stocking rate around the turn of the century, and indeed than the flock size run later by Lachie Fletcher (Roddy Mor's nephew) when Lachie managed the Estate from the late 1950s to the late 1970s. Roddy Mor's limited stocking rate may have been dictated by the Estate as a condition in his tenancy agreement in an attempt to improve the quality and productivity of the deer, and particularly the offtake - the size and calibre of the heads (the antlers) of the stags as well as the numbers shot.

Roddy and Lizzie's tenant's stock, including their limited machinery and farm implements, along with the cattle and sheep stock, were valued by the valuers - MacDonald Fraser and Company of Inverness in May 1952 - and Roddy Mor relinquished the tenancy of Arnisdale Home Farm in the May Term (Whitsun) on 28 May, 1952.  The MacLeod tenancy of the Home Farm had lasted for fifty momentous years - spanning the two World Wars.

Just before the end of Roddy's tenancy, the Kitsons appointed Jimmy Mitchell, from Alford in Aberdeenshire, as the Estate Manager. Jimmy was much more a cattleman than a shepherd and set out to increase the cattle stock and, through time, changed the method of conserving surplus summer's grass for winter feeding from hay to silage. When Jimmy started his stint as Manager he had among his staff the Estate workers - Ludovic Fraser, Kenny Fletcher and young Iain MacKenzie. Later Jimmy Mitchell, who was resident at Glenfield, appointed Jimmy Ritchie and later Bob MacRobbie as his Cattleman/Tractorman and Bob and his family lived in the Farm House, next to the steading. A few years after Jimmy's appointment, the Estate changed hands, the Kitsons selling out to the Richmond Watson family.

Jimmy was succeeded as Farm Manager in 1959 by Lachie Fletcher. Between them, Lachie and Mr Richmond Watson decided on increasing both the cattle and sheep stocks. Lachie gradually built up a herd of mainly Aberdeen Angus cross Hereford suckler cows. These were mated to Hereford bulls to calve in the springtime, with weaned calves being sold at the Autumn sales. Lachie was a great sheep man and built up a flock of 3000 Blackface ewes on the Arnisdale hill. Thus, the 9500 acres of the estate - about 98 per cent of it rough hill ground - carried a considerable number of stock in the summer - 3000 ewes and their lambs, 70 suckler cows and their calves and almost 1000 red deer, with the hinds producing their calves in the June/July period. The winter stocking was the same - except for the calves and lambs sold at the autumn sales - but the deer numbers were even higher in winter, with many stags moving in from colder, more exposed, areas in Glen Shiel and Glen Quoich to the warmer, more sheltered areas near Loch Hourn for the toughest of the winter months.

Lachie's staff on the farm was boosted the year after he started when Mr Richmond Watson, the laird, managed to persuade Lachie's younger brother, Peter, that he should come back to work in Arnisdale as Estate Handyman. Peter was a self-taught craftsman at all the jobs that required attention on the Estate - the maintenance of the Lodge, the other buildings, joinery, mason work, roofing, plumbing and electrical; the repair and maintenance of the many miles of estate dykes and fences, the bridle paths and bridges, the servicing of tractors and the estate vehicles for going up the hill paths to bring home the shot stags and hinds, the maintenance of the engines and the general sea-worthiness of the boats - and many other jobs besides. Peter was also great company, had a ready wit and could get many 'fine tunes' out of his fiddle. He was a superb 'catch' for the estate and provided great support for all. At about the same time as Peter's appointment, another old Arnisdale native had returned to the village to 'retire' after a long career as a police constable in Glasgow - George MacDougall. Although George was of retiring age, he did not believe in growing old. George, whose daughter Chrissie was married to Lachie, knew the Arnisdale hill very well from his boyhood years, he was good with his sheep and he was appointed as one of the shepherds. He was still 'running' up and down the formidable Arnisdale hills at the sheep gatherings when he was well into his 80s and he was still grafting away at the silage making and other jobs down at the farm when he was in his early 90s. George was made of good stuff. Lachie's farm staff was completed when he managed to recruit Iain MacKenzie as shepherd/cattleman/stalker from his work on the Kylerhea ferry, and then with the appointment of Danny Mackay as tractorman/cattleman. Danny hailed from the Balquhidder district of West Perthshire. By this time, of the old squad of stalkers/ghillies/gamekeepers/shepherds, Ludovic Fraser had now retired but Lachie's older brother, Kenny, was still in the squad. Although slowing up a bit by now, Kenny was still a good stalker and adept at other estate jobs too - but at his own pace. Kenny had a great fund of stories, and was a fine singer of Gaelic songs when in the mood at evening ceilidhs - and was good company.

The Arnisdale Farm consists of approximately 35 acres of permanent grass fields, suitable for hay and silage making, along the shore line on either side of the farm steading with some additional small fields at the bottom of Glen Arnisdale bordering the river. Then there is Achadh a'Ghlinne (about 50 acres), the big fenced flat in the cradle of the surrounding hills, part of which was used for silage making in

Lachie's era as farm manager. Beyond the Achadh as you travel eastwards up Glen Arnisdale there are the flats of Blar An Each (the field or moor of the horses) on the south side of the river on the lower slopes of Druim Fada and another 'blar' on the north side of the river below Beinn Chlachach. Above these flats is the Coille Mhor (the big wood) on the south facing slope of Beinn Chlachach. This wood is very largely made up of natural oak.

These flats to the east of the Achadh are good productive areas for the summering of cows and calves while the Coille Mhor is a wintering area for a large red deer hind population.

Before describing the Arnisdale hill ground, it might be useful to list the names of the hills, the corries and other features within and just outside the Arnisdale Estate march:

Beinn na h-eaglaise - The Church hill

Beinn Bhuidhe - The yellow or dun hill - probably named from its colour in the Autumn when the predominance of deer grass provides a basic dun or light brown colour to the slopes.

Beinn Chlachach - The rocky ben

Allt Utha - The Burn flowing steeply down the valley between Beinn Bhuidhe and Beinn Chlachach. The spectacular waterfall on this burn is called Eas an Cuin.

Coire Chorsalain - The Corrie between Beinn nan Caorach and Beinn Chlachach

Beinn nan Caorach - The hill of the sheep

Druim nam Bo - The ridge of the cattle - runs due northwards from the top of Beinn na h-eaglaise

Beinn Aoidhdailean -

Bealach Aoidhdailean - The pass of Beinn Aoidhdailean

Sgurr-na Laire Brice - The pinnacle of the speckled mare. (Possibly the speckled mare gave birth to her foal there or was born there herself)

Druim na Firean - The Ridge of the Eagle

Spidean Dhomhuill Bhric - The peak of speckled Donald. Why was Donald speckled? Did he have a heavily freckled face or was his face pitted as typified those who had survived the scourge of smallpox?

Bealach a'Chasain - The Glen from the top of Glen More which runs southwards to cross the Bealach (pass) between Druim na firean and Spidean Dhomhuill Bhric to join the old drove road from Kylerhea and Glen Beag near Crionaich. Chasain are the 'feet' and the name Bealach a' Chasain might signify the very steep climb up to the Bealach at the south side of this long Glen.

Sgurr Leac nan each - Leac - a flat or flag stone or tombstone. The pinnacle of the flagstone of the horse. Did a pack horse or riding horse break a leg or die from other causes here and was buried below the flat stone?

An Diollaid - The Saddle. When this hill is viewed from the east - the Kinloch Hourn side, the raised section in the middle is like a saddle with the long ridges on either side resembling the neck and rear end of a horse.

Allt a'Choire Odhar - The grey or dun coloured corrie. Was it grey because of the rocks or does the name refer to the light colour of the withered grasses in the autumn, winter and early spring?

Mullach Gorm - The green top

Allt Coire Mhalagain - The burn of the Malagain Corrie

Mam an Staing - The bealach of the market stance

Carn nan caorach - The cairn of the sheep

Lochan Carn nan caorach - The lochan of the cairn of the sheep.

Lochan nan Crionaich - Crionaich loch

Gleann Dubh Lochain - The glen of the black lochs

Dubh Lochain - The black lochs

Druim Fada - The long ridge

Caolas Mor - The big firth or strait (The firth with the big (fast flowing) current in Upper Loch Hourn).

Sgurr Mor - The big pinnacle (on Druim Fada).

The Arnisdale Estate March starts on the west side at the Scots Pine trees by the roadside between Rarsaidh and Arnisdale (Eilanreach Estate is on the other side). The march then runs eastwards across the lower slopes of Beinn Sgritheall and along the top of the Camusban croft lands. It then goes up the west shoulder of Beinn na h-eaglaise and over Bealach Arnaisdail between Beinn Sgritheall and Beinn na h-eaglaise. From there it runs down the spine of Druim nam Bò before moving eastwards across the north facing slope of Beinn nan caorach. It then runs on to the top of Sgurr na laire Brice and continues eastwards across the ridge of Druim na firean before it crosses the highest point of Bealach a'Chasain to the top of Spidean Dhomhuill Bhric (it now has Glen Shiel estate to the north). After this it runs just below the highest point of the Saddle across its south facing slope and down into Allt Coire Mhalagain (now the Kinlochourn Estate is to the east). The march then swings westwards to Crionaich and climbs up the north facing slope of Druim Fada at the Dubh Lochain. It continues over the ridge of Druim Fada and moves down the south facing slope towards Loch Hourn, reaching the sea about half a mile west of Caolas Mor. The estate to the east is that of Kinlochhourn.

It is tough but very interesting territory. Despite the very high rainfall, it is fairly productive - as judged by the high stock numbers it carried in the 1960s and 1970s - with reasonable annual productivity from the sheep, cattle and deer populations.

In the years of the 3000 ewe stock, the regular sheep gatherings throughout the year for such operations as dipping, marking lambs, shearing and weaning took a lot of time, required good fit, skilled men who knew the territory, good dogs and clear weather.

There would usually be six gatherings over six suitable days to get the sheep in. The approximate numbers coming in on each of the gathers were as follows:

Day 1        Beinn nan caorach - 300 ewes

Day 2        Sgurr na Laire Brice and the mosses towards Druim na firean - 400 ewes

Day 3   Spidean Dhomhuill Bhric, over to the Saddle, then south into Coire Mhalagain and Mullach Gorm - 600 ewes

Day 4   Beinn Chlachach.   This was a particularly difficult gather because of the extremely rocky nature of the hill and the Coille Mhor on the lower south facing slopes        - 700 ewes

Days 5 and 6   Druim Fada. This was a very extensive territory which took two days to gather -1000 ewes.

On good clear days for gathering, over 95 per cent of the sheep on a particular hill area would be in the final gather. With the natural cunning of Blackface sheep and the nature of the territory, it was virtually impossible to achieve a 100 per cent gather, despite the high quality of shepherds and dogs. When gathering the northernmost reaches of the estate - the Sgurr na Laire Brice, Druim na firean, Spidean Dhomhuill Bhric, the Saddle and the Coire Mhalagain areas, Iain Mackenzie would start his day's gathering from Glen Shiel. Peter Fletcher would run him to Achnagart - usually around 5 o'clock in the morning, Iain and his dogs would come up Allt Coire Mhalagain on the Glen Shiel side and come in on the Saddle, Spidean Dhomhuill Bhric and the other far distant Arnisdale hill grazings from the Glen Shiel end. Lachie, Kenny, George and sometimes Danny Mackay would be waiting in pre-arranged positions for Iain's arrival with the Arnisdale sheep which he had found on the Glen Shiel side of the march, and then together, they and their dogs would sweep the rest of the territory to be gathered. That gather would be taken into the Arnisdale Glen near Crionaich and from there down the Arnisdale Glen into Achadh a'Ghlinne. On arrival there - sheep, dogs and shepherds would heave a big sigh of relief and - if any refreshing tea was left in the thermos flasks - they would have it there. The sheep would be left there in the Achadh overnight to await the operation - dipping, clipping - or whatever was in store for them the next day.

So the shepherds would set off on the gather around 5 a.m., they would be up on the tops at first light to start their gather - and often it would be 8 o'clock in the evening before the haven of Achadh a'Ghlinne was reached. It was a very long day - but also very satisfying for all - if the weather had remained reasonable, the mist had not descended on the tops and the gather had gone well.

At lambing time, all the ewes would be taken down to the Achadh a'Ghlinne, the inbye fields and the flats east of the achadh so that they could receive more attention and assistance as required. Ewes and lambs which were well bonded - and where the lamb had got off to a good start in life - would be let out to the hill within one week of lambing. The mother would then gradually lead her lamb to her own regular grazing area on the hill - her own heft. The lambing percentage - the number of lambs sold at the autumn sales (or retained as replacement ewe hoggs) for every 100 ewes that were there at tupping time - would be 80 in a good winter and spring and 75 in a bad season. About 5 or 6 ewes out of every 100 would not be in lamb for one reason or another. Lamb losses would range between 15 and 20 for every 100 born. Some would be lost through the depredations of foxes or a rogue golden eagle. But

Iain MacKenzie is of the firm opinion that most lambs die due to chilling or hypothermia in cold, wet, windy weather at lambing and because of the diseases which are transmitted by the ticks - such as tick pyaemia and joint ill. It is a tick infested hill and the ticks and the diseases they transmit also affect the deer.

The preventative measures used against the tick were the regular twice a year dipping - the first about three weeks before lambing to minimise the tick infestation transmitted to new-born lambs and the second was in November.

The tupping took place on the hill, with the rams being put out around 28 November so that the first lambings - some 145 days later - would not be expected until around the 20 April. By that time all on the farm would hope that Spring had begun, the soil had warmed up, the conditions were somewhat warmer and the first blades of new spring grass would be pushing themselves up invitingly above ground level to satisfy some of the nutritional needs of ewes in late pregnancy and those which had just lambed - and were trying their best to produce enough colostrum and milk to meet the needs of their new lambs for survival, growth, fitness and good health.

The replacement tups were purchased in Inverness for an average of £100 per head. They had to be tough to do their work on the Arnisdale hills at mating time. Lachie was a very thorough working manager/shepherd, Iain MacKenzie remembers. They were among the sheep on the hills every day at tupping time, ensuring that the tups, which were clearly marked with copious bright coloured paint, were well spread out among all the ewes - so as to ensure that the maximum number was mated and had a chance of producing a lamb to cover her year's keep on the farm - and perhaps leave a little extra profit besides.

The rams were kept for about four years, spending the first two years on one hirsel (grazing area) and then being transferred to another hirsel for the next two years. This prevented the rams from mating with their own progeny and thus resulting in in-breeding, with consequent degeneration in the quality of the stock.

The lambs were weaned from their mothers in late August and sold soon afterwards at the Autumn sales. Iain remembers that, in general, the weaned lambs were a fine, well grown and uniform crop - which indicated that the ground was certainly not over-stocked.

When the ground carried over 3000 ewes, there was no evidence that the performance and quality of the deer suffered in any way. The mineral status of the hill also appeared to be good - as indicated by the good teeth in the ewe stock. By the time they weaned their fourth crop of lambs on the hill (at five and a half years of age) almost every ewe had a full set of incisor teeth - her main mechanisms for harvesting the hill forage. The old ewes were culled at this stage and most went on to produce further lamb crops on low ground farms.

Lachie believed in rearing the replacement ewe hoggs at home in their first winter - rather than wintering them away on low ground farms in the east coast - which is a very common practice in hill sheep farming. From around early November, the replacement ewe hoggs (about 800 of them) would be confined to the sheep pens in the fank and offered silage and water - at first most of them would show very little interest in the stuff - but soon they would be driven by a combination of hunger and curiosity to investigate and nibble at the silage. It would not be long before they were all eating silage and then they would be released to the inbye fields - where silage would be made available to them throughout the winter months - with limited amounts of bruised oats in addition.

Regarding the deer population on the Arnisdale Estate, Iain MacKenzie estimates that there is a regular population of approximately 450 hinds and 250 stags - with another 300 or so stags making their way on to the estate over the worst of the winter months from tough exposed and colder areas of Glen Shiel and Glen Quoich. As well as better shelter, they almost certainly enjoy better feeding in the more sheltered areas of Arnisdale near the sea and especially in wooded areas on south facing slopes.

Iain estimates that just under half of the hinds produce calves in a year and, as in all areas, calves suffer fairly high mortality - some from diseases transmitted by ticks - but most of the deaths occur in their first winter - mainly through malnutrition and exposure. Having calved in June and July, many are just not sufficiently well grown before the tough months of winter arrive. It is not the scarcity of herbage in their natural grazings which is the problem but the low digestibility of the material available to them in winter. This, combined with cold, wet, windy conditions is just too much for them and they succumb. Only the fittest survive to adulthood to produce the next generation - and this, of course, is the way of the wild - and the basis of maintaining the strong genetic constitution of wild species. It is sad - but it is reality. The offtake from the Arnisdale deer forest is an average of 50 stags and 50 hinds per year. This offtake is designed to maintain a constant breeding population. Of course, if approximately 200 calves are born in an average year on Arnisdale - it indicates that only about half make it to adulthood.

Stags in the Arnisdale Forest reach prime condition for shooting at anything over five years of age. However, despite the stags being very well grown and in excellent condition when shot in season, the quality of the heads (the antlers) is generally disappointing.

Hinds are culled at anything from 18 months of age (poorly grown, ill - thriving youngsters which are unlikely to survive the winter) - up to 20 years of age. Some hinds breed regularly and rear a calf year after year. When old hinds fail to thrive, this is partly because they are losing their incisor teeth and their efficiency of harvesting their daily requirements of forage is deteriorating. Some hinds in the Arnisdale Forest will start to lose incisor teeth from about 12 years of age.

Has Iain seen any unusual hinds or stags in the Arnisdale Forest? No, there are some hinds with white markings but nothing else unusual. But early this century a white male deer calf was born at the back of Donald MacAskill's house on Achadh a'Ghlinne on the lower slopes of Beinn Clachach when Donald, his wife and his family (Lachie, Allan, Maggie, Mary and Jessie) stayed there. It grew into a fine white stag which graced the Arnisdale Forest for a few years. However, at the time of the rut one Autumn, it set off to more inviting territory to find new hinds. It never returned and the bush telegraph indicated that it had been shot in Glen Affric.

Has Iain seen anything else of interest in all his many wanderings over almost every spot in the Arnisdale Forest? "Well, early one morning, I was walking up the path at the Dubh Lochain setting off on a sheep gather, I was totally sober, and I met this very smart lady in full Highland Dress coming towards me. She wore a plaid, and had cock feathers in her Glengarry bonnet. As we passed I looked at her and wished her good morning. She did not respond to my greeting. She was a nice looking lady and I turned round wondering that she did not return my greeting. When I looked round, the path on her route was empty - she had disappeared! I never could explain that experience".

Iain has seen many remains of small buildings over many parts of the estate - on top of some of the hills, on the slopes and in the corries. . They are probably the remains of small sheilings where folk in the past stayed in the summer while herding the cattle, the goats and the sheep.

What about the salmon fishing in the Arnisdale river? In the past, the river used to provide an average catch of over 50 salmon per season but the catch has been very disappointing in recent years. Iain speculates that the fish farming on Loch Hourn may have had an influence on this decline, there being theories that caged salmon may send out distress signals to their wild fellows, just as the dolphins and whales have their elaborate communication systems. The Estate is trying to redress the damage of recent years, whatever the causes, by 'seeding' the river with salmon fry - 57,000 fry each year having been released into the upper reaches of the river below Coire Mhalagain in recent years.

The trout in the Dubh Lochain are small but fairly plentiful. Of course, the dam on the Dubh Lochain has been deliberately breached in more recent years because it was becoming unsafe. It had been built by a proprietor in the early part of the century - Valentine Fleming - to help create a 'spate' in dry weather in the late summer and autumn to entice the salmon and sea trout massing at the mouth of the river - to come up the river so that the fishing would be enhanced and, later, those which escaped the lures of the fishers could spawn and regenerate the stock. The man in charge of building the dam was Donald Sheorais (Campbell) from Camusban and Iain tells an amusing story involving Donald and his father 'Willie the Post' during the dam building, which will be related later.

What about the eagles and the foxes? Iain knows of three pairs of eagles which nest regularly on the estate and he reckons that they live pretty much in harmony with the environment, mainly feeding on deer carrion. Only occasionally does a rogue eagle cause depredations among the lamb crop in the spring time. Foxes too are kept in balance. There are good official and unofficial fox hunters around who do a good job. Rabbits on the lower reaches of Glen Arnisdale provide part of their food source. However, they have to be kept in check because they have plenty of hiding places, dens and potential dens in the rocky fastnesses of the estate and they could soon get out of hand if they are not carefully controlled. Iain, and others, suspect that some 'do gooders' from the south may be transporting young semi-tame foxes up to the Highlands and releasing them to what they hope, in their naivity, might be a perfect lifestyle in the hills. When Iain and his cronies come across a fox in the hills which appears to present itself as a 'sitting duck', obviously lacking in the extreme cunning of the native stock, they suspect that it might have a southern 'twang'.

The Arnisdale Estate hill country relates mainly to deer, sheep, wildlife and a great deal of history - about people and places - of travellers along the mountain highways - through the glens and over the bealachs, of gamekeepers, stalkers, shepherds - and poachers. Much of that history is lost and we can now only speculate on the origin of the names of the bens, the ridges and the valleys.

What of the lower ground on the Arnisdale Estate and the folk there? After the eras of Bob MacRobbie and Danny MacKay, Iain and his family took up occupation of the old farmhouse home of folk like Coinneach MacLeod and his family, and later Roddy and Lizzie. Iain married Dorothy Jane Morrison, the sister of the then estate handyman, Len, in 1963. Iain and Dorothy's son, Jon was born in the following year. By the time Jon reached school age the Arnisdale school had closed so Jon travelled daily to Glenelg for his primary schooling and he had his secondary education in Plockton, where he boarded for the week and returned home at weekends. Jon is now married (to Carine) and is a member of the Banking Profession in Edinburgh, where he is an under-manager with the Clydesdale Bank. Jon has a close attachment to Arnisdale, its culture, history, its people and its beautiful places - and he and Carine come back to visit the haunts of his boyhood as often as they can.

Iain recalls the early days of the big clippings when the hill was carrying 3000 ewes. He was the only one who had adopted shearing using the electric shears. All the others - Lachie, Kenny and old George MacDougall were using hand shears and still clipping on the stool - which involved the laborious delivery of each ewe to the shearer by the 'crogger' (the catcher), turning the ewe over on its back on the platform of the stool, tying the two front legs and one back leg together to 'secure' the ewe, then proceeding with the shearing, and completing the job by untying the cord to release the legs, buesting and then the final release of the shorn beast. Not only could you get the fleece off more quickly using the machine but the ewe was being shorn on the ground, in a much more comfortable position for the ewe and it involved a lot less 'hassle' for shearer and ewe combined. Iain remembers one morning when they started clipping at 9 and finishing at 12 for their lunch and with a 15 minute break for a smoke and some tea in between. The fleeces were fine and dry, the sheep were in good condition and Iain had 92 shorn to show for his morning's work. He was not sure how many Kenny managed to do but he remembers Kenny being a bit mesmerised by Iain shouting almost constantly for the 'buest' and Danny Mackay moving like lightning between holding pen and Iain's shearing site to keep Iain supplied with new sheep to shear. Either Kenny's concentration on his own job was being somewhat upset or he was enjoying the 'entertainment' of rough sheep being delivered to Iain and leaving him fully shorn not too many moments later. It was not part of the leisurely pace which had characterised the clipping from Kenny's earliest years - with plenty of time for story telling and leg-pulling of each other, which was the way of making the work more acceptable - and much more enjoyable!

All the workers on the farm had a cow at that time which was part of their perks. All the cows - those of Lachie, Peter, Iain, Danny and George - were kept on the farm and their summer grazing and winter fodder were provided by the estate. They also kept a few extra cows - so that when Mr Richmond Watson and his family came up for their season's shooting and fishing, there would be surplus milk to supply the lodge. The regular supply of milk for their respective households and the sale price of their calf at the annual calf sales in Inverness provided a useful extra 'bonus' to their regular wages.

In addition, they had a regular supply of venison in season and they were also allowed to fish the river for salmon and sea trout. Soon after Mr Richmond Watson, Senior took over the estate, he invited all the crofters in Arnisdale to a meeting and gave all of them the opportunity to get a hind in the shooting season and to fish the river. The only stipulations were that they could not fish the river for three days before the arrival of himself and his family to fish, and if they were going to the hill for a hind for their own pot (and to be shared with neighbours who were unable to go to the hill), that they should let Lachie know in advance so that they would not spoil an intended stalk by the laird and his family. The following were the contents of the offer sent out by Mr Richmond Watson to all Arnisdale residents in 1961.

**Hind Shooting in Arnisdale 1961/62 Winter.**
Hinds may be shot by:-
    1. Anyone on the Arnisdale staff
    2. Crofters from Corran
    3. Crofters from Camus Ban.
The Ponies and harness may be borrowed to bring the hinds in if required.

Arnisdale staff should be given a reasonable portion of the venison, the rest only to be consumed at Corran and Camus Ban; No venison to leave these areas.

Lachie Fletcher in charge of these arrangements and nobody can shoot hinds without first obtaining his permission.

Lachie Fletcher will use his own judgement in deciding which part of the Forest will be stalked at any time and will forbid certain areas if he thinks that too many are being killed in these areas.

No more than 30 hinds to be shot.    Mr Richmond Watson - 14.12.61

This gesture by Mr Richmond Watson was greatly appreciated by the local folk.

There was a general saying in neighbouring localities at this time that 'all the folk in Arnisdale are gamekeepers'. There was no further need to do any poaching on the part of the locals and they would all be on the lookout for any 'outsiders' who came in to raid 'their' deer and salmon stocks!

In addition to this generosity, it was very customary when Lachie and Iain were at the hind shooting, rather than sell all the hinds shot, some would be cut up on the estate into joints and a good supply of venison would be provided to all the folk in the village. It is perhaps little wonder that Mr Richmond Watson was tagged with the nickname of 'Sunny' by the local folk.

The 1960s and 1970s, when the estate was under Lachie's management, were the last 'heydays' of the Arnisdale Estate in more recent times. The estate employed a lot of people, some with young families, and the whole community benefitted from the buoyancy and generosity of the estate and, despite a high wage bill and other expenses, the estate was profitable - with reasonable income being obtained from the output of lambs, calves and venison. However, just before the special European Community (EC) Sheepmeat Scheme was launched in the early 1980s, hill sheep farming was becoming less profitable and, on Lachie's retirement as Estate manager, the decision was taken to sell off the sheep stock of 3000 Blackfaces. While being a wise decision at the time, in the light of 'knowledge after the event' and the great boost to sheep prices and the profitability of sheep which followed the launch of the new EC Sheepmeat Scheme, the decision to sell off the sheep was, in retrospect, unfortunate.

After the sheep were sold off, the economy of the estate depended primarily on the cattle and the venison production. In more recent years, the cattle have been all but phased out, so that now the shot hinds and stags provide the estate's main income. With the phasing out of the sheep, and then the cattle, from the estate's activities, the staffing has also been reduced - with Iain being the sole remaining local employee - as the working manager.

Iain MacKenzie, in his long period of working alongside Lachie and Peter Fletcher on the Arnisdale Estate, developed expertise in all aspects of estate management and maintenance. He was the obvious successor when Lachie and Peter retired. If Lachie and Peter were alive today they would have glowing tributes to what Iain has achieved on the estate and within the Arnisdale community as a whole. In the circumstances, there are probably few others who could comment as knowledgeably at Iain's contribution than young Peter Fletcher, Lachie and Chrissie's son, who had considerable experience of the working of the estate - from accompanying his relatives and friends on gatherings, the stalking and the whole spectrum of activities associated with the running of a west Highland estate. Peter speaks in glowing terms of Iain's prowess with the rifle and the shotgun. Iain it was who was one of the main organisers of the Arnisdale Clay Pigeon Shoot which was a very popular event for many years among the gamekeeping and shooting fraternity. Iain himself was invariably well up the prize list.

Iain made an excellent job of teaching himself many of the skills required to keep a remote Highland estate and its equipment in good working order. Thus, in the repair and maintenance of engines for farm equipment or the boats, Iain was at the forefront of saving the estate considerable costs. Where there was a need for mason work, joinery, plumbing and electrical work, Iain learned much from Peter Fletcher (Senior) and he learned things thoroughly and well.

Iain regularly comes to the rescue of the Arnisdale folk when hazards such as wind, rain, snow and lightning play havoc with the Arnisdale TV reception. He sets off up the shoulder of Beinn Sgritheall to the mast - and works away at the mechanisms until perfect reception is restored. He has been Arnisdale's self appointed, unpaid, Television Engineer for the past seventeen years, having detected the best site for a mast along with his great friend Tom Swanney from Barrisdale.

He has been greatly supported in his work on the estate and for the community, first by his wife Dorothy Jane and son Jon and then later, over many years, by his partner, Chris Lea. His deep friendship with both Dorothy Jane and Chris continues.

Iain has a fund of stories about Arnisdale which have been gleaned from many people - his father - the first 'Willie the Post', from Lachie and Peter Fletcher and from his other working mates - these two characters - Kenny Fletcher and George MacDougall. George had a great knowledge of the hill and would cite old Gaelic names of places which do not appear on any modern maps. Iain remembers these names very clearly, but while he is a fluent Gaelic speaker, he would not claim to be a Gaelic scholar. Writing down these old place names which he gleaned from old George - and spelling them correctly in Gaelic - is not something that comes easily to Iain.

He remembers his father relating a story about the building of the dam on the Dubh Lochain. Donald Sheorais (George) Campbell was the foreman in charge and Iain's father, Willie, was labouring on the scheme as a young lad before the start of the 1914-18 war. Apparently every tool and wheelbarrow was clearly stamped with the initials of the laird - 'H.B.' for 'Harmood-Banner'. Willie had been barrowing gravel for the cement making all day long over a very long working day - and Donald Sheorais was a great worker himself and relentless in what he demanded of those under him. Willie trudged along with what he thought would be almost the last barrowful of the day and, as he emptied the barrow in the big heap he had created, he nonchalantly threw the upturned barrow down on the heap. However, the barrow moved down the heap - slowly at first - but gathered pace and - before Willie could stop it - down it tumbled towards the edge of the dam wall and over the precipice it went to crash on to the rocks far below - and went into a thousand bits. Donald Sheorais was furious at such youthful carelessness and - as he was about to launch into young Willie, Willie dived in first, "Look here", he said, "H.B. stands for - 'Tha (pronounced 'Ha') e briste!' (it is broken!). That means that it was broken before it fell over there!" In the moments it took for Donald to work out Willie's interpretation of the letters 'HB', Willie had bolted to escape Donald's wrath, hoping that he would have calmed down again by the following morning!

It was George MacDougall who told Iain about the prospecting for gold which took place on the estate in the latter part of the last century. One of the Foster family was reputed to have found a fair sized gold nugget in the shingle of the river just below the bridge linking Achadh a'Ghlinne with the Glen Arnisdale path to Corran. The story goes that the gold found by a prospector - a man named Cliff - was of high quality but not available in
commercially viable amounts. The same prospector was reputed to have assessed the quantities of 'soap stone' available on the banks of the burn which tumbles down the steep slope between Beinn Bhuidhe and Beinn Clachach into the Achadh a'Ghlinne. The interest in this stone was for the manufacture of Talcum Powder. However, once again, the material was assessed not to be available in workable quantities. The soap stone in the Achadh burn was well known to, and used by, the old Arnisdale folk. They would get a piece of the 'Clach Cuilleann' and use it to keep a white and clean, tidy appearance on their doorstep and hearth stones.

When Peter Fletcher, Junior, became old enough, he would accompany his seniors - including his father Lachie and grandfather George MacDougall - on stalks and at sheep gatherings. He remembers one amusing incident when he was accompanying his Uncle Kenny and each was leading a pony (Ginger and Sally) up the hill to take home two shot deer. There was a fair spate in the mountain streams and as Kenny came to this particular burn, leading the pony, he took a great leap across the raging torrent beneath his feet. However, Ginger the pony never moved from the other side, the rope tightened and Kenny landed right in the middle of the spate. Peter could not hide his extreme amusement. But Kenny was not amused! Ginger, wisely, made no comment and did not convey his innermost thoughts to his master, Kenny!

Peter Fletcher also tells the story of himself as a little boy, and a young friend, hunting for and finding fresh water mussels in one of the hill burns and on the very first day of such searching they found a lovely big pearl. They were so excited that they ran home to report the find to their family and friends. On seeing their exciting find, another friend thought he would join in the search and also make a quick fortune. The latter set off very early the next morning on his own - but he was spotted on his way to the 'treasure'. The two pearl fishers of the previous day then armed themselves with a heap of imitation pearls from a sister's necklace and quickly caught up with their friend. As they got down to their 'fishing', the two who had started the 'gold rush' on the previous day would excitedly claim to have found 'another beauty' on regular occasions. When the new 'prospector' asked to see their find - he could not believe his eyes as he viewed the handful of magnificent large shiny round pearls found by his friends! Boys will be boys - they might not make a fortune - but they have great fun!

Now let us return to Iain MacKenzie. Iain adopted one of his favourite hobbies not so many years ago and surprised himself, as much as others, with his talent in the making of fiddles. He liked fiddle music very much but had no inclination to play himself - probably because he was totally unaware of this latent talent. When Iain's old friend Peter Fletcher died, Lizzie, Peter's widow, gifted Peter's fiddle to Iain. On a visit from his friend and Peter's first cousin - Jimmy Forbes, from Inverness, Iain asked Jimmy, a noted fiddler, to have a go at his new fiddle. Jimmy could not make much of it but asked Iain if he could take it away with him to tune it. Jimmy returned in defeat. Iain asked Jimmy if he thought it would help if he made a new top for it. Jimmy thought that this might help - so Iain got a piece of white pine from a redundant church pew and shaped a new top for the fiddle. Iain was helped by a book on fiddle making which he had borrowed from his friend Ricky Rohde from Lea. When Jimmy Forbes returned and tried the fiddle, he could not believe it was the same fiddle - now with Jimmy's skill, it played some 'fine tunes' once again.

Iain has not looked back since then and is now widely recognised as an expert in the fine art of making fiddles. Among his many friends and admirers of the fiddle playing fraternity, is that great Shetland fiddler, Ali Bain, who Iain says is 'hard to beat'.

Iain's fiddle has had an interesting history. Apparently Peter Fletcher received it as a gift from his grandfather Coinneach MacLeod, proprietor of the Lochcarron Hotel in the 1920s. Coinneach, in turn, had bought it from one of the Travelling Folk by the name of Miller, who was trying to raise some money for himself. One day fairly recently, some travelling people came to Iain's door in Arnisdale. They were selling clothes pegs and other useful household goods. One of them asked Iain if they could see his fiddle, and when he agreed to show it to them, they asked if they could photograph it. Iain again consented. They explained to Iain that they were related to the girl, Henrietta Stewart, who just after the turn of the century, was drowned in the Arnisdale River when in spate, and who lies buried in the Arnisdale graveyard. They also explained that they were related to Miller, the original owner of the fiddle. They had kept track of its movements and were glad to meet up with an old family friend once again.

Iain claims that when he and his friends are having a good ceilidh in the house, with the old fiddle playing out its fine tunes, sometimes he sees the door opening slightly as if Coinneach or some of the other previous inhabitants of this happy house are coming to join them and enjoy the company. Iain thinks that the Farm House, along with the house at Lea, are the two oldest houses in the district, being built before the 1745 Rising. Iain has always found the house to provide good 'vibes' and it has been a very popular ceilidh house over the decades from the time of Kenny (Coinneach) MacLeod at the start of the century, followed by Roddy Mor and Lizzie, then the MacRobbie and Mackay families up to the current era of Iain and his own family.

Iain has benefited greatly from spending his working life with such interesting folk and from all the ceilidhs in which he has been a very active participant. He is well versed in the history of the place and knows the hill grazing areas of the Corran and Camusban crofts, the farmed areas of the estate and the deer forest as well as anybody. There are few corners that he has not explored.

He considers that the conservationists are having an excessive influence in turning localities such as the Loch Hourn area into wildernesses, with little thought given to the livelihoods of the folk who reside in these places, as their forebears have done for generations. The so-called conservationists are very concerned about the flora and the fauna, but seem to be totally unconscious of the need to preserve other extremely precious assets - the language, the culture, the music, the history and the ways of living of a people who have lived and worked in these parts for centuries, always with a great consciousness of sustaining resources for the benefit of the current and future generations.

He considers that the old crofting system should be modified to form more viable units for keen and competent youngsters, farming their cattle and sheep at sustainable stocking rates, as in the past. He sees considerable opportunities for a range of sporting and leisure pursuits involving fishing, shooting and sailing. He would also like to see more focus, as tourist interests, on the great range of flora and fauna of the district and also on the many places of historical interest. So that while tourism might provide the largest component of a rejuvenated economy, he favours a wider spectrum of activities to establish a sounder base which will provide better prospects in the longer term.

As Iain prepares for his retirement from his post as Estate Manager, he displays a strange mixture of pessimism and optimism about the future of Arnisdale and its environs but when, as devil's advocate, one supports his pessimistic scenario, he then begins to think and talk positively about his optimistic viewpoint - and he has plenty of good ideas as to how the old place might be re-invigorated to prepare itself for the twenty-first century. "It is far too good a place to let it die", he asserts with that look of determination dominating his whole expression. His forebears have played a very important role in serving and supporting the Arnisdale community for many decades and he wants to ensure that his followers will continue to play an important role in its future growth and development. Iain MacKenzie has always been a very determined and able fellow.

**Top Left.**  On leaving school at the age of 14, Iain MacKenzie's first job was as a ghillie/handyman on the Arnisdale Estate.  Iain is on the far right with L to R. Donald Fletcher, Iain's sister Flora and Sheena Stewart.
**Right.**  Iain MacKenzie (left) and Charlie MacTavish reminisce about their young days together on the Barrisdale Estate

**Middle Left.**  George MacDougall (left) who worked as a shepherd at Barrisdale in the 1970s had his own theories about the fabled beast of Barrisdale and the weird noises which some folk heard from time to time in that location.  **Right.**  Iain MacKenzie worked for a few years on the Kylerhea Ferry, assisting his cousin Murdo MacKenzie.

**Bottom Left.**  Lachie Fletcher at the Dubh Lochain in Glen Arnisdale.  After Lachie was appointed as Manager on the Arnisdale Estate, he recruited Iain MacKenzie as a shepherd/ghillie/stalker.   **Right.**  As well as greatly increasing the sheep stock, Lachie built up the suckler cow herd to around seventy breeding cows.

**Top Left.** Peter Fletcher with his wife Lizzie and children Tina and Jean. Peter was enticed back to Arnisdale to the job of Estate Handyman in the early 1960s.  **Right.** A view of the low ground part of Arnisdale Estate from Druim Fada showing the shoreline fields, the fields on the north side of the River Arnisdale from Corran (below) in the lower part of the Glen and eastwards (to the right) towards Achadh a' Ghlinne and Blar nan each further up the Glen.

**Middle Left.** The Coille Mhor (the big wood) mainly of native oak to the north of Blar nan Each and on the southern slopes of Beinn Clachach.  **Right.** The burn – Allt Utha which tumbles down the precipitous slopes between Beinn Bhuidhe on the left and Beinn Clachach, and then flows through Achadh a' Ghlinne to join up with the Arnisdale River.  The special stone Clach Chuilinn or 'holly stone' is found in this burn.

**Bottom Left.** Map of main features of the Arnisdale Estate and the adjacent territories.  **Right.** Some of Arnisdale's red deer stag population of the present era pasturing at Glenfield in the late spring/early summer period.  The view is eastwards up Glen Arnisdale.

**Top Left.** Iain MacKenzie at the oars, making up Loch Hourn for a stalk on Druim Fada with Antony Sheppard (left) and Chris. **Centre**. Iain MacKenzie (centre) with Lachie Fletcher (left) and Kenny Fletcher check on the location of the deer to work out the best strategy for their stalk. **Right.** Culmination of a successful stalk and shot on Beinn na h-Eaglaise for young Dan Richmond-Watson (left) and Iain MacKenzie.

**Middle Left.** Fishing for salmon and sea trout on the Arnisdale river, in common with most rivers around Britain is not as productive as formerly. In an attempt to rectify the situation the Estate have initiated a policy of 'seeding' the upper reaches of the river with salmon fry. **Right.** The dam on Dubh Lochain which was built by proprietor, Sir John Harmood-Banner, to help create an artificial spate in dry weather in late summer and autumn to entice salmon and sea trout up the river to spawn.

**Bottom Left.** Donald Sheorais Campbell (seated) with his nephew George MacDougall. As a young man, Donald Sheorais was in charge of building the dam on the Dubh Lochain. **Right.** The bridge across the river at Kinloch Hourn – another of Donald Sheorais' achievements as he was the foreman in charge.

**Top Left.** Iain MacKenzie has been one of the main organisers of the Arnisdale Clay Pigeon Shoot and has been a regular prizewinner over the years. **Right**. Alan MacAskill of Glenelg (centre) with a group of fellow competitors. **Below** (L to R). Donald Fletcher and John Arthur. Ewan Cameron and Roddy MacRae. Roddy Cameron. Freddie Main and Johnny MacLean.
**Middle Left.** Interested spectators at a Shoot – Rena MacDonald, Chrissie Morrison (nee MacCuaig) and Chrissie Campbell. **Right.** A trio waiting their turn to compete – L to R. Willie Douglas, Willie's grandson Eddie Pryce and Uisdean MacLure.
**Bottom Left.** Another group of competitors. L to R. George Stoddart, Charlie MacTavish, Alex Boyd, Billy MacKenzie, Willie MacKenzie, Peter MacRae, Roddy MacRae and Donald Fletcher in front of Arnisdale Lodge.
**Right.** George Stoddart collects his prize at a shoot in Barrisdale.

94

**Top Left.** Iain MacKenzie working on Arnisdale's TV receiver high up on the slopes of Beinn Sgritheall. Iain is Arnisdale's self-appointed, unpaid TV engineer. **Right.** Young Jon MacKenzie, son of Iain and Dorothy Jane, beside the Corran River with his friends Daniel MacDonald (left) and Angus Stewart.

**Middle Left.** Iain MacKenzie (seen here at the top of Beinn Sgritheall with sister Flora (left) and Morag MacIntyre) has developed a great interest in fiddle music and since he received a gift of the fiddle belonging to his good friend, the late Peter Fletcher, he has started to make fiddles himself. (Picture in House with friend). **Right.** Iain has found out that the fiddle inherited from his late friend Peter Fletcher has had an interesting history. It was once owned by the relatives of Henrietta Stewart who was drowned in the Arnisdale River while in spate in the early 1900s. Henrietta is the little girl in this picture taken in Quarry, Glenelg.

**Bottom Left.** Henrietta, who was one of the travelling people who plied their skills as tinkers in mending pots and pans on their annual rounds, is seen here outside the family's summer camp at the Bernera Market Stance, Glenelg. **Right.** James Forbes from Inverness, Grandson of Kenneth MacLeod visits Iain MacKenzie fairly regularly to play some fine tunes together.

# Chapter 7

**The Camusban Crofting Township and Charlie MacTavish**

Charlie is now one of the two active crofters left in Camusban, the other being Len Morrison who is now the Camusban Crofting Township Clerk. After a working life as a stalker, ghillie and head gamekeeper, Charlie and his wife Mary Kate returned to the old family home several years ago.

Charlie's father, Angan, was for a long time employed as a boatman by the Barrisdale Estate and later in the same capacity by the Arnisdale Estate before working in the Mialairidh Forest in his later years. Angan's mother was a Mary MacPherson from Camusban who married Archie MacTavish from Lochgilphead, a fisherman, in Barrisdale Church. When the children were still very young, Charlie's grandfather was drowned. Granny MacTavish then came back home from Glassary in Argyll to Camusban with her five children to make their home with her brother Angus MacPherson, who was a fisherman and bachelor. Angan was the youngest of that young family (being only a few days old when his father was drowned) while his brother Duncan was only 2 years older. Duncan was born in 1882 and in the early 1960s he made a fine written record of his memories of Camusban and all its people during his childhood in the later part of last century.

This extremely useful historical account of Duncan's is reproduced elsewhere in this book (Chapter 32).

Charlie's mother, Maggie Douglas before her marriage to Angan, was popularly known as Bean Angan (wife of Angan). In her youth she worked for Cameron of Lochiel in the Shooting Lodge in Glen Dessary where one of her neighbours was Maggie Stewart (nee MacPherson), the wife of the head shepherd in Glen Dessary, Angus Stewart. 'Auntie Maggie' as the author's wife Anne calls Mrs Stewart, was one of the MacPhersons of Moyle, Glenelg, and sister of Mrs Charlotte Chisholm of the Glenelg Post Office, of Peter MacPherson who was shepherd at Sandaig for the Eilanreach Estate in the 1930s and of Donald MacPherson, the Postmaster in Glenelg before Donald Chisholm. Maggie Douglas later worked in Barrisdale Lodge and it was there that she met Angan.

Maggie was a light-hearted person who enjoyed life to the full. She loved her croft and all her animals, the dogs, cats, hens, sheep and especially the cows. She was the last to have a milking cow in Camusban and in summer she could be found milking it in the byre, on the shore or on the hill - wherever she and Rosie happened to meet each other around milking time!

So Maggie and Angan were the last to work their croft in the old traditional way in Camusban. They were therefore part of the history of crofting in the village.

Following the deliberations of the Napier Commission in 1883 (which included the evidence provided by the two Camusban crofting representatives, Archibald Fletcher MacGillivray and John McIntyre) and the subsequent Crofting Acts, the Camusban Crofting Township was divided into 22 crofts with cattle, 17 of which had a souming for sheep. The maximum stocking allowed per croft or 'souming' was one cow and follower and ten ewes and two hoggs (young replacement ewes). The author is indebted to Charlie (the nephew of Duncan, who provided the excellent 1890s summary of the houses and people in Camusban) and his wife Mary Kate for the following summary of the 22 crofters with cattle and the 17 of these who were also allowed the 'souming' of sheep. These figures are based on Charlie's memories from his boyhood. They differ from his Uncle Duncan's memories from the 1890s because, in the interim, crofting tenancies had changed hands through inheritance and re-assignment.

| Croft No. | Name of Crofter | Cattle Souming Cows | Sheep Souming Ewes | Hoggs |
|---|---|---|---|---|
| 1. | John MacLean (Johnny Ruadh). | 1 | 10 | 2 |
| 2. | Andrew Fraser | 1 | | |
| 3. | Donald Sinclair | 1 | | |
| 4. | Angus MacTavish | 2 | 10 | 2 |
| 5. | Archibald MacGillivray | 1 | | |
| 6. | Duncan MacTavish | 2 | | |
| 7. | John MacGillivray (Iain Beag) | 1 | 10 | 2 |
| 8. | Alick MacIntyre | 2 | 10 | 2 |
| 9. | Johnny MacGillivray | 1 | 10 | 2 |
| 10. | Andrew Fraser | 1 | 10 | 2 |
| 11. | Alick Fletcher | 3 | 20 | 4 |
| 12. | Archie MacLean | 2 | 20 | 4 |
| 13. | Ludovic Fraser | - | 10 | 2 |
| 14. | Sweyn MacIntosh | - | 10 | 2 |
| 15. | Angus David MacIntosh | 1 | 10 | 2 |
| 16. | Mary MacGillivray (Mary Thormaid) | 1 | 10 | 2 |
| 17. | John MacCuaig | - | 10 | 2 |
| 18. | Angus Donald MacIntosh | 1 | 10 | 2 |
| 19. | Donald Sheorais Campbell | 1 | 10 | 2 |
| | Total cattle | 22 cows | Total sheep 170 | 34 |
| | | 22 calves | Ewes | Hoggs |

<u>Note</u>  On the original allocation of crofting tenures, each household had only 1 cow (+ followers) and 10 ewes (with lambs) plus 2 hoggs. However, by the time of Charlie MacTavish's boyhood some households had acquired an additional croft through inheritance or re-assignment.

The Camusban inbye land for producing their hay and growing their potatoes and oats lies behind the houses and the perimeter is deer fenced, thus preventing the deer from getting access to the inbye land in the old days. However, since the 1960s the deer fence has fallen into a state of disrepair and now the stags in particular roam the inbye land and even plunder the gardens in Camusban in winter and early spring.

The hill grazing land for the Camusban crofters' sheep was on Beinn na h-eaglaise while their cattle also had access to hill grazings on the lower reaches of Beinn Sgritheall between the west end of Camusban (Peggy Ann's) and Rarsaidh. This included the rough land down to the shore and Eilean Tioram (The Dry Island).

The division of the inbye land between the crofters was in two main sections. One section was on the west side of Allt an t-Siucair (the Sugar Burn) which runs into the sea between Johnnie Sinclair's house and the Mission House (formerly Maggie and Jessie Li's house). Each crofter had about one acre of this section. The other section was between Allt an t-Siucair and Allt an sgoil (the School Burn) or the wall on the west side of this burn. This section is described as 'church land' and was leased to the Camusban crofters along with the Beinn na h-eaglaise grazings by the then generous proprietor of Arnisdale estate, Mr Birkbeck of Kinloch Hourn. The rental from these inbye lands and grazings was paid to the Free Church to support the church. The Arnisdale estate retained the shooting rights on these areas. The inbye 'church lands' was subdivided between most of the Camusban crofters, with about one quarter of an acre being allocated per croft. The ewes were not allowed into the inbye land except at tupping and lambing time but all sheep had to go out to the hill by early May to allow the grass to grow for hay and for the land to be prepared for potatoes and any other crops, such as oats. The forty or so ewe lambs kept as replacement stock spent their first winter in the inbye croft land during the day but were shepherded on to the dry island at low tide before darkness, being taken back to the fields in the morning. After the end of the tupping season in early January, the tups were taken into the croft land and given a supplement of hay and sometimes a little oats. In March, the tups were taken to Rarsaidh Island (Eilean Rarsaidh) and they would remain there until clipping time in July.

The only time the cows were allowed on to the inbye ground was after the hay was secured and safely in the barn. By this time the grass would have recovered and some crofters would tether their cow on their own land at this time, the aftermath grazing usually giving a good boost to the milk yield. Apart from this brief period tethered in their own field, the 20 or so cows went out all together to the rough grazing west of the village towards Rarsaidh. The target was to get all the cows to calve in April. So when they came in season at the appropriate time they were haltered and taken on the rope to Roddy Mor's Aberdeen Angus bull at the farm to be served. After suckling the colostrum for the first few days after calving, the calves were then taken from the cow and bucket fed three times per day at first on a mixture of skim milk and oil cake. They would continue to be fed milk in this way until about August. When a few weeks old the calves would be tethered in the field during the day and they would start eating the young spring grass. When they were 6 or 7 weeks old they just joined the cows on their hill grazings between the two milkings (morning and evening). By this time, they had lost their suckling instinct so they would not suckle their mothers.

The lambing percentage was usually around 75 so that there were usually about 75 wether lambs to sell at the Inverness or Dingwall sales from the 200 or so ewes. The Camusban calves were usually bought privately by Roddy Mor in late September or early October. The income from the lamb sales would be divided equally among the crofters, while each crofter would get the sale price of his or her own calf in private dealing with Roddy Mor.

For some time before the last War, the Camusban crofters leased the Beinn Sgritheall grazing from Mr Scott of the Eilanreach Estate and had a 'Club' stock of about 300 pure bred Blackfaces on Beinn Sgritheall. They were identified differently to the Crofting Township Beinn na h-eaglaise stock in terms of colour mark, ear mark, and horn brand. The Township stock were a mixture of Blackfaces, South Country Cheviots and crosses between the two. In the 1930s in particular, very poor prices were being obtained for lambs and wool so before the 1939 war the whole 'Club' stock on Beinn Sgritheall was sold privately to Knoydart Estate.

The Camusban crofters had their own fank just above the deer fence which surrounds the inbye land on the lower slopes of Beinn na h-eaglaise. It is strategically sited close to the stream 'Allt an t-Siucair' which can be readily diverted when required to fill the dipper without having to carry water for the sheep dipping. Charlie remembers helping to instal the last dipper made of stainless steel in the 1940s. Although the fank is now dilapidated, the dipper is still intact to 'tell some of the old tales' - and some fine ones there were!.

Days at the Camusban fank for dipping, dosing, marking lambs, clipping or weaning were always big, exciting days in the calendar. There would be a big squad of all age groups up to help, especially at clipping time when there are plenty of jobs for all - the gathering, shedding, clipping, buisting, folding and packing the wool and, of course, making the tea. Charlie asserted that the water from Allt an t-siùcar made the finest tea imaginable, and there was full consensus on this by all the Camusban folk. Possibly, this may have been the reason why it was given the name 'The sugar burn'. Charlie, nor Maggie Li ( who had lived beside this burn at the Mission House for many years of her life) can give no other basis for the name given to this burn from time immemorial.

In addition to the sheep clipping, another big communal day on the crofts remembered by Charlie was the potato planting. This traditionally took place around mid May when the soil had dried up from sodden winter and early spring conditions and the weather was suitable. Roddy Mor would come down with the horses and plough - and the men, women and children would be ready with their graips, barrows, dung, seaweed and seed potatoes to first line the opened furrow with dung and seaweed and then plant the drill. Roddy Mor would then turn over two more furrows before the dunging and planting would start in the next drill - and so on until the area required by each croft was planted. Then the whole squad would move on from croft to croft repeating the process until all the crofts would be planted within the day if the weather remained fine. There would be stops for tea, oatcakes, scones and pancakes in mid morning, for dinner soon after mid-day and for more tea and goodies in mid afternoon. Charlie recalls on one occasion when he would be about 8 years of age that dinner time arrived when they had just finished the planting on their croft, Roddy Mor and the rest came in for their dinner. It was a fine day and it was in the middle of a fine dry spell of weather and the little burn (Alltan beag) which flowed through the deep channel under the little bridge just outside their garden gate only had a trickle of water gurgling towards the sea. At the end of the soup, meat and tatties and a cup of tea, Charlie's mother Bean Angan produced a bottle of liquid from a hiding place which Charlie had not seen before. She proceeded to pour some of this liquid into glasses and all present got a glass of the stuff except young Charlie. The latter was very disappointed but was too polite to say so - although Peggy Anne sold lemonade in the Post Office next door it was only on rare occasions that a bottle was purchased and you got a little drink of the stuff.

When, after a good dinner, the squad rose from the dinner table and made their way to get on with the job on the next croft, Charlie stayed behind. He had watched carefully where his mother had placed the bottle after dispensing some of the contents to each of the company, except himself. He was determined to have his share, so when the last of the folk had left the house, Charlie made his way to the cupboard, located the bottle, took out the cork and had a good swig of the contents. He remembers little after that until he heard voices of the folk moving around the place as he lay in the channel of Alltan beag just below the little bridge. He seemed to be just wakening from a sleep and his feet seemed not to obey the inclinations of his mind. At last he heard somebody say - 'Here he is, lying in the burn - the poor boy must have taken a fit!' Charlie remembers getting quite a lot of sympathy and attention as he was helped to his feet and out of the burn until his mother found the root cause of the illness which came over him so suddenly - especially when he seemed to have had such a good appetite for his dinner and was perfectly normal at the end of it!

Charlie's first paid employment was from Roddy Mor at the farm. From the time he was about 12 years old he would go up to help with the work at the fank with the sheep and on other jobs. Roddy was good at giving him a shot of things such as ploughing and Charlie learned a lot. His job at the clipping was the crogging - catching the sheep in the holding pen and bringing them to each clipper as they sat on their clipping stools, helping to turn each sheep over on its back on the clipping stool until the two front legs and one hind leg were roped together to control the ewe as the clipper proceeded to remove the fleece. Charlie remembers one day after all the sheep had been clipped when Roddy remembered about a Blackface tup which he had put into the pig shed and it was not yet clipped, so he went with Charlie to get the tup. Charlie remembers the tup with its big handlebar horns standing at the far end of the shed as he and Roddy reached the door. Charlie was quick to accept the challenge of catching the tup and taking it down to the clipping area. Just as he got inside the door with Roddy guarding the entrance - the tup - 'a big wild brute' charged for Charlie, head down. Charlie had to think and act like lightning if he was not going to be impaled to the door. With a great twisting leap such as he never achieved before or since, Charlie was on the tup's back and, as Roddy opened the door, Charlie managed to get a grip of the handlebars and away tup and rider careered across the steading square, through the gate, down past the fank and away down to the bottom of the field at the shore. Roddy, always ready for a bit of fun, was in stitches of laughter, but probably quietly impressed by the tenacity of the bareback rider as he caught up with the pair and together they got the wild beast back to the fank to relieve it of its heavy winter coat!

Roddy would give Charlie ten bob (fifty new pence) a day for his toil which Charlie thought was OK because when he started to work in the Forestry on leaving school his wage for a five and a half day week was thirty shillings and, after tax and insurance deductions, he was left with just over £1 for his week's work.

Charlie's next job after leaving the Forestry was with Her Majesty's Forces. Charlie served in the Royal Engineers and, among other places, served in Kenya towards the end of the Mau Mau rebellion. After demob, he got the job of Handyman/Ghillie/Stalker on the Barrisdale Estate. There he met up with the local teacher, Mary Kate Campbell, one of a family of the finest of Gaelic singers from Greepe in Skye. He and Mary Kate married in 1953 and they left Barrisdale in 1955 when Charlie got the job of Head Keeper in Strathvaich in Wester Ross where their children Margaret and James were born. On retirement, Charlie and Mary Kate returned to the old family home in Camusban.

Charlie is still active with his sheep on the croft and in keeping his boat and outboard motor in good trim. He is very pleased to take parties of tourists for sailing trips to whatever location they wish on Loch Hourn. He knows the loch and all its moods very well, as his father Angan did before him. Perhaps his own favourite sail is up the loch to Barrisdale where his grandparents were married, his mother was employed in the Lodge in her youth, his father was employed as the boatman and he himself met his good wife, Mary Kate.

**Top Left.** Charlie MacTavish, Camusban Crofting Township Clerk, outside his house in the village.
**Right.** Charlie in his days as head keeper on the Strathraich Estate in Wester Ross with his wife Mary Kate and their children Margaret and James. (Photograph taken in Camusban).

**Middle Left.** Charlie (second from right) and Mary Kate (far right) in their Barrisdale days when Mary Kate was the side school teacher and Charlie the stalker/ghillie/shepherd. With them is Barrisdale Head Stalker Bob MacRae, from Avernish in Kintail, his wife Chrissie (nee Morrison) (a native of Harris) and their children. **Right.** The view from Charlie and Mary Kate's home in Camusban looking across Loch Hourn to Knoydart and Barrisdale. Charlie's boat lies peacefully on a calm sea while the camera captures the snow capped tops of Luinne Bheinn, Sgurr na Ciste and Coire Dhorcail.

**Bottom Left.** Barrisdale Lodge and Policies and the Knoydart mountains beyond. **Right.** Remains of the little church in Barrisdale where Charlie's grandparents were married. Photograph taken from the adjacent tidal island of Eilean Choinnich. Willie MacKenzie beside the gravestones in this ancient graveyard.

**Top Left.** Charlie's father Angan who was employed for a long time as head boatman on the Barrisdale Estate with a fine Loch Hourn lobster.  **Centre.**  Charlie's mother Maggie (nee Douglas) in her days working for Cameron of Lochiel in Glen Dessary with (behind) Angus Stewart (head shepherd) and Angus' wife Maggie (nee MacPherson) from Moyle in Glenelg.   Angus is about to get a little dram to celebrate the completion of the big sheep dipping.  **Right**.   Maggie Douglas in her days working in Barrisdale Lodge.

**Middle Left.**  The wedding of Angan MacTavish and Maggie Douglas.   **Centre.**   Angan (right) with Daniel MacDonald in his later years working as boatman on the Arnisdale Estate.   **Right.**   Maggie catching up with her cow for the milking on the hill grazings above the Camus Ban crofts.

**Bottom**. Camusban in the late 1890s.  The original thatched houses in Camusban were very close to the shore and were flooded in the great high tide of 1881.   The estate proprietor, Lord Burton of Dochfour, financed the building of houses with slated roofs on slightly higher ground.  The photograph shows the transition between the line of new houses and the old since some of the old thatched houses still remain much closer to the shore.  The croftlands give the appearance of being worked very intensively – for the growing of potatoes, oats and hay in particular.

**Top Left.** The Camusban enclosed croft lands at the base of Beinn Sgritheall and Beinn na h-eaglaise. Each croft had a strip of arable land behind the house on which the byre and adjoining barn for the hay was sited. In addition, most crofters had a share of the church land behind the Free Church. **Right.** A view of the arable lands behind the houses in Camusban with the little byres and haysheds. The Free Church is on the extreme right of the picture.

**Middle Left.** The Church land behind the Free Church (lower right hand corner) which was subdivided between the crofters. In the middle of the picture is Eilean Tioram (The dry island) to which the ewe hoggs were shepherded each evening for their overnight stay in winter time. The church lands are bounded by the two burns – Allt an t-Siucair and Allt na Sgoile. **Right.** The remains of the deer fence which at one time prevented the deer from entering the arable areas on the Camusban Crofts.

**Bottom Left.** Johan MacLean on the Camusban road with the red deer stags in the background now free to plunder the arable areas on the crofts. **Right.** The remains of the transverse drain (in direct line with Arnisdale Lodge) on the lower slopes of Beinn na h-Eaglaise which diverted the copious water flowing down the steep slopes into Allt an sgoil, thus keeping the lower arable areas drier.

**Top Left.** The Camusban Crofting Township hill grazings on Beinn na h-Eagliase with the fank at the base just above the deer fence and the arable areas. Allt an t-Siucair makes its way down the mountainside towards the fank. **Right.** The fank from above looking down on the arable areas, Loch Hourn and Knoydart beyond. Eilean Tioram is to the right. The stream flowing past the fank, Allt an t-Siucair provided the water to fill the dipper and, of course, water for the tea. The Camusban folk were unanimous that the water from Allt an t-Siucair made the best tea!

**Middle Left.** Coopers Swim Bath - the Camusban dipper installed in the mid-1940s still remains. **Right.** Now the old Camusban fank and dipper have been abandoned. The fine tea from Allt an t-Siucair is savoured no more. All sheep handling is now done at the fank up at the farm. Here Charlie MacTavish (centre), Willie MacKenzie and Charlie's son-in-law Dan MacKenzie (left), are busy at the dipping (Autumn 1990).

**Bottom Left.** Roddy Mor ploughing the croftlands in preparation for the tattie planting. **Right.** The squad of ladies graiping the dung and seaweed into the opened drills just before planting the precious potatoes are (L to R.) Annie MacIntyre, Gwennie Stoddart, Mary MacIntyre and Bean Angan (Maggie MacTavish).

**Top Left.** Eilean Rarsaidh which was the home of the Camusban tups each year from March until they were sailed home for the clipping in July.   **Right.**   Mr Robert Birkbeck the proprietor of the Arnisdale and Kinloch Hourn Estates (purchased in 1890) who leased the church lands to the Camusban crofters with the rentals being payable to the Free Church to help its upkeep.

**Middle Left.**   A squad of mainly Camusban folk keeping the Arnisdale graveyard tidy (around 1930).
L to R. are Kate Fletcher, John MacGillivray, Mary MacLean, Annie MacIntyre, Ludovic Fraser Sen., Kirsty MacKintosh, Archie MacLean, Archie MacGillivray, Andrew Fraser, Mary Ann MacCuaig and Angan MacTavish.   **Right.**   This group photographed at the roadside just outside the graveyard may be another squad about to tidy up the graveyard. It was probably taken in the 1910-1920 era. The gentleman on the far right may be a missionary and the group may include Aonghas Dhaidh MacKintosh, John Kelly, Mary Anne MacCuaig, Mary MacIntyre, Johan and Ina MacLean.

**Bottom Left.**   Charlie MacTavish in his schooldays.   L to R.  Teacher Joan Kennedy, Alistair Fletcher, Calum Kennedy, Willie Stoddart, Mary Anne MacKintosh, Rena MacDonald, Willie MacKenzie, Charlie MacTavish, Flora MacKenzie, Johan MacDonald, Nellie MacKenzie, District Nurse Boyd (who belonged to the Uists), Frances Kennedy and Iain Sinclair.

**Right.**   Charlie, who knows Loch Hourn and its moods as well as anybody, is now running sailing trips for those who want to explore the loch or reach any destination within reach.   Here Charlie sails a group of tourists up the loch to Kinloch Hourn.

# Chapter 8

**The Corran Crofting Township and Willie MacKenzie (Willie the Post)**

Willie was not the first MacKenzie to act as the Arnisdale postman and he is not to be the last. His father - the first 'Willie the Post', delivered the Arnisdale mail from 1922 to 1955, when he was succeeded by the present Willie. Willie the second retired from the job just four years ago in 1995 and David, his son, has now taken over the reins.

Willie is the oldest of the MacKenzie family, followed by Nellie, Flora and Iain. In turn, Willie and his wife Christine (nee MacLaren) have 5 children (Billy, Shona, David, Alan and Roderick) and now the grandchildren are beginning to appear.

The first 'Willie the Post' was in the Lovat Scouts in the First World War and served throughout, seeing active service in the Dardanelles, Gallipoli, Egypt and France. Having survived that dreadful war, Willie then sought a job and the means to survive because his parents could barely keep themselves on the produce of the croft at Corran combined with what they could harvest from the sea in the form of fish and shellfish. At the time, there appeared to be reasonable opportunities for tough young men who had experience in handling cattle and horses, to go to Montana in the USA and work the huge cattle ranches there. Willie, along with other young men from Arnisdale, Lochcarron, and other localities in the area took up the challenge. He was accompanied, among others, by Donald Sinclair (father of Johnnie - later the Arnisdale-Glenelg mail carrier), Donald and Murdo MacLeod (sons of Kenny and brothers of Roddy Mor at the Arnisdale Farm). These tough Arnisdale 'cowboys' made as 'good a go' of the Montana ranges and their cattle as anybody could do for a year or two. Then they were overtaken with a terrible drought and this (possibly combined with an element of overstocking of the range with cattle and the resulting depletion in the quality and quantity of available grazing) resulted in starving, emaciated cattle. The humane and only common sense response in the circumstance was to shoot the worst affected of the cattle and there were vast numbers of these. Shoot them they did and made themselves redundant - at least until the rains came and cattle numbers could be built up gradually again.

Willie and a few of his friends decided that while it was difficult to make a living in Arnisdale, things were even tougher in Montana - so home they came again. It was just about this time (around 1922) that Arnisdale experienced the tragedy of the drowning of the local postman - Duncan Campbell of Corran. Duncan had been sailing his little boat up Loch Hourn, delivering the mails to Li, Barrisdale and Coalasmor when the terrible accident occurred near Coalasmor and Duncan's body was found only a matter of yards from the shore. Duncan may have been turning his boat round or hoisting his sail when a fierce gust of wind caught the boat, causing it to overturn. Although Duncan was a very strong swimmer it was thought that he suffered from epilepsy so that may have been the reason for Duncan failing to make it to the shore after the sinking of his little boat.

When Willie got home to Arnisdale, the postman's job was therefore vacant and he applied for and got the job. At that time, the Arnisdale postman's job involved being at the Post Office at Camusban when the mails arrived from the Glenelg Post Office by pony and trap. It was then the postman's job along with the Postmaster or Postmistress (Peggy Ann MacLean's father Johnny Ruadh, and later Peggy Ann herself) to sort out the mails and then deliver them to the householders in Camusban, then the Lodge, the farm, Glenfield, Achadh a'Ghlinne and then finish up in Corran. It was a late afternoon and evening job because it was often 4 to 6 o'clock in the afternoon before the mail car would reach Arnisdale. This timing suited Willie fine because he could combine it with helping to work the croft and fishing in the daytime.

Then four times weekly, at a time to suit his work on the croft, Willie would set off to deliver the mail across the Loch, to Croalig, Red Point (Rudha Ruadh), Li and Barrisdale and then further up the loch on the Arnisdale side to the Paterson (and later the MacRae and MacDonald) families at Caolasmor.

'Young' Willie who was to take over from his father as the postman in 1955 had a long apprenticeship in the job as he often accompanied his father on the trips across the loch and up to Caolasmor. He was about 12 years old when he had an experience which still causes palpitations when he recalls the incident when he is on the loch and especially when it is dark. He and his father had reached the Landing Place at Barrisdale when his father secured the boat and set off to the Barrisdale Lodge and the other houses to deliver the mail. Willie sat on the knoll to survey the scene and think his own thoughts until his father returned, when they would set off for Caolasmor.

As young Willie's eyes scanned the shoreline and the water over towards the shore on the Druim Fada side, he noticed a disturbance in the water and then emerged, rising to a considerable height above the surface, the head and long neck of a 'beast', the like of which Willie had not seen before or since - nor does he wish to witness such ever again. It seemed almost like a monster eel and Willie watched it in disbelief for what appeared to be about a minute or so before gradually, without apparent fuss or undue turbulence of the water, from his point of vision, the huge head and neck submerged again. When his father returned, Willie told him of his unique experience and his father had considerable difficulty persuading the youngster to get back into the boat for their journey on to Caolasmor and then back along the coast to Corran.

Willie claims that still when he is passing that spot of the inexplicable sighting, now well over half a century later, he still feels a tenseness, a bit of a cold sweat and if he had a heart rate monitor operating on him, it would record a noticeable rise in the heart beat. Understandably, he is even more nervous when on the loch in the darkness.

When the relieved youngster eventually got his feet on dry land again on arriving back at Corran, his experience and sighting was, of course, the major topic of conversation. His Granny, Mairi Bhan and neighbours Daniel MacDonald and Robert Foster had all made similar, individual sightings in the past.

Marie Bhan's sighting had been in her early twenties when she was making her way up the Corran to Caolasmor shoreline path gathering driftwood on the shore for the fire. She, like her young grandson, was terrified by what she saw fairly close to the shore. Daniel MacDonald's sighting was in the early 1920s but the location of his sighting is uncertain. Robert Foster made his sighting as he was fishing in deep water off the little island - the Sgeir Leathann - up the loch a mile or so from Corran. Robert was very keen on his fishing but Willie claims that after that experience, Robert was so shaken and nervous that he never returned to fish at that spot, and all his subsequent fishing was along the coast in shallower water within easy reach of the shore. Other sightings of a very large strange 'beast' in Loch Hourn have been reported by the Rev. John MacRae and a young friend as they sailed up Loch Hourn as far back as 1875. John, like young Willie, described what he saw as being like a very large eel, or sea serpent, and he reported up to nine 'humps' as the beast, with head and neck well above the water line, made its way through the water. The location of John MacRae's sighting again is not certain but there is an indication that it was somewhere in the area of the sightings of Marie Bhan, Robert Foster and young Willie. Roddy MacPherson from Glenelg (in the early 1930s), the MacDiarmid boys (Sandy, Tom and Alan) and Bobby MacLean (in the mid to late 1930s) have all reported sighting a large unidentified strange 'beast' in Loch Hourn in the Port Luinge area. These sightings are described elsewhere in this book (see also Chapter 34).

When young Willie took over as postman from his father in 1955 his duties in serving Arnisdale and the habitations across Loch Hourn and up the loch were similar to those of his father. However, Croalig and Red Point were no longer inhabited. The Paterson family had left Caolasmor but this beautiful little corner was inhabited by a Mr MacDonald and his wife. He was employed as a ghillie and 'watcher' by the Kinlochourn Estate, the 'watching' entailing the discouragement of poaching, the fishermen on the many boats plying Loch Hourn for herring in particular also being partial to a good bit of venison in season. The MacDonald family continued to work the croft, having 2 cows and 20 or 30 sheep and making hay on the fine fertile coastal strip of land just westwards of the 2 houses, barns and byres.

Bringing the mails from Glenelg to Arnisdale in Willie's early days was Johnnie Sinclair. However, by this time Johnnie had replaced the pony and trap with his car. When Johnnie retired, these deliveries were taken over by Roddy Mor after he and Lizzie retired from Arnisdale Farm and set up home in Glenelg. Roddy Mor, in turn, was succeeded by Calum Iain Lamont from Glenelg.

In the late 1960s, Willie, supplied with a Post Office van, began to collect the Arnisdale mails from Glenelg himself, and still later in the early 1970s, he collected the mails at Inverinate after the regular daily mail boat service run by Calum Garde (and his father before him) and later by Donald John MacLeod, from Kyle to Glenelg, ceased to operate.

Soon afterwards Willie went all the way to Kyle to collect the mails and then became the Glenelg as well as the Arnisdale postman. This was a full day's work and left no time for Willie to get across to Li, Barrisdale and Croalig. The Post Office then arranged for the folk in these localities to collect their mail from the Post Office in Arnisdale, providing them with a modest annual fee for such self help. After Peggy Ann, the Arnisdale Post Office was successfully run in turn by Willie's sister Nellie, Willie's mother Christina, and Rena MacDonald (all in Corran). Now, with the great loss to her family, Arnisdale and all her friends with Rena's passing, the Post Office has returned to Camusban, with Len Morrison as the Postmaster.

With Willie's retirement as Postman in 1995 after 42 years of uninterrupted service to the Arnisdale and Glenelg communities, Willie has been succeeded in the job by his son David. 'Willie the Post' (first and second), not only delivered the mail and collected outgoing mail, but they both provided almost a social service to the folk and brought everybody up to date with the main up to date news. Couthy characters both, they always had time to ask after the well-being of the folk in each household and to pass on relevant pieces of news. Thus they played a very vital role in spreading awareness of illness and problems, but also the good news, which is so essential in generating continuance of the strong community spirit and neighbourliness which has always prevailed in these localities, and still does. There is little doubt that young David will continue the fine 'community service' of his father and grandfather.

The posting was but half of the work of Willie the Post, both first and second. The other half was the crofting and that too still goes on. The MacKenzies are almost the last bastions of the old crofting system in Arnisdale, with some support still from Iain MacKenzie and Betty MacRae in Corran along with Charlie MacTavish and Len Morrison in Camusban.

The Corran crofters experienced very tough times before the Napier Commission met in Glenelg in August 1883 to hear the evidence of the Arnisdale and Glenelg Crofters, and of the farms and estates which interacted with them. The Corran Crofters' evidence to that Commission was provided by their representatives John MacCuaig ('Crofter and Fisherman') and John McPhee ('Crofter'). They had some very revealing evidence to provide about the very limited areas of land allocated to them from which they were expected to make a living, the poor quality of much of this land, and the excessive rental charged for essential additional grazing land leased from Arnisdale Farm.

The evidence of John MacCuaig and John MacPhee did not fall on deaf ears. The membership of Lord Napier's Commission had been put together with a degree of sensitivity which had not hitherto prevailed in listening and reacting positively to the totally justifiable complaints of very many crofters in the Highlands and Islands. Among others, it included the MP, Donald Cameron, Esq. of Lochiel. He and his family have had a good reputation over the generations of being able to 'listen carefully to the crofters' and to respond accordingly.

There is no doubt that the honest and sincere evidence of John MacCuaig and John MacPhee, along with that of Archibald Fletcher McGillivray and John McIntyre who represented the Camusban crofters, and that provided by those who represented the Glenelg crofters, played its full part - when combined with the evidence from crofters in many other areas of the Highlands and Islands, in establishing the basis of the new Crofting Acts which were firmly based on the evidence obtained by the Napier Commission. These Acts, which provided considerably improved conditions for many hitherto extremely hard pressed crofters and their families, in terms of extra grazing land, control of rents and security of tenure, came into force before the end of the 1880s.

It appears from the evidence provided by the Corran and Camusban representatives that the Camusban crofters had not been quite as hard pressed as those at Corran. This may well be the reason why the 'deal' which the Corran crofters obtained afterwards seemed to be much better than that won by their counterparts in Camusban. The stocking allowance or 'souming' for each of the 20 or so Camusban crofters is 1 cow plus one follower and 10 ewes plus 2 hoggs (young replacement ewes); whereas the souming for the 10 or so Corran crofters is 2 cows plus 2 followers and 30 ewes plus 6 hoggs.

The Napier Commission also proposed and established the basis for the democratic management of crofting townships, with one of the crofters being elected to be the 'Township Clerk' or 'Manager' who acts as Chairman at the meetings of all the crofters in the township to decide on policy, e.g. when to gather, dip, clip, wean lambs, sell lambs, purchase replacement tups etc. and to settle any disputes which arise.

Four Township Clerks have served the Corran crofters well over a very long period of years - Angus Murchison, Angus Stewart, Willie's brother Iain and the current Clerk is Willie's son, Billy. Willie himself has been appointed for two terms of office as Crofting Assessor for the Crofters' Commission serving the Glenelg Parish (Glenelg, Arnisdale, Loch Hourn, Knoydart, Inverie and north Morar). Willie succeeded Neilly MacLure, Glenelg in this role.

There are two areas of fenced inbye land at Corran, one on each side of the village with one part adjacent to the shore and the other area running along the riverside. This is subdivided into 9 lots - not by fences but by well known boundary lines. It is in these areas that the hay for the winter feeding of the cattle was made as well as the land used for growing the potatoes and oats. Up to recently, all work was done by hand apart from the preparations of the land for planting potatoes. The planting of the potatoes was always a big day in Corran when all crofts were being worked. In Roddy Mor's time at the farm, he would open the drills with his own horse and one of the Lodge horses yoked to the plough. He would turn two furrows with the plough. Then the 'squad' of the Corran folk of all ages and both sexes would get to work lining the base of the open furrow with dung and seaweed. The seed potatoes - Kerrs Pink, Golden Wonders, Home Guards, Duke of York, Edzell Blues, Sharpe's Express, or whatever, would then be planted Then two further furrows would be ploughed before the process of dunging ad planting resumed. When the required amount of potatoes had been planted on one croft, horses, plough and folk would get to work on the next croft in line until the planting had been completed. Of course, there were regular stops for tea and scones, dinner, more tea and perhaps at the end of a long and satisfying day, a little dram might be dispensed. The potatoes were a tremendously important and treasured crop. The varieties grown and the fertiliser treatment used ensured a dry, flavoursome potato which made up a precious component of the daily diet. It was a truly organic product.

In the case of the folk who wanted to grow some oats, these were usually broadcast, following surface cultivation, on the potato ground of the previous year. After this, sometimes after undersowing the oat crop with grass seed, the ground would revert to grass for hay. It might be 10 years or more before the same piece of land was used for potatoes again. This gave the soil plenty of time to build up fertility and structure again to help to ensure a fine potato crop once again.

Hay was cut with the scythe and much work was involved in winning the hay from the mainly natural meadows, with the frequent showers and general dampness which prevailed for much of the time. The midges were always a pest and Willie MacKenzie comments that the Corran midges are so irksome on the face, neck and arms that you would think that they were wearing tackety boots! After the hay was finally won, then it was a case of getting it into the barns, most of which were built adjacent to each croft's patch of land.

For the most part, the cattle and sheep grazed on the hill areas allocated to the Corran crofters. Part of this area was at the base of Druim Fada (the long ridge) behind the village and along the river bank and part was on the other side of the glen on Beinn Bhuidhe (yellow hill or mountain). A total of 920 acres bounded by a deer fence was allocated to the Corran crofters on Beinn Bhuidhe while they had a total 226 acres along the base of Druim Fada. This was separated from the main hill (the deer forest) by a deer fence which came down at the boat house just about half a mile along the shore south of Corran. The Beinn Bhuidhe grazing was used by the sheep and the Druim Fada grazing by the cattle. In addition, the Corran crofters had a 4 acre park surrounded by well built dykes adjacent to Achadh a'Ghlinne. This, the 'round park', was mainly used for the tups outwith their breeding season.

The inbye area within the Corran hay and potato land carried the sheep only at lambing and tupping time while the cows sometimes got into this area after the land recovered from the hay harvest, when cows would be tethered on their own croft area to harvest the fresh growth of foggage which always gave them a boost in their milk yield.

When all the crofts were being worked, the Corran grazing areas were carrying up to 20 cows, 20 calves and about 300 ewes. Of course, the land was rented from the estate and the same annual rent was payable by each crofter.

Part of the agreement between the Corran crofters and the Estate was that they had the use of the fank built by the estate at the farm. Thus, after gathering, the sheep would be taken to the fank at the farm for such operations as dipping, marking the lambs, clipping, weaning and sorting the lambs for sale.

The weaned wether lambs, along with the cast (culled) ewes, would be taken for sale to places such as Dingwall or Inverness in September. Usually the lambing percentage was around 80, that is, 80 lambs weaned per 100 ewes that ran with the tups at mating time. This gave a total output of some 240 lambs per year, half of which (120) were wethers for sale. The 6 month old calves from the Corran cows were sometimes sold at the Inverness or Dingwall markets but, more usually, they were bought privately in Corran by local people such as Arnisdale's Roddy Mor, or Glenelg's Neilly MacLure or Angus Morrison (Moyle). The prices obtained for each calf would go directly to the owner, whereas the prices received for the lambs and cast ewes were pooled and divided equally between the crofters after the deduction of transport and other expenses.

Willie MacKenzie is still an active crofter. Along with neighbour Betty MacRae, they still grow their own potatoes and Willie is also kept busy with his own sheep and those of neighbours. He is one of the few in Arnisdale left with working collie dogs, so he is much in demand. He and his wife Christine are also strong church goers and do their best to maintain the old standards in their daily living.

Despite his busy-ness, he takes time to relate some of the old stories about Arnisdale, his own memorable experiences and thinks a lot about the future of Arnisdale and how it might be developed in the most balanced and acceptable way.

He remembers the days when almost all the Corran crofters were very dependent on peat for fuel. One of the peat mosses was on the lower slopes of Druim Fada close to the old drove road. The dried peats would be carted home to Corran in barrows and in creels carried on the back. Some people went as far up the Arnisdale Glen as Blar nan each (The flat grazing area of the horses) to cut their peats so they had a long distance to cover to get them home (over 2 miles). He speculates a bit about the origin of the name, Blar nan each. Just across the Glen bridle path from the Blar are the ruins of several buildings. Willie was told that one of these buildings was a smiddy which had a forge, horse shoes and other implements and utensils would be made and horses would be shod. How much trade did the smith get and how much of this came from the local population and how much from those passing on horseback and with their packhorses on this main route? What fuel did they use for the forge? Was it peat or wood or a combination of the two?

One thing to remember in trying to answer some of these questions is that, in the droving of cattle from the north and west to the great markets at Crieff and Falkirk, the cattle were shod - otherwise considerable damage to the hooves and serious lameness and losses would have resulted. So that shoeing the cattle of drovers as they made their long way from the district to the main markets far distant would undoubtedly have provided some of the smith's business at Blar nan each. It is likely that there was a considerable number of pack horses passing by this way, not only accompanying the cattle droves, carrying the essential supplies of the drovers, but also transporting goods to market from the west and taking to the folk of Arnisdale and communities further westwards essential materials and articles which were not available locally. These pedlars played a very important role in bygone days in the conduct of their little bit of private enterprise.

What about the fuel for the forge? Possibly it was mainly peat, cut, dried and harvested from the adjacent Blar. It is possible also that one of the buildings, only the ruins of which remain, was an inn, where travellers could have their night's rest before proceeding on their journey after their horse had been re-shod and perhaps some of their cattle too. While the horses waited their turn to be shod, they would spend their time grazing on Blar nan each, probably accompanied by the horses which belonged to the smith, the inn keeper and the other residents of this clachan.

One or more of these residents might have been a horse dealer so this spare supply of horses might also be among those grazing on the Blar. What about the food supply of the folk in this place? Well, they undoubtedly had their cows and goats, grazing the adjacent hill pastures and turning them into milk and meat and skins and processed butter and cheese. The deer would also be around to be harvested in season and in times of need. The river, close by, would have yielded plentiful trout, and salmon in season. They would have also grown their potatoes and oats, made their oatmeal and made hay for the wintering of their horses and cattle. Further back in time it is likely that the adjacent forest of oak, birch, alder, aspen, rowan, willow and other trees would have provided cover and fodder for wild boar. The folk from this little township, on a major thoroughfare, would have developed ways of obtaining and feasting on the meat of the wild boar. Perhaps in winter this route might be busier because the alternative route from Crionach round the back of Beinn Sgritheall into Glen Beag and then on to Glenelg and Skye, with its high mountain pass (Bealach Aoidhdailean), might be considered to be too cold, hostile and dangerous - and perhaps impassable during snowstorms.

All these possibilities about Blar nan each and the little clachan there is sheer speculation, but possible and maybe probable.

Willie MacKenzie also did some speculating about an incident which occurred as he was making his way in his little boat up Loch Hourn one day. As he sat in the stern controlling the outboard engine, a jet fighter plane went roaring overhead and up the fjord of Loch Hourn. He had not proceeded on his way much further when the jet returned, this time zooming very low over his head. When it returned for a third time, he made up his mind that it must have been somebody who knew him. His conviction was that it was his old friend, Sandy English, who at that time was a Fleet Air Arm Officer. When Willie later confronted this pal of his teenage years, Sandy denied all knowledge of the incident but Willie was not convinced!

When the question of the disappearance of the Loch Hourn herring is raised with Willie, he had no hesitation in placing the blame fairly and squarely on the twin trawlers, mainly from the East Coast of Scotland, carrying out mid-water trawls, scooping up everything within reach. He remembers as many as 50 boats engaged in this 'hoovering' of the sea, scooping up vast quantities of fish and throwing back - dead - those species of fish and the small fish for which they had no market. He remembers coming across areas of the loch and shoreline which were stinking with such putrefying fish. He deplores these tactics which totally disregard the need to conserve fish stocks and the integrity of spawning grounds. The wise people and generations of the past placed tremendous emphasis on such conservation measures in their fishing policy and that is why Loch Hourn and similar areas in the west coast maintained the quality of the local fishing which catered for the needs of local populations for so many generations.

While Willie considers that there has been much wanton destruction of fish resources with no consideration given to conservation of breeding stock on traditional spawning grounds, he feels that conservation of land resources especially in the Loch Hourn and Knoydart areas has gone to the other extreme. He is not enamoured with the policies and practices of the John Muir Trust in Knoydart, deer fencing off huge tracts of land almost to the shore line. They have been planting native tree species within the deer fenced area but they have also been carrying out their planting on the Sabbath, and that Willie considers, displays no sensitivity whatsoever to the beliefs and culture of the native people. It is good that precious components of nature should be preserved but so too should the native folk along with their history, culture and religious beliefs. He sees the scope for crofting and medium scale farming on the Loch Hourn side of Knoydart at least, being eliminated. Cattle and sheep enterprises provided a living for a large population in the past and could do so for a smaller number of enthusiastic, competent young folk now and in the future without upsetting the balance of nature.

He fears that the John Muir Trust may have alienated some of their best advisers with their extreme, unbalanced policies.

In Arnisdale, he sees an urgent need to see the old deer fences restored which prevented the deer coming into the inbye croft lands and so that the grazing of sheep and cattle could be more effectively controlled. He sees the need to amalgamate the smaller crofts which are not being worked, into medium sized, more viable farming units. While he sees good opportunities to develop tourism, he also feels that there is a danger in these areas of 'putting all the eggs into one basket'. The advent of in-bag silage is a great development for the high rainfall areas of the West Coast, he asserts. Trying to make hay has been the most soul destroying job of any in the West Coast - the hard work, the frustration and the midges destroyed the spirit of many good men, women and children. The opportunities for medium sized farming units, with fair quotas of cattle and sheep, and winter keep in the form of bagged silage, when combined with part-time tourist-related occupations could see many areas in the west being revitalised by enthusiastic competent young men and women who are native to these localities and therefore have a vested interest - almost a calling - in seeing these places providing steady, gainful, satisfying employment and making the localities more attractive and welcoming to the tourists at the same time.

Such revitalisation of beautiful places and villages with the fine community spirit of old, maintaining the old cultures and beliefs, preserving history and sharing resources and burdens is Willie MacKenzie's concept of conservation - not turning once very attractive places, vibrant with people who were doing very useful things for each other and for society in general - into wildernesses. The danger of creating wildernesses, Willie asserts with a twinkle in his eye, is that some people may get lost therein, including some land use planners from high places, especially when wearing their rose-tinted spectacles!

**Top Left.** The village of Corran beside the mouth of the Arnisdale River with the arable croftlands in two areas – to the right of the village along the shoreline and to the left of the village along the south side of the river. Each crofter in the Corran crofting township had a strip of arable land in both areas. The sheds for the fishing gear can be seen on the extreme right while the row of 14 byres can be seen behind the village stretching towards Druim Fada. **Right.** In Corran village, there is one house to the north of the river while the houses on the south side are divided by the burn flowing at right angles into the river close to the bridge. To the left of the burn are a few houses which was called Cosaig in the old days. After crossing the bridge there are two homes on each side of the access road and at the end of this the Corran 'street' goes off at right angles to the right.

**Middle Left.** The row of thatched houses close to the river around 1890. After the great high tide in 1881, these houses were badly flooded and it was decided to rebuild on higher ground to prevent another calamity.
**Right.** Mr Robert Birkbeck, proprietor of Arnisdale and Kinloch Hourn estates at the time, financed the rebuilding programme.

**Bottom Left.** The row of little byres for each of the crofters behind the village which were also provided by Mr Birkbeck. **Right.** The row of sheds close to the tidal mouth of the river were also built by Mr Birkbeck for the fishing gear of the crofters. These were also used by the crofters to provide extra storage space for hay.

**Top Left.** The Corran crofters had 226 acres of rough grazing at the base of Druim Fada for their cattle which was separated from the Estate's deer forest by a deer fence. The crofters also cut their peats in this area. In the distance is Achadh a' Ghlinne and Beinn Clachach. **Right.** Beinn Bhuidhe viewed from the Corran riverside croftlands with the tree lined river below and the glenside fields of the farm beyond. The Corran crofters had 920 acres on this hill for their sheep grazing, again separated from the Camusban sheep grazings on adjacent Beinn na h-Eaglaise and the deer forest by a deer fence.

**Middle Left.** The Corran Crofting Township has had only four Township Clerks in almost 100 years. These (L to R.) are Angus Murchison, Angus Stewart (on right of photograph), Iain MacKenzie (right of photograph) and Billy MacKenzie, the present Township Clerk.

**Bottom Left.** The present Willie MacKenzie, or the second 'Willie the Post' (left) combined his posting and crofting duties before his recent retirement. Willie's father, the first 'Willie the Post' (right) had the same combination of jobs. As well as daily postal deliveries in Arnisdale, Willie delivered the mail three times weekly to the other Loch Hourn locations of Caolasmor, Barrisdale, Li, Red Point and Crowlick.

**Top Left.** A good gather of the Corran sheep off Beinn Bhuidhe in the 1930s as they make their way through the hill gate behind Arnisdale Lodge on their way to the fank. **Right.** The first Willie the Post (left) dipping the Corran sheep at the fank at the Home Farm in the 1930s along with Angus Murchison (centre) and Lachie MacAskill (right).

**Middle Left.** Youngsters Johnnie Murchison (left) and Angus Stewart busy at the clipping of the Corran ewes (1930s). **Right.** Another squad of Corran Crofters at the clipping at the communal fank at the Home Farm in the 1930s. L to R. Sandy MacAskill, Angus Murchison, Willie MacKenzie (Senior), young Angus Stewart, Granny MacKenzie (Mairi Bhan) and Johnnie Murchison.

**Bottom Left.** Preparing the ground for the potato planting around 1940 are L to R. Willie the Post Senior, his mother Mairi Bhan, Willie's wife Christina and young Willie. **Right.** The present Willie MacKenzie with sisters Flora and Nellie and brother Iain, the youngest member of the family (around 1940).

**Top Left.** An idyllic scene from the mouth of the Arnisdale River looking eastwards towards the bridge, the arable croft lands to the right of the river beyond the bridge and on the left to Beinn Bhuidhe, the Corran Township hill sheep grazing area. To the right is Beinn Clachach. **Right.** The MacKenzie boat at its landing and mooring place to the south of Corran in full view of Beinn Sgritheall.

**Middle Left.** The present Willie MacKenzie with his young family (around 1980). L to R. David, Alan, Shona and Billy. **Right.** Willie is still an active crofter. He is seen here with neighbour and fellow crofter Betty MacRae, Betty's daughter Rosamund and grandchildren, Shane and Lewis at the tattie planting on the riverside fields.

**Bottom Left.** A view of the riverside fields at Corran from the lower slopes of Druim Fada. **Right.** Willie and his wife Christina at the wedding of their son Alan to Carol Sword in 1995 with the other members of the family (L to R.) Billy, Roderick, Willie, Christine, Alan, Carol, David, son-in-law Willie Frame, Shona and their children Lisa and Ross..

**Top Left.** The ruins at Blar nan Each near the sentinel holly tree in the Arnisdale Glen. Willie had heard stories from the old folk that there was a smiddy and possibly an inn there at one time. **Right.** The view from the slopes of Druim Fada down to the ruins and across the blar to the Arnisdale River with its lining of alder trees, and thence to the lower slopes of Beinn Clachach.

**Middle Left.** Looking eastwards towards the Coille Mhor (mainly natural oak) and the zig-zag part of the hill track to Kinloch Hourn. **Right.** The view of Blar nan each from the north side of Achadh a' Ghlinne looking across the Achadh burn (Allt Utha) across the tree lined Arnisdale River and the blar to the ruins at the base of Druim Fada.

**Below.** An artist's impression of how the inn, smiddy and other dwellings at Blar nan Each may have looked in the busy times in past ages of passing droves of cattle, pedlars and other travellers with their pack horses. Closer scrutiny of the area above the ruins has located a well and possible charcoal burning sites. (Drawing by Blair Anderson).

# Chapter 9

**Schooldays as recalled by Morag, Flora and Sheena**

**Morag MacIntyre.** Morag's people have been in Arnisdale for a considerable time. It was one of her forebears, John MacIntyre ('Crofter's son and Fisherman') who, along with Archibald Fletcher MacGillivray ('crofter and Fisherman'), represented Camusban in giving evidence to the Government's Napier Commission when that body, which was examining the plight of the crofters and their families at that time, met in the Glenelg Hotel in August 1883. The evidence received by the Commission, under Lord Napier, and their subsequent deliberation, lead to Acts of Parliament which greatly improved conditions for the crofters, including security of tenure.

Morag's nursing career saw her serving in the Royal Northern Infirmary, Inverness, Ipswich, Kilmarnock and Aberdeen. Morag served as a Nursing Sister in the Granite City for a number of years before her retirement and her return to the old home a few years ago.

Her first taste of school in Arnisdale in the early part of the last war was with Martin Kennedy as the teacher, followed by Miss Ferguson, Miss Cruickshank (later Mrs Norman Cameron, Glenelg), Ann MacRae (later Mrs Bobby MacLean) and latterly Lexy Campbell (later Mrs Iain MacCuaig).

It is not surprising that some of Morag's early memories relate to wartime activities in the village and the Arnisdale Home Guard. The local 'Dad's Army' consisted of such characters as Roddy Mor as the Lieutenant, Archie MacLean, Kenny Fletcher, Lachie Fletcher, Andrew Thomson, Johnnie Sinclair, Donald Fletcher, Jimmy Kennedy and Johnnie MacGillivray. Willie MacKenzie and Daniel MacDonald with their extensive surveillance of land, and especially the sea, in their everyday jobs, acted as 'special constables' during the war years. Young Alistair Fletcher, who was around 14 to 15 years old at the time, aspired to be a member of the formidable Home Guard squad but although he volunteered his services, he was too young to be taken in. However, Alistair followed the squad wherever they went to do their exercises and he would then come back to report the 'goings on' to Morag and the other young children in school. He would shoulder a brush and give a fine demonstration of presenting arms, charges with fixed bayonets and the whole spectrum of drill and military manoeuvres!

Morag remembers the squad training in the park in front of the Lodge, on the field opposite Eilean Tioram (The Dry Island) and sometimes on the Dry Island itself. They would practice their drill, have their shooting practice at targets, go crawling around on their bellies with rifles and fixed bayonets, have mock fixed bayonet charges, and use dummy hand grenades when attacking 'key positions' which made quite a bang as they 'exploded' on impact. The children would have a grandstand view of all of this exciting activity from a stance up the Arnisdale brae overlooking Eilean Tioram. Morag also remembers a Regular Army Officer coming to inspect and train the unit as they performed their drill and carried out their exercises around the Dry Island. The Home Guard members also had a rota of night duty, keeping an eye on Loch Hourn for any suspicious naval activity, the Naval Base at Kyle and the fuel stores at Ardentoul being targets for enemy attack.

Work on the croft was quite enjoyed by Morag, except for the tattie lifting - it was too cold and messy. But she liked the work on the hay - despite the midges and also the work with the cows and the milking - taking them home, the milking itself, feeding the calf and then making the crowdie, butter and sometimes cheese. The old cheese press is now a feature in Morag's flower garden. The last cows they had on the croft were Missie and Sheila, the latter being bought from Colin Campbell in Glenshiel. There was always a good sense of sharing in the village - if somebody's cow was newly calved they would supply milk to those whose cow was drying off or in the dry stage. Roddy Mor was the man to be called out if anything went wrong with the beasts. Although she wasn't very enthusiastic about lifting the tatties, Morag acknowledges how important a part of the diet the Kerrs Pink, The Golden Wonders, the Edzell Blues and the Duke of Yorks were. She remembers that Johnny MacGillivray, their next door neighbour on the east side, used to like to experiment, growing different varieties of potatoes to the old faithfuls. Slightly further eastwards from the MacIntyre croft is the burn from which most folk in Camusban drew their water - Allt a'Mhuilinn or the Mill Burn. The mill had obviously been for the processing of oats to produce the oat meal for the porridge, brose and oatcakes which formed an extremely important part of the diet of the local people and probably also of the hordes of fishermen who were around in the herring fishing season. No trace of this mill beside the burn now remains although a neighbour did find one of the mill stones on the shore and it now adorns his front doorstep.

At school, Morag recalls the fine summer days when Ann MacRae was the teacher. All the activities would be transferred outside. They would get their lessons seated on the big benches in the open air or they would do nature study along the shore or up the side of the School burn (Alltan Sgoil) looking at the flowers, the insects and the life in the water. Sometimes the girls would get sewing and the boys would go into the Schoolhouse garden to build and plant a rockery. When back in the school room, if the teacher had to leave for any reason, a common pastime among some was to chew blotting paper, work it into wet 'cannonballs' and then, using the ruler as a propulsion force, the missiles would be sent skywards to the varnished ceiling above, where they would stick. This must have been a fairly regular custom for generations of Arnisdale pupils for apparently the ceiling was peppered with these 'missiles',

After Ann MacRae married and became Mrs Bobby MacLean, she was replaced as teacher by Lexy Campbell By this time, Morag and her lifelong friend Flora MacKenzie (now Mrs Bob Crombie) were the senior pupils and, being very responsible young ladies, they were trusted to go into the Schoolhouse to develop their cookery skills.

However, the three Rs were not neglected and Morag has good cause to remember a fairly dull reading book which provided no excitement whatsoever to herself and Flora. This book they shared as not even the teacher appeared to have a copy. One day they hatched an evil scheme. At playtime they made their way surreptitiously across the school burn, purporting to engage in some private nature study but when they reached Roddy Mor's field behind the Nurse's house, the cunning pair dug a hole and buried the detested book. When school resumed and it was time to perform their combined stint on reading, the totally mysterious loss of the book was reported to Lexy. Greatly to their surprise, Lexy appeared to be not one whit concerned - but made her way to the storage cupboard, opened the door and there - facing her and in full sight of the two trusted young ladies was a whole row of copies of the book which Morag and Flora felt would never trouble their young lives again! 'The best laid schemes gang aft agley' and so it was in this case!

What about the cookery and baking lessons? Well, the two of them were often left in the schoolhouse very much to work things out for themselves as Lexy attended to the other pupils in the schoolroom. One day, the two experimenters were trying to make pancakes, they made what appeared to be a good mix but they were failing to get nice round pancakes on to the girdle - they were spooning the mix on and the resulting pancakes had weird and wonderful shapes. Unexpected guidance came in the form of Iain MacCuaig paying a visit to the schoolhouse in a break from the Lodge gardens (before he and Lexy were married). On finding Morag and Flora struggling with the pancakes, he immediately detected where they were going wrong. After he showed them the way, pouring the pancake mix from the bowl on to the back of a spoon and thence on to the girdle, the two ladies had 'cracked it' and pancakes of excellent shape materialised thereafter.

In another culinary experience, as Halloween approached, the two girls were assigned to make a dumpling. At first, things were going according to plan. Morag was busy mixing the dumpling while Flora was sitting on a chair sewing a hem on the muslin cloth which was to be wrapped round Morag's mix before being put in the pot of boiling water. Morag was taken by surprise when she noted a sudden change in Flora's behaviour who had up to now been totally cool, calm and collected as she prepared her muslin cloth. Flora seemed to panic, jabbed her finger with the needle, quickly scalded the muslin cloth in hot water to try to rid it of the blood which was now dripping from her finger and told Morag to get the mix into the cloth as quickly as possible. Morag, although taken aback, obeyed Flora's instructions as quickly as she could. Flora then bundled the muslin encased dumpling into the pot of boiling water, announced that she had heard the noise of the ghost in the adjoining passage way and, with that, both girls rushed to the door, abandoning the boiling dumpling, as they fled to the safety of the outdoors!

The reason for the panic was that the girls had many times in the past heard the stories about the ghost in the Schoolhouse. This story had its origins in a teacher who had a brother in the war (possibly the Boer War) who took home a piece of shrapnel. The teacher put this on her mantelpiece and from that moment she would from time to time, hear mysterious noises in the corridor. When the teacher's father (a Minister) came to visit her, he became ill at ease to see this article on the mantelpiece and persuaded her to take it outside and bury it in the garden. However, after this, while no further noises were heard in the corridor, knocking on the outside door occurred periodically. When the door was answered, nobody stood outside. It was stories about such reported strange occurrences which went through Flora's mind as she was putting the finishing touches to sewing her muslin cloth for the Halloween dumpling when she heard the suspicious noise in the passageway. When Morag became aware of the reason for Flora's panic, she sought no further explanation as both of them bolted outside. They were very relieved to get back into the 'safety' of the classroom on this occasion to engage in more academic pursuits!

Another group of folk had similar experiences when in the Schoolhouse. In practising little sketches for the forthcoming ceilidhs, Mary Ann MacCuaig, Mary MacIntyre, Lizzie MacLeod (Bean Roddy), Katie Foster, Maggie MacAskill and Johan MacLean would meet in the Schoolhouse with the resident teacher at the time. Those who had heard the knock at the door for the first time and found that nobody stood on the threshold after opening the door, blamed mischievous characters like Roddy Mor for knocking and then disappearing into the night. So, on successive nights, the ladies set a trap for the suspected culprit and took turns to stand behind the door and open it immediately the first knock was heard. For the first few nights 'on guard', no knock came. But they kept up their vigil and when eventually the knock was heard and the door was opened immediately - nobody stood there! So even the mischievous Roddy Mor was not always responsible for the mysterious happenings around the district.

For Morag, Flora and their friends, going out guising on Halloween was always great fun. They would visit the Camusban houses, call at the Lodge where they would get home grown apples from Mr & Mrs Thomson and their next call was at the farm. If Lizzie (Mrs Roddy) was in on her own, this registered with them, for there was no doubt as they made their way to Corran in the dark that somewhere along their route, a figure (Roddy Mor) would come bounding out of the whins at the side of the road. He was always playing tricks on them as he knew that they would be on the move doing their guising. One year, they got a little of their own back when they managed to lift Roddy's bicycle up to the rafters above the old lorry in the cartshed and tied it to the rafters. Roddy apparently spent days trying to find his bike!

After visiting the Corran houses, they would finish up at Granny MacKenzie's (Flora's Granny). She always made a dumpling for the children at Halloween and after doing their party pieces they would all be rewarded by partaking of Granny's fine dumpling.

Morag recalls the discipline imposed on her young life, especially on the Sabbath, with regular attendance at morning and evening services in the church, with the precentors leading the singing over the time that she remembers being Sweyn MacKintosh, Roddy Mor, Willie and Post and Donald Li. She also remembers the excitement of the ceilidh - dances and 'welcome homes' in the school for all the returning ex-servicemen and women - and the long tables laden with sandwiches, home-made scones and cakes for the feast to celebrate the home comings.

Just after the end of the war when Alistair Fletcher had left the village to obtain work in England, Morag tells the story of Alistair phoning home on New Year's Day to find out how his own folk and all the Arnsdale folk were and to wish them 'A Happy New Year'. At the time, the only telephone in Arnisdale was Peggy Ann MacLean's at the Post Office. When Alistair asked the Operator to put him through to Arnisdale Post Office, the Operator apologised, stating that this would not be possible, since all Post Offices in Britain were closed on New Year's Day. But Alistair held the line retorting politely to the Operator "Thank you, but although all other Post Offices in Britain may be closed, Peggy Ann is always there!" The Operator duly dialled the correct code, Peggy Ann responded very promptly, Alistair proved his point, had a good blether with Peggy Ann, exchanging good wishes, finding out about all his folk and friends and sending them all, through Peggy Ann, all his best wishes for the New Year!

In recent years, Morag has been in contact with an old school friend and neighbour who no longer has his home in Arnisdale - Iain MacGillivray. Iain comes to visit the old home and his old friends as do also some of his family - his wife Jessie and their family of Elizabeth, Catherine and John. They too have a bonding with the home of their ancestors and with its culture and history.

After a busy career in the nursing profession which she found very satisfying, Morag is home again and a few doors along the Camusban 'street' is her bosom pal from her earliest years, Flora, with her husband Bob Crombie. The two have just picked up again where they left off, doing many things together as before - attending the church services, climbing Beinn Sgritheall, going on their nature trails and, at the same time in these pursuits, taking wonderful photographs, capturing Arnisdale and its environs in all its moods and in all its splendour.

**Flora Crombie (nee MacKenzie)** Many of Flora's memories of her young days are similar to those of Morag MacIntyre, which is not surprising. They started school in the same year, they were always in the same class, they were great pals, and now they are back in Arnisdale together - almost as next door neighbours.

As a little girl, Flora had a great way with the animals. She liked working with and milking Rosie and the other cows and she would catch little wild rabbits, feed them and nurture them and they would soon be running around outside the house as pets. She also reared orphaned seagull chicks which she found and they too became bonded to the MacKenzie household. She also fancied Roddy Mor's new little pig and commissioned George MacDougall to try to smuggle it and take it home for her.

Then there was Molly, the little Shetland pony which was later joined by Beaver, an Icelandic pony belonging to Arnisdale Lodge, which came to Corran for its retirement after it was no longer fit to go to the hill to bring home the shot stags and hinds.

Molly had a mind of her own and would only do what suited her. When Flora's little friend Morag got astride Molly one day, Molly showed her disapproval by turning round and biting Morag's leg! For this reason, Flora's older sister, Nellie was not the best of friends with Molly, to say the least. However, Flora would ride her bareback and Molly usually obliged, except on one occasion as she was all ready to trot sedately around the field when Nellie came along and, with a firm slap on the haunches, goaded her into a gallop - Flora ending up prostrate on the ground as Molly careered into the distance.

Children were expected to be useful in carrying out necessary chores on the croft from their early years, such as taking buckets of water from the river. Flora did not enjoy working at hay because of the midges! However, she liked fetching the cows in the evening from their grazing areas on the lower slopes of Druim Fada. By watching the direction the cows took as they went out through the hill gate in the morning, you had a fair idea of where they might be found in the evening. Sometimes they would be up the shore towards Caolasmor near the Rudha (headland) opposite the island - Sgeir Leathann. At other times, they might be away up Glen Arnisdale at Blar nan Each but they might be found just beyond the Corran crofts up beside the river on the Eilan Mor.

A regular component of the diet which Flora quite liked was salt herring but the salt venison was not so palatable! Her father used to catch huge skate which Flora did not get too excited about but she liked the other fresh fish which were often available - either caught by themselves or shared from the catch of neighbours. Sometimes a fine salmon would appear on the table but there would be little or no discussion about its origins. Granny MacKenzie used to collect mussels and winkles and boil them in a big black pot but again Flora was not enamoured by the product. The winkles were too much like the snails which crawled around the garden and she didn't fancy eating them!

In her early schooldays, Flora has many memories of wartime activity, in addition to the exercises of the Arnisdale Home Guard. There was the day a German plane flew low over Corran as they were working at the hay. Granny waved to it enthusiastically, and on being reprimanded by her son Willie (Flora's father) for such friendly gestures towards the enemy, she responded that probably by showing such friendliness towards it had saved them all from getting shot! Flora also remembers one school day when, returning to school after her lunch, they witnessed a naval confrontation out in the Sound of Sleat with tracer bullets being fired from an allied cruiser at some unseen (to Flora) enemy vessel - perhaps a surfacing submarine. With rumours of the threat of bombing of allied ships in the area involved in the defence of the Naval Base at Kyle or other objectives, Flora's father briefed the children on the location of their 'air-raid shelter'. This was the fairly deep valley of the burn which flowed past the Corran byres and past their house. Nestled deep in this recess any impact from enemy bombing might hopefully pass above their heads. There was a pleasant experience one day when they all went in the little family boat to Camusban and Peggy Ann's store for their weekly rations. There, berthed in the bay close to Peggy Ann's, was an allied boat with guns. When the children (Flora, Nellie, Iain and Willie) waved to the sailors, they were invited on board, each was given an empty shell case while father received a supply of sugar and syrup - very useful in the tough days of rationing.

Ration books for the folk in the district were delivered to the school for distribution and Flora, along with Morag, recalls being given the job to sort out the ration books by the teacher. Not only did they do the sorting out process to get the books ready for delivery to the folk, but they took the chance to check up on all the ages of all they knew in the village. People were always very secretive about their age to children, so studying the dates of birth on the ration books yielded much interesting information!

As the end of schooldays approached, there were useful locations for playing cards and working the 'tumbler' out of sight of parental surveillance. Thus the young gang of Flora, Morag, Nellie and Iain MacKenzie along with Donald Fletcher and Iain Sinclair spent many evenings in the Camusban Casinos (various barns) playing cards with matches as the stake money.

Flora's family have been associated with the Post Office in Arnisdale and Loch Hourn almost continuously for over 75 years. Willie, Flora's father, was succeeded as postman by her brother Willie and he, in turn, by her nephew David. In addition, after Peggy Ann retired as Postmistress in Arnisdale after many years, Flora's sister Nellie ran the Post Office at Corran for many years before being succeeded in that role by Flora's mother, Christina. Christina in turn was succeeded by the late Rena MacDonald, with Len Morrison being the present Postmaster.

Flora's father, Willie the Post, not only delivered the Arnisdale mail but several times weekly, set off in his boat with outboard motor, to deliver the mail to Li, Barrisdale and Caolasmor up Loch Hourn. Her father liked a little dram on special occasions and Flora remembers on one occasion returning from Barrisdale or some such place visited, with a bottle of clear liquid which he sampled on his return. Flora remembers that he was never his usual self after taking a few 'samples' from this precious bottle. In his 'unwell' state after much 'sampling' he would attribute his 'illness' to a recurrence of his malaria - which both he and Roddy Mor had contracted during their active service in war zones such as the Dardenelles, Gallipoli and Egypt in the First World War.

After leaving school, Flora's first job was in Ayr and then in Arnisdale Lodge and thereafter she worked in Boat of Garten, at the last location being joined by her friend, Morag. She then worked in Skye before meeting Bob Crombie, getting married and setting up house in Bob's home territory in Morayshire where he had a long career in the employment of British Rail. Their family of Christine, Robert, Duncan, Johnnie and Gordon were all born in Morayshire. In frequent holidays in Arnisdale, Bob soon acquired a bonding with Flora's original home and in 1993 they retired to Camusban, where Bob has always enjoyed his fishing, gardening and other pursuits. Flora, of course, is back where she belongs and, in addition to joining Bob in his favourite activities, she teams up again with her neighbour and lifelong friend, Morag, to go climbing, rambling and hunting with her camera. The photographic products are of excellent quality.

Both Bob and Flora are disappointed that the old crofting system has virtually disintegrated and see the need for a modified approach to meet present day circumstances. They visualise good opportunities for the development of tourism and feel that the provision of public toilet and camping facilities in Arnisdale is a first essential step in this direction.

At the time when Flora and Morag were the senior girls in Arnisdale School, with Flora's younger brother Iain and the author in the middle of the 'peck order', the youngest pupil was Sheena Stewart from Corran.

**Sheena Nash (nee Stewart).** Sheena is another Arnisdale native who has returned home to the old family home in Corran where she runs a tea-hut in the spring, summer and autumn months.

Sheena's paternal grandmother was Sheena Thomson from Camusban while her paternal grandfather, Angus Stewart, worked for the Arnisdale Estate, his people in turn having come from Inverie in Knoydart. It was Grandfather Angus who was responsible for building the fine dry stone dykes on the Arnisdale estate, round the fields, the inbye land and separating the inbye land from the hill land. Grandmother Sheena ran a shop at her Corran crofthouse home and Sheena still has her bell which customers rang so as to get attention. As always in any community, there was a bit of pilfering in the shop by a few young vagabonds, who are long gone, but who shall still be nameless in print, whose 'helping themselves' tended to reduce the economic viability of the business!

Sheena's father, also Angus, apart from Army service in the Second World War, spent all his life in Arnisdale. Angus ran the croft and also worked in the Forestry, being the Forestry ganger in the later part of his career. While most of the Forestry workers made their way to the Mhialairidh Forest on foot or on their push bikes, Angus always had his motor bike to get him around.

Sheena's mother, Ina, was a MacLean before her marriage and hailed from the Kiltarlity area where she attended Culburnie and Tomnacross Schools. Ina was a nurse before her marriage, spending most of her nursing career in Edinburgh. After her marriage and making her home in Corran, she was always in demand as a fine singer at the Arnisdale ceilidhs. At the time of writing, Ina is still with us, she is in fine fettle and resides with Sheena in the old family home at Corran.

Sheena married Hamish MacLeod from Eilanreach, a fine young man who was killed tragically in a road accident while their family - 3 daughters (Lorraine, Kim and Helen), and one son (Stuart) - were still very young.

Sheena still has the family croft but sublets it to her neighbours, Willie MacKenzie and Betty MacRae.

She has great memories of her upbringing in Corran and Arnisdale and although there were very few contemporaries in Corran, she did have one special young friend. While a decade or two previously there had been many youngsters growing up together in Corran with the families of MacDonalds, MacCuaigs, Murchisons along with Jimmy Campbell and Sheena's own father Angus, now there was only the MacKenzies - Willie, Nellie, Flora and Iain. The first three were considerably older than Sheena but Iain was only three years Sheena's senior so they were always good pals. They had the 'little girl' pursuits of 'housies' and Sheena's 'housie' was up on the hill at a very favourite place - the Cnoc Ruadh (Red Knoll). She would collect interesting things from the shore, and along with redundant pots, pans, crockery and ornaments of her Mam's, she would arrange and rearrange things in her upstairs and downstairs among the rocks in the Cnoc Ruadh. Sometimes, but not often, she and her friend would 'fall out' and the order and tidiness in her 'housie' would be disrupted somewhat but, after a while, peace and harmony would once again prevail in the partnership. When they wanted a change from their 'housie', on the trees neighbouring Cnoc Ruadh the two of them would engage in games of Tarzan and Jane as they swung from branch to branch. Then at night they would get up to other ploys together such as sparking white stones to get that unique sniff of fire which is generated by clashing stones, along with the sparks which light up the darkness of the night. Another game, they had, perhaps generated by her friend, was 'Tick Tack'. This involved attaching a knocking device such as a stone suspended by black thread on a door, running the thread a considerable distance away to a hiding place, then pulling the thread, so that when the door was answered to welcome the caller, nobody stood in the darkness on the threshold and nobody was in sight. Was the knocking just imagination or was it that ghost which made a habit of such visits every other night? Such questions might go through the minds of those who were less familiar with the ploys of the two youngsters in the village!

Sheena treasured her upbringing on the croft, in Corran, and in Arnisdale in general. She appreciates particularly the fine community spirit which prevailed. She liked the work with the cows, going to collect them from the hill in the evening, and she was helping to milk Daisy and Rhona by the time she was 5 years old. She would often do the milking before she went to school. She enjoyed going to school in Arnisdale and her teachers included Ann MacRae (later MacLean), Lexy Campbell (later MacCuaig), Mrs Roddy from the farm for a short period and also Mrs MacInnes, a sister of Lexy Campbell.

In her current piece of private enterprise, Sheena can be quite busy in her little tea-hut on some days in high summer but Arnisdale's visitors tend to come and go fairly quickly. Public toilets would be a considerable asset, she thinks, to give visitors the opportunity to look around all the places of interest. She would also like to see some young families settling down in the district but she highlights the great change in the availability of work locally from the heyday of the Arnisdale Estate, when many local people were employed, to the present time when there are no such employment opportunities.

Decrofting part of the crofting lands might encourage relatives of the current population to set up their homes in Arnisdale. She also sees scope for more bed and breakfast enterprises and, recognising the 'craft' talents of local people in making such diverse things as violins, furniture, shepherd's crooks and walking sticks, she visualises such 'cottage industry' type opportunities. The wonderful scenery and the merging of mountain, moors, the river and the intriguing shoreline of Loch Hourn, generates further ideas in terms of nature trails, conducted tours to places of historical interest and scenic beauty, and even pony trekking. Two of the crofters in Camusban currently have boat trips on offer up and down the loch and with a wider range of attractions and activities available in the district, these facilities would undoubtedly be in greater demand. She also wonders whether the crofting system itself could be revived in a modified form.

Over the decades and centuries, different forms of employment first attracted people to Arnisdale and Loch Hourn and then helped them to become established in these places. Undoubtedly first it was the great fishing in Loch Hourn, and particularly the herring fishing, which attracted and settled the people; then there was the era of the great estates, employing many people in the shooting lodges, in the gardens, on their yachts and sea-going vessels and on the estate - for the fishing, stalking and shooting; perhaps now, Sheena thinks, it is time to provide for the tourists and she considers that Arnisdale and its environs have a great potential in this respect.

**Top Left.** The three subjects of this Chapter attended Arnisdale School together and are all now back residing in Arnisdale. L to R. Iain (Ruaridh) MacLeod, Calum MacLeod, Morag MacIntyre, Iain MacGillivray, Willie MacLeod, Nellie MacKenzie, Sheena Stewart, Iain MacKenzie and Flora MacKenzie. (Photograph around 1945). **Right**. When Lexy Campbell came as teacher to the school in 1946, Morag and Flora, being senior pupils and responsible young ladies, were entrusted to conduct their own self-learning cookery lessons in the Schoolhouse. However, when they were having difficulty in producing pancakes with normal shapes they were rescued by Iain MacCuaig. Later, Lexy was to become Mrs Iain MacCuaig. The picture of Iain and Lexy is taken in front of the Arnisdale School and Schoolhouse.

**Middle Left.** Morag (far right) with a group of friends and neighbours in Camusban. L to R. Donald MacCuaig, Jackie Morrison, Nellie Leitch, Christina MacKenzie and Morag with the youngsters, Donald and Morabelle Morrison, in front (1960-70 era). **Right** Morag and Flora at the site in Rarsaidh where they collected sphagnum moss in their wartime schooldays. The sphagnum moss was used to prepare wound dressings. This was also the area where the Camusban folk cut their peats, transporting them home by boat.

**Bottom Left.** Morag now spends time exploring Arnisdale mountains and other interesting places with her great friend Flora. Here Morag is making steady progress up Beinn Sgritheall. **Right**,. Now the summit is reached it is time to rest and admire the view. L to R. Flora, Morag and Iain MacKenzie.

**Top Left.** Morag (right) treating some friends to a dram on a fine Summer's day in Camusban. L. to R. Donnie Leitch, Tom MacDiarmid, Hugh Barron and Nellie Leitch (nee MacKenzie). **Centre.** Flora MacKenzie (left) and sister Nellie in their schooldays. **Right.** Flora with Donald Fletcher (left) and Angus Stewart. As Flora, Morag and Nellie came towards the end of their schooldays in Arnisdale they teamed up with other youngsters – Ian Sinclair, Donald Fletcher and Iain MacKenzie and played cards, with matches as stake money, in various barns in Camusbun (The Camusban Casinos) – away from parental surveillance.

**Middle Left.** One of Flora's first jobs on leaving school was in Arnisdale Lodge. She is pictured here with other Lodge and Estate staff (around 1948). L to R. Chrissie MacCuaig, Flora, Ian Sinclair, Ludovic Fraser, Katie Foster and Angus Beaton. **Right.** Flora's husband Bob Crombie (left) joins the 100th Birthday celebrations of Mrs Mary Anne MacDonald at Corran with the wonderful old lady's daughter Rena (centre).

**Bottom Left.** Flora on one of her climbing expeditions with Morag. **Right.** Flora at the site, Cnoc Ruadh, of a favourite play area for Corran youngsters. This was the location where they played 'housies' and organised an upstairs and downstairs in their play and imagination.

**Top Left**.  Sheena Stewart with a group of Corran youngsters around 1950.  L to R. Leslie Aldridge, Sheena, Johan Macdonald, Margaret Robertson, Iain MacKenzie and Morag Ann MacDonald.  **Right**.  Sheena with her little friend Pam MacLennan, daughter of Rev. Mr MacLennan and his wife.  Mr MacLennan was the last active Church of Scotland Minister to reside in Arnisdale.

**Middle Left**.  Sheena's mother, Ina – a fine singer at the Arnisdale ceilidh dances.  **Right**.  Sheena and her mother, Ina, relax after winning the battle to secure the haycrop.

**Bottom Left**.  Sheena's father Angus Stewart during his wartime service period.  **Right**.  Angus Stewart on his motorbike in Camusban on his way to the Mialairidh Forest.  Angus was a ganger in the Arnisdale Forest for many years.

**Top Left**. Angus Stewart (right) and his friend enjoy a dram together.   **Right**.  Angus' father (also Angus) with one of the Arnisdale Estate ponies.  Old Angus worked for the Estate for many years.   He was a fine stone mason and built most of the fine dykes around the estate.

**Middle Left**.  Old Angus Stewart (right) with Robert Foster.   **Right**.  Sheena's wedding to Hamish MacLeod of Eilanreach.  Hamish was killed tragically in a road accident when their family of Lorraine, Kim, Helen and Stuart were still very young.

**Bottom Left**.  Sheena (centre) is now back in Arnisdale at the old family home in Corran.   Her mother Ina is on the left while daughter Helen is on the right.   Sheena's house is the furthest west in the Corran street, is close to the line of sheds built to store the fishing gear of the Corran Crofters and there is a splendid view up Loch Hourn towards Skye and the Cuillin.   **Right**.   Sheena runs her tea hut adjacent to her home.   On fine days she is kept very busy as tourists drop in for a cup of tea in a unique environment.

# Chapter 10

**The memories of Nellie Leitch and her history searches**

The recollections of Nellie Leitch (nee Mackenzie) of her treasured upbringing in Arnisdale are very similar to those of her sister Flora and brothers, Willie and Iain.

She certainly remembers the nightly ceilidhs where the villagers (mainly the men folk) would adjourn to one of the ceilidh houses and the children would follow. As their elders would discuss, in the Gaelic, the events of the day, local history, genealogy, mythology, the supernatural and that very wide range of topics that would come up at the nightly ceilidhs, the children would listen, learn and enjoy themselves thoroughly. On some occasions the children would become less passive and would be invited to give a song or do a dance together which they had been going over in school or in their daytime play together at Corran.

Nellie remembers Sandy MacAskill's house best as a ceilidh house and the likes of Colin Murchison, Alan MacAskill, Angus Stewart and Willie MacKenzie (Nellie's father) would walk in one by one, at intervals, without a knock on the door but with their usual Gaelic greeting to announce their arrival to join the gathering of the local 'parliament'. Often the entry was accompanied by the rhetorical question "Bheil duine stigh?" (Anybody at home?) to which there was the immediate response of "Thig a stigh" (Come in!).

Another neighbour arrived home on holiday just in time, on an occasion when Nellie was becoming quite ill as a ten year old. This was Surgeon Captain Ewen Murchison and as soon as he was spotted in the street, he was 'apprehended' and escorted into the MacKenzie household. Pleurisy was diagnosed, appropriate medicinal treatment was applied immediately and Nellie was soon on the mend. Although many of the established medical protocols were broken, it was the essence of common sense and practicality - and the problem was resolved very quickly. While the District Nurse was resident in Arnisdale, the Doctor (Dr Devon at the time) was resident in Glenelg and a call there might have found her far away on her rounds, not contactable, and it might have been long enough before she made it to Arnisdale to examine the ailing little Nellie. However, Doctor Devon did come to Arnisdale fairly quickly when, soon after recovering from her pleurisy, Nellie tripped coming out of Sandy MacAskill's ceilidh house, fell heavily and felt such great pain in her leg that she was quite unable to put any weight on it. Dr Devon diagnosed a fracture, put a splint on the leg and telephoned the Children's Ward at the Royal Northern Infirmary in Inverness to arrange for the admission of the injured child. Meanwhile Roddy Mor was contacted at the farm and he soon got the little Austin Seven started and was off up to Corran to collect Nellie and her Mam. Then they were off on their long, circuitous, bumpy journey - gravel roads to Glenelg, over Mam Ratagan, into Glenshiel, past Cluanie and they did not reach a smooth tarred road until they reached Upper Glenmoriston.

Was the child in agony with all the potholes, bumps, Z bends, steep braes, precipitous descents and many other hazards? Nellie has no such traumatic memories but rather of the pleasures of the jaunt, seeing much of the beautiful terrain for the very first time. Nellie was tough, Dr Devon must have made a good job of the splint, while her Mam and Roddy Mor must have been having interesting conversations about places, people and history, Nellie would be 'lugging in' and be pleasantly diverted from any of her aches, pains and childish worries about where she was going and the fear of the big hospital in the Highland Capital.

After leaving school, Nellie had to seek employment further afield in the Highlands and she eventually met and married Donnie Leitch from Inverness. Nellie and Donnie have four children - Sidney, Raymond, Iain and Mary and now have many grand children - and the first great grandchild (Nadine) has now arrived on the scene.

Soon after they got married, Nellie and Donnie inherited Jimmy MacDonald's croft in Corran and made their way back to the old clachan. Donnie got a job with the Forestry Commission in the Mialairidh Forest and Nellie took over the Arnisdale Post Office. Peggy Ann had, reluctantly, decided to call it a day at her well known and much loved little shop in the first house at the base of the Arnisdale brae in Camusban, so Nellie set up as Postmistress in her little croft house in Corran. She provided this very useful service for Arnisdale and its dependent communities for eight years before her mother succeeded her as Postmistress.

Donnie has many amusing tales to tell of his days in the Mialairidh Forest such as the time when there was an unusually heavy snowfall and the Arnisdale to Glenelg road was completely impassable to vehicular traffic. All able bodied men, including the forestry workers, set to in starting to clear the road using their tried and tested old shovels. They made slow but steady headway as they tried to find a way out to the great world beyond. They had fought their way up the Arnisdale brae, down the other side, past Rarsaidh, into the Mialairidh Forest, up the Carr Ruadh, out the other end of the forest - when up at the top of the Gorstan, in full view of Isleornsay, the Isle of Skye, the Cuillins and looking down the Sound of Sleat to Eigg, Rhum and Canna beyond - they saw their rescuers approaching up the Sandaig brae. This was the Glenelg Forestry squad who had been 'commandeered' to help in solving the crisis by the road foreman on the Glenelg side, John Mor (MacDonald). Stranded in 'no man's land' between Glenelg and Arnisdale was John Donald MacLeod, road foreman on this stretch of road, who resided at Sandaig and was unable to make progress in either direction such was the depth and extent of the snow drifts. As John Mor battled to find a way through from Glenelg and Eilanreach along with his assistants Willie MacLeod, Archie MacLean and Donnie Lamont, he had the brainwave that the quickest way to rescue John Donald at Sandaig was to call the Glenelg Forestry squad into action and get them by boat to Lower Sandaig so that once they reached John Donald's house they could first try to clear the way to meet up with the Arnisdale squad and after that to work back towards Glenelg to rendezvous with John Mor and his fellow rescuers operating from that end. The problem of finding a boat to get the Glenelg Forestry squad to Lower Sandaig was solved by Donald John MacLeod from Glenelg. Donald John was operating the mail service between Glenelg and Kyle at the time on his Kelvin Cabin launch, 'The Gobhar'. Since the mails between Arnisdale and Glenelg could not be delivered by road, Donald John was asked to deliver and collect the Arnisdale mails by sea after returning from his regular morning run to Kyle.

So along with his assistant ferryman, Norman (Tosh) Elder, they got the Glenelg forestry squad of Donnie MacPherson, Alistair MacDonald, Tommy Moffat, Johnny MacLean, Ewan MacKinnon (Diesel) and John MacLeod on board and headed for Lower Sandaig. There, Donald John and Tosh off-loaded the relief workers into a dinghy, and the bold lads rowed ashore, and then made their way, shouldering their shovels, past Gavin Maxwell's house, up alongside the Sandaig burn, eventually reached John Donald's house and - after a quick check on the well-being of John Donald MacLeod and his wife Mary - they immediately set off clearing the road towards Arnisdale. They made good progress up the Sandaig brae and, as they were approaching the top of the Gorstan, they saw the Arnisdale squad of forestry workers - Angus Stewart, Donald Fletcher, Jackie Morrison, Donnie Leitch and the Arnisdale roadman John Arthur, shovelling their way towards them.

Eventually the two formidable squads met face to face, they had been 'tunnelling' from different directions in each other's direction and, amazingly, the tunnels were joined at exactly the right point - a great feat of civil engineering! Greetings were exchanged, legs were pulled mercilessly, the experiences of the rival gangs were exchanged, they had their tea and their piece and then, reluctantly, after a most enjoyable mid-day ceilidh at the top of that great vantage point and viewpoint at the Gorstan, they had to turn their backs on each other and retreat to their respective clachans - but bringing home to their folk the full story of the great liberation!

However, the way home was not as clear for the Glenelg boys as it was for their Arnisdale brethren. Once they got back down the Sandaig brae to John Donald's house, they had to clear the way from Sandaig, past Tormor and on to the top of the Eilanreach brae until they met up with John Mor's squad of himself, Willie, Archie and Donnie coming up the brae from the Glenelg direction.

Soon after they met, the forestry landrover arrived on the scene from Glenelg and in two runs it got them all back to Glenelg. There they all adjourned to the pub to get some 'anti-freeze', as they called it, so as to recover their composure and strength and to relate to their friends there their valiant deliverance of the Arnisdale folk in connecting them once again with the outside world!

It was too good a story to remain untold and Tommy Moffat, one of the liberators in the Glenelg Forestry squad, duly penned the following lines so that the tale of the famous occasion would be sure to feature at Arnisdale and Glenelg ceilidhs and in the local folklore for generations to come!

**The Sandaig Landing (by Tommy Moffat)**

1. The snow lay heavy on the ground
   'Twas deep mid Winter all around
   The road to Arnisdale was blocked
   Even the Whisky van was stopped

2. The roadmen toiled from break of day
   To try to open up the way
   It was a losing battle tho'
   To clear so many drifts of snow

3. So John took the best way no doubt
   He called the forestry workers out
   He asked them if they would agree
   To being landed by the sea

4. It was Donald John who saved the day
   The Gobhar sped swiftly through the bay
   They landed on the Sandaig shore
   And some used their shovels as an oar

5. When Major Maxwell saw the sight
   I hear he got an awful fright
   He went and hid below the bed
   He thought his otters would be dead

6. They were a fearful looking band
   Approaching with shovels o'er the strand
   What on earth could the meaning be
   Roadmen arriving by the sea

7.     They clambered up the Sandaig track
   In order that they could attack
   The very many drifts of snow
   That stopped the whisky getting through

8.     MacLeod who had been snowed in for days
   Stood in the doorway in a daze
   He said, if only he had known
   He would have cleared it on his own

9.     They set to working with a will
   And dug their way up round the hill
   The thought of whisky getting through
   Put extra strength into the crew

10.     When at last the crews did meet
    They did with joy each other greet
    So roadmen now from toil may cease
    And forestry workers rest in peace.

(Author's note: Nobody appeared to have a copy of the late Tommy Moffat's poem but Hugh Ian (Uisdean) MacLure and the same Donald John MacLeod, erstwhile skipper of 'The Gobhar' which played a key role in the rescue mission, pressed their memory banks and duly resuscitated Tommy's poem).

Now, let us return to Nellie's story. As their children grew up, Nellie and Donnie made their way back to the Inverness area to take up employment themselves and to increase the chances of the children finding suitable further education and work opportunities.

Nellie and Donnie and their family return to holiday at Corran at every opportunity and Nellie has been very active in recent years in researching family and local history. Her Granny in Corran (Mairi Bhan) had told her as a child that the MacKenzie part of her ancestry had close associations with the 1745 Rising and that Roderick MacKenzie, whose grave and memorial stone are close to the roadside at Ceannacroc in Upper Glenmoriston, was one of her forefathers. Nellie, as with most children, was interested in this association at the time of her Granny's story-telling, but gave it scant attention at the time. However, in recent times, her Granny's story, in those childhood years, came back to her more strongly and provided the urge to investigate matters further.

Nellie's research, aided by very helpful friends in the Inverness Library (and particularly from the resident genealogist, Alasdair MacLeod) and also from the Scottish Records Office has fairly conclusively proved her family's direct line of descent from the Roderick MacKenzie whose feats on behalf of Prince Charlie are commemorated by the Ceannacroc monument.

In the early part of the 18th Century, the MacKenzies were in the Hilton district of Easter Ross and their tenancy of a farm holding at Mellon Udrigle is mentioned in the records. Roderick MacKenzie's grandfather was Colin of the same name from Easter Ross and his father's name was Kenneth. Kenneth went to Edinburgh and started a business as a Deacon of Goldsmiths and jeweller. His son Roderick is classified in the records as a 'Writer' to his father which indicates that he dealt with the correspondence pertaining to the business and did the book-keeping. He also appeared to act as a traveller on behalf of the business, obtaining orders for watches and other jewellery. Since a branch of the MacKenzie family had gone to Eilanreach before the 1745 Rising, Roderick happened to be at his relatives there when the news of the raising of the Jacobite Standard at Glenfinnan came through. Nellie's Granny's story was that he was sitting on a stool shearing sheep when this news came. Roderick decided that he must join Prince Charlie's Regiment and made his way back to Edinburgh, possibly joining the Prince's army before the Battle of Prestonpans.

He followed the Prince thereafter and was still there in the Culloden aftermath in the protection of his leader until he fell to Cumberland's Redcoats when acting as a decoy when the Prince was in hiding in the well appointed cave in the Coire Dho in Upper Glenmoriston.

Nellie has also carried out research on a military warrior of later years - her father ('Willie the Post'). At the outbreak of the First World War, Willie, at the age of 20, volunteered to join the Lovat Scouts. He was joined by two other 21 year olds from Arnisdale - his brother Norman and Roddy MacLeod (Roddy Mor) from the farm. The three Arnisdale boys were allocated to K Squadron and carried out their cavalry training at Kimbolton in Bedfordshire. Nellie remembers that the name of her father's horse was Stella. It was not long after somewhat rushed initial training that they were all on their way to support the Dardanelles campaign against the Turks. It was the toughest of campaigns against a formidable enemy fighting on their familiar home territory. At the end of that successful campaign, K Squadron and the three Arnisdale boys joined the war in Egypt and France. But, praise be, the three lads survived the War and all made it back to their beloved Arnisdale. All three contracted malaria but had to fight on regardless. Norman received serious shrapnel wounds in 1916 and was hospitalised in the field hospital for a time and then was shipped home to Britain for more specialist treatment. He ended up in D3 Ward, Alder Hay Hospital, Liverpool and soon after arrival there he received a picture postcard from his 17 year old sister, Peggie Ann, in Corran. The picture was of a group of Norman's fellow Scouts whom he had had to leave behind and included brother Willie and Roddy Mor.

The postcard read:
___

                                          Corran
                                          21 November 1916

Dear Brother,
I have no envelope to hold it but I hope you will get it alright. You will know them alright - they look very well. Good bye dear. Try and get another taken and send to Flora.
        Your loving sister
            Peggie Ann MacKenzie
___

(Footnote. Flora was Norman's other sister who was 20 years of age at that time).

Willie had sent home the picture to his mother Mairi Bhan and sister Peggie Ann. The family were obviously reassured by how well Willie, Roddy Mor and their other mates were looking in their summer combat kit in Egypt.

Although the Scouts may have been looking well when the picture was taken, things could not have been tougher for these boys. When eventually they got home, at the end of the war, they discussed little of the detail - they were only too glad to put these terrible times behind them and get on with their lives in their own pleasant and peaceful land. However, Roddy Mor sometimes confided to those closest to him that among his innermost thoughts when things were at their very worst was that, if he ever was lucky enough to get back to Arnisdale, he would never leave it again. When he did get back, these thoughts in his darkest hours prevailed and he always took a lot of coaxing to go away for a little holiday or jaunt - and then it would only be for a few days or even a few hours. He was the essence of contentment among his own beloved people, on the farm, shepherding the sheep, herding and caring for the cows, tilling the land, making his hay, planting and harvesting his crops - and getting up to his own boyish brand of mischief at frequent intervals - even into his old age.

Perhaps the best hint of Willie's innermost feelings in the prolonged battles against the enemy in the Dardanelles, Gallipoli and Salonika (in Northern Greece), Egypt and France have been best described in another medium - in the verses of a Gaelic song. The story was as follows:

The officer in charge of K Squadron of the Lovat Scouts was Captain William MacKintosh, a native of Nairn who, after the war, owned and ran in turn the Lochmaddy Hotel, Glenelg Hotel and then the Roy Bridge Hotel. Captain William had joined the Lovat Scouts at the age of 16 when Lord Lovat first raised the Regiment for service in the South African War.

After emigrating to New Zealand in 1913, he raised a troop of New Zealand Scouts at the outbreak of the Great War in 1914, came back to fight for the cause and distinguished himself in battle, winning the Military Cross. Captain William was promoted to the rank of Major when the Lovat Scouts moved on from the Dardanelles and Egypt to the war in France.

In the long and bitter fighting in which the Lovat Scouts were engaged at the height of the Gallipoli Campaign, conditions were very tough, fatigue was prevalent among the highly trained, fit young soldiers and morale was quite low at times. The battle hardened Captain William, like all good leaders, was sensitive to the physical and mental state of his men, and decided on a little ploy to turn minds away from the bitterness of war, in their limited off-duty hours in the trenches. The challenge he gave them was to compose a Gaelic song and the prize to the winner was to be a bottle of whisky. What a prize in the circumstances! What a challenge! The boys went for it and Willie won the bottle. One can imagine how Willie and his mates enjoyed their precious dram.

What of the song? Well, Willie gave his manuscript to brother Norman when both of them got back to Arnisdale at the end of the War. Norman eventually went to work in Inveraray, settled and died there in the 1970s. About ten years after Norman passed away, Willie's song was translated into English by the Rev Dr Roderick MacLeod, who was Minister of the Cumlodden and Furnace congregation in Lochfyneside and a native of North Uist.

Ethel MacCallum (nee Woods) of Inveraray, a native of Tiree and a Mod Gold Medallist, set a tune to the Gaelic song and has recorded it in both Gaelic and English. Nellie has these recordings of the song and also a tape of the song sung in the Gaelic by Norman MacKinnon, Campbeltown (a Mod Gold medallist) who has Glasgow, Campbeltown, Inveraray and Tiree connections and is a grandson of Nellie's Uncle Norman and a grand-nephew of 'Willie the Post'. The words of Willie's song composed in the trenches at Gallipoli are as follows:

> You speakers of Gaelic hear what I say
> In Greece I'm so journeying but with grief and dismay
> Europe's war is still raging and no ending is near
> With no hope of returning to Scotland so dear.
>
> Drink a toast from the bottle, round the table be gay.
> To Glenquoich and Kintail is my greeting today
> Get a deer in the autumn, in the winter a hind

> Colonel Roberts' great heroes leave their warfare behind.
>
> Go to battle with foes, strong on land and at sea.
> With great guns so destructive the soldier's lot seems to be
> But in the annals of history it will all be revealed
> How Arnisdale's poachers cause the bold Turks to yield.
>
> Give me as my watchman MacPherson so true
> And our own Captain William no panic he knew.
> Fearless and with valiance to fight they did go
> All mates in conflict and heroes renowned.
>
> The pipes and the trumpets sound reveille again
> For our great Highland soldiers who in battle will be slain
> To guard Britain's homeland was the price they did pay
> Our fine worthy heroes kept the Germans at bay.
>
> Let's expel all the landlords who have emptied our glens
> We'll possess their deer forests and inherit the bens
> Fill their lands with your cattle, fish the rivers once more
> At the cost of the heroes who the peace did restore.

---

Author's note. Although in verse 4 MacPherson is referred to as 'my watchman MacPherson so true' the Gaelic version refers to Mac a' Phearsain na Maòil (MacPherson of Maòil or Moyle in Glenelg). This, almost certainly is Rory Macpherson, a granduncle of the author's wife, Anne. Rory was considered to be one of the best shots in the Lovat Scouts and would be Willie's usual companion on paired scouting missions to assess enemy positions and movements. Both had excellent training for these dangerous assignments through their stalking and shooting experience on the Arnisdale, Knoydart, Kinloch Hourn and Glen Quoich hill and mountain territories.

These verses of Willie's song provide the best record the MacKenzie family have of their father's thoughts at a time when undoubtedly there were feelings of despair, of misery, hunger and great fatigue - but always also of hope. Undoubtedly as young Willie's mind concentrated on composing the song, the hardships were lightened somewhat and the spirits, hopes and determination were raised to a higher level for a while.

Willie's dreams were that his people at home would be enabled to re-possess their hills and glens, farm their land and their cattle, fish their rivers and hunt their deer once more.

When Willie eventually got back to Arnisdale after that dreadful war, the hopes expressed in his song of having the chance to farm, hunt and fish the lands of his fathers were, of course, not fulfilled. Instead Willie, along with several other fit young men from the area made for the ranges of Montana in the United States where there were opportunities for setting up cattle and sheep ranches on cheap land. For one reason or other, Willie came back home within a year or so of going out to 'test the water'. Perhaps the call of home was just too strong. Or perhaps he had heard from home of the opportunity to obtain regular paid employment in his native haunts. After the tragic drowning of Duncan Campbell at Caolasmor in the course of his duties as postman, the job of Arnisdale and Loch Hourn postman was advertised, Willie applied and in a letter of 13 August 1920, Alex Anderson, Postmaster at Kyle wrote to Willie as follows:

"Dear Sir,

I am pleased to inform you that you have been appointed Arnisdale, Corran and Barrisdale Deliverer at wages of 17/- a week, all told. I shall be glad if you will be good enough to commence duty at Arnisdale on Monday the 16th instant.

The Sub-Postmaster will instruct you in your duties.

Alex Anderson

Postmaster."

Author's note. The wage of 17/- (shillings) per week is equivalent to 85 pence per week.

Thus, from 16 August 1920, Willie became the first 'Willie the Post'.

In his memories of his early days in Arnisdale, Surgeon Captain Ewen Murchison, now resident in Gibraltar, penned the following lines about Willie MacKenzie.

'I must also comment about Willie MacKenzie who, in my opinion, was the outstanding character of his era in the entire Arnisdale complex. My earliest recollections of him are as a small boy sitting by a winter's peat fire in Corran enthralled with his detailed description of trench warfare both in the ill conceived Gallipoli landings and on the Western Front. At the time, I am sure that many thought he was exaggerating but history has proved that the fearful conditions required few embellishments.

I enjoyed his company immensely and spent many happy days with him stalking the mountains of Knoydart! His nocturnal expeditions were not discussed openly in our house, but were nevertheless very much in evidence when a salmon was surreptitiously handed in at our door in the early hours of the morning!

He made quite an impression on tourists and I recall that, by some strange coincidence, I met some of them on my travels in the Middle East and Southern England, who remarked on his versatility and loyalty - a small world indeed! On National Commemorative Days he always proudly displayed the Union Jack from the stern of his boat as he delivered mail round Loch Hourn.'

So ends Ewen's tribute to Willie.

If we return to the last verse of Willie's winning Gaelic song, although he did not literally come to 'possess the deer forests' and 'fish the rivers once more' openly, Willie made sure in 'his nocturnal expeditions', as Ewen Murchison puts it, that his family and his friends got the opportunity to enjoy some fresh salmon and roast venison now and again!

But let us now return to Nellie's story and her thoughts on the future of Arnisdale.

Rather than think of the future, perhaps Nellie is more interested in delving further into Arnisdale's history and that of its people, including her own. She and Donnie get back to their little cottage in Corran as often as possible, as do their expanding family. But the family have no interest in crofting, so the croft land has been passed over to nephew Billy and grandson of the first 'Willie the Post'. The latter, with more land resources to croft and farm on a more realistic scale, to combine with his other local work, is one of Arnisdale's big hopes for appropriate future development and the re-invigoration of life and activity in the community.

Although the hopes expressed by soldier Willie as he penned the last verse of his song in Gallipoli did not materialise for his generation, who is to say that Willie's hopes might not come to fruition in future generations?

**Top Left**.   Nellie Leitch (nee MacKenzie) outside the Mission House in Arnisdale.   The gable of the Free Church with its intriguing circular window is behind her.   **Right.**   Nellie in her young days in Corran (front left) with sister Flora (front right) and Johan MacDonald (left) and Frances Kennedy behind.

**Middle Left**.   The ceilidh house in Corran best remembered by Nellie in her young days was that of Sandy MacAskill.   In this group taken during a break working with the Corran Township sheep at the Arnisdale fank are L to R.  Angus Campbell, Archie MacLean, Sandy MacAskill, Fay MacLaren, Donald MacLaren and Betty MacLaren.   **Right**.   Surgeon Captain Ewen Murchison who was commandeered by Nellie's father immediately he arrived home on holiday on one occasion to diagnose her illness and prescribe a remedy.

**Bottom Left**.   Nellie's husband Donnie Leitch (second from left) at Corran with (L to R.) Nellie, Hector MacKinnon  with his wife Mary (Nellie's first cousin), Nellie's mother Christina and brother Willie.   **Right**.   Deep snow on the Arnisdale road near Rarsaidh on one occasion which blocked the Arnisdale road to all but foot traffic.   (Maggie Lea in photograph),.   This was similar to the famous road block a few decades later which was commemorated by Tommy Moffat's poem.

**Top**.  Donald John MacLeod who helped in the rescue of snowbound Arnisdale by sailing the Glenelg Forestry Squad in his boat 'The Gobhar' to lower Sandaig armed with their shovels to clear the way through the deep drifts.

**Middle Left**.  John 'Mor' MacDonald (arrowed in centre) who was battling with his road squad from the Eilanreach end to help relieve Arnisdale's isolation from the world and Tommy Moffat (arrowed left) who penned a famous poem to commemorate the incident.
**Right**.   John Donald MacLeod who was marooned with his family at Sandaig and according to Tommy Moffat's immortal lines indicated that 'If only he had known, he would have cleared it on his own'.

**Bottom Left**.   Nellie's grandparents Allan and Mary (Mairi Bhan) MacKenzie.   Mairi Bhan's father and mother died during the typhoid epidemic around 1890 in Arnisdale.   **Right**.   A later picture of Nellie's Granny Mairi Bhan MacKenzie with her daughter Peggie Anne.  Mairi Bhan was a survivor of the typhoid epidemic which also claimed the life of the local Doctor Graham from Glenelg.

**Top Left**.  Nellie's history searches have found a family link with Roderick MacKenzie, a follower and defender of Bonnie Prince Charlie, who was shot and killed by Cumberland's troops and whose feats on behalf of the Prince are commemorated in the cairn in Upper Glenmoriston.  An ancestor of Ewen Grant (standing beside the Cairn) was one of the Seven Men of Glenmoriston who protected the Prince.  **Right**.  The cave in Coire Dho in Upper Glenmoriston where Prince Charlie was hidden and defended in the early summer of 1746 by the seven men of Glenmoriston and other followers including Roderick MacKenzie.

**Middle Left.**  Nellie's father Willie (rear on right) and his Arnisdale pal Roddy Mor (middle row right) in desert kit during their First World War service with the Lovat Scouts.  **Right**.  The Lovat Scouts on their cavalry training at Kimbolton, Bedfordshire before sailing to support the Dardanelles campaign against the Turks in World War 1.

**Bottom Left**.  The Lovat Scouts before embarkation for Turkey.  Willie MacKenzie is on the extreme right of the middle row.  **Centre and Right**.  Willie MacKenzie (right) and Captain (later Major) William MacKintosh (centre).  Captain Willie set his troops a challenge during a lull in the Gallipoli Campaign for the best composition of a Gaelic song.  The competition was won by Nellie's father Willie and the song has now been recorded for posterity.

142

**Top Left**. Nellie's Uncle Norman (right) at Inveraray where he spent most of his working days and retirement. **Right**. Norman's daughter, Mary, with her husband, Hector MacKinnon, a native of Tiree. Their son Norman, a Mod Gold Medallist, has recorded Willie the Post's winning Gaelic song from the first World War.

**Middle Left.** Rory MacPherson, of Moyle, Glenelg (seventh from left in the back row) who was reputed to be the best shot in the Lovat Scouts. It is almost certain that Willie and Rory worked as a pair in scouting missions during the Gallipoli Campaign. **Right**. The wedding of Nellie's father Willie and mother Christina in the late 1920s.

**Bottom Left**. A welcome home to Arnisdale for the young couple from Mary Ann MacCuaig (left) and Willie's lifelong friend Roddy Mor with his bagpipes. **Right**. Willie MacKenzie (Willie the Post) delivers the mail to the Loch Hourn clachans on Coronation Day 1937 (King George VI and Queen Elizabeth) and flies his flag in celebration. The photograph was taken by a visitor from Glasgow who sent Willie the picture with the caption 'Loyalty in lonely places'.

## Chapter 11

**War Time and the Welcomes Home**

There are many reports in these pages of the experiences of Arnisdale and Loch Hourn folk both at the battle fronts and at home during the two world wars. Lachlan Fletcher, Donald Cameron, Rarsaidh and Major Fleming, the new owner of the Arnisdale Estate made the supreme sacrifice in the First War while Donald MacIntosh, Rarsaidh, a nephew of Donald Cameron, died for his country in the second. Many others served their country in both wars and survived these terrible times to return to their homes and loved ones.

At the end of the First War, returning ex-servicemen had hopes that their valiant service would be recognised by being granted more land to rent on their crofts and small farms to enable them to make a living for themselves and their families.

The following account in the Oban Times of 2 April 1921 reports on the resolution made at a meeting of the Arnisdale 'Land Leaguers':

**"Arnisdale, Loch Hourn**

A meeting of the ex-Service men was held this week, when the following ex-Service men took part and delivered strong and stirring speeches in respect of the land policy before and after the war: Mr John McIntyre, D.C.M.; Mr Roderick MacLeod, Mr Andrew Fraser, Mr Angus McTavish, Mr John Sinclair, Mr John MacGilivray, jun., and Mr Alick MacLeod. Mr John McIntyre, D.C.M. moved the following resolution, seconded by Mr Roderick MacLeod, and carried unanimously:

> That this meeting of ex-Service men pledges itself to continue to agitate and to demand the promise of the Government to settle them on the land - and that at an early date - and urges upon the Board of Agriculture for Scotland to take immediate steps in this direction, using the full powers conferred upon them. That nothing short of the land for ex-Service men will ameliorate their condition or satisfy their demands.

Copies were ordered to be sent to the Secretary for Scotland, the Lord Advocate and the Board of Agriculture for Scotland."

So that the three Johns, Roddy Mor, Andrew, Angan and Alick made a bold bid to claim more land to rent but there are no subsequent reports of a response from the powers that be.

On first reflection, it is surprising that neither Willie MacKenzie or his brother Norman was at this meeting in Arnisdale in 1921 but probably they had already sought a future in Montana where they went to work in the great cattle ranches there in the early 1920s. Willie, Norman and Roddy Mor had served throughout the war together in the Lovat Scouts in Gallipoli, the Dardanelles, Egypt and France and the dream of obtaining more land at home if they survived the war was obviously with them as they served their country on these foreign fields. This is evident from Willie's Gaelic song, written in Gallipoli, which won him first prize - a precious bottle of whisky - in the competition organised by their commanding officer - Captain William MacKintosh (Captain Willie).

The translated last verse of Willie's winning composition reads:

> 'Let's expel all the landlords who have emptied our Glens,
> We'll possess their deer forests and inherit the bens,
> Fill their lands with your cattle, fish the rivers once more,
> At the cost of the heroes who the peace did restore.'

The strong aspirations of the local boys to make more efficient use of the 'lands of their fathers' was certainly there but they apparently received no response from officialdom. So they received no material rewards but they had played their noble part in winning freedom for their country and their people.

That hard-won freedom was often evident in the free spirits of Arnisdale, and rarely more so than in a 'hen party' organised with great secrecy in Arnisdale Lodge on Christmas Eve 1918. The following lines composed by the author's Aunt Lizzie, who had only recently (1917) arrived in Arnisdale as the new teacher, captures the spirit of that obviously very memorable get-together which excluded the returned ex-Servicemen and all others of the same sex.

**Composed by Lizzie MacDonald in memory of a party in Arnisdale Lodge on 24 December 1918**

These simple lines which here I write
just tell the little tale
of but a very jolly night, I've had in Arnisdale
with Nan and Teenie, Kate and Flo and Katie Foster too,
just the six of us you know and
we didn't prove too few
Should I live for four score years and ten
I ever shall remember
the time we had without the men
on the 24th of December.

And let me tell you of our plan
and how we had to dodge
every woman, child and man
and sneak over to the Lodge
We managed to get safely in - unseen by man and beast
and then began oh! such a din
which I enjoyed at least.
Nan made a fire so warm and bright
and locked the doors behind
Not a soul could see our light
for we'd a dust sheet for a blind.

Then Kate started off to play
such tunes so gay and sweet
that ere a moment passed away
we all were on our feet
and there we danced about the hall
with swiftly flying feet
Kate and Flo and Nan and all

not one could keep her seat
and when of dancing we had enough
we thought it would be fine
to have a game of Blind Man's Buff
to pass away the time.

So from our chairs we all did rise
for Kate's scarf Teenie ran
and bound it round and round the eyes
of good old jolly Nan.
And oh! how quickly she did run,
nor did she stop at all
till she had caught us one by one
and we were like to fall
And when we all had got our chance
For it didn't take too long
we were too tired for a dance
so called out for a song.

'Twas Kate we asked to give the first
She jumped up with a will
and sang tho' she was like to burst
The "Rustic Bridge by the Mill".
Then when we all in merry glee
had sung our songs so bright
we called out for a up of tea
I think 'twas only right.

But ere the night came to an end
we'd something to do yet
for we had a good old stalwart friend
whom we must not forget
And as this was his wedding day
We thought it very right
we should remember Big MacRae
as this was "his first night".
We drank his health in blood red wine
as good as any whisky
and though it tasted very fine
it didn't leave us frisky.

The last part of our happy night
turned out to be a wedding,
tho' some may think it wasn't right
we hadn't got the bedding
But then you see 'twas of no use
for the couple was Flo and Nan
And if dear friends you'll me excuse
the bedding needs a man
As bridesmaid, Teenie looked quite sweet

Kate stood on Nan's right side
As Minister, Katie played her part
I, father to the Bride.

Seeing this night was Christmas Eve,
the clock struck half past one,
before we felt inclined to leave
so much we enjoyed the fun -
then three loud cheers with all our might
For good old Jolly Nan
who gave us such a splendid night
Unknown to every one.

Tho' future years then may us sever
how far apart we cannot tell
that very happy night will ever
fondly in my memory dwell.

For distance may divide
But friendship will abide.

Surgeon Captain Ewen Murchison who was a young pupil of the new Arnisdale teacher in 1917 and is now resident in Gibraltar commented as follows when he read the poem recently.

"The poem from my much loved and respected erstwhile teacher is exceptionally good and epitomises the spirit of those days and its contrasts with the modern age with its dependence on TV and canned music".

In addition to the poetess, who was later to become Mrs 'Roddy Mor', the other 'characters' who made this great 'hen party' were Nan, who was the Caretaker at Arnisdale Lodge (and a sister of Jimmy MacDonald from Corran and an aunt of the late Jimmy MacMorran, Glenelg), Flo was Roddy Mor's sister and later became Mrs Jeck MacKenzie, Lochcarron, Katie Foster came from Corran as did Teenie MacAskill who later became Mrs Norman MacKenzie. The Kate referred to in the poem may have been a sister of John MacGillivray or Kate 'Hearadh', a native of Harris who worked at the farm.

In the Second War, Arnisdale and Loch Hourn had ten of its young people - both male and female in the forces, serving the needs of their country both at home and in foreign fields.

The older folks at home also had to play their part because they were living in a restricted area. The Naval Base at Kyle of Lochalsh and the naval fuel stores at Ardentoul were obvious targets for enemy activity. So the Arnisdale Home Guard was formed under the command of Roddy Mor while Willie MacKenzie and Daniel MacDonald had special reconnaissance responsibilities in their daily seagoing activities.

Like everywhere else, all the inhabitants were issued with Identity Cards which had to be produced on demand. In addition the Arnisdale fishermen had to be issued with a 'Permit to Fish' by the Admiralty which prescribed allowable fishing activities. For example, Donald Sheorais Campbell's fishing vessel 'Roe' (Port Letters and Number BRD 281) was licensed for coastal fishing in 'Sleat Sound and Loch Hourn (during daylight only)'.

Naval ships patrolled the area regularly and often berthed in the bay at Camusban for a few days. The sailors and the local Arnisdale folk soon got to know each other. One such naval ship that many remember was HMS Foss. A ceilidh dance was organised to welcome the sailors and two of the local bards composed poems which they duly recited at the ceilidh.

The composition of Andrew Thomson, head gardener at the lodge, went as follows:

**The HMS Foss Dance**

>The Navy came to Arnisdale
>A dance the reason why
>For Red Cross and for charity
>To swell the funds they'd try
>A likely lot of lively lads
>From North, South, East and West
>To entertain the local folks
>They did their very best.
>
>There were twa fine loons frae Aberdeen
>Clydeside was there of course
>From Hebrides and even Wales
>And English Jacks in force
>E'en Harry Lauder paid a call
>Charlie his name all right
>He looked a bonnie Highland lad
>Although his knees were white!
>
>They sang and danced the whole night through
>As merry as could be
>Perhaps the memory they'll recall
>When they are far at sea
>The best luck to the sailor lads
>When they go we'll feel their loss
>Best thanks from all at Arnisdale
>To the boys of H.M.S. "Foss".         (Andrew Thomson)

John MacGillivray dedicated his poem to 'The Crew of HMS Foss'. These are the lines penned and recited by John:

**Dedicated to the Crew of H.M.S. Foss**

>**T**hey are the boys who never say die
>**H**appy where ever they be
>**E**ast or West wherever they roam
>**C**omrades merry and free
>**R**oaming over the stormy waves
>**E**ager to meet the hun
>**W**atchmen of our native shore
>**O**ur shield till the battle is won
>**F**earless, undaunted in storm or calm

> They never complain of their lot
> Heaven to them a night spent
> Enjoying a waltz or a fox trot
> Fortune us favoured when we did them meet
> Ours when they go, is the loss
> So now I will end my simple effusion
> Saying - Good Luck to the crew of the Foss
> (John MacGillivray)

Not to be outdone, the crew of the Foss replied with the following poem 'Dedicated to the folk of Arnisdale':

**Arnisdale**
> Alone thou shall stand, deep impressed in my mind
> Reflecting with splendour your motives so kind
> Niched snug in the bosom of lovely Loch Hourn
> Inspired by your homeliness, friendship is born
> Spirit of Gaeldom breathes sweet from your shore
> Delightful to Scotsmen the whole world o'er
> Ah!  give me a lilt in the tongue of the Gael
> Let me mix with the hill-folks, with hearts ever hale
> Expressed in this hamlet of sweet Arnisdale.

Obviously the Arnisdale folk brightened things up for the sailors during the wartime strains while the sailors in turn reciprocated in style.

The Arnisdale community spirit was even greater in wartime than usual and every effort was made to keep morale high.   This spirit is portrayed in Andrew Thomson's account in verse of the Hogmanay Dance of 1941.

**The Arnisdale Hogmanay Dance 1941-42**

> At Arnisdale on Hogmanay
> A dance we thought we'd hae
> Wi song and dance to pass the night
> It was the proper way.
>
> From near and far the dancers came
> To join us in our fun
> They fairly did enjoy themselves
> Before the night was done.
>
> From Kinlochourn and from Glenelg
> From Sandaig and Glenmore
> Some even thought it worth their while
> To come from Aviemore.
>
> We'd some grand songs to help along
> With no time to be dull
> To have a song was understood

If e'er there was a lull.

The old time dance is fav'rite here
Though new are not debarred
We'd try the latest, never fear!
And wouldn't find it hard.

To the accordion and fiddles' lilt
We'd pipers there galore
As every dance came to an end
The cry was aye for more.

The lads and lassies did their bit,
To make it fairly go
They never got much chance to sit
Indeed 'twas really so.

The night wore on, we all were blythe
A knock came to the door
Old Father Time complete wi' scythe
Came tottering up the floor.

Then twelve was struck, his task complete
"Farewell Old Forty One!"
A sprightly Miss came tripping in
Twas Forty Two begun.

On with the dance a great big V
To cheer us on our way
"A Guid New Year to one and a!"
That's what we all did say.

We kept it up to break o' day
Now good times have to end.
Sure everyone was loathe to leave
But home we'll have to wend.

Then "Auld Lang Syne" to finish up
We'll meet some other night
To end it all with that grand tune
You'll all agree was right.
(Andrew Thompson)

As the Arnisdale servicemen and women returned home on leave they always received a great welcome and very special 'Welcome Homes' were arranged for each one of them when the dreadful war ended. There was great relief, thankfulness and joy as each returned home. VE Day was celebrated at a gathering of all able bodied men, women and children at a bonfire at the Crudh Ard. The crowd assembled at the farm steading and were led to the Crudh Ard by Donald MacLaren and Roddy Mor playing stirring tunes on the pipes.

## The Welcome Home ceilidh dances

Those returning ex-servicemen and women who were welcomed home to Arnisdale were Angus Stewart, Iain and Chrissie MacCuaig, Morag, Jessie and Mary Macdonald, Jimmy Campbell (all from Arnisdale), Roddy MacRae from Kinlochourn and two of the Glenelg boys who had close associations with Arnisdale - Kenny MacRae and Roddy MacPherson. Roddy from Kinlochourn, along with Kenny and Roddy from Glenelg, had been 'regulars' at the Arnisdale ceilidh-dances before the war. In those days when transportation was difficult, all possible means including the 'Shank's Pony' was deployed to get themselves to the great Arnisdale dances.

Roddy MacPherson, of course, had spent many nights in Arnisdale as a young boy with his old friend Donald Sheorais (Campbell) as he made his way between his home in Glenelg and his relatives up Loch Hourn - the MacMillans at Runival and the MacRaes at Kinlochourn. He had also worked after leaving school with the Arnisdale folk in the Mialairidh Forest.

Roddy was in the 4th Battalion Seaforth Highlanders from the outbreak of hostilities and he was captured at Abbeville, near Dunkirk on 4 June 1940, as Allied troops were being evacuated. The assignment given to his battalion was to try to stop the Germans advance so as to achieve a more successful evacuation from Dunkirk. During a fixed bayonet charge up an occupied knoll with a view to gaining a stronger position, they suffered heavy casualties. The bren-gunner was hit and Roddy took over the bren-gun from his fallen mate. But they realised that they had gone in too far when they were surrounded by enemy tanks and the 12 surviving Seaforths were captured. As well as Roddy, the twelve included Duncan MacRae from Drumbuie near Kyle. They were marched towards Germany through France and Holland, they spent 4 nights on a barge going up the Rhine during which they received neither food nor water. On reaching their first Prisoner of War Camp in Germany they were interrogated. They entered a room one by one and immediately on entry a German Officer addressed them 'Cia mar tha thu?, to which the instinctive unthinking response of the Gaelic speakers was 'Glé mhath'. This was the German's technique of detecting and isolating the Gaelic speakers after 3 Ballachulish Gaelic speaking boys in the Argyll and Sutherland Highlanders (Ginger Wilson, Willie Kemp and Alistair MacDonald) had escaped from their POW camp and through enemy held territory by never speaking in English but always in the Gaelic, causing much confusion to enemy interrogators as to their origin. (Ginger, Willie and Alistair had been in the same regiment as Mabel Fletcher's late husband, Peter Campbell). After the initial interrogation had been completed in the case of Roddy and his mates, the 24 Gaelic speakers were confined in a small room for further questioning. Roddy and his mates were captured on 4 June 1940 but his folk in Glenelg, Arnisdale and Loch Hourn were not aware that he was alive and in a POW camp until the following October. However, Donald Chisholm, then Postmaster at Glenelg and a great friend of Roddy's, in a fine act of faith and hope, penned a very simple brief letter to his young friend on 13 July 1940. The letter and the envelope in which it was sent are reproduced later. The POW number of Roddy and his Camp number were left blank for they were unknown to Donald who did not even know if Roddy was still alive - although Donald's hopes were high. It was, of course, the first letter received by Roddy after his capture. One can imagine just how lifted Roddy was in his spirits when he received and read Donald's letter. It is little wonder that Roddy has preserved it with tender loving care through the 60 intervening years. Roddy believes that the letter (without a POW or Camp number) came to him by wonderful coincidences. Roddy's Seaforth Number was 2823377; by pure chance, the POW number he was allocated was 377 and even the number of the German Officer who censored (Geprutt) and stamped Donald's letter with the Stalag IX C Official Stamp was 37. There is little wonder that Roddy still has a special affinity for the figures 3 and 7.

Roddy's first POW Camp was at Ruddelstat and he and his mates were transferred from camp to camp thereafter according to where they were assigned to work. The first work was in a sand quarry (probably for the production of fine glass) and later they worked in a salt mine. The salt mine was christened 'Salt Lake City' by Roddy and his mates. Roddy recalls that there were older Nazi German workers in the mines and also communists, the latter being despised by the Nazis. One old communist worker had a greater affinity with the Scottish boys than he had with his Nazi German colleagues. The old fellow would light a cigarette and then lay it on the dyke for Roddy to pick up and have a smoke. Roddy, who did not smoke, would have a little puff to please his old German friend, then nip the fag out and keep it for one of his own POW smoking buddies. The likes of the late Duncan MacRae from Drumbuie, near Kyle of Lochalsh, used to think that Christmas had come when Roddy would hand him the cigarette which he had saved for him. The consecutive days of total starvation after capture and their POW Camp diet of bread and lard almost certainly induced the severe duodenal ulcer and serious internal bleeding from which Roddy suffered during these months and years. His pale, emaciated appearance must have made him a very sorry sight.

However, despite their problems, Roddy and his mates were good at keeping up eachother's morale by diversions such as games of football in their spare time. There were quite a few shinty boys in the group and they started making camans using tree branches which were lying around. Soon, therefore, playing their shinty on foreign fields became a pleasant pastime.

But Roddy's internal bleeding from his ulcer was taking a heavy toll and eventually he became so ill that he was hospitalised and he did not eat for three months. He was receiving tiny doses of liquid containing milk at frequent intervals. The decision was taken to repatriate him in 1944 when it was considered that he was dying. After reaching British shores, Roddy was hospitalised for a considerable time and recovered very gradually through excellent nursing and his own willpower. That same willpower and lust for life are still there in his octogenarian years - everybody who knows him will tell you that it is a job to keep him quiet and impossible to keep him down!

When eventually it was time for Roddy to make his way home to Glenelg, he was accompanied on the train to Inverness by many of his fellow POWs.
When they came off the train at Inverness one can just imagine their feelings. Before getting their connections to their own precious homes, they had time to look around their old haunts in their Highland Capital. They made their way to Eastgate and in a sheltered doorway they came across an old fellow playing the accordion with his bonnet placed in front of him hoping to get some pennies from the passers-by. They commandeered the old fellow and he was thrilled to oblige. They asked him to play for an Eightsome Reel and he played probably as well as he ever played before as the bold lads in uniform danced their reel in the middle of Eastgate - stopping all the traffic in the process. Nobody cared because the reel and its sheer enjoyment by the participants, the old fellow on the box and all the spectators, was everybody's priority for these precious minutes.

Roddy's first 'Welcome Home' was in Glenelg. The local GP, Dr Devon, volunteered to arrange to have the cake made. She heard that a young lady from Lochcarron, Mimmie Beaton, who was an excellent cook and baker was visiting her sister, Mrs Lolla Garde (wife of Calum Garde who operated the Glenelg-Kyle mailboat service) in the village. Dr Devon asked Mimmie to bake the cake. Mimmie duly obliged and produced one of her 'Specials' for the occasion. Later Mimmie was to become Roddy's wife and, at the time of writing these lines, they are still with us - a very special couple.

The Welcome Home ceilidh dance in Glenelg and all that went with it were very special. Soon afterwards, the Arnisdale 'Welcome' was organised. Roddy remembers that singers at the ceilidh included his cousin Fachie MacRae from Kinlochourn, Roddy Mor from the farm and his wife Lizzie (Bean Roddy), Mary MacIntyre and Ina Stewart. The musicians at the dance included Peter and Donald Fletcher, the MacLaren family (Jessie, Donald, Effie and Betty) and his great mates from

Kinlochourn and Glen Quoich, Peter MacRae and Do MacKillop. After a splendid night which lasted until after the dawn broke, there was no better way to keep the ceilidh going than to set off up Loch Hourn in the boat for Runival, Kinlochourn and Glen Quoich with Peter, Do and Fachie. There is no doubt that there were many more welcomes up the loch from the folk who could not get to the dance and were so relieved to see their young fellow back on home soil.

The other Glenelg youngster who received a great welcome home in both Glenelg and Arnisdale were Kenny MacRae (Kenny 'Wilson'). Kenny was also a Seaforth Highlander and was captured along with the rest of the 51st Highland Division at St Valery in 1940. Kenny was a POW for the remaining five years of the war. Along with his fellow Seaforths he spent the main part of this time in occupied Poland. At first they worked in a factory and their food ration was very meagre. Kenny's widow Betty (nee MacAskill), now resident and still crofting in Corran, remembers Kenny commenting to her that they were all 'as thin as skeletons'. When the boys got the chance, one or two of them would nip out to the adjacent Polish fields and pinch some potatoes which they would smuggle in and bake in the factory ovens and have a special feast.

Later the Seaforth POWs were sent under armed guard to work on farms in Germany in the planting, weeding and harvesting of the crops. Their pale, emaciated appearance must have made Kenny and his mates a very sorry sight. While war is associated with so much senselessness, cruelty and injustice, compassion can also be found in abundance. As Kenny worked with his mates in the German fields at their planting and weeding, they were accompanied by German women. Often when Kenny, at the end of the working day, picked up his jacket which he had left at the end of the field, he would find a raw egg in a pocket. The donor could not provide openly such excellent food to a young man who was obviously suffering from serious malnutrition but 'she' or 'they' found a way of helping a young fellow human to survive. They had their own youngsters fighting and in danger in some foreign field and they knew that this pale, emaciated young man also had loving relatives and friends back home.

After the traumas and hardships of these six years, Kenny eventually got back to the people and places that were nearest and dearest to his heart - and to the official 'Welcome Home' at the special occasions organised by the Glenelg and Arnisdale folk.

Kenny gradually recovered and it was not long before he was gracing the local football and shinty fields again - he was a fine exponent of the arts, crafts and skills of each of these games. He married Betty, they raised their family at their homes in Eilanreach, and later Upper Sandaig, and they began to work their croft in Arnisdale. Kenny died suddenly in his early 70s. He was engaged at the time in one of his favourite ploys - fishing in perfect peace on the Eilanreach River.

The great feelings of relief and joy at the Arnisdale 'Welcome Homes' for the returning ex-servicemen and women are still very clear in the memories of the folk who experienced these uplifting occasions of thanksgiving and gladness.

Some of the Arnisdale and Loch Hourn young folk who served in World War 2.

**Top** (L to R.) Angus Stewart, Peter Fletcher and Farquhar Fletcher.
**Row 2** (L to R.) Chrissie MacCuaig, Morag MacDonald and Jimmy Campbell
**Row 3** Left – Jessie and Mary MacDonald (seated) with sisters Rena and Johan.
   Right – Roddy MacRae (far right) with L to R. Peter and Ewen MacRae, Katie Murchison, the Arnisdale Missionary, and Peggy MacRae.

**Row 4** Left – Iain MacCuaig with his wife Lexy (nee Campbell)
   Right – Kenny MacRae (right) and brother Finlay. Finlay was wounded at St Valery in 1940, evacuated and hospitalised in England. Finlay, on recovery, rejoined the war and made the supreme sacrifice at El Alamein in the Desert Campaign.

154

**Top Left**.  Roddy MacPherson with fellow prisoners of war in Germany.  Roddy is fifth from left in the back row.  **Right**.  Another group of POWs with Roddy 'standing tall' in the back row to the right.

**Row 2 Left.**  Roddy (seated centre) with four of his mates in the Prison Camp.  **Right.**  Roddy's Third Class 'Free Leave Travel' home to Kyle and Glenelg dated 19 September 1944 on his repatriation.

**Row 3**  A larger group of POWs with the emaciated and seriously ill Roddy in the middle of Row 3 from the rear being propped up by two of his mates.

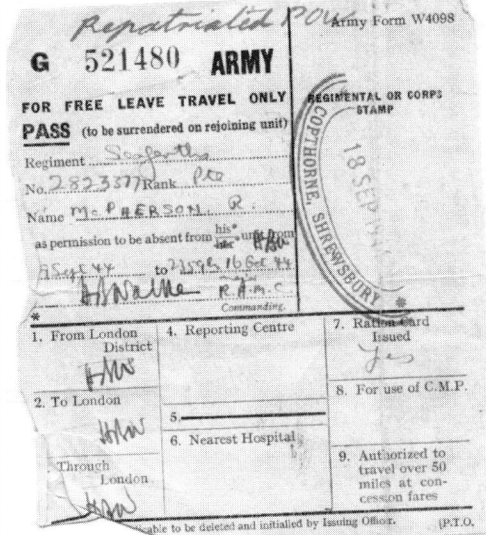

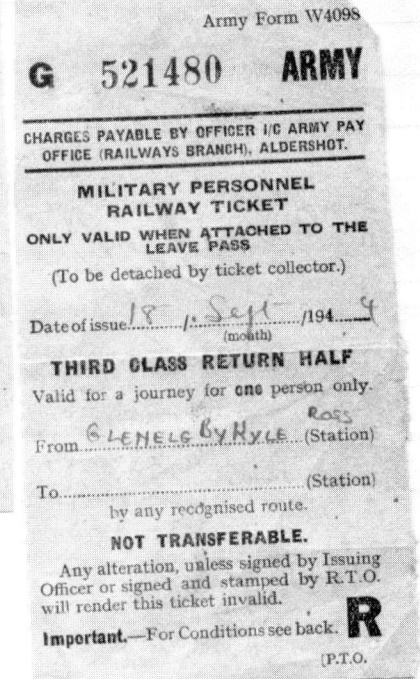

155

**Top Left**.  A group of ex POWs from the same Prison Camp. L. to R. Iain MacKinnon, Skye, Duncan MacRae from Drumbuie near Kyle, Roddy and Willie Watson from Falkirk who later became a gamekeeper on the Kinloch Hourn Estate.  **Right**.  When the homecoming POWs reached Inverness, they made their way to Eastgate, 'commandeered' an old fellow (who had been playing his accordion to make a few pennies for himself) to play an Eightsome Reel.  The joyful lads danced an Eightsome in the middle of Eastgate, stopping all the traffic.  (Drawing by Blair Anderson).

**Middle Left**.  Roddy's wife Mimmie.   It was Mimmie who, before their marriage, baked his 'Welcome Home' cake.  **Centre.**   In the Prison Camp the lads were excellent at keeping up each other's morale.  When they got the chance of diversions they played football and shinty, making their own camans from branches lying around.  Gregor MacBain (from Kincraig) and Roddy reminisce about their days on the POW Camp and about making their camans at a get-together in 1992.  **Right**.  Donald Chisholm, Postmaster in Glenelg, and a great friend of Roddy's who wrote Roddy (when he was reported missing in 1940) a fine letter of faith and hope which Roddy still has in his possession.

**Bottom Left**.   Kenny MacRae (fourth from left in back row) in a post war Glenelg Football team.   Kenny was captured at St Valery and spent the rest of the war in a Prison Camp – mainly in occupied Poland.   Other team members are Back Row (L to R.) Charlie Cochrane, Neilly Gordon, John Don MacKenzie, Kenny MacRae, Murdo ??? (shepherd at Ardentoul), Ala MacRae.   Front (L to R.) Willie Gordon, Y MacLeod, Calum Garde, Davie Miles, Jocky O'Kane.  **Centre.**  Kenny MacRae in later years with his wife Betty (nee MacAskill) and grandson, Douglas.     **Right**.   Johnny MacGillivray (right) with John MacCuaig and Maggie MacTavish.   Johnny, who doubled up as local roadman and running his shop in Camusban, was  one of the Arnisdale 'bards' who composed and recited poems at the Arnisdale Ceilidh Dances.  One such poem was dedicated to the crew of HMS Foss, a Naval Patrol ship which spent a few days in Arnisdale Bay during the war.   Johnny had served in the Armed Forces during World War 1 and was one of Arnisdale's 'Land Leaguers' at the end of the war.

The letter of faith and hope from Donald Chisholm, Postmaster in Glenelg, written on 12 July 1940 to his young friend, Roddy MacPherson. Roddy had been captured at Abbeville, near Dunkirk on 4 June 1940. He was reported missing and his family in Glenelg were not aware that Roddy was in a POW Camp until October, over four months after his capture. The envelope is reproduced below with blanks opposite the POW Camp number and POW number. The POW number turned out to be 377 - the last 3 numbers in Roddy's Seaforth number. Roddy is sure that this coincidence was responsible for the safe delivery of a treasured letter.

**Top Left**.  Andrew Thomson, the Arnisdale Lodge Gardener, and Mrs Thomson.  Andrew was another of the local 'bards' who composed poems for recitation and entertainment at the wartime Arnisdale ceilidh dances.  **Centre**.  Peter MacRae and Do MacKillop of Kinloch Hourn, two of the regular music makers with bagpipes and fiddle at Arnisdale ceilidh dances.  With them is Mrs Urquhart who was the Housekeeper at Kinloch Hourn Lodge for over fifty years.  **Right**.  Donald Sheorais Campbell (seated) with his nephew George MacDougall and his wartime 'Permit to Fish' which was issued by the Admiralty.

**Middle Right**.  On VE Day in 1945, all able bodied men, women and children in Arnisdale assembled at the farm steading and with Donald MacLaren and Roddy Mor leading the party, playing stirring tunes on their pipes, all marched and danced along the Corran road to the Crudh Ard where the bonfire was lit and the celebrations greatly
enjoyed by all.   In the picture, the Crudh Ard is the promontary to the right of the Corran road.

**Bottom**  Mabel Fletcher's 'Identity Card' during wartime.  All such Identity Cards had to be produced on demand.

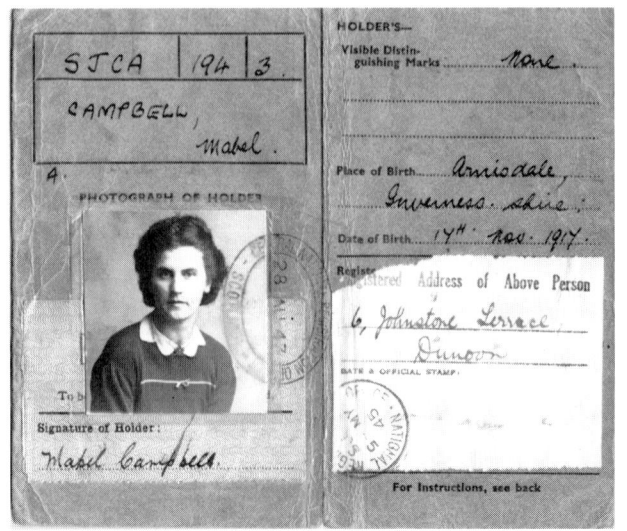

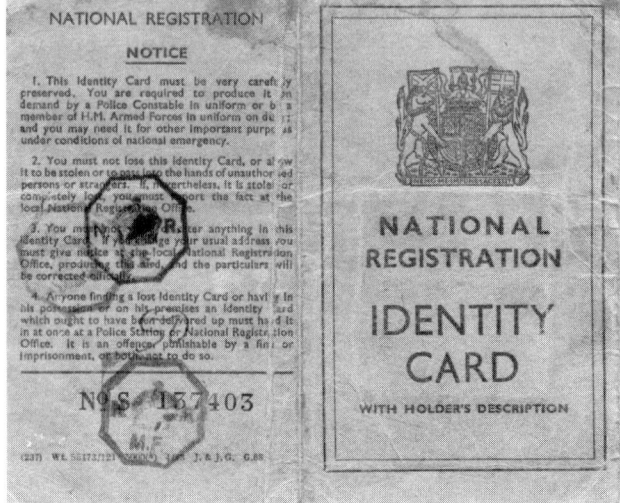

# Chapter 12

**Some recollections and experiences of visitors to Arnisdale over the years.**

**Memories of a beloved place (Lally English).** To this day, nearly sixty years after the first holiday in Arnisdale which I remember, I still have the same feeling of excited anticipation while waiting to top the rise and see Arnisdale from the peak of the brae. I had been taken to visit Aunt Lizzie and Uncle Roddy several times as a very young child, by my mother, father and other relatives but my memory of these early visits is very hazy.

Then when I was eight years old I went with Aunt Chrissie (sister of Aunt Lizzie) for a whole two weeks. Now, in memory, the car in which I am travelling comes to the bottom of the Càrr Ruadh brae, along past Rarsaidh to the sharp turn between the two sentinel Scots Pine, past the Balla Mòr, up the incline with rocks on either side and - at the top - there is Arnisdale spread before me.

Corran just visible to the right; Glenfield gables glimpsed through the conifer windbreak. The farm waiting to welcome me, local boats anchored in the bay and some pulled up on to the shore above the high tide mark. As we go down the brae - there is the Lodge with the conifer plantation on the right. MacDonald's shed, - for me it will always bear that name - because each time I passed, that dear man with the twinkling eyes shouted a teasing greeting.

The Nurse's Cottage and over the burn the school, where I had so many happy times with Maggie Lea, Rena MacDonald and Ann MacLean (nee MacRae); then the churchyard and the Free Church. Past the Mission House where Maggie and her mother Jessie lived on moving from Lea. Of Maggie's wedding to John Angus MacDonald in the Free Church and reception in the school I have the happiest memory. In more recent years, Rick and Hillary Rohde with their two children lived in Lea. They made so many friends in the area, all of whom shared their heartbreak when their son Leif was so suddenly taken from them following a car accident.

Then the Sinclairs' house beside the road where John and Mrs Sinclair and their son Iain lived. There is Angus David (Aonghas Dhaidh) sitting by John MacGillivray's shop. Nora MacDonald's house and when first I used to visit, her mother and aunt lived with her. To Mary Ann MacCuaig's where I spent so many happy evenings ceilidhing - were we really **always** laughing - the crowd of us there? Next door was Jessie "Rarsaidh", I always wondered how on earth they climbed the steep ladder-like stairs opposite the front door to the 'attic' room above. Then comes Sweyn MacIntosh's and Kelly's and the MacLeans - and each time I see a garden filled with dahlias I think of theirs. To the Fletchers, I knew them all and always thought of them as kind of cousins, since they are Uncle Roddy's nieces and nephews. Across the burn to Ludovic's and John MacGillivray, his mother and "Gingie". Mary MacIntyre's is next, Mary with her kindly smile and always a warm enquiry about my folks at home. Dear Annie and wee Morag - as she was then. On to Duncan MacTavish who always seemed so contented. Then to Angan MacTavish , Bean Angan and Charlie.

Peggy Ann and Mary - even now I can get that wonderful aroma as I opened the Post Office and shop door. It was a mixture of bread, cheese, cakes, biscuits, sweets, soap, paraffin, paper, ink - one would have to experience it to understand. Eyes twinkling, Peggy Ann would first ask how I was, then add "and how is Uncle Roddy?" because, jocularly as ever, she said he was her boyfriend. Mary her sister, would then come through to greet me in the same lovely soft Arnisdale accent. On that visit in 1938 when we arrived at the Farm - Uncle Roddy and Aunt Lizzie having met us at Cluanie Inn - Mary and Rena MacDonald were waiting with a welcome, and a lovely meal. It was my first meeting with Rena to start a friendship which lasted for almost sixty years. Rena was a friend in the truest sense of that word. Rena was a vital part of the very soul of the Arnisdale community and all felt a great sense of personal loss with her death in 1995. I also had a warm friendship with Rena's dear parents and sisters. How often I have wished my visitors who stay overnight "Good Sleep", as Mrs MacDonald did to me.

To arrive at Estate Cottage in Corran where the MacDonalds lived, I passed the kindly MacAskills, Alan and Maggie. Over the bridge I remember Angus and Ivy Campbell and Mary Ann who had as many cats as I now have. Granny MacKenzie's house up on the left and next Chrissie and Jimmy Campbell and then the MacKenzies (Willie the Post), Sandy MacAskill, the MacCuaigs where Chrissie (now Morrison) lives still. Past the Murchisons' house to Katie Foster's and the Stewarts - Angus, Ina and Sheena. I can still hear Ina's beautiful voice as she sang "Castles in the Air", with "Two eyes of Blue" for an encore at ceilidhs.

Visits to Glenfield with Aunt Lizzie to the MacLarens, these talented musical folk, Betty, Fay, and their parents. How I loved to watch and listen to Betty play that organ - she would belt out "Leaving Glenurquhart" especially for me.

So often when I hear the song of a blackbird or thrush I think of Mrs Thomson at the Lodge. Her dear husband was gardener and they were also caretakers. I loved to go there and, on summer evenings, we would walk in the garden listening to the birdsong. Mrs Thomson recognised the song of each bird which I thought was very clever, as I could not do so then.

Now back to the Farm and so many memories of that very dear place. The day the pig got out of its sty and we all tried to get it back. Jimmy Kennedy, who helped on the Farm, fell full length in the wet "dung" of the Square running so fast. The noise of barrows and hand carts trundling past the house when MacLennan's boat was spotted at the point on Tuesdays with the weekly Arnisdale supplies from Mallaig. The first time I tried my hand at milking, I loved it and the warm moist smell of the byre.

Getting a "lift" home on Dick's (the Highland Garron) back after a day at the hay. Going to the Crudh Ard for bunches of honeysuckle - and it is still there.

Picnics up the Glen on the day of the Scottish Six Day Motor Cycle Trials, the bikes making their way down the Arnisdale Glen from Kinlochourn and beyond. And lastly, but not least, the welcome and fun during holidays at the farm from Aunt Lizzie and Uncle Roddy, who made these memories possible.

**Some memories of Isabella Mackay (nee Macpherson, Riverfoot, Glenelg).** When I was twelve years old I paid my first visit to Arnisdale. Mr & Mrs MacLaren, Glenfield were friends of my mother and father and their two daughters, Effie and Betty, were ages with myself. At that time in the 1920s we all competed at the Kyle Mod where our friendship began. To get to Arnisdale at that time, the mode of transport was by Johnny Sinclair's Horse and Trap. Johnny collected the mail for Arnisdale at Glenelg which came via the mail boat from Kyle. I duly joined Johnny and his trap at the pier in Quarry, Glenelg. He had one other passenger that day - Mary Ann MacCuaig who was going home to Arnisdale. To make it easier for the horse climbing the steep braes, Mary Ann (who was in her twenties at the time) was made to walk up the braes, whereas I was allowed to remain on the trap! Mary Ann was certainly not offended - but highly amused by this treatment from Johnny. She was a lovely lady. Our only coverings were travelling rugs and a large waterproof sheet to protect us from the rain. To me, this was a great adventure and there was such a nice welcome when I reached journey's end. I am now 82 years of age and can recall it all still with the feelings of a child's excitement and pleasure.

**Recollections of Christina MacKenzie (nee MacLaren).** I came to start work in Arnisdale on Saturday, the second of February 1957. I had visited Arnisdale earlier as a child to holiday with the MacLaren family at Glenfield as Donald MacLaren, the head gamekeeper/ghillie/shepherd working for the estate, was my uncle. On the day I arrived in Arnisdale in 1957, the west coast had been struck by a ferocious storm the previous day and when I arrived by hired car from Kyle in the evening, seaweed and various flotsam was strewn all along the road in Arnisdale. Seaweed, driftwood and stones also littered the pathway up to the Schoolhouse. I had come to Arnisdale as the new teacher. The school was reopening after being closed for about a year. The teacher before me was Mrs Effie MacInnes, sister of Lexie Campbell who had been teacher before Mrs MacInnes. Lexie had married Iain MacCuaig from Corran and they had moved to the Lothians where Lexie got another teaching appointment. There were only two pupils in the school when I came - Fraser MacRobbie (9) whose father was the Farm Manager, and Joseph Saflain (5) (Polish parents), whose father was gardener at the Lodge. However, there were five other children who were under school age so there were prospects for an expansion in the school roll.

The following is a list of the homes occupied in Arnisdale at that time. I will start at west end of the Camusban village and list the homes in order as we move through Camusban to the lodge, then the farm and Glenfield and from there to Corran.

Camusban
Peggy Ann and Mary MacLean, two elderly sisters. Peggy Ann was Postmistress.
Angus and Maggie MacTavish.
Duncan MacTavish.
Willie Stoddart (retired stalker from Barrisdale) and his daughter Gwennie.
Mary and Annie MacIntyre (sisters).
Ludovic Fraser and his wife.
Kenny, Donald and Roddie Fletcher (brothers).
Archie and Johan MacLean (brother and sister).
Donald and Liza MacKenzie.
Jessie (Rarsaidh) MacIntosh.
Mary Ann MacCuaig.
Nora MacDonald (Nora was away at work for most of the year).
George MacDougall (George's wife Chrissie had died just before I arrived in Arnisdale). Angus MacIntosh (who died soon after I came).
John and Annie Sinclair.
A missionary who stayed in the Mission House only at weekends. I think he was Neil Cameron.
Two Miss Thompsons (sisters), one being the District Nurse.
The Saflain family (father, mother and two small boys).
Harry and Ginny Kitson (in the Lodge).
Bob and Cathie MacRobbie, son Fraser (daughter Mary, who was older, came home only on school holidays) at the Farm.
Hughie and Rita MacLean (and four small children) at Glenfield.

Corran
Alan, Lachie and Maggie MacAskill (brothers and sister).
Mr & Mrs Daniel MacDonald and daughter Rena.
Mrs MacKenzie and sons Willie and Iain.
Chrissie Campbell.
Sandy MacAskill.
Mrs MacCuaig, daughter Chrissie and son-in-law Jacky Morrison.
Angus and Ina Stewart, daughter Sheena and Ina's aunt, Miss MacLean.

Thus, there were 26 residents in Camusban, 6 at the Lodge, 10 at the farm and Glenfield and 18 in Corran. This made a total Arnisdale population at the time of 60.

Later, as many previous Arnisdale teachers had done, I married a local man - Willie MacKenzie, or 'Willie the Post'. I was to be the last teacher in Arnisdale - in the twentieth century at least, the school being closed in 1959. So that when our own five children reached school age, all of them - Billy, Roderick, Alan, David and Shona - travelled daily to Glenelg School for their primary education and went to Plockton for their secondary education. At Plockton they boarded during the week, returning home to Arnisdale for the weekends and holidays.

Two of our children - Billy and David - have made their homes in Arnisdale. When I do a 'census' on the resident Arnisdale population now, the total is just 32 - considerably fewer than the 60 residents when I first came to teach in Arnisdale just over 40 years ago now. The present population includes only three children, all under school age at the time of writing.

Thus, Arnisdale has been in decline over the period of my residence here. The number of residents have declined, it has an ageing population, the school has been converted into a private house and the only public place left for the Arnisdale community is the Free Church.

Despite the current situation being a somewhat sombre one, Arnisdale has much to offer in many ways, so perhaps the new Millennium will see a revival of activity and of the community.

**Memories of Arnisdale and Thoughts for its Future**
**by Frances Kennedy**

I remember Arnisdale between 1932 and 1939. Being hardly three years old when I arrived, it seems as if I had been born there. After a lifetime of faraway places, it's wonderful to be reconnected to the village where I went to school, and with the playmates and schoolmates of those days. Not less so, is the sense of exhilaration I feel at its constant though ever changing beauty – magnificence even, when one thinks of Beinn Sgriol – in sun, mist, and rain.

When I came back in 1990 after 50 years, Arnisdale hadn't changed, and even the stones in the walls were familiar. However, there was a difference in the contours of the shore, and in the spread of the mill burn over it. And the dam away up the school burn on the Church Beinn had filled with debris from the mountain.

Memories of my childhood there are still clear. The impressions of nature can never be forgotten, for they imprinted in me then a fascination with Earth's landscapes, and respect for its laws, which are over and above the laws of man. Patterns of frost on the windowpane and on the morning grass; thin crystal plates of patterned ice over the burn, which tinkled on the dry stones below, when you broke them; the scent of spring hyacinths, and primroses by the burn; the silvery underside of sycamore leaves held under the water; bracken in autumn. These lovely images filled the mind.

There were always musical sounds of water – from the culvert, from the waterfall and from the sea. One night, there was a fearful storm which washed away the road in three places, and cast the Noressian from her moorings up onto the shore. I lay awake in the dark, ears tingling with the sound of the raging gale.

One winter, when there was a sizeable snowfall, my father made a sledge. Up the brae behind the schoolhouse went Dad, my brother Callum and I. What wild excitement it was, to come tobogganing downhill with such hitherto unimaginable speed!

The people of Arnisdale were gentle, kind and soft-spoken. On passing by, you were likely to be called in to someone's house and given a fresh scone, an oatcake or even an egg. Children going to Peggy Ann's shop usually received a black-striped ball to suck, out of a tall glass jar. There was kindness everywhere.

However, the village dogs were a different matter. Occasionally I had to go to the shop for Dad's cigarettes (with cigarette-cards). I would feel quite nervous about the big black 'towlers' as they were called. From time to time they would get into an appalling dogfight – a great snapping and snarling, rolling black heap of six or seven dogs, with agonized yelping now and then as some sensitive part got punctured by sharp teeth.

Personalities remembered were Sweyn, Lexie, Ludovic, Maryann; Johan MacLean with the happy smile and dark braids coiled over her ears; Mrs McTavish with her cheery face and colourful garden full of dahlias, fuchsia, marigolds and forget-me-nots; Angan with the limp; the Fletchers, Nurse Morrison, Lizzie MacLeod in the dairy and the farmhouse kitchen. In Corran: the Murchisons, Angus Stewart with the little fawn he rescued one spring; Kitty Foster, and an old lady in the house of the eventual Post Office; Granny MacKenzie, hirpling along with her rheumatism; MacLaren the gamekeeper over at Glenfield, in his kilt; the MacDonalds and dear, warm-hearted Rena, with her sense of humour, who told me about the MacAskills, where Betty MacRae now lives. They liked to be tidy and well-dressed, and kept their barn and outhouses very neat. "Even the manure-heap was tidy", said Rena. "It looked like a big ginger-cake. And when the snow fell, it looked like a ginger-cake with icing on it".

So there you are!

A high point still vivid to me was a visit to Corran, to the wee MacKenzies. Willie, Nellie, Flora (perhaps Iain was too small) and Frances were all in the sitting-room – shy at first, then abandoned to a wonderfully thrilling game: 'You can't catch me!' The running in and out became faster and faster, the laughter and screams even louder, and someone – would it be Willie? – even scrambled over the table. Willie Senior and Mrs MacKenzie might have been expected to come in and put a stop to it, but no – they just left us to enjoy ourselves. Though I could have been no more than eight or so, I still recall thinking that they must be very good-natured people. All that din wouldn't have been put up with in my own house.

Late one Friday night, there took place one of the strangest experiences of my entire life. I had been put to bed in the room next to the school, and had fallen asleep. Later however, a blasting of strange noises abruptly awakened me. It was coming through the wall, from the classroom. What could it possibly be? Was it …? Could it be …? Yes, indeed – it was the grown-ups! No doubt about it. But what on earth could they be doing? A queer feeling rose from the pit of my stomach at the realisation that the grown-ups were by no means the sane and sensible people they had always appeared to be. My father was sawing away at the fiddle for dear life. It sounded as though the people were actually galloping up and down the room, jumping rhythmically on the floor with heavy feet and sturdy frames. From time to time a horrible scream would make me still with fright. My hair almost stood on end. My hands were icy cold. And I was all, all alone in the darkness.

This would be followed by loud and animated talk and laughter. Then would come a deafening skirl from the bagpipes and in no time they were jumping and screaming again upon the floor – hoo-oo-ooch! HOOCH!

What a dreadful, terrifying night! Exhausted by this enigma of the adults' split personality, I finally feel asleep.

And next day – all was quiet, all was normal. The days proceeded, and it was never mentioned that anything in the least unusual had ever happened.

A memory to treasure was when Roddy MacLeod – Roddy the Farmer – was sowing oats on a mild spring day in the field below the farmhouse. This field had been ploughed and harrowed, and Roddy strode up and down its length and breadth, scattering seed rhythmically with each hand in turn, the handfuls drawn from a shallow basket-type contrivance tied around his waist and suspended from his broad shoulders. During the whole life of mankind since farming began, until the relatively recent industrialisation of agriculture – farmers must have sown their seed in this way. I am thankful for the privilege of having seen this primordial activity, which so closely united man with the soil and his food supply.

Another spring day, Roddy was ploughing with the big bay horse and his dark brown consort, Nancy, in the field now occupied by the fish farm. It was time for the potato planting. There were pails of potatoes which had been cut so that each piece had an 'eye' that would sprout and eventually yield the new crop of potatoes. We had to follow the plough, and press a piece of potato into the furrow at regular intervals. Perhaps my family were to have one or two rows of potatoes for ourselves. The earth was fresh and brown, seagulls were flying overhead and people bending attentively over the furrows, while the two big horses stamped their way heavily across the field. Damp earth, pink worms, air fresh and pure, and cheerful people all working together – what could be more pleasant, more healthful?

My happy childhood in Arnisdale went on for seven of the most impressionable years of my life. There – was experienced real brotherhood. People lived, and still live, in true sharing of their lives. Perhaps only in such a remote place is this possible, where nature in all its phases is the fundamental.

Regrettably, the new arrivals in Arnisdale have not had the richness of this experience. Nor have they any links with the people of past generations who were thrown off the arable land in favour of sheep, and made to struggle for a mere subsistence, in the barren places and along the margins of the sea. The stones in the one-room cottages they built along the Highland shores were used in Arnisdale, after the disastrous high tide of 1881, to build the present homes – except for the ruin to which the Post Box is attached, in Camusban. But in Rarsaidh, as Chrissie MacCuaig (now Morrison) has told me, there are the fallen-down remains of those primitive stone houses in the bracken, just above and along the high-tide mark.

Let's always remember the earlier generations of Arnisdale – their suffering and deprivation, their simplicity, their struggle to survive. For all of that – let's respect them! Let's not turn Arnisdale into a mere playground for those with holiday homes. Let's retain, natives and incomers alike, that priceless sense of community found among the people of Loch Hourn, and today undreamt of, it appears, in much of the outside world. Out there, more and more, it's each for himself and devil take the hindmost. But in remote areas, we can only pull together. To everyone's enrichment.

It's a pity about the fish farm. Arnisdale Estate couldn't have had any idea, at its beginnings, that it would develop in the way it has done. Two picturesque features of the village were the avenue of sycamores in Flora's postcard dating back at least a hundred and twenty-five years, and behind them Daniel MacDonald's round roofed green boatshed, which housed the Noressian for the winter. One's pleasure in these features is now robbed, one's attention diverted – by a disgusting smell, unpleasant litter on the shore, ugly equipment in full view and the partially dismantled old, old wall, which reveals a dismal sight in the once fertile field behind it. And a disturbing clatter accompanies any vehicle or incautious foot passing over the metal contraption in the roadway. With a region officially classified as 'of outstanding scenic beauty' – it's amazing that this commercial blight should be allowed.

Why not move down the coast, Fish Farm? There are several slip roads leading from the shore up to the main road, though the latter was not built to accommodate such heavy vehicles as yours. From there, you could transport your fish directly to Mallaig and the railhead by sea, as was done not so long ago.

There are also the nettles. I don't remember any when I was little. Why not have a Nettle-pulling Day? It could be fun, with tea and scones outside for everyone at the end of it.

Well, we've had Arnisdale past and present. What about its future? Peter's idea of 'The Book of Arnisdale' is great. Its proceeds, after the deduction of expenses, are to be for the benefit of the village. As they are to be disbursed by a committee of Arnisdale folks, hoary now in wisdom, we can be sure the proceeds would be well spent – possibly on a hall, a place to get together.

May I, also, suggest something? It is: an annual Arnisdale Village Festival of about a week or even a few days, where people interested in village life and self-sufficiency could come to learn and participate in all sorts of useful and simple technologies, crafts and skills. Perhaps each house could spare a bed or two, with meals here or there, or at Sheena's Tea Hut – all at a nominal price. The hosts (everybody, hopefully) could pass on their knowledge of crofting; keeping a cow, hens, goats, sheep; gardens fertilised with seaweed; scone and pancake making; gathering whelks; rowing a boat; fishing with rod, sgriben or net; cleaning, carding and spinning wool; sawing and chopping wood; making (and playing!) violins; dancing, of course; singing Gaelic songs and having ceilidhs; and lots more. There's plenty of talent.

What about a museum of old farm implements, no longer in use and hidden away in the barns and outhouses, or lying neglected on the crofts e.g. Archie MacLean's old tractor, and the harrow up on the old tin shed? Where are the creels, so useful for seaweed, manure or peat – and so good for the back?! I'm sure a lot of interesting things could be unearthed! What **is** there exactly, locked up in Corran's mysterious sheds?

All could have a happy and absorbing time together, with sheep-dog trials; what to do and not to do in the mountains, by young and not-so-young Arnisdalers; Iain at the fiddle; Gaelic songs; and lots of tea, friendship and home-baking. And the proceeds after expenses would go to the Arnisdale Fund.

It might even be infectious, and set off a chain of village festivals all around the Highlands!
What a lot we could learn, teach and practise together, both natives and incomers! Then, when due to global warming the seas inexorably rise and swallow up the low-lying lands, when Earth is devastated by human greed wedded to super-technology, there will remain in the high lands a few of us, prepared – ready to carry on and help transmit some knowledge of ourselves to the far future.

Shall we try it?

Let me end by quoting to you a haunting poem by my brother Alex:

Summer Sunday

Lovely Loch Hourn at eve
Ebb tide flows out
Like a silent swathe of silk
Leaving wet the darkened receding shores
Like a face after weeping.

God knows
How many strong, dark
And stealthy tides
Flow outward from my heart
Grasping for something gone astray
On a long, cold, grim, unending horizon
Ever before my eyes.

Without the sense of warm interlinking in a community, as we have all known it in the life of this one, something has indeed gone astray – maybe our very civilization – leaving but a future long, cold, grim and empty, like the horizon.

So, on with Arnisdale! Long live its descendants, and may they always remember their antecedents!

**Footnote**
A few details of my family, at the author's request:

My father, Martin Kennedy, was brought up in Lochaber in sight of Ben Nevis. He served in France in the last two years of the Great War. After that he taught in Kinlochleven, and in 1924 was appointed to Dunan School, Isle of Skye. My mother, Johan MacInnes, from Breakish, Skye became his Assistant. They were married at the King's Arms Hotel in Kyleakin, on Christmas Day, 1928.

In 1929, they moved to Struy, Strathglass. In 1932, my father enrolled in Glasgow University to study towards an MA Degree, while my mother held the fort in Arnisdale until he took over in 1936, I believe. Alex was born in Skye, before we moved to Dochgarroch School on Dochfour Estate, near Inverness – just after the War broke out. In 1943, we left for Glasgow, where David was born.

My uncle, the Rev. Neil MacInnes of the Parish of Glenshiel, who retired to Inverinate, was briefly in Arnisdale as a missionary. He used to go fishing up the loch with Willie MacKenzie the Post – the present Willie's father and David's grandfather.

The author wants me to include some observations of mine in a letter to him. Here they are, regarding China: 'There was great beauty and interest, even magnificence in many places. But the area I was most attracted to was a remote valley, away in the mountains in a bend of the Yang-tse River, only a few hundred miles from Tibet. Why did I like it so?

Because of its several hamlets, the friendliness and hospitality of the people. "Come in. Sit down. Drink tea". My Chinese could stretch as far as understanding that.'

'I loved it there, because of Arnisdale. With all those migrations around the planet, I never lost my identity, my self, which was formed by the simple life and loving-kindness of people far removed from economic manipulation, living as best they could from the land and the sea, and all in a mutually sharing lifestyle'

**Top Left.** Memories of visits to Arnisdale. Lally English on her first visit to Arnisdale which she remembers with L to R Uncle Roddy Mor, Aunt Chrissie and Jimmy Kennedy who worked on the farm. The horse-drawn hayrake is about to start its work in the shoreline fields.. **Right.** L to R. Lally (right) with her great friend Rena MacDonald behind, Aunt Lizzie, and young brother Bob with a new collie pup.

**Middle Left.** Great friends (L to R) Jessie, Rena, Mary and Johan MacDonald. **Right.** The 100th Birthday party of dear friend Mrs Mary Ann MacDonald, Corran with (L to R.) Morag Ann, Johan, Jessie, Mary, Rena and Morag.

**Bottom Left.** Peggy Ann and Mary MacLean in their garden with a summer visitor. Mary kept a beautiful and productive garden while Peggy Ann's shop and Post Office had a wonderful atmosphere. **Right.** Other great friends – Mary Ann MacCuaig and her mother Lexy with young next door neighbour, Iain (Ruaridh) MacLeod..

**Top Left.** Maggie 'Lea', a few days after her marriage to John Angus MacDonald (left) in Arnisdale in 1952, set sail along with mother Jessie to her married life in Eigg. Maggie and Jessie's 'Mission House' in Arnisdale was a very popular ceilidh house. **Right.** Mrs Thomson and her husband Andrew who was gardener at the Arnisdale Lodge. Mrs Thomson was an expert on birdsong.

**Middle Left.** Aonghas Dhaidh MacKintosh (left) with Mary Kate MacTavish and Uncle Roddy Mor..
**Centre.** Mary Ann Cameron at the doorway of her home just across the Corran Bridge. **Right..** There was keen excitement in Arnisdale every Tuesday when the boat came from Mallaig with the weekly supplies.

**Bottom Left.** Standing on the pier awaiting the delivery of goods are (L to R.) Lachie MacAskill, Uncle Roddy Mor, Allan MacAskill, Aonghas Dhaidh, Daniel MacDonald, Corran and the old farm collie, Whisky, who always wanted to be among the 'action'. **Right.** The Scottish Six Day Motorcycle Trials which came down the Arnisdale Glen from Kinloch Hourn also created much excitement.

**Top Left.** Isabella Mackay (nee MacPherson) (second from right) in her childhood days with L to R. brothers Donnie and Roddy and sister Janet (Mrs Nettie Campbell). **Right.** Isabella with her husband Tony Mackay. Tony, a native of Durness, Sutherland was a young Forester involved in the planting of the Mialairidh Forest in the late 1920-1930 period.

**Middle Left.** Fay (left) and Betty MacLaren (right) with Annie Fletcher in the 1930s. Fay and Betty lived with their parents at Glenfield. The MacLaren family were friendly with the MacPherson family in Galtair, Glenelg and there were occasional exchanges of visits. **Right.** Johnny Sinclair (left) who had the mail contract between Glenelg and Arnisdale. Johnny first used a pony and trap but later bought a car to do the job. With Johnny (L to R.) are Archie MacLean and Willie Campbell.

**Bottom Left.** Mary Ann MacCuaig visiting her cousin Johan MacLure in Riverfoot, Glenelg. On the way home to Arnisdale on Johnny Sinclair's pony and trap, Mary Ann had to walk up all the steep hills to make it easier for the horse. Mary Ann did everything that was asked of her with a light heart and the best of humour.
**Right.** Christina MacKenzie (nee MacLaren), husband Willie and their family at the wedding in 1995 of son Alan to Carol (Sword). L to R. Billy, Roderick, Willie, Christine, Alan, Carol, David, son-in-law Willie Frame, Shona and their children Lisa and Ross.

**Top.** Christina MacKenzie (nee MacLaren) was the last teacher in Arnisdale School before it was closed. These were the last Christmas Parties to be held in the Arnisdale School before the closure and sale of the school. As well as Christina, Chrissie Morrison and Santa, the group (left) includes Lizzie, Tina and Jean Fletcher, Chrissy and Peter Fletcher, Donald Angus and Morabelle Morrison, the Mackay children from the farm, Christine Crombie, Nellie, Sidney and Raymond Leitch and Billy MacKenzie. **Right**. A similar group enjoying a subsequent Christmas Party with the addition of the children of Flora and Bob Crombie – Christine, Robert, John and Duncan.

**Middle Left.** After Arnisdale School closed the Arnisdale children travelled to and from Glenelg School each day. Glenelg teachers Mrs Cameron and Miss Clarke are seen here with the pupils from both districts in 1970 at the opening of the new Glenelg School. Back Row (L to R.) Catriona MacPherson, Margaret Fletcher, Myra MacLeod, Fay MacAskill, Marion MacDonald, Duncan MacLeod, Billy MacKenzie, Calum MacKenzie, Donald Morrison, Charles MacDiarmid, Miss Clarke. Middle Row: Dorothy MacAskill, John MacAskill, Donald Dunlop, William Lamont, Morabelle Morrison, Raymond Chisholm, Mairi MacDonald and Rosey MacRae. Front: Donald MacAskill, David MacKenzie, David MacLeod, Roddy MacPherson, Kathleen MacLean, Helen Chisholm, Shona MacKenzie, John MacKenzie and Dougald Dunlop. **Right.** Christina MacKenzie enjoying one of Arnisdale's fine days along with her children, Shona, David, Billy and Alan in their toddler days.

**Bottom Left.** The Arnisdale School complement during Frances Kennedy's period there. L to R. Mrs Joan Kennedy (Teacher), Alistair Fletcher, Callum Kennedy, Willie Stoddart, Maryann MacKintosh, Rena MacDonald, Willie MacKenzie, Charlie MacTavish, Flora MacKenzie, Johan MacDonald, Nellie MacKenzie, District Nurse Morrison, Frances Kennedy and Iain Sinclair. **Right.** Callum Kennedy (Frances' brother) at a clipping at the farm fank with Archie MacLean (left) and Roddy Mor (1938).

# Chapter 13

**The MacDonald Family - Memories of Jessie, Mary and Johan**
**(Mrs Jessie MacGowan, Mrs Mary MacDonald and Mrs Johan Smith)**

We all have many happy memories from our Corran and Arnisdale childhood in the 1920s and 1930s - at work and play. We all had our share of the chores - both in the house and outside, such as bringing home water from the river before we got tap water in the house. Although we had no croft ourselves, we always had fun helping our friends milking the cows, putting them out to the hill in the morning after milking and then bringing them home in the evening. Then we would help Willie MacKenzie with the hay and he would often give us a sixpence or a shilling which was a lot of money in those days. We also went round the neighbours asking them if they wanted any messages from the shops. This would give us an excuse to go down to Peggy Ann's shop in Camusban.

In the summer time all the boys and girls would often play shinty at the back of Alan MacAskill's house - we used to make our sticks from drift wood on the shore. After a big shinty match in Arnisdale against Glenelg, one of the real sticks got broken and our father spliced it for us to use in our own shinty matches. We also played rounders even when it got dark. We used to put candles inside jam jars - these were our floodlights! We also went sledging on the steep slopes at the bottom of Druim Fada above the fields - even when there was no snow at all! At Christmas one year, all the children organised a Christmas Party in Granny MacKenzie's house. We cut up covers of old jotters, glued the strips into rings, made yards of decorations and hung them all up around the room. We got a big branch of an evergreen pine tree as a Christmas Tree and also decorated that. Then we got little presents, packed them up and put them in a "Santa" bag. Johnnie Murchison got dressed up as Santa, wearing our mother's red coat and then came into the room and handed out the presents to everybody. Granny MacKenzie was great fun. Granny's English was not too good and we children used to write letters for her, with her dictating what she wanted to say.

At Christmas, all the Arnisdale folk got presents from the Kitsons at the Lodge. The men folk would get tobacco, the ladies tea and the children would get sweets. The Kitsons also held great parties for all the Arnisdale children at the Lodge at Christmas. The sailors on the Golden Hind, Kitson's yacht, were also very kind and one of them, Willie MacLean, sent sweets to Johan and Charlie (MacTavish) one Christmas.

There was great fun at King George V's Silver Jubilee in 1935 and at the Coronation of King George VI in 1937. The men built a big bonfire on the Crudh Ard, mainly using whins and some driftwood from the shore. It was lit after dark and made a great glow with all the Arnisdale folk from the youngest to the oldest round about. We had fireworks and Angus Campbell played the pipes as we all danced around the fire. There was also a dinner dance at the Lodge to celebrate these great events.

The Kitsons at the Lodge employed a lot of people - 10 to 12 between house staff and gardeners. Then there would be 3 to 4 stalkers/ghillies/shepherds and 8 to 10 sailors on the Golden Hind, their yacht. With all the Lodge staff and the Arnisdale folk, there was a big crowd at the dinner dances.

Before they got the Golden Hind, the Kitson family had 2 boats - the Morag and the smaller Noressian. Our father was responsible for these boats and also the small boats and outboard motors. Dad's main base was the Boat Shed in Camusban near the Lodge where he spent lots of time working on the engines and in the general maintenance of the boats. Helping in this work were Angan MacTavish and Allan Murchison. Every summer when we were children, father would take our mother and ourselves to visit our many relatives on the Island of Eigg (both mother and father belonged to Eigg) on the

Morag. The journey from Arnisdale to Eigg would take 3 to 4 hours and father would deliver us and then return to Arnisdale. We always had a great time in Eigg for 3 to 4 weeks and at the end of our holiday we didn't like to see the Morag coming into view to collect us as that meant the end of our great summer-time in Eigg.

At the end of the season, the Noressian would be winched up the slipway into the Arnisdale boatshed while the Morag had to be taken to Roseneath for the winter. Our father, Angan and Allan would set off with it from Arnisdale, take about two days to reach Roseneath and then they would return by train to Mallaig and get the boat from Mallaig to Arnisdale. In the Spring they would do the reverse journey to collect the Morag for the season's activities.

Our father had come to Arnisdale in 1912 as the Church of Scotland Missionary and the first funeral service he conducted was that of Aonghas Dhaidh's father. Father and mother were married in Glasgow in 1918. After several years as the Missionary, father got the job with the Estate and the boats. He loved the sea, he respected it, and sailed in all weathers except when it became just too dangerous. When he was sailing either his small boat or bigger boats around Arnisdale he was always accompanied by what became a pet seagull. He was very fond of the birds, and the animals, and people. A little wren used to nest in a leather covered seat in the boat house every year. Our sister Rena also had this great love for, and way with the birds.

Life always seemed to be interesting in our young days. There was always something to talk about whether it was the lady (Mrs Cameron) who lived at Skiary who was supposed to have the gift for healing or the time Bobby Robertson, the tramp, claimed that he saw a ghost when spending a night in the byre at Rarsaidh and was so terrified that he never returned to that place for his night's rest! It took a lot to terrify the tramps! There was also always great rivalry between the Corran and Camusban folk. The nicknames were the Coulags (the Corran folk) and the Lonacs (the Camusban folk). There was always plenty of leg-pulling and Donald Fletcher used to give the Corran folk a hard time, but the Coulags got their own back when Donald went to Kyle for his motorbike test. There was no need to use hand signals in Arnisdale, Donald had never heard of such, and duly failed his test. That provided plenty of ammunition to Johnnie Murchison, Angus Stewart, Willie MacKenzie and others of the Coulag fraternity to give Donald a tough time with their 'leg-pulling'!

With the outbreak of the Second World War, as well as the Arnisdale Home Guard being formed with Roddy Mor in charge, the children and others got involved, among other activities, in collecting sphagnum moss from the moors. The moss was collected, dried, dressed and packed into gauze bags as wound dressings for the injured troops and bombing victims. After preparing a good quantity of such packs it was taken to the Nurse's cottage in Camusban for collection. The Glenelg folk took their material to Dr Devon's and Mary, who worked for Dr Devon at the start of the war, remembers Dr Devon rewarding the folk as they brought in their supplies with tea and pancakes.

Earlier, in 1938, after working in the Lodge for a season, Chrissie MacCuaig and Mary went with the Kitsons to work in their winter home in Maidstone, Kent and returned with them for the next summer and autumn season in Arnisdale As a big dance was being planned for the Lodge to mark the end of the 1939 season (before war broke out), tragedy struck the Kitson family when the eldest son (JB) was killed in an air accident. A large cake had already been prepared in the form of the Golden Hind, but when the tragedy occurred, the dance, of course, was cancelled and the cake was given to the school to be shared by the children.

Mary was working at Ardverikie House on Loch Laggan in the early part of the War and in 1942 she volunteered to join the WAAF. However, she was posted to the WRENS and the following poems relate some of her activities and ports of call including Tullichunan, Balloch and Scapa Flow.

**Naval Terms**

When first we joined the WRENS we learned a thing or two
We learned to drill as sailors drill and talk as sailors do
We learned the ropes and other things that we had never known
We found out that the Navy has a language of its own
We were taught to say we've gone ashore when we have been in town
and when its time to go to bed we turn in and pipe down
We never have a grumble but instead we sometimes drip
and if we take French leave, well - then we've broken ship
We talk about the starboard watch instead of evening shift
and if we stay out late we say we must have gone adrift
We call our bedrooms cabins and a bed we call a bunk
We talk of being bottled but that doesn't mean we're drunk!
The kitchen's called a galley and the dining room's a mess
We call our officers - oh well - we better let you guess!
A waitress is a steward and a clerk is called a writer
The cook is sometimes called a 'B' - we mean of course a 'blighter'
We say we've had a Friday wild when on weekend we've been
We speak of leave as liberty and washing as dhobying
We find its no good being haughty for naval terms are nautical
and sometimes - oh so naughty!
We are not made to wash the floor - we have to swab the deck
We call the soldiers 'Pongos' and Marines are leather necks
A sailor is a matelot but don't think cadets are men
An officer in training is a male seagoing wren
We would not dare to say it loud or write it with a pen
But we leave you to imagine what the sailors call the WRENS.

**Its a long, long way to Tullichunan (Sung by the Wrens on their many route marches in the Balloch area)**

Its a long, long, way to Tullichunan
Its a long, long, way to go
Its a long, long, way to Tullichunan
To the mud and rain and snow.
Goodbye to all the glamour
Farewell to high heel shoes
Its a long, long way to Tullichunan
And we've all got Balloch Blues.

**The following poem was composed by Mr Andrew Thomson, Arnisdale Lodge gardener, as Mary's 'Welcome Home' at the end of the war.**

When Mary joined the Services
A WREN she said she'd be
She'd join the Royal Navy
and sail the deep blue sea.

A sailor's life is the life for me
Heave-ho and 'Ship Ahoy'
We'll cruise along quite merrily
In every Port a boy
And though the ship a mine might hit
and on the rocks be cast
She wouldn't change her place a bit
She'd sail before the mast.
Off to a depot she did trek
A sailor's life to share
But before she'd trod the Quarter deck
She'd to tramp the Barrack Square.

She soon passed out as a bold AB
The Navy said she'd do
And on the good ship Cochrane
She signed on with the crew
And now for a cruise on the open sea
They're off to Baltimore
They were all as merry as could be
When they left old Scotland's shore

They'd visit every foreign port
and think of home, - well whiles
but instead of reaching Singapore
They reached the Orkney Isles.

Now - the Orkney Isles - there's nothing new
except some ENSA show
and nothing else to listen to
but the sound of Scapa Flow.

They were soon fed up and wanted away
To somewhere more merry and blithe
So they sailed one morning at the break of day
and landed at Rosyth.

Now life afloat in Rosyth Bay
can be very drab and stale
So Mary said as she drew her pay
I'm going back to Arnisdale.

Now Mary served for two years and more
She says no more she'll roam
She has done her bit so its up to us
To give her a Welcome Home.

While Mary joined the WRENS, sisters Morag and Jessie were in the WAAFS. Their Corran friend, Chrissie MacCuaig, joined the NAAFI.

At the end of the war, the Arnisdale folk were very quick off the mark to "Welcome Home" the returning service personnel - both male and female. Among those were ex prisoners of war - Roddy MacRae from Kinlochourn, Kenny MacRae and Roddy MacPherson from Glenelg as well as the big Corran contingent of Mary, Morag, Jessie and Chrissie MacCuaig along with Angus Stewart and Jimmy Campbell.

Mary relates two further little stories about her Dad. He knew Loch Hourn very well and had seen it in all its moods and thought that he knew most of what there was to know about its marine life. But in the early 1920s he saw something as he was sailing up the loch which he could never easily explain. Out of the water, fairly close to the boat, emerged a head and then a long neck of a 'being'. As it swam, its head seemed to turn from side to side as if surveying the scene. It transpired afterwards that similar sightings had been made before. The Rev John MacRae of Glenelg, accompanied by a young boy, as they sailed up Loch Hourn in their little yacht in 1872, reported seeing a very big animal, black and round like a herring barrel. When it rose quite close to them, it sent a wave aboard the yacht, causing them great alarm. It wriggled through the water like a huge eel and they counted 8 or 9 humps showing above the water. A similar sighting was reported earlier by their good friend, Granny MacKenzie. As a fairly young girl (probably around 1880-1890), she was moving up the shore of Loch Hourn between Corran and Caolas Mor gathering driftwood for the fire. Suddenly there emerged from the surface of the water a huge head and neck very similar to what Mary's father described he saw. Granny MacKenzie said that she was terrified, she ran home as fast as she could and did not return up that shore until weeks afterwards. Neither Mary's father nor Granny MacKenzie were given to imagining things. Both of them were realists. The mystery remains.

Elsewhere in this book similar sightings of a very unusual marine 'being' have been reported by Granny MacKenzie's grandson, Willie MacKenzie (Willie the Post, the second), very close in terms of location, in fact, to the earlier sighting of his Granny. Robert Foster, while out fishing on his own, had a similar experience in this location in the 1920s. Willie Campbell made a similar sighting in his youth at Crowlick, while close to Sandaig, both Roddy MacPherson and his friends, and also the MacDiarmid brothers on another occasion saw a strange, large aquatic 'beast' (see also Chapter 34).

Mary continued the story of her father's sighting: 'The earlier sighting of a strange 'being' in Loch Hourn by our father was recalled by Mrs MacTaggart, the Minister's wife in Glenelg, when sightings of a 'Loch Ness Monster' were reported by the large squad of workers (mainly incomers) building the Loch Ness - side road in the early 1930s. Mrs MacTaggart wrote the following letter to our Dad and at the end made some simple drawings of what people had reported seeing in Loch Ness and Loch Hourn. Unfortunately we do not have a copy of the reply which our Dad undoubtedly sent to Mrs MacTaggart.'

The Old Manse<br>
Glenelg<br>
19/12/33

Dear Mr Macdonald

Since the sensation caused by the mysterious creature in Loch Ness, I have often thought of writing you to enquire about what you saw in Loch Hourn some 10 years ago or so.

I have a vague idea that you saw a long neck rise out of the water, turn its head from side to side as if looking round about, then sinking into the water again. The other day I got the enclosed article from an old gentleman in Glasgow. He wanted to know if I had heard of the Rev. John Macrae of Glenelg seeing the Sea Serpent in Loch Hourn in 1872. I got the story of that event a good many years ago, from an old man, who, as a boy was along with Mr Macrae, helping to sail the little yacht when they saw a very big animal, black and round like a herring barrel. When it rose quite close to them, it sent a wave aboard the yacht, causing them great alarm. It wriggled through the water like a huge eel, and they counted 8 or 9 humps showing above the water. You will see a sketch of it in the cutting I enclose.

It seems to me that the sketch of the creature seen at Fort Augustus by Mr Russell is very like what you saw in Loch Hourn. It looks as if it is a sea-serpent that is in Loch Ness.

Will you be so kind as to write and describe to me what you actually saw, and about what year. And will you please return this article as I want to send it back to the old gentleman.

Mr MacTaggart is in Edinburgh just now, but will be home on Saturday.

With kindest regards and wishing you all a very Happy Xmas.
Yours very sincerely

Mary MacTaggart

Another story told by Mary related to her friend Chrissie MacCuaig's engagement ring (she became Mrs Jacky Morrison). Chrissie was not in the habit of wearing her ring. However, she went to Glenelg one day, wore the ring, and on her return, she milked the cow. Soon afterwards, she missed the ring. Mary's father, who had established a garden for potatoes and vegetables on Sandy MacAskill's croft, received a load of cow manure from Jacky Morrison as he was preparing the ground for planting his potatoes.

On harvesting the crop, the following Autumn, his eye caught sight of a glossy object. He picked it up, thought it was a child's ring that came out of a Christmas cracker but took it home, cleaned it and - lo and behold - it turned out to be Chrissie's ring - as good as new. It was almost like finding the needle in the haystack!

We have so many happy memories of Arnisdale but there are also the very sad ones. The saddest of our young days was when our sister Flora died at the age of 6 years. Flora was born on Christmas Day and she was christened 'Florence Noel'. She died in the January after her sixth birthday from peritonitis. Flora's death affected everyone (old and young) in Arnisdale. Shirley Temple was a child star at that time and Flora was just like her. In fact, people were always telling our mother to send her photo to the press as Shirley Temple's double. Flora started school at the same time as Calum Kennedy (the son of Mrs Joan Kennedy and Martin Kennedy, the schoolteachers). Calum and Flora were great pals and, after school, little Calum used to convoy Flora up the road to Corran. Mary continued: 'When I worked at the farm, Lizzie and I used to watch Calum and Flora walking up the road on their way to Corran. I also remember little Calum saying to his sister Frances when he saw little Flora in her coffin "She is like your doll, Frances"'.

What was also strange at the time Flora died was that John MacGillivray's wife (Lizzie) was not well and she woke up the morning Flora passed away and saw a light at the foot of her bed and said to John: "Something has happened to Flora" and all the clocks in their house stopped at that time. Lizzie was the next one to die in the village. We also had the sad news of sister Jessie and Willie's baby, Donald, passing away at 5 months of age. Both Flora and Donald are buried in Arnisdale. Then we lost Dad and Mum and then there was our great sorrow when we lost our dear sisters Morag in 1993 and Rena in 1995.

Bessie Lamont (nee MacDonald) from Glenelg often said that our father had a big influence in retaining a resident doctor in Glenelg at a time when there was pressure to have the nearest doctor in Kyle or Kintail. Mother had had a stillborn baby boy (a breech birth) between the births of Rena and Johan and it was often said that, if a Doctor had been more quickly available, our brother could have been saved. Likewise with our darling little sister Flora who died of peritonitis as a result of a burst appendix, if diagnosis of the appendicitis had been more prompt, Flora's life might have been saved. Therefore, at the meetings discussing the residence of the Doctor serving Glenelg, Arnisdale and the other local communities, our father was able to put forward a very strong case for the doctor to be readily available at short notice to serve our communities.

Another thing we remember is that no one in Corran had water in the house when we were young. We were the first to have tap water and then a tap was put at the top of the Corran street for the Village. The tap water supply failed during the war and that was when everyone had to go to the river again for it. That was when our niece Morag Ann was small. We had to make sure that the tide was out before we went for water to the river or we would have had salt water in our bucket! Dad was also the first to have a radio. It was worked from a wet battery which he re-charged at regular intervals at the power house beside the school burn. Before that he had to send the battery over to Kyle to be re-charged. We had earphones to begin with and then he got a loud speaker. At New Year, or if there was anything special on, he would open the sitting room window and put it on the window for the First Footers or the Village folk to hear.

The most important ones at the dances were Peter and Farquhar MacRae along with Allan Murchison, Peter and Donald Fletcher and Do MacKillop as they were the ones who supplied the music and they were also good singers. (They played the pipes, box and violin). The MacLaren family used to help as well as they all played violin and piano. We used to keep the dances going till daybreak as the boys could not go back to Kinlochhourn with the boat until it was light enough.

As kids we were all fond of spending time with the old folk around and had we only thought of writing things down then we would have so much more to pass on. Alas, when you are young these things don't occur to you.

Johan recalled her teachers as follows: My first teacher was Mrs Joan Kennedy and they must have gone to Arnisdale about 1932. Her husband Martin was at University doing a degree course and when he finished he took over the teaching. They left in 1939 and after that we had Miss MacAskill, and then Miss Cruickshank for a short time on relief from Glenelg. She later became Mrs Cameron, Glenelg. We then had a Miss Forsyth followed by a Miss Ferguson, and my last teacher was Miss MacRae who belonged to Glenelg. I think it was Lexy Campbell who came after that. I think Lexy's sister Mrs MacInnes came after her and then Christine, Willie MacKenzie's wife, and, if my memory serves me right, Christine was the last teacher in Arnisdale before the school was closed.

The last wedding in Arnisdale to my knowledge was Margaret Cameron (Maggie Lea), who married John Angus Macdonald from the Island of Eigg on 4 April 1952, in the Free Church and the reception was in the school. I cannot remember any baptisms in the church. I was baptised in the school as that is where the Church of Scotland held their services in those days but all the rest of our family were baptised in our home.

Although it was hard work at all the regular seasonal jobs such as peat cutting, stacking and carting, the sheep clippings, the planting and lifting of the tatties and working at the hay, our memories are of the fun that we had together on these occasions rather than the strenuous work involved. The Corran folk used to cut peat on their own ground (Druim Fada) and then it had to be dried and carted home to provide winter warmth. They used to tell us that old Granny Murchison often carried peat in a creel on her back from well up the Arnisdale glen.

It used to be a big day at the farm when all the Corran crofters were shearing their sheep and all the ladies went along to fold the fleeces. The ladies would take along baskets of sandwiches and home baking and there would be regular stops for tea and goodies during the long day it took to complete the shearing of the three hundred or so in the Corran Township sheep flock and to pack the fleeces into the woolbags at the end of the day.

**Other Memories of Mary MacDonald from the 1920s and later period.**

In our young days all the families (except ourselves) had crofts and they worked them fully. All had sheep, cows and hens - the cows being milked twice daily. They made hay, they grew potatoes and some grew some oats (for the hens). My brief recollections of various activities are as follows:

The farm: Roddie and Lizzy MacLeod had the farm and there was a chap called Jimmy Kennedy working for them before the 1939-45 war. Roddie was also our butcher.

The Lodge: The Kitsons had the Lodge and Estate from the 1920s to the 1950s. Captain and Mrs Kitson came from the South (Maidhurst, Sussex) every season. They had five of a family - J B (John Buller), Margaret, Robert, Ruth and Harry. They had a ladies' maid, two girls in the kitchen, two in the dining room, two in the house and another woman in charge. There was also a gardener and his assistant.

Free Church: As stated earlier, the last wedding there was that of Margaret Cameron (Maggie Lea) and John Angus MacDonald from the Island of Eigg. The only other wedding I remember being there was that of Mabel Fletcher and Peter Campbell in 1940.

The Church of Scotland: The Church of Scotland services were held in the School. Daniel Macdonald (our Dad) was the first preacher I remember there. After him it was mostly students who came to preach. Among the names I remember are those of Smith, Gillies, Macdougal, a retired Minister (Mr Milne) and then I think it was the Glenelg Ministers who took the services. Among these ministers were Neil MacInnes, Norman Macdonald and Angus MacKinnon. Before them there was Tommy Murchison and the first one that we can remember was Mr MacTaggart.

The School: The first teacher we had was Miss Logan and she was followed in turn by Miss Fletcher, Donald Finlayson, Mrs Kennedy and Martin Kennedy, Ann MacRae (Mrs MacLean), Lexy Campbell (Mrs McCuaig), Mrs MacInnes and Christine MacLaren (now Mrs Willie MacKenzie). When we were at school we were taken every summer before the holidays for a school picnic and games to some place; I think we went mostly down to Rarsaidh or up the Arnisdale Glen. It was the highlight of our school days. We also loved it when it was a lovely day and we got our lessons outside sitting on wooden benches.

The Scholars: The ones at school when we went were Johnnie Murchison, Angus Stewart, Iain and Chrissie MacCuaig, Jimmy Campbell, Effie and Betty MacLaren, Margaret Cameron, Ian Sinclair, Mabel, Roddie, Donald, Farquhar and Alistair Fletcher, Charlie MacTavish, Ian and Donald MacCuaig (at times) and six Macdonalds (Morag, Jessie, Mary, Rena, Johan and Flora).

Shops:  Peggy Ann MacLean had the shop and Post Office and then John MacGillivray opened one which Willie Gordon from Glenelg took over later and our sister Rena worked there during the war and later on.

The Mail Car:  John Sinclair ran the mails with a horse and trap before he got a car.  At that time the only ones in Arnisdale who had a car were Roddie at the farm and John Sinclair while my Dad had a motorbike.

The Mallaig Boat:  The Boat which came in with supplies every Tuesday and also carried passengers was run by Mr MacLennan of the Marine Hotel, Mallaig.  It was the highlight of the week and you would see most of the folk in both villages at the pier to meet it.

Winter Evenings:  All we youngsters gathered in the evenings at homes such as that of Mary Ann Cameron, Jessie MacIntosh, Robbie and Katie Foster, Norman Morrison, Granny MacKenzie or Sandy Macaskill and we played games of cards, sang and danced and told stories.  Later we used to go to 'Jessie Lea's', as we called her, when Jessie and Maggie moved from Lea to the Mission House in Arnisdale.

Potato Planting:  Our potatoes were planted in the field beside the boat shed in Camusban where Dad spent his time when not working on the Estate or away on the boats.  As children, we helped to plant and gather them.

The Forestry:  Several people from Arnisdale worked in the Forestry including my sisters Morag and Rena for a while.

The Roads:  I only remember John Donald MacLeod from Sandaig being the roadman at Arnisdale for a long time, helped at times by Johnny MacGillivray and then latterly John Arthur did it.

The Herring:  Our Dad fished a lot for herring and used to salt barrels of them for a lot of folk.  Loch Hourn yielded 90,000 crans of herring in 1882.  Everyone liked Loch Hourn herring because they were small and tasty.  There were between 700 and 800 herrings to the cran so this catch in 1882 exceeded sixty million herring.

Peats:  Most of the Corran folk cut peats up on the south side of the river on the hill grazings for the Corran cows.  Allan MacAskill cut his peats between his house and the cross roads - the road going to Glenfield.

The Coal Boat:  That was how all the coal came in when we were young.  The boat would beach at Camusban and then the coal would be distributed to all the households by horse and cart and later by lorry.

These, then, are the memories of Jessie (Mrs Willie MacGowan), Mary (Mrs Donnie MacDonald) and Johan (Mrs Peter Smith).  It is a matter of sadness to the author, to all the Arnisdale residents and a host of Arnisdale friends now located in many parts of the country, that the MacDonald family no longer have a foothold in Arnisdale since the great loss which the community suffered with Rena's death in 1995.

Daniel MacDonald had come to Arnisdale from the Island of Eigg as a young Church of Scotland missionary in 1912.  Soon afterwards he married his life's partner, Mary - who was also a native of Eigg.

The entire family contributed a great deal to the Arnisdale and Loch Hourn communities for over eighty years. They had their share of great sadnesses, especially with the loss of two of the children - one at birth and little Flora at six years of age. However, they all remained strong in the faith and did so much to help others.

Daniel was an inspirational leader in the community, both spiritually and practically, and was held in great respect by all who knew him. He was an expert seaman, an able mechanic and a leader of men in his own quiet, humble way. Mary ran her ever welcoming home and tended her devoted family with great grace and loving care. She retained her wonderful serenity to the end of her days at 102 years of age, tended by the ever devoted Rena and the rest of the family.

The girls, Morag, Jessie, Mary, Rena and Johan, followed the fine example of their parents. They were always at the very heart of all that was going on in Arnisdale - the school and the ceilidh dances in their earlier years, the work at the lodge, on the farm and in the Arnisdale Forest, and in serving their country in the last war. They were active in, and very supportive of, church activities, while Rena worked in John MacGillivray's shop and for many of her later years was the local Postmistress operating from her little office at Corran. Rena also made time to keep a wonderful flower and vegetable garden which was a source of admiration to all who passed by.

The MacDonalds were a very kindly, joyous and inspirational family. They were indeed a very important component of the spirit and the soul of Arnisdale for most of the century. The younger generations will undoubtedly be returning at regular intervals to visit the special place that they have all heard so much about from their folks. It would be good to think that there will be many places in Arnisdale - both private and public - that will spontaneously provide 'Ceud Mile Failte' to them all as they pay their nostalgic but fleeting visits 'home' to Arnisdale in the years to come. A community hall or tea-room in Arnisdale with basic facilities would be a boon to Arnisdale residents and visitors alike.

**Top Left.**   The MacDonald family home faces the traveller as the Corran Bridge is crossed.   Rena, the last member of the MacDonald family to stay in the old home, ran the Post Office in part of the building to the right and also kept a wonderful garden – both picturesque and productive.   **Right.**   Daniel MacDonald came to Arnisdale in 1912 as the Church of Scotland Missionary.   He conducted services both in Arnisdale and Kinloch Hourn.   He is seen here at the helm of his boat at the landing place at Kinloch Hourn after a church service attended by the Kinloch Hourn, Glen Quoich, Runival, Skiary and Caolasmor folk.

**Middle Left.**      Daniel and Mary Ann were married in Glasgow in 1918.   **Right.**    The children (L to R) Mary,  Jessie, Johan, Morag, Flora and Rena.    The family lost little Flora (front centre) when she died tragically from peritonitis at the age of 6 years.

**Bottom Left.**     The girls during World War 2.    L to R seated.   Jessie and Mary.   Behind (L to R) Rena and Johan.
**Right.**    Morag, during her wartime service in the WAAFS

**Top Left.** Daniel MacDonald was later appointed by the Arnisdale Estate to maintain and operate the estate boats. Daniel (far left) is with (L to R) his brother-in-law Archie MacDonald, Allan Murchison and Angan MacTavish. Allan and Angan assisted Daniel on the boats of the Kitson family, the estate owners. **Right.** Commander Kitson's 114 tonne yacht The Golden Hind, seen here anchored in Arnisdale Bay close to Eilean Tioram, had a separate crew of nine sailors and Captain Tait.

**Middle Left.** Daniel and Angan at the controls of Commander Kitson's boat, the Noressian. **Right.** The other estate boat, the Morag.

**Bottom Left**. The Morag (left) and the Noressian anchored in the bay at Camusban. **Centre.** Wherever Daniel sailed on Loch Hourn he was always accompanied by his pet seagull. Here it awaits his arrival on his little boat with outboard motor which he used between his home in Corran and his boathouse in Camusban. **Right.** Daniel in typical pose as he plied Loch Hourn at the helm of the Noressian.

**Top Left.**  A break from the schoolwork for L to R.  Mabel Fletcher, Jessie, Mary and Rena MacDonald, Chrissie MacCuaig and Morag MacDonald (early 1930s).  **Right.**  A fine day in Arnisdale in the early 1930s so lessons are transferred to the fresh air.  L to R. Mabel Fletcher, Mary, Jessie, Rena and Morag MacDonald, Chrissy MacCuaig, Angus Stewart, Farquhar Fletcher, Willie Stoddart and Donald MacKintosh.

**Middle Left.**  Enjoying a fine day away from school on a picnic in Barrisdale in the 1930s are L to R. Mary, Rena, Johan and Jessie MacDonald, Chrissie MacCuaig and, front left, little Angus Murchison.  Those having fun in the background are Hector, Ewen and Johnnie Murchison.  **Right.**  One of the annual parties for all the children at Arnisdale Lodge in the late 1920s.  Standing L to R. Teacher Miss Bessie Logan, Roddy Fletcher, Johnnie Murchison, Miss Bean (Governess to Kitson children), Chrissie MacCuaig, Miss Ruth Kitson, Annie Fletcher, Jessie MacDonald, Robert Kitson, Margaret Kitson, Effie (Fay) MacLaren, Mabel Fletcher, James Buller (JB) Kitson, Betty MacLaren, Angus Stewart, Mary, Rena and Morag MacDonald, Commander J B Kitson.
Seated: Jimmy Campbell, Donald and Farquhar Fletcher, Iain MacCuaig and Harry Kitson.

**Bottom Left.**  Thinking of going off for a sail are Corran youngsters L to R. Angus Stewart, Morag and Jessie MacDonald, Chrissie MacCuaig, Johnnie Murchison, Mary MacDonald, Iain MacCuaig and Rena MacDonald (1930s).  **Right.**  An idyllic scene at Corran looking up river towards the bridge, the Corran croftlands with Achadh a' Ghlinne and the mountains beyond.

**Top Left.** The annual summer holiday in the Island of Eigg for Daniel and Mary Ann with the children. L to R. Jessie, Mary, Rena and Morag (late 1920s). **Right.** Many hands make the work light at the Corran clipping at the Arnisdale fank in the late 1930s. L to R. little Nellie and Flora MacKenzie, Granny MacKenzie (Mairi Bhan) Mary and Johan MacDonald, Ina Stewart, Christina MacKenzie, Chrissie MacCuaig and Rena MacDonald.

**Middle Left.** Now it is time to get the tatties lifted (mid 1940s). L to R. Ina Kennedy, Morag and Rena MacDonald, Aunt Lizzie. Seated Roddy Mor and Whisky, the fine old collie. **Right.** Arnisdale Lodge staff in the late 1930s. L to R. Jessie MacDonald, Mrs Christina Thompson, Phyllis Cooke, Maggie 'Lea', Mary Ann MacCuaig, Beatrice Haines, Winnie Windsor and Connie Galloway.

**Bottom Left.** Some members of the Kitson family, owners of the Arnisdale Estate. L to R. Miss Bean (Governess), Mrs Robert Kitson, Miss Ruth Kitson and Mrs Kitson (daughter of Lord Strathcona and Mount Royal). **Right.** Next door neighbour to the MacDonald family at Corran was Mary Ann Cameron seen here with Willie Macdonald, a policeman in Glasgow who was a nephew of Mary Ann's neighbour Daniel MacDonald.. Mary Ann's was a favourite ceilidh home for the MacDonald children.

**Top Left.** Norman Morrison, Cosaig, Corran. The Corran children were always made welcome at Norman's house. He was an old man who was young at heart. **Right.** There was always excitement at the annual Scottish 6 day Motor Cycle Trials. Here a competitor, having just come down the rough track from Kinloch Hourn, approaches the Corran Bridge and the gravel road to Glenelg ahead (1930s).

**Middle Left.** The MacDonald girls played a key role in organising Arnisdale's famous ceilidh dances. They always got good support from the music makers such as Donald Fletcher (left) and the Kinloch Hourn pipers and fiddlers – Peter MacRae and Donald MacKillop (right). The forebears of Donald (Do) had once occupied the MacDonald's house at Corran and ran it as a pub in the great days of the herring fishing.

**Bottom.** The pupils in Glenelg School at the same time the MacDonald girls were attending school in Arnisdale in the 1930s. The boys (L to R.) are back row: Murdie Lamont, Ronnie Lamont, Donnie MacLennan, Donnie Lamont, Kenny Garde and Tommy Moffat. Front L to R. Hector MacKenzie, Billy Thomson, Iain Campbell and Alasdair MacRae. The girls back row (L to R.) Cathie Thomson, Margaret Garde, Teenie Lamont, Mary Flora Cameron, Molly Sharp and Annie Lamont. Front. Christina MacRae, Morag MacKenzie, Janet Chisholm, Betty Gunn, Cathie Campbell, Chrissie Elder and Ishbel Chisholm.

185

**Top Left.** Daniel MacDonald (left) in his latter years at Corran with neighbour Angus Stewart and little Jon MacKenzie. **Right.** The 100th Birthday Party of Mrs Mary Ann MacDonald (seated right) surrounded by her loving family. Standing. Morag Ann, Jessie, Rena and Morag. Seated Johan and Mary.

**Middle Left.** The extended family came from far and wide to join in the birthday celebrations of a wonderfully serene and graceful old lady. **Right.** Rev. Mr MacKenzie and Ewan Cameron from Glenelg call to pass on their very best wishes.

**Bottom Left.** The view from the MacDonald household down the road past Donnie MacDonald and Peter Smith standing at the Corran Bridge with the bonfire fully prepared on the field behind the MacAskill's house. This was the area where the MacDonald children and all others used to engage in their games of rounders, shinty and football, sometimes with the help of candlelight when it was getting too dark! **Right.** The wonderful old lady had full view of the bonfire to commemorate her 100th birthday through the living room window from which she had viewed Beinn Sgritheall and its varied moods for more than 70 years. Mary Ann's grand-daughter Ellen Smith shares the moment with a very special Grandmother.

# Chapter 14

**Chrissie Morrison (nee MacCuaig) and the Corran of her youth**

Chrissie, who has been widowed since her husband Jackie Morrison died several years ago, spends the summer months in the old family home at Corran. Her granduncle, John MacCuaig, was the representative of the Corran crofters (along with John McPhee), who gave evidence to the Napier Commission in Glenelg Hotel in August 1883 when the plight of the crofters in the Highlands and Islands was being examined. This evidence provided the basis for the later Crofting Acts which ensured for the crofters a fairer deal and security of tenure. In the Napier Commission evidence, Chrissie's granduncle was described as a 'crofter and fisherman'. There was not enough work for Chrissie's father - Donald MacCuaig (born in 1880), in Arnisdale and he left as a young man, obtaining work in the Clyde shipyards and leaving his widowed mother to work the croft. He married Marion Anderson from Ardvasar in the Sleat district of Skye and Chrissie and her brother Ian started school in Glasgow. When Chrissie was 3 years old, Granny MacCuaig died and the family returned to the old family home in Corran to work the croft and live as best they could.

Chrissie has great memories of her schooldays in Arnisdale in the late 1920s and 30s and of her young life in Corran. Her teachers included Miss Logan, Miss Fletcher, Mrs Joan Kennedy and Martin Kennedy. There were many children in Corran in those days - her brother Ian, the MacDonalds - Morag, Jessie, Mary, Rena, Johan and Flora (who died tragically at the age of 6 years), Angus Stewart, Johnnie Murchison (and his older brothers and sister, Katie), and Jimmy Campbell. There were also many children in Camusban - the Fletchers, Donald MacKintosh from Rarsaidh, Charlie MacTavish, Willie Stoddart and Ian Sinclair, as well as Effie and Betty MacLaren from Glenfield.

They had plenty of work to do as children but they treated most of it as fun. There was water to be taken in buckets up from the river when the tide was out, firewood to be collected from the driftwood on the shore , the work with the cows and sheep and in the planting and harvesting of the crops.

The gathering, clipping and dipping of the sheep and the planting of the potatoes were great Corran community events in which everybody participated and helped. This was also the case when the peats were cut, stacked to dry and carted home in bags and creels. These were times of great excitement for the children. But the hay making was less fun. Father would scythe the hay and after a few days in the swath, if the weather was reasonable, then would start much laborious turning and shaking, making prapags and small coles - later converted into bigger ones. All the hay making was interrupted very frequently by the rain and the dampness - and the midges always seemed to pervade the air and annoy the children in particular. However, following hay cutting in July, eventually it would be ready to take into the barns in September - at the same time often as the potatoes were being lifted. The hay was carted to the barns in wheel-barrows, ropes and often by a few folk fixing their hay forks or graips into the bottom of the cole and 'sledging' it along the ground towards the barn. Once in the barn, that was the winter fodder for the cows secured. Later on, Chrissie's husband Jackie introduced the 'Glenelg' technique of drying the hay on the fences and this was easier and more effective than making prapags.

Working with the cows was also good fun. There were 14 byres in the row behind the village - almost everybody had one or two cows. After milking in the morning, the cows would be let out of each byre and they would automatically make their way to the hill gate behind the byres - out they would go and the gate would be closed behind them. They had the range of the lower slopes of Druim Fada and they would go where they felt inclined on the day, harvesting the hill grasses and herbs and converting them into the precious milk. Then any surplus milk would be made into crowdie, butter and sometimes cheese.

Going to bring home the cows at night was always a pleasure because many of the children would go - Chrissie, Rena, Morag, Mary, Jessie, Johan and others. They would be calling 'Trobhad' to try to locate the position of the cows which always kept together on their expansive range. Once located, they would be rounded up for the homeward journey - from time to time checking the number to make sure that all 18 were there. This was often tricky in the autumn and winter when it would be almost dark when taking them home. After coming through the hill gate, the cows would make their way each to the correct byre and correct stall. Then they would be given their reward of hay in winter and the milking would be carried out. There was a fine relationship between the folk and the cows and gentle conversation in the Gaelic from the folk, much of which the cow probably understood. When anything went wrong with the cows or calves, the first thought was to go for Roddy Mor at the farm - he was the unofficial local 'vet' and the folk had great faith in his abilities to diagnose and cure most problems which arose. The MacCuaig (and later Morrison) byre was No. 10. Chrissie remembers many of the cows they had over the years, the most recent ones being Daisy and Shorac, the latter originating in Moyle, Glenelg.

Getting away to take home the cows was particularly enjoyable on a Sunday. The Sabbath was observed strictly with regular church going, no noise or frivolity and all chores possible were done on the Saturday in preparation for the 'day of rest' and worship. When the children got away for the cows, there was relief as they got out of earshot of the village, for now they could let themselves 'go' a bit. They could collect nuts off the many hazel trees in the autumn, look for little fish in the river and streams, play 'hide and seek' and other games. Sometimes the cows were as far away as Blar nan each (the moor of the horses) which was east of Achadh a' Ghlinne on the Corran side of the river.

At night after the chores had been completed, a favourite house for the children was that of Sandy MacAskill - his was the 'ceilidh house' and the children would always have good fun there with all the story telling. 'Lachie's parlour' across the river was also very popular. This was the MacAskill's barn, where Lachie preferred to hold his ceilidhs rather than in his house with his brother and sister. Lachie had been in the Artillery in the First World War and volunteered for service again in the Second World War. He was a very pleasant, couthy man who was very fond of children. He had a primus stove in the barn to warm it up a bit and provide a little light at the same time on autumn and winter nights.

Katie Foster's house next door was also a regular port of call for Chrissie and Ian as children. Katie was a lovely neighbour as were the Murchisons on the other side. Mrs Murchison, like Chrissie's mother, came from Skye - Katherine Sutherland before marriage from the Braes district near Portree. Johnnie Murchison, the youngest of the seven Murchison children, used to give the two Skye ladies - his own mother and Chrissie's mother - a hard time of it. He would tell them that Skye should be blown up because that's where all the Arnisdale rain was coming from. The two Sgiathanachs used to give as good as they got - asserting that if Skye wasn't there, Arnisdale would be blown away by the Atlantic gales!

Chrissie remembers Robert Foster, Katie's brother as a very fine man who died when he was still quite young. When he was not working on the croft or the estate he would be out in his boat catching cuddies. He would catch enough for all the folk in Corran and when he got back he would go round all the houses sharing out his bounty from the sea.

Other memories which Chrissie has of her schooldays include Jimmy Kennedy from the farm swearing away at the horses as he prepared the Corran ground on the big day of the potato planting. There was also the excitement of the Scottish Six Day Motor Cycle Trials as the motor bikes made their tortuous way down Glen Arnisdale from Invergarry and Kinlochourn, negotiating the precipitous zigzag below the Dubh Lochain and then fording the river below Glenfield. There were also very pleasant memories of the Arnisdale dances, with the Kinlochourn boys - Peter, Roddy and Fachie MacRae and Do MacKillop providing the music along with the Arnisdale musicians including Allan Murchison, Peter and Donald Fletcher and the MacLaren family. She also recalls neighbour Granny Murchison going away up the Glen Arnisdale track from Corran with a creel on her back to carry the peats home, knitting as she went. Her father told her of the heyday of the herring fishing on Loch Hourn when it was claimed that people could cross Loch Hourn by walking from one boat to another, there were so many boats gathering in the bountiful harvest of the Sgadain. Arnisdale and other Loch Hourn clachans provided essential facilities for the fishermen including shops, pubs and religious services. It was at that time that the Arnisdale folk went from boat to boat collecting the funds which contributed to the building of the Free Church.

When Chrissie left school at the age of 14, her first job was as a kitchen maid in Arnisdale Lodge with the Kitson family. Chrissie stayed in the servants' quarters in the Lodge, sharing a room. It was hard work but they were well fed and it was great fun. The Lodge and the Estate employed many people at that time before the Second World War. The Kitsons had their 144 ton yacht, the Golden Hind, which brought them up from their home in Devon each season for the fishing and shooting. Captain Tait and nine sailors manned the Golden Hind and they also had smaller boats - the Noressian and the Morag - which were manned by the local men - Daniel MacDonald, Angan MacTavish and Allan Murchsion. In addition, eight staff were employed in the Lodge including from time to time Chrissie, Mary Anne MacCuaig, Maggie 'Li', and Jessie MacDonald. The head gardener, Andrew Thomson, usually had two or three assistants and, at various times, local folk such as Chrissie's brother Ian, Donald MacCuaig, Jimmy MacDonald and Maggie Li worked in this capacity. Then there were the stalkers /gamekeepers/shepherds, including Ludovic Fraser, Donald MacLaren, Angus Campbell and Kenny Fletcher. Thus, considerable employment was provided for the local folk and many romances blossomed between the Golden Hind and house staff and the local folk.

Chrissie also worked for the Kitson family at their other homes - Torling House in Devon, Lower Farm, Mannion House in Sussex and their flat in Kensington, London. Chrissie found the Kitson family fine to work for. She was also accompanied at the various homes by other Arnisdale folk such as Amy Thomson and Mary Ann MacCuaig, who was always fine, humorous company and very good at her job.

At the outbreak of war, the Kitson boats - the Golden Hind, Morag and Noressian - were commandeered for war service and the activity at Arnisdale Lodge during the season was reduced considerably.

Chrissie was in the NAAFI during the war and spent a considerable time stationed at Achnacarry - the base for the training of the Commandos. There were as many as 1000 soldiers there at a time including many American volunteers. The job of Chrissie, as one of the cooks, and her NAAFI colleagues, was to ensure that commandos undergoing their ultra tough training schedule were as well fed as possible. The accommodation for the troops were nissen huts and tents and the wintry wet, cold conditions were pretty tough. Chrissie recalls hearing about the training using live ammunition and several casualties during exercises on Loch Lochy.

After the war, Chrissie went back to work for the Kitsons again in Arnisdale Lodge and their other homes before settling down again in the old home at Corran and becoming Mrs Jackie Morrison, Jackie hailing from Moyle in Glenelg. Their children, Donald and Morabelle are now both married and settled not far away in the Dornie area. Chrissie now joins her family in that locality for the winter, returning to the scenes of her childhood and of her forebears for the summer months.

Among her many amusing stories are two about Roddy Mor from the farm. Roddy was, for a long time, the precentor in the Free Church, and his little box and seat - from which he led the singing - was just below the pulpit so, along with the minister, he faced the congregation. On one of the 'frequent' very wet days, Chrissie, of course, made full use of her umbrella as she walked the mile or so from Corran to the church in Camusban. Despite violent shaking of the umbrella at the church door to get rid of as much moisture as possible, it was obviously still pretty saturated when Chrissie laid it down on the floor beside the aisle near the front of the church. As the sermon began, a little 'river'; of liquid started trickling down the aisle from Chrissie's position towards Roddy's box. He was very quick to spot such things and Chrissie had great difficulty in keeping her composure, as the smirk came across Roddy's face and he caught her eye with an expression which told her all that he was insinuating without any words being mouthed or spoken. While Roddy could smirk with impunity as he had his back to the minister, poor Chrissie found it very difficult to remain serious and concentrate on the sermon. Of course, at the end of the service, Roddy was not slow to comment on the problem that some people must have in controlling their 'water works' even in the church!

Chrissie exacted some revenge when herself and Rena (MacDonald) found an old enamel bed pot on the shore and quietly placed it in the boot of Roddy's car but, inadvertently, failed to close the boot properly. The next morning Roddy set off over to Glenelg with the Arnisdale mails and his first stop was at Eilanreach to collect the mails from there. Ali Beag (MacRae) met Roddy to hand over the mails and noticed that the boot of the car was not properly closed. As he lifted the boot a bit to gain the necessary momentum to close it properly, he noticed the interesting article therein! "What kind of dishes are you carrying around with you here?" he asked mischievously. Roddy alighted and came round to investigate the subject of Ali's enquiry. As soon as he saw the article, he 'twigged' immediately who the culprits were! There can be little doubt that Chrissie and Rena were the victims of the next Arnisdale prank!

When her brother Ian and his wife Lexie (nee Campbell) a former teacher in the Arnisdale School - retired to Arnisdale after completing their careers in Carrington, Midlothian, Chrissie and her family were delighted to welcome them home to their new house in Camusban. There has always been a great urge for Arnisdale folk who have moved away for all or part of their working lives to return to their home heft for their retirement.

Chrissie, who remembers the place when it was probably in its prime, is somewhat pessimistic about the future of Arnisdale. Apart from the fish farm, there is now virtually no local employment - not even in the Lodge and Estate. Yet, Arnisdale and its environs has much to offer in terms of its rugged beauty and its history to interest and excite the tourist. There is also potential for sporting pursuits and adventure. But these possibilities remain to be exploited.

**Top Left.** Chrissie Morrison (nee MacCuaig) who was in the NAAFI in World War 2 and was stationed for most of the time at Achnacarry in Lochaber where the Commandos trained during the war. **Right.** Chrissie's husband Jackie Morrison belonged to Glenelg and spent most of his life working for the Forestry Commission. On his retirement, Jackie received presentations from next door neighbour and Forestry Ganger, Angus Stewart (centre) and from the local Head Forester, Hugh Mackay.
**Middle Left.** Chrissie as a toddler with brother Iain, her father Donald, her mother Morag (nee Anderson) and Grandmother Mrs Kirsty Anderson (nee Robertson) from Tarscavaig in the Sleat area of Skye. **Right.** Chrissie and Jackie's children, Donald and Morabelle make the most of a fine sunny day in Arnisdale by having a dip in the river with their friends – Jon, Billy, Roderick, Alan, David and Shona MacKenzie.
**Bottom Left.** A summer picnic at the shore for Chrissy and Jackie Morrison with children Donald Angus and Morabelle and for Chrissy's cousin Donald MacCuaig with Iain and Mairi. Donald is now resident in Islay. **Middle.** Arnisdale School pupils, all dressed up in their 'Sunday Best' in the late 1920s, about to depart for a special summer outing. **Right.** Chrissie's brother Iain married the local teacher Lexy Campbell in the early 1950s. After spending much of their working life in Midlothian, Iain and Lexy (on the right) came home to Arnisdale for their retirement. Their good friends on the left are Victor and Margaret Corbett from Belfast.

**Top Left.** The hill gate through which the Corran cows went out to the hill pastures each morning and were brought home each evening for the milking and their overnight stay. The MacCuaig family byre was No. 10 in the row of 14 byres at Corran. In her childhood, Chrissie greatly enjoyed going out to the moor and hill with her Corran friends to take the cows home for the milking. **Right**. Work at the hay Chrissie found much less enjoyable. Jacky 'imported' the Glenelg technique of drying the hay on the fences to Arnisdale – instead of the chore of making prapags. Chrissie and Jacky get a helping hand from brother Iain and Iain's wife Lexie to win the Corran hay.

**Middle Left**. Granny MacKenzie (Mairi Bhan) carrying water from the river accompanied by a little friend. The river is tidal to above the bridge so it was safer to draw water when the tide was out and there was less distance to carry it. **Right**. Roddy Mor was looked upon as the local vet to cure problems among the cows and also did the ploughing to prepare the ground for the potato planting.

**Bottom Left.** Chrissie and her fellow Lodge and Estate workers at Arnisdale Lodge in 1950. (L to R.) Johnny Kennedy (brother of Mrs Margaret Beaton), Chrissie MacCuaig, Ian Sinclair, Ludovic Fraser, Katie Foster and Angus Beaton. **Right** Another group of friends at Arnisdale Lodge. Standing (L to R.) Chrissie MacCuaig, Amy Thomson, Jessie MacDonald, Jean Thomson and Mrs Thomson. Kneeling: Mr Thomson (Head Gardener) and Iain MacCuaig. Immediately behind Mr Thomson and Iain are two Austrian girls who worked in the Lodge during the season.

**Top Left**. The Scottish 6-day Motor Cycle Trials created excitement in the 1930s and 1940s especially when the bikes forded the Arnisdale River on the way down the Glen from Kinloch Hourn. **Centre.** Popular ceilidh houses in the evenings in the 1930-1940 period were those of Sandy MacAskill and Lachie MacAskill (seen here in his First World War Royal Artillery uniform). **Right..** Chrissie (left) with her great Corran friends Rena and Johan MacDonald.

**Middle Left**. Chrissie (left) at the Mod in Kyle with Rena MacDonald and Margaret Beaton from Glenfield. **Centre.** Fine next door neighbours were the Murchisons, Stewart and Foster families. In the photograph is Adam Foster and his wife who were paying a visit to the old home. In the centre is young Angus Stewart. **Right**. Johnnie Murchison seen here (left) clipping the Corran sheep along with young Angus Stewart in the 1930s used to tease the two Skye ladies – his own mother and Chrissie's mother that all the Arnisdale rain was coming from Skye and that Skye should be blown up. The two ladies gave as good as they got!

**Bottom. L to R.** Neighbours Robert Foster, Katie Foster and Sandy MacAskill, (having just completed the shearing of the black sheep).

# Chapter 15

**Donald MacCuaig, Glasgow. Arnisdale holidays and ceilidh stories.**

Donald's father, John MacCuaig, was a native of Corran who went away to Glasgow to find work as a young man. John met his future wife, Mary MacDiarmid there, and eventually John and Mary had two sons, Donald and Iain. Here Donald, in his own unique way, recalls his holidays in Arnisdale and some of the many ceilidh stories he heard there.

"My older brother Iain and I were brought up in Glasgow. My father was at sea and came home every two weeks or so. When we went to school, we spoke English only, as my mother and father considered it best, but as it was Gaelic which was mainly spoken at home, and most of our visitors were Gaelic speakers, it was not long before we became fluent in the language. My mother (Mary MacDiarmid before her marriage) belonged to Glendale in Skye, and could remember some of the things that happened during the 'Land League' movement.

At our home in Glasgow, we looked forward to Colin Murchison from Corran arriving on a Friday night, as he often did, and were allowed to sit up and listen to Colin and my father relating old stories about Arnisdale and Loch Hourn.

The highlight of the year came when the school holidays were about to start - but more of that later. One year, on the very day the school was due to close for the summer, the teacher found out that I was in a Gaelic choir, and suggested that I would sing two songs to the afternoon class; now I knew that I would be the 'joker' of the day at four o'clock, as none of the class had Gaelic, so I enlisted the help of a boy in the class, who was the best fighter in the school, and he warned the class that if anybody tried to make fun of me, they would have to fight him at 4 o'clock, and this is how I survived a very awkward situation - without too much leg pulling!

**Arnisdale holidays.** That same night the big green trunk was taken out of its usual storage corner and packed with all the clothes we would need for six glorious weeks in Arnisdale.

A tea chest of various food and baking items would be ordered at Andrew Cochrane's grocery store to be sent to Mallaig by train and then from there on board MacLennan's boat 'The Bounty' to Arnisdale on the regular Tuesday run with the Arnisdale provisions. When the trunk was packed, we would be sent to order a taxi to take us to the Railway Station in the morning. We would be packed off to bed early, and would have to rise from our beds at about half past four in the morning, the taxi arriving at about quarter past five, and off we would set to Queen Street Station to catch the 5.50 a.m. train to Mallaig. On arriving at Mallaig about noon, the one thing that seemed to catch our attention were the seagulls - they seemed to be everywhere!

Then we were off down the pier, and aboard the 'Bounty' and off to Arnisdale, calling at Airor and Crowlick on the way and then into the jetty at Arnisdale. There, in Camusban, as always, would be Lexie Campbell, that kind old soul, waiting for us with tea and fresh eggs and a scone or two and oatcakes, and then would commence for us six weeks of pure bliss.

**The Loch Hourn monster.** Now, with reference to the many stories about the Loch Hourn monster, I remember hearing about the minister from Glenelg who reported seeing a monster in the loch, and as far as I can remember, this was being discussed in, I think, Lexie Campbell's house in the presence of Angus David MacIntosh (Aonghas Dhaidh). A few days later, Angus David borrowed a boat to go fishing at the Rarsaidh Islands and, somewhere past the Dry Island (Eilean Tioram), he remembered the discussion relating to the monster - and immediately turned the boat round and, as fast as he could row, he made back for Camusban and safety - probably having bread and cheese for his tea instead of the nice fresh fish which he had fancied earlier in the day before the ceilidh stories came back to him!

**Aonghas Dhaidh's attempt to beat the tobacco famine.**   While on the subject of Angus David, he was a very heavy pipe smoker and, during the war, tobacco became scarce, and Peggy Ann in the shop - Post Office, instituted a form of rationing within Arnisdale, so that all pipe smokers got a fair share. This was quite in order for moderate smokers, but the heavy smokers found that they were going short. This affected them in many ways - they became disorientated and their personality changed.   For example, Willie the Post would be putting on his shirt collar, and then attempting to put a second collar on top of the first;   Archie MacLean became so moody that his sister Johan went to great lengths to obtain tobacco from other sources to try to change his mood!

Angus David, however, obtained a copy of the 'Christian Herald' from someone, and noted an advert for 'smoking herbs'.   He decided that this was just the thing, not realising that this was for 'asthma sufferers'.   I was in Arnisdale at the time and he came into our house, and asked me to go to the Post Office for him, and get 25 one penny stamps.

This was a rather extraordinary request from a man who was seldom known to have written a letter, and as there were a few in the house for a ceilidh when he called with his request, eyebrows were raised! When he went out, a discussion arose as to what he was going to do with 25, one penny stamps!

The stamps were duly obtained from Peggy Ann and delivered to Angus and eventually forgotten about - until one day a parcel arrived at the Post Office, addressed to Angus David, which Willie the Post duly delivered to Angus.   When Angus received the parcel, he asked Willie the Post into the house and explained about the contents of the parcel.   On opening the parcel, the smoking herbs were revealed, and, producing his pipe, he proceeded to fill the bowl, lit a match, and took one long puff - inhaling deeply in excited anticipation of a good long satisfying smoke at long last!   Willie later described the consequences in graphic detail.   Almost immediately Aonghas Dhaidh choked, his face turned red, his eyes bulged, and he lost his breath, and Willie, getting exceedingly alarmed, was very relieved when Angus David got over the fit, and so ended the idea of the smoking herbs to relieve the Arnisdale tobacco famine!

**Another Loch Hourn monster.**   As far as I can remember, I think it was Angus David that told me of an incident that happened when Duncan MacTavish and John Kelly were fishing with long lines.   After the lines had been laid on the floor of the Loch for some time, they decided to lift them, and in the process of doing so, they felt something heavy on the line and, eventually, the head of a fish broke the surface.   They said it was, in circumference, about the size of the rim of a bucket, and they immediately cut the line and let it go.   Angus David was of the opinion that it was a huge conger eel.

**An explosion on the Fast Day.**   Now, at some time during the summer months the communion season came around, and started with the 'Fast Day' on the Thursday, and on the following Sunday the communion was to be held in Glenelg.   One time when we were on holiday, we found that if you got a key with a hole in the bore and a nail, a piece of string and red matches, and by scraping the red end of the match into the hole, then inserting the nail and tying nail and key together and banging this contraption against a stone or wall, it gave a sharp report - very like a shot from a gun.   One Thursday, and being a Fast Day -which was observed like a Sunday, I decided to try out this contraption that I had heard about. I obtained the necessary key, nail, string and matches, and assembled the device. I took the contraption to the end of Angus Donald MacIntosh's house, not realising that Angus was having a dose at his fireside.   I hit the contraption against the side of his house, and 'Bang'! went the noise through the village. Then out of the house rushed old Angus Donald and gave me a slap in the ear; as he said himself, the slap was for causing a noise on the Fast Day - but that was nothing to what I got when my mother found out about me profaning the Fast Day in such an irresponsible manner!

**Bravery awards!** When I was about four years old, and playing in front of the house at Camusban, I fell onto a stone and gashed my head, and my mother rushed me to the nurse - up the village to her house next to the School. The nurse took one look at it, and told my mother that it was a case for the Doctor. John Sinclair was then alerted and cycled to Corran where Daniel MacDonald immediately contacted Kitson at the Arnisdale Lodge. The estate boat the 'Morag' was made ready and my mother, brother, myself, with one or two others to help, boarded the 'Morag' at the jetty and it was 'Full Ahead' for Glenelg. In the Doctor's surgery there, and while sitting on John Sinclair's knee, five stitches were inserted, and I remember getting a bag of sweets from the Doctor for being brave! When we arrived back in Arnisdale, Angus Donald was waiting for us - a very worried man, as he had been told that it was his dog 'Watt' that had bitten me! He was a very relieved man when my mother explained the true story to him. A week or two later, Roddy Mor from the farm took us to the Doctor in Glenelg in his horse and machine to get the stitches out, and I was presented with another bag of sweets for being brave. I think the Doctor must have kept a big stock of sweets in for this purpose!.

**Kirsty in a panic at the mischievous false alarm.** When the Kitsons owned Arnisdale Estate, they had for a while, as housekeeper, a Lily MacDonald, who had first come to the Lodge some years previously from England with the Kitsons and she later married Jimmie MacDonald who stayed in Corran. Daniel MacDonald was the engineer for the boats and handyman at the Lodge at that time, and a Kirsty MacIntosh was employed as laundry maid, usually when the Kitsons were in residence. One morning Kirsty was out at her gate, when she noticed MacDonald aboard the motor yacht 'Noressian' which was moored a short distance from the jetty. As she was watching MacDonald working, Andrew Fraser was passing, and Kirsty enquired as to what MacDonald was doing out in the 'Noressian'. Andrew mischievously replied that she should know, as the Kitsons were coming up the following week!

When Kirsty heard this, she totally panicked, as the beds were stripped, the curtains were folded away and a host of other things had to be done to prepare for the arrival of the gentry. Kirsty took off for the Lodge at a great pace! A short while later, Mrs Jimmie MacDonald the housekeeper, as she was passing the laundry room, heard a noise and, on entering, found Kirsty working her heart out, preparing bed linen, table linen, and curtains. Mrs MacDonald enquired as to what was happening - to be told that the Kitsons were arriving the following week, and MacDonald was getting the 'Noressian' ready, and she did not know how she was going to cope with such short notice!

When Mrs MacDonald heard this, she became very annoyed that MacDonald knew all this and she, as housekeeper, was not told, so off she went to the jetty. On arriving at the end of the jetty, she shouted to MacDonald to come ashore immediately as she wanted a word with him. Obliging gentleman that he always was, Daniel duly clambered into the dinghy and, on arriving at the jetty, was met with a tirade, about the Kitsons coming the next week, and why he had not told her! When MacDonald explained that he had no knowledge of them coming and all he was doing was his usual check on the engines, Mrs MacDonald calmed down enough to explain her side of the story.

The two of them then went up to the Lodge and approached Kirsty, enquiring as to her source of information regarding the imminent arrival of the Kitsons. After poor Kirsty's breathless explanation, it was then realised that all the panic, stress and strain was the result of the jocular and mischievous reply by Andrew Fraser to Kirsty in the passing. So it was all a big false alarm - but it all made a fine story which caused much discussion and hilarity at the ceilidhs - and still does to this day!

**Gifts from the teacher and a scolding from mother.** During the short period I went to school in Arnsdale, the school teacher was a Bessie Logan, who came from Spean Bridge. Bessie was being wooed simultaneously by John Sinclair and Willie Fraser and, at this time, I was under the influence of John Sinclair. I would do anything he told me to do, much to the annoyance of my mother, and Johnnie's amusement. One night he told me that I was to ask Miss Logan next morning when at school for a penny and a piece and jam. The next morning at roll call, when my name was called, I stood up and told her that John Sinclair told me to ask her for a piece and jam and a penny, and was immediately told to sit down, be quiet and behave myself. When we were out in the playground at playtime, Miss Logan called to me from her house, took me in, and gave me a piece and jam, put a penny in my pocket, with instructions to tell John Sinclair. When I told John Sinclair what had happened he started to laugh, but I am afraid my mother was a different proposition, and I was taken to task in no uncertain manner!

**Double tragedy in successive generations.** While reading through the Arnsdale school roll, I noticed No. 78, Lachlan MacTavish, Camusban, and recall how he became a Master on the Clyde Steamers, and sadly was drowned at Gourock Pier, leaving a son, two daughters and a widow. When I was employed by MacBraynes and sailing as Second Mate, with a Mate's Ticket, I decided to apply for study leave to sit for a Master's Certificate. Twelve weeks study leave was granted, and I duly enrolled in the Nautical College in John Street in Glasgow. Approximately a week later, the late Lachlan MacTavish's son, Duncan, also enrolled for his Master's Certificate, and the last time I had seen Duncan previously, was in Arnsdale at a time when he was employed with the Caledonia Steam Packet Co. as Mate on the Railway Steamers. It was a pleasant surprise to meet up with him again at the Nautical College, and after eight weeks intensive studying we decided to take the plunge and sat the exam, starting on the Monday and finishing on the Thursday. We both finished up on the Thursday afternoon with our Master's Tickets. Some years later, Duncan left the Railway Steamers and transferred to international lines. Sadly he met the same fate as his father, being drowned in Crete.

**Calum Rarsaidh. Master craftsman and strongman.** Many years ago there resided at the house at Rarsaidh a family of Camerons, the mother being commonly known as 'Cailleach Rarsaidh', Calum Cameron, the son, also known as Calum Rarsaidh, and Jessie Cameron, again known as Jessie Rarsaidh. They were a very kindly family and Calum had a flair for carving and joinery; he once carved a walking stick, creating two serpents entwined up the shaft and, finishing up with the heads as the handle. Calum could turn rough bits of wood into works of art. At one time, the County Council decided to renew the bridge at Rarsaidh and Calum took the old planks, sawed them into thinner plans, planed them and out of this emerged a kitchen dresser, complete with drawers, presses, and plate rack. Although Calum walked with a limp, he was a very fit man, and Donald Fletcher told me that Calum and Donald's father were out on the hill stalking for Eilanreach estate and shot a stag in the vicinity of Rarsaidh; however, by the time they dragged it down to the road side, the time was getting on in the day. It was near five o'clock and time to go home, so it was decided to leave the stag, and pick it up in the morning. When Donald's father arrived at the spot the next morning, the stag was gone. He immediately made for Rarsaidh Cottage, and on reporting to Calum that the stag was missing, Calum explained that he did not like the idea of leaving the stag by the roadside all night, so after his dinner, he hoisted the stag onto his back, and carried it some seven miles or so to the Eilanreach lodge larder - up all the formidable hills and down the steep braes.

**The Rarsaidh Ghost.** When old Mrs Cameron died, Calum and Jessie remained at Rarsaidh for a short time, but eventually Calum left to stay across at 'Lea' and Jessie came to Arnsdale, and stayed in a small house next door to Lexie Campbell and her daughter Mary Ann. Now, shortly before the Camerons left Rarsaidh Cottage, and for some time afterwards, stories started circulating around

Arnisdale that a ghostly figure was to be seen in the vicinity of Rarsaidh, and some folk thought it was in the form of old Mrs Cameron. Now, Lachie Fletcher told me that at this time, he was paying some attention to a girl at Eilanreach called Gertie MacLean, and one night there was a dance in Arnisdale Schoolhouse. Lachie collected Gertie at Eilanreach and took her on the pillion of the motor bike to the dance. When the dance finished, he took her back to Eilanreach and, when he was returning home, and approaching Rarsaidh, his thoughts circulated around the ghostly figure reported at Rarsaidh. As he was approaching the house, he opened up the throttle, and as the bike gathered speed, a terrifying rattling noise commenced behind him. When he heard this, he increased his speed, but the noise got even more terrifying - keeping pace with him! In desperation, Lachie decided to stop, investigate and face up to the rattling noisy ghost in close pursuit. He was never so relieved when he diagnosed the cause of the ghostly rattle. When he had suddenly increased his speed, the motorbike stand had come off its catch, fell down backwards on to the road, causing the terrible rattling sound, which got even worse as Lachie increased his speed to the limit of his motorbike's capacity, in a desperate attempt to escape from it.

**Tracing roots and family likenesses.** In 1840, my grandfather's brother emigrated to Roxburgh, Ontario in Canada and I still have a copy of a letter sent to my grandfather at Corran in 1880, asking after the health of all those at home in Corran and reporting on the Arnisdale and Glenelg exiles in his vicinity in Canada. Some two years ago, I read a request from a Mr Ferguson from Ontario seeking information regarding people of that name in Islay, from where his forebears came. I answered his request, giving details of Fergusons currently resident in Islay whom he could contact, and explained that I was interested in MacCuaigs who emigrated to Ontario, enclosed details from the letter sent to my grandfather in 1880 from his brother in Ontario. There was no immediate response but, one night I received a phone call, and this was Mr Ferguson, phoning from a Bed and Breakfast house in Bowmore, Islay. He and his brother then came to visit us, and it turned out that he was a Minister of a Baptist Church in Canada. He explained that he did some research on my behalf, but could not find any trace of our family at the address in Ontario where our people first settled. After that, in the summer of 1960, I was sent to join the MacBrayne Steamer, the Loch Seaforth, as Mate - sailing between Kyle of Lochalsh and Stornoway, and my future wife Bella and I had decided to get married on the First of September. About a fortnight before the wedding date, I came down to Glasgow for a long weekend and thence to Islay for Saturday and Sunday to finalise some details of the wedding. On reaching Islay, I was told that Bella received a phone call from an Alex MacCuaig from Canada who had been in Arnisdale and then he contacted the Loch Seaforth and eventually got Bella's phone number. He phoned the hotel where I was staying and we made arrangements to meet on the following Monday at my house in Glasgow at 7.30 p.m.

I had a brother, Iain, who died when he was 25 years old, and when I answered the door to the Canadian, I was struck by the close resemblance he had to my late brother, but he had so much detail and facts and figures that there was no doubt at all that a relationship existed between us. Both he and his wife were teachers, and the only thing that I regretted was that I could not spend a longer time with them - they were a very interesting couple. Chrissie, my cousin in Arnisdale, met them there and she also saw the resemblance to my late brother.

**Not dumb dogs that cannot bark!** Ewen Murchison's reference to the story of the plums stolen from the Arnisdale Lodge Garden in the 1930s brings to mind a story related to me by Donald Fletcher, regarding old John MacGillivray (Iain Beag) who was present at the inquest about the stolen plums. On rising up to address Captain Kitson, who was making rash accusations and was tending to intimidate, Iain Beag made his famous eloquent statement - "Do you think we are dumb dogs that cannot bark, I thank God that we are not". (See Chapter 18 for the full story).

**Precarious highway and the learner driver.** I also remember Roddy Mor telling me that when he first drove a car over the Glenelg to Arnsdale road, he picked up a couple of hikers outside Glenelg, and as they drove along, one of the passengers said to him, that it was 'some road' and only an experienced driver would attempt it; Roddy Mor said that he never replied but kept quiet about the fact that it was his own baptism of driving over the precarious thoroughfare.

I greatly enjoyed the Arnisdale fireside ceilidhs from my earliest years and the following varied tales are my memories of these regular ceilidhs involving a gathering of neighbours and friends around the Camusban and Corran firesides on many highly entertaining evenings.

**Location of the old pier.** Some folk have enquired about the location of the pier or jetty before the present jetty was constructed but I have no recollection of any mention of an old pier, other than the present jetty; however, I will relate a story I was told by Angus David MacIntosh that might have some bearing on the subject. When the "Herring Fishing" was at its height, there was a fisherman, who had the nickname of "Wingy" because he had only one arm, with only a stump in place of the other, and on one occasion he was drinking in the pub at Corran, when an argument ensued. This resulted in "Wingy" being chased along the road to Camusban. Now, it seems that at the bottom of the field below Roddy Mor's farmhouse was stored a large number of barrels, filled with brine, and "Wingy", realising he could not face his pursuers with only one arm, made for the barrels of brine. When his pursuers caught up with him, he steeped his empty sleeve in the brine and commenced to slosh his pursuers across the eyes, leaving them in agony. Now, whether or not the old pier was in that vicinity can not now be confirmed.

**Curing the herring.** With regard to the herring fishing, Angus David mentioned about a firm of curers who came to the Loch with fishing smacks by the name of O'Brian Brothers from Bristol, and if one reads the "Tales of Para Handy", by Neil Munro, mention is made of this firm of curers.

**The Loch Hourn Pubs.** With regard to licensed premises in Arnisdale and Loch Hourn, there was a licence at Skiary, approximately half way up the loch between Barrisdale and Lochhournhead, and also a similar licence in Corran. I understand that the Corran licence was where the MacDonald family resided, and the last person to hold this licence at that house was a man by the name of MacKillop. 'Do' MacKillop from Glen Quoich who was a great musician (violin and pipes) at the Arnisdale ceilidhs in the 1930 to 1960 period was descended from this family. As Duncan MacTavish explains in his memoirs, there was another pub close to the burn (Allt a'mhuilinn) at Camusban, one at Glenelg and the final one was at the Glenelg side of the Kylerhea Ferry, making a total of six hostelries from the Head of Lochhourn to Kylerhea Ferry - not bad going for those days!

**The Corran School.** At the bottom of the Corran Brae, and on the shore side, was situated a school, and I would presume that it was organised and run by the Free Church. While staying for a few days at Carrington Schoolhouse in Midlothian where my late cousin Iain resided with his wife Lexie, who was the teacher, I came across a book which related to the life story of an eminent Free Church Minister, who was commonly known as "Big MacRae of Kintail". It stated that at one time he taught at the school at Corran, Arnisdale, and on departing from Arnisdale to go to Edinburgh to study for the ministry, the good people of Arnisdale presented him with a home-made white shirt as a gift of appreciation.

**Open Air Worship in the old days.** While on the subject of Ministers, I was also told that when the Free Church separated from the established Church in 1843, they had no place to worship. Now, when you approach Arnisdale from Glenelg, and just before you climb up to the top of the Arnisdale brae, there is a form of bridge crossing a gully and called the "Balla Mòr" or the "Big Wall" and it was in this gully that the services were held until the Free Church was built in the latter half of last century.

**Origin of the MacCuaigs.** I was led to believe that the MacCuaigs came to the Arnisdale area from Dunvegan, where they were the Banner Carriers for the Clan MacLeod. It seems that after the death of a certain Chief, his successor had a different attitude to the Clan System and departed from the old order. This resulted in the Bard, who was known as the "Blind Minstrel" taking up residence at a place near Glenelg called "Tobhta Mor" and the MacCuaigs, MacLeods and MacCrimmons followed suit.

**Cosaig, Corran and its folk.** As you cross the bridge at Corran, and approach the end of the main access street, turn left, cross a small bridge, go up a short brae and you will come to a row of houses, this area being called "Cosaig". The first house belonged to a family by the name of Campbell, and another house was occupied by a Norman Morrison who was blind. Norman had a beautiful dog called "Help" which was similar to a Saint Bernard in size. The end house belonged to a Granny MacKenzie (Mairi Bhan), mother of the first 'Willie the Post'. Mairi Bhan was a survivor of the great typhoid epidemic in Arnisdale towards the end of last century.

**Neil the master gardener and Anna Park's ducks.** There was also a Neil MacCrimmon who resided at Corran. Neil, it seems, spent the best part of his life at sea, and had a brother John, who, according to my father, lived in the Hamiltonhill area of Glasgow, and was employed as a carter (I think that our great grandmother was a MacCrimmon). Now it seems that when this Neil MacCrimmon retired, he passed his time in gardening, in which he took a great pride, but living beside him in Corran was a woman called "Anna Park" who kept hens and ducks. It seems that her ducks were annoying Neil, by disturbing his garden. One day Anna heard a knock at her door, which was unusual in Corran in those days as most people just walked in without knocking, so tidying herself up, she opened the door, and standing in the door, was Neil with a duck in each hand held by the neck. He threw the ducks in her door and said that the next time they came into his garden, she would get them back in a pot of soup! Anna Park's son, Jimmie MacDonald married an English girl called Lily who came to the Lodge with the Kitsons and was for a while the housekeeper at the Lodge while Jimmie worked in the Lodge garden.

**Mr Phipps' devoted servant.** The first house on entering Corran and before crossing the bridge, was occupied by the MacAskill family, Allan and Lachie, Mary, Maggie and Jessie whose grandfather was known as "Ailean Iain Mor" or "Allan the son of Big John" and was head gamekeeper to Mr Phipps who owned Arnisdale Estate. It has been said that he was such a devoted servant to Mr Phipps, that when Phipps died, he left his entire estate to Allan his gamekeeper, but the will was contested and the relatives retrieved the Estate and possibly some of the monies.

**Mr Phipps' Highland funeral.** It seems that Mr Phipps requested a Highland funeral and his relatives, having a vague idea as to what constituted a Highland funeral, supplied a quantity of biscuits and cheese and whisky - so much so, in fact, that quite a few began to feel its effects. The service it seems, was held in the schoolhouse and was attended by shepherds, ghillies, keepers and stalkers. The service commenced by the minister taking his text from the book of Exodus, explaining to his congregation of mourners, how, although Abraham had gathered together a large flock of sheep and goats, he was still a godly man - when, from amongst the mourners came a voice, probably encouraged by the amount of spirits consumed, appealing to the preacher to talk less about sheep and goats as they had enough of them in their daily work! The minister being rather taken aback at this outburst, asked the precentor to sing a psalm, and some young blade shouted to him to sing a song as they had heard him singing the psalm tune Kilmarnock too often before and they wanted a change! When they reached the Cemetery, they had to wait for some of the mourners, and a Colin MacGillivray addressed the folk present by offering to sing a song about the Black Watch. On the road back to Corran, they found

Jimmie MacDonald asleep by the roadside. On asking where he was, Jimmie was told that he had been at Phipps' funeral but Jimmie retorted that this was nonsense as Mr Phipps' funeral was due the next day! So ended the Highland funeral of Mr Phipps.

**The typhoid epidemic.** The original thatched houses in Arnisdale were situated at the side of the existing road at Camusban and also at the bottom of the gardens at Corran. I think the only sign of those buildings at Camusban is between the Fletcher's house beside the burn and Archie MacLean's house. You will probably find that the letter box is fixed to what is left of the wall which is the remains of what was known as "Seann taigh Lex" or "Lexie's old house" (Lexie Campbell - mother of Mary Ann). Lexie Campbell and Mrs Mary MacKenzie (Mairi Bhan), the mother of Willie the Post, as he was known, were sisters of a family of five. At the latter end of last century, typhoid fever swept through the Highlands and took its toll of Arnisdale people, and I was told that in one week, sixteen coffins crossed the Corran Bridge, and Mary MacKenzie told my cousin Chrissie, that her father and mother died at Camusban with this fever when they were young and because of the fear of others contracting the disease, Mary had to return home from Glasgow to coffin her own father and mother.

**Marathon walks.** My father spoke quite often about the Foster family who lived next door to them in Corran. My father seemed to have a great liking for this family and especially a Sandy Foster. He used to relate the story of when he was a young ghillie at Glenquoich in the service of Lord Burton. He left Glenquoich on a Saturday afternoon and walked down the lochside to Corran, arriving in time for tea and then went to a ceilidh. He arose early on Sunday morning and, in the company of Sandy Foster they crossed over the shoulder of Beinn Sgritheall by Bealach Arnasdail and then went down into Glenshiel for the morning communion service at Glenshiel Free Church. After the evening service they returned to Corran by the same route, and, rising early on Monday morning, my father walked up the Glen until he reached Glenquoich (a distance of about 12 miles) in time for the start of his day's work at 7 a.m..

**Clever psychology.** At the top of Arnisdale glen are two lochs, which are called the "Dubh Lochain" or the "Black Lochs", presumably because of their depth and they seemingly abound with trout. My father told me that when he was a boy, it was decided by a number of them to go fishing in the lochs. With this in mind, they commenced to shape some rods from the hazel wood and, while engaged in this work, an old man passing by asked them what they were doing. They explained to him about their intended fishing trip. Now the old man nodded his head and, on leaving, warmly invited the boys to come and ceilidh with him that night - and the boys were delighted to do so. As the night wore on, the old man started to relate a tale, of how he was herding cattle one day at the lochs where the boys intended to go fishing. After a short while, a large beast arose out of the loch, which was half bull and half fish. On mixing with the cattle it served some of the cows, and eventually it returned to the loch. In quite some fear, the old man related that he moved his cattle away from the loch, and some months later, the cows had calves, and instead of ears, they had fish gills. When the boys heard the story, they gave up the idea of going fishing, and my father always maintained that this story had more effect on the boys than telling them not to go. The old man was obviously wanting to keep all the fish for the estate, on whose behalf he was acting.

**Kenny Fletcher's yarns.** There was many a night when Kenny Fletcher would come to our house in Camusban for a ceilidh. Kenny was a very knowledgeable man in relation to Arnisdale, and he mentioned that the names of Foster, Stoddart and MacMorran came up with the sheep at the time of the clearances and how a ship lay in the loch for approximately three weeks to take families away from the Arnisdale and Knoydart sides of Loch Hourn. My cousin Chrissie told me that if you walk along the coast line in both directions from Rarsaidh Cottage, you will find the ruins of houses by the shore and that the folk from all of these houses were evicted at that time and loaded on to the ship. Kenny also told me that at one time there was a cattle reiver at Barrisdale by the name of Macdonald who took up arms along with his followers in the Jacobite cause and was captured by Cumberland's army. As a result, the lands of Barrisdale were given to the Earl of Moray. Now, there was a woman at Barrisdale whose seven sons were also taken prisoner. One day, it seems, the mother of the seven sons, who was a widow and living off shellfish from the shore, was confronted by the Earl of Moray. He asked after her welfare, and the old widow replied, "You have taken my seven big sons, but thank God, I still have the big shore of Barrisdale". When the Earl of Moray heard the old lady's words, he gave orders that the Barrisdale shore be ploughed, so that even shellfish would be denied to her.

(See A. Carmichael 'Carmina Gadelica' VI, page 65 where it is said that Colla Bàn, second of Barrisdale, caused the strand to be ploughed up thus allowing the shellfish to rot. The old widow had said that she still had the shore after he had taken her cow from her).

Kenny also related that after the '45 and Prince Charlie's escape to France, there were messengers going through the Highlands, collecting money for the Prince in France. He also said that one such man was in Coire Dhorcuill on the Knoydart side of the loch and, in fear of being caught by the Redcoats, he buried the collected money below a beech tree. Kenny also told me that a chief of the MacDonalds who resided in Coire Scamadail on the Knoydart side of the loch and fought for the Prince, was ordered to appear in London to receive a pardon. On appearing before the King, he was asked if he was sorry for his actions; the reply from MacDonald was that he was not, and that if he had been supporting the King he would have done the same for him. The story goes that he was pardoned.

**Ceitag na stoirm (Kate of the storm).** Many years ago there was a nurse in Arnisdale by the name of Lisa Graham whose father before her was a Doctor in Tobermory, and later in Glenelg. Lisa was considered to be quite outstanding in her nursing duties. During her period as a nurse there was a family of MacPhersons staying at Red Point or the "Rudha Ruadh" on the Knoydart side, approximately two miles from Li towards the mouth of the Loch. One very wild winter's night, a light was seen in a window at Red Point, and this was an indication that medical help was required; when the nurse was informed she indicated that she must at all costs get across, as the woman (Mrs MacPherson) was expecting a child. A boat was immediately launched, and as far as I know, Angus Murchison, Donald MacCuaig, and two other men, whom I cannot name, manned the boat, with the nurse lying in the bottom and covered with a sail. Using four oars, they crossed the loch. I never heard how long it took them, but I was told that some way across one man suggested going back, but another advised to carry on, as turning the boat around with the gale that was raging, would be fatal. However, they reached over and after a while a girl was born, who was always known as "Ceitag na stoirm" or "Kate of the storm". Shortly after the birth they attempted to return across the loch, but had to come back to Red Point until daylight came, when they eventually managed to return to Arnisdale.

**A drowning tragedy. Effie Stewart.** In the late twenties or the early thirties, a number of tinkers were travelling from Kinloch Hourn to Arnisdale down the Glen on a day of continuous rain, and in the evening, one of the men appeared at Corran in a distressed condition, asking for help, saying that his wife had fallen into the Corran river, near the top of the glen (Gleann Dubh Lochain). A number of men from Arnisdale immediately made up the glen to see what could be done, but very sadly, they found the lady's body at the side of the river. It seems she attempted to cross the raging torrent and lost her footing. She was 28 years old and her name was Effie Stewart and came from Balallan in Lewis. Her remains were taken to the Free Church and later buried in Arnisdale Cemetery.

**Eilidh Hay from Corran. Lost and found.** When the herring fishing in Loch Hourn was at its height, there was a family by the name of Hay living at Corran. I think the man's name was Donald, his wife's name was Eilidh, they had a son called John and, living in the same house, was Donald's sister.

It seems that Donald's wife Eilidh and the sister did not agree, and one night there was a terrible row between wife and sister which resulted in the wife walking out of the house and disappearing. A search of the area was conducted but to no avail; some people said that she went away on a fishing boat, others had various suggestions but there was no trace of her. Eventually, the Hay family left Arnisdale and went to stay in Cathcart on the outskirts of Glasgow.

As a young man, my father decided to leave Arnisdale and go to sea and the day he left, in the company of Willie Fraser from Camusban, was the wedding day of Alexander Fletcher (Ally) and Christina (Tina) MacLeod, from the Home Farm. My father and Willie arrived in Glasgow and my father joined a ship called the Mountaineer and Willie obtained work, I think, as a gardener with John Stirling Maxwell at Pollok Estate outside Glasgow. Now Glasgow was like a foreign land to my father, but he became friendly with a sailor from Mull who was on the same ship. One Saturday evening in Glasgow, this sailor coaxed my father to go with him to the Jamaica Bridge where most Highlanders congregated, and on arriving at the bridge and talking to some other Highland people, a man approached my father who he immediately recognised as John Hay from Corran, and he invited my father to Cathcart to visit his father and give him all the news of Arnisdale.

Now John Hay, the son, married a girl from Glendale in Skye, who was a great friend of my mother, and it was at the Hay's house in Glasgow that my mother and father met. My father was eventually shifted to a ship called the "Claymore" and on the Claymore was a foreman stoker by the name of Beaton who came from Glenelg and knew the Hay family quite well. I think Beaton's first name was Donald. The Claymore berthed at Lancefield Quay in Glasgow and one day Beaton took a walk ashore and was walking along Argyle Street which is always a busy place. As he walked, a couple passed him, and in the passing he thought he recognised the woman, so he stopped and looked back, and noticed her looking back at him. Then he suddenly realised that he was looking at Eilidh Hay who had disappeared from Corran a few years before. He immediately turned back to speak to her, but unfortunately lost sight of her in the crowd. That solved the mystery of Eilidh's disappearance.

**The stretched stories of Cailean Iain.** In Camusban there was a man by the name of Colin MacGillivray who was known by the Gaelic name of "Cailean Iain" or "Colin, the son of Iain" whose stories were considered to be rather far fetched. One story relates to another man from Arnisdale who was a shepherd, herding a flock of sheep from Arnisdale to Strathcarron to be loaded on to the train there for sale at Dingwall market. It was at this time that the railway line from Strathcarron to Kyle was being laid and a considerable amount of rock blasting was in progress when this shepherd arrived with his sheep. Now, this man never heard such a noise in his life, and when he returned to Arnisdale, he started to relate the story of the blasting, and how the noise re-echoed through the hills. Colin was listening, and - not to be in the background, he started to relate about a blast that went off at the head of Loch Hourn which was so strong that it was a week later before the stones started to come back down from the heavens!

A wedding took place in Arnisdale Schoolhouse at which the same Colin MacGillivray was present, and a David MacIntosh who was related to our family, was asked to say the Grace. Now it seems the Grace was quite lengthy, blessing this and that person and - after a while, David said "Amen". Colin lifted his head remarking that it was about time the "Amen" was said as the Grace was too long. David replied that it was not as long as the eel that Colin was supposed to have seen, when the head of the eel passed the mouth of the Loch on Monday and it was Saturday before they saw the tail!

**The Lonacs and the Coulags.** There was a friendly rivalry between the folk of the two villages Camusban (The Lonacs) and Corran (the Coulags) and one day the Camusban men were engaged in shearing sheep at the Camusban fank and some of the Murchison boys from Corran arrived at the fank.

Seemingly, there was some good natured banter going back and forth, and Johnnie Murchison made the remark that if there was a contest as to which village had the laziest men Camusban would win. An answer was immediately given by Angus David MacIntosh, that this would probably be quite right as the Corran men would be too lazy to enter!

Having written what I can remember, I would say that Arnisdale was a very tight-knit community and if illness came to any family, they were not alone, as the whole community became involved. If any young person was leaving to take up employment, money was usually donated to help them on their way.

These are some of my memories of Arnisdale and my only regret is that we did not listen and take more heed of what was happening and all the stories told around the fireside. I was brought up in Glasgow and sometimes when Colin Murchison's family were away from home and he was on his own, he would come down for a ceilidh, which would usually last into the early hours of Saturday morning. The talk, of course, was almost all about Arnisdale and Loch Hourn.

**Top Left**. Donald MacCuaig, now resident in Islay with his wife Bella, daughter Mairi, grand-daughter Kerry and son Iain.  **Right**. Donald's father John MacCuaig (left) with Maggie MacTavish (Bean Angan) and Johnny MacGillivray,. Johnny had his shop in Camusban and was also a part-time roadman.

**Middle Left.** Donald's mother Mary (nee MacDiarmid), who came from Glendale in Skye (centre) with Jessie 'Lea' (left) and Maggie 'Lea' at the Mission House in Arnisdale.  Mary's family were very involved in the Land League Movement in Skye which eventually won better rights for the crofters in the 1880s.  **Right**. Donald's brother Iain who died at the age of 25.

**Bottom Left**. Donald (far left) with a group of Arnisdale friends around 1960.  L to R.  Donald, Jackie Morrison, Nellie Leitch (nee MacKenzie), Mary Leitch, Christina MacKenzie and Morag MacIntyre.  **Right**. Donald and brother Iain experienced great excitement as boys in Glasgow when the school holidays arrived and it was time to set off on the train to Mallaig and board MacLennan's boat on the regular Tuesday run to Arnisdale. The culmination came when the Bounty finally arrived at the Arnisdale pier and the 'Ceud Mile Failte' received from a crowd of Arnisdale friends.

205

**Top Left**. A group of Lonacs on a fine day in Camusban in the 1920-30 era. Seated L to R. Kenny, Peter and Lachie Fletcher, Molly Fraser, Nora MacDonald, Mary MacCuaig, Iain MacCuaig. Rear. Donald and Farquhar Fletcher, Johnny Sinclair and Donald MacCuaig (with head bandage). The Lonacs were the Camusban folk while the 'Coulags' were the Corran folk. There was always friendly rivalry and witty banter between the two villages. **Right**. Donald MacCuaig (left) and Roddy Fletcher having a short break for a cup of tea at the haymaking on the Fletcher family croft.

**Middle Left.** Aonghas Dhaidh MacKintosh (left) with John MacCuaig outside Johnny MacGillivray's shop (1930s). When the stories of the Loch Hourn monster came in to his mind, Aonghas Dhaidh returned to shore very quickly from his intended fishing trip. His experiment with 'substitute tobacco' during wartime rationing did not work out too well either! **Centre.** Aonghas Dhaidh (left) with Mary Kate MacTavish and Roddy Mor. **Right**. Johnny Sinclair (centre) with Donald's father John MacCuaig (left) and Donald Sheorais Campbell. Johnny was one of Arnisdale's practical jokers.

**Bottom Left**. Next door neighbours to the MacCuaig's family home in Camusban, were the very kindly Mary Ann MacCuaig (right) and her mother Lexy. Lexy had very poor eyesight which was attributed to the typhoid epidemic in Arnisdale around 1890 which claimed the lives of both of her parents. **Right**. 'Seann taigh Lex' or Lexy's old house. This ruin at the roadside close to the Fletcher and 'Archie MacLean' family homes in Camusban was that in which Lexy's parents succumbed to typhoid. The house was abandoned and the ruin left untouched through fear of infection. It is now 'home' to the Camusban letterbox.

**Top Left**. A faded photograph of the line of the old thatched houses in Camusban which were situated very close to the shore and were flooded by the great high tide in 1881. 'Seann Taigh Lex' is the only remnant of these houses remaining although 'Johnny Sinclair's' house on the west side of Allt an t-Siucair was also rebuilt in the 1930s on the site of one of these old houses in the Camusban 'street'.
**Right**. Nurse Graham (left) doing her District Nurse rounds in Arnisdale (around 1930s). With her is Mrs Jane Campbell (centre) and Mairi Bhan both of whom lived in Cosaig, Corran. Nurse Graham's father, the local Doctor resident in Glenelg, also died during the typhoid epidemic after visiting his patients in Arnisdale. Nurse Graham was also involved in the rowing boat crossing across a raging Loch Hourn to attend at the birth of 'Ceitag an stoirm' in Rudha Ruadh after the 'distress signal' was noted in Camusban.

**Middle Left**. The lone house at Rudha Ruadh directly across from Camusban on the Knoydart shore where 'Ceitag an stoirm' was brought safely into this world. The island just offshore is Eilean a'Phiobaire. **Right**. A group of Arnisdale Estate gamekeepers/ stalkers/ghillies in the 1910-20 period in the days when Mr Phipps was the shooting tenant. L to R. John MacCuaig, Rory Foster, Angus Murchison, Jimmy MacDonald and Allan MacAskill. (Ailean Iain Mor). Allan was head gamekeeper and a very devoted servant to Mr Phipps.

**Bottom Left**. Jimmy MacDonald, Corran at his wedding to Lily Rosier who worked at the Lodge. Others standing are (L to R.) John MacCuaig, Mr and Mrs MacMorran, and Donald MacCuaig. Seated on the right is best man Colin Murchison. Jimmy 'featured' in Mr Phipps' Highland Funeral. Jimmy's mother, Anna Park, was 'not popular' with her master gardener neighbour, Neil MacCrimmon when her ducks raided his immaculate garden! **Right**. Effie Stewart as a young girl in Glenelg with her older sister Mrs Isabella MacDonald. Effie was drowned in 1905 when trying to cross the Arnisdale River when in spate at the age of 28 years. Effie is buried in the Arnisdale Churchyard.

**Top Left**. Arnisdale churchyard and the Free Church which was built around 1880 in the great days of the herring fishing and financed by donations of the local folk and collections among the very large numbers of fishermen on the herring drifters and other boats massed on Loch Hourn. The squad of volunteers keeping the graves and churchyard tidy are L to R. Kate Fletcher, John MacGillivray, Mary MacLean, Annie MacIntyre, Ludovic Fraser, Sen., Kirsty MacKintosh, Archie MacLean, Archie MacGillivray, Andrew Fraser, Maryann MacCuaig and Angan MacTavish. **Right**. The Balla Mor or big wall just over the Arnisdale brae on the road to Glenelg. After the Free Church separated from the Established Church in 1843 and the Free Church folk had no place of worship they often worshipped in the sheltered little Coire to the left of the road in this picture.

**Middle Left.** The Balla Mor which was erected to support the roadway at this point. **Right**. The view looking westwards at the Balla Mor with the Coire in which worship took place on the left, the Balla Mor and the vista towards Knoydart and the Sound of Sleat. The remains of the old road to Arnisdale at this point runs between the trees in the middle of the picture and the rock on the right.

**Bottom Left**. Andrew Fraser (front row, second from right) who mischievously caused great panic among the Arnisdale Lodge staff, and old Kirsty MacKintosh (sixth from left in top left hand picture) in particular, by asserting that the arrival of the Kitsons at the Lodge was imminent. Others in this Mialairidh Forestry squad of the 1930s are Back row (L to R.) Peter Fletcher, Tony MacKay (Forester), Ludovic Fraser, Iain Elder, Jimmy Campbell. Front (L to R.) Donald MacKintosh (Rarsaidh), Bobby MacLean, Archie MacLean, Andrew Fraser and Angus Stewart. **Right**. Ally Fletcher with his wife Christina (1920s). When Ally went to Rarsaidh to find the stag he and Calum Cameron, Rarsaidh had shot the previous day to carry it to Eilanreach it had disappeared. Calum 'Rarsaidh', despite his limp, had carried it the 7 miles to Eilanreach himself the previous night!

# Chapter 16.

**The Murchison family. Their achievements and memories.**

The story of the Murchison family from Corran would require several volumes to relate in full so this coverage can only provide a flavour of the background, character and achievements of this crofting family.

Fine accounts have already been written about members of this family and some of these will be reproduced later as they epitomise the character of the family as a whole and also help to provide a picture of their roots and ideals. The personal memories of two members of this family are presented at the end of this chapter and they help to preserve the unique spirit which prevailed in the past in the Corran community, but perhaps more particularly in the family home.

As a prelude to these accounts and family memories, some brief details of family history along with aspects of the author's recollections of, and continuing communication with, members of the Murchison family will be outlined.

The main focus of this coverage is the family of Angus Murchison (1874-1953) and of his wife Catherine (nee Sutherland) (1875-1962), the latter being born and brought up in Portree. Angus' mother was Christina Murchison (nee MacCuaig) who was born in Arnisdale and could remember the sailing ship, the Liscard, coming into Loch Hourn in 1849 to take on board 314 inhabitants of the Glenelg, Loch Hourn and Knoydart areas, most of whom were cleared from their crofts to make way for the letting of the vacated lands by the laird to tenant farmers and their large flocks of sheep. Christina's husband, Colin Murchison, came from Glenelg.

Angus and Catherine had seven children - Colin, Hector, Alan, Katie, Angus Duncan, Ewen and Johnnie in that order. The wherewithal to sustain the large family came from the small croft and fishing on Loch Hourn, while Angus also at various times had part-time employment from the County Council in maintaining part of the Arnisdale-Glenelg road and also as part-time factor to one of the Arnisdale lairds - Sir Harmood Banner. Angus also acted as Corran Crofting Township Clerk for over 50 years but this was an honorary unpaid post, which involved administrative work on behalf of his fellow crofters which Angus performed with diligence, skill and considerable initiative. Angus derived great pleasure and satisfaction from these honorary duties on behalf of his fellows.

The family attended the local Arnisdale school for their primary education and through determination, hard graft, and self-sacrifice, ways were found to enable the children to obtain a secondary education, some in Fort William and others in Portree. The children, in turn, responded magnificently to the efforts of their parents and their outstanding achievements in elevated positions in the professions and public service are highlighted later.

To provide for their large family, the small croft and the garden had to be well worked and the two cows along with their sheep in the township flock had to be well husbanded. The sale of lambs and weaned calves provided a large part of the family's meagre annual income while milk from the cows, potatoes and garden produce constituted a vital part of the food requirements of a hard grafting, energetic family. The garden ground and croft land had to be kept in good heart with the help of dung from the byre, seaweed from the shore and a good crop rotation. No waste could be tolerated. This applied also, of course, to the sea fishing. If unthinking youngsters went out to fish, and in the excitement of pulling in big catches on their lines, caught more than was required by the family and all the neighbours, so that surplus fish were wasted, they would get a severe scolding from Grandma Murchison. She would spell out to them in gentle but very firm tones about the necessity to avoid waste and to conserve for 'tomorrow'. Crofters like Grandma Murchsion were always preaching the need to conserve fish stocks and other vital natural resources - and they practised what they preached with great diligence. If only their preachings were heeded by those whose main motives are greed and 'self' without thought of tomorrow, next year and the next generation!

Fuel for working and winter warmth had also to be won from the cutting and curing of peats often far distant from the homestead. Neighbour Chrissie Morrison (nee MacCuaig) remembers the great creel loads of peat Grandma would be carting home on her back, often from as far away as Blar an Each - almost 2 miles away from Corran. Driftwood from the shore was another source of fuel and was harvested meticulously and regularly.

When the author first visited and spent time in Arnisdale in 1946, Grandpa and Grandma Murchsion were still running the croft. However, while all members of the family by this time had set up their own homes in the cities and were in elevated positions in the professions and public service, they would all come back 'home' for their summer vacation. No doubt, they regarded their summer sojourn in Arnisdale as a holiday because they would be ceilidhing with their old friends, catching up on the news, relating new yarns, going out in the boat for a row or a sail, and fishing of course, but they would also have plenty of work to do. The hay had to be scythed and 'worked' a great deal before it could be won and carted into the barn for the winter sustenance of the cattle, the sheep had to be gathered from the hill, clipped and the wool packed and despatched for sale, peats had to be taken home and stored for winter, the cows had to be milked twice daily, water carted from the burn and the river and there was a host of other daily chores to be done.

On meeting up with the Murchisons for the first time, one got the impression of a very lively, interesting family. The boys such as Colin and Johnnie would appear at Roddy Mor's sheep clipping unannounced, armed with their shears, there would be hearty reunions with Roddy and Lizzie and the rest of the clipping gang - and then they would just get down to work. With the quiet snip-snip tones of sharp shears on the dry wool of sheep with a good 'rise' on the fleece, conversation - almost invariably in the Gaelic - was clear and incessant. There would be exchanges of bits and pieces of news interspersed with considerable 'leg-pulling' and laughter. Johnnie, the youngest of the Murchsion family was a master of repartee. There was always great rivalry between the Camusban and Corran folk and with representatives from both of the Townships usually present at the clipping, the 'crack' was always highly entertaining. It made the work light! The exchanges between Johnnie, as the Corran spokesman, and Donald Fletcher from Camusban, when these two got together were a source of great amusement to all and many of their witticisms are still well remembered.

The Murchison's neighbour at Corran, Chrissie Morrison (nee MacCuaig) relates the story of Johnnie teasing the two Skye ladies - his own mother who belonged to Portree and Chrissie's mother who hailed from Ardvasar. Johnnie was telling them that the incessant Arnisdale rain was all coming from Skye and the island should be blown up to get rid of it altogether. The two ladies gave as good as they got, claiming that, if Skye was not sitting there protecting Arnisdale from the Atlantic gales, 'Arnisdale would be blown away out of the universe altogether!'

Johnnie had attended Secondary School in Portree, residing with his Sutherland relatives there. There Johnnie got the shinty 'bug', playing the game with his cousin Johnny Sutherland and his other schoolmates. He became a fine player, representing his University and later the Glasgow Skye Club in local and national competitions. Later Johnnie became a top administrator in the game and was elected as President of the Camanachd Association, the sport's ruling body. It was during his tenure of this high office that he met his very untimely end in a tragic road accident. Johnnie was highly respected in the medical world as a General Practitioner and he is well remembered as one of Arnisdale's entertainers.

As well as their academic, professional and public service accolades, the Murchisons, in addition to Johnnie, are well remembered for their sporting achievements; four of the brothers - Colin, Hector, Angus Duncan and Ewen formed a formidable team of rowers, winning many major competitions, including the Scottish Fours Rowing Championship in the 1930s. This quartette represented the Clydesdale Amateur Rowing Club in these Championships and often their closest rival was a Glasgow University team which included their youngest brother Johnnie.

The sole survivor of the family at the time of writing is Surgeon Captain Ewen Murchison who had an outstanding career as a surgeon and in the Royal Navy. He is now living in retirement in Gibraltar. Ewen remembers very well a famous Arnisdale incident which took place after his first year in Glasgow University as a young medical student. This story about the stolen plums from the Arnisdale Lodge garden is told in detail in Chapter 18. Briefly, the local people had been accused by the laird of 'pinching' all his plums on the Sabbath Day. The local folk were appalled by such an accusation and harnessed the skills of young Ewen as the Chairman at a 'Court of Enquiry' which they called with the laird. Ewen contrived to prove the innocence of the locals and to extract an apology from the laird.

Another amusing incident involving Surgeon Captain Ewen occurred in the Mediterranean in May 1967. The author's elder brother, Sandy, a Naval Officer on board HMS Hermes with 826 Squadron, ended up in sick bay at the Royal Naval Hospital, Gibraltar. In the recovery phase following a small operation, Sandy had occasion to meet up with the Surgeon Captain in a formal meeting. After formalities were covered, the Surgeon Captain remarked "I see that you are an Inverness man. I'm an Inverness man myself". Something went 'click' in Sandy's mind and he asked: "Do you know Lizzie MacLeod, Sir?" "Goodness gracious man, she taught me at school", retorted the Surgeon Captain. "Well, she's my aunt, Sir", said Sandy. That was the prelude to mutual Arnisdale friends being remembered and tales of Loch Hourn retold.

The first of the Arnisdale brothers to leave Arnisdale to work was Allan. Older brothers Colin and Hector had already left home to attend Secondary School in Fort William and Allan insisted on going to Portree on leaving Arnisdale school to be apprenticed to his uncle, Bob Sutherland, Carpenter and Boat Builder. Allan spent 5 years in Portree and his wage of £8 per year was a great help to family finances at home in Corran. When Allan returned home he was employed by the Arnisdale Estate, where he helped Daniel MacDonald and Angan MacTavish to look after and crew the Estate boats - the Morag and the Noressian. As well as using his building skills on other jobs around the Estate he also helped his father to put a second floor on the family home in Corran. Such tarrying in the old home paid dividends for Allan, for a young Skye girl, Cathy Finlayson, came to work in the Lodge and in due course Cathy became Mrs Allan Murchison. Camina, Allan and Cathy's daughter, relates her wonderful memories of Arnisdale, the old family home and of her Grandma and Grandpa later in this chapter.

The best appreciation of the character and achievements of the Murchison family is in the press cuttings containing tributes to individual members following their death and reports on others of accolades received. From those available, the ones selected to be reproduced here are those reports following the death of old Angus, the patriarch of the family and of Colin, the eldest of the family. Thereafter, reports on prestigious appointments and honours for Hector and Ewen are presented.

**Loss to Arnisdale.  The late Mr Angus Murchison, Corran**

**(From The Oban Times, December 1954)**

The death occurred on December 2 at Corran, Arnisdale, Inverness-shire, in his 81st year, of Angus Murchison, the last of the three sons of the late Mr and Mrs Colin Murchison.  Mr Murchison lived all his life at Arnisdale and besides attending to a croft, he in his early days was engaged in fishing;  and for many years he was a road contractor on the Arnisdale-Glenelg Road.

He also at some time or another was in the employ of all the proprietors of Arnisdale within the past sixty years, including the present proprietor, Captain Kitson, and in that of the late Sir Donald Cameron of Lochiel at Achnacarry.

Blessed with an intelligence and memory above average, Mr Murchison could draw on a vast fund of local folk-lore and incident to illustrate a point or enliven conversation and it was rare that he would not add a verse or two from a well-known song or poem or even the doggerel lines of some local rhymester.  His knowledge of natural history was extensive for one who made no special study of it, and his particular interests were game birds and deer.  Having gone over any ground but once he seemed to be able to retain an almost photographic record of it and this, combined with an uncanny facility for estimating heights and distances, meant that in conversation he was informative as well as interesting.

He was secretary of the local crofting township for over fifty years and in fact only relinquished this office at his death.  He was much interested in communal improvements and enlargement of holdings and, as secretary, much of the effort to secure these fell upon him;  in this respect those of us who are left owe him a real debt.  He took an active part in all church matters, and until a few years ago when his rich tenor voice began to fail, he led the praise at the Arnisdale church services.

It is almost certain that Mr Murchison would have gone South or even abroad but for the death of his father at a comparatively early age;  by not going away he met and married Catherine Sutherland, elder daughter of Hector Sutherland who had a boat building business in Portree.  This marriage proved a most happy one;  it lasted just over fifty-three years and they reared a family of seven.  Both parents were ambitious for their family and, by dint of striving and sacrificing, they gave them the opportunity of acquiring a higher education.  Three of the family chose a University career and it must have been of gratifying satisfaction that, long before he died, he and his wife saw each one of the seven holding a position of responsibility in their several careers.  He is survived by his widow, daughter Catherine and six sons, Colin, Hector, Allan, Angus, Ewen and John.

The funeral was to the local graveyard.  The chief mourners being his six sons;  Angus the eldest grandson;  Mr Lachlan McLaren, nephew;  Messrs Alex and Robert Sutherland, brothers of the widow;  Mr Ewen MacRae, brother-in-law;  and Mr Thomas Fleming, nephew.  The funeral service was conducted, as the departed hoped it would be, by the Rev. A MacKinnon, former parish minister at Glenelg, assisted by Mr Daniel Macdonald, former missionary at Arnisdale.  As is customary in the Highlands, a service was conducted at the house on the evening of the death and this was done by the Rev. A MacLennan, present missionary at Arnisdale.

And so ended the tribute to Angus, the patriarch of the Murchison Family.

The following tribute was to Colin, the oldest of the family.

### Education Convener dies.   Mr Colin Murchison, MBE, MA.   Arnisdale

(From "The Oban Times", 6 October 1966)

Inverness-shire education convener, Mr Colin Murchison, Arnisdale, Glenelg, died last week at his home.  Son of a crofter, he was a former Glasgow headmaster.  In the General Election of 1959, Mr Murchison unsuccessfully contested Ross and Cromarty as a Liberal.  In 1963 he was elected to Inverness County Council and in the following year was appointed chairman of the education committee.  Mr Murchison's many qualities and interests are referred to in the following appreciation received by the editor of the "Oban Times":-

It is with regret that we announce the death of Mr Colin Murchsion, MBE, MA., on September 27.  He died at his home in Arnisdale where he was born and brought up and where he and Mrs Murchison retired three years ago.  By profession he was a teacher in Glasgow; a member of the science department of North Kelvinside School and latterly headmaster of Miltonbank, one of the new schools of the city.  Many of his contemporaries followed a similar course but withdrew from the game to become spectators.  Colin Murchison was elected by his peers to represent his area in the County Council of Inverness, and spent much of his retirement as convener of the Education Committee.  To close the book at this point and say "This is your life", would be true, but so far short of the whole truth as to be quite misleading.  He was far from being a one-track "educationist".

On the wall of the board room of the Clydesdale Rowing Club is a faded photograph from which a crew of four Murchison brothers look out with folded arms and solemn countenance over a silver cup and a diminutive cox.  The memory of that regatta and of that Murchison Four is as dim as the photograph, but Colin Murchison never ceased to be an active, fully-committed member of the club.

In 1942, when there was every excuse for postponing difficult undertakings, he instituted the Glasgow Schools Rowing Club.  He overcame the doubts of the Clydesdale committee, the inertia of authority and the sceptism of colleagues.  He lived to see a membership of 700 boys and a fleet that two boathouses held with difficulty.  He never accepted the peerage but served under successive presidents as humbly and as eagerly as the newest enthusiast.  He played golf with pleasure and badminton with formidable skill;  he was for three years president of the Partick Camera Club;  but the Glasgow Schools Rowing Club was his life work - the corner stone of his memorial.

All this is true and still misleading.  People who are efficient and successful can often be dull or heartless or both.  Colin Murchison was never dull.  His talk was always quick and lively and wide-ranging.  He was an appreciative listener too - which is the rarer gift - one for whom his friends saved up the joke or the witty saying.  His successes in various fields never and in no way went to his head.  His shrewd common-sense seemed always to be deployed on behalf of someone or some object other than himself.  His was not the vague benevolence that says, "If there is anything I can do...", but the firm-edged kindness that says "I shall call round at 2.30" or "Leave that to me and I'll send you the information tomorrow".

By the same token his affection for his native shire and his native tongue was as unequivocal as the granite of which his house is built.  He was not the kind of exile who sits in one of the four cities singing "'s truagh nach robh mi . . .".  He lived the city life to the full but his land was never neglected; the educationist had a goodly flock of sheep on the hill; the honorary president was crofters' secretary.  His Gaelic was not for Ossianic laments about the "Gleann 'san robh mi og", but for the telephone and the wool-clip and the social crack.  On the Mallaig train it would take him a good half-hour in Gaelic or English to make his way from one end of a Pullman coach to the other.

His house in Arnisdale was like one of those mysterious castles in Campbell's Tales which the Younger Son finds of an evening at the end of a houseless road. It needs little trans-position to see him and his wife as the lord and lady of it. More people from widely separated walks of life must have visited that house beyond the "End of the Road" sign than ever called at any house within the reach of a corporation bus or the Blue Train. One did not cross Mam Ratagan nor thread the Arnisdale road for morning coffee or afternoon tea. As in Campbell's Tales there was "food in the place of eating and sleep in the place of sleeping" and good crack until far too late.

His was a personality rich in fine qualities. In his wife, in his son Angus and in his daughter Mary - three differing personalities - are to be seen the same admirable common factors. In them and in their households a full and varied life was rounded off and completed. He lived in two worlds and made the best of both of them. The final proof, if proof were needed, was the close knit company of friends at the Gaelic service of farewell in Arnisdale, and the great gathering of many groups from many circles at the Western Necropolis in Glasgow.

His was a personality rich in fine qualities, he was "fervent in spirit"; and though he never advertised the fact, he was all his life "serving the Lord".

**An Appreciation by Dr MacLean**

Dr J A MacLean, Director of Education for Inverness-shire, writes in appreciation:

"It was with profound regret and sadness that his wide circle of friends in his native Glenelg and elsewhere learned of the sudden death of Mr Colin Murchsion. Born in Arnisdale on the northern shore of Loch Hourn towards the beginning of the century, Mr Murchison completed his school education at Fort William at a time when pupils and parents from remote areas made great sacrifices for the sake of education. It was certainly so for Mr Murchsion for in those days when public transport was unknown he frequently made the long journey on foot across the Rough-bounds of Lochaber between his home and the school.

In due course he went to Glasgow University where he took a degree with a strong bias towards mathematics. His long career as a teacher was devoted entirely to service in Glasgow, and during the latter part of this he was headmaster of one of the city's newest schools. In that position he was much loved by teachers, parents and children. His single-mindedness and his regard for his fellows ensured for him a place of respect and affection wherever he went.

It was obvious during those long and happy years that Mr Murchison constantly dreamt of the day when he would return to Glenelg and this he did as soon as the retiral regulations permitted. The preparations that he made for his return to the old family house along with his devoted wife, herself a fellow-student of his and a teacher in Glasgow, were unmistakable evidence of his desire to spend his latter days among his people. Sad it is that these days were so few.

Before his retiral he was already representing his native parish on the County Council of Inverness and two years ago he became Chairman of its Education Committee. This appointment - which came to him entirely unsolicited - gave him great satisfaction. His enthusiasm for the work of the committee was unbounded and nothing was ever any trouble to him if it was for the good of the children and those who taught them.

This handsome, genial and kindly Highlander will long be remembered for his devotion to the cause of the young, his loyalty to his fellows, and above all, the kind and generous attitude that he displayed to others at all times. It was indeed a privilege to have known him."

Following these glowing press tributes to Colin, there follows press reports on the achievements of two of Colin's younger brothers, Hector and Ewen.

**Superintendent Hector Murchison - Native of Arnisdale**

**(From 'The Oban Times - 1947)**

The youngest, aged 43, of the three senior police officers recently promoted in Glasgow was Supt. Hector Murchison, second son of Mr and Mrs Angus Murchison, Arnisdale, Inverness-shire. Mr Murchison received his early education at the village school at Arnisdale and then at Fort William Secondary School where he took his Leaving Certificate. After leaving school he served with the L.N.E. Railway Company as a junior clerk before joining the Glasgow Police Force in 1926.

In police work he found plenty of scope for his interests and his energies, and showing early promise of a high sense of duty and of organising ability, his promotion was rapid. While still a constable, this trait for organising was recognised when a scheme he submitted for the reorganisation of the Glasgow Police Force was largely used in the scheme that was finally adopted at that time. But perhaps the biggest tribute to his ability came in 1941 when he was seconded to the Ministry of Civil Defence and appointed Chief Fire Guard Officer for the city. This department had to be built right from the bottom, and an idea of the magnitude of the task may be gathered from the fact that the organisation under him contained more than 100,000 Fire Guards with a further 3300 or so of promoted ranks, and a secretarial staff of three dozen. He was informed he had organised the largest unit in the whole of Britain.

Two years ago he was on the short leet for the post of Chief Constable of Greenock, and last year he was on the corresponding leet for the Aberdeen post. Mr Murchison now goes from the Govan Division, where he was appointed second in command on his return from Civil Defence duties, to the Southern Division, and as Police Superintendent of that Division will be directly responsible for the handling of the biggest sporting crowds in the world - the Hampden football crowds.

Superintendent Murchsion, enriched by a wealth of experience in all branches of police work, including nearly seven years at Headquarters, strikes one by his quiet, confident demeanour as being ideally equipped to address the very formidable challenges of this prestigious and responsible undertaking."

**"Surgeon Captain Murchison appointed Hon. Surgeon to the Queen.**

(From The Oban Times - 18 May 1966)

"Surgeon Captain E H Murchison, R.N., medical officer in charge of the Royal Naval Hospital, Gibraltar, and surgeon-consultant for the Navy, has been appointed honorary surgeon to Her Majesty the Queen. Educated at Portree High School, the Surgeon Captain, who is the second youngest son of the late Mr and Mrs Angus Murchsion, Arnisdale, Glenelg, Inverness-shire, after a brilliant studentship, qualified at Glasgow University in 1935 and joined the Royal Navy in 1936.

His first appointment found him casualty surgeon on the Spanish coast during the civil war helping refugees under the non-intervention agreement. During the Second World War he was seconded to work with Sir Harold Gillies as a plastic surgeon on blitz casualties. He was subsequently in charge of the Royal Naval Hospital at Hvitanes, Iceland, and then went to the Royal Naval Hospital, Sherbourne, where he did plastic and orthopaedic reconstructive surgery. Thereafter he moved his unit to the Royal Naval Hospital, Haslar, and there founded "Orthopaedics" in the Navy.

Surgeon Captain Murchsion was awarded the O.B.E. in 1949. He is a founder member of the Association of Plastic Surgeons, and a Fellow of the Association of Surgeons. When time permits the Surgeon

Captain holidays at his cottage at Balmacara, Ross-shire."

These reports speak for themselves and reflect a wonderful collective package of endeavour, talent, initiative, achievement and service of their fellows emanating from a home humble in nature but rich in terms of purity and spirit.

There now follows some personal recollections of Ewen of his boyhood days, and of the memories of Camina, niece of Ewen and daughter of Alan, of her holidays in Arnsdale.

**Ewen's recollections of his boyhood days in Arnisdale - penned at his home in Gibraltar in June 1997**

Within the limits of the memory of my boyhood I have appended a list of houses in Corran with names of occupants at that time. The house in Achadh a'Ghlinne and the one by the lochs at Crionach in the Arnisdale Glen were not occupied in my time but were well known and used by the nomadic fraternity.

The story of the plums seems to have travelled far and wide!! On arrival back from my first year in the University (Glasgow), I was entreated by the community to attempt to exonerate them from Captain Kitson's accusations that some of the local people had stolen his prize plums - a rated product of his garden. To add insult to injury the alleged crime occurred on a Sabbath.

As the folk all seemed so upset about the whole affair, I decided to challenge the Goliath - Kitson to a confrontation in the Schoolroom. The outcome of the meeting was a retraction of the accusations, and an apology for the outrageous suggestion that any local person was capable of such a heinous deed on the Lord's Day.

The Sabbath was indeed a Special Day but whether this was strictly in observance of the dictates of the Almighty or merely to impress one's neighbours is open to question. Be that as it may, everyone turned out in their best bib and tucker, with the occasional deferential sign coming from the elderly. Although the denominations were confined to Wee Frees, United Frees and Church of Scotland (Moderates), there was considerable rivalry between them, but to the best of my knowledge, no one was actually burnt at the stake!

The advent of radio created quite a problem as listening on Sunday was confined to the "news" and a religious sermon, provided the latter emanated from the appropriate spiritual source. This accurate timing demanded trustworthy clocks and watches as the accidental emission of a musical note etc. was not allowed to disturb the sanctity of the day. We youngsters managed to let off steam in some remote area, well away from the prying eyes of our mentors.

Despite the solemnity of the occasion, and the absence of material thoughts, in some mysterious way, a promising weather outlook on Sunday guaranteed the assembly of all fit males before 6 a.m. on Monday for sheep gathering and shearing. The sheep gathering itself was arranged with military precision; the oldest were given positions at the foot of Beinn Bhuidhe and the rest strategically placed, some at the summit depending on their agility, experience, and the quality of their dogs. Until we left them at baseline, the old timers - Angus Stewart (Snr) and Norman Morrison invariably amused us with their vituperative arguments, delving into the past without thought of legal reprisals for slander! If they showed any signs of wavering, Willie McKenzie or Sandy MacAskill would 'throw them a sprat' to get them reignited! I thoroughly enjoyed those outings away from hard work and city grime.

As a sideline, I suppose my father could be referred to as Crofting Township Clerk as he undertook the administration of all community requirements both public and sometimes private as well, including the financial and all other arrangements associated with the township sheep flock. When an outbreak of "scab" occurred, he represented the "township" in Court at Portree where the Crofters were fined for omitting 'secondary dipping'. It was a much bigger affair than the O.J.Simpson trial!! He also acted as local factor to Sir Harmood-Banner and thus oiled the infrequent queries that arose between squire and tenants.

Our family livestock consisted of fifty sheep plus lambs, two cows plus followers (kept for market), one pig, numerous hens, two collies (Wilson breed) and two Persian cats. As far as I can recall, Johnnie Sinclair (Camusban) who ran the Glenelg-Arnisdale Mail Service prior to Roddy McLeod was the only one who owned a horse. I believe that at one time Loch Hourn herring was famous for its medium size, excellent quality and amazing abundance, confined to this particular area. The appearance of trawlers at the early part of the century completely destroyed the local herring industry.

In my medical student days, I attended a wake of someone who shall be nameless. In the early stages I got the impression from various remarks that he had been a most exemplary character, but as the evening wore on and the golden liquid got lower in the numerous bottles around the place he and his forebears became somewhat less commendable!

I attended only one wedding in the Highlands and it was so subdued with a preponderance of soft drinks, that it might well have taken place long before the days of "Whisky Galore". However, the practice of welcoming the newly-weds back to their homestead with a fusillade of musketry could be very bewildering for the bride, particularly if she hailed from "foreign" parts!

It would take volumes to describe the virtues and idiosyncrasies of the individuals living in Arnisdale and its environments, but I doubt if this would be appreciated or understood in the so-called sophisticated society we live in today.

Returning to my own family, we were exceptionally fortunate in having such magnificent parents. My father was a highly principled and firm but kindly disciplinarian, whereas, with hindsight, one can say my mother was much more modern in her outlook. We were taught to respect the successful and, if possible, to emulate them. In this respect my parents were great friends with the author's Aunt Lizzie, who was a frequent visitor to our house. As my teacher, I deeply respected her and truly loved her. At the age of nine or ten she must have been my first girlfriend. She and Roddy Mor were a superb couple held in the highest esteem by all and sundry.

Regarding my student days in Glasgow, I will always remember the universal warm welcome in Arnisdale when the four Murchison brothers arrived back with the Scottish Rowing Championship Cup.

In the years 1933, 1934 and 1935 we managed to win the Junior and Senior Rowing Championships, and in our final regatta at one stage we were up against the Glasgow University crew including our youngest brother John, a medical student, and duly beat them!!"

These, then, are Ewen's memories. Now for those of Ewen's niece, Camina.

**Recollections of Camina Brown (nee Murchison)**

My memories of Arnisdale are a treasury of happiness and security: raspberries in Crown Derby bowls, crowdie in muslin cloths; sweet williams and tiger lilies, gooseberries and blackcurrants in the garden; the arch of yew over the path down the garden to the rose-covered gate that led out to the green sward of the river side; the corn barrel for feeding the hens; the warm musty reassurance of the byre; Grandma's deft hands squeezing jets of warm, creamy milk into a pail; fresh scones, home-made butter and rhubarb jam; the butter churn; great, brass paraffin lamps in the summer evenings; the varnished, pine-combed bedrooms with dainty floral ewer and basin, the soap dish and chamber pot to match;

going out in the boat, its gleaming, varnished hull smacking the waves; the vast grandeur of the landscape dominated by the sheer, square-topped majesty of Beinn Sgritheall; the mackerel leaping in the loch.

I could go on and on recalling the countless features that made life in Arnisdale so marvellous to me as a child. Was ever a place more perfect for a child to grow in? It was a busy daily round of activities I couldn't know anywhere else: the range lit by 6 a.m., the cows to be milked, the water to be fetched from the river. My gallant little Grandma off to the fresh spring upstream of the bridge so the rest of us could have a ewer of hot water for our morning ablutions. By breakfast she'd have made warm scones, porridge or switched egg. It was a treat to get asked to feed the hens or to follow down to the boat shed to fetch some oars and then off on the loch for a spot of fishing. Oh, how still I love the sound of an outboard way out on the loch.

Arnisdale filled up my senses. I held my breath, mentally, every year, hoping that "this year" we would go to Arnisdale. The incredible elation I felt once I knew we could, was only surpassed by the relish I had for every familiar sight and sound that confirmed I was truly there. From the shriek of the seagulls over the pier at Mallaig to the sturdy 'put-put' of MacLennan's ferry as it rounded that unique buttress rock at the mouth of Loch Hourn, my happiness mounted. It reigned supreme from the time we landed ashore at the jetty till the final day of the holiday when my idyll had to end. Only as a child can one 'hone' in on the sensory detail. I loved the rumble of the planks on the bridge; I loved the scent of honeysuckle and the musty odour of the old hedge; I loved the myriad colours of the tiny shells down the shore; the rusty line of lichen round the high-tide mark on the rocks, the smell of the hay, the fat, climbing roses on the cottage walls, the motionless line of the boat on shining, clear water - everything! And first thing in the morning, as I lay in my bed and looked toward the little window in the varnished coombed ceiling, I knew for sure I was truly in Arnisdale by the sound of a great 'shh' that comes from all the corries and streams and mountain sides. Now I rationalise it as the sound of all the water rushing through them, but then it was just an integral, unnamed presence, that together with the quiet swish of the river and the 'crou-crou' of the hens was inimitably proof I was magically in Arnisdale.

I have lovely memories of all the family - uncles and aunts, grandparents, my parents, cousins, my brother and I - out at the hay, particularly in the field by the shore at Corran, lunching by the stone wall on scones and fruit cake and lashings of tea from a huge ten-cup teapot, against the backdrop of sparkling loch, hazy green mountains and distant purple Cuillins. The voices around me lulled and fascinated with their musical Gaelic, soft and humorous. It was a perfect happiness I felt then and it chills me to see that same wall which afforded and symbolised protection of the way of life then, is now breached in several places and the high tides of recent years threatening to erode the little cultivable land left in Corran.

It seems extraordinary to me that Loch Hourn (Huirbhne?) should be named in Gaelic the "Loch of Hell". I know my grandfather used to use a sail on his boat in the past but found the sudden squalls on the loch treacherous, even "hellish"! Such a terrible name, however, seems more likely to commemorate some terrible event far back in history. Since some Norwegian friends assured me years ago that the name ARNISDALE meant ARNE'S DALE (glen/land) in Norwegian, it seems certain that some powerful Viking, called Arne, fought his way to taking the area under his control. It is not hard to imagine the horror of such an event. The Vikings were known for their cruel ways. Perhaps this made some people want to remember the loch as the "Loch of the Devil" and maybe his name was "ARNE"!

No doubt there will have been other dire sufferings which could have led to such a breathtakingly beautiful place deserving such a name, but they remain unchronicled. However, I have been told by my father and uncle that in my great grandmother's time, people were cleared from crofts up the loch as far as Kinloch Hourn and put on board a ship for Canada. But owing to bad weather and other delays the ship did not leave the loch for two weeks and the "emigrants" were forced to remain on board. This event was spoken of as being greatly distressing to those on board and to their former neighbours who were not allowed to alleviate the privations endured on such a crowded boat. Apparently the "authorities" in charge were afraid their "cargo", if allowed ashore, would not return! One or two of the abandoned homes of these local emigrants are still to be seen as ruins at the loch side. I think this event happened around 1850. For those who remained, a daily living meant hard work. A crofter and his wife had to be able to turn their hands to making almost everything they needed to sustain life. My grandmother got the milk from the cow, helped it calve or tended its wounds. She made her butter, crowdie, preserves, and grew her own potatoes, fruit and vegetables. She knitted, sewed, embroidered, fetched the cows or peats or the water - two pails at a time - cooked, washed and ironed for a family of ten, her six sons and daughter, her husband, herself...and her mother-in-law! My grandfather crofted, strode the hills for the sheep, repaired fences, boats, dykes, roads, built another storey on his cottage and found time to be honorary unpaid secretary for the local crofters' association.

Theirs was a full life - no holidays - they had one trip to Glasgow together in 1937! My grandmother only came south again to join the family in 1954 because my grandfather had died. She attended only one wedding of her children, that of her eldest son Colin. That was only possible because it was held nearby in Glenelg. They simply could not leave their livestock. Theirs seemed such a good life to me as a child, but there are so many questions I would ask them now, as an adult, of what dreams were unfulfilled, what strains they felt, never getting a break from the diurnal round of hard labour. I feel they were two very contented, proud people. Years later when I stayed with my grandmother and aunt in Glasgow, I found my grandmother a benign and cheerful, sweet soul who never talked of herself, her woes or wants, but who began her day with a reading from the Bible and ended it with another.

It is certain that the values and personal example of my grandparents inspired their sons and daughter to lead exemplary lives, characterised by hard work and achievement. I'm sure my grandmother's years in-service for the well-to-do and minor gentry, taught her to encourage her family to strive to 'get on' in life. Three sons went to University: Colin, the eldest, became a headmaster, was a founder member of the Glasgow Schools Rowing Club, served as councillor for the Arnisdale/Glenelg area and was Chairman of the Education Committee for the Highlands and Islands when he died in 1966. Hector, the second son, rose to Chief Superintendent in the Glasgow Police and finally a security officer for the Atomic Energy Commission. Allan, my father, was a skilled carpenter and boat builder, inspector of works, a fine tenor (he often precented in the church services in the Arnisdale school). He also played the fiddle at the dances in Arnisdale in the "thirties". He was always active in the church and in community service. Kate, the only daughter, became a catering manageress. Angus, son No. 4, became a detective inspector in the Glasgow Police and worked as a security officer for the Army Recruitment Service. Ewen, the second youngest, won medals as a bright medical student and had a very successful career as a plastic surgeon in H.M.'s Navy. John, the youngest son, also became a doctor and had a practice in Glasgow till his tragic car accident in 1969. Colin, Hector and Ewen all received recognition for their public service in the Queen's Honours List. There must have been a lot of good in the upbringing and quality of life they received in their early years in Arnisdale. It would be wonderful if youngsters nowadays could enjoy a happy, simple childhood in Arnisdale today.

---

So ends Camina's idyllic memories of her grandparents, the family and of Corran and Arnisdale.

When one considers the tough, basic existence of old Angus and Grandma Murchison, of their strong character and spirit, their determination to do their very best for their family - and the great response of all the family to their example and inspiration, one is reminded of the Biblical phrase 'By their fruits shall ye know them'. What wonderful satisfaction in their advancing years the old couple must have derived from the achievements of their 'fruits'.

Now the succeeding generations of Murchisons are spread around the world, they have multiplied but none are permanently resident in the old home, although Angus, the oldest grandson, spends as much time there as his other commitments allow. Angus' sister Mary (Mrs Ian Ross), now resident at Inverinate in Kintail, is not too far distant from the old family base. Other grandchildren, such as Camina, and great grandchildren have their own spiritual attachments to Corran and Arnisdale.

So while the Murchison family contact and nostalgic interest is still there, in many ways, relative to the firm home base of the first half of last century, the attachment is now more tenuous - the Murchisons have moved on.

It is interesting, although futile, to speculate on the likely impact on Arnisdale, and on similar places, of the application of the energies, talents and initiative of the outstanding family members of Angus and Grandma Murchison to the development of Arnisdale itself and its environs - and of similar families in other Highland locations. The Murchison family obviously felt that Arnisdale had no basic resources to develop, to provide them with a challenge which they could address using their undoubted talents. Or perhaps the available resources were too tied up in other activities. Possibly also they arrived on the scene too early - before the days of the Highlands and Islands Development Board and the Enterprise Companies. The basis of development in any area to create industry and employment and a vibrant community is the matching of good people, good ideas and adequate resources.

For whatever reason, the Murchisons moved on to address challenges and to help meet the needs of folk in many walks of life in other parts of the world. Arnisdale's loss was compensated by considerable gain in other places and in many other sectors of society.

However, although the Murchisons have moved away from Arnisdale in a physical sense, many of them, such as Camina, are spiritually, still in Arnisdale. Few will wonder why.

**Top Left.** Corran from east of the bridge with Mary Ann Cameron's house just across the bridge, the MacDonald home on the extreme left and the Corran street extending to the right. The line of sheds built for fishing gear is on the extreme right. The fence above the rocks behind Corran was designed to keep the more adventurous of the Corran cows from falling over the rocks. **Right**. Corran from behind with the row of 14 byres in the foreground and the Corran 'street' stretching leftwards. The two storey house is the Murchison home with its fine view down Loch Hourn towards Skye.

**Middle Left**. The Murchison family about 1919. Seated. Angus Murchison, Ewen, Grandmother Christina Murchison (nee MacCuaig), Johnnie and Mrs Catherine Murchison (nee Sutherland). Standing. Allan, Angus Duncan, Colin and Kate. (Hector, the second eldest is absent). **Right**. The family at Colin's wedding in 1932 to Nettie Currie. Standing L to R. Colin, Angus Sen. Katie, Ewen, Mrs Catherine Murchison, Hector. Seated Allan, Johnnie and Angus Duncan.

**Bottom Left**. A faded photograph of Arnisdale School pupils in 1916 with their teacher (Catherine MacLean). Standing. Colin Murchison (second left), Katie Murchison (fourth left), Hector Murchison (third right), Allan Murchison (second right). Front. Kenny Fletcher, Angus Duncan Murchison and Lachie Fletcher. Others in the photograph cannot be identified but the pupils who where enrolled in the school between 1908 and 1916 were Katie Ann Henderson, Mary MacIntyre, Johan MacKenzie and Mary Miller (1908), Jessie MacAskill, Angus Campbell and Johan MacLean (1909), William MacKintosh, Ina MacLean, Allan Murchison and Maggie MacAskill (1911), Archie MacLean (1912), Annie MacMorran and Norah MacDonald (1913), Janet Anderson (1914), Susannah McCallum and Mary Kennedy (1915) and Cathie Ann MacInnes (1916). **Right**. Arnisdale School pupils around 1919 with the new teacher Lizzie MacDonald (Aunt Lizzie) on the left and her youngest sister Lily (mother of the author) on the right who was visiting. L to R. standing. Archie MacLean, Nora MacDonald, Ina MacLean, Kate Murchison, Amy Henderson, Annie MacMorran, Allan Murchison. Seated – Angus Duncan and Ewen Murchison, Peter, Lachie and Kenny Fletcher.

**Top Left.** A view from behind the riverside inbye croft lands at Corran across the river to the blar and from there to Camusban and the Arnisdale brae, and the start of the road to Glenelg. The Murchison hay barn in the foreground is one of a series of barns where the cured hay for each croft was stored for winter use.
**Right**. Some hay is already in coles and some lies in the bout, newly scythed. Mary and Angus Murchison do their bit in the 1940s and have no time to admire the view across the river to the Glenside farm fields, Beinn Bhuidhe to the left, Beinn Chlachach to the right and the ravine of Allt Utha between.

**Middle Left**. The laborious job of making prapags which was the first stage in the hay making process when the hay in the scythed bout was reasonably dry. Grandma Murchison beavers away as her daughter-in-law Nettie does the raking. A fine view down Loch Hourn from the shoreline field.   **Right**. All the Corran crofters are busy at their hay on the shoreline fields on a fine day with the Knoydart hills across Loch Hourn beyond looking somewhat dark and with ominous indications of rain later.

**Bottom Left.** Grandpa Murchison has a brief stop for a 'breather'.   **Right**. A well deserved cup of tea as the haymakers reach the culmination of the process and get the made hay into the security of the barn (the row of sheds originally built for the fishing gear beside the shore at Corran). L to R. Grandma Murchison at the entry point of the hay into the barn, Johnnie, Mary, Colin, Angus, Nettie, Katie and Grandpa.

**Top Left**. The Corran sheep gathered off Beinn Bhuidhe make their way through the hill gate behind Arnisdale Lodge on their way to the fank for the clipping. **Right**. Having been herded down to Glenfield, the Corran flock now reach the main road and are guided into the farm field towards the fank.

**Middle Left**. 'All hands on deck' as the clipping gets under way. L to R. Iain MacCuaig, Angus Murchison, Ewen Murchison, Donald MacCuaig and Norman Morrison. **Right**. The work continues while some of the squad have a refreshing cup of tea L to R. foreground. Angus Stewart, ? , Angus, Johnnie, Katie and Nettie Murchison and Sandy MacAskill.

**Bottom**. There was always great banter at the clipping between old Angus Stewart (left) and Norman Morrison (centre) aided and abetted by Willie MacKenzie and Johnnie Murchison (right), Sandy MacAskill and others. The great community spirit and the 'crack' made the work light and turned it into a fine social occasion – a veritable ceilidh!

**Top Left**. A group of Corran crofters at the four acre 'Round Park' next to Achadh a' Ghlinne which was used, among other purposes, to confine the tups outwith the breeding season. L to R. Sandy MacAskill, Johnnie Murchison, Willie MacKenzie, Allan MacAskill and Colin Murchison. **Right**. The Corran ewes being herded over the bridge at Corran making their way to the shoreline fields which they occupied at key times such as lambing.

**Middle Left**. Grandpa Murchison and young Angus at the row of byres behind the village. Each byre also had its own dung pit (right) to store the manure until the Spring time when it was used on the potato ground. **Right**. A haircut on the village street for young Ewen Murchison by his father.

**Bottom Left** Ewen Murchison in his young days in Corran – later to become Surgeon Captain and Hon. Surgeon to the Queen. **Middle**. Ewen and family enjoy a picnic along the Corran shore with Colin, Angus, Nettie, Johnnie and Mary. **Right** The author's brother Sandy – surprised Surgeon Captain Ewen at a chance meeting when in sick bay in the Mediterranean – at the mention of the word 'Arnisdale'.

**Top Left**. Allan Murchison rowing the family boat on Loch Hourn in the late 1920s. This picture triggers special memories for Allan's daughter Casmina – 'the joys and excitement of being 'out in the boat'. I can hear the sound of the oars in the rowlocks and smell the varnish on the boat every time I look at this!' **Right**. Camina's mum as Cathie Finlayson (second left) came from her home in Skye to work in Arnisdale Lodge and met and married Allan Murchison. Others having a break from the hay making are L to R. Nora MacDonald, Roddy Mor and Aunt Lizzie. (Early 1930s).

**Middle Left**. Cathie Finlayson and Allan Murchison before their marriage. **Centre.** Camina Murchison and her brother Angus during their schooldays. **Right**. Camina (right) on holiday in Corran with next door neighbour Chrissie Morrison (nee MacCuaig) in 1998.

**Bottom Left.** Camina and Michael's daughters Michaela and Kiri pose as mermaids at the mouth of the Arnisdale River at Corran in 1984. Brother Ruaraidh was engaged in other ploys. **Right**. Grandma Murchison (1875-1962) in the garden at Corran. Camina's 'ideal grandmother'.

**Top Left**. The Murchison brothers Colin, Hector, Angus Duncan and Ewen practice on Loch Hourn for the Scottish Rowing Championships, coached by their father (early 1930s). **Right**. Scottish Rowing Champions for several consecutive years in the 1930s. L to R. Angus Duncan, Ewen, Hector and Colin. Cox D D MacLean.

**Middle Left**. The Scottish Rowing Champions with their trophies. L to R. Colin, Hector, Angus Duncan and Ewen. Cox D D MacLean. **Right**. The Scottish Champions got a great welcome from all the Arnisdale folk when they arrived home with their trophies. A celebratory picnic in Barrisdale for the MacDonalds, MacCuaigs, Murchisons, Stewarts and other Corran and Arnisdale folk (early 1930s).

**Bottom Left**. Returning Murchison family members over the decades have rejoiced when that unique buttress rock (Creag an t-sagairt) near the entrance to Loch Hourn is reached bringing Arnisdale and Corran into full view. **Right**. Holidays in Arnisdale. 'My happiness reigned supreme from the time we landed ashore at the jetty till the final day of the holiday when my idyll had to end'. (Camina).

# Chapter 17

**Childhood holidays in Corran. Memories of Mary Catherine Ross (nee Murchison)**

As a child, I remember being somewhat envious of the author of this book. He came on his summer school holiday to Arnisdale and was allowed to attend the village school for almost a year. I did not have this privilege. My own visits were restricted to the school holidays - about twelve weeks every year. But I was able to join in and appreciate much of the seasonal changes in the community activities and the enduring constancy of my grandparents' lifestyle - both spiritual and secular. I readily and easily slipped into this alternative life after arriving from the town (Fort William) or the city (Glasgow).

My long stays in Arnisdale were possible because my father - Colin - was a schoolmaster in Glasgow and had the long summer, Easter and Christmas holidays. Perhaps it was because he was the eldest son and would inherit the croft that he never went anywhere else. I know that it was also the deep affection he had for his parents and the knowledge that his father was not in the best of health to run the croft himself. Like many others of his generation in the area, Grandpa Murchison suffered from TB - surviving on only one half lung. Grandma Murchison herself did most of the work on the croft and I saw how totally he relied on her strength. Because of Dadda's commitment, a very large part of every holiday was taken up with work on the croft. His brothers and sister helped when available. His hands would be soft on arrival but by the time he returned to Glasgow they were hardened and calloused. He always acknowledged and was very appreciative of the support and help he got from the other Corran crofters over the many years when circumstances forced him to be an 'Absentee Crofter' until he retired and came 'home' to Corran.

Preparation for our summer migration started early with the packing of the large trunk and hamper with our summer needs - these were sent "Luggage in Advance" to Mallaig where they would be waiting for us following our train journey from Glasgow. En route to Arnisdale we embarked at Mallaig either on the "Bounty" which made a weekly trip to Arnisdale with provisions and other materials for the crofts, farm and lodge, or on the "Royal Scot", the elegant motor launch hired specially. (If visitors or tourists could be persuaded to join us for a sail up Loch Hourn, the hire fee was reduced). As soon as the school gates closed for the holidays we were 'on our way' to Arnisdale. My brother Angus and I would go to bed but my mother would be up all night attending to all the things necessary when leaving our own home for the long holidays in Arnisdale. We would be wakened at 4 a.m. for the train leaving the Glasgow Queen Street Station at 6.05 a.m. - our eyes would be heavy with sleep but excitement always kept us fully awake. Our welcome from the MacLennans at the Marine Hotel in Mallaig was always so warm that one felt that they had been waiting all year for our family to call! Their daughter Grace (Robertson) inherited that special gift of hospitality.

Transferred by the dinghy to the shore at Corran or disembarked at the Lodge jetty, our first desire after greeting our Grandparents was to reassure ourselves that nothing had changed since our last visit. Contact would be made with the MacKenzies - Willie, Nellie, Flora and Iain; Sheena Stewart; and the Campbells - Donald and Eric when they were visiting their Aunt there. Funnily enough, during the summer the Corran and Camusban youngsters led separate lives. (Peter and his brothers and sisters were acceptable to both because during the holidays they lived 'halfway' between the two villages - at the farm).

I loved being with Grandma and helped her feed the hens on our way to the byre to milk the cow. It upset me when she selected one of the hens for the pot, and she herself was sad when the selected hen was found to be still in lay with many eggs in the 'pipeline'. Grandma's incredible culinary art impressed me when I was still quite young. She was able to present satisfying and tasty meals for so many from so little. There was never any waste with her and somehow she managed to do several jobs at the same time in the house - and seemed tireless outside coping with the demands of animals, the crops and the land.

Milking the cow was not as easy as Grandma made it look and the cow could and would withhold her milk if not happy with my milking technique. After the calf was fed, my brother Angus given warm milk to drink (my share was turned into junket), he and I would collect the rest of the cows and escort them to the pasture up the Glen. They would be brought back in the late afternoon for milking. The cows all knew their own byre so this was not too difficult a job for us. Sometimes the cry would go up - "The cows are on the rocks" and we would be sent to rescue them and either bring them home or direct them back to the pasture - before any calamities occurred as the cows sought out nibbles of lush grass at the edge of a precipice.

Another interesting and different task was helping to cut and stack the peats for fuel. I understand that the peat we were able to cut was of poor quality due to the heather and bog-myrtle roots. The other source of fuel was coal, brought by a "Para Handy" style puffer - the Glen Gloy. (This was the glen close to Spean Bridge where my maternal Grandpa Currie was born and reared). The coal-boat was run up onto the shore at high tide and the supplies for the various homes would be delivered by horse and cart or lorry.

The ewes were brought down from the hill and put in the fields at the 'Back of Corran' for lambing. As lambs were born their identity would be established according to the mother it suckled and buisted (marked with special paint). The mark for each croft was on a different part of the anatomy - back of neck, right/left hind leg, above the tail etc. Any lambs which were not identified would become common property and given the Township mark. After lambing was completed towards the end of April, all the ewes and lambs would be returned to the hill, allowing the natural meadows to grow hay for harvesting in July.

In early July the decision would be made to gather for the clipping. The area to be covered in the gathering on Beinn Bhuidhe by each crofter and his dog or dogs would be worked out in advance so that all corners of the hill would be covered and all the gatherers would work in unison. They needed to be out at the gathering very early in the morning in the hope that the clipping would be completed in good time and while it was still dry. Later on in late August, the sheep would be gathered again for dipping, sorting and the selling of surplus lambs. Often after a gathering the sheep were held overnight in the 'Round Park' which was next to Achadh a' Ghlinne. At the gathering for the shearing, excitement would mount back home when we heard the bleating of the sheep several hours after the men had gone out to the hill. This was the signal for the womenfolk to gather together the food baskets and meet up with the men and the sheep at the fank after the sheep and lambs were securely penned.

Shearing was a community activity and the sheep were clipped by everyone for each other - with the appropriate buist applied and the fleeces stacked according to ownership. The men did the clipping either with the sheep on the ground or held on special stools - in the open air or inside in the steading if the weather was wet. Before the advent of electrical clippers the procedure was very Biblical - the sheep would be restrained with a tie holding three legs together, held in front of the shearer who sat astride the stool. After the appropriate buist had been applied and that sheep released to graze, another would be brought by the "crogger" - a young lad or youth with sufficient strength and agility to manhandle the ewe from the pen to the shearer. There was a special way for the rolling of the fleeces - the Blackface fleeces with rough side out; Cheviot and Cheviot Cross fleeces were rolled with the smooth side out. It was important to roll neatly and tightly in complete fleeces, dirty pieces of wool being removed before rolling. The special large wool sacks would be suspended from the rafters in the barn of the farm steading and packed tightly by someone standing inside the bag. Rolling fleeces was women's work and I loved the feel of lanolin on my hands. Sheep dipping caused me much distress - perhaps more than the sheep - because I felt sorry for the discomfort they must have felt when their heads were forced under the surface of the sheep-dip in the bath.

After the clipping was completed, it was time to think of making the hay. In mid-July, once the field had fully recovered from grazing of the ewes at lambing time, the hay would be ready for harvesting. Dadda would start hand scything the 'Back of Corran' field. The pressure to get the hay cut, dried and stored was intense and the weather dominated this activity. If the days were sunny and dry with a good breeze, hay making could be completed quickly with the minimum of handling. However, in damp overcast weather we were thwarted; instead of going from swathe to spreading, turning, then raking together for making into larger ricks, we would be 'deeved' with spreading, turning, raking together to build small 'coilies' or 'prapags' - followed by even more spreading, turning, and raking for making into larger ricks. Often the process seemed to be locked into basic and tedious prapags. After getting the hay into ricks it would tolerate some rain! Once the shore field was secured, and sometimes in tandem, the field at the barn up on the south side of the Arnisdale river would be scythed, and the whole process repeated. Whole days would be spent haymaking, interrupted by Grandma's superb picnic refreshments, scones, pancakes, clootie dumpling, oatcake and crowdie. Although tea was the great thirst quencher and most welcome fluid, it was the oatmeal water in its special pail that I found the most delicious. It really did slake my thirst.

Haymaking would never be done on a Sunday. As I got older my commitment also grew and one of my enduring memories before I left home to take up nursing, was working alone with Dadda up at the Barn field with Grandpa Murchison 'supervising'. We had reached the stage of bringing completed hay-ricks up the slope from the river side to be spread and finally aired before being packed into the barn. Although it had seemed a promising day, the clouds were gathering and I almost sweated blood. As the rain that we could see approaching from the head of Loch Hourn finally fell on us we had secured the last rick.

Arnisdale 'holidays' were not all work! Every family in Corran owned a boat and used it for many purposes - work and pleasure. Our boat, the "Catherine", had been built by Grandpa and we used it for sails on the Loch. This was the boat used by the four Murchison brothers for practice for the forthcoming Rowing Championships in Glasgow in the 1930s.

When we were very young, my brother Angus and I loved exploring the seashells and other treasures on the Barrisdale Sands, and when we got older there was great delight in swimming in the warm water that came in over the sun warmed sands. The whole day would be spent there, since departure from Barrisdale and arrival back at Corran was very dependent on the state of the tide. For me, the perfect end to a sail was the return journey with 'bumps' from the wind whipped waves. We sometimes went for a long sail to the head of Loch Hourn through the fast running currents at Caolasmor. At high tide, negotiating the currents was easy but at low tide, this was formidable and tricky. In later years my husband Ian and I would sail our Mirror Dinghy to the same places Dadda had taken us as children. Very occasionally as children, Angus and I would take the oars and row, but we somehow failed to reach that high standard of wrist and blade control which was a hallmark of the Murchison rowers! We preferred the delight of an out-board motor. The boat was never used on a Sunday and my memory tells me that there were very many perfect sailing Sabbath days.

This brings me to thoughts of Arnisdale Sundays. It was very much a Day of Rest, observed and appreciated by the hard working community. Once the animals had been attended to in the early morning, the day assumed its own tranquillity. We all dressed in our best Sunday clothes and time was spent reading the discussing the Scriptures. Grandpa had a special interest in the singing of the Psalms as he was Precentor in the Church of Scotland for almost fifty years. There were also animated discussions about the various interpretations of certain passages in Scripture. From this I learned to be cautious of selective and out of context quotes from the Bible. Our denomination (Church of Scotland) met in the school for our Sunday services and we walked there and back. Walks up Glen Arnisdale were permitted - not my favourite because the way back always seemed so long and the midges so ferocious. I was, and still am, the favourite meal for all biting insects - midges, clegs and mosquitoes. From preference on these walks up the Glen and back I would stay behind with Grandma to hear further from her about her source of strength and endurance. She found it easy to quote Scripture to me at the right time - feeding the hens, rolling the fleeces, milking the cow, making hay, working in the garden, at the housework and whenever I came to her with personal and relationship worries. She simplified for me the different concepts of 'turning the other cheek' - 'wind tempered to the shorn lamb' - 'sapling bending with the wind' - and the difficult one of 'heaping coals of fire' - not in revenge but in love. For me, she lived her faith, was trusting and naive in it.

Grandpa and Grandma Murchison were not idle in the winter months and took this time to repair items inside the home and use their individual handicraft skills. Grandpa made beautiful handles for shepherd crooks out of horn; Grandma made rag rugs - nothing was wasted - making most attractive designs from the different colours and fabrics. She made sheets and pillowcases from flour and sugar bags, the sacks no longer used as backing for the rugs. She was a good seamstress and made attractive quilt covers from odd pieces of fabric joined with crochet inserts. She crocheted the lace curtains for the windows and she told me that she thought she might have strained her eyes when she crocheted the fine edging for them. The garden was a surprisingly beautiful one - the Estate had given a selection of unusual plants to each crofter and among the shrubs were hydrangeas, escallonias and fuchsias. Interspersed between these were fruit bushes - black currants, gooseberries, red currants and raspberries. I have never seen or tasted such wonderful strawberries to compare with Grandma's!! My own mother added other treasures to the garden when my father died.

Electricity was not brought into Corran until 1952. In many ways, water piped to the house would have been preferred by Grandma. Dragging the water in pails from the burn for domestic use, or from the river for drinking or cooking was a frequent task. For the drinking water, the tide had to be out, for the river was tidal up to where we collected it. One year Dadda attached a piece of string to the rone so as to direct some of the overflow into a pail for household use. The rain was so heavy that the pail would soon be full and then our trips were for drinking water only. The source is now from an everlasting spring from Beinn Sgritheall. Perhaps because of my experience of carrying buckets of water for Grandma in my childhood in all weathers, I am aware of its value and try hard not to waste it. Uncle Ewen forecast in 1947 that we in Britain should be making provision for husbanding water, for drought could become severe even here. Already his forecast is proving to be correct. The well is not missed until dry.

The remoteness of Arnisdale remains a handicap whenever urgent medical aid is required. Before the Mountain Rescue Teams and available Helicopter Service were set up in the area, any victim or casualty relied and depended on local skill and ability. The nearest hospital was Raigmore in Inverness - Broadford Hospital on Skye did not open until the 1960s - and the road there was mostly single track until the 1990s. Even now parts are still single track. An episode in 1957 highlights the problem of such remoteness. Sandy MacAskill from Corran was out stalking on Druim Fada that October. Near the top he tripped and fell down some forty feet. It is not clear whether he had had a heart attack but it was not until 10 p.m. that day that he was brought down by stretcher to the shore at Camus na gall. Next day he was taken to Raigmore Hospital - 90 miles away - where he died not having regained consciousness.

I was still quite young when the War in Europe ended and the Welcome Home Parties were arranged for the returning folk in the school. I remember well the huge bonfire we made and burned on the Crudh Ard for the Victory over Japan celebrations. My grandparents had made a rare visit to Skye and because of certain circumstances had had to walk back to Arnisdale from Glenelg. Despite their fatigue after such a strenuous walk, they joined us at the bonfire before making their way home to Corran for a well earned rest.

My parents met when they were attending Fort William Senior School. Dadda was thirteen and Mamma twelve years old and they shared a friendly academic rivalry throughout their school years. For his further education, Dadda resided with his father's sister in Banavie. The first time he went to Fort William School, Grandpa Murchison walked with him from Barrisdale, after crossing by boat from Corran. They walked from Barrisdale up Glen Barrisdale, over into Glen Còsaidh, across the western shores of Loch Quoich, up Coire Reidh, over into Glen Dessary, along the north shore of Loch Arkaig to Achnacarry and thence to Banavie. Grandpa probably knew that route very well for he had worked at Achnacarry for the Cameron of Locheil in his younger days and that would have been his route to and from Arnisdale. Dadda's education was hard won and he physically worked on the land and roads with and for his Uncle in Banavie. He won a scholarship to Glasgow University, where Mamma followed him one year later, and there he got his Master of Arts Degree in Philosophy and Mathematics. Dadda and Mamma married in Glenelg Parish Church in 1932. The following year, my brother Angus was baptised there.

My love of Arnisdale goes beyond my early years to the time when my father inherited the croft in 1954 and remains as strong as ever to the present day. My father's love and appreciation of his inheritance drove him to serve the community politically. He stood as Liberal candidate for Ross and Cromarty in 1959. Later he became the Local Councillor and Convenor of the Education Committee on the Inverness County Council until his sudden and unexpected death in Arnisdale in 1966. Mamma, who had relatives of her own residing at Kinloch Hourn at one time, stayed on in Corran after Dadda's death and accepted the challenge to also serve as Local Councillor. She was a good Councillor and enjoyed the work and travel involved. Although a non-driver, she never missed a meeting of either the Inverness meetings or the Lochaber District Council Meetings.

My longing and desire to return and live in Arnisdale were not destined to be fulfilled but my wish to return to live in Scotland was after Mamma died in 1985. The family croft is now Angus' and his son Colin shows a real love of the place. With Arnisdale neighbour Chrissie Morrison's encouragement and with favourable outcome, Ian and I purchased St Conal's in Inverinate and have retired here. In the extended Parish of Glenelg and Kintail we are in the Parish where it all began for me spiritually. I am the Organist for Glenelg and, when called on, I also play in the Kintail and Dornie Churches. On special occasions when Ian preaches I go with him to Arnisdale. I am humbled at the thought that Ian, my husband, is a lay preacher and elder in this Parish. He has always indulged my need of spending time here and since we were married has been happy to visit Corran - when Dadda was alive and when Mamma stayed on.

As I have pressed my memory bank and looked through the old family photograph albums to prepare these notes, many of the magic memories and feelings of my childhood days spent in Arnisdale have returned to me strongly. My Grandma and Grandpa worked so hard to subsist and bring up their family, but I remember them as being so very contented. They lived a simple life, they kept the faith, they led by example, they made little of their hardships and were always counting their blessings. It was uplifting for me to journey back in time and remember.

**Top Left**.  There was always great excitement when the summer holidays arrived and immediate preparations were made for Mary and Angus Murchison to travel from Glasgow via Fort William and Mallaig to Arnisdale.  The culmination came when the Bounty or Royal Scot was about to dock at the Arnisdale pier.  **Right**.  Mary and Grandma packing the hay in the barn at the 'Back of Corran'.

**Middle Left**.  Mary and Angus as toddlers in the hay meadow beside the Murchison barn on the riverside fields, with the tree lined River Arnisdale below, the farm glenside fields across the river and Beinn Bhuidhe, the Corran Crofters' sheep grazing beyond.   **Right**.  Johnnie and Ewen Murchison working at the hay on the riverside field with Mary, Nettie, Angus and the collie Flossie providing moral support.

**Bottom Left**.  Becoming more useful.  Angus and Mary fully armed for work at the hay.  Achadh a' Ghlinne is just across the river.  To the left is the east end of Beinn Bhuidhe with the ravine of Allt Utha separating it from the mass of Beinn Chlachach to the right.  **Right**.  The welcome break for a well deserved picnic of refreshing tea and home baking at the door of the barn on the riverside field.  L to R.  Grandpa,  Nettie, Grandma, Mary Angus and Katie.

**Top Left**. Helping to roll the fleeces at the fank. L to R. Angus, Aunt Katie, Mother Nettie and Mary (around 1940). **Right**. Having fun on the Barrisdale sands looking westwards to the island group Corr Eileanan L to R. Nettie, Mary and Angus (late 1930s).

**Middle Left**. A sunny day along the Corran shoreline for L to R. Sheena Stewart, Angus, Cousin Betty Murchison, Mary and the ever faithful Collie (early 1940s). **Right**. Mary and Angus with Mother Nettie on a walk up Glen Arnisdale (late 1930s).

**Bottom Left**. Angus and Mary stop for a brief rest on a Sunday walk up Glen Arnisdale with Uncle Johnnie. **Right**. Neighbour Sandy MacAskill has just finished clipping the black sheep at the fank. In his day, Sandy was a great wit and his home was a popular one for evening ceilidhs.

**Top Left**.  A rare little treat for Grandma and Grandpa Murchison – a picnic on a fine day up the shore beyond Corran.  L to R. Grandpa, Allan, Grandma, Mary, a family friend and Nettie.   **Right**.  The Glen Gloy – the coal boat which delivered Arnisdale's annual coal supply, beaching at Camusban.  Glen Gloy in Lochaber was the place where Grandpa Currie was born and brought up.

**Middle Left**.  Colin Murchison, who was elected as the Local County Councillor and was appointed as Convener of Inverness County Council Education Committee after his retirement.  Colin was also an excellent photographer and many of his fine photographs are reproduced in these pages.   **Right**.  Commander Kitson's 144 tonne yacht 'The Golden Hind' anchored in Arnisdale Bay with Daniel MacDonald's boat house in the trees just to the left of the yacht.  To the right is the pier and the Lodge.  Further right is the Farmhouse with the little hump of Cnoc Or almost immediately behind.

**Bottom Left**.  A little celebration to commemorate '60 glorious years' together.  Grandpa and Grandma Murchison.  'By their fruits shall ye know them'.   **Right**.  Off to church on their weekly pilgrimage with joy and gladness (1952).  'They began each day with a reading from the Bible and ended it with another'.

## Chapter 18

**The Fletcher Family - their links and their contributions.**

The Fletchers have had a major impact on the Arnisdale community. They have been around for a long time and ran the Camusban pub in the heyday of the herring fishing. They are related through either bloodlines or marriage to many of the other Arnisdale families - to the MacGillivrays, the MacAskills, the Campbells (Lexy, Mairi Bhan, Anne (Mrs MacLure) and Donald Sheorais), the Mackenzies and to Roddy Mor and the rest of the MacLeod family of the farm. The Fletcher family which undoubtedly has had the biggest impact on Arnisdale was that of Ali and Tina - Kenny (born 1908), Lachie, Peter, Annie, Roddy, Mabel, Donald, Farquhar and Alistair (born 1925). They all went to school in Arnisdale, they were staunch members of the Free Church, they worked on the estate as shepherds, ghillies, stalkers, gamekeepers, estate handyman, and manager - and some of them worked in the local forest. They provided music in song, fiddle and accordion at the ceilidh dances, they were great wits, very friendly and supportive folk in the community, as well as being enthusiastic and interesting house ceilidh participants. That family now has many progeny who continue their close association with, and support for, the Arnisdale community.

The original Fletchers may have come from Glen Orchy and may have been among the early Highland shepherds as the sheep came in from the south in the middle of the last century to displace the goats and, to some extent, the cattle - which for centuries had been a very important component of the subsistence living of the people and of the rural economy.

The Camusban Innkeepers who are best remembered in Arnisdale are Lachlan Fletcher and his wife Janet (nee MacLeod). Their inn was just on the east side of Allt a'mhuilinn, the site of the current Fletcher family home and croft. A story which Lachie MacAskill of Corran used to relate indicated that Janet was in charge of the inn or at least of the finances! Lachlan may have been too busy as a fisherman/crofter/shepherd. Lachie's tale was that Janet ran a very successful business when the herring fishing was at its height, made a lot of money and to secure her takings, buried a bag full of sovereigns on the croft. Banks were too far away and Janet obviously decided that it was safer to bury it on the croft than to keep it under the bed! Did Janet remember where she buried it? Is there a treasure chest still in hiding in the Camusban croftlands awaiting to be discovered?

Lachlan and Janet had six children - Jean, Peggy, Martha, Duncan, Alistair and Peter. Duncan's son Farquhar never fully recovered from being gassed in France during the First War. Farquhar did manage to get home but was extremely ill for a time before he died. The added sadness of Farquhar's illness was that very few people were allowed to visit him because it was feared that he had a transmissible illness. It was not until he died that it was realised that the entire undermining of his health was due to the terrible scourge of gassing in that dreadful war.

Of that family, Alistair (Ali) was the one who remained in the old home. Ali married Christina (Tina), the eldest of the MacLeod family from the farm in 1907. Their wedding took place in the roadside house at Sandaig. This house was occupied by one of the Eilanreach shepherds and the choice of venue for the marriage ceremony was a compromise worked out with the Free Church Minister. The Minister had to travel all the way from Ardelve to marry the young couple and he obviously had been very aware that the toughest section of the Arnisdale to Glenelg road was that between Sandaig and Arnisdale.

In their courting days before the marriage in Sandaig, Tina had been working in the Glenelg Hotel for the princely sum of £7 for each six months period, while Ali was employed as a shepherd/stalker on the

Arnisdale Estate, as well as running the family croft and also doing some fishing. After his hard day's toil, Ali would, as often as he could, walk over to Glenelg to visit Tina. Nora MacDonald's mother Flora, who was one of Ali's neighbours, once asked him during his courting days "Do you not find the time long going all these miles to Glenelg and back?" Ali replied "Well, Flora, I never feel the time long on the way over to see her, but I do feel the time very long on the way back home again!"

Ali, Tina and their young family left Arnisdale for four years between 1920 and 1924 when Ali got a job as a Gamekeeper in Glenmallie where their nearest neighbour was three miles away at Invermallie on the southern side of Loch Arkaig. Farquhar was born in Glenmallie and Alistair, the last of the family of nine, was born when they returned to Arnisdale.

The family lost their loving mother and father within a period of 17 months of each other while Alistair and Farquhar were still at school. Both parents died in the Royal Northern Infirmary, Ali on 31 July 1935 (aged 61 years) and Tina on the first day of February 1937 (aged 53 years). These were dreadful double tragedies for the young family. However, the family were, and have always been, very closely knit and mutually supportive. They needed each other's love and care more than ever now. They all set their hands to the plough and came through these very difficult times very much together.

There follows brief pen pictures of the family, progressing from Kenny, the oldest, to Alistair - the 'baby' of the family.

Kenny
Kenny, on leaving school, got a job in England on the Countess of Warwick's estate. He did general work on the farm and on the estate. It was not a happy work situation because there were regular sackings for no obvious reasons. After observing these almost random dismissals for a while, Kenny thought he should leave before he was the next to be fired, so off he set back to Arnisdale. After a few weeks Kenny received a letter from the Countess commenting that she was very pleased with his work and inviting him back to work for her. Kenny declined politely, feeling that he was much more secure in Arnisdale where he was already working as a shepherd/ ghillie/stalker on the estate. Kenny stayed in Arnisdale, working for the estate and helping to run the croft until the end of his days. Donald MacCuaig, in his Arnisdale reminiscences, speaks very highly of Kenny's participation in the house ceilidhs and his great memory of old stories and events in the history of Loch Hourn and its environs. Stories about Kenny occur regularly throughout these pages.

Lachie
Lachie, the second oldest of the family, was always a great worker who would turn his hands ably to all kinds of tasks, being particularly fond of his sheep, but he was good at handling all kinds of stock from cattle, to horses, to dogs. Among his earliest jobs while at school and soon after leaving school was as a shepherd at the lambing on the Eilanreach Estate which carried several thousand sheep at that time. Lachie died a few years ago but many of his early memories were tape recorded by his family, Peter and Margaret in his later years. In this tape, Lachie talks of his early shepherding at Swordland, which lies between Glen Beag and Glen Mor in Glenelg. Lachie also remembered, and participated in, the droving of big herds of Skye cattle from Kylerhea to Glen Dessary and Spean Bridge, before handing the drove on to the local drovers there who would take the drove over the hills to the south of Spean Bridge and into Glen Coe - and onwards to the main market places at Crieff and Falkirk. There were 200 to 400 cattle in the droves when Lachie was employed in the droving. They had their regular overnight stops where the cattle would graze and rest and the drovers would shelter for the night. As a young boy, Lachie remembered taking a horse from Glenelg to Lochaber via the old drove route all on his own.

Lachie's prowess as a drover and his knowledge of the old drove roads also came in handy when a friend of his had an altercation with the Arnisdale laird's wife and resigned from his post on the Arnisdale Estate. The laird at the time (1920) was Sir John Harmood-Banner, MP for Everton and Lord Mayor of Liverpool. Alick Campbell, the estate head gamekeeper resident at Glenfield, was obviously riled by some incident which involved the laird's wife and told her in no uncertain terms that he was just as independent as she was and perhaps even more so. So he resigned there and then. Alick had prior knowledge that the laird was about to sell the Arnisdale Estate in any case and feared that he might lose his job in the change-over. He may already have secured another job in the Lochaber area by the time he had his row with the laird's spouse. Alick was a tough character - a member of a family of 13 children - born and brought up on the Fannich Estate at the Nest of Fannich in Ross-shire where his father was also a gamekeeper. All thirteen of the family survived to maturity. Alick and his wife Mary had two of a family, Mary and Duncan, and they were soon on their way to their new home at Mucomir at the south east end of Loch Lochy opposite Gairlochy. The farmer there at the time was the well known heavyweight athlete, A. A. Cameron, of caber-tossing, shot-putting and Cumberland wrestling fame.

Alick Campbell, as part of his perks as a gamekeeper in Arnisdale, was allowed to have three cows and followers, and the most logical and easy way to get them to Lochaber at that time was to take them via the old drove roads. It was Lachie as a young boy and Duncan MacTavish who got the job and the little drove was soon on the move and was delivered safely to Mucomir. There Alick was probably employed as a shepherd rather than a gamekeeper, for A A Cameron had a large flock of sheep and also a fold of breeding cattle. The old Fort William to Fort Augustus railway line ran through the farm lands.

In his recording, Lachie tells the story of A A Cameron's son who was a strong man like his father. One day, the son casually lifted a big barrel of herring into a cart. The father, who was present, was asked by an observer if he was not very proud of his son's great strength. A A Cameron's reply was that he had never seen his son do anything that his mother could not do!

Alick and Mary's daughter, also Mary, is well remembered in Arnisdale and was a good friend of the author's mother and aunt, a friendship which continued throughout their lives.
Daughter Mary later married Sandy Campbell, the Gairlochy postman, who hailed from Glen Shira where the River Spey has its source. Mary and Sandy had four sons, John, Davie, Roddy and Bernard who were all stalwart shinty players with the Lochaber Camanachd Club and played regularly in their time against teams such as Lochcarron, Kinlochshiel and GlenUrquhart, all of which contained players with strong Arnisdale connections. Arnisdale itself may now be a rapidly dwindling community - but the Arnisdale and Loch Hourn web is extremely wide and grows bigger by the day as these lines are penned.

After delivering Alick Campbell's cattle to Mucomir, Duncan MacTavish and young Lachie set off through the hills back to Arnisdale. Duncan knew the Loch Quoich and Kinlochourn territory and its people very well and there is no doubt that the two drovers found very welcoming and comfortable accommodation for the night in these parts before completing their journey home on the following day.

Lachie's clear memories of the cattle droving and his knowledge of the droving routes proved to be extremely useful to the folk involved in a re-enactment of a drove (filmed by BBC Television) through Skye, across the narrows of Kylerhea and then via the old drove route up Glen Beag, behind Beinn Sgritheall, by Kinlochourn, Glen Kingie and Glen Dessary to Spean Bridge and beyond. Authors of books and other publications on droving also found Lachie's experiences and memories to be extremely useful in describing the old system of getting the cattle from the Outer Hebrides and Skye all the way to the fattening pastures and markets in the south.

In tape recording his memories, Lachie was asked his opinion about the Kitson family and if the local people presented a united front in trying to win better conditions from the estate. Lachie commented that while there may have been minor disagreements among the local folk, they were never too serious and he expressed general admiration for the Kitson family. However, he went on to relate in detail one incident which resulted in a complete closing of ranks among the Arnisdale folk and a confrontation with the laird.

The reason for the bitter conflict had nothing to do with the wholesale poaching of deer or salmon, or the wanton desecration of the laird's property, or anything of that sort - but involved the theft of Victoria plums from the lodge garden! This occurred just before Andrew Thompson was about to harvest the beautiful fruit and present it with justifiable pride to the Kitson family for them to savour and enjoy.

So when the harvesting was about to start - the beautiful plums had flown - every one of them!

The local folk were under immediate suspicion. The only question to be answered was - which of the locals were responsible? Was it the youngest of the Fletcher boys from Camusban or the young Murchisons from Corran? Or even Roddy Mor? Or Johnny Sinclair?

Kitson summoned Andrew Thompson and the rest of the Lodge hierarchy for a summit meeting to cope with the crisis. The Estate Factor was summoned forthwith from Edinburgh and was ordered to get to Arnisdale with all speed. All possible culprits were considered and the course of further enquiries and actions was planned meticulously.

The first step in the criminal investigation was to interrogate two young lads who often roamed about the lodge precincts and the nearby farm in their spare time, to find out if they had spotted the thieves. One of them was the 'Boots' (possibly 'Jackson' to name) in the lodge who attended to general cleaning duties, while the other was Jimmy Kennedy from the farm. Jimmy originated from the Glasgow area and he helped Roddy Mor at the farm. Jimmy was rather short sighted and he wore spectacles which only partially corrected his eyesight problem. Did they see anything or anybody suspicious around the lodge gardens? - they were asked. The 'Boots' had seen nobody around, while Jimmy indicated that he thought he had made out a figure near the garden on the previous day but had no idea of the identity of this figure. Who might have this person been? Letters were despatched immediately to the representatives of the two villages - the Crofting Township Clerks - Angus Murchison in Corran and John MacGillivray (Ian Beag) in Camusban. The letter was to the effect that all the people of Arnisdale had to stay away from the lodge garden forthwith and that a crisis meeting was to be held in the school on a specified date, with a view to determining which of the local people had stolen the hallowed plums. The demand from the laird was that every inhabitant of both villages must attend the meeting.

The locals were absolutely furious at the accusation. They all respected the Kitson family to date, they never went near the lodge and, while some of them might get a salmon, or a bit of venison for the pot on the quiet, from time to time - they would never dream of going near the lodge garden. And the absolute need for total honesty and integrity was drummed into the children continuously - and the children knew in turn where the boundaries of acceptable and unacceptable behaviour lay and dared not breach these codes.

Agreement was eventually reached between the lodge and village representatives for the conduct of the meeting. It was agreed that one of the villagers would act as the Chairman of the meeting - this would provide Commander Kitson, his factor and gardener full opportunity to interrogate freely in their quest to find the culprit. Posters announcing the meeting were nailed to Archie's shed door in Camusban and to the equivalent 'notice board' in Corran. One phrase on the notice indicated that 'this was an opportunity to clear this community of this suspicion as a whole'. Excitement rose to fever pitch in the community as zero hour drew near. Word spread to other districts about the crisis meeting in Arnisdale. Lachie, currently working in Eilanreach, was determined not to miss it, so he made sure that his motor bike was in good trim to negotiate the formidable braes and Z bends of the precipitous Arnisdale road. His mate, Ali MacRae (Ali Beag) from Eilanreach, got caught up in the excitement and insisted on coming over on the pillion with Lachie so as not to miss out on any entertainment! Zero hour came. The school room was packed to the door. The atmosphere, according to Lachie, was very tense! The villagers had made a somewhat surprising choice as Chairman - young Ewen Murchison, fifth son of the Corran Township Clerk, who was in his early years of a medical degree course at Glasgow University. The Chairman opened the meeting with an invitation to Commander Kitson to speak, make his accusations and initiate his interrogations.

According to Lachie's account, there were 'great speeches' by some of the local people, who felt as one, and were totally confident within themselves that it was not one of their number who was guilty of the crime. Kitson persevered with his accusations and enquiries in an attempt to break the united front of the locals and to isolate the culprit.
John MacGillivray (Ian Beag), a learned and eloquent man, made his ever famous statement - oft quoted in the Arnisdale folklore - as Kitson continued on the offensive - "Commander Kitson, you think we are dumb dogs that cannot bark, but I thank God that we are not!" - and old John thumped the table with a resounding thump to drive home his point. Another of the local people made the comment that the accusations seemed to be based on 'the blind seeing' (referring to Jimmy Kennedy and his short-sightedness) 'while the one with sight saw nothing' (referring to Jimmy's mate - the 'Boots' from the lodge).

Andrew Thompson, the gardener, tried to appease the locals by referring to the 'democratic' approach that Kitson and the lodge hierarchy were adopting and enquiring of the very large assembly of local folk - with all households represented - "Would you have preferred if we had sent for the 'polis' so that they could come and look into every nook and cranny in all of your houses?" Angus Duncan Murchison then asked the Chairman if he could respond, and on being granted permission to speak from his young brother, stood up and said calmly "I happen to be a Police Constable and it is not my duty to look into every nook and cranny in any person's house without having a search warrant!"

Kitson and his factor were getting increasingly rattled by the total solidity of the local people and their presentation of a cool, firm and logical defence against the accusations levelled against them. He was losing his cool in frustration and at one point referred to your 'so-called Chairman'. Young Ewen, as Chairman, waited for the Commander to complete his statement and then quietly but pointedly intervened: "Commander Kitson, I may only be a poor crofter's son, but I refuse to be referred to as a 'so-called Chairman'.

Commander Kitson, basically a very honourable and kind man, and a good laird, realised that, while the locals were totally rational, cool, polite and resolute in their defence, he was losing his cool and, at the same time, rapidly losing his case and his credibility - and perhaps some of the considerable respect felt in the community towards himself and his family.

The Commander apologised to the Chairman and said that he had lost his temper and was sorry.

After further debate, now conducted more calmly and rationally by the accusers, it became very clear that the two young lads who had been first questioned - the short-sighted Jimmy from the farm and the 'Boots' from the Lodge - were the real culprits. The 'Boots' did not appear with the rest of the regular staff when they returned to the lodge in the following season!

Lachie commented in his tape recording that the most painful experiences were the suspicions which fell on the locals, the inference that they were in disgrace and that they were criminals. High moral codes had been instilled into them all continuously and resolutely from their earliest years. They had total confidence that it was not one of themselves who was the guilty party. They were greatly hurt that Kitson thought that they would have stooped to such petty theft.

However, Lachie's final comments on his tape indicate the nature of his lasting memory of the crisis meeting. "Oh, it was great. We all enjoyed it. There were great speeches!" Honesty and diplomacy had won the day and helped to solve the little problem!

But little problems often make good stories which are well worth recounting.

And just one final footnote to this incident which regularly crops up in the reminiscences at Arnisdale ceilidhs. Mrs Thompson, the gardener's wife, whose husband was very much in the line of fire from the villagers during the vigorous debate, also saw the funny side of things. A friend enquired of her, after all the furore had abated, what she had thought about the meeting in the school. "Oh," she said, "I was intrigued because the man who could hear couldn't speak - and the man who could speak, couldn't hear". Apparently two of the ablest leaders of the crofting communities had experienced difficulty at the meeting. One of them used to get so excited that he would cough and stammer slightly and had difficulty in expressing himself. The other was a great orator and speech maker who could express himself very clearly, eloquently and pointedly. However, as the debate raged, the latter was desperate to enter into it but was not catching what other speakers were saying and kept asking those sitting next to him "What's he saying? What's he saying?" Perhaps it is best to complete the story of this famous incident with these amusing observations of the gardener's wife. The Thompson family were all very popular and made notable contributions to the community over many years.

After working at Eilanreach as a shepherd, Lachie came back to Arnisdale after his parents died to support the family. He worked in the Arnisdale Forest at Mialairidh during this period. However, there was no keeping Lachie away from his sheep and soon afterwards he took a job as a shepherd on a hill farm in the Loch Lomond area. After the end of the war, Lachie went to a shepherding job in the Largs area. There he gained considerable experience, not only on the shepherding side but on all aspects of stock farming and farm management. When the job of Manager of the Arnisdale Farm and Estate was advertised in 1959, Lachie applied for the post along with about one hundred others and he was the one selected by Mr Richmond Watson on the basis of his interview, but more particularly on his track record. The sheep stock had been run down before Lachie took over at the expense of more cattle and Lachie's first move was to get the sheep numbers up to nearer the carrying capacity of the land.

Lachie was the only one of the Fletchers who married a native of Arnisdale - Christina MacDougall - daughter of George MacDougall and his wife Margaret (nee MacDonald - who belonged to Skinidin, Glendale in Skye). George, who was a police constable in Glasgow, was a nephew of Donald Sheorais (Campbell) and was also related to Lexy Campbell and Mairi Bhan (mother of the first 'Willie the Post'). Lachie and Chrissie were married in 1958 in the Free Church Manse in Dunoon with Lachie's great friend and Arnisdale neighbour, Archie MacLean, being his best man. So when Lachie landed the Manager's job on the Arnisdale Estate, both he and Chrissie were coming back home again. By the time their family of Peter and Margaret came along, the Arnisdale School had closed, so Peter and Margaret had their schooling in Glenelg, Plockton and Inverness.

Peter and Margaret still have very strong ties with Arnisdale and would dearly love to see a revival of

its fortunes and a renewal of vigour and activity in the community. Both Peter and Margaret are experts with their cameras and have captured some wonderful pictures
depicting Arnisdale and its environs in all its glories through the seasons - with its unique combinations of mountains and sea, flora and fauna.

Peter
The teacher who Kenny, Lachie and Peter had for most of their schooldays was Lizzie MacDonald from GlenUrquhart who, later, was to marry their Uncle Roddy (Roddy Mor) from the Farm. During some of Peter and Lachie's school holidays they would set off for Lochcarron to spend their holiday with their maternal grandfather, aunts and cousins. The game of shinty, as at present, was very popular in Lochcarron at the time and Peter and Lachie were soon developing the skills and tricks of the old game. These skills obviously came to the fore at a great shinty match played between Arnisdale and their great rivals Glenelg on the Crudh Ard field in the early 1930s. The game was described in the following terms in the Shinty Yearbook of 1972-73 by a great friend of Lachie and Peter - Tony Mackay, who was one of the young Foresters in the Mialairidh Forest at the time of the great game.

**An Old Time Local Derby (by Tony Mackay)**

"During the past half century I have enjoyed many games of shinty, but the one which comes to mind for sheer entertainment value, if not for skill, is that memorable match forty years ago on the Crudh Ard field of Arnisdale, Loch Hourn.

The contestants were Arnisdale and Glenelg, not a cup-tie, not an organised league game, but a challenge match. No old firm confrontation aroused such fervour at Parkhead or Ibrox as did this clash of local rivals by the shores of Loch Hourn. Over in the Clachan, argument and speculation of the outcome was the main topic as the bodaich reminisced on games of their youth.

Time has dimmed one's memory of the names of many of the players. Some are no longer with us - Doctor Johnnie Murchison, who lost his life tragically in a road accident three years ago while President of the Camanachd Association; Ali Beag, Eilanreach; Malcolm Garde the Glenelg Ferry Man, all of them remembered as great sportsmen and champions of the ancient game. There was also Donald Rarsaidh who gave his life during the last war.

There were no distinctive club colours - they were unnecessary, the "Enemy" was known and for each half you played Sios or Suas (down or up) depending on the spin of the coin tossed up by Ruaridh Mor from the farm whom one is happy to relate is still a sprightly octogenarian. I know that he will forgive me saying that in addition to being in charge of the whistle, he also acted as coach to the home team. His shouts of encouragement and advice could be heard at creag an t-sagairt on the south shore of the Loch.

"Naire air do chulthaobh" (Watch out behind you). - his warning yell relieved many a dangerous situation for the Arnisdale side!

Fouls were few or perhaps one should say infringements of today's rules were overlooked, no quarter was asked or given, and strange to relate - no serious casualties resulted. One remembers the big stalker from up the Loch, caman held aloft, in an extremely hostile and
aggressive attitude in hot pursuit of Iain from Glenelg, a torrent of Gaelic expletives proclaiming that retribution was imminent and only by Olympic standard sprinting was Iain able to escape.

The finer points of the game were exhibited by our old friend, Lachie Fletcher and his brother, Peter.

Perhaps not surprising - having spent part of their boyhood in Lochcarron. There was Angus Campbell from Corran, a stonewall custodian, flourishing a formidable caman hewn from an old ash in Achadh a'Ghlinne. It took a powerful man to wield this weapon and strong and powerful Angus was.

What of the result? Arnisdale were the victors although the actual score is forgotten. After the match, lavish and generous hospitality was dispensed at the Farm and soon all the earlier arguments, quarrels and clashes were forgotten, soothed by the mellowing influence of copious measures of 'stags breath' and fortified by venison sandwiches.

Victors and vanquished joined forces and - far into the night - Beinn Sgritheall and Druim Fada re-echoed with rousing Gaelic Chorus." (From Shinty Yearbook 1972-73).

---

So Arnisdale, with the help of their usual recruits from up Loch Hourn - the MacRae boys (Ewen, Roddy, Fachie and Peter), Do MacKillop and Angus MacKintosh - triumphed on the day. The complete neutrality of the referee - Peter and Lachie's uncle - Roddy Mor from the Farm - might not have been total - but obviously a great time was had by one and all! No doubt Glenelg would select their own referee for the return game!

After leaving school, Peter worked in the Mialairidh Forest and then took a job on the Estate of Ardtaraig near Dunoon. Young brother Donald went to work with him there and soon sister Mabel was also on her way to keep house for both of them and to work in the shooting lodge at the same time. They were a musical trio. Mabel's teacher, Mrs Kennedy, used to tell her that she had a good singing voice and Mabel also tried to master the accordion. However, she did not persevere beyond being able to play 'The Skye Boat Song'. Donald and Peter were more persevering, Peter on the fiddle and Donald on the 'Box'.

As well as developing their musical talents, both Peter and Mabel met their other halves while at Ardtaraig. An attractive young girl from Greenock, Lizzie Turner, came to work at the shooting lodge, Peter and Lizzie soon fell for each other, and they were married in October 1939. Peter volunteered for war service soon afterwards and he found himself in the thick of hostilities in France within six weeks of joining up.

With regard to Mabel and her fate, a handsome young postman, Peter Campbell, was delivering the mail in the Ardtaraig area and soon another of the Fletcher family had found her life's partner. Peter Campbell was called up to the 8th Battalion Argyll and Sutherland Highlanders on a Friday and war was declared two days later on the Sunday. Mabel and Peter Campbell were to be married later in Arnisdale in January 1940.

At the end of the war, Peter and Lizzie set up home first back at Ardtaraig and then later in Strathnairn where Peter was appointed as Estate Handyman on the Farr Estate. Peter was an excellent craftsman, his skills coming to him almost naturally.

Peter, like Lachie, was to finish his working life in Arnisdale. In 1960, just one year after Lachie returned to the village, Peter and Lizzie had come to Arnisdale on holiday. The laird, Mr Richmond Watson, had heard all about Peter's character and skills and asked Lachie if he could arrange for Peter to pay him a visit. Peter duly obliged. Mr Richmond Watson offered Peter a job on the estate, outlined the terms of employment, including accommodation available. Peter was taken aback and asked if he wished to see his testimonials from other jobs. The laird responded that he knew all about him from Lachie and he did not require to look at any paper work.

So the Arnisdale Community was further enriched by the return of Peter, Lizzie and their daughters Jean and Christine to Arnisdale. However, Jean and Christine arrived too late to follow in their father's footsteps by attending Arnisdale School, for the school had been closed in the year before their arrival - in 1959 - because of the shortage of pupils. So Jean and Christine had their secondary schooling in Inverness, returning home to Arnisdale at holiday time.

Annie
Annie, being the elder of the two Fletcher daughters in the family of nine, had plenty of work to do in the house from her earliest years as she helped her mother with the housework and in looking after her younger brothers and sister. This experience was to serve her well when her mother and father died in the mid 1930s - Annie answered the call and came home from her work in Glasgow to help the family through the crisis.

Soon after leaving school, Annie had obtained work in domestic service in England but, of course, returned to Arnisdale regularly on holiday and to help out in the home. There was, at that time, plenty of activity and excitement in an Arnisdale summer. Not only would the many local exiles be returning for their summer holidays but the lodge staff would regroup for the season. This would include not only the eight or ten house staff which was made up almost equally of Arnisdale folk and staff such as cooks and butlers whom the Kitson family would bring with them from their permanent residence in the south; but it would also include the eight or so 'sailors' - the Captain and crew of 'The Golden Hind' - the Kitson's yacht.

Of course, when all the local folk were home on holiday - and the Lodge, the Estate and the Kitson's seagoing vessels were buzzing with people, activity and excitement - that was the time to organise one of these famous Arnisdale ceilidh dances. At one such dance in the latter half of the 1930s, as the folk - young and old - gathered in the school, those unfamiliar to one another began to weigh each other up (that is, the new Lodge staff and the Golden Hind crew who were on their first visit to Arnisdale, on the one hand, and the Arnisdale regulars on the other). As this process continued with sideways glances and inaudible comments, Annie's next door neighbour, Archie (MacLean) queried in whispered tones: "Do you fancy any of them, Annie?" "Not really", responded Annie, "except for that big dark fellow over there". The big dark fellow was Alick MacCallum from Tighnabruaich on the Kyles of Bute - home of that famous shinty team - Kyles Athletic.

Well, Annie obviously fancied Alick and Alick obviously fancied Annie and, when such unity of purpose prevails, there is but one outcome. Annie and Alick were married in 1939, they made their home in Tighnabruaich and raised their family of Sarah, Christine and Anne there. The family and their progeny continue to have very close associations with Arnisdale and the old family home.

Annie's sister Mabel has very clear memories of one telegram which Annie and Alick received on their wedding day. It read:
   "Here's good luck to the Arnisdale bride
   Who captured her mate on the Golden Hind".

Roddy
Roddy worked in the Mialairidh Forest at the planting of the young conifers and at weeding around the fledgling trees after he left school in the early 1930s. He also worked in the Glenelg Hotel. But Roddy also enjoyed the work on the croft - with the cows and the sheep, making the hay and attending to the potatoes which were such a vital part of the diet for all the Arnisdale folk. The ground had to be prepared in the springtime, the open drills had to be lined with dung from the byre and seaweed from

the shore - and the Kerrs Pink, Golden Wonders and Edzell Blues had to be planted.  Then weeding had to be done before the plants were 'earthed up' to provide plenty of soil and plant food around the developing tubers - and to protect the tubers from the greening effects of sunlight.  Then, of course, as things came to fruition, there would be the regular daily lifting of the 'new' potatoes.  This was one of the highlights of the year as the new tubers would be inspected for individual size and numbers per plant - but the real excitement would come as the steaming first potful was emptied into the dish in the middle of the dinner table.  That is when the new arrivals would be really savoured and it mattered little what the other component of the meal comprised - from basic to exotic - the total conversation and the analysis of the meal would centre around the new potatoes.  No matter how overfilled the dinner dish was with the new fruits of the earth, there would not be one, not even a scrap, left at the end of the meal - to be thrown out to the always expectant hens.  The scraps from the table were always one of the daily joys of the hens on the croft - but they did not get the opportunity to savour the new potatoes!

So Roddy loved the work on the croft and in the house, he was very good at it - and he had impeccable manners and grace.  So it was that when the family suffered the double tragedy of losing a loving mother and father within a 17 month period between 1935 and 1937, considerable weight and expectation fell upon Roddy.  Roddy rose to the challenge of running the home and the croft, helped greatly in the early years by a family united in grief but also in shielding and looking after each other.

The author remembers during his young life in Arnisdale in the 1946-48 period that when Roddy Mor and Aunt Lizzie would be away for a night or two, his 'lodgings' were always with Roddy in the Fletcher family home.  He could not have been made so welcome, so comfortable and so well looked after in any other place in the land.  Roddy was one of his great Arnisdale 'pals' - a veritable fine little Highland gentleman.  Roddy was often termed 'Roddy Beag' - probably to identify him in general conversation from his uncle at the Farm - 'Roddy Mor'.

Roddy, like the rest of the Fletcher family, was very musical and was an outstanding dancer.  From the overheard comments of the ladies after many Arnisdale schoolroom dances, Roddy was as graceful a dancer as ever graced the Arnisdale schoolroom floor.  All the ladies - young, middle aged and those in more mature years - always thoroughly enjoyed and savoured the dance they got from 'Roddy Beag'.

Mabel
Mabel was still in her teens when her mother and father died.  She was a very important 'brick' in the family efforts to cope with their grief and to pull together to find their way ahead.  Mabel is still around - and still very much of a 'brick' - totally enthusiastic from her home in Dunoon about this venture of producing a book on Arnisdale and Loch Hourn.  She has been pressing her memory bank, thinking, writing, telephoning and generally enthusing and fuelling the author - and many other people besides - Jessie MacGowan (nee MacDonald), Margaret Fletcher, Donald MacCuaig, Effie MacLaren (now Mrs Haggart) in Carnoustie - to name but a few.  Mabel has recorded her own memories of Arnisdale and Loch Hourn elsewhere in this book so only some brief memories will be recorded here.

Mabel enjoyed her schooldays and liked life in general.  Sometimes school and 'life' did not mesh together such as on the occasion the teacher banned the children from attending a Friday night ceilidh dance in the school to welcome home 'Willie the Post' and his new bride, Christina.  Mabel could not resist missing out on all this Friday evening excitement, so defied the teacher's ruling - and paid for it on the following Monday morning!

Mabel was obviously a very sensitive young lady and as her father lay during his final illness in the Royal Northern Infirmary in Inverness, she had a dream one night that her father was on the hill at his stalking and gamekeeping and as she, in her dream, entered her house, there were two telegrams lying on the table. On the following day, in reality, two telegrams appeared on their kitchen table and her Uncle 'Roddy Mor' was there with them. One was for her mother and the other was for Roddy Mor but both had been delivered to Roddy on her father's express wishes. Ali, her father, a great friend of Roddy Mor, had asked the staff in the Infirmary, that, when his time came, the messages about his passing should be sent to Roddy, who, in turn, would come to break the news to Mabel's mother (Roddy's sister) and the young family.

Just seventeen months later, Mabel's mother, aged 53 years, was in the same Infirmary recovering from what the family thought was a routine operation. But then a telegram came through to the effect that their mother was very ill and the family should come as quickly as possible. They moved immediately. Mabel and Lachie set off on the four hour journey with Uncle Roddy Mor in his little Austin 7. They made all possible speed but, alas, the news which met them on their arrival was that their dear mother had passed away a few hours previously. Young Mabel, Lachie and Uncle Roddy had to return home to their new responsibilities - along with the rest of the close-knit young family to look after each other and try to get their lives together again and move forwards. Through great mutual support and love, the Fletcher family succeeded.

After helping the family over the trauma of the loss of their dear mother and father, and reorganising their ways for coping and running the household, the croft - and their lives - in positive ways, Mabel's first job away from home was to go to keep house for her brothers Peter and Donald in Ardtaraig Estate, near Dunoon. There Mabel met her husband-to-be, Peter Campbell, who was the local postman. Before they could get married, Peter, who was already in the Territorials, was drafted into the 8th Battalion Argyll and Sutherland Highlanders and, within two days of joining up in 1939, war was declared.

Mabel and Peter were eventually married in the Free Church in Arnisdale on the first of January 1940. The officiating Minister was the Rev. Peter Munro Chisholm from Ardelve. Everybody in Arnisdale - from both Camusban and Corran - were invited - and many more besides . After the marriage ceremony, the whole company marched from the Church to the Fletcher family home. Leading the party was Angus Campbell, playing the tune 'The Campbells are Coming' on his bagpipes. Then followed the bride and groom and all the guests. The family and neighbours had been very busy preparing a great feast for days previously and, despite the shortage of space in the croft house, all managed to squeeze in and a great wedding meal and ceilidh was enjoyed by all. It was the first wedding which took place in Arnisdale for 40 years - Sheena Nash's (nee Stewart) grandfather and grandmother being the last one.

Mabel and Peter had two of a family - Jeanette and Sandra, and now the grandchildren and great-grandchildren are with us.

The family lost Peter in 1971 at the age of 66 years. The expanding Campbell-Fletcher family still have very strong ties with Arnisdale - but none more so than the vintage matriarch herself - Mabel!

Mabel has been very enthusiastic about the current Arnisdale book project. Her memories are still very clear and she still retains her fine singing voice. She was not only able to recall the popular songs sung at the Arnisdale ceilidhs of old but she proceeded to sing them all to provide a taped record of many of the old favourites of Roddy Mor, Mary MacIntyre, Fachie MacRae, Tony Mackay and many others.

Donald
Donald kept the old family home and the croft going as long as he was able and he is now resident in the Home Farm House, Portree where he is happy and comfortable and greatly enjoys the regular visits

of his family and his very many friends.  Donald always savoured the yarns and the ceilidhs and there are few better at telling a good story than himself.  Donald was always a great wit and a 'leg puller' and in the 'repartee' which was a great source of amusement in past days between the rival clachans of Arnisdale-Camusban and Corran - there were few better than Donald at keeping up the end of the Lonacs (the Camusban villagers) against the jibes of the Coulags (the Corran folk) - such as Sandy MacAskill, Willie the Post, Johnnie Murchison and Angus Stewart.

Donald has always had a great interest in the Highland Games and particularly the heavy events - the caber, the shot, the weight over the bar and the Cumberland Wrestling or the 'Catch as Catch can'.  He loves to talk about the great feats of the legendary Donald Dinnie and A. A. Cameron and other great heavies of the past such as Clark, Hunter, Cameron, Lochearnhead, Anderson, MacLellan and Jay Scott from Inchmurrin on Loch Lomond - an outstanding all-rounder in both light and heavy events.

Another great interest of Donald's is the boxing and particularly at the heavyweight level again - and he still talks enthusiastically and knowingly of Joe Louis, Tommy Farr, Rocky Marciano, Cassius Clay and the like.

Donald's first job on leaving school was with big brother Peter on the Ardtaraig Estate near Dunoon.  After army service, Donald spent most of his working life in the Mialairidh Forest where his wit and stories brightened up many a wet, misty, dreich, midgie-infested day for his working companions.

However, Donald is probably best remembered in Arnisdale for his music making and his playing of 'fine tunes' on his 'boxie' for the dancing at the Arnisdale ceilidh dances.   While there was always some uncertainty whether the boys from up the loch - Do MacKillop with his fiddle or Peter MacRae with his bagpipes - would manage to get to the dances in wet, stormy weather - Donald could always be relied on to be there.  The musically talented MacLaren family from Glenfield and Donald's brother Peter (when available) with his fiddle, were others who gave Donald great support in providing the fine music and tempo which always prevailed at the Arnisdale dances.

Donald could fill a book on his own with all his amusing stories about Arnisdale, about the Mialairidh Forestry squad and about the exploits and life in general of the Loch Hourn folk.

Farquhar and Alistair
Farquhar and Alistair had seven older brothers and sisters to care for them in their early years and they needed them very badly when they lost their mother when only 15 and 12 years old respectively, especially with their father's death only seventeen months previously.

Among the very pleasant memories of the youngest members of the family was the dancing of the Camusban - and also the Corran - children on the old wooden bridge below their house which spanned Allt a'mhuilinn.  The music for the dancing was the puirt a beul (the mouth music) sung by their older sister Mabel and others.  They also remember their brother Donald practising and perfecting his melodeon tunes sitting on a stone on the shore.  Donald used to say that the music would attract the seals.

When they left school, both Farquhar and Alistair worked in the Mialairidh Forest for a time and also got jobs on the Arnisdale Estate during the season.

In the early part of the war, Farquhar, still too young to be accepted for war service, tried to join the local Home Guard - the Arnisdale 'Dad's Army'.  Although he was not accepted because of his age, he followed them on their exercises and manoeuvres and would then give a full report of all exciting activities to the other youngsters in the village.  As soon as he was old enough, Farquhar joined the army and it was during the war years that he met his wife to be, Brenda, who belongs to Coventry.

After the end of the war, Farquhar and his new bride settled in Coventry and it was there that their son, Keith, was born. Later, younger brother, Alistair, joined Farquhar in Coventry and they worked in the car manufacturing industry there throughout their working lives.

Of the original family of nine, three are still with us at the time these lines are being penned - Mabel, Donald, and Farquhar. Mabel, a bit like mother hen, stays in touch with her younger brothers on a regular basis, keeping the close-knit family together.

As Mabel's generation of the Fletcher family thins out, the succeeding generations are around in expanding numbers, many with a very healthy interest in Arnisdale, with good ideas on how to halt its present decline, revitalise it and to make it grow and bustle again, always trying to build firm new foundations on the basis of culture, the faith, the history, the language, the honesty, integrity, industry - and the great sense of community - which prevailed among Arnisdale and Loch Hourn folk in the past.

**Top Left**. Ally Fletcher and his wife Tina (nee MacLeod) were married in the shepherd's house in Upper Sandaig in 1907 so that the Minister from Ardelve did not have to travel all the way to Arnisdale.  **Centre**.. Ally Fletcher in his Lovat Scout uniform (around 1900). **Right**. Ally Fletcher (right) after a successful stalk on the Arnisdale Estate.  The pony with its burden arrives at Arnisdale Lodge for the stag to be off loaded and hung up in the larder for skinning and further processing (1920s).

**Middle Left.** The first six of the nine children of Ally Fletcher and Christina (Tina) L to R.  Roddy, Lachie, Kenny, Annie, Peter and baby Mabel.  **Right**.  The three eldest of the Fletcher children in Arnisdale School around 1919.  Front Row. L to R. Angus Duncan and Ewen Murchison, Peter, Lachie and Kenny Fletcher.

**Bottom Left**.  A later Arnisdale School photograph (around 1930).  Back Row (L to R.) Iain MacCuaig, Jimmy Campbell, Roddy Fletcher, Morag MacDonald, Teacher Miss Fletcher, (no relation to Arnisdale Fletchers), Mabel Fletcher, Angus Stewart and Donald MacKintosh.  Front Row (L to R.) Jessie MacDonald, Chrissie MacCuaig, Mary and Rena Macdonald, Farquhar and Donald Fletcher. **Right**.  L to R. Farquhar, Donald and Alistair Fletcher outside the family home in Camusban on the east side of Allt a Mhuilinn.

**Top Left**. Ally Fletcher (centre) lends a hand at the Corran Township clipping at the farm fank. Others (L to R.) are Allan MacAskill and Johnnie Murchison (around 1930).   **Right**.  This Camusban group in their 'Sunday best' relax on a fine summer's day. Seated L to R. Kenny, Peter and Lachie Fletcher, Molly Fraser, Nora MacDonald, Mary MacCuaig, Iain MacCuaig.   Rear. Donald and Farquhar Fletcher, Johnny Sinclair, Donald MacCuaig (with head bandage).

**Middle Left**.  Another Camusban group on a Sunday afternoon stroll to Rarsaidh.   Front (L to R.) Peter and Farquhar Fletcher, Archie MacLean and Donald Fletcher.   Back. Annie and Mabel Fletcher (around 1930).
**Centre.**  Annie Fletcher was 'the Arnisdale bride who met her mate on the Golden Hind'.  Annie's husband was Alick MacCallum from Tighnabruaich who was one of the sailors on Commander Kitson's yacht.
**Right**.   Annie's husband Alick MacCallum, Tighnabruaich,  and their little daughter, Sarah.

**Bottom Left**.  Annie Fletcher (centre) with her friends Fay (left) and Betty MacLaren about to board the estate boat the 'Noressian' for the annual sail and party which the Kitson family put on for the local folk (late 1930s).
**Right**.  Joining the same sailing trip on Loch Hourn are (L to R.) Mabel Fletcher, Morag MacDonald, Maggie MacAskill and District Nurse Morrison.

**Top Left**. Having a spy to locate the stags on a stalk on the Arnisdale hill are L to R. Kenny, Peter and Lachie Fletcher and Iain MacKenzie (1960s). **Right**. On the bridge over Allt a Mhuilinn with their rebuilt house in the background are Kenny (left) and Donald Fletcher (right) with Mrs Sheila Campbell, daughter of Donald and Lisa MacKenzie, Lea. (1960s). The old house had been destroyed by fire.

**Middle Left**. Lachie Fletcher at his home at Glenfield around 1980. Lachie was appointed to the job of Arnisdale Estate Manager in 1959. **Right**. Lachie married Chrissie MacDougall (right) in 1958. Chrissie is seen here with her parents, Margaret and George MacDougall. Margaret was a native of Skinidin, Glendale, in Skye. George was still working on the Arnisdale Estate into his nineties.

**Bottom Left**. Lachie and Chrissie's family, Margaret and Peter with Chrissie (centre) and Christine Hastings (left) at Glenfield, Arnisdale. **Middle**. Peter Fletcher with his wife Lizzie and daughters Tina and Jean. Peter was appointed to the post of Arnisdale Estate handyman in 1960. **Right**. Donald Fletcher along with brother Peter (on the fiddle) and others were the regular musicians at the Arnisdale ceilidh dances.

**Top Left**. L to R. Lachie, Peter and Kenny Fletcher on an October stalk make their way up Druim na Firean with snow capped Druim Ealasaig to the right. **Right.** L to R. Lachie, Peter and Kenny Fletcher on the top of Mullach Gorm have got the stags in their sights. Below, the River Arnisdale makes its way into the Dubh Lochain. To the left is Druim Fada with Ladhar Behinn's top showing on the south side of Loch Hourn.

**Middle Left**. Peter Fletcher checks for any sign of deer on the north face of Beinn Chlachach from Coire Chorsalain between Beinn nan Caorach and Beinn Chlachach. To the right is the shoulder of Beinn Bhuidhe and in the distance Beinn Caillaich in Knoydart. **Right**. The old house at Crionaich at the junction of the hill track from Kinloch Hourn, with one branch making for Glen Beag, Glen Mor and Glenelg and the other branch making its way to Arnisdale. The Fosters were the last family of shepherds to stay in the Crionaich house and tend their large hirsel of sheep in this area.

**Bottom Left.** L to R. Lachie Fletcher, Iain MacKenzie and Kenny Fletcher have a good spy of the territory as they progress on their stalk on a fine late Autumn day. **Right**. George MacDougall who did his good share of stalking, shepherding and everything else which had to be done on the farm and the estate. George was still working into his nineties. He liked to be in the thick of the action

**Top Left.** Lachie Fletcher in his young days was involved as a drover in taking the big herds of cattle which were swum across the 'Narrows' at Kylerhea from Skye. **Right**. A small drove passing Galltair in Glenelg on the long route to southern markets via Glen Beag, Glen Kingie, Loch Arkaig, Spean Bridge, Glencoe and Glenlyon.

**Middle Left.** Lachie's skills as a drover and his knowledge of the drove route was used in the 1920s when the cattle and sheep stock of the Arnisdale Estate head stalker/gamekeeper, Alick Campbell, were moved via the ancient drove route from Arnisdale to Mucomir in Lochaber. The wedding day picture of Alick Campbell and his wife Mary (early 1900s). **Right** Alick and Mary Campbell at a later stage of their lives.

**Bottom**. Duncan MacTavish (left), another experienced Arnisdale man who knew the drove route and the folk along the way very well, accompanied young Lachie in taking the small drove from Arnisdale to Mucomir. L to R. Mary and Duncan Campbell, daughter and son of Alick and Mary. Far right. Peter Fletcher, son of Lachie and Chrissie, a keen runner and climber who has good knowledge of the old drove route.

**Top**. Lachie and Peter Fletcher were great shinty enthusiasts. As boys, they had spent holidays with their grandfather and their aunts (Mrs Jeck MacKenzie, Mrs Dan Mackay and Mrs Donald Forbes) and cousins in the Lochcarron-Stromeferry area. Along with their cousins there they developed their shinty skills and both played in the great shinty battles between Arnisdale and Glenelg in the 1920-30 period. Naturally, they were great supporters of the Lochcarron Shinty team. Their cousins Kenny and Tommy MacKenzie were members of the fine Lochcarron team of the 1960-70 period. This Lochcarron team defeated Lovat in the first Dewar Shield Final (1970). Front. L to R. Murdo MacLean (Monty), Lachie MacKenzie, Tommy MacKenzie (Jeck), Kenny Cameron, Alasdair MacKenzie (Ham), Jimmy Cushnie and son Gregor. Back. L to R. Roddy MacLennan, Hugh Matheson, David Ross, Calum MacKenzie (Cappy), Kenny MacKenzie (Jeck), Willie MacKenzie (Dula), Kenny John Stewart, Norrie Matheson, Ronnie Ross.

**Middle**. Lachie and Peter also took a keen interest in the performance of other shinty teams which had players with strong Arnisdale connections such as Lochaber Camanachd (with the sons - Davie, Roddy and Bernard of Mary Campbell formerly of Glenfield and her husband Sandy Campbell – the postman at Gairlochy and also **Below** in the Glasgow Kelvin team which contained the other Campbell brother, John and none other than old Arnisdale friend, Johnnie Murchison, as the team manager. **Middle Right**. Lochaber Camanachd. Winners of MacGillivray Junior League Cup 1966. Back. L to R. Clifford Millen, Alister MacDonald, John Andrews, Colin MacFadyen, Tom (Nick) MacDonald, Hector Millen, Billy MacLachlan. Front. L to R. Ronnie MacKintosh, Tommy MacGregor, David Campbell, Roddy Campbell and Ian (Beanie) Murray.

**Below**. The Glasgow Kelvin Club 1969. Back Row (L to R.) Finlay MacRae, John A MacGregor, John MacLeod, John Campbell, Dr J D Murchison (President of the Camanachd Association), Donald Buchanan, Andy Dunn.
Front (L to R.) Archie Fraser, Murdo MacKenzie, Alistair Clark, Allan Hoey, Gregor Denoon, Allan MacPherson.

Lachie and Peter Fletcher also followed the fortunes of Straths Athletic from the Stratherrick district (with the Sandaig quartet of Bobby MacLean, Sandy, Tom and Alan MacDiarmid) and also GlenUrquhart which contained another batch of players with strong Arnisdale connections (Tom MacDiarmid, Bob and Peter English, and Peter MacDonald). Lachie and Peter would have taken great pleasure in forming an Arnisdale Shinty Team from those 'eligible' players in these Lochcarron, Lochaber, Glasgow Kelvin, Straths Athletic and GlenUrquhart teams. There is no doubt that they would have backed them against old rivals Glenelg and many other teams besides.

**Top**. Straths Athletic. Winners of the MacGillivray Junior League Cup 1951. Back Row (L to R.) Mrs Mary MacKintosh, Tim Pow, Ewan MacDonald, Johnny Kennedy, Angus MacGillivray. Middle Row. Father Thain, Hughie Fraser, Sandy Campbell, Robin Fraser, Tom MacDiarmid, Alan MacDiarmid, Ali Fraser, Dick Ogilvie, Roddy MacKintosh. Front. Wolstan MacPherson, Peter Grant, Bobby MacLean, Col. Sopper, Willie Cooper, Fachie MacDonald and Iain MacDonald.

**Below**. GlenUrquhart. Winners of the Scottish Junior Championship (Sutherland Cup) and MacGillivray Junior League Cup 1963. Back Row (L to R.) Danny Fraser, John MacLean, Andrew Iain MacDonald, Calum Fraser, George Stewart, Tom MacKenna, John MacKintosh, Peter English, John Alick MacKenzie, Bob English, Murdo Campbell. Front. Sandy MacDonald, Kenny 'Tosh' MacKintosh, Bob MacDonald, Jocky MacDonald, Tom MacDiarmid, Roddy Mackintosh, Jimmac MacKintosh, Bob MacDonald and Ken Fraser.

Lachie Fletcher had very clear memories of a major confrontation around 1930 of the Arnisdale folk with the laird – Commander Kitson. The Kitson family were kind and widely respected but when the estate gardener and the laird accused the local folk of stealing the prime Victoria plums on the Sabbath day from the lodge garden this called for urgent action. The local folk, many of them employees of the estate, demanded to have a crisis meeting in the school in an attempt to clear their name. Notices were posted about the 'Court of Enquiry' and almost the entire population of Arnisdale, as well as many from Glenelg, made their way to the school. Kitson had summoned the Estate Factor from Edinburgh to support himself and the lodge gardener, Andrew Thompson at the meeting. **Top Left**. Johnnie Murchison (left) reads the notice for the meeting attached to Archie MacLean's shed door along with Archie (right) at the Camusban roadside. **Right**. Young Ewen Murchison, on holiday from University, was elected by the local folk to be chairman at the meeting.

**Middle Left**. After many accusations from Commander Kitson and Andrew Thompson and very stout defence by the local folk, it emerged that the culprits were not the local folk but the 'Boots' from the lodge aided and abetted by Jimmy Kennedy (far right) who worked at the farm. **Right**. Andrew and Mrs Thompson in front of Arnisdale Lodge. Mrs Thompson, wife of the lodge gardener, despite her husband 'getting a hard time of it' at the meeting saw the funny side of the proceedings. She observed the plight of the respective Crofting Township Clerks, Iain Beag MacGillivray (Camusban) and Angus Murchison (Corran). Her comment was that 'the one who could speak couldn't hear while the one who could hear, couldn't speak'. Apparently Ian Beag, desperate to engage in the debate, could not hear what others were saying while Angus, with good hearing, was getting so excited that he was unable to gather himself sufficiently to put across the points he wished to make!

**Bottom**. Ian Beag MacGillivray (left) and Angus Murchison (right) who were both desperate to have their say in the heated debate.

# Chapter 19

**Mabel's special memories**
**(Mrs Mabel Campbell (nee Fletcher) - now resident in Dunoon)**

Here I go to tell you some stories that I can recall from the olden days back home in Arnisdale; although I left there almost 60 years ago, there is a lot still fresh in my memory.

I shall start off with the dances held in Arnisdale in my teenage years in the 1930s. The dances always had to be held on a Friday night, as they took place in the School, and the School had to be scrubbed on the Saturday for the children to go back into on Monday. In those days the dances did not start in earnest till maybe ten o'clock at night, as we waited or hoped some would come from Glenelg and Kinlochourn - so we would stand at the School door watching for a light of a car coming down the brae or the noise of a motor-boat from Kinlochourn. The cars were very few in these days and usually the first, and I think the only car that would arrive, would go back for more folk. The dances took the form of a ceilidh dance, and usually, someone would be asked to sing. My most vivid memories of the singers were Mary MacIntyre, Roddie Mor and Tony MacKay. Mary would usually sing "Danny Boy". Roddie Mor was sure to sing "Soraidh" (Farewell) or "Caisteal a'Ghlinne" (Castle in the Glen) and Tony would always sing "Grannie's Hielan Hame". I never hear these songs now, but I think on these three people. The next day (Saturday), the ladies all met to scrub out the School, and we would be down on our knees, with a pail and scrubbing brush, and the usual topic of conversation was, who gave you a certain dance? and who saw you home? And if a young man saw you home, the whole village would know about it. I remember one dance in particular that took place - I think it was a welcome home dance for Willie MacKenzie and his new bride, and we looked so much forward to it, but the teacher told us at School, that she did not want to see any of her pupils at the dance - but this was too much for me, so I went to the dance, and when we went back to the School on Monday the teacher said "stand up the girl who disobeyed my orders, and went to the dance". So I stood up and got a right dressing down; all I can remember is her final words, "you have gone down to the depths of my estimation". Well, that is enough about the dances.

Now about ceilidhing in the houses; one of our favourite houses was Lexy Campbell's, and when we saw her taking the clock down to wind, we knew that was a hint to go, but we just ignored it, until she would say to us "Have none of you a bed to go to tonight?" So we finally left, but went back the following night - no offence taken! Lexy had a daughter Mary-Ann who used to be in domestic service in Glasgow. She used to tell us that when she went for an interview for a job, she had only one question to ask - have you any beetles in your house? And if they had, she would not accept the job, as she had an awful fear of beetles. She always used to tell us that when she went down Hope Street in Glasgow on a Saturday night to go to the "Hielan Man's Umbrella", she just felt as much at home, as if she was walking down the Arnisdale brae back home.

Lexy had very bad eyesight which she developed in her early years after nursing her mother and father during the dreadful typhoid epidemic in Arnisdale. Lexy's mother and father died along with many others in Arnisdale. Although Lexy and her sisters Mairi Bhan and Anne survived, Lexy's vision was badly affected afterwards. When I was a young girl, Lexy used to ask me to read her Gaelic Bible to her. Although I was not very good at first, that's the way I learned to read Gaelic. It was almost 50 years later when I visited Mary Ann in her latter years on one of my return visits to Arnisdale that I was reading some stories in Gaelic to Mary Ann. By this time Mary Ann herself had gone blind and she asked me where I learned to read in Gaelic. "It was in this house fifty years ago when I used to read the Bible to your mother", I replied.

Another house we liked to visit for a ceilidh was Mary Ann Cameron's house in Corran, and the attraction there was that she had an old gramophone that she played for us. No matter where we visited, we always had to be back home by ten o'clock, as my father took out the Bible and read it to us at that time. The only day we went for a walk was a Sunday, as there was hardly any work done on a Sunday. We usually took a walk down to Rarsaidh and back. We had to carry all the water in on the Saturday night, but we were near the burn so it was no bother. The sermons in the Church in those days lasted for 2 hours in the morning and at night for another 2 hours.

We often talked about the drowning tragedy in 1905 in the Arnisdale river up the Glen, of Effie Stewart. Effie belonged to the travelling people and as she and her family tried to cross the raging river, Effie lost her footing and was swept away. Effie is buried in the Arnisdale churchyard. My brother Farquhar told me that he remembers hearing that a few days before Effie was drowned, that our father was riding on horseback up the glen, and when they got to a certain spot, the horse refused to go further, and a few days later Effie was found drowned - not far from the spot where the horse refused to move further.

Another story about my father - one night he was wakened out of his sleep, with someone shouting 'Eirich, Ali' (get up, Alick); this was repeated three times and my father got up to the window, but there was no one there. However, three nights later, he heard the same voice again, and this time there was a man there to tell him that some man (a neighbour) had died suddenly.

As kids we were all fond of spending time with the old folk around and had we only thought of writing things down then we would have so much to pass on. Alas, when you are young, these things don't occur to you.

Now, I will get back to my schooldays in Arnisdale. Our family were away from Camusban from 1920 till 1924, as my father got a job as a gamekeeper in a place called Glenmallie - and the nearest house was 3 miles away at Invermallie, and then Spean Bridge was beyond that. Farquhar was born at Glenmallie, and Alastair was born after we got back to Camusban. I still remember the morning Alastair was born - we were all taken into the bedroom to see the new baby, all wrapped up - only his face was showing - so Farquhar kept saying "Bheil casan air?" (Has he got feet?).

I would have been seven years old when we came back from Glenmallie and I think the first teacher we had was a Miss MacLean, who later married one of the Fosters, then there was Miss Logan from Spean Bridge, and then Miss Fletcher from Skye, and the last teacher I had was Donald Finlayson, also from Skye. He was a very fine teacher. I left school before Mrs Kennedy came; she too was from Skye, and her husband, Martin, came from Roybridge. At the time, Mrs Kennedy's husband was doing a degree course so as to enter the teaching profession and, after completing his Degree, he did some teaching in Arnisdale for a time.

I remember one morning when we got to school, the teacher could not get the door opened, so she sent for one of the local men, Donald McIntosh. Donald managed to get the door opened, and inside in the lobby was a tramp. Poor soul, he got short shrift! The tramps I remember were Buffalo Bill who played the pipes, Bobby Robertson, and there was one called 'daft George'. He would say "Some are daft, and they don't know it, but I am daft, and I know it!" And then there was the MacAllister family from Campbeltown, who came every year, and they were greeted as long lost friends; they were tinsmiths and they had a tent down near the dry island (Eilean Tioram). They would get plenty of work repairing all the pots and pans and milk pails of the Arnisdale folk.

Just after Morag MacDonald and I left school, Mrs Kennedy was organising a school concert and she asked Morag and myself to take part. The day after this concert everybody said to us "you acted everything so very well" so we fancied ourselves as actresses for some time afterwards! Below is the report of the concert which appeared in the Oban Times in 1931.

**School Concert in Arnisdale**
A successful concert was held in the school at Arnisdale on Friday last to raise funds for the Children's Xmas Treat. Rev. T M Murchison presided. An interesting programme of English and Gaelic songs, recitations, plays and dancing was carried through by the schoolchildren. Humorous dialogues (Gaelic) were given by Misses Mabel Fletcher and Morag MacDonald. The play "Bloaters" was performed by the children, spirited dancing and eightsome reels were performed by junior children to the accompaniment of the organ played by Miss Amy Thomson and violin music was rendered by Messrs Peter Fletcher and Donald MacLaren, and on the close the Chairman commented on the creditable performance by the children.

Pupils who took part were Morag, Jessie, Rena and Mary MacDonald, Effie and Betty MacLaren, Chrissie and Ian MacCuaig, James A Campbell, Donald and Farquhar Fletcher and William Stoddart. Singing was rendered by a choir of 8 children. Their teacher, Mrs Joan Kennedy is to be congratulated for her training of the children.

Hearty cheers were given on the call of Mr Murchison and thanks to the chairman were proposed by Mr Daniel MacDonald. A happy evening was brought to a close by the singing of "Oidhche Mhath Leibh". A handsome sum was realised in the collection taken".

So ended the press report on the fine concert provided by the children and now Mabel proceeds with her memories.

The Kitsons, who were the landlords at that time, used to take all the schoolchildren for a sail up the loch on the Noressian each year and then we went back to the Lodge for tea and played games on the lawn. When we had our school picnic every summer, Mary Campbell (whose father was the gamekeeper and stayed at Glenfield) always helped at these picnics, so when she was leaving Arnisdale we collected money to give her a gift. I was asked to present her with the book we got for her and I can still remember the name of the book presented to her - 'The Key above the door'. At Xmas, Mr Andrew Thomson (gardener on the estate) came round all the houses with gifts from the Kitson family of tobacco for the men, and tea for the ladies, and I think it was sweets for the children.

There is another story which I have never forgotten, though it happened about seventy years ago. I found a penny on the road and I knew it was wrong to keep money that did not belong to you; but I thought it would not matter because it was just a penny, and I was thinking on all the sweeties I could buy, so I went home and held out the penny in my hand to my father; he looked at me and said in a firm voice "Where did you get that penny?" "Go and put that penny back where you found it and maybe the person who lost it will find it". So I replied, "It is only a penny" and then he said "If you keep that money, that is stealing, and stealing a penny is just as bad as stealing a pound". So the penny went back on the road where I found it! Well, to this day, every time I find a penny on the road, or various sums of money, I think on my father's words, I pick up the penny or whatever amount lies there, take it home, put it in a jar, and when there is a reasonable amount in the jar, I give it to charity.

I can remember when it was a horse and trap that John Sinclair had for the mails. It took 3 hours to get from Arnisdale to Glenelg and then 3 hours back. I do not remember when the mail car arrived, but often it was very late at night. One Saturday evening, very late at night, when John Sinclair arrived with the mail from Glenelg - the year was 1940 - he reported possible enemy activity en route. I think John liked a bit of excitement; his story was that as he was coming towards Eilanreach, he saw two men going up Eilanreach brae but when he got to that spot there was no trace of them, so the Home Guard was called out, as John gave the impression they might be German spies. However, it turned out that they were two hikers. However, as the Arnisdale Home Guard set off to investigate, I remember Archie MacLean's old mother saying to me "It will be terrible if they are Germans, and our boys have nothing to defend themselves with".

I remember one day as a little girl, Uncle Roddie took me down to the Post Office on his bicycle and, as I waited outside, Peggy Ann's dog bit me on the bottom; in those days, the dog had to be destroyed immediately for such an unprovoked attack on a child. I felt very sorry for the dog.

I had a dream one night, and I have never forgotten it. It was the night before my father died in the Northern Infirmary at Inverness (31 July 1935). I dreamt that my father was out on the hill and when I walked into our house, there were two telegrams lying on the table. In the morning, my mother sent me to the Post Office to post a letter to my father, and Peggy Ann said to me "Who is the letter to, Mabel?" I replied "To my father", to which she responded, "Do you think you should post it?" I said "Yes, my mother says that he will worry if he doesn't get a letter". So Peggy Ann said, "Just put it in the box". When I went back home, Uncle Roddie was in the house and there were two telegrams lying on the table - one had been sent to Uncle Roddie, as my father told them in the hospital, that when his time came, they were to send the news to Uncle Roddie, and he in turn would break the news to my mother. However, the hospital also sent one telegram to my mother, so Peggy Ann sent them both to Uncle Roddie. I realised then that Peggy Ann had already known the sad news when I arrived with the letter for my father, as she was the only one who had the phone in Arnisdale at the time and, of course, the bad news had come via the Post Office.

In those days, all the funerals took place from the home, and a few men and women would take turn about sitting up all night with the bereaved, as they seemed to think it wasn't right to go to bed to sleep, while the remains of the departed family member were in the house.

There was always strict observance of the Sabbath day in the village especially among the older folk. One Sunday morning, Morag MacIntyre's mother, Mary, walked into Archie MacLean's mother's house, and as she walked into the house, she said to Ina the daughter, "My, Ina, your doorstep has remained nice and clean over the weekend" and Ina replied "Yes, it has, hasn't it?" So when Mary left, Ina's mother said to her slowly in a most solemn voice "Ina, did you do these steps this morning?" - to which Ina replied "Well, yes I did, but nobody saw me" - to which the old lady replied "Oh, but God saw you" but Ina responded "No, He never, He is away up to Kinlochourn with the Missionary for the service up there"!

When we went up to Arnisdale on holiday, when our children Jeanette and Sandra were small, I would tell them that they weren't to play outside on the Sunday, as the missionary would be coming to conduct the service in the Free Church, so when they saw his car coming down the Arnisdale brae they used to hide down below the bridge over Allt a' mhuilinn which flowed past our house.

One night when we were children, we were in church at the evening service, and the missionary kept talking about the war in Abyssinia, and repeated the word A-BIS-IN-IA many times, so when we came out of the church, my brother Alastair, who was just a little boy at the time said to my father "Why did the missionary keep saying "I'll be seeing you, I'll be seeing you".

I still remember the crisis meeting in the school about the plums that the local people were accused of stealing from Captain Kitson's Lodge Garden. (See Chapter 18 for the full report on this major 'incident' in Arnisdale).

Ewen Murchison was the Chairman, and carried out his duty in a most professional manner. I can still remember Ian MacGillivray or Ian Beag, as he was known, who stood up and banged his hand on the table, and said to Commander Kitson "You think we are dumb dogs that cannot bark, but thank God we aren't". I thought for a few minutes that he said 'damn dogs', and I thought it was terrible uttering a swear word to Commander Kitson as, in those days, the toffs were very much looked up to; however, I realised afterwards that it was 'dumb' he said, and not 'damn'.

That reminds me of another story I heard, that Roderick Cameron in Rarsaidh would walk the three miles or so up to the farm to see my grandfather (Choinnich MacLeod), and my grandfather would walk back down with Roderick to Rarsaidh, and they would keep convoying one another backwards and forwards for hours. They were obviously very fine friends and greatly enjoyed each other's company as these 'Scotch Convoys' indicate.

Recalling all these stories about Arnisdale for this book has been a great pleasure for me. We had our share of sadness but it is the fun that we had together and the great community spirit which prevailed which are uppermost in the memory chest now. It has been great fun reminiscing over the phone with my great friends such as Jessie MacGowan, Donald MacCuaig and many others. It has just been like having one of these great Arnisdale ceilidhs once again.

**Top**. Mabel Campbell's (nee Fletcher) memories of the regular singers at the Arnisdale ceilidh dances in the 1930s – her uncle Roddy Mor (left), Mary MacIntyre (centre) and Tony Mackay (back row, second from left). The others in this picture of the Mialairidh forestry squad in the 1930s are: Back row L to R. Peter Fletcher, Tony Mackay, Ludovic Fraser, Iain Elder, Jimmy Campbell. Front Row. Donald MacKintosh, Bobby MacLean, Archie MacLean, Andrew Fraser and Angus Stewart.

**Middle Left.** A group of Arnisdale School pupils in the 1920s. L to R. Mabel Fletcher, Jessie, Mary and Rena MacDonald, Chrissy MacCuaig and Morag MacDonald. **Centre**. Mabel (left) with Morag MacDonald on the Arnisdale Estate boat, the Noressian, as they sail to Glenelg for a Sports Day to celebrate Coronation Day, 1937. **Right.** Mabel's wedding to Peter Campbell in 1940 in Arnisdale's Free Church with brother Donald as best man, Morag MacDonald as bridesmaid and the Rev. Peter Munro Chisholm, of the Free Church of Lochalsh as the officiating minister.

**Bottom Left**. The bridal party led by Angus Campbell on the pipes playing 'The Campbells are Coming', make their way from the Church to the Fletcher family home for the reception and feast. **Middle**. Mabel and Peter's daughters Sandra and Jeanette. **Right**. Mabel's younger brother Farquhar's wedding in the late 1940s to Brenda Cleaver in Coventry. Brother Lachie is second from right in the back row.

# Chapter 20

**Sandaig and its people**

The old name for the area or headland at the junction of the north shore of Loch Hourn and the Sound of Sleat is Mialairidh (Meolary in present day usage). A large area of Mialairidh was planted with conifers by the Forestry Commission in the late 1920s and 1930s and later by the Eilanreach Estate in the 1960s. Human habitations are scarce in this area. There is the house at Upper Sandaig beside the main Glenelg-Arnisdale road while there was also a house and croft at Lower Sandaig and a Lighthouse out on the Sandaig Islands. This Lighthouse along with its equivalent across the Sound at Isle Ornsay in Skye, helped to guide the boats and ships through the Sound of Sleat on their way to ports of call such as Kyle of Lochalsh, Mallaig and the Inner and Outer Hebrides. Round further into Loch Hourn there is Port Luinge, the now ruined house there being last inhabited by the MacLeans (Peggy Ann's people) who later established their General Store and Post Office in Arnisdale. Still further round the Mialairidh shore the Forestry Hut was situated, which was the temporary home of such well loved and remembered characters as Tony Mackay and Jimmy MacLean. They were young foresters with the Forestry Commission who helped to plant and establish the Mialairidh Forest in the 1930s. Further round the shoreline still is Rarsaidh with its many islands and after that Arnisdale is reached.

When many outsiders hear reference to Sandaig they will think of the late Gavin Maxwell, his pet otters and his fine books. The book 'Ring of Bright Water' and the later film of the same name featured the pet otters Mijbil and Edal. Thus, the great naturalist Gavin Maxwell made his Camusfearna world famous. Before leaving Camusfearna, the old croft house there which was Maxwell's home, went on fire, was burnt to the ground and has never been rebuilt. Prior to its occupation by Maxwell, Lower Sandaig was occupied by a succession of local crofter shepherds who were employed by the Eilanreach Estate, being responsible for the hirsel of the large Eilanreach sheep flock which grazed the Mialairidh area and the lower slopes of the mountains above (Beinn a'Chapuill and Beinn Sgritheall) throughout the year.

Among the shepherds who occupied Lower Sandaig in earlier years along with their families were the MacKinnons and Robert (Rob) Moffat. At these times in the early 1900s, the children had their own special teacher, Donald Chisholm, late postmaster in Glenelg, having spent some of his early years in this role at Lower Sandaig. Around the late 1920s - early 1930s the Lower Sandaig croft was run by Peter MacPherson from Glenelg along with his wife Katie (nee MacLure), also from Glenelg, and their children Ian, Donald and Jessie Ann. The teacher was Katie Ann MacDonald from Moyle in Glenelg. Peter worked as a shepherd for Eilanreach Estate which was then owned by Mr Scott of Fearn, Ross-shire and Peter was also responsible for servicing the Sandaig Lighthouse.

Working in the Mialairidh Forest in the early 1930s, as well as the Arnisdale boys, were a few from Glenelg such as Archie MacLeod and 14 to 15 year old youngsters who had just left school including Ewan Cameron, Watty MacIntyre, Bobby MacLean and Roddy MacPherson. Roddy, after finishing work half-day on the Saturday would often go to spend the weekend with his Uncle Peter and Aunt Katie in Lower Sandaig.

Roddy remembers that Peter's pay from Eilanreach at that time in the 1930s was £50 per year with the perks being occupation of the house and croft, along with a boll of meal and a boll of flour each year. In addition, Peter received £26 per year for servicing the Lighthouse. Peter and Katie kept one cow for their supply of milk and of crowdie, butter and cheese when the milk was plentiful, they grew their potatoes and made hay for the wintering of the cow.

One job which Roddy was given during the weekend visits to Lower Sandaig was the servicing of the Lighthouse which had to be done every 3 weeks. Although his Uncle Peter was a great shepherd who loved his sheep and walking and working on the moors and mountains, he hated the water. Peter was a big man (about 6ft 2in and 16 stones in his heyday) but was always nervous in the boat as they would make their way out to the Lighthouse on the island. As Roddy rowed out, Peter would sit in the middle of the boat holding on to the sides and would panic at the least rocking. The servicing of the Lighthouse included the polishing of the brasses, cleaning the outside glass and taking the ash off the carbide burner. The Lighthouse Ship came in every 6 months to renew the canister of carbide and service the water tank to provide the regular drip of water to generate the carbide gas for the pilot light and the on-off main light (a stationary light - not a revolving one). Peter was always relieved to get the job done, to get on to dry land again and to get back to working on the croft and with the sheep on the hill - he was not a sailor! Nor did he fish or shoot. However, Roddy spent a lot of time shooting rabbits with a .22 rifle and fishing around the Islands. It was a great place to fish at the time and you could always guarantee a good catch if you went to the right places.

One of the Sandaig Islands served another purpose - grazing ground for the 40 or so Eilanreach Estate tups from the spring to the start of the next tupping season in late November. No fences were required - the tups, like Peter, not being very fond of the water!

Roddy remembers as a young lad helping Peter and Katie with the flitting to Sandaig. The furniture was taken in on the Eilanreach Estate boat with Ali Beag (MacRae) at the helm. The flitting was straightforward except for a large wardrobe which would not go up the staircase. Katie was very keen to get this wardrobe into an upstairs bedroom but the task seemed impossible. Peter had to go to the hill to check the sheep as it was lambing time, so young Roddy suggested to Katie that if they took out one of the upstairs windows, they might get it in that way. Katie thought it was a chance worth taking but what would Peter say if he came back to find one of the upstairs windows missing? They decided to have a go. Roddy managed to get the window out. Then they took the big strong kitchen table and placed it below the open window. They put a wool bag on the window sill and wrapped wool bags round the wardrobe so as to reduce the risk of scratching the wardrobe and then encircled it with a rope. There was discussion as to whether it was best for Katie to stand on the table and push the wardrobe up or else go upstairs to do the pulling on the rope. It was decided that Katie would stand on the table, lift and push while Roddy would go upstairs and pull. Katie and Roddy were right in the middle of this very delicate and potentially disastrous operation when who did they see coming down the path beside the burn but Peter returning from the hill! He saw what was happening and the panic could be seen written all over his face, and he started to run as the big precious wardrobe dangled above the head of his beloved wife, with the youngster above directing operations and trying to keep a cool head in the deepening crisis! Well, they say, when the going gets tough, the tough get going! Katie and Roddy, with one final massive wonderfully synchronised push and pull, managed to get the base of the wardrobe to the edge of the window and the wardrobe was just disappearing inside the open window when the distraught Peter arrived below. The exhaustion of Katie and Roddy was a small price to pay for managing to get the formidable job done while the going was good! Later, when the film 'The Ring of Bright Water' was being shown on television, Roddy told two of his colleagues on the Carsegrey Estate in Forfar (where he was Estate Manager) to be sure to watch it so that they could see the upstairs window of the house through which he performed such a great feat in his early years. Unknown to Roddy, the film had been made in Argyll and not at Lower Sandaig (Camusfearna) and the house featured had only small skylights as upstairs windows! So Roddy's colleagues found it impossible to believe how he had succeeded in getting such a huge wardrobe through such tiny windows!

Roddy remembers Sandaig as a beautiful place and it was little wonder that Gavin Maxwell fell in love with it and performed his finest literary works there.

Close to Lower Sandaig, Roddy had an unforgettable experience of a different kind as a young lad of about 14 – around 1932. On a boat trip he accompanied Donald MacKinnon, stalker at Kylerhea and a man from Glenelg who was in the habit of shooting a seal, cutting the fat into small cubes, suspending it in the sun in muslin or cheesecloth bags and collecting the oil which dripped slowly from the mass into a clean jar below. He would treat his boots and other leather goods with this fine, odourless oil and this provided excellent waterproofing, as well as keeping the leather fine and supple. They rowed their boat past the Sandaig Islands and were making for the island – Eilean a' Chlamhain which is mid-way between the Sandaig Islands and Port Luinge. This island, just offshore, was well known to be used frequently by seals to bask in the sun as they lay on the rocky slopes on its eastern side. On the ebb tide, the ploy was to approach the island from the west (out of sight of the basking seals) and then for the rifleman to clamber up the rocks as quietly as possible to the highest point, to check the location of any seals and then to shoot the most suitable adult, so positioned that it would not slither into the sea on being shot.

Roddy and Donald MacKinnon waited in the boat and watched as the other Glenelg man with the rifle reached the vantage point and they could see him carefully scanning the eastern slope. Usually they did not have long to wait until they saw their friend taking aim and very soon afterwards they would hear the shot of this excellent marksman. But this time there was an unusual delay as their friend continued to scan the rocky eastern slope of the island. After some time there was a rifle shot and the rifleman shouted to Roddy and Donald that he had shot something which was huge. Roddy and Donald thought that a huge seal had been the target and rowed as quickly as they could round the southern edge of the island to the east side. When they reached about 20 yards offshore from the island as the rifleman directed them towards where the 'beast' had gone after the shot, Roddy and Donald noticed a considerable amount of bloodied water in the vicinity. As they studied the water further at this point – lo and behold! – about a further 25 yards to the east a 'thing' broke the surface of the water and started to rise vertically to form a 'long black shiny column' which Roddy reckoned was 10 to 12 feet above the surface. They were terrified and in their terror Donald MacKinnon shouted 'get out of here' and fired two shots from his 12 bore shot-gun (which he always carried with him) to 'frighten the beast' as Roddy 'rowed like blazes' for the safety of the island where the rifleman awaited them. Roddy reckoned that the shots from the 12 bore would have done the beast no harm at that range but Donald fired the shots to 'frighten the beast' so that it would not approach them before they reached the safety of the island.

Before proceeding with Roddy's description of the 'huge beast', the rifleman's experience will be related.

When he had reached the vantage point at the highest point of the island to view the eastern slope and hopefully the seals that would be basking there, he was most surprised to spot not one seal. This had never happened before in their long experience. As he scanned all the nooks and crannies of the face just to make sure no seal was lurking therein, his attention was attracted to what at first he thought was a large black wet shiny rock about three feet high just at the water's edge which was exposed as the tide ebbed. However, as his curious eyes focussed on this unusually black 'rock' he thought he saw the 'rock' moving. As it moved more and started to slither into the water it was then that he instinctively fired his rifle shot. Immediately he shouted to his 'boatmen' about this huge thing at which he had fired. Thinking it was a huge seal, the boatmen responded by rowing round immediately to the east side of the island to get their unforgettable experience of the blood in the water and the column rising vertically out of the water just about 25 yards away from them.

In such circumstances, studies of anatomy were out of the question – survival was the top priority for

Roddy and Donald and, in their terror, they could not reach that shore quickly enough!

What does Roddy remember of his momentary frightening view of the beast? Roddy estimated that it cleared the water's surface by ten to twelve feet, the diameter of the 'tapering column' was around 4 to 6 feet at its base and one foot at the top. Roddy got the impression that the top was swivelling as if it was a head but 'the head was small in relation to the size of the body'. Roddy noticed nothing that resembled flippers and there was no indication of a neck – it tapered gradually to the top. It was 'one big black glossy mass'. It did not remain above the surface for long so there was no chance to study it in detail when they reached the safety of the island. "It was one big black glossy mass – it was the queerest thing anybody could see" said Roddy.

"When it submerged, it did not dive forwards or sideways – it just seemed to go down vertically and gradually without causing much of a wash as it disappeared. It was like a huge tapered shiny bottle as it rose out of the water and as it submerged again." The Glenelg man and Donald MacKinnon, used to the sea and very knowledgeable regarding its contents over a lifetime, had never seen anything remotely resembling their Loch Hourn sighting before. The mystery remains, with Roddy now the sole survivor of that experience. (See also Chapter 34).

Now let us return to more mundane happenings at Sandaig.

At the time in the early 1930s when Roddy worked as a young lad in the Mialairidh Forest, apart from Archie MacLeod, Ewan Cameron, Bobby MacLean and Watty MacIntyre from Glenelg, Archie MacLean from Arnisdale was in the squad as well as youngsters Donald Fletcher from Arnisdale and Donald MacKintosh from Rarsaidh. The ganger was Andrew Fraser from Arnisdale and, as ever with youngsters, they would try to get what licence they could from Andrew to have a rest now and again - especially on wet drizzly days when the midges were bad. They knew that Andrew was terrified of thunder and lightning and as they weeded around the young trees using their sickles to cut brackens and tall grasses, if Andrew heard thunder he would throw the sickle from his hand lest the lightning caught him holding a metal tool. Aware of this frailty, the young boys would often pretend that they heard thunder so that Andrew might decide to stop work temporarily because of the dangers of subsequent lightning! The head forester at the time was a Mr Bill Stoddart and he would come to check unannounced from time to time that progress with the weeding was satisfactory. Bill Stoddart smoked the pipe almost constantly and the whiff of his 'Black Twist' as he approached preceded any sight or sound of him. Therefore, when Andrew thought the youngsters in the squad were slacking a bit, one of his chief weapons to get the boys beavering away again was to stop momentarily, put his nose in the air and warn the squad 'I can smell Stoddart's tobacco - we better get going'!

But, let us return to Peter MacPherson, the Sandaig shepherd. Peter was appointed to a shepherding job in Knoydart around 1936 and so he and his family moved away from Lower Sandaig. Selected as Eilanreach shepherd in his place in charge of the Sandaig hirsel, was a young man who was born in Greenock who had strong Arnisdale and Glenelg connections. He was the son of Mr and Mrs Hugh MacLean. Hugh had been born and lived all his life in Greenock while his forebears had come from Stein in the Vaternish district of Skye. Mrs MacLean was Ada Moffat before her marriage (daughter of Tom Moffat and his wife Agnes (nee Foster)). Thus Bobby was related to the Moffats of Glenelg (and to Rob Moffat, a former shepherd at Lower Sandaig) and to the Fosters who were at Crionach in the Arnisdale Glen and later at Corran. Bobby had learned much of his sheep lore from his Uncle Rob Moffat who was by now Sheep Manager on the Eilanreach Estate. Bobby had a sister, Gertie, and their father had died suddenly as a young man, after playing football. After a few years, Ada, Hugh's widow, married Sandy MacDiarmid from Easdale in Argyll and they had three sons, Sandy, Tom and Alan. Around 1932 they came home to Glenelg, at first living in the Glenelg village at Kirkton. When

Bobby left school, he first worked in the Mialairidh Forest and later in the Aluminium Factory in Fort William, but when he got the job as a shepherd on the Eilanreach Estate he moved along with his whole family to Lower Sandaig. While his sister Gertie had left school by this time, the young MacDiarmid boys had their own teacher at Lower Sandaig - first Katie Anne MacDonald from Moyle in Glenelg and later Cathie Thomson from Quarry, Glenelg. In addition to being devoted to and highly competent at his shepherding, Bobby and his brothers Sandy, Tom and Alan, sometimes accompanied by their cousin Tommy Moffat, found time for sport and many other ploys. Bobby had developed his early footballing skills in Greenock and the whole family were great supporters of Greenock Morton. While working in the Aluminium Factory at Fort William, Bobby's football talents saw him quickly gain his place in the Factory team. Scouts from a Scottish First Division Team were soon on his trail and, were it not for the outbreak of war, Bobby might well have graduated to the highest level in Scottish football. So there was plenty of football played at Lower Sandaig but they were all equally keen on the shinty and, with home made camans, prepared from the plentiful alder and hazel woods within reach, fine shinty skills were also developed by the boys Tom remembers making a good caman from a holly branch. But there was also plenty of work to do. Father Sandy had a fine garden and produced all the vegetables and fruit which they required, they grew potatoes and some oats and made hay to provide the winter fodder for their four cows and followers and the goat which was also kept for its milk. They also kept hens and ducks. They used to try to get the cows calving in sequence so that they would always have milk, but since they had to take the cows (when in season) on the halter and rope to the nearest bull at Eilanreach, it was often difficult to get this good spread of calving which they sought. However, making butter and crowdie were fairly regular chores, while mother also had a cheese press to make their own cheese.

They were very dependent on their animals for milk and eggs and, of course, on the dung for the garden and for the potatoes and oats on the croft. The croft animals were well looked after, as were the wild birds. Father Sandy, while digging in the garden, was often accompanied by the pet buzzard eating worms close to his feet. Occasionally, as he would come down the path beside the burn from Upper Sandaig, the buzzard would come swooping down at his head and knock his bonnet off. They also had a sparrow hawk and when Ada called it to offer it a tit-bit of meat, it would come diving down from the heavens to collect its reward almost out of her hand. On one occasion the buzzard witnessed this operation and pursued the sparrow hawk, caught up with it over the Sandaig Islands, gripped it and dispossessed it of its titbit. However, although deprived, the sparrow hawk was otherwise none the worse.

For fuel, the family were dependent on peats which they cut on the moors on both sides of the Sandaig burn - on the south-east Arnisdale side and on the Tormòr side on the north-west. They also got firewood from the plentiful nearby supplies of birch and alder and from the driftwood on the shore. Peats were carted home from the moor in bags and creels on their back while the hay was taken to the barn in rope bundles when it was fully cured and won from the elements. Later on, Bobby bought an old Riley car from a friend at Eilanreach with a view to 'mechanising' some of the operations at the croft. The car was driven to Upper Sandaig on the main road and then began the delicate operation to get it down to Lower Sandaig. Bobby and his brothers set off down the old cart track on the Arnisdale side of the Sandaig burn, passed the fank and lower down managed to get across the burn at the old ford, and - bit by bit edged the vehicle down the track and succeeded in getting it down the final bank to Lower Sandaig. There the old car was converted into a little truck and was ideal for collecting the hay from the field and taking it to the barn - that is after they got it started - and it usually took a lot of cranking of the starting handle before the old engine purred into life!

Spring cultivation work was sometimes assisted by the appearance of Willie MacLeod with the Eilanreach horses. The plough would be brought from Eilanreach in the boat and Willie would plough the area set aside for the potatoes and oats. Willie was a brother of John Donald MacLeod - the nearest neighbour at Upper Sandaig. John Donald often planted a few drills of potatoes for his own family in the Lower Sandaig ground. While others planted the medium sized potatoes, John Donald always kept his biggest ones for planting, firmly believing that this policy gave him his biggest harvest. One of Bobby's additional jobs, as always with the Sandaig shepherd, was the servicing of the Lighthouse on the Sandaig Island, for which a boat was supplied. This boat was handy for the fishing and cod and saithe, with mackerel and herring in season, were a regular part of the diet.

There was a good cod bank along towards 'Joe's cave' on the Glenelg side. This was located by rowing along the shore towards the cave, then moving out at right angles to the shore. When the top of Beinn Sgritheall was seen, that was the spot to drop the anchor and it never failed to provide a good harvest of cod - except once!

On this occasion, the anchor had just been dropped when a great dull roar was heard towards the shore such as none of them had ever heard before. When they glanced shorewards towards the roar, there was some sort of great sea beast making its way along fairly near the shore in the Glenelg direction. It was creating great foam and turbulence as it moved along. The boys had seen the blow of whales before and also plenty of basking sharks but never before did they hear or see anything like this! They were terrified, up came the anchor as it had never been raised before, they made directly for the shore, rowing at breakneck speed. They were never so relieved in their young lives before to hear the keel of the boat hitting the stones on the shore. Alan remembers that on their way home to Sandaig, one oar was touching the stones on the shore as they rowed and the keel of the boat was touching the bottom all the way to Sandaig. They wanted to be ready to abandon ship and get on to dry land immediately if they saw any sign of the huge beast again with its frightening roar. It was a long time before they went fishing for cod at that favourite spot again!

There was also plenty of fish in the Sandaig burn - good little brown trout - while the little elvers would appear in their droves and make their way up the burn, negotiating the waterfall with great persistence and skill. One Sunday there was added excitement when, in one of the deeper pools, a fresh run salmon was spotted. Both sides of the pool were 'dammed' with stones to prevent the escape of the fish and the wiles of the squad of young hunters eventually succeeded in capturing their quarry. Their elation was dampened by the realisation that this was the Sabbath and Mother would be horrified to think of fish being caught on a Sunday when only works of 'necessity and mercy' were permissible. The boys killed the fish and with a string through the gills secured it to an alder root in a pool further up the burn. On the Monday morning, the fish was brought home in triumph as being freshly caught, mother was delighted and the family feasted with mother and father totally unaware about the timing of the catch, while solidarity prevailed among the hunters and the truth never was divulged!

While sometimes food for the family would materialise unexpectedly as in the case of the salmon captured on the Sabbath, much planning by mother and father had to go into ensuring that the family would not go hungry - because the nearest shop was six miles distant. A boll of meal and a boll of flour were brought in just before the previous supply had run out, there was always the barrel of salt herring and there might be the occasional luxury of a bit of venison from the estate. Once a year, mother would order a supply of essentials from a Glasgow store. This would come in a big tea chest by train to Kyle and by Calum Garde's boat from Kyle to Glenelg. Father MacDiarmid and the boys would then row to Glenelg to transport the big wooden box and its contents back to Sandaig. It would contain essentials such as salt, sugar, some dried fruit (currants and prunes), tea, spices, lard and other materials for baking and one bottle of whisky for medicinal purposes - and for a token celebration at New Year. Mother was always baking - oatcakes, scones and pancakes to keep her big family well nourished. On some fine autumn days, after all the daily chores had been completed, the family would set off armed with kettle and picnic supplies (tea, sugar, milk, oatcakes and syrup) along the shore towards Arnisdale - often as far as Port Luinge. There the fire would be lit on the shore, the kettle would be boiled and all would enjoy the picnic. The fact that this was combined with bramble picking to provide a large part of the family's jam supply for the year was not considered as a chore but as a special part of the whole adventure.

There was a grave by the shore along towards Port Luinge. The unidentified body of a man had been washed up there during the first World War and the body was buried there and marked with a stone. Mother would take the boys along there regularly to put flowers on the grave.

Mother would also take the family to Glenelg every Sunday for the evening service in the Free Church and for the whole day at the time of Communion. This was a major exercise. In the summer, the boys would set off barefoot across the moor to join the main road, with mother carrying shoes, stockings and a towel in a bag. When the burn was reached between Culindune and Quarry as Glenelg was approached, feet would be washed in the burn, dried and the stockings and shoes put on. The bag was left at this point and the exercise was reversed on the return journey, proceeding from the changing point on the barefooted journey home. There were no objections whatsoever to these regular pilgrimages to church, it being accepted by all as a standard part of the way of living, along with daily worship in the house and the Grace before and after all the meals.

The atmosphere and life in general changed at Lower Sandaig with the outbreak of the Second World War. To protect the Naval Base at Kyle of Lochalsh against attack from enemy submarines, a boom defence was constructed between Sandaig Island and the nearest point on the Skye shoreline across the sound of Sleat. A trawler armed with a gun mounted at the bow was anchored close to Sandaig Island all the time to control the shipping by opening and closing the gate on the boom close to the Sandaig Island shore. The Lower Sandaig house was totally isolated, there was a constant awareness of the possibility of enemy infiltration into the area, heightened by the knowledge of the land and sea defences in place at all possible entry points to the area and to Kyle in particular - and there were always the rumours, some based on well founded sightings of suspicious personnel or of the sound of gun fire - and some triggered by more mischievous members of the community who wished to generate a bit of excitement - and perhaps also increased alertness.

The existence of the booms guarding the seaward entrances to the Kyle base and the barrage balloon defences of the naval fuel stores at Ardentoul between the Kylerhea Narrows and Loch Duich, heightened the tension. Tom MacDiarmid also remembers seeing the cruiser down the sound near the mouth of Loch Nevis close to Inverie dropping depth charges - having detected the presence of an enemy submarine. Willie MacLeod, formerly of Upper Sandaig, remembers his father, John Donald, telling him that some windows of their house were shattered by the reverberations from these blasts at sea.

At the height of the tension, one can imagine the thoughts which went through minds in the Lower Sandaig household when one night after midnight there was loud knocking on the Lower Sandaig door. As all occupants waking from their sleep realised that these sounds were real and not part of their dreams, gradually one by one the occupants took up arms in self defence. Tom grabbed the poker, Alan a walking stick while Sandy and Bobby each got one of the chairs. Alan remembers that all were terrified, including their young cousin Tommy Moffat, whose survival strategy was to hide under his bed. As the knocking continued and the inner defenders/attackers mobilised, but did not answer the door, those outside probably became aware that the inmates had now risen from their slumbers and wondered why their knocking was not being answered so they gave the call 'Anybody in?' There was wonderful relief among the defenders to recognise the voice of Ali Beag (MacRae) from Eilanreach. The door was unlocked and opened as the great tension began to find a release valve, and there standing in the darkness were the figures of Ali Beag and the local Glenelg bobby, Constable Sharpe.

The midnight visit had been triggered by the following sequence of events. Earlier that day, young Neilly MacLennan from Glenelg had been visiting his pals at Lower Sandaig. On making his way home across the moor on to the main road as the day was darkening, he had spotted a white object some distance away which he thought might be a tent (in fact it was one of the Eilanreach cows - a white Highlander). When he got on to the road as he progressed towards Glenelg, he saw two figures coming down off the hill, cross the road and make their way towards the shore below. He thought that one of them might have been carrying a stick or a rifle (apparently a cargo boat was anchored below just off shore and two of the crew might have fancied having a look up the hill to get some venison for the pot).

As Neilly made his way home through Quarry in Glenelg, Sharpe the bobby was standing at the pier and he always liked to have a 'news' with all he met. In the course of casual conversation with young Neilly, he got all the news about Lower Sandaig and about the suspicious tent and the two armed furtive figures crossing the road. That was enough for Sharpe (apparently one of his Ayrshire forebears had bred the Sharpe's Express potato) to alert the local Home Guard. So late at night, Ali Beag was mobilised and off the two of them set to investigate the suspicious movements and sightings in the Sandaig area.

Over the tea and scones which had soon been laid out on the table by the relieved folk in Lower Sandaig, the mystery sightings were soon solved in terms of the white Highland cows grazing in the area, the cargo boat anchored in the sound and the common custom of the sailors or the fishermen, who had time to spend and who knew a bit about the hills and the stalking, to deploy their time usefully in sporting pursuits and get some variety to their diet.

On another occasion, young Sandy MacDiarmid after leaving school, had got a job in the Mialairidh Forest and was working with those Arnisdale worthies, ganger Andrew Fraser and Angan MacTavish. They were weeding, cutting the bracken and tall grasses with their corrans (sickles) around the young trees. Sandy happened to be working a little distance away from Andrew and Angan when, in the course of his weeding, he came across an old holly tree which seemed to be rotten and hollow in the middle but very sound on the outside. He struck the trunk nonchalantly with his corran and, it being hollow in the middle, it made a very interesting and satisfying sound. So he gave it a few more cracks in fairly quick succession which seemed to reverberate around the hillside with interesting echoes coming back. Almost immediately he heard a shout from Andrew to come down. Obeying the instructions of his ganger, down Sandy came to join Andrew and Angan to get his further instructions. They were both looking tense and worried, saying that they had heard a succession of shots and were not sure from which direction they were coming. Since it was not the shooting season for the deer, they were very suspicious and the Home Guard should be informed immediately. So Sandy was instructed to go home to Lower Sandaig as quickly as he could while they would make their way back to Arnisdale on their bikes with full speed to alert Roddy Mòr and the local Home Guard. When they reached Arnisdale and Roddy Mòr, the Glenelg Home Guard were alerted by telephone, the Arnisdale Squad mobilised and both forces set out to investigate the source of the gunfire - to no avail! Meanwhile, Sandy had managed to escape temporarily from the very boring job of weeding in the forest. Perhaps Andrew and Angan were also quite grateful for this respite from their tedious job among the drizzle and the midges, while both Home Guard forces got in some practice, in what they all thought was a serious active service exercise!

Although there was often tension in the air, there were many compensations during the war. There were usually about 12 sailors manning the defence trawler at the boom gate off Sandaig Island. There were Irish, Welsh, English and Scottish boys and they were good neighbours. There were great games of football in the hayfield, sometimes involving brother-in-law Tommy Cartwright (Gertie's husband) when he would be home on leave. Mother would have even more baking to do and they enjoyed her teas of scones and oatcakes. In turn, the family would get gifts of condensed milk and tinned meat from them. They would also help at the haymaking and Tom remembers one Irishman even helping at the peats. It was a very hot summer and obviously he had been lying around on deck or on the shore and got sunburnt. When he was helping mother and the teacher, Cathie Thomson, at the peats, Cathie told him jocularly, that if he rubbed peat on his sunburn it would soon cure it. So they lathered him with wet peat! While it was soothing as long as it was wet, when it dried and he tried to get it off, he was in even greater agony than ever!

The MacDiarmid boys had their own teacher at Lower Sandaig until they were eleven years of age at which stage they walked the six miles to and from Glenelg School daily until they left at the age of fourteen. Among the memories when in Glenelg School is going down to the shore when the herring shoals were in. The shore would be a mass of herring sprats with the dogfish and mackerel coming in to feast on them. Armed with hay forks, graips and even sticks, the boys used to 'shovel' the dogfish and mackerel on to the shore - they were so plentiful and so overfed with sprats.

At lambing time, even as young as 12 to 13 years, Tom and Sandy were allowed to have 2 weeks off school to help with the lambing. Tom's beat was the Sandaig hirsel above the road towards the lower slopes of Beinn Sgritheall. Sandy was responsible for the upper Tormòr hirsel towards Beinn a' Chapuill, while Bobby took responsibility for the Sandaig and Tormòr areas below the road which carried most of the sheep, because of the better grazing in these parts.

Near the end of the MacDiarmid and MacLean family's stay in Lower Sandaig, John Donald MacLeod, his wife Mary and their young family of 3 boys, Paddy (Ruaridh), and the twins Willie and Calum, made their home at Upper Sandaig. John Donald had the responsibility for maintaining the road from the top of Mam Ratagan to Arnisdale. Tom, as a young 14 year old, worked for John Donald for a while. It was a gravel road at the time with little quarries in operation all along the route as a source of road metal. John Donald set young Tom to work at one of the little quarries one day as he went away to attend to another job. Tom hacked away at the quarry face, separated the big stones from the mass and built up his heap of prepared metal. It was hard, slow, tedious work and it took a long time to see the fruits of your labours. When John Donald came back, he looked at Tom's work for the day exclaiming "Well, Tom, you haven't done very much but it is quite tidy!" - that well tempered note of admonition flavoured with a little praise was the hallmark of wise men like John Donald as they tried to cajole youngsters into being more productive at their work, while at the same time taking care not to demoralise but to motivate to greater effort tomorrow!

As time during the war progressed at Lower Sandaig, Bobby began to pay regular evening visits to Arnisdale on his 'most rickety old push-bike which could be heard a long way off and was forever breaking down'. There was now a young teacher, Ann MacRae from Glenelg, in Arnisdale and Bobby could not disguise his visits to Arnisdale such was the rattle from his old bike! Later Ann and Bobby were to marry in 1946. Their wedding reception was to be the last one in the fine Glenelg Hotel before it was totally destroyed by fire in January 1947.

In addition, despite all the work which had to be done, the Lower Sandaig boys always found time to play their football and shinty, the preference being football when their neighbours the sailors came up for a game. But the shinty got its due prominence when the boys were on their own. Bobby was a very fine footballer, and played for the Glenelg team both before and after the War. He, along with his brothers were also very fine shinty players. Although Glenelg did not have a shinty team, the Sandaig boys were later to find full opportunity to express their shinty talents in playing for very successful teams in other districts.

In 1945, just before the end of the War, Bobby (as Farm Manager) and Tom (as shepherd) were successful in getting jobs on the Farraline Estate in Abersky, Stratherrick, then tenanted by Mr Campbell, who later moved to farm in Strachur. After this move to Abersky, Bobby, Sandy, Tom and Alan were soon in the formidable Straths Athletic Shinty Team and were highly successful in winning most of the North of Scotland competitions as well as the Scottish Junior Cup (The Sutherland Cup). Donald Cumming, a Skyeman, who owned the Cumming's Hotel in Inverness, took over the tenancy of Abersky from Mr Campbell and, as a great shinty enthusiast, became a very active official in the Straths Shinty Club. Later, when the MacDiarmid family moved across Loch Ness to Borlum Farm, Drumnadrochit, Tom transferred his allegiance to the Glen Urquhart Shinty Club. From a group of keen fledglings, aided by the experience, great skill, determination and leadership of 'Big Tom', this Glen Urquhart team containing others with very strong Arnisdale connections, won every competition open to them, including the Scottish Junior Cup in 1963. Some of their best and most enjoyable tussles on the shinty field were against Kinlochshiel, Lochcarron and Skye. Bobby and Alan, after their Straths Athletic days, graced the ranks of Kinlochshiel, while Alan was also a key player in the Glenelg team which entered the north competitions for a few years in the 1960s. As well as Alan, the other Glenelg players of that time included Ewen Cameron, Hugh Ian MacLure, Malcolm (Tosh) Elder, Y MacLeod, and Alan MacAskill. So that all the sporting skills developed on the machair at Lower Sandaig, both in shinty and football, were put to good use later and graced many sports fields in the west, north and further afield.

After the MacDiarmid and MacLean family left beautiful Lower Sandaig in 1945, the next tenant in his beloved 'Camusfearna' was to be Gavin Maxwell; the world knows much of his thinking and activities there through his writings and the film "The Ring of Bright Water" which was based on what was considered to be his finest literary work.

The house at Upper Sandaig beside the Arnisdale-Glenelg road is of more recent origins than that at Lower Sandaig. It was built by the Eilanreach Estate as a shepherd's house to tend the sheep on the Tormór and Sandaig hirsels and the main sheep fank in that area was just on the other side of the Sandaig burn from the house. However, later the house became available for general leasing and it was during the War around 1941 that John Donald MacLeod, the road foreman on the Arnisdale to the top of Mam Ratagan stretch of road, his wife Mary and their three young sons, Paddy (Ruaridh), Willie and Calum, made Sandaig their home. Prior to moving to Upper Sandaig the family had their home in Bernera in Glenelg. John Donald was a Glenelg man while Mary was born and brought up along the Arnisdale road at Rarsaidh. Before marriage, Mary had worked for the Scotts of Fearn in Easter Ross. The Scotts were proprietors of Eilanreach Estate for a time and Mary later worked for the family at Eilanreach House. When Ruaridh was 18 months old, Mary was due to give birth to her second child and the local GP, Dr Devon, made the judgment that Mary should go into hospital to have her second baby. When the imminent signs of impending delivery materialised, it was Dr Devon herself who set off with Mary for the Royal Northern Infirmary at Inverness. However, things were happening quickly as they drove up Glen Shiel, then past Cluanie and into upper Glen Moriston. As they approached Invermoriston, the judgment of Mary and Dr Devon was that they were not going to make it to Inverness in time so they sought help at the Invermoriston Hotel. The good folk there offered them all possible facilities and soon afterwards little Willie was delivered into this world. There was great relief that they had made it - and all seemed well until the realisation that Willie was not the only baby who was about to see the light of day. So immediately Mary and Dr Devon realised that the delivery had not been completed, off they set - accompanied by the fledgling Willie, of course, - and, this time, reached the Royal Northern Infirmary in time. There, four and a quarter hours after Willie, little twin brother

Calum was born. A headline in one of the papers next day announced 'Twins born 25 miles apart'.

John Donald, as road foreman for a 20 mile stretch of road, with some of the steepest braes and worst Z bends in the country to negotiate, was totally dependent on his push bike to cover his territory. His road maintenance equipment consisted of a pick, shovel and wheelbarrow - or several such sets - distributed at intervals and left in little quarries along the route. On the Glenelg stretch, big John MacDonald (John Mor) assisted him while John MacGillivray, and later John Arthur, provided some part-time assistance on the Arnisdale stretch. Willie Campbell of Letterfearn also provided help now and again on a part-time basis. The team did its very best to avoid too many potholes as they battled against some of the wettest weather in Britain, with the roadway tracks becoming little streams at regular intervals, hurtling down the steep braes and taking the finer particles of road metal with them into the side drains. Of course, these many miles of roadside drains also had to be cleaned and maintained at regular intervals.

In his off-duty time, John Donald, along with Mary, established and maintained a big vegetable garden - of about a quarter of an acre - all worked by the spade and other hand tools. Both of them had the green fingers and grew enough vegetables to keep the family, and many friends, also in fresh vegetables throughout the year. Mary also kept a flower garden which was a joy to behold in the summer and autumn.

Mary was also a great animal lover - a bit of a St Francis of Assisi - as she nurtured her dogs, cats, ferrets, ducks, hens, goats and sheep. She kept the goats for milk and had about a dozen sheep. When the stags and hinds were driven down from the high tops on Beinn a' Chapuill and Beinn Sgritheall in winter by the harshness of the weather, there would often be three to four hundred of them in the vicinity of Sandaig. They would not be long in the Sandaig environment before Mary would have some of them eating titbits from the garden out of her hands.

Although the Upper Sandaig house was very isolated, the family never felt lonely. Willie 'Sandaig' (the Invermoriston Hotel baby) looks back with great fondness on what he considered to be a wonderful upbringing. With the Arnisdale road virtually passing their front door at that time (since then the road has been re-aligned and passes behind the house), it was common for most local traffic to stop and call to exchange greetings and news. Mary was ever hospitable and it was no easy task to be persuaded to proceed on one's journey without being entertained beforehand to a cup of tea and her fine home baking.

In addition to the daily chores and the garden, both John Donald and Mary were great readers. John Donald enjoyed poetry and could recite reams of the great classics. As one old friend said 'John Donald was bookish above his station and was very learned'. He had collected a considerable library and the long winter evenings after his hard day's toil and his supper, would often see him immersed in the classics. It was little wonder that when Gavin Maxwell made Lower Sandaig his home that he found great soul-mates in his neighbours Mary and John Donald at Upper Sandaig. Intellectually and in relation to their way with animals they had a great deal in common.

One of the first books which Gavin Maxwell wrote at Camusfearna was 'Harpoon at a Venture' which was based on the fishing for basking sharks in the Minch and the Atlantic from his base on the island of Soay just after the War.

Willie 'Sandaig' remembers three of Maxwell's otters., There was Mijbil which he rescued as a baby in the Arab marshes in Iraq and Edal which he acquired from passers-by as he sat in the Lochalsh Hotel in Kyle. The owners of Edal had been looking for a good home for their otter at the time, as they were about to depart for Africa.  'Teko' was the last otter at Camusfearna.  Willie remembers being out fishing off the Sandaig Islands when all of a sudden one of the otters would come clambering up an oar and slither all over his back.  They had a great empathy with humans.  Among the otter keepers Willie remembers at Camusfearna are Jimmy Watt and Terry Nutkins in their younger days.

The Sandaig boys first went to school in Arnisdale, in the early days being transported to and from school by Johnny Sinclair's car and later by Roddy Mòr.  Sometimes, the boys would stay with their Granny (Mrs Jessie MacKintosh) in Arnisdale for the week and come home just at the weekend.  Later on the boys transferred to Glenelg School.  Their Granny had been born and brought up in the lone house at Rarsaidh which lies between Sandaig and Arnisdale.

After Willie's family left Upper Sandaig, they were succeeded there by Kenny MacRae, his wife Betty (nee MacAskill) and their family.  Kenny had been a prisoner of war in the Second War and later worked for the Eilanreach Estate.  He had been a fine shinty player in his day and a noted goalkeeper in the Glenelg football team.  He died suddenly when partaking in another favourite pastime - fishing in the Eilanreach River.  Betty is now resident in Corran, Arnisdale and is still active in working her croft.  Betty is a Glenelg MacAskill, daughter of the late and famous 'Gaffie' and his wife Isobel (nee MacDonald).

Alas, Sandaig is now deserted with nobody resident in the house at Upper Sandaig while the house at Camusfearna was totally destroyed by fire while Gavin Maxwell was still resident there.  Therefore only the Sandaig memories remain - and there are many of these - mainly very happy ones.

**Top Left.** The location of Sandaig in relation to Kyle, Glenelg, Mialairidh, Arnisdale, Knoydart and Skye.. **Right**. The house, croftlands, byre and barn at Lower Sandaig, the Sandaig Islands and Lighthouse, and Skye to the west across the Sound of Sleat.
**Middle Left**. The house at Lower Sandaig with Mrs Agnes Moffat (nee Foster) at the doorway. Agnes' husband and son Rob worked as shepherds for the Eilanreach Estate on the Sandaig - Tormor hirsel in this area in the early 1900s. **Middle.** Donald Chisholm in his Cameron Highlander's uniform during the First World War. In his earlier days Donald was a side school teacher in Lower Sandaig.
**Right**. Mrs Agnes Moffat in her later years busies herself with her knitting while sitting at the Monument in Glenelg.
**Bottom Left.** The shepherd who succeeded Rob Moffat at Lower Sandaig in the 1920s was Peter MacPherson from Moyle, Glenelg and his wife Katie (nee MacLure) also from Glenelg. L to R. Johan MacLure, Donald MacPherson, Isabella MacPherson, Donnie MacCrimmon, Peter MacPherson, Duncan MacPherson, Katie MacLure, Janet (Nettie) MacPherson, Anne MacLure and Roddy MacPherson (early 1930s). **Centre**. There was a major 'incident' soon after Peter and Katie flitted to Lower Sandaig involving a large wardrobe which Katie and her young friend Roddy MacPherson (Peter's nephew) had to manoeuvre through an upstairs window because it would not go up the staircase! **Right**. A later resident of Lower Sandaig – his treasured 'Camusfearna'. Gavin Maxwell reclining with pet otter Edal of 'Ring of Bright Water' fame.

274

**Top Left**.  Roddy McPherson worked in the Mialairidh Forest with many other Glenelg and Arnisdale youngsters on leaving school.  Back (L to R.) Peter Fletcher, Mr Stoddart (Head Forester), Ludovic Fraser, Iain Elder and Jimmy Campbell.  Front. Donald MacKintosh, Bobby MacLean, Archie MacLean, Andrew Fraser and Angus Stewart.  **Right**.  Just south of the croft at Lower Sandaig is Eilean a'Chlamhain close to which young Roddy MacPherson along with Donald MacKinnon from Kylerhea and a Glenelg man witnessed a huge 'sea monster' around 1933.

**Middle Left**.  Eilean a Chlamhain photographed from the high ground above - the Gorstan - with views south to Knoydart on the left, the Sleat area of Skye on the right and the Islands of Eigg and Rhum beyond.  **Right.**  Donald MacKinnon of Kylerhea (third from left) after a successful white hare and ptarmigan shoot in the Kylerhea area of Skye in the 1920s.  Others include L to R. Mr Douglas (Shooting Tenant), Donald MacPherson (Glenelg), Donald MacKinnon, Lachie MacInnes of Kylerhea and ??????.

**Bottom Left**.   Peter MacPherson was to be succeeded as shepherd in Lower Sandaig by Bobby MacLean, a grandson of Agnes Moffat seen here with her grandchildren, Bobby and sister Gertie.  **Right**.  Bobby and Gertie were the children of Agnes Moffat's daughter, Ada and her husband Hugh MacLean.  Hugh was a native of Waternish, Skye, and he worked in Greenock.  Hugh died as a young man.

**Top Left**.  A few years after the death of her husband Hugh, Ada married Sandy MacDiarmid (centre), a native of Easdale in Argyll.  **Right**.  The first of the MacDiarmid children, Sandy, being tended by sister Gertie and brother Bobby.

**Middle Left**.  The other members of the MacDiarmid family (L to R.) Sandy, Alan and Tommy with their cousin Tommy Moffat. (Late 1930s).  **Right**.  Bobby MacLean after his appointment as Sandaig shepherd in 1936.

**Bottom Left**  There was always plenty of work to be done at Lower Sandaig on the croft.  Here Tom is working with the cattle and shearing the sheep.  Also hay had to be made and peats cut and carted home;  but there was time too for leisure (right) L to R.  Tom, Sandy and Alan MacDiarmid with a favourite pet.  There was also time to play football and shinty, catch fish and do many other exciting things in this wonderful environment.  The sailors resident on the nearby trawler which operated the boom defence between Sandaig and Skye also joined in the fun and games as often as they could.

**Top Left**. A boom defence stretched from Sandaig to Skye across the Sound of Sleat during World War 2. **Right**. There was nervousness during wartime and a watchful eye was always kept for anything unusual on land and sea. There was real fear one night around midnight when loud banging was heard on the door in this very isolated place. Resolute defences were prepared by the boys but great relief was felt when they heard the voice of Ali Beag MacRae from Eilanreach. Ali was checking along with the local policeman on suspicious sightings earlier in the day. Ali Beag is fourth from left (back row) in this pre-war Glenelg Football team. Others (L to R.) back row are Kenny MacKenzie, Ewan Cameron, Jimmy Murchison, Ali 'Beag' MacRae, Roddy MacPherson, John 'Mor' MacDonald, Donnie 'Skibo' MacLeod. Front (L to R.) Malcolm Garde, Bobby MacLean, Johnnie Murchison and Alick MacPaik.

**Middle Left**. An innocent incident triggered off by Sandy MacDiarmid while working as a young lad in the Mialairidh forest resulted in gangers Andrew Fraser and Angan MacTavish abandoning planting work for the day and calling out the Glenelg and Arnisdale units of the Home Guard such as Archie MacLean (left) and Roddy Mor in Arnisdale. The young lad helping at the clipping is Callum Kennedy. **Centre**. Ann MacRae (left), the Arnisdale teacher in the 1940-46 period with her friend Teenie Lamont from Glenelg in the Arnisdale School Garden. **Right**. Bobby MacLean on a visit to the Arnisdale teacher, Ann MacRae who belongs to Glenelg.

**Bottom Left**. The wedding of Ann and Bobby in Glenelg in 1946 with Bessie MacDonald as bridesmaid and Sandy MacDiarmid as best man. **Middle**. The growing Sandaig lads around 1945. L to R. Sandy, Alan and Tom MacDiarmid. **Right**. The MacDiarmid family at Borlum Farm, Drumnadrochit in the 1950s with their mother and father. L to R. Tom, Alan and Sandy.

**Top Left**. After moving from Lower Sandaig to Stratherrick, Bobby MacLean and the three MacDiarmid boys became key members of the very successful Straths Athletic Shinty Team in the late 1940-early 1950 period. The Straths Athletics team of 1951 – Winners of the MacGillivray Junior League Cup. Back row (L to R.) Mrs Mary MacKintosh, Tim Pow, Ewan MacDonald, Johnny Kennedy, Angus MacGillivray. Middle Row. Father Thain, Hughie Fraser, Sandy Campbell, Robin Fraser, Tom MacDiarmid, Alan MacDiarmid, Ali Fraser, Dick Ogilvie, Roddy MacKintosh. Front. Wolstan MacPherson, Peter Grant, Bobby MacLean, Col. Sopper, Willie Cooper, Fachie MacDonald and Iain MacDonald.

**Right.** On moving to GlenUrquhart in the mid-1950s, Tom MacDiarmid was a leading player in the GlenUrquhart team which achieved a high level of success in all competitions in the late 1950s –-early 1960s period. The GlenUrquhart Team of 1963 – Winners of the Scottish Junior Championship (The Sutherland Cup) and MacGillivray Junior League Cup. Back Row. L to R. Danny Fraser, John MacLean, Andrew Iain MacDonald, Calum Fraser, George Stewart, Tom MacKenna, John MacKintosh, Peter English, John Alick MacKenzie, Bob English, Murdo Campbell. Front. Sandy MacDonald, Kenny 'Tosh' MacKintosh, Bob MacDonald, Jocky MacDonald, Tom MacDiarmid, Roddy Mackintosh, Jimmac MacKintosh, Bob MacDonald and Ken Fraser.

**Bottom Left**. Bobby MacLean and Alan MacDiarmid later became key members of both the Kinlochshiel Shinty Team and the Glenelg Football Team. The players in this Glenelg team of 1950 – Winners of the Macleod Cup are: Back (L to R.) Roddy MacPherson, Y MacLeod, Kenny MacRae, Ala MacRae, Roddy MacKenzie and Bobby MacLean. Front. Hamish MacLeod, Neilly Gordon, Jocky O'Kane, Willie Gordon and Malcolm Garde. **Right**. The three MacDiarmid boys in their maturing years. L to R. Sandy, Tom and Alan.

**Top Left.** John Donald MacLeod, a native of Glenelg, who came with his family to Upper Sandaig in 1941.
**Centre**. John Donald's wife Mary (right) with Mary's mother Mrs Jessie MacKintosh (Jessie 'Rarsaidh') on the left with friends L to R. Jessie 'Lea', Elizabeth Stevenson and Maggie 'Lea' in Arnisdale. **Right**. Mary with the boys L to R. Calum, Willie and Iain (Ruaridh). Twins Calum and Willie were born 25 miles apart – Willie in Invermoriston Hotel and Calum in the Royal Northern Infirmary, Inverness.

**Middle Left**. Mary with her pet goats. She had a great way with all the animals – both wild and domesticated.
**Right**. Gavin Maxwell with his pet otter, Edal.

**Bottom Left**. Gavin Maxwell (centre) found great soul mates in John Donald and Mary during his years in Lower Sandaig – his beloved Camusfearna. **Middle**. Terry Nutkins, who was one of Gavin Maxwell's first otter keepers at Camusfearna and below - Jimmy Watt, another of the otter keepers at Camusfearna with Edal. The large herd of Eilanreach cows graze the croftlands below. **Right**. Lower Sandaig in more recent times from one of the Sandaig Islands, looking on to the meadows of the old croft, the conifer plantation and Beinn a' Chapuill in the distance.

# Chapter 21

**The Mialairidh (Mealory) Forest**

The area between Sandaig and Rarsaidh which was important in history but is no longer inhabited is called 'Mialairidh'. The Ordnance Survey maps of the area produced in the 1890s have the following interesting names depicted in this area: Beinn Mhialairidh (1799 ft), Coille Mhialairidh, Creag Ruadh, Creag a' Chàise, Tobar a' Chaisteal, Torr an tuirc; and then down at the shore moving from the Sandaig to Rarsaidh areas are Rudha a' Chaisteal, Ruadh Bhuidhe, Glas Eilean, Port an tarbh and a 'Cave' indicated just above the shore line before Eilean Rarsaidh is reached.

So although no humans currently reside in this area (apart from temporary campers down at the shore), the old Gaelic names tell us a little about the past importance of this locality: the Coille (wood) refers to the great wood of natural oaks in this area, Tobar (a well), Caisteal (Castle), Torc (the pig), Tarbh (bull) and, of course, the Port (Harbour).

Probably the last semi-permanent inhabitants of this area were the late Tony Mackay (father-in-law of the author) and the late Jimmy MacLean of Glenurquhart. In the 1930s, Tony and Jimmy were young foresters with the Forestry Commission who were involved with forestry workers from Arnisdale and Glenelg in establishing a pine forest on the site of the old oak forest (Coille Mhialairidh). The home of Tony and Jimmy was a hut just above the shoreline in a location close to the spot marked 'Cave' on the Ordnance Survey Map and within sight of Eilean Rarsaidh. Very close to the site of this hut, the remains of a line of oak posts can still be seen in the water. This is where the oak lengths, which were cut from the forest, were transported at low tide and secured between the posts so that at high tide, the boats could come in alongside to load and transport the oak to form the keels of boats and ships in ship building havens such as Isleornsay and Mallaig locally and other ports much further afield.

Along the bank just above the high water line which was previously occupied by Tony and Jimmy's forestry hut are the ruins of a row of houses. Alan MacDiarmid was told that one of these houses was a shop. Moreover, Penny MacLeod who lived in Kirkton, Glenelg to the age of 104 and died in the mid-1950s, remembered spending part of her first wages earned at the Eilanreach Lodge at this shop. Some of Penny's relations lived in that little clachan by the Mialairidh shore.

Further along the shore from this site towards Sandaig there are the remains of a dwelling house which was built and occupied by the forebears of the Arnisdale MacLeans - Peggy Ann and Mary at the old Post Office and Archie, Johan and their family further up Camusban close to Allt a'mhuilinn. The grandfather of Peggy Ann and Archie was the 'watcher' in Coille Mhialairidh, being employed by the estate to prevent seagoing raiders from Skye and the adjacent coastlines coming in to help themselves to a supply of fine oak for their boat building. The MacLeans also worked a croft here and probably had a general store to provide the needs of those harvesting and loading the oak and probably also of the herring fishermen working in Loch Hourn. The origins of the Caisteal (the castle), the tarbh (the bull) and the torc (the pig) are uncertain. However, oakwoods and pigs often go together with the autumn and winter fruits of the oak forest forming a major food source for wild pigs in many areas of the world. One can only speculate again about the Caisteal. Alan MacDairmid knows of the remains of a building at this site which has a commanding view down the Sound of Sleat, and Alan has also seen what may be the remains of Pictish Brochs in this area as well as stone circles.

There was the risk of invasion in this area from time immemorial, perhaps first from the Vikings and later during the great era of the Lords of the Isles. Then there were the periods of clan warfare, particularly between the MacLeods and the MacDonalds when defences and lookouts in this strategic area were probably extremely important in defending those settled on the mainland from the marauding of the seafarers.

Another ancillary industry, which was almost certainly in operation when the oakwoods were being harvested, was the burning of the oak bark for the production of tannins, used in the tanning of leather.

In the 1890 Ordnance Survey Map, the only Port listed on the Map is Port an tarbh (Port of the Bull) while Port Luinge (Luinge = boat) is not listed as such. Are these ports one and the same, being given these different names at separate points in history? Others may know the answer to this question. Tony Mackay, were he alive today, would undoubtedly make an informed comment on this question.

It is possible that Port an tarbh played its part in a famous historical event in the district. The story goes that a wild bull, of which the natives had lived in dread, lived in the woods of Glen Elg. At the time, the Glen Elg territory was in the possession of the MacLeods of Harris and Skye or the MacLeods of Dunvegan as they were often called. Malcolm, one of the younger sons of a MacLeod chief, encountered the wild bull in the Glen Elg woods. Armed only with his sgian-dubh, Malcolm engaged the wild animal, held him fast by the horns, and eventually managed to cut off its head. Thus, the story goes, the bull's head was adopted as the crest of the MacLeods and 'Hold Fast' became their motto. The story further asserts that Malcolm cut off one of the horns and this became the drinking-horn of Rory Mor, a MacLeod chief, and is still preserved at Dunvegan Castle. Was the severed head of the wild bull of Glenelg loaded on to a MacLeod galley at Port an tarbh on the Mialairidh Peninsula for its triumphant journey to Dunvegan? One can now only speculate on this possible origin of the name of this landing and loading location on the Loch Hourn shore.

Tony Mackay and Jimmy MacLean are still well remembered in the area, especially Tony, who later married Isabella MacPherson from Glenelg, and Isabella, the much loved and respected mother-in-law of the author is now resident again in her native Glenelg. Tony, a native of Durness in Sutherland, was a regular singer of Gaelic and English songs at the Arnisdale and Glenelg ceilidh dances and it is one of the great regrets of the author that this work was not undertaken many years previously so that Tony and many more scholars and characters like him could have guided the work and provided much information about old Gaelic place names and their origins as well as much detailed history and stories which have been lost forever with the passing of these interesting, learned, couthy and humble folk.

Despite the use of alternative names such as Port Luinge, Tony always referred to this area as Mialairidh and he had a host of stories about the work in the forest, about the great characters who worked with him and about all the ceilidhs in Glenelg and Arnisdale.

Mialairidh was very dear to 'Grandpa' as he was lovingly known to young and old in the family.

After completing his training as a Forester in the Forestry School near Dunoon, Tony's first posting was to the Drumdelgie Forest, near Huntly. He was not long there before being transferred to the Mialairidh Forest. Bill Stoddart was the Head Forester and he had as his young assistants Tony and Jimmy MacLean from Glenurquhart. As stated earlier, Tony and Jimmy had as their home for several years the Forestry hut down at the Mialairidh shore - just across from Crowlick and within sight of Rarsaidh Island. Tony and Jimmy soon got to know very well the boys in the Forestry squad and were quickly integrated into the full social life of Arnisdale and Glenelg. Tony played football for the Glenelg team and was in demand as a singer at the ceilidhs, he met his life's partner in Glenelg and he had nothing but pleasant memories of his sojourn in the area. He went back there to visit all his old friends as often as he could and had a host of stories about his time there with all the local characters. He told these stories frequently in different company, he told them well - with a twinkle in his eye and with that great sense of boyish humour which was so typical of him. The family heard his favourite stories many times and never tired of these repeats - because Tony would bring them very much alive in his telling - as if they happened just yesterday. Tony's son Donald here recalls some of his father's tales of Arnisdale and the Mialairidh Forest.

**The Mialairidh Sea Monster.** Although gregarious by nature, Tony Mackay was quite happy with his own company and especially so when his Forestry Commission posting led to him living in a bothy by the shore at Mialairidh.
He loved trees, perhaps because he had been deprived of much contact with them during his childhood in Durness, Sutherland and, after all, they were his living. He adored the mountains and loved to climb them. Again the geography of his birthplace did not permit direct contact with mountains but the memories of the distant spectacular Sutherland hills of his youth probably lent an additional enchantment and created the longing to climb. Above all, Tony loved the sea and spent most of his waking hours as a child playing in or beside it when he was growing up in Durness. At Mialairidh, he had all three virtually on his doorstep - the mountains, the trees and the sea.

Fear was an emotion of which Tony had little experience. He was a rational man who listened to ghost stories with a sceptical interest. Living alone in a remote place certainly held no fears for him. He was familiar with most of the sights and sounds of nature, at any hour of the day or night, and any which could not be accounted for there and then did not trouble him unduly, as he knew he would discover the reason sooner or later. However, one night when alone in the bothy, he heard a sound which was so far outside his experience - that his rational mind raced - unsuccessfully - to find an acceptable explanation and real fear took over. The sound was like footsteps on the shingle of the beach but much too loud and irregular to be made by any human feet. Stories of sea monsters flashed through his mind. Could they be true? The bothy was very near the water after all! As he gazed apprehensively at the uncurtained window, towards which the sound seemed to be approaching, the noise stopped and he was aware of a pair of huge nostrils almost touching the glass. When his rational self had gained sufficient control over his fear, he picked up the paraffin lamp and moved towards the window for a closer look. The increased illumination revealed a huge pair of eyes above and behind the nostrils. So the stories **were** true! He nearly dropped the lamp when the creature suddenly snorted and shook its head. In that familiar movement, it revealed its true identity and Tony's fear turned to mirth when he realised that the sea monster was really old Dick, the work horse used in the forest for transporting materials such as pine seedlings and fencing materials!

**The delayed lunch break.** The squad in the Mialairidh Forest were all busy planting one fine day and, helped by the good soil conditions and fine weather, were making good progress. With a 7.30 a.m. start, they had a ten minute stop for their morning tea at 9.30 and many were no doubt looking forward to their break at mid-day for their lunch-time 'piece'. Tony was the only one with a watch and, perhaps carried away a bit with the fine progress they were making, he did not check the time as often as usual. When he eventually looked at his watch - lo and behold - it was not mid-day but a whole hour later - one o'clock! Tony was amazed how the time had passed so quickly and wondered if the squad had been aware that 'piece-time' was now long overdue. So, as he expressed his amazement, he asked the relevant question - 'Good life, boys, its one o'clock - did you think it was as late as this, Roddy?' 'Oh', said Roddy, 'I thought it must have been about 3 o'clock!'

Tony, although the ganger, was very much one of the boys but there was always respect; and although many others may have felt that, by the way their tummies were rumbling, it was well past the due time for their mid-day piece, they expressed no such feelings. They just carried on with their planting, patiently awaiting the lunchtime call of their friend Tony.

**The Islander and the boots.** The Arnisdale Forestry squad were all getting a bit fed up with the claims being made for the accomplishments of Island women folk by a native of the Outer Isles who was forced, by circumstances outwith his control, to spend his exile in their midst.  If someone remarked on how good the home-made jam on his lunch-time 'piece' was, he was promptly told that no-one could make jam like the women of the exile's native isle.  The qualities of the local scones, pancakes, oatcakes, dumplings, or whatever, were similarly put in their rightful inferior place if anyone dared to mention them to the islander.

One lunch-time, a compliment on someone's particularly fine 'plus four' stockings led to a discussion of hand-knitting and its most highly regarded practitioners.  Everyone, of course, expected the abilities of the local women to be set at nought compared to those of their island sisters.  In due course it was, but one of the Arnisdale boys, sitting downhill, spotted a weakness in the Islander's armour, in the form of a hole in his boot, and when the latter played his usual hand, immediately trumped it with a quiet, sly "Isn't it a pity that the .....women are no good at mending boots!"

**Lachie, the Hearach and the Bicycle.**  This story is of an Arnisdale man making his way to his day's work on his bike in the Mialairidh Forest and a Harris man cycling in the opposite direction to his job repairing the road.  It was a stormy day and Lachie was ascending the brae as the Hearach was speeding downhill in the opposite direction.  If the brae hadn't been so steep and the day so stormy - with the west wind blowing into his face, Lachie might have seen or heard the approaching speeding bicycle before it was too late but, as he laboured head down on his upward way, his first awareness of it was the Hearach's warning shout when they were within a few yards of a head on collision!

The gradient of the brae near Rarsaidh and the momentum of the descending cyclist meant that there was only one strategy if disaster was to be avoided, and that was evasive action.  Unfortunately, there wasn't much time for decision making and although there were only three decisions open to each of them - maintain the present course or move to the left or to the right, the selection of any one of them depended for its success on the appropriate corresponding decision by the other party.  One could say that the two cyclists were spoilt for choice, because the three options open to each of them gave rise to nine possible outcomes, six of which would have avoided trouble with only three resulting in a collision course!  With twice as much choice of getting it right than getting it wrong, one would have thought - but no - life's not like that!  What happened next must have occupied three or four seconds, at the most, but to the participants it seemed like a slow-motion film in which they were the main actors.  As each of them realised that he, or the other fellow, had chosen the wrong strategy, time ran out for evasive action and the inevitable happened.

To lessen the consequences of the collision, Lachie, just before the Hearach's bicycle struck him, leapt upwards, legs apart, and threw his arms round the Hearach whose reflex response was to do the same to Lachie.  As the two rolled over and over in tight embrace down the steep slope on the seaward side of the road, the silence which had ensued since the initial warning yell, was broken by Lachie asking the Hearach "Ca bheil thu dol?"  (Where are you going?)!  For as long as their embrace lasted, of course, wherever the Hearach was going, Lachie could not but go in the same direction!

**The tough seal.**  Shooting was an important pastime, not to say a preoccupation, for some members of the Arnisdale and Loch Hourn community.  In fact, it could be said that they thought of little else and would shoot anything that moved, or even some things that didn't move, such as table legs - but that's another story.  Any seal which strayed within sight and range of the shore was a likely target for the hero of our tale and, one day, spying a particularly large head bobbing among the waves, he blasted off a shot with his 12 bore - just before he realised that "the seal" was really an iron fishing net buoy.  The loud ricochet immediately confirmed his blunder and also, unfortunately for him, drew it to the attention of a neighbour.  Some days later his neighbour commented to him casually "My, you must have had a hard job skinning that beast you shot last Tuesday!"

**The Flitting.** An Arnisdale character went to clean his gun in the kitchen one night and discovered, too late, that he had committed the unforgivable error of leaving a cartridge in one of the chambers. Fortunately, as he tested the trigger and the shot blasted off, no one was in the direct line of fire so the damage was limited to the conversion of a four legged kitchen table to one with only three legs - and a shot-riddled floor and chairs in the vicinity of the table leg, which had taken the brunt of the discharge. The consequential damage was of less concern to the 'marksman' than the consequential embarrassment, should details of the incident leak outwith the four walls of the house. In due course it did, as such events usually do. Not long afterwards, two Glenelg fellows were getting ready to travel by steamer to Mallaig and were watching a flitting being loaded at the pier before they could set sail. The sight of this forest of table and chair legs, sticking up invitingly in the air in all directions, prompted one of them to turn to the other and comment "Nach eil e bochd nach eil.....an seo". "Nach aig esan am bitheas an spors!" (Isn't it a pity (Arnisdale character) isn't here. Isn't it him that would have some fine sport!).

**The C.O.D. (Cash on Delivery).** An Arnisdale man was very proud of his sea-faring son. The boy had gone off to join one of the deep sea lines as a deckhand and, by diligence and determination, made steady progress in his chosen career. He kept his father well informed of his progress in his letters home, from various parts of the globe, and the old man eagerly passed on the information to the bodaich (old friends) at the daily "parliament" in Camus Ban. In fact, the subject of his son and his achievements was almost his sole contribution to the proceedings. The progression from deckhand to first officer had been reported in detail and the merit of each step in that progression duly extolled.

Thereafter, there was a long period during which there was nothing to report because the sailor was on his way home for one of his rare visits to his native village. The proud father, however, had no doubt that the homecoming would be a source of news of further advancement. The day the son arrived home there also arrived a parcel containing some goods he had ordered from his landfall ports. When the old man heard the post say "There's a parcel here for your son, C.O.D." he puzzled for a long time - as he'd never heard of 'C.O.D.' before.

At last the penny dropped and he couldn't get to that day's "assembly" in the village quickly enough. When someone enquired if his son had got home all right and asked about his welfare and career he wasn't slow to enlighten them. "Oh, he's fine and there's no holding the boy! A parcel arrived for him this morning addressed 'C.O.D.' - Commander of the Deep"!

It is certain that the natural oakwoods of Coille Mhialairidh provided employment and contributed to the local economy for centuries. The pinewoods planted in the 1930s to replace the natural oak also provided considerable employment for Arnisdale, Sandaig and Glenelg folk over several decades. Alas, now, the Mialairidh Forest employs no local people on a regular basis. The necessary work of harvesting, is carried out by contractors who sometimes employ some of the local men on a part-time basis. So this is yet another industry which is now contributing very little to the local economy and local employment. However, Mialairidh has had a proud role in the long history of these parts. Moreover, the location, as the sentinel monitoring the seafarers in the Sound of Sleat over many centuries is unsurpassable. It will continue to have this spectacular role for admiring tourists in the years ahead.

**Top Left**. The Mialairidh Peninsula, uninhabited now, but the place names on old maps indicate that this location had been very active in history. This was the southern boundary of the kingdom of the kings of Man, from whom it passed to the MacLeods of Harris and Dunvegan. To the immediate south were the lands of Somerled's line which included the Macdonalds of Clanranald, the MacDonells of Glengarry, the MacDougalls, MacRuaris and the MacSorleys. Over the centuries from the demise of Norse political control of the Hebrides in 1266, the MacLeods had fought a rearguard action against the northern expansion of Somerled's family (Rixson, 1999). **Right**. The expansive view from the high ground on the Mialairidh Peninsula to Knoydart (left), Skye (right) and down the Sound of Sleat towards Eigg and Rhum. Threats to security from naval invasions could be detected very early from the 'look-out' posts in this area. **Middle Left**. The last permanent inhabitants of the Mialairidh area were Tony Mackay (left), a native of Durness, Sutherland and Jimmy MacLean from GlenUrquhart (right), young Forestry Commission foresters who helped to plant the area with conifers in the late 1920-1930 period. **Centre..** The Forestry Commission hut on the Mialairidh shore looking across Loch Hourn to Crowlick on Knoydart and within sight of Eilean Rarsaidh. **Right**. Tony Mackay about to have a dip in the sea at Mialairidh. **Bottom Left**. The hut was situated close to the remains of a row of houses inhabited at least up to the 1860 era. **Right**. Flora Crombie (nee MacKenzie) and Morag MacIntyre seated on the bracken and bramble infested remains of the walls of the Mialairidh clachan, which included a shop.

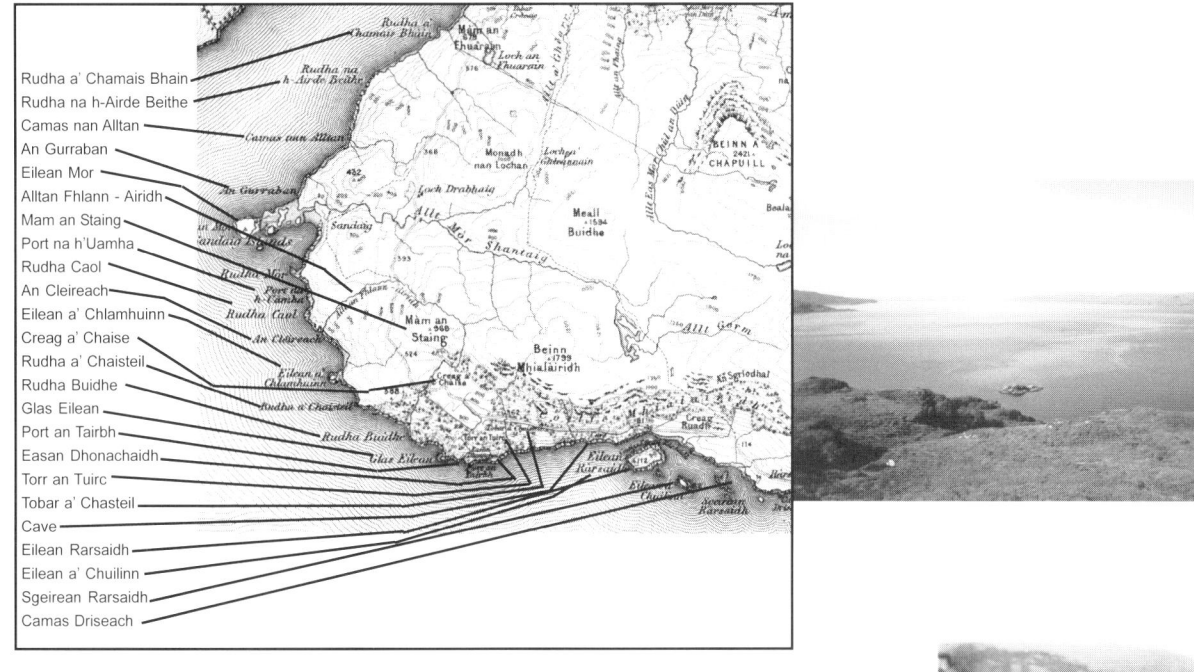

**Top Left**. The line of posts stretching into the sea close to the site of the former Forestry Commission hut on the Mialairidh shore. In harvesting the oak from the Coille Mialairidh, the logs were piled between the posts at low tide and loaded on to the boats at high tide. Across Loch Hourn on the Knoydart shore are the tiny clachans of Coilleshubh and Crowlick. **Right**. The Forestry squad members who were planting the Mialairidh Forest with conifers in the late 1920-1930 period. Back (L to R.) Peter Fletcher, Tony Mackay, Ludovic Fraser, Iain Elder, Jimmy Campbell. Front Row. Donald MacKintosh, Bobby MacLean, Archie MacLean, Andrew Fraser and Angus Stewart.

**Middle Left**. Tony Mackay, a regular singer at the Arnisdale ceilidh dances in the 1930s and member of the Glenelg football teams of that era. **Right**. Tony Mackay and his wife Isabella (nee MacPherson) - 'Grandpa' and 'Granny' to the author's children.

**Bottom Left**. Donald Mackay, recorder of some of the many tales of Mialairidh, Arnisdale and Glenelg of his late father. **Right**. The remains of the house just above the high water mark at Port an Tarbh or Port Luinge on Mialairidh which was the home of Duncan MacLean and his family. Duncan, grandfather of Peggy Ann of Arnisdale Post Office and of Archie MacLean of Camusban, was the 'Watcher' of the oakwood, a remnant of which is seen behind the house.

## Chapter 22

**Rarsaidh and its mysteries**

At the present time, there is only one house in Rarsaidh but, as in all other localities in the Highlands, there was a much larger community there in bygone days. There was a dwelling on Rarsaidh Island (Eilean Rarsaidh) and other dwellings just above the shore line between the present house and the Rarsaidh burn and also to the east towards Arnisdale. It is believed that the people were cleared from these houses around 1849 at the time of the great evictions from the area and the transportation of the folk who survived the sea passage to a new life in Canada, aboard sailing ships such as the Liscard.

In the early 1900s, the present house and croft was occupied by Ewen Cameron and his wife and family. Mrs Cameron's mother was one of the MacRaes of Kishorn where her family were well known boat builders and this skill in boat building and wood working in general was handed down to succeeding generations. However, Ewen Cameron was employed by the Eilanreach Estate as a shepherd and the crofting and boat building activities were spare time occupations. Ewen was succeeded as shepherd by his son Roddie and the next generation included Jessie, Malcolm and Donald. Jessie married Donald MacKintosh of Arnisdale and she suffered the tragic loss of her brother Donald in the First War and of her son (Donald Rarsaidh) in the Second War. Jessie in her later years, came to stay in Arnisdale and her grandsons from Sandaig - Ruaridh, Willie and Calum MacLeod, often stayed through the week with their Granny while at school in Arnisdale, going home to Sandaig at weekends. Willie 'Sandaig' remembers the enjoyment of many walks to Rarsaidh with his Granny to visit all her old haunts when they stayed with her in their Arnisdale schooldays.

Jessie's brother Calum was an excellent craftsman, making boats and furniture such as sideboards and dressing tables to a very high degree of finish. One of his excellent boats is still in use in Arnisdale. It was made, as Willie 'Sandaig' was told, from the old planks from a redundant bridge.

There was a house on Eilean Rarsaidh which was last occupied by the forebears of the late Ludovic and Andrew Fraser of Camusbàn. They probably made their living there by working the land to grow potatoes, make hay and for the grazing of their stock - perhaps a cow and a few goats.

The man who was most associated with Rarsaidh in more recent times was Archie MacLean of Camusbàn who worked as the shepherd/stalker for the Eilanreach Estate in this area. Archie's people had originated in Port Luinge where his grandfather was the watcher in the great oak wood of Coille Mhialairidh. As well as summering the Camusban Crofting Township tups on Eilean Rarsaidh, Archie also kept goats on the island for a time.

Archie was a great local character and passed away just after this book was conceived, taking his wonderful fund of memories and stories with him. He had a great affinity with the old haunts of the MacLean family around Mialairidh and Rarsaidh. In his early days in the 1930s he had worked in the conifer planting of the Mialairidh Forest, and he was the semaphore expert in the local Home Guard during the war. He was also a crack shot with the rifle. After he finished working for the Eilanreach Estate, knowing the territory so well, he was partial to getting some venison for the pot at the due time. The story goes that on one occasion he was on the Sandaig ground and, after a very careful stalk, he got himself into a great position with a fine stag well within shooting distance. As he lined up his rifle and was about to pull the trigger, the stag dropped to the ground like a stone and in the next fraction of a second which it takes for sound to travel, he heard a rifle shot. Archie, almost in disbelief, remained motionless and kept his eye on the spot where the stag fell. After a further few moments, over a rise walking towards the beast strode Ali Beag (MacRae) from the Eilanreach Estate, stalking on behalf of the Estate. Archie continued to 'freeze' as he lay motionless in his shooting position until Ali Beag had done his work on the stag and left westwards with his kill. When Ali was out of sight, Archie proceeded eastwards to Arnisdale, experiencing a rare hunting failure on this occasion. In relating the story to a friend, Archie was asked "Do you think that Ali spotted you?" "Well, if he did," said Archie, "he was too polite to let on!" Archie would undoubtedly have behaved likewise if it had been Ali Beag who had been caught in the act. That was the way between these fine honourable people.

There is an unofficial graveyard at Rarsaidh on a plot to the north side of the road on the lower slopes of Beinn Sgritheall. The graves are marked by flat stones which Willie MacKenzie, Corran, located within recent years. The story is, that buried there are the victims of a smallpox epidemic in the Rarsaidh district - perhaps in the early to mid-1800s. The Rarsaidh folk were not allowed to bury their dear ones in the official graveyard in Arnisdale because of the fear of transmission of infection to the Arnisdale folk. A few may have survived the dreaded disease. One of the survivors may have been Alasdair Breac (Breac = spotted or marked with smallpox) who later lived and worked at Barrisdale. Alasdair plied the shore in his canoe doing his fishing. Maggie Lea said that her mother remembered Alasdair well. Maggie also relates the story of the lady from Airor who spent a summer's night sleeping in the open air on Eilean Rarsaidh and was reputed to have died as the result of a snake bite. It was said that it was found curled up in her mouth in the morning as she wakened from her open-mouthed slumbers!

Of all the places around Arnisdale, there are more tales of the supernatural about Rarsaidh than in any other location in the district. Bobby Robertson, that toughest member of the 'men of the road' brethren who had spent his nights sleeping in many strange places as he proceeded on his well trodden and familiar circuit, after spending a night in the Rarsaidh barn, reported that he had a frightening experience during the night and vowed never again to return to the place for a night's rest. Johnny Sinclair, always out for a bit of excitement, and good at telling his own stories and adorning and enhancing those of others, claimed to have seen the apparition of a lady as he was opening the Rarsaidh gate on the way home from Glenelg with the mails. Another report referred to a female 'apparition' crossing the road in the darkness of an autumn evening with a haunch of venison on her back! Could it have been one of the local poachers, cleverly disguised?

Regarding Bobby Robertson, Alan MacDiarmid recalls that Bobby was a frequent caller at Lower Sandaig to get a good meal from his Mother and a good night's rest on the hay in the barn. When Alan's family moved from Lower Sandaig to Abersky in Stratherrick, Bobby duly found them there and when the family moved later to Borlum at Drumnadrochit in Glenurquhart, they had not long got settled in when they had a visit again from their old friend Bobby. Bobby claimed to some that he was a Fifer where his father had run a coal business. As a young man he went to work in Canada for a number of years but returned to the old country and took to the road, visiting all his hospitable friends on a rota basis. 'Bobby Robertson' was a name he had given himself. Alan was never aware of his correct name - Bobby liked his friends but he wanted to be anonymous in relation to his original identity.

So the Sandaig, Mialairidh and Rarsaidh areas, now virtually deserted, have had a very interesting history. Each location has its own particular charms and very picturesque corners. With such history and scenic beauty one cannot help feeling that these attractive, intriguing places will live again in the future, if not literally in terms of restored dwellings and families of people, then at least in the minds and memories of the current and future generations.

**Top**.  The Mialairidh, Beinn Sgritheall and Rarsaidh areas around 1900 including Eilean Rarsaidh on the right.  A magnifying glass will help in spotting the house at Rarsaidh and the different lines of the old road beyond Rarsaidh to those of the present day (George Washington Wilson).

**Middle Left**.   Rarsaidh at sunset from behind the house looking westwards to Eilean Rarsaidh, the corners of the Mialairidh peninsula (right), Knoydart (left) and Skye beyond.   **Right**.  Views of Rarsaidh from the west near Eilean Rarsaidh.

**Bottom Left.**  The Rarsaidh house and adjacent road from the shore.   **Centre.**  Mrs Jessie Mackintosh (centre) with Gwennie Stoddart (left) and Chrissie Campbell.  Jessie 'Rarsaidh' was born and reared in Rarsaidh but spent her later years in her little house in Camusban.
**Right**.  Archie MacLean feeding the Eilanreach Estate hoggs on the Rarsaidh croft.  Archie had great affinity with Rarsaidh.  His grandfather had been the Watcher in the nearby Coille Mhialairidh – the big oak forest.

**Top Left**. Eilean Rarsaidh and Caolas Eilean Rarsaidh looking westwards from the slopes of Beinn Sgritheall to Knoydart across the loch. **Right**. A closer view of Eilean Rarsaidh which was once inhabited, the last to occupy the island being a family of MacAskills. At a later date the Camusban tups were 'incarcerated' on the island from March to July each year.

**Middle Left**. The remains of the Rarsaidh garden situated in a sheltered spot on the east side of the house towards Arnisdale. The view looks westwards to Barrisdale and the moss in the foreground was where the Camusban folk cut their peats and collected sphagnum moss for wound dressings in wartime. **Right**. Rarsaidh once had a much bigger population and, on closer examination, along the shoreline and in the brackens, ruins are to be found. Some of the population were cleared off the land and on to the sailing ships bound for Canada and other faraway places around 1850. Many others died in a smallpox epidemic around the same time.

**Bottom Left**. The relatives of the victims of the smallpox epidemic were not allowed to bury their dear ones in the Arnisdale graveyard. So they were buried close to Rarsaidh. Here Blair Anderson, Tom MacDiarmid and Willie MacKenzie search for the lost graves of the Rarsaidh folk on the lower slopes of Beinn Sgritheall above Rarsaidh and Eilean a' Chuilinn directly across the loch from Rudha Ruadh on the Knoydart shore. **Right**. A view of the coastline at Rarsaidh looking westwards from the oak woods high up on the western slopes of Beinn Sgritheall.

# Chapter 23

**Caolasmor and the Paterson family.**

The distance from shore to shore on Loch Hourn is shortest at Caolasmor. The word Caolas means a 'firth' or 'strait' or 'ferry'. The narrowness of Loch Hourn at this point results in a swift flow of the tide or current as it ebbs and flows. A sound knowledge of sailing and boats, while being important when covering all parts of Loch Hourn, is particularly vital when going through the big strait or the Caolas Mor. A more appropriate translation for the name might be 'powerful current'. The locality on the north shore, with two houses, outbuildings and croft land has the same name as the strait - Caolasmor.

Traditionally, this locality has been part of the Kinlochourn Estate with a gamekeeper/ ghillie/stalker/ shepherd/watcher in the employment of the estate being resident at this location. The term 'Watcher' refers to that part of the employee's responsibility which involves watching for and discouraging poachers (of the deer), particularly from the many fishing boats (and particularly the herring drifters) which were plying their trade in the loch over the many decades of the herring fishing. The fishermen, whether from nearby places such as Mallaig, Lochcarron (The Caranachs), or more distant locations such as Ullapool, the East Coast or even from Barra or other islands in the Inner or Outer Hebrides, were all partial to a bit of roast venison; it provided a fine change from the usual diet of fish and more fish. And many of the fishermen had considerable experience of the habits of the deer, of scanning the shore line and hillsides with the 'glass', and of stalking. Many of them were also crack shots! So they had to be watched!

The resident Watcher at Caolasmor also worked the croft. They would usually have two or more cows, a few sheep and plenty of hens. They would grow their own potatoes, cabbage and oats and make hay for the winter feeding of the cattle. With the plentiful supply of fish and shellfish available on their doorstep, their barrel of salt herring and their share of estate venison in season, they could live a reasonably independent existence. When they required supplies, they could walk to Corran and Arnisdale down the path along the shore, or take the boat down the loch themselves, or ask the Arnisdale postman such as Duncan Campbell, Willie the Post (the first) or Willie the Post (the second) to bring up their requirements the next time they came up the loch with their mails. To get their cows served so as to produce the next year's calves, and get a new bountiful supply of milk after calving, they would take the cows on the rope and halter as they came into season along the shoreline path to the bull down at Arnisdale Farm.

The family which the older Loch Hourn generation associate most with Caolasmor are the Patersons. The last Mrs Paterson to reside at Caolasmor back in the early part of the twentieth century (a Chisholm before her marriage) was a cousin of Peter and Roddy MacRae of Kinlochourn. Mrs Paterson's husband's (John) family were born and brought up in Caolas Mor, John's father in turn having come from Glenelg. John, along with his sisters Mary and Flora were enrolled as 14 to 15 year olds at Arnisdale School between the years 1893 and 1895 and boarded in the Schoolhouse with the Arnisdale teacher of the time, Isabella McKay. They had probably received their earlier education from their side school teacher at Caolasmor.

The last Patersons to rear their family at Caolasmor had ten children - Hugh, Elizabeth, Roddy, John, Annie, Sandy, Roderick, Helen, Hannah, Farquhar and Mary. The children had their own resident teacher at Caolasmor. It was a fine place to be brought up with great scope for adventure along the shore, on the hill and in the woods which thrive in the sheltered recess in which the house and croft lands lie. There was also plenty of work to be done to occupy all the children - in the house, in the byre and barn, on the croft land, collecting firewood in the woods and on the shore, cutting and carting peats and at the fishing.

However, when they reached the end of their education at their own Caolasmor side-school at the age of 13 or 14 years, there was no local paid employment for them. So they had either to proceed to further education (which was out of the question financially because of the basic subsistence level wage earned by their father) or to seek employment.

Farquhar emigrated to Bermuda and Mary to New Zealand, Roddy joined the Merchant Navy, Hugh went to London to join the bank and had a distinguished career in banking. As a young man, John drove the mail coach between Shiel and Kyle, then emigrated to South Africa, joined the South African Scottish Regiment at the start of the Great War in 1914 and made the supreme sacrifice at the Battle of Ypres. Young Sandy decided to make a move to Kinlochleven. There was the prospect of plenty of work there because the huge project of building the reservoir to provide the hydro electricity to serve the needs of the aluminium factory (smelting the bauxite for the manufacture of aluminium), was about to start. Sandy took up residence in Foyers Road, Kinlochleven in 1912. There were 3000 navvies working on the building of the reservoir and Sandy soon got a job in this huge squad. Sandy married Flora Kennedy (who was born in Plockton) in 1913.

This employment was fine for about 2 years until the outbreak of war in 1914 when Sandy and his brothers answered the call of their country, Sandy joining the Argyll and Sutherland Highlanders. In the Loch Hourn area, the Paterson family had the reputation of being fine specimens of manhood and womanhood and young Sandy was no exception. The Recruiting Staff of the Argylls, in seeking as many suitable recruits as possible for their regiment, obviously wanted to portray the Argylls as strong, athletic, handsome and dashing young men. From all their fine young men, it was Sandy Paterson's photograph which they selected for their Recruiting Poster. Sandy fought in the trenches in France from the outset of the war in 1914. He was machine gunned and wounded in 1917 and, suffering also from cholera, he was invalided out of the Army in 1917.

Following prolonged hospitalisation on home soil, he was nursed back to a reasonable state of fitness. He eventually got back to Kinlochleven and his wife Flora and to his work in the Smelter. Sandy and Flora had nine children - Mary, Duncan, John, Ewen (Hugh), Ruth, Ruby, Anne, Fiona and Billy.

The author in preparing this book, sought relatives of folk who had once resided and worked in those locations on Loch Hourn which are no longer inhabited on a year round basis, one such being Caolasmor. Many older people, such as Peter MacRae, Isabella Mackay, Maggie Li, Mary MacDonald, Roddy MacPherson and Nettie Campbell had referred to the Patersons of Caolasmor. Were any of their descendants traceable?

Among many extremely useful allies in this venture has been Maggie Li (Mrs John MacDonald) now resident in the Caol area. Maggie has got libraries of relevant information on Loch Hourn filed away in her head and she is a most impressive Gaelic scholar, although she vehemently contradicts such a claim with her usual graceful humility. "Have you any idea about the Patersons of Caolasmor - are they still around?" she was asked. "One of them, Fiona, stays fairly near here and I will speak to her to find out if she is interested about Caolasmor", was the reply. The author fully expected such a response from Maggie - the storage capacity of her computer is infinite and she always seems to know which buttons to press to answer all sorts of questions and to supply all kinds of information.

Maggie duly contacted Fiona who certainly was interested, but indicated that her younger brother Billy was even more interested to trace his roots, and perhaps also supply some relevant family information and photographs of the days at Caolasmor.

So Billy was duly contacted by the author. Some family member had drawn up a detailed family tree a considerable time ago but it had been lost or destroyed and, with the old folk gone, the roots of father Sandy (who died in 1956) were now becoming very elusive, despite visits to graveyards in an attempt to find relevant gravestone inscriptions at places such as Glenelg and elsewhere. Billy was delighted to make the contact and sought guidance as to the Paterson roots - somewhere in the Glenelg area. The author could not oblige, but indicated that Isabella Mackay and Peter MacRae would almost certainly provide Billy's detailed genealogy. Peter MacRae, now at Invergarry, had it all worked out in a jiffy and this information was conveyed to Billy Paterson, now resident in Inverness. Who was Billy, anyway, where did he spend his working life and what kind of work did he do?

Oh, as a young lad of 16 he played football for Inverness Thistle, then he was transferred to Doncaster Rovers. He captained the Scottish B International team, he was transferred to Newcastle United and later to Rangers and played for them for many years. After finishing a long and illustrious playing career with Rangers, he set off to 'chase the dollar', as Billy put it himself, coaching youngsters in soccer skills in Canada (Niagara Falls and Toronto) and America (Montreal, Buffalo and Detroit).

Now Billy is working out that his father's mother was a Chisholm and her mother in turn was a MacRae - a sister of the grandmother of Peter MacRae and Roddy at Invergarry. He wanted Peter and Roddy's address and phone number. He now knew exactly where his old long lost cousins resided. He was soon off to visit them, to catch up on lost time to get the genealogy sorted out - and all the old stories about Caolasmor at the same time! Peter and Roddy greatly looked forward to Billy's visit! They had a very memorable reunion.

'The blood is strong.'

**Top Left**. Map. The caolas at Caolasmor is evident, through which the tide rushes each time it ebbs and flows. **Right**. A glimpse of Caolasmor as Billy MacKenzie sails up the loch towards Kinloch Hourn.

**Middle Left**. One of the houses at Caolasmor with the adjoining remains of the barn and byre – looking westwards. **Centre**. The second house at Caolasmor looking eastwards. A wide variety of trees flourish in this sheltered little corner. **Right**. The adjoining arable croftland looking eastwards up Loch Hourn towards Runival and Skiary.

**Bottom Left**. Willie MacKenzie of Corran on the fine fertile coastal strip of land at Caolasmor which helped to sustain the families resident there over the years with the production of oats, potatoes, vegetables and hay for the cows and sheep. The view is across to Knoydart and westwards down the loch. **Centre.** Some of the Paterson family members at Caolasmor around 1900 – the children of John and Mrs Paterson (nee Chisholm). Standing. L to R. Hugh, John, Roddy and Sandy. Seated. Helen and Hannah. Several members of the Paterson family gave their lives for their country during the two Great Wars. John was killed in the Battle of Ypres in World War 1. Sandy's son John, who was serving in the Scots Guards, was killed on the Anzio beaches in World War 2, while Hannah's son John, a fighter pilot, also made the supreme sacrifice in World War 2. **Right**. The route of the shoreline path (The Stone of meal road) from Caolasmor to Corran below the slopes of Druim Fada. The Corran shoreline fields are evident with Camusban and Beinn Sgritheall beyond.

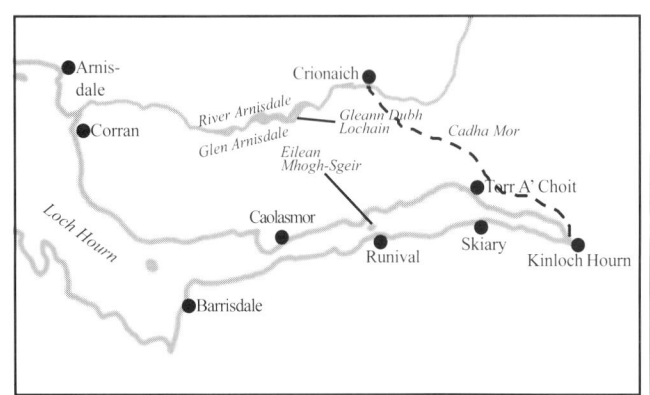

**Top Left**.  Hugh Paterson at a function of the London Gaelic Society in 1913.   Hugh was born and reared at Caolasmor in a family of ten.  He left Caolasmor in his early teens soon after 1900 to seek employment.  Hugh had a distinguished career as a Company Secretary in London and retired to Balmacara.  **Centre**.  Sandy and Flora Paterson with one of their nine children.  Sandy joined the Argyll and Sutherland Highlanders at the outbreak of the Great War in 1914.  It was Sandy's photograph which was used on the Recruiting Poster for the Argylls.  Sandy was machine gunned and wounded in 1917, but survived and died in 1956.  **Right**.  The youngest of Sandy and Flora's nine children, Billy, had a distinguished career as a footballer.

**Middle**.  Billy Paterson (middle of second row) with the rest of the Rangers squad in season 1960-61.  Current Scotland Team Manager, Craig Brown, is fifth from the right in the front row.

**Bottom Left**.   Rangers, winners of the Scottish Cup in the 1950s.   L to R. Niven, MacMillan, Scott, Bill Paterson, Millar, Wilson, skipper Eric Caldow, Shearer, 'Slim Jim' Baxter, Brand and Davis.
**Right**.  Peter (left) and the late Roddy MacRae of Kinloch Hourn to whom Billy Paterson made a 'beeline' to catch up with his long lost cousins and to be brought up to date with his genealogy.

# Chapter 24

**Kinloch Hourn, Torr a' choit and Glen Quoich - Memories of Peter and Roddy MacRae.**

No family are better remembered in the upper reaches of Loch Hourn than the MacRaes of Kinloch Hourn. They have been connected with the Home Farm of Kinloch Hourn on the Glen Quoich Estate for well over 100 years. Ewen MacRae first came as tenant of the Home Farm on the Estate in 1888. Ewen was one of the MacRaes of Ardentoul in Kintail and he married Janet MacRae - also from Kintail. They had 4 sons (Farquhar, John, Peter and Donald) and 4 daughters (Anne, Flora, Helen and Isabella). Anne, Flora and Isabella were later to become, respectively, Mrs Hugh MacMillan of Runival, Mrs Robert MacRaild of Arisaig and Mrs Donald MacPherson of Glenelg. Helen died of meningitis when only 15 years of age. The second son, John, succeeded his father as tenant of the Glen Quoich Estate Home Farm. John married Jessie Gillies from the neighbouring Kinloch Hourn Estate and they in turn had nine children, Ewen, Helen, Angus, Jessie, Roddy, Peggy, Dolly, Peter and Farquhar (Fachie) in that order. At the time these lines are being penned (1997), Peter and Roddy are still with us - now retired in their little cottage at the Home Farm, Invergarry. They are a mine of information, history and stories ('sgeulachdan') about upper Loch Hourn and the Glen Quoich and Kinloch Hourn Estates. That is a huge sweep of country and while now largely deserted, except by the hill walkers and those who like to explore such wildernesses, within the memories of Peter and Roddy, the area bristled with folk - certainly during the months of the stalking and the herring fishing.

The Glen Quoich and Kinloch Hourn Estates are divided by Coire Sgoireadail on the lower slopes of Bhuidhe Bheinn and by the river which flows from Loch Quoich into Loch Hourn. The Kinloch Hourn Estate also marches with Glen Shiel Estate to the north and that of Arnisdale to the West. Glen Quoich Estate stretches towards Cluanie to the north, Lochiel Estate to the south and at one time reached Invergarry and Loch Oich to the east.

The changes in the area which Peter and Roddy have witnessed in their lifetime are immense - the Loch Hourn herring fishing is no more, the halcyon days of the big sporting estates employing a great number of local folk as gamekeepers, ghillies, stalkers, watchers, shepherds, gardeners, chauffeurs, butlers, housemaids, cooks and the many others required to run the shooting lodges are but a memory, while there have also been great changes in the landscape. Notable among these are the destruction of the once magnificent Glen Quoich Lodge and its adjacent wooded policies, the remnants now submerged some 100 feet below the new extended Loch Quoich. The Hydro Electric Dam built in the 1950s more than doubled the area of the loch - from 3 to 7 square miles, helping to harvest the water in this very high rainfall area for the generation of electricity. The Loch Loyne Hydro Scheme to the east and the raising of these waters cut off the centuries old road connecting Cluanie and Glen Shiel to Tomdoun and Glengarry. In addition, the magnificent wild splendour of this countryside is now punctuated by the line of pylons conveying electricity to the Island of Skye. Also, Arnisdale - the traditional mecca for Kinloch Hourn and Glen Quoich folk in days gone by - for their weekly or monthly shopping and for their wonderful twice yearly ceilidh dances - no longer provides these services and entertainments of past days.

But despite the natural sadness over the 'desecration' (as Peter refers to many of the changes) of once magnificent virgin landscape and of the welcoming homes and beautiful garden policies created by local craftsmen, Peter and Roddy are readily diverted to recalling joyfully the great days and stories from the past.

Perhaps Alastair Scott, in relating part of the Kinloch Hourn story in a fine article in the Scots Magazine, managed to capture the true feelings of Peter about what had been so special about his lifetime at

Kinloch Hourn - he surmised: 'It was independence and solitude, and a love of mountains and sea. It was also, I guessed, a sense of conquering a place which could be so intimidating, and of belonging to a place where the senses could soar'.

Now for some of Roddy and Peter's memories. On the home farm at Kinloch Hourn, they ran a flock of 200 Cheviot ewes on the hill, and had five cows to keep the family and neighbours supplied in milk, butter, crowdie and cheese. They never kept a bull, the cows being taken when in season all the 8 miles or so down to Arnisdale to Roddy Mor's bull there or the 6 miles along the shore track to Barrisdale. Sometimes they had breeding cattle and a bull at Glen Quoich lodge so that was a slightly shorter trek to get the cow served and in-calf. The calves were reared mainly on skim milk and butter milk with some oil cake added to the bucket of their twice daily liquid feed, supplemented with their home cured hay. They also kept chickens and ducks and preserved the surplus eggs from the spring and summer period of plenty in water glass to tide them over the winter period of scarcity.

Two Highland garrons were usually kept, being used to carry home the deer from the hill to the Glen Quoich and Kinloch Hourn Lodges in the stalking season and they teamed up for the cultivations in the spring time, while being used for carting throughout the year. Normally 3 acres were ploughed, oats were hand sown out of a home made sowing 'box' held in front of the sower just below waist height by straps suspended from the neck and shoulders. The resulting crop was harvested with the scythe while still fairly green so as to improve its feeding value. It was bundled into sheaves, stooked and carted into the barn when dry enough for storage. Making hay and getting the stooks in dry was a formidable challenge at Kinloch Hourn with its 100 to 150 inches of annual rainfall. Some of the oats were threshed and cleaned using a hand powered threshing mill and fanners. The rest of the oat sheaves were fed whole to the cattle and horses. The sheep received no supplementary winter feed - they had to live off their store of body fat stored in the summer period of plenty and what they could harvest themselves on the hill from the withered forage left over from the summer season.

The family had to be as self sufficient as possible, and , of course, grew their own potatoes - Kerrs Pinks, Golden Wonders and Edzell Blues were the main ones grown with some Sharpes Express and Duke of York as earlies to yield these wonderful new potatoes which provided such a greatly anticipated culinary treat each summer.

The farm garden provided plentiful quantities of apples, pears, blackcurrants and gooseberries from which mother would make the year's large supply of jam. To accompany the potatoes, there would be fish from Loch Hourn, including fresh herring when the silver darlings arrived on their annual migration. Later there would be salt herring and there was always plenty of venison. Venison was not sold before the last war - the Estates gave it away and when there was a surplus of fresh venison, this was salted for later use. On occasions too, a fat wether would be slaughtered in the late Autumn, the carcase would be hung up in an outside airy larder and it would be in prime condition for weeks afterwards. Of course, neighbours would always receive their due share - 'we looked after each other in those days' said Roddy. Peter comments about the attitude of some visitors to their home produced milk - some were suspicious of it, preferring the so-called 'dairy milk' they were used to purchasing in bottles in the grocer's shop. He chuckled 'If you ask me, I think listeria and salmonella have only been invented to keep the hospitals full!'

The main sales from the sheep flock were wool and two to three year old wethers sold at the Autumn sales. In the hard times of the 1930s, wool was fetching only 4 old pence per pound weight (about 4 new pence per kg) with hogg wool (from one year old sheep) sometimes making a penny more. Each year, Roddy Mor from Arnisdale would buy around 20 of these well grown wethers for butchering - he used to supply Arnisdale and also had a weekly run in his pony and cart to sell meat in Glenelg. The wethers would be taken from Kinloch Hourn between shearing time in July and the compulsory August winter dipping. They would load them 10 to a boat and row them down to Arnisdale. The wethers were big strong sheep by this, their third to fourth summer, and Peter estimated that they would yield a well finished carcass of around 70lb (about 32 kg). On a few occasions when the loch was too stormy, Roddy 'Loch Hourn' and Roddy Mor would shepherd the wethers down the hill track from Kinloch Hourn and down the Arnisdale Glen. Sometimes cattle would also be herded down the same track on their way to the annual auction market in Glenelg.

However, up to the 1930s, most of the wethers, surplus weaned calves and farrow cows were herded by Peter's older brothers, Ewen, Angus and Roddy, by road to Invergarry and then on to Fort Augustus - a distance of 32 miles, which took them 2 days. At Fort Augustus they would be loaded on to the steamer for their onward journey down Loch Ness and the Caledonian Canal to the market in Inverness. The drovers would return by the same route - almost one week later, with the main annual income of the farm in their pockets which would have to keep the family in essential supplies for the following year.

In 1930, transportation of goods and livestock became a bit easier for the MacRae family. Ewen and his brothers went to an auction sale near Fort William and purchased a Ford lorry (a 3 way hand tipper) for £25.

As well as being adept at travelling overland, the MacRaes also had to be able seamen. The main food store was in Arnisdale - John MacLean's shop and Post Office - later run by John's daughters Peggy Ann and Mary. The Arnisdale supplies came weekly by MacLennan's launch from Mallaig. The nine miles row from Kinloch Hourn to Arnisdale - about once a fortnight - had to be carefully planned - going down on the ebb tide and back on the flow was a great help to the oarsmen. Two or three boats would set off together with representatives from all dwellings in the district to get their 'messages' - essential supplies of commodities such as salt, flour and oatmeal, tea and tobacco. Peter remembers two brands of oatmeal - one for making the porridge and the brose and a special meal for the oatcakes. The meal came from the Inverurie Meal Mill in Aberdeenshire and Peter remembers the 'advertisement' on the bag - 'Meal - the marrow of men'. Many in the old days would certainly agree with that slogan - such was the importance of oat meal in the daily diet.

The main outer clothing needs of the folk in the district were met by the half yearly visits of MacLennan the Tailor from Fort William. He would come to measure for the tweed suits - for both the women and men folk - and 6 months later would return with the finished garments. Often each estate had its own Harris Tweed check - a distinguishing mark for the estate 'team'. Peter remembers that folk were then paid twice yearly so if the tailor came just before the next pay was due, he would have to go home empty handed and await the payment some six months later on his next visit. MacLennan's nickname of 'The Robber' was certainly undeserved as he provided an excellent service and also good credit terms! But he went off with some of their hard earned cash and the nickname was merely a source of amusement - probably as much enjoyed by the tailor himself as by those who gave him that tag in the first place!

The schooling of all the MacRae children started in the loft of the Kinloch Hourn Farm Steading. Peter remembers that there were 8 in the school there when he started and their teacher was a Joan MacInnes from Breakish in Skye. Roddy chipped in with his memory that 'She was a bad b...... but that her sister was super'. Perhaps most small boys had similar opinions of teachers who kept strict discipline and were making valiant attempts to educate children whose wont was to escape into the wilds and get away from the inevitable restraint within a small group of like-minded youngsters under the close surveillance of a dedicated teacher. After 2 years, the 'home' school closed because of the low number of pupils and Peter 'graduated' to Tomdoun School (with 13 pupils) for the remainder of his Primary Education. Some pupils stayed on at Tomdoun until the school leaving age of 14 but Peter progressed to Fort William for 3 years from the age of 12. He stayed in lodgings at both Tomdoun and Fort William so he spent most of his schooldays away from home, apart from weekends and holiday time. He was glad to get back 'full-time' to Kinloch Hourn when his schooldays were over. There is no doubt that Peter's family and many others in that era could have made a name for themselves in the professions and in elevated positions in industry if the finance and educational opportunities of today were available to them. However, both Peter and Roddy exude great joy in relating their memories - life was tough at times but the lasting memories are those of lives which were very satisfying and fulfilling.

Apart from sheep farming on their own account, there was extra seasonal work to be done on the neighbouring estates, especially at stalking time. In addition, the MacRae boys maintained the seven mile stretch of gravel road between their home and Loch Quoich bridge, they acted as the local postmen, collecting the mail three times weekly from Tomdoun and delivering locally, including the clachans of Torr a' choit, Skiary and Runival. They also fished and collected mussels, their 'catch' being picked up at regular intervals by boats from Mallaig or Kyle. They also had the contract for organising the annual supply of coal for the district. Coastal puffers belonging to Hamilton Brothers from the Clyde, loaded with 100 to 110 tonnes, would call at Arnisdale to take on board a pilot such as Alex MacIntyre or Duncan MacTavish who well knew the hazards and moods of Loch Hourn, to guide them up the loch, through the narrows at Caolasmor (taking their usual bearing from the old Scots Pine on the southern shore which is marked on the Admiralty Sailing Directions) and thence cannily to the end of the loch. They would beach the boat almost beside the road only about 400 yards from the farm steading. The Arnisdale pilots would be joined by the local squad which included the MacRae boys, Donald (Do) MacKillop, Neil MacPherson from Li and Johnnie MacMillan from Runival. A pair of them would take turns of going into the grime and dustiness of the hold and filling the bucket with shovels. When full, the bucket would be hoisted up using a system of ropes and pulleys and swung sideways into the waiting carts. The coal was stored in the big shed at the farm and the supply for the lodges and cottages in the district was delivered as required. The lodges went through a lot of coal in a year, while each estate employee got between 1 and 3 tonnes as a perquisite along with their tied cottage, the exact amount varying with their estate 'rank' and whether they were full or part-time employees.

Among the coal boats that Peter remembers are the Glen Gloy, the Lochranza and the Loch Fyne. They did not go back to the Clyde empty - usually loading up with sand for glass-making at the Lochaline sand quarry on the Ardnamurchan Peninsula.

Coal was an essential fuel since fire wood was not available in the district and, surprisingly, peat was also very scarce.

As well as for household use, the coal was required in days gone by in the smearing sheds. Smearing was a forerunner of dipping to control external sheep parasites such as ticks, keds and blowfly. It was also possibly designed to provide some added protection against the elements over the wet and cold winter period. The commodities used were Archangel tar, imported in casks from Russia and kegs of cheap butter - of British origin, according to Peter. A mixture was made of the butter and tar with the help of the heat of a coal fire. Each sheep was treated in turn around the month of August. The wool was parted, exposing the skin and the mixture was smeared on the surface, meticulously covering the entire skin surface of each beast. It was slow, back-breaking work, Roddy remembers, taking two men a good 20 minutes to cover each sheep.

Peter has nostalgic memories of the herring fishing in Loch Hourn and laments the overfishing which undoubtedly contributed to the demise of this industry which, more than any other, contributed to the development of the Loch Hourn clachans, provided considerable local employment and helped to make a fortune for some in places far removed from the district, and with no interest in conserving stocks, nor the welfare of local folk or the development of the area.

At the height of the Munich Crisis in 1938, Peter remembers counting 65 herring drifters in the upper reaches of Loch Hourn and by that time the great herring fishing was almost on its last legs relative to the great 18,000 tonnes per year catches of past eras. The shores of Knoydart in these days, Peter asserts, must have been thronged with the Klondykers' squads of curers. The Klondykers or merchant ships which purchased the catches of the drifters, in Peter's memory, were mainly of British origin but they supplied many parts of Europe as well as the home market. Roddy recalls the self-imposed discipline of the old days of the herring fishing. With the onset of dusk, the horn of one of the Klondykers would be sounded. That was the signal for the boats to set their drift nets, they remained set overnight and the catches would be lifted in the morning. There was to be no movement of boats while the nets were set between dusk and the hauling in of the nets soon after dawn on the following day. Roddy commented that when the old drift nets were replaced by ring nets - with the resulting 'hoovering' of almost all the fish in the loch - that spelled the end of the annual migration of the new generations of the great shoals of Loch Hourn herring into what had been the haunts of their progenitors for centuries past.

Regarding the salting of the herring, this curing did not start until after the end of September, the herring being marketed and eaten fresh up to this time of the year.

Although Kinloch Hourn is very remote and isolated, the MacRaes were never short of entertainment at any time of the year. The nearest neighbours over the long winter period were at Runival (where a family of MacMasters resided before the MacMillans while Johnny Campbell and his family were the last residents there); Caolasmor (where the Paterson family were succeeded by the MacRaes), at Torr a' choit (the home of Angus MacKintosh and his family) and Skiary - the nearest clachan to Kinloch Hourn. In the heyday of the herring fishing there was a pub at Skiary to supply the needs of the hordes of fishermen and herring curers. Peter's family remembered 5 or 6 families at Skiary - MacMillans, MacPhersons, Stoddarts, MacCallums and Camerons, all with their own crofts - but also getting employment from the estates and at the herring fishing. The MacRae family would venture the 3 miles to Skiary for an evening ceilidh along the coastal track but the other locations were either too far distant or too hazardous to reach in the darkness. However, daytime visiting to these locations took place when other duties such as fishing, stalking or sheep gathering took them into these locations. Johnny Cameron was the last resident Peter remembers at Skiary, Johnny dying in 1941.

Somewhat surprisingly, many 'men or the road' were regular callers or perhaps this is not so surprising, for these vagrants, as some wish to call them, remembered well the places where they received a welcome and sustenance and trod the same welcome paths on their annual pilgrimages to visit their kindly friends in faraway places. The MacRae family never questioned them and they were never turned away from the farm without some tea, a bed in a barn and some breakfast the next morning. Some had a pedlar's licence and sold pins, needles, razor blades, shoelaces, and such like. Some liked to work, others didn't. Most avoided the cities where there was little charity.

"I remember Alfred Simmons, a Cockney. Alfred had a syrup tin made into a mug, a 'drum'", said Peter. "It was held over the fire on a walking stick. 'A drum of tea' was the common expression. There was Johnny Jones, too - he was a Welshman, and a thief. He was hard to catch, but they caught him stealing a pheasant at Cluanie Lodge. He was very indignant and protested that it had been a mistake. 'I thought it was a hen', he said - and Peter laughed at the audacity of Johnny's defence.

"There were others who remained nameless. One was reputed to come from a good family in Lochaber. He was a piper, always cheerful, full of humour and nonsense. These travelling people performed a useful service at a time when communications were so poor, by bringing news of friends and relatives on neighbouring estates".

Another regular visitor to Kinloch Hourn whom Peter remembered well was Ronald Burn, now famous for the incorporation of his wonderful diaries into the book "Burn on the Hill" by Elizabeth Allan. Ronald was a renowned hill walker in the early part of the century, including the time of the Great War and the 1920s. He called unexpectedly at the homes of hill farmers, shepherds and stalkers on his walking exploits on Highland hills, and expected a welcome, sustenance, a bed for the night and a good breakfast the following morning.

Ronald got all that he expected at most of his ports of call, including the farm at Kinloch Hourn. He would be on his route between his other popular 'supper, bed and breakfast' calling points such as the Stewart home in Glen Dessary in Lochaber and the MacPherson household at Moyle in Glenelg. Ronald would often go from there - to expect and duly receive - another welcome at the Scott's cottage in upper Glen Affric at Alltbeithe and from there he would make for other old friends in Glen Strathfarrar. And so - on Ronald would march every summer holiday, escaping from the hustle and bustle of London.

Ronald, like the men of the road, would carry news from place to place, to and from folk who were sometimes related, but always knew each other well and had a common bond of mutual interest in each other's well-being. He was interested in all the ways of the hill men and women, he learned Gaelic and Peter MacRae remembers how entertaining he was when he called at their Loch Hourn home. Peter remembers on one occasion he was finding out about all the distinctive marks of the hill sheep which belonged to different hill farms and estates. Ronald took notes in his diary as Peter's father explained to him the different keel colours and their locations on the fleece as one means of distinguishing each other's sheep. He then went on to explain the horn branding in the Blackface breed. When he started to explain the different lug (ear) marks, Peter's father found it very convenient that the cat jumped up to have a snooze on his lap. As the cat lay there in perfect peace and comfort, Peter's father, as he fondled the cat's head and its ears, demonstrated to Ronald the placement and shape of the different lug marks on the sheep belonging to neighbouring farms and estates. This helped to identify stray sheep that came in with the hill gatherings to the fank for sorting and whatever treatment (shearing, dipping etc) was the main objective of the gather.

In the summer months especially, there were many other hill walkers passing by on the fine hill tracks making for Knoydart, Arnisdale, Glenelg, southwards to Lochaber or northwards to Glenshiel and Kintail.

With all these comings and goings, the activities on the estates and at the fishing, things were never lonely or boring for the MacRae family at Loch Hourn.

Church Services were held at Kinloch Hourn every two to four weeks or so. Church of Scotland missionaries based in Arnisdale, such as Daniel MacDonald, would come up on his boat for a mid-day service and get back down the loch before darkness fell. The services were held in the school at the farm - the little room at the top of the outside stairway which later became the farm's hay loft. The folk would come from all around to the services - from the Glen Quoich Estate houses, the staff in the three neighbouring Lodges and from Skiary, Runival and Torr a' choit. Along with the MacRae family contingent, there were often up to 30 at these services.

With regard to medical services, perhaps it was just as well that, in general, the Glen Quoich and Kinloch Hourn folk kept pretty healthy. When emergencies arose, medical attention took a long time to materialise by the time messages were relayed and the Doctor or Nurse could respond. Kinloch Hourn did not get its first public telephone until the late 1940s. Roddy recalled a case in the 1920s when estate worker Johnny Cameron who lived at Skiary sustained a serious arm injury. A messenger was sent to Glen Quoich Lodge (8 miles from Skiary) where there was a telephone, and the nearest doctor was summoned. Dr Brander of Fort William grabbed his pushbike and took the first train to Invergarry. He then cycled 26 miles of gravel road to Kinloch Hourn, was rowed two miles to Skiary where he treated his patient, and then set off on the long return journey.

It was only in dire emergency that anyone went to hospital in those days, for the attitude persisted that "if you went to hospital, you went to die". Later that decade all those who could afford it contributed one or two shillings per year to the Loch Hourn, Glenelg and Arnisdale Nursing Association which employed a roving nurse, based in Arnisdale. "Ach, it never worked. By the time you had rowed to Arnisdale to fetch her, likely as not she had been called to Glenelg" said Roddy.

In addition to the permanent residents of the district, such as the MacRaes at the farm and the permanent staff on the estates, many extra folk were employed in the main stalking and fishing season. So the summer and autumn saw a big influx of extra stalkers and staff to run the various estate lodges such as Kinloch Hourn, Glen Quoich and the Locheil Lodge which was at the west end of Loch Quoich. For a long time when Glen Quoich Estate was owned by the Ellice family, Glen Quoich Lodge along with the associated fishing and shooting rights, had been leased at intervals to such as the Williams family. Charles Williams was a Cornish tin magnate and MP who eventually purchased the estate in 1945. Lord Burton of Dochfour also leased the Glen Quoich Lodge and adjacent estate for a considerable period in the early part of the century. A long term tenant of Lochiel Lodge and the adjacent sporting estate was Lord Belper. These estates provided regular employment for many local people, many of the Arnisdale folk being employed on a seasonal basis, the women folk working in the lodges and the men on the estates.

Many of the MacRae family also obtained gainful employment on the estates both seasonally and on a regular basis, the girls working in domestic service in the lodges during the season and also being engaged by the lease holders, such as Lord Belper, to staff their country houses in the south at the end of the stalking season.

Another group of seasonal workers who descended on the area each year in the days before the last war were the stonebreakers. The MacRae family had the contract for maintaining the 7 mile stretch of gravel road between Kinloch Hourn and Loch Quoich Bridge, their employers being the County Council.

They would dig sand and gravel out of adjacent quarries and transport rocks for breaking to the roadside. The stonebreakers would arrive in the late Spring and using large hammers at first and then smaller hammers, knappers, they would reduce the rocks to metal. A bing of metal made the foundation of the road, and the breakers were paid by the cubic yard. Some cheated and placed turf or rocks under the bings, but they seldom dared show face another year! Peter commented "Peter Campbell from Ayrshire, he was the best of them. He usually had to be paid off when he began drinking at the end of the season. After months of work the stonebreakers suddenly seemed to develop itchy feet. They would ask for their pay and just disappear". However, payment was not made until the County Council surveyor appeared to inspect the standard of the work.

During the summer and the stalking season Glen Quoich Estate had many illustrious visitors. Among these was the famous artist, Landseer and 'Landseer's Rock', which lies adjacent to the road before

Kinloch Hourn comes into view commemorates his visit. He was reputed to have set up his easel at this point to paint the glorious scenery and possibly even the famous 'Monarch of the Glen' which is believed to be set in Glen Quoich.

An even more illustrious visitor in the stalking season was King Edward VII who would sail in the Royal Yacht up Loch Hourn, transfer to a small launch at the head of the loch and would be welcomed at the specially constructed stone jetty at Kinloch Hourn before proceeding to Glen Quoich Lodge. The stalkers and other estate workers, by skilled stalking and herding of the stags in that area would ensure that the King got every chance to shoot a 'royal' from a comfortable stance on the hill.

So the Kinloch Hourn folk were seldom idle or lonely and they always had plenty of talking points. The oral tradition was very strong and on the long winter evenings around the coal fire and the light of the paraffin lamps, there would be plenty of talk about current affairs, about family and friends, about history and stories of characters and happenings from the past.

One such local character whom Roddy and Peter never met but heard a lot about in the winter evening fireside stories was Murchadh nan gobhar (Murdo of the goats). Murdo (MacLennan) was a native of Glenelg who lived between about 1800 and 1881 and who obtained the sustenance of himself and his family from his goat herd. His humble house was in Glen Loyne between Cluanie and Tomdoun and he had the grazing for his goats free of rent on the Glen Quoich Deer Forest. His main sustenance was the milk from his goats which he mixed with a little barley meal when such was available. At one of his visits to sell some of his goats at the great Fort Augustus cattle sales at Tom na Feille (Market Hill) he was asked why he ate this rather unappetising looking gruel. "Well", replied Murdo, "if it was good enough for the Earl of Mar, it is good enough for me!" Then he would relate the story how such a gruel, gifted by an old herd-woman in the Lochaber hills, had saved the Earl's life when he was fleeing after a defeat of his forces in a battle at Inverlochy in the thirteenth century. Such oral tradition provided a powerful record of history in the stories handed down over the decades by the likes of Murchadh and the MacRae family. Another story told of old Murdo by the late Alexander Campbell of Fort Augustus was about the occasion at a Fort Augustus market when an inquisitive fellow asked the old man "How many goats have you got all told, Murdo?" "Ah", retorted Murdo, "if there were as many bugs in your shirt, you wouldn't get any sleep tonight"!

Another story handed down about old Murdo was on a rare occasion when he joined his friend Neil Campbell from Arnisdale, who was a fox hunter on the Glenelg Estate, on a New Year's day poaching expedition. They had a successful stalk, duly shot a good hind but then there was the challenge of getting the haunches home past the crowd gathered at the annual great shinty match in the district. Murdo, who had a heather-thatched roof on his humble dwelling was up to the challenge. He doffed his plaid, surrounded the haunch with moss, stuck long lengths of heather in at both ends of the haunch, wrapped things up in the plaid and slung the bundle on his back. As they made their way past the big crowd watching the shinty, an acquaintance shouted to Murdo and Neil "What on earth have you got there?" "Just a puckle thatch for the roof", said Murdo, never breaking his step!

Murdo was reputed to have a great way with his animals, he remained very fit and healthy all his days, he was a great local character and the stories of his exploits are well remembered by Roddy and Peter.

Other stories handed down to the MacRaes from the past relate to the overland trading which took place in the heyday of the Loch Hourn herring fishing. Peter remembers hearing from the old folk how men from as far away as Glenurquhart would come in October to Kinloch Hourn with their horses and carts loaded with potatoes and they would barter their potatoes for barrels of herring. Peter reckoned that the journey from Glenurquhart up the Great Glen to Invergarry and thence via Tomdoun to Kinloch

Hourn would take all of three days and of course the same time to return. The author recalls hearing about this annual pilgrimage from Glenurquhart to Loch Hourn from Rory the Miller (Rory MacDonald) and his wife Mary who crofted at Mill of Tore in Glenurquhart. Rory could trace back his family at Mill of Tore for several hundred years. While Loch Hourn was certainly famous for its herring, Glenurquhart was equally well known for its fine potatoes so it was little wonder that this bartering trade was so common and was probably carried out for centuries.

Hugh Barron of Inverness relates that he was told by the late Donald MacMillan, Wester Balnagrantach in Glenurquhart that Donald and other Glen folk would take three days to travel to Kinloch Hourn and three days to return to the Glen. Donald also said that at night they slept 'fo na cuirn' (underneath the carts). Kiltarlity people also went to Loch Hourn for their winter supply of salt herring.

Regarding this traditional trading route from the Great Glen to Loch Hourn, it is of interest that when the author's grandfather and grandmother made their first visit to Arnisdale in the early 1920s to their newly married daughter, Lizzie and their new son-in-law Roddy Mor, they travelled via Invergarry and Kinloch Hourn and by boat down the loch to Arnisdale rather than take the now normal route via Glen Moriston, Glenshiel, over Mam Ratagan and via Glenelg.

At the outbreak of the 1939-1945 War, Roddy MacRae joined the Royal Artillery while Peter's work on the farm and the estate was classed as an essential service and he continued to run the farm along with his eldest brother, Ewan. They had a motor lorry by that time to relieve the work of the ponies, and the Ministry of Agriculture sent round a man with a tractor to increase the area under plough. A modest grant ("one pound, or maybe thirty shillings") was paid for each extra acre ploughed, and the farm made an extra three acres of crop though the new land taken in was of poor quality.

Apart from the ubiquitous rationing, the war touched the Kinloch Hourn area in two unexpected places. One dark night, a lone German plane dropped two bombs on Knoydart. It is thought that a keeper had been burning heather and the German air crew mistook the glow for the aluminium smelter at Fort William. The bombs landed about three miles from Inverie House - one very close to Lord Brocket's monument - but caused no serious damage. Peter heard the explosions, and the people living by Loch Quoich saw flashes.

The other incident occurred in 1943 when an ailing Boeing Fortress flew into the glen. Its American crew had lost their way on a flight from Newfoundland to Northern Ireland, and were almost out of fuel. The wing tips narrowly missed the ground as the pilot, finding himself in a cul-de-sac of mountains, wrenched the plane into a tight turn. Four men evacuated before the pilot realised they were now over water. He brought the plane down on the surface of Loch Quoich and it floated for long enough to allow the six remaining crew to escape. Only one life was lost, that of the fourth parachutist, who was drowned. Peter commented: "I saw the plane going down, but it passed out of sight beyond a hill. I knew it was going to crash into the loch. We drove to where the survivors were and helped them. They were a nice bunch. The parachutists all had survival kits with machetes, fishing tackle and things like that. They had wonderful flying jackets, too - I was given a present of one and it lasted for years".

The Ministry of Defence recovered the plane for diplomatic documents which were supposedly aboard. They cut up the wreckage and then removed it. Cases of cigarettes and chocolate were washed up on the loch shore, but it was no *Whisky Galore*, for the produce was all ruined.

While the activities of the estate and the farm, along with the needs of the home, took the MacRae boys in all directions - to Glen Quoich and Lochiel lodges, to Tomdoun and Invergarry, to Cluanie to the north, Glen Dessary to the south and Barrisdale to the west, one got the distinct impression that Arnisdale was their favourite destination. They went there for their fortnightly shopping, they traded sheep and cattle, they went down to play for Arnisdale in the great shinty matches with Glenelg and they never missed any of the unforgettable Arnisdale ceilidh-dances. They went to ceilidh, to dance and to provide the music - on the pipes, the melodeon and the fiddle. In addition to the MacRae boys, their great friend Donald ('Do') MacKillop from Glen Quoich (along with his fiddle), was always a regular at the Arnisdale dances. The MacKillops originally came from Arnisdale, having had a pub in Corran at one time. All these Arnisdale memories are recalled with great enthusiasm by Roddy and Peter, and in talking about these escapades, you can almost see them mentally casting aside octogenarian and nonagenarian attitudes and reliving in their minds the fun of their youth.

Peter recalled a livestock auction sale held at Glenelg Hotel in 1925. Roddy and 'Do' MacKillop took down from Kinloch Hourn, through the Arnisdale Glen, a Beef Shorthorn farrow cow, a black weaned bullock called Murdo, while 'Do' MacKillop had a stirk. The stirk made thirty shillings, Murdo made £11 and Roddy Mor from Arnisdale bought the farrow cow for £9. They then had to take the cow all the way back to Arnisdale. Roddy and 'Do' often thought afterwards that if they had done a private deal with Roddy Mor in Arnisdale on their way to Glenelg - this would have saved the cow and themselves a great deal of hassle. After getting back to Arnisdale with the cow, Roddy and Do walked up the shore path to Caolasmor and then got the boat home from there to Kinloch Hourn.

Roddy Mor was at the butchering in Arnisdale at that time and not only did he supply the Arnisdale folk with their meat but he went over to Glenelg once weekly with the horse and dog cart to sell his beef and mutton in Glenelg. Roddy Mor often purchased 2 to 4 year old wethers from the MacRaes and also from Jimmy Mackay at Li, to supply his butchering needs when he ran out of his own home grown Arnisdale Farm wethers for this purpose.

The shinty matches provided another excuse to go down to Arnisdale. Often there would be five or six from up the loch in the Arnisdale team - Peter, Fachie, Roddy and Ewen MacRae, Do MacKillop and sometimes Angus MacKintosh from Torr a' choit. They would also raise a team to play Invergarry on New Year's Day. They would make their own camans of ash and birch. The regulars mentioned above from the Arnisdale games would be in the team to play Invergarry. Then they would have Johnny Campbell from Runival, Tommy Taylor from Loch Hourn, Angus Mackintosh from Torr a' choit (who had played for Lovat), Alan Grant from Tomdoun Hotel, Neil Stewart from Inchlaggan, Archie MacLean from Ardachy and the Invergarry policeman, MacInnes, who came from Ballachulish. They would have their game against Invergarry - no quarter was asked or given - and afterwards the two teams would retire together for a ceilidh. There would be singing, dancing and they would have a fine tea before they would set off on the old lorry back to Kinloch Hourn in the early hours of the morning.

Among Peter's many great memories of the Arnisdale dances, he remembers in particular one dance during the war in 1944 when the Kinloch Hourn contingent was not expected to make it to Arnisdale for the dance. It was impossible to buy petrol at that time, except for really essential services - so going down the loch by boat was out of the question. In addition, there had been torrential rain for days and going down the Glen and getting across the raging torrent of the Arnisdale River in the Glen seemed an equally forlorn hope. However, Do MacKillop and Jimmy Mackay, along with Peter, were not going to give up easily. This was partly because they didn't want to miss such a great occasion, as all the Arnisdale dances were, but, in addition, the Kinloch Hourn contingent was a key part of the music making for the dance.

In addition to the three local worthies, two of the soldiers who were posted strategically to guard against enemy infiltration to the key Naval Base at Kyle, were also keen to sample the Arnisdale dances

- they had heard so much about them! There was one Sergeant (Shields) stationed at Tomdoun and a Private (Melville) at Kinloch Hourn. The two custodians decided to take a chance of being AWOL, so the party of five set off down the Glen. The Sergeant was not terribly fit for such a strenuous and potentially dangerous journey so he was put astride the pony - led by Jimmy Mackay. The rain was torrential and was not letting up, and when they got to the usual crossing of the Arnisdale River at Crionach, the situation was hopeless.

The river was a raging torrent - hurtling down the Glen. No human would ever survive any attempt to get across. The thought momentarily crossed the minds of the experienced trio that they would turn back and concede defeat. But they had never conceded defeat on such an important mission before and they were not going to start now.

They saw the only hope as making their way along the precipitous left bank of the Dubh Lochain but this would be an impossible route for the pony. So the pony was put into the old fank and secured as well as they could. The sergeant now had to prove his mettle on foot! Apart from his fitness (or lack of it in the conditions), one of the great worries of the Sergeant was that he would slip on the rocks and smash the half bottle of whisky (a prized possession at the time) in his hip pocket. Protecting the dry stockings, shoes, bagpipes and fiddle they carried in their haversacks as best they could, the formidable troop groped their way along the banks of the Dubh Lochain and eventually reached the path on the Kinloch Hourn side of the Zig-Zag descent to Arnisdale. As they reached the top, now the target was in sight and apart from negotiating the swollen burns as best they could, they were almost 'home' - but certainly not dry!

On reaching the promised land, 'Do' made a beeline for the MacLarens to get partially dried off and at least get into his dry socks and shoes. Jimmy, Peter, the Sergeant and Melville made for Jessie and Maggie Li's. They got a great welcome for they had made it against all the odds. The Sergeant's long johns were the most difficult to wring dry - or semi-dry!. Their trousers and shirts were soaking wet but, as Peter said, they were dry by the morning after all the dancing and the feasting in the school.

Whenever day broke on the Saturday morning, Peter and Do, after a great night but with their thoughts now on the pony, set off up the Glen. The pony was as tough as themselves. When they reached the fank it was awaiting them - so off they set up the path for Kinloch Hourn.

Jimmy and Melville stayed another day and night with Jimmy's relatives, Jessie and Maggie, and walked back up the Glen to Kinloch Hourn on the Sunday - by which time the storm had abated. What of the Sergeant? He waited until the Monday, the Arnisdale folk didn't chance setting him off up the Glen on his own. Somebody found some petrol, got the outboard motor going and gave the Sergeant a lift up the loch. As Peter accompanied the Sergeant to his deserted army post at Tomdoun, there was the thought that his superiors may have been trying to contact him - only to find that he had deserted his post. The enemy may have slipped through in the interim! Ten minutes after the Sergeant got back into his post on the Monday afternoon, the telephone rang. He answered it immediately and dealt competently with the queries of his superiors, reporting honestly that he had seen no suspicious people or movements around Tomdoun over the whole weekend period. It was the first call that had come through since the post was abandoned three long days and nights before. For the experience and enjoyment of a dance in Arnisdale, the Sergeant deserved his bit of luck!

While soldiers such as Private Melville and Sergeant Shields were doing their wartime duty in the Tomdoun and Kinloch Hourn areas, Roddy MacRae was serving his country in foreign fields.

Roddy was in the Royal Artillery during the War. All the practice he had at the deer stalking made him an excellent shot. During the North African Desert Campaign he was captured at Tobruk in 1942. As prisoners of war, he and his fellows were shipped from Benghazi to Salerno in the south of Italy to a prison camp there. Later they were transferred to a German Prison Camp. Towards the end of the War, as the Russians advanced from the East, the Germans released them with a rucksack and blanket as their sole possessions. They were on the move westwards for a month before they met up with the Americans. During this time, as they moved, speaking German, they would sometimes get bread and biscuits from the ordinary German folk and, on their way, they would take their share of potatoes from the fields to supplement their diet. They slept under the open sky at night. It was usually much warmer and drier than Roddy had been used to previously when tramping through the frequent torrential downpours on the Glen Quoich and Kinloch Hourn hills! Roddy and his mates were generally in good spirits and were always optimistic that they would reach the promised land. Roddy eventually reached home in May 1945, and it was not long before a big 'Welcome Home' was being planned for him in Arnisdale. When the big day arrived later in the summer, Daniel MacDonald from Arnisdale took the Kinloch Hourn boys down to Arnisdale in the estate boat - Roddy, Peter and Fachie MacRae and Do MacKillop. At the Dance and Welcome in the School, Roddy Mor was the Chairman and Do, Peter, Fachie, the MacLarens and Donald Fletcher supplied the music. It was a great night. Roddy was so pleased to meet up with his many old friends again and they, of course, with him. Old Kelly was there and Duncan MacTavish - great friends with whom he had worked on Glen Quoich Estate at the stalking and general estate work before the war.

The dancing went on until daybreak on the Saturday. Then Daniel MacDonald ran them up the loch to Kinloch Hourn in the boat. Maggie Li, Ann MacRae and a few others went up the loch with them for the jaunt. As the Arnisdale Estate launch made its way up the loch, Do and Peter were playing the pipes and all the favourite Gaelic and English songs were being sung in between. There was heaps of food left over from the feast at the Welcome and Dance, so venison sandwiches and home-made dumpling kept them all going as they made their way up the loch past Barrisdale, Caolasmor, Runival, Skiary and Torr a' choit on their way to Kinloch Hourn. It had been a great night for Roddy and it was fine to be home and to meet all his great old and young friends again.

Peter has not seen too many changes in the landowners in the area over his lifetime. At the end of last century, the Ellice family for a long time owned the Glengarry and Glen Quoich Estates. Edward Ellice had made his fortune in the Hudson Bay Company in Northern Canada and built a luxurious house at Invergarry (now the Glengarry Castle Hotel). He in turn was succeeded by his son, Major Edward Ellice, who lost his three sons in the First World War. After this triple family tragedy the estate was divided and leased out. Lord Burton took over the lease of the Glen Quoich Estate which used to yield a bag of 30 stags in an average season. After Lord Burton's era, a Cornish tin magnate, Charles Williams leased the estate and he eventually purchased the estate in 1945. Glen Quoich and Barrisdale Estates are currently owned by the Gordon family.

Kinloch Hourn Estate has been owned by the same family - the Birkbecks of banking fame, since the 1870s. The estate lodge is situated near the head of the loch in a magnificent stand of eucalyptus trees introduced early this century by Robert Birkbeck, a very enthusiastic gardener and botanist. Peter remembers going to tea parties given by him in the 1920s. He also recalls that Robert labelled every tree and shrub in the spring and removed the labels in the winter. Roddy remembers the Birkbecks as kindly folk. Just before Christmas, a big box of tea would be delivered to the Lodge along with paper bags. Mrs Urquhart, the housekeeper, would fill the bags and Donald MacRae the gardener would take them down to Arnisdale on the boat. There he would be met by Duncan MacTavish and together they would deliver a bag of tea to each household. This went on from the end of the first war to the beginning of the second, when rationing of tea and other foods came in.

Lord Burton and his family were also kind. Among other gifts, the old folk used to get woollen semmits each Christmas. One of Lord Burton's staff down in England by the name of Grant used to organise these gifts but he was drowned and after this the gifts to the folk stopped. It was later discovered that Mr Grant's replacement was embezzling the money which had been set aside to buy these Christmas gifts for the Loch Hourn folk.

In terms of the use of the hill land, the emphasis on both the Glen Quoich and Kinloch Hourn Estates was on red deer rather than sheep. In the middle of last century, however, both estates carried very large sheep stocks, some of breeding ewes but a large proportion was made up of wethers (castrated males) which were often kept up to 4 years of age before they were fat enough to be marketed for meat, with surplus fat being used for the manufacture of candles. The wethers, of course, provided a good fleece each year for the wool trade. These were tough hills, especially with the cold and very high rainfall in winter and, while breeding ewes would struggle, the wether stock had a much greater change of surviving the rigours of winter, subsisting on what they could glean from the withered hill pastures supplemented by drawing on their fat stores which had been deposited in the summer period of plentiful and fresh hill forage. One of the last shepherds on the Kinloch Hourn Estate was the grandfather of the late Angus Macdonald who for many years farmed at Balvraid in Glen Beag, Glenelg. Angus' daughter, Catriona, is still resident in the area. In the era of the large sheep stocks, there was considerable investment in hill fencing round the borders of each estate to prevent sheep straying on to neighbouring property and to facilitate the gatherings for operations such as lamb marking, shearing and dipping.

While the memories of Roddy and Peter of the lifetime they spent at Kinloch Hourn are of a very happy and fulfilling life, despite (or perhaps because of) the prevailing tough conditions, both feel a great sense of sadness at the destruction of the properties and policies of both the Glen Quoich and Lochiel lodges, the remains now submerged some 100 feet below the waters of Loch Quoich since the construction of the Hydro Electric dam in the 1950s. As they traverse the old route and they come on the roadside rhododendrons below which Glen Quoich Lodge once stood in all its glory, they experience a natural nostalgia because of their memories of a once vibrant estate and of all the folk who made it such. They feel a sense of disappointment too at how the natural grandeur of the hills and moors have been tarnished by the giant pylons transporting electricity to the Island of Skye.

However, as they relive their memories around the fireside and comfort of their retirement home, there is little doubt that uppermost in their thoughts and conversation will be the satisfaction and fun of overcoming challenges, in the company of great friends, in an extremely interesting environment.

**Top**. Map. Kinloch Hourn with routes to the neighbours on the east and the west.

**Middle Left.** Kinloch Hourn or Loch Hournhead from the east with the road on the left passing the Glen Quoich Estate Home Farm steading and proceeding to the landing place in Loch Beag. Thereafter the track proceeds to Skiary, Runival, Barrisdale and across Knoydart to Inverie. The road to the right goes to the Kinloch Hourn Lodge and thereafter the track continues up the hill and then to Arnisdale and other locations. **Right.** John and Isabella MacRae of Kinloch Hourn with their mother Janet MacRae (early 1900s).

**Bottom Left**. John MacRae (left) with his wife Jessie (nee Gillies) who were tenants of the Home Farm (early 1900s). Donald MacRae of Barrisdale is on the right. **Right.** The MacRae family and friends in the Home Farm steading at the base of the steps leading to the loft which doubled up as the school and the 'church' where regular Sunday services were held. Back (L to R.) Jessie MacRae, Mary Ann MacKenzie, Peggy and Ewen MacRae. Front. (L to R.) Angus, Dolly, Roddy and Peter MacRae, Johnny Cameron (Skiary), the boys Fachie MacRae and Donald (Do) MacKillop, John MacRae with his wife Jessie (nee Gillies) in front of him.

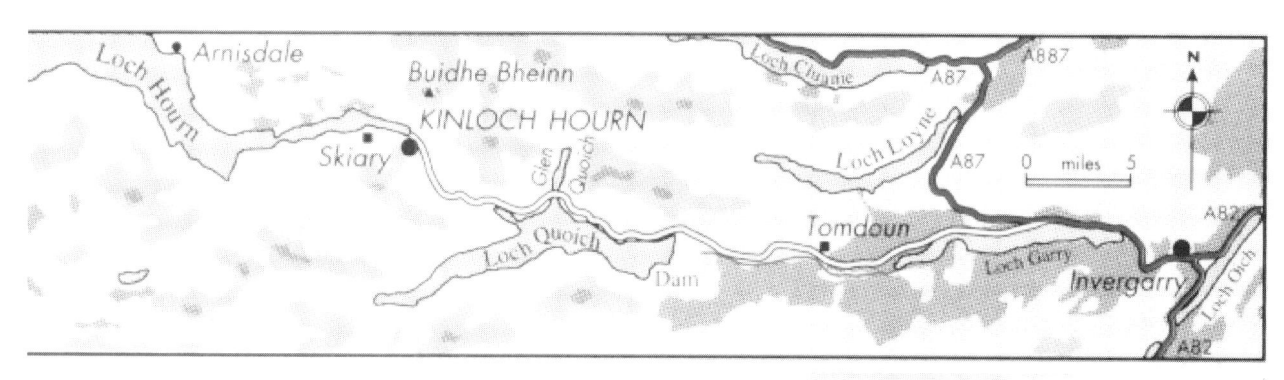

**Top Left.** Isabella MacRae (centre) leaving Kinloch Hourn for the sail down Loch Hourn and on to Glenelg for her marriage to Donald MacPherson of Moyle, Glenelg (early 1900s). **Centre.** The marriage of Isabella MacRae and Donald MacPherson in Glenelg (early 1900s). **Right**. Mrs Jessie MacRae (nee Gillies) and Mrs Isabella MacPherson (nee MacRae) with Mrs Janet MacRae and the latter's new grandchildren Roddy MacRae and Duncan MacPherson at Kinloch Hourn (early 1900s).

**Middle Left.** Donnie, Roddy, Isabella and Janet (Nettie) MacPherson, the children of Donald and Isabella MacPherson (about 1920). **Right**. The loft at the Kinloch Hourn steading which doubled up as both the 'Side School' and for church services.

**Bottom Left**. The MacRae family, their father and other Kinloch Hourn residents bid farewell to their friends about to set off down from the Kinloch Hourn landing place to their homes at Skiary, Runival, Caolasmor and Arnisdale after a mid-day Gaelic church service (early 1920s). L to R. Mary Ann MacKenzie, Jessie, Peggy and Dolly MacRae, Ewen MacMillan, (Runival), Fachie MacRae, John MacRae (father), Roddy, Ewen and Peter MacRae, Donald (Do) MacKillop, Sandy MacRae (Keeper at Caolasmor), Chrissie MacMillan, (Runival), Flora Kennedy (side school teacher at Kinloch Hourn who married Hughie MacMillan), Hughie MacMillan, Duncan MacRae, Caolasmor (Sandy's father), Daniel MacDonald, Church of Scotland missionary from Corran, Arnisdale.
**Right**. Peter and Fachie MacRae, the youngest members of the MacRae family. In the early 1920s the Kinloch Hourn side school was closed and thereafter the children had to attend Tomdoun school which was over 20 miles away.

**Top Left**. Kinloch Hourn viewed from the west in the 1890s (George Washington Wilson). **Right**. The estate was purchased by Robert Birkbeck in 1890. Robert was a keen botanist, erected fences to exclude the deer and sheep and began a comprehensive tree and shrub planting programme.

**Middle Left.** The fruits of labours over more than a century by the Birkbeck family and their employees. The thriving woodlands on the right surround Kinloch Hourn Lodge at the present day. (Photograph by Aileen Cameron). Some of the employees at Kinloch Hourn Estate over the century. **Right.** Stalker Peter Angus Gillies.

**Bottom Left.** Mary Urquhart and Lena Stoddart (housekeepers) and Donald MacRae (gardener). Donald was related to the MacRaes at Caolasmor. **Centre**. Peter MacRae (left) and Donald MacKillop who helped with the stalking and were the main musicians at the Arnisdale ceilidh dances. With Peter and Donald is Mrs Mary Urquhart who was housekeeper at Kinloch Hourn Lodge for over fifty years. **Right.** Aileen and Donald Cameron who are the current residents of Stalker's Cottage next to the Lodge. Donald has been the stalker on the estate for several years now. Like his predecessors, he is an able musician on fiddle and accordion.

**Top**. The magnificent Glen Quoich Lodge which was built by Mr Edward Ellice (right) who made his fortune when working for the Hudson's Bay Company in Northern Canada. The Lodge and policies are now under water following the erection of the Glen Quoich Dam in 1955 and the raising of the level of Loch Quoich in one of a series of hydro-electricity schemes completed around that time.

**Middle Left**. King Edward VII (seated in front) as a guest at Armadale House in Skye. He proceeded in his yacht from Skye up Loch Hourn to Glen Quoich Lodge as a guest of Lord Burton who was the shooting tenant of Glen Quoich Estate at the time. The Landing Place at Kinloch Hourn was erected to help the King get ashore without risking wet feet. **Right**. The hill paths were improved for the King's shooting forays and a shooting stance was prepared complete with a stone picnic table. Charles MacKay (left) (youngest son of Tony Mackay of Mialairidh Forest fame in the 1930s) rests with his friend Brian Gardiner on the shooting stance on Gleouraich above Loch Quoich in 1990. The small army of ghillies and stalkers drove the stags in to within shooting distance in the Coire Fraoch below to make sure King Edward had a successful day.

**Bottom**. The large squad of stalkers and ghillies on the Glen Quoich Estate around 1910. **Back row** (L to R.) Neil MacCuaig, Corran; ???; Alick (Sandy) MacPherson, Skiary. Went to Glenkinglas; ???; Sandy Stewart. (Father is No. 4 in middle row); Footman in Lodge; Roddy McPherson, Moyle, Glenelg, (best shot in Lovat Scouts in 1914-1918); John Alick MacLean, Cosaig, Glenelg; Hugh MacRae, Glenelg (Ghillie); Sandy Foster, Corran; ???Foster; ???MacPherson, (died young. Widow worked at Achnacarry in dairy). **Middle row.** Roddie Matheson ('Roddie Shieldaig'. After married was at Camuslinnie); Sandy Foster (Was in Lochan. Stalker in east end of Glen Quoich (Glen Kingie)); John Kennedy (was in AlltBeithe in Glen Quoich - came from Guisachan, Strathglass); Jimmy Stewart (father of No. 5 back row); Johnnie Henderson, Kinloch Quoich (married to Peggy Ann's sister). **Front row**. Neil Stewart, Inchlaggan at Tomdoun. (brother of Jimmy Stewart – No. 4 middle row); Donald MacRae (brother of John MacRae, Kinloch Hourn); Robert Henderson, Stalker (brother of Johnnie, No. 5 middle row); James Henderson, Head Stalker (son Robert, No. 3 front row succeeded him); ??? MacKintosh (belonged to Grantown on Spey).

**Top Left**.  While King Edward and his friends had their pleasure, the work had to proceed on the Kinloch Hourn Estate Home Farm.  Clipping in progress with young Peter MacRae (right) and sister Dolly (left).
**Right**.  After the Kinloch Hourn side school closed in the early 1920s, Peter, Fachie and the other Kinloch Hourn children had to attend Tomdoun school which was on the other side of the road from the Tomdoun Hotel.

**Middle Left.**  Peter MacRae proceeded from Tomdoun School to secondary education in Fort William.  In this photograph taken in 1933 Peter is in the back row, third from the right and on his left is Donald Stewart from Glen Dessary on the Lichiel Estates which marched with Glen Quoich.  Joey Henderson, niece of Peggy Ann at the Arnisdale Post Office is in Row 3 from the back at the extreme left.
**Right**.  When Peter MacRae left school he returned to Kinloch Hourn to help his father and brother Ewen on the farm.  Here they are loading the wool clip on the little farm lorry.

**Bottom Left.**  Fachie MacRae (left) working on the outboard engine on the boat.  The main shopping was done at Peggy Ann's store in Arnisdale.  Two or three boats would set off together on the ebb tide and return on the flow.  The shopping for essential supplies was done fortnightly.  **Middle**.  The main supplier of clothing was Peter MacLennan from Fort William.  He would come round to show materials, take measurements and return in a few months with the tailored suits.  Here Peter MacLennan with his van calls at Maggie MacTavish's house in Arnisdale.   **Right**.  Glen Quoich estate workers in the Home Farm steading.  L to R.  Neil MacPherson (Lea), Mr Grant (gardener at Glen Quoich Lodge) and John Kelly (Arnisdale).

A fairly regular caller at Kinloch Hourn during and after World War 1 was Ronald Burn whose hill walking exploits are recorded by Elizabeth Allan in her book 'Burn on the Hill'. Ronald spent the night with the MacRaes as he tramped his well trodden route each year.
**Top Left.** He was a regular caller at the home of Angus Stewart and his wife Maggie (nee MacPherson) in Strathan on Cameron of Lochiel's estate near Loch Arkaig which marched with Glen Quoich Estate. L to R. Donald, Isobel, Maisie and Janet with Uncle Donald Stewart. **Right**. Angus Stewart with daughter Maisie.
**Middle Left.** Duncan MacPherson, Moyle, Glenelg with his daughter Maggie – later Mrs Angus Stewart. **Right.** The Scott family at Alltbeithe in Glen Affric. Ronald was usually offered free hospitality at his regular ports of call but his hosts always found him interesting and he brought news with him about the wellbeing of friends in remote hill country places.
**Bottom Left**. Ronald Burn greatly enjoyed the stories about characters such as Murchadh nan Godhar (Murdo of the goats) who lived from around 1800 to 1881 and who ran his goat herd in Glen Loyne between Cluanie and Tomdoun. **Right**. The stories about the exploits of another local character – Niall Brocair (Neil the fox-hunter) from Arnsdale were also enjoyed by Ronald Burn.

**Top Left**. Peter MacRae (left) with some of his brothers and sisters and other friends at Kinloch Hourn in the late 1920s. L to R. Peter and Ewen MacRae, Katie Murchison (Arnisdale), the Church of Scotland Missionary in Arnisdale, Peggy and Roddy MacRae. The MacRae family had been tenants of Glen Quoich Estate Home Farm for in excess of 100 years. **Right**,. The MacRaes had traded their livestock both eastwards to Fort Augustus and Inverness and westwards to Arnisdale and Glenelg. They had supplied fat wedders over many years in the 1920 to 1946 period to the Arnisdale butchery business of Roddy Mor and Lizzie MacLeod (second and fourth from left) seen here with L to R. Lizzie's parents, Ali Ban MacDonald and his wife Jessie from GlenUrquhart, Calum Finlayson, and Jessie 'Rarsaidh' (far right). Ali Ban and Jessie had travelled from GlenUrquhart to Arnisdale by car via the old trade route up the Great Glen to Invergarry and thence to Kinloch Hourn and boat to Arnisdale. This was the route taken over the centuries by GlenUrquhart folk carting potatoes and oatmeal to Kinloch Hourn to be bartered for salt herring which filled the cart for the return journey. The two way journey by horse and cart in the old days took 6 days to complete.

**Middle Left.** Henry Anthony Birkbeck, who inherited Kinloch Hourn Estate from his Uncle Bob, having a row in Loch Beag at the head of Loch Hourn. The Birkbecks have cared for the estate and its folk for well over 100 years. **Middle**. Henry Anthony Birkbeck's grandson Henry Birkbeck having a spy with current Kinloch Hourn Estate stalker, Donald Angus Cameron to try to spot the location of the stags – despite the mist on the tops. **Right**. Another successful stalk for Donald Angus Cameron and ghillie Stephen Russell.

**Bottom Left.** Donald Angus Cameron and his wife Aileen find time to relax on a fine day outside Stalker's Cottage overlooking the mouth of the Kinloch Hourn River and Loch Beag. **Right**. Peter MacRae (second from right) although now resident in Invergarry, never misses the opportunity to visit his old haunts. These are in good hands with Margaret Potter (left) and her husband Joe spending each summer in the old Farmhouse. In addition, Mieke (second left) and Ruurd Groot (right) from the Netherlands visit for three month each summer to savour the natural riches of the area and to record and conserve much of the beauty, the culture, language, the flora and the spirit for the benefit of others.

# Chapter 25

**Runival and Skiary - the MacMillans and their visitors.**

The family which was associated most with Runival, while it was still in its heyday in the early part of the twentieth century, was the MacMillans. In the early 1900s, Ewen MacMillan was the stalker/ gamekeeper/watcher/shepherd at Runival employed by the Barrisdale Estate. He had married Anne MacRae, a sister of John MacRae (father of Peter and Roddy from Kinlochourn) (see Chapter 24). Another sister of John and Anne had married Robert MacRaild from Arisaig - more of that family later! Ewen MacMillan and Anne had eight of a family - Ewen (Hughie), Murdo, Sarah, Chrissie (Jessie), Helen, Bella, Annie and Johnnie (resident in Letterfearn during his retirement). The second oldest son, Murdo, later took over from his first cousin, Willie MacRaild, as a shepherd/stalker on the Arisaig Estate, some time after Willie and his family had emigrated to Australia.

As well as acting as gamekeeper for the Estate, Ewen MacMillan and his family worked the croft at Runival, keeping 2 to 3 cows and followers, 30 to 40 ewes on the hill and, of course, kept hens like everybody else. They made hay for the wintering of the cattle, grew potatoes and some oats, with the grain being used for the hens and the straw for the cattle. They also fished on Loch Hourn to catch fish in season when required, salted a barrel of herring for winter requirements and got their share of venison in season from the estate. For requirements such as salt, sugar, flour and oatmeal they did their 'shopping' at the MacLean's store in Arnisdale (see Chapter 30).

The late Jock Hunter of Corpach, who was at one time factor at Barrisdale, told the story about how the young MacMillan boys were trained for the stalking by their elders from their earliest years. A Blackface ewe would be spotted grazing up the hill slopes and each child in turn would be challenged to stalk the ewe, and as they got close enough, they then had to try to catch the unsuspecting ewe by the leg. Now, Blackface ewes are always wary and, without winter feeding and close regular handling, they are as wild and cunning as the deer themselves. While it is very unlikely that any of the children succeeded in stalking a wild and wary Blackface hill ewe so successfully as to catch its leg, the objective set for the child was very clear and, as they moved stealthily towards the ewe against the wind and for periods crawling along wet areas slithering on their belly quietly and gradually, they would undoubtedly have learned many tricks of the trade necessary for the successful stalking of the deer.

Young Murdo's first job was with the Belpers on the Glen Quoich Estate as a shepherd/stalker but he was called to service in the armed forces at the start of the 1914-18 War. After surviving that dreadful war, Murdo resumed his job at Glen Quoich, but in 1920 he got a shepherding job in Glenlyon. The job of shepherd/stalker on the Arisaig Estate of Sir Arthur William Nicolson came up in 1925, Murdo applied for it with 117 others and he was the successful one. He married Isabella (Bella) MacDonald from Invergarry just before starting his new job at Arnipol on the east end of the Arisaig estate. Their son Ewen (E.D.) was born at Arnipol and when Ewen left school, he also got a job on the estate under Murdo his father, who had in the interim been promoted to Estate Manager. While Murdo proved to be very able and successful in this position, he was very much a man of the hills and glens and the open fresh air, and was much less at home doing office work and attending sales to sell lambs and cast ewes and to purchase new tups. The late Jock Hunter told another story about accompanying Murdo and E.D. to the Perth Sales to buy a required number of Blackface tups for the hill flock. Setting off from Arisaig for Perth early on a crisp October morning, the car had hardly got going when old Murdo wound down all the windows to provide 'plenty of hoxygen' as he said himself. While Murdo appreciated the great crispness and sharpness of the Autumn air as they sped along, Jock and E.D. were considerably less enthusiastic about the chill, almost gale force, winds as they ripped through the car on the long journey. Since the tup sales lasted 2 to 3 days, accommodation was reserved in Perth's Salutation

Hotel for the Arisaig trio, with Murdo and his son E.D sharing a room. As soon as they were shown into the room, predictably, Murdo's first reaction was to open all the windows as wide as possible to ensure that there would be 'plenty of hoxygen' coming in and - not only for a few minutes after entry - but all through the night the cold air continued to blast into the room. This suited old Murdo just fine and, as was his wont, he was up as fresh as a daisy, 'before the lark' in the morning and he was soon down in the hotel foyer looking very fresh and smart, looking (in vain) for signs of staff being 'on the go' preparing the morning tea and breakfast.

By the time E.D. and Jock arrived on the scene, Murdo was none too pleased, to say the least, at not even a cup of tea being on offer at such a late hour as 7 a.m. 'I don't know what's keeping them with the tea and the breakfast' he would mutter to his 2 friends. The day was good, work had to be done and Murdo wanted to get on with things. Meanwhile E.D. confided to Jock that the bedroom was like an ice box during the night with the windows wide open and the cold damp night air belching in. Jock immediately thought of a plan to save his friend E.D. from hypothermia. Jock would offer his room to old Murdo, while he (Jock) and E.D. would go into the other room - with windows fully closed. Murdo had no objections to this suggestion and graciously accepted Jock's offer. He could have the windows as wide open as he wanted with no ill effect on others.

However, in the interim, a former acquaintance of Jock Hunter had spotted him from a distance in the Salutation Hotel and decided to play a trick on Jock to 'get his own back' on Jock who, in his rugby playing days and afterwards as an NFU member and official, had played many practical jokes on his acquaintances. This fellow, knowing how much Jock liked to sleep very peacefully and not to rise too early in the morning, found out from the Hotel Receptionist the room number Jock had reserved for himself at the Hotel and, on Jock's behalf, ordered tea to be brought to him at the unearthly hour of 4 a.m.

When the next morning came, the night porter made his way at 4 a.m. with the tea to Jock's (now old Murdo's) room and knocked at the door. Murdo was already awake and was just thinking of getting up. 'Come in' he said immediately and he was absolutely delighted to welcome the arrival of the early morning cup of tea.

When Jock and E.D. finally rose and made their way downstairs for their breakfast, the first person to catch their eye was old Murdo - strutting around like a peacock. 'How are you today, Murdo?' Jock enquired. 'Just fine, just fine' said Murdo, 'this is the best hotel I was ever in - you get a cup of tea at 4 o'clock in the morning!' So sometimes even the best laid practical jokes miss their intended target! However, old Murdo was delighted, and Jock, not for the first time, had escaped the wily scheming of his old acquaintance, and ended up having a very peaceful and undisturbed long night's sleep - just what he wanted!

The Runival story will now be switched to Murdo's Aunt Flora (Mrs Robert MacRaild) and his cousins (Willie, Jessie and Hugh) in Arisaig. Robert MacRaild died from tuberculosis when the family were young. Within the next few years, three of Robert and Flora's six children also died from TB and, soon after the end of the Great War, another became very ill from the same problem. The prospects for survival were not good and the local GP advised them to try to get away from the rain and damp winter cold of Arisaig and seek a warmer climate to help the ailing youngster. Mrs MacRaild took this advice and made arrangements to emigrate to Australia (the Melbourne district in Victoria). Meanwhile Willie MacRaild, as a nineteen year old, was just finishing the season as a stalker on the Arisaig Estate and decided to visit his relatives on Loch Hourn. It was mid-October and the days were shortening. He set off on the first train from Arisaig to Mallaig and then got the boat to cross Loch Nevis to Inverie in Knoydart. He left Inverie at 3 p.m. on the hill path across the Knoydart Peninsula on the long route to Barrisdale. It was getting dark as he descended the precipitous Mam Barrisdale, he had a quick cup of tea in the old church in Barrisdale on the shore of Loch Hourn and then set off eastwards on the lochside path to Runival. It was pitch dark when he reached his Aunt Anne's (Mrs MacMillan) house at Runival and, as was his wont, he would play a trick when the door would open in response to his loud knocking. As Aunt Anne came to the door in the blackness of the night, the figure at the door put on the best Englified accent he could muster: 'Excuse me, how can I get to the MacRae's house at Kinlochourn?' The reply came from Aunt Anne 'Oh, you can't get down there tonight, it is pitch dark, the path is too dangerous and there is no boat here to take you down!' 'But I have to get there tonight', retorted the caller who proceeded - 'Have you got a torch that I could borrow?' 'No, I'm sorry, I have no torch', said Aunt Anne, 'would you like to come in for a cup of tea?' 'Thank you very much, I will be very glad to accept your hospitality', the visitor responded. As Willie made his way in and reached the candlelight, Aunt Anne was able to study the shape and then the features of the 'stranger'. There was almost instant recognition - 'Oh, you rascal!', she exclaimed. After they exchanged welcomes, the tea and a good meal were soon on the table. There was no need for any torch or boat to assist the passage to Kinlochourn that night. All the news was exchanged and the ceilidh proceeded into the night before they all retired for their night's rest.

The year was 1922 but the story was not related (to the author) by Willie until 62 years later in Melbourne. This was to be Willie's last visit to his Aunt Anne's at Runival and to his Uncle John MacRae's at Kinlochourn the next day. Soon afterwards, Willie, his mother, his brother Hugh and only surviving sister, Jessie, were on the long voyage by ship to Australia and Willie, much to his regret, was never able to return to the scenes of his youth and to visit again his many relations on Loch Hourn and elsewhere.

On the author's first visit to Australia in 1984, after lecturing commitments in Western Australia (Perth), New South Wales and Victoria, the MacRaild home in Melbourne was visited one Saturday afternoon. Willie, now 84 years of age, was not at home. His wife, Olive, indicated that he was 'at the races' but would be home soon. Was he a betting man? Had he become an Australian? were questions which occurred in the mind. Then the old gentleman appeared. He was a car park attendant at the Race Course which earned him some Australian dollars to supplement his old age pension. He was a fresh, spry octogenarian, with fore and aft, just as in his young days as a ghillie in Arisaig and treading the Inverie path to Barrisdale and then up Loch Hourn to visit his relatives. He spoke as if he had never left Arisaig, he was the Chieftain of the Melbourne Gaelic Society and Chairman of Melbourne and District Pipe Band. He indicated that Donald MacPherson of Glenelg (who married his Aunt Isabella - nee MacRae) had taught him to play the pipes and how to make reeds for the pipes. He had never managed to revisit the old country - he could not afford it. A big part of his heart and soul was still in Arisaig and Knoydart and Loch Hourn. He was very pleased to see his visitor, although undoubtedly he would have preferred if his caller could have conversed with him in the Gaelic. However, he was delighted to get news of his cousins the MacRaes (at Kinlochourn) and the MacPhersons (Nettie, Donnie, Isabella and Roddy) and about Arnisdale and Loch Hourn. He related the simple story told above, and appeared to relive the whole experience of his journey that October day in 1922 from Arisaig to Mallaig to Inverie to Barrisdale to Runival and then to Kinlochourn as if it had happened in the previous week. There was a great twinkle in his eye as he made his way in that Runival door 62 long years before, from the darkness of the Knoydart night, and anticipated once again the recognition and the wonderful welcome of his Aunt Anne to her very basic but lovely home and family.

As for the author, it was one of these periods of just a few hours in a lifetime that seemed very special to both participants of the ceilidh as they shared something very special to their hearts and souls.

Another visitor from home whom Willie had on more than one occasion, and greatly enjoyed, was

Fachie MacBeath, now farming in Glenbeag, Glenelg. Fachie was sailing the seven seas in these years with the Merchant Navy.

Another story which Willie MacRaild told the author during those very special few hours together may have less relevance to Loch Hourn but is none the less interesting in these days when most phenomena are explicable and fewer mysteries remain.

Willie related that his Uncle Sandy MacRaild was employed at Fort Augustus as the resident diver with the Caledonian Canal Company, where it was his responsibility to make sure that the lock gates on the canal were kept in good working order and the whole sequence of lock gates between Loch Ness and Loch Oich worked efficiently to aid the passage of the boats to and fro. His residence was at Apple Cottage, Fort Augustus. Sandy had been on duty when a terrible tragedy occurred on Loch Ness. This is how Willie MacRaild related the story to the author.

A gentleman, who was one of the local gentry, was out on Loch Ness in his rowing boat, accompanied by two ghillies. He was fishing and also had his gun with him, just in case any wild ducks came within shooting distance. The loch was flat calm but, suddenly, as the gentleman fished, there was a great upheaval, the boat rocked and then capsized and all three were drowned. People had witnessed the tragedy from the shore but no boat could be launched in time to attempt a rescue. As the local diver, Sandy MacRaild was called upon immediately to try to find the bodies. Sandy responded to the call and that same day he submerged into the dark waters, located the boat, recovered the bodies of the two ghillies and even found the fishing rod and the shot gun. However, the body of the gentleman could not be found before darkness. The search therefore was abandoned for the night and was resumed at first light on the following day. Sandy submerged at the spot located on the previous day and was not long down when tapping on the air tubes indicated that Sandy may have found the body. Soon afterwards Sandy surfaced. The inevitable first question to Sandy was: "Did you find the gentleman"? "No", said Sandy, "and I will not find him now". "Why not?" the question came back. "Because I am not going down there again", retorted Sandy.

Willie MacRaild said that his Uncle Sandy never dived again. He retired there and then as the resident diver on the Fort Augustus locks. A few days after the tragedy, Sandy made his way to visit Willie MacRaild's family in Arisaig. He was given the usual fine welcome which most visitors, friends and relatives enjoyed in those days. For Sandy, however, this was not a fleeting visit. Sandy, who was a bachelor, told Willie's mother, brother and sister about the tragedy, said that he had decided to retire and asked if he could spend his retirement with them, sharing their home. This was a normal request from a relative at that time and, as Willie said, 'Uncle Sandy would have been welcome to share our home but we had to tell him that we were due to leave for Australia in just a few weeks'.

Sandy had told the MacRaild family that he refused to go down at the site of the tragedy on Loch Ness despite the pleading of the family involved and the estate workers 'even supposing they would give me half of Scotland'. Willie said that it was a characteristic of the MacRailds in general that they would not make any statement about a subject unless they were sure what they were talking about. He felt that if his Uncle Sandy made any attempt to explain his reaction to whatever he may have experienced on that last dive close to Fort Augustus - if he gave anything away at all - he might be subject to ridicule.

Suffice it to say, in conclusion, that Sandy MacRaild had an experience or a sensation on that last dive which he did not want to have again. Did he spot a strange object, did he experience an inexplicable turbulence of water round about him? Only Sandy could have attempted to answer such questions and he was not prepared to do so because, like the rest of the MacRailds "they would not make any statement about a subject unless they were sure what they were talking about."

Another octogenarian who takes great pleasure in recalling visits in his youth to Runival and the upper reaches of Loch Hourn is Roddy MacPherson from Glenelg. Roddy remembers great holidays visiting his relatives at Runival, Lochournhead (Kinlochourn) and Glen Quoich when he was in his early teens (early 1930s). He would get a lift from Glenelg to Arnisdale on Johnny Sinclair's pony and trap as Johnnie took over the mails. He would stay overnight with old family friend Donald Sheorais (Campbell) - and neighbour Mary Anne Lex (MacCuaig) would make sure that the two of them were well fed. The next morning they would be up early to get Donald's boat ready for the row up the loch. Roddy would row the six miles up the loch because Donald would have to row back on his own. Sometimes they would make for Lochournhead and land at the jetty that was specially built for King Edward VII to land for his regular stalking and shooting visits to the Glen Quoich Deer Forest. At other times the boat would make for Runival.

At Runival, Roddy would get a big welcome from his Aunt Anne and Uncle Hugh (MacMillan) and he would spend a few weeks of his holiday there. Hugh was employed on the Barrisdale Estate and he and Anne ran the croft so that the family of ten were as self-sufficient as possible. Roddy remembers that apart from the little croft house they had the little byre and barn situated in the field quite close to the house. They had two cows and always seemed to have plenty of milk and made butter, crowdie and cheese. They also had hens so eggs were a common part of the diet and, of course, were used in the baking of scones and pancakes. They grew their own potatoes and made hay for the winter feeding of the cows.

Although the nearest house at Skiary was about two miles away via the shoreline and mountain path, Roddy never felt lonely at Runival. There was great company there, lots of fun and plenty to do. There was good cod fishing close to the island (Eilean Mhosgeir) just out from the croft. Roddy and his brother Donnie would go out in the boat with Uncle Hugh, collect mussels off the rocks, anchor the boat above the known best fishing areas and use the mussels as bait for the cod. Roddy remembers that their Uncle Hugh sometimes did not appear very keen to take them out fishing especially at high tide, making the excuse that the Big Beast (Hugh had a Gaelic name for it) might be up the loch. On further enquiry with their Aunt Anne about the 'Beast', she confirmed that her husband had seen the 'Beast' up the loch on several occasions when there was a high tide. Hugh's explanation was that it was only at high tide the beast could negotiate the 'narrows' at Caolasmor.

On Roddy and brother Donnie's holidays at Runival they would have frequent visits from cousin Ewen MacRae from Lochournhead as he delivered the mails three times per week.

Roddy's MacMillan cousins who had moved away from home as they completed their schooling would also sometimes pay visits to their parents and the old home at Runival. For example, Murdo MacMillan and his wife Bella would come from their new home in Arisaig on the motorbike to Kinlochourn and come down the loch to Runival on cousin Ewen MacRae's boat.

Up the loch between Runival and Kinlochourn was the holding of Skiary run by Johnnie Cameron and his mother Mary. They had quite a lot of sheep and some cattle while Johnnie was also employed as a stalker in the shooting season to supplement their income. In the old days, at the height of the herring fishing on Loch Hourn, their house at Skiary had served as a pub to meet the liquid and social needs of the great number of fishermen who were around at the time. Mrs Cameron was reputed to have the gift of healing and is reputed to have helped one of the noted Glenelg athletes prepare for an important Highland Gathering. Norman Cameron, who was a good all-round athlete (running, jumping and heavy events), had sprained his ankle very badly in practising his vaulting in the 'Nursery Park' just opposite the school in Glenelg. He wrote to Mary Cameron at Skiary telling her of his problem and seeking her help. Annie responded by sending him a piece of string with instructions to tie it very tightly round the severely swollen ankle. Norman carried out her instructions to the letter and the morning after the string had been applied, all swelling had disappeared from the ankle. Norman was now fully convinced about the gifts of his clanswoman and was fully fit for his competitions a few days later!

(Hugh Barron of Inverness quotes as follows from A Carmichael's 'Carmina Gadelica' Volume IV, pages 230-231: "Mary MacMillan was renowned in the countryside for removing the mote from a person's eye" and "A descendant of hers, Mary Cameron of Skiary had 'Eolas an sguchaidh' - the charm for sprain").

On another occasion in the early 1920s, Katie MacLean the young Arnisdale teacher got an eye infection which proved to be very painful and persistent. Due to there being no resident District Nurse at the time and because of the difficulty of getting over to Glenelg to the Doctor there, Mrs Cameron was consulted about Katie's problem. Katie was unable to get up the loch to Skiary and Mrs Cameron was too old to make the journey to Arnisdale. When the problem was explained to Mrs Cameron, the latter 'analysed' the situation but concluded that there was nothing she could do to help because 'what was in her eye was visible and could be removed'. When this message was relayed to Katie, her eye was examined closely. Under Katie's eyelid they detected a rose thorn which was the focus of the infection. This was removed and Katie was soon on the mend. Some time earlier Katie had been pruning the roses in the School Garden so a stray thorn must have pierced Katie's eyelid without her being aware of it. So much for Skiary.

There was a house at Torr a' choit on the opposite side of the loch from Skiary and in Roddy MacPherson's early visits to Runival it was occupied by Angus Mackintosh, a native of Kiltarlity who worked as a stalker and watcher for the Kinlochourn Estate. He was a fine shinty player and, along with the MacRaes (Roddy, Ewen, Peter and Fachie) from Kinloch Hourn, was a key player (wearing a pair of his wife's bloomers as shorts) in the Arnisdale team that had battles with caman and ball against Glenelg on regular occasions.

Roddy MacPherson, of course, was on the opposite side to his cousins and recalls the great games, usually played on the Crudh Ard field in Arnisdale around New Year's day. Roddy also remembers a very wild rocky bay between Kinlochourn and Skiary called the Carn Mor and Angus Mackintosh remarking on one occasion that the place was so wild that he would not be a bit surprised to find tigers in it!

After spending a week or two at Runival, Roddy would then go up on the boat with his cousin Ewen to spend a further holiday with his Uncle John, Aunt Jessie and cousins Fachie, Peter, Ewen, Roddy and their sisters, Helen, Jessie, Peggy and Dolly, at Kinlochourn. There was always plenty of fun there getting involved in the estate work, helping on the farm with haymaking, shearing and milking the cows, playing shinty and fishing.

A grocery van used to come to Kinlochourn from Invergarry, as did the mails. The nearest Post Office was at Glen Quoich - about seven miles from Kinlochourn. Roddy would often
go down the loch with cousin Ewen in the boat to deliver mails and other requirements to his relatives and friends at Runival, Skiary and Torr a' choit. This annual holiday kept Roddy in touch with his many relatives up the loch. He savoured this holiday greatly at the time - and still does when he talks about it.
So Runival, Skiary and Torr a' choit were vibrant places in the heyday of the large active estates and of

the herring fishing. When the herring fishing declined, there was no further need for the watchers to keep an eye on fishermen who fancied a bit of venison from time to time. Eventually also the estates got rid of their sheep stock and employed considerably fewer people over time for the stalking. So these little clachans at the upper reaches of Loch Hourn are no longer occupied permanently and some are falling into disrepair.

However, these homes are revitalised when those octogenarians who are still with us - such as Peter MacRae, Roddy MacPherson and Maggie Lea get together for a ceilidh. Their memories of the hard working, happy folk who toiled, had fun and reared their large families there are still vibrant.

**Top Left**. The fiord of Upper Loch Hourn with the wooded policies around the lodge and the home farm at Loch Hournhead to the left. This photograph taken from Carn nan Caorach at the east end of Druim Fada looks down on Lochan Charn nan Caorach and directly across the loch to Skiary (Sgiath Airidh) with the burn splitting the old croft lands in two. The track from Kinloch Hourn to Skiary hugs the very rocky coast line.
**Right**. The view from behind the croftlands at Skiary looking westwards down Loch Hourn. Round the first promontory on the left (Runival Point) is the Runival homestead.

**Middle Left.** The landing place on the east side of the Skiary croftlands. Peter MacRae of Kinloch Hourn remembers up to five occupied dwellings and families at Skiary. The last family which was permanently resident at Skiary was that of Johnny Cameron (died 1941) and his mother, Mary. Mary had the gift of healing and helped to alleviate the ailments of a few local folk. **Right**. Only one home remains at Skiary now – that of John and Christina Everitt who run a very special little hotel there in the summer months. In this group are (L to R.)
Christina and John Everitt, Tom and Alan MacDiarmid, Billy MacKenzie and Marion MacDonald.

**Bottom Left**. Three honoured guests from Wester Loch Hourn enjoy their morning coffee at Skiary. L to R. Billy MacKenzie from Coran and Alan and Tom MacDiarmid from Lower Sandaig. **Right**. The remains of the old pub at Skiary which was a very busy place during the great days of the herring fishing. L to R. Christina Everett, Marion MacDonald (nee Birkbeck), Oona Arnott and John Everett.

**Top Left**. Approaching Runival from the east. Part of the name is believed to be derived from the Norse word Fjall which means a hill, being equivalent to the Gaelic Beinn (Rixson, 1999). **Right**. A view from the lower slopes of the hill above Runival with the house on the left beside the burn, the remains of the old byre and barn in the centre foreground and the island Eilean Mhosgeir not far offshore. The croft lands, where potatoes, oats and vegetables were grown and hay made, were enclosed by a deer fence. This area was also protected from the deluges of rain coming down the mountain side by a deep perimeter drain which channelled the water into the sea on each side of the croft land.

**Middle Left**. The view westwards down Loch Hourn with the projecting spit of land on the right being that at Caolasmor with the Corr Eileanan beyond. **Right**. Alan and Tom MacDiarmid examine a gravestone just above the high water mark on the Runival croftlands. There are many such gravestones around the coast of Loch Hourn. Torr a Choit can be seen directly across the loch.

**Bottom Left**. A view from Runival of Torr a Choit with its single house and outbuildings. This little home and croft was once occupied by Angus MacKintosh and his family. Angus was a stalker/watcher on the Kinloch Hourn estate in the 1930s era. A native of Kiltarlity, near Inverness, he was a fine shinty player who was a team mate of the four MacRae brothers and played for Arnisdale and Glen Quoich in the great battles against Glenelg and Invergarry respectively. **Right**. Ewen MacMillan who was a stalker/watcher/gamekeeper/ shepherd on the Barrisdale Estate and operated the croft at Runival, in his spare time, along with his wife Ann and their family in the 1900-1930 era.

**Left**.  Ewen MacMillan, his wife Anne and daughter Annie at Runival and right – Ewen and Anne with Farquhar MacRae, Peter MacRae, Kinloch Hourn, Farquhar's married daughter Jean Mitchell and Anne MacMillan.  Farquhar was a brother of Ewen's wife Anne (early 1930s).  Other siblings in this family included John MacRae of Kinloch Hourn, Isabella, wife of Donald MacPherson of Glenelg and Flora, wife of Robert MacRaild of Arisaig.

**Middle Left**.  A stalking party at Barrisdale in the early 1900s.  L to R. Angus Stewart (Arnisdale), Ewen MacMillan, (Runival), Major Smith-Ryland, Willie Stoddart, Willie Douglas and Kenny Fletcher.    **Right**.  Stalking at Barrisdale often involved journeys up Loch Hourn in the Barrisdale boat to offload the folk engaged in the stalk and later in the day collecting them - hopefully along with the stag which they had shot.  L to R. Ewen MacMillan on the extreme left with Jimmag Stoddart from Crowlick second from the left.    The Barrisdale boat man was Angan MacTavish (around 1910).

**Bottom Left**.  Hughie MacMillan, the eldest of the Runival family of Ewen and Anne with his wife Flora (nee Kennedy).  Flora was once the teacher in the Runival side school.  Hughie and Flora spent their retirement in Dochgarnoch near Inverness.   **Right**.  Murdo MacMillan, the second oldest of the Runival family of Ewen and Anne with his wife Isabella who was born and brought up in Invergarry.  Soon after the end of the first World War Murdo was appointed as shepherd/stalker on Arisaig estate.  He later became the manager.

**Top Left**. Ewen (ED) MacMillan, Arisaig who worked under his father, Murdo, on the Arisaig Estate and later succeeded him as manager. **Middle**. The late Jock Hunter, Factor of Lochiel Estates, of Arisaig Estate and many other properties in the West Highlands, proudly shows the Champion Blackface tup belonging to Lochiel Estates at the 1976 Lochaber Show. Jock had a way of playing practical jokes on folk but was difficult to catch out himself. **Right**. Margaret MacMillan at her graduation from Aberdeen University with her father (ED) and mother Elsbeth. Loch Hourn 'natives' were discovered in diverse places in the compilation of this book. The author discovered Maggie sitting in front of him in a University class.

**Middle Left.** The wedding of Maggie MacMillan to Euan Hart with Mrs Elsbeth MacMillan and Ewen. **Right**. Euan and Maggie Hart with their children – E D. and Katie.

**Bottom Left**. A family get-together for the MacMillans of Borrodale, Arisaig at the 70th Birthday Party of Ewen. Back Row. (L to R.) Emma Morrison, Derek Morrison, Murdo MacMillan, Angus Ross, Euan Hart, with little Ewen. Middle Row. Margaret Hart (nee MacMillan), Alasdair Ross, Arlene Morrison (nee MacMillan), Calum Morrison, Jane Ross (nee MacMillan), Ailsa Ross, Ewen MacMillan, Kirsty Morrison. Front Row. Katie Hart, Elsbeth MacMillan and Ewen MacMillan. **Right**. Roddy MacPherson from Glenelg (Left Back Row) who worked on Arisaig Estate with his cousin ED for a period in his young days and who also enjoyed visiting his cousins, aunts and uncles at Kinloch Hourn and Runival in his teenage years. With Roddy is brother Donnie, sisters Nettie (left), Isabella (right) and in the centre their mother Isabella (nee MacRae)

**Top Left**. Robert MacRaild and his wife Flora (nee MacRae) and two of their six children. Robert was a stalker on the Arisaig Estate and died while a comparatively young man in 1903. Flora was one of the Kinloch Hourn MacRaes whose sister Anne was married to Ewen MacMillan at Runival. **Right**. Flora MacRaild with her three surviving children, L to R. Hugh, Willie and Jessie. Following the death of her husband and three of their young children, the family Doctor made a strong recommendation that they emigrate to a warmer and drier climate. This advice was taken and they duly emigrated to Australia.

**Middle Left** Before emigrating around 1922, Willie as a young man of about 20 years set off to pay a last visit to his relatives on Loch Hourn (that of his Aunt Anne at Runival and his Uncle John at Kinloch Hourn. His day's journey involved the train from Arisaig to Mallaig, the boat to Inverie and walking the remaining twelve miles on the hill track from Inverie to Runival via Barrisdale. **Right**. Willie stopped for a quick cup of tea in the little church beside the track in Barrisdale, seen here with the tidal Eilean Choinnich and its ancient island graveyard to the right and the Corr Eileanan in the middle..

**Bottom Left**. After emigrating in 1922, Willie MacRaild was never able to return to these haunts which he knew and loved so well He greatly enjoyed visitors from the old homeland such as Fachie MacBeath now farming in Glen Beag, Glenelg. The photograph is of Fachie (left) taken at Ballarat, Victoria in 1954 during one of his visits to Willie MacRaild. With Fachie is Glenshiel exile, James MacRae – a fine piper and a good friend of Willie MacRaild. **Right**. Donald MacPherson of Glenelg, piping tutor to young Willie MacRaild. Willie after 62 years in Australia was still holding fast to the culture and ways of his youth in Arisaig and Loch Hourn. He was a leading light in both the Gaelic and Piping Societies in Melbourne. He had great respect for the piping tutor of his teenage years who also taught him to make reeds for his pipes.

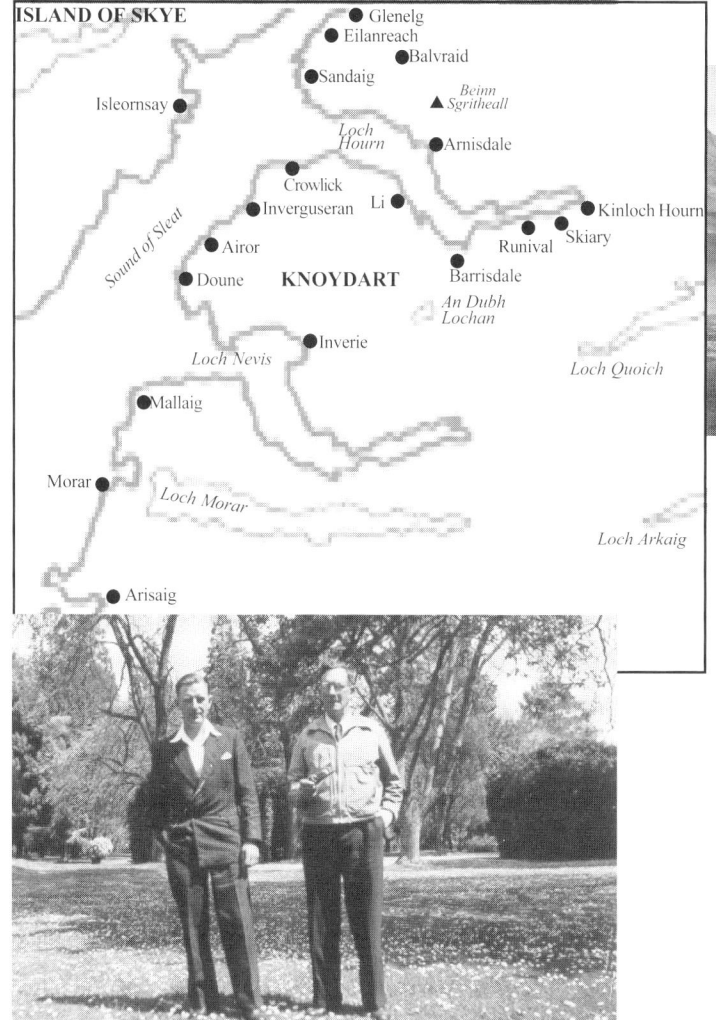

# Chapter 26

**Barrisdale and its people.**

Barrisdale was always considered to be part of the Arnisdale 'community'. It always lay there below the majestic Ladhar Bheinn in sight of both Camusban and Corran, it got its mails through Arnisdale and many Arnisdale folk over the generations got work there as ghillies, stalkers, shepherds, estate handymen, boatmen and as cooks, table maids and housemaids in the shooting lodge.

Charlie MacTavish from Camusban, whose grandparents Archie MacTavish and Mary MacPherson were married in the little church there, whose father Angan worked there as the boatman, whose mother worked in the lodge, who worked there himself as a ghillie/stalker/handyman and who met his wife Mary Kate there, recalls several owners of the Barrisdale Estate.

His first memories are of Major Smith-Ryland, followed by Major Bell-Irvine. Then there was Charles Williams and Mrs Williams, who also owned Glen Quoich Estate. Charles Williams bequeathed both estates to a nephew and then Barrisdale was purchased back by Mrs Williams. It is now owned by Major Sandy Gordon who also has Glen Quoich Estate.

Willie Stoddart was the gamekeeper/stalker at Barrisdale for many years before he and his wife retired to Arnisdale with daughters Gwennie and Lina in the late 1940s. It was soon after Willie Stoddart retired that Charlie MacTavish, on demob from the Army, was appointed to the Barrisdale Estate staff. The head keeper at that time was John MacRae from Avernish in Nostie, near Balmacara. John and his wife had three children and they had their own little school in Barrisdale. Their teacher was Mary Kate Campbell of that famous family of Gaelic singers from Greepe, near Dunvegan in Skye. Mary Kate and Charlie were later to become man and wife before Charlie got the job of head keeper at Strathvaich in Wester Ross, and they left Barrisdale in 1955. For a time before his marriage, Charlie shared the bothy with his young friend from Arnisdale, Iain MacKenzie, who helped on all the estate jobs. Charlie remembers the Barrisdale deer forest as being very well managed, the stocking rate matching very well the deer carrying capacity of the hill. At that time there was no sheep stock on Barrisdale but later Mrs Williams stocked the hill with sheep and she appointed as her shepherd that tough old character from Arnisdale, George MacDougall who was around seventy years of age at the time. That was young for George who was still gathering sheep from the high tops around Loch Hourn when he approached 90 years of age. George's uncle, Donald Campbell (Donald Sheorais) from Arnisdale, had himself spent much of his working life on the Barrisdale Estate, not only working in the deer forest and with the sheep but in building projects on the estate.

The origin of the little church at Barrisdale is not very clear. This church is close to the shore and the island graveyard of Eilean Choinnich (Kenneth's Island). It appears to be interdenominational, may be associated with the graveyard and was possibly built to serve the spiritual needs of the hordes of fishermen working on Loch Hourn and its shores over the many generations when Loch Hourn was famous for the bounty and quality of its herring. Willie MacKenzie, from Corran, who remembers the church when the roof was still intact and very tidy inside, with its pulpit and seating, believes that the church and the graveyard are still under the jurisdiction of the Bishop of Argyll which would indicate that the origins are more of the Catholic persuasion. Peter MacRae, from Kinlochourn, supports the view that the graveyard at least has been mainly associated in the past with those of the Catholic faith. He and his brother Roddy remember attending a funeral there in the 1920s along with other members of their family from up the loch. The funeral was that of Jean (Sineag) MacGillivray from distant Druim Chosaidh near Loch Quoich on the Barrisdale Estate. The remains were transported down the hill track and road to Kinlochourn and then by boat down Loch Hourn to Eilean Choinnich. The officiating priest walked from Inverie up the hill track to the top of Mam Barrisdale and then down the Loch Hourn side to the graveyard. Peter remembers that as they came down Loch Hourn in the boat wearing their blue serge suits, made to measure for them by MacLennan the Tailor (The 'Robber') in Fort William, by the time they reached Barrisdale, their suits were almost white as a result of the salt spray generated in their sail down the loch in stormy conditions.

Willie MacKenzie thinks that the Barrisdale Church may have doubled up as a school for some time. Willie MacRaild, a first cousin of Peter MacRae of Kinlochourn and whose Aunt Anne (nee MacRae) was Mrs Ewen MacMillan of Runival at the time, remembered making a brief call at the Barrisdale Church around 1920 on his journey on foot from Inverie to Runival and receiving a cup of tea there. The author met Willie when he was in his 84th year (in 1984) in Melbourne, Australia. Willie had emigrated there with his family around 1922 when he was a young man of about 20 years. Before he left for Australia he had been working as a ghillie on the Arisaig Estate and at the end of the season he decided to pay a visit to his relatives in Runival and Kinlochourn to say his farewells. He left Arisaig early one October morning, got the train to Mallaig and then the boat from Mallaig to Inverie. He reached Inverie at 3 o'clock in the afternoon and then set off on the path to Barrisdale. He thoroughly enjoyed and appreciated his cup of tea in the Barrisdale church before setting off as quickly as he could to try to reach Runival before it got too dark. Who provided hospitality for Willie in the Barrisdale Church? Was it a caretaker, or missionary or teacher? Willie did not say, the question was not put to him at the time and he is no longer with us to answer it now. But he got his tea, enjoyed it and it set him on his way with renewed vigour towards Runival - and he remembered that Barrisdale cup of tea after sixty-two long years in Australia.

Another who trod these wonderfully constructed hill paths from Kinlochourn to Barrisdale and then up Mam Barrisdale over to Inverie was Mary Ann MacCuaig, that wonderful lady from Camusban who was always so full of fun and grace. The author, along with brother-in-law Doey MacLean and youngsters Ali and Ewen (MacLean) and Martin (English), made the pilgrimage around 1980 along the path from Arnisdale up the Glen to Crionach and then on to Kinlochourn, past Skiary and Runival to Barrisdale, then up Mam Barrisdale, down the other side of the Knoydart ridge to Inverie and from there across Knoydart again, past the ruined house at Fholaich, up Mam Li and then down by the side of Alt Li to Li. There, by prior arrangement, the party were met by young Billy MacKenzie who sailed them back to Arnisdale.

On visiting Mary Anne after arriving back in Arnisdale, she was very interested in the author's account of the trek as it recalled many happy memories of her own. She recalled that when she was working as a youngster in Barrisdale Lodge, when the evening's work in the kitchen had been completed on a Friday evening and the 'gentry' had been fed and fully catered for, she and her pals would set off up the Mam Barrisdale path and down the other side to Inverie for the Dance. After a great night and early morning of dancing, the Barrisdale crowd would set off back up the path in the darkness; as dawn was breaking they would be making their way back down Mam Barrisdale and they would arrive at the Lodge in plenty of time to start their day's (Saturday) work by 7 a.m. Mary Anne recalled these days with great joy.

Like most other places, Barrisdale has its fables and its mysteries, such as the Big Beast of Barrisdale and Druim Fada which, according to Peter MacRae, was supposed to resemble a huge bird with three legs. In more recent times, weird, inexplicable noises resembling human laughing and screams have been heard both within the buildings and out in the open beside the river and up the Barrisdale Glen. These have been reported by Iain MacKenzie and members of the Swanney family who came from the Orkney Islands. Some associate these strange experiences with a fatality which occurred when a large squad of workers were resident in Barrisdale in very cramped conditions while working on the building and maintenance of all those fine mountain and lochside tracks.

The Swanney family of Tom, Ivy, daughter Sheena and son Brian are remembered in Barrisdale with much respect and affection. Tom, Ivy and Brian are not with us any more, Ivy having died at a comparatively young age, while Tom and Brian were drowned tragically in 1992 while fishing off Skye when their boat sank almost without warning. They liked and respected Barrisdale, worked for the estate and at their fishing and lived very much in harmony with the Barrisdale and Loch Hourn environments. They were greatly missed in the area. Sheena trained as a nurse and is now married and resident near Aberdeen.

The Swanneys first went to Barrisdale in 1967 when Sheena was five years of age and Brian one year younger. Dad Tom, who belonged to the Orkney Mainland, got the job as estate handyman with Mrs Williams while Mum Ivy (a native of the Island of Hoy) was engaged to look after the Lodge - to attend to internal maintenance and cleanliness and also to do some of the cooking at times.

The Swanneys settled down well at Barrisdale and soon became vital cogs in the local and Loch Hourn communities. As estate handyman, Tom was responsible for the boats and the vehicles used to bring home the shot deer from the hill. He also attended to the maintenance of the lodge and the other buildings as well as fencing and the upkeep of roads, mountain tracks and bridges. He found time to do some fishing on Loch Hourn for lobsters and white fish on his own account, while Ivy collected whelks along the shore line - she was unsurpassed at this job - very few could fill the bags as quickly as Ivy. The whelks were sometimes collected by a van from Arnisdale while at other times Tom took them with his fish and lobster catches for sale in Mallaig.

Sheena remembers Mrs Williams and Miss Buchanan (Mrs Williams' secretary) with respect and affection. The estate had a stock of about 200 Blackface ewes on the hill and a fold of about 20 breeding Highland cattle as well as the two hill ponies, Toscar and Lucy. Old George MacDougall from Arnisdale was the shepherd/cattleman and his home through the week was the Barrisdale bothy. At the weekend George would go back to Arnisdale to relax with his daughter Chrissie and son-in-law Lachie Fletcher and his grandchildren Margaret and Peter at Glenfield. Old George's strength would be fully restored over the weekend and Willie MacKenzie would sail him back to Barrisdale early on the Monday morning.

At the times of the Barrisdale sheep gathering, clipping, dipping and stalking, Tom Swanney would take the estate boat - the 'Eider Duck' down to Kinloch Hourn to collect folk such as Peter and Roddy MacRae, Lea MacNally and George Stoddart who would come down to Barrisdale to lend a hand. Sometimes Duncan MacHardy would also be brought in for a few weeks at a time to help with fencing and other estate jobs.

Mrs Williams sold the Barrisdale estate to Major Sandy Gordon in the early 1970s and after that Mrs Williams and Miss Buchanan would stay at their holiday home at Skiary during their visits to their old haunts. Their renovated house at Skiary had served as a pub at the time of the great herring fishing in Loch Hourn.

When Sheena Swanney first arrived in Barrisdale she was just ready to start school and so as to increase the number of pupils at the Barrisdale 'side school' from one to two, brother Brian was enrolled at his more tender four years of age. The school was the old Barrisdale bothy and Maureen Clark was their first teacher. The next teacher after Maureen Clark left Barrisdale was Mrs Katie MacInnes. Katie's husband Matthew worked on the estate and their two children, Penny and Marion, were babies at the time so they did not bolster the Barrisdale School roll. Mrs MacInnes was later succeeded as teacher by

Mrs Keith. Most of the teachers stayed in the 'White House' at Barrisdale. When the Swanneys first went to Barrisdale, Tom succeeded James Fraser as the estate handyman. Although James, his wife Margaret and their children, Sandy, James and Linda left Barrisdale soon after the Swanneys arrived, the two families became very friendly in that short time and this friendship was later to prove very valuable for the Swanney family.

Mrs Williams' successor as the proprietors of Barrisdale Estate were Major Sandy Gordon and Mrs Gordon whose main base was in Blair Atholl, Perthshire. Major Gordon would arrive at Barrisdale in his Tiger Moth and land in the field beside the shore. If the Swanney family did not anticipate his arrival, Major Gordon would circle above the Swanney household until he was heard and spotted. Then there would be a mad rush to get the cows and ponies out of the field so that the field was clear of 'obstacles' to make possible a safe landing for the Tiger Moth. Although the field was often very wet, Sheena remembers, the Tiger Moth always got down safely and managed to take off again without any trouble.

Among the others who worked at Barrisdale during the Swanney family era were Andy Rogerson who was the stalker for about four years and Victor Cerfice who came as ghillie during the stalking season for several years. Victor belongs to Ireland and is a fine artist - especially of the scenes so typical of Barrisdale and Knoydart with its intriguing mixture of sea and mountain, hill lochs, red deer, Highland cattle, blackface sheep, beautiful, still and sunny days on the Barrisdale sands or wild storms raging down Loch Hourn. In the last months of Ivy's terminal illness, Victor painted a special picture for Ivy which was dear to her heart. It featured the Highland cows paddling on the Barrisdale sands with a back drop of Eilean Choinnich and Fraoch Eilean and the varied face and autumn colours of Carn Mhàiri behind. This gift was treasured by Ivy and it now adorns the lounge of the home of Sheena, husband Gary and six year old Murray near Aberdeen.

The great wounds suffered by the family with the loss of Ivy at the age of forty one years and later by Sheena with the tragic loss of her Dad and Brian have been healed somewhat through the years and Sheena can now look back on what she describes as the idyllic childhood she and Brian had in Barrisdale.

While her Dad was always busy on the estate and at his fishing, her Mum was never idle, running the home, helping at the lodge and tending her very productive garden. The family had been given a share of the sheltered and fertile walled garden at the lodge by Mrs Gordon and Ivy was always busy harvesting the autumn fruits and making enough jam to keep them going until the next harvest time came round - and they certainly did not want for choice - with homemade strawberry, raspberry, blackcurrant, rhubarb, gooseberry, plum and bramble jam in the store. The garden produce also ensured that they were self-sufficient in tatties and a full range of vegetables throughout the year, some preserved in the freezer and others in the shed - well protected from the occasional winter frosts. On wet days when they were not at the fishing, Sheena's Dad and Brian were often to be found in the big shearing shed servicing the engines and other equipment.

So the Swanneys were fairly self sufficient in terms of many of their food requirements especially in terms of fish and garden produce. They also had the use of Carol - one of the Barrisdale Estate cows. Sheena remembers that Carol gave a good yield of milk and mother Ivy made her weekly supplies of fresh butter and crowdie while Carol was in milk. However, all essential provisions could not be grown or harvested in Barrisdale so there was twice weekly shopping in Glenelg. This took the form of sending a list of required provisions via 'Willie the Post' to the Glenelg shop. Alistair Davidson and Cathie MacDonald would make up the order, Willie would collect the boxes for his return trip to Arnisdale and deliver them to Barrisdale on his twice weekly sail across Loch Hourn with the mails.

When the Swanneys first went to Barrisdale they were dependent on the diesel generator for their electricity, but later 'Jock' and 'Charlie' from Major Gordon's Blair Atholl estate, along with Tom and two students, built a dam on one of the hill burns and installed a turbine to generate their power. While the copious rainfall at Barrisdale almost always ensured enough hydro power, on odd occasions after a dry spell they would temporarily run out of electricity. For fuel - 'to keep the home fires burning' - the Swanneys used
coal, peat and wood. The wood was harvested from the trees which blew down from time to time while the peat was cut from the flats across on the Lea side of the Barrisdale river. Sheena remembers their good neighbours - the Rohde family at Lea, the Carrs at Crowlick and, of course, their friends in the little Barrisdale community.

Sheena and Brian had their schooling at Barrisdale until she was nine years old and after that they attended Glenelg School until the age of twelve, after which she and Brian went to Millburn Academy in Inverness. Mrs Cameron was their teacher in Glenelg.

The children had a long day when they started at Glenelg School. They would leave Barrisdale in the estate boat (the Eider Duck) with their father soon after 7 am and about one hour later at Arnisdale they would catch Calum Ian Lamont's landrover - the school bus - for the journey to Glenelg along with the contingent of MacKenzie children - Jon, Shona, David and Alan. When they made the return journey at night, Sheena and Brian had an arrangement to stay with either Maggie MacTavish (Bean Angan) or Mary MacIntyre in Camusban until their father finished work and could cross Loch Hourn to collect them. The time Sheena and Brian spent with Maggie and Mary was treasured as they were always treated to tea, pancakes and other goodies while they awaited their Dad. On the return journey to Barrisdale which would take almost an hour, Sheena would always complete all her school homework in the little cabin of the boat and they would usually arrive home to see the last of the BBC 1 children's programmes on their black and white TV before 6 o'clock.

Often for long spells during winter, when twice daily crossings of Loch Hourn in darkness and stormy weather was difficult, Sheena and Brian often stayed during the week with Ian and Dorothy MacKenzie and their son Jon at the farm house in Arnisdale and they would go home to Barrisdale for the weekend if weather conditions were suitable for the crossing. On such occasions, Sheena's great friend and classmate, Shona MacKenzie from Corran, would often spend the weekend at Barrisdale with them. With no telephone line to Barrisdale, around this time a radio telephone link was set up so that friends could be alerted about Barrisdale emergencies such as family problems or climbing accidents on Ladhar Bheinn and the other Knoydart mountains. Dad Tom and 'Willie the Post' in Corran would have their daily chat on the 'walkie-talkie' to keep each other informed about relevant matters. After such 'business' matters were attended to, Sheena and her Corran friend Shona would take over the radio from their Dads and catch up with each other's news. Now - a full quarter century after their early schooldays together, Sheena and Shona still keep in touch with each other over the 'air waves' on a regular basis.

At the time mother Ivy fell ill, Sheena and Brian had just completed their secondary schooling in Inverness. When the extreme seriousness of Ivy's illness was established, Ivy faced up to it with great courage and grace. After she came out of hospital, Ivy stayed in Inverness at the home of former Barrisdale friend Margaret Fraser and was cared for by Margaret and Sheena. One thing Ivy was determined to do as the nature of her illness and her life expectancy was known, was to return to Barrisdale for a few days to savour the little Knoydart haven where the family had such happy times working and enjoying themselves together. However, with the extreme difficulty of obtaining regular and appropriate medical attention at Barrisdale, alternative provision had to be made. In these parts, friends were never slow in providing all possible comfort and help. Iain MacKenzie, partner Chris and his son Jon invited the Swanney family to share their home in Arnisdale at the Farm House. This offer was accepted graciously so that Ivy spent her last days in Arnisdale surrounded by her loving family and friends and with the ever caring support of Dr Carnachan from Glenelg, the District Nurses and many very kind neighbours.

All of the Swanney family found Barrisdale greatly to their liking. Tom enjoyed the variety of the work on land and sea. Ivy was often asked by the many visitors to Knoydart if she found it a lonely existence. Her reply was invariably that she was always too busy ever to feel lonely. The children, Sheena and Brian, found Barrisdale to be a veritable adventure playground. They would go rock climbing, explore the shore, swim in the 'byre pool' which was fairly close to their home and create their own games and challenges. When Sheena recalls her childhood with great enthusiasm she sums it all up as 'an upbringing of freedom and adventure'.

One of the things which made Sheena's childhood so interesting for her was their regular visitors who would come to climb Knoydarts's great mountains and explore the fascinating territory of the peninsula. She recalls the Earnshaw family from Yorkshire who visited year after year. Connie and Norman would go off on their daily climbing expeditions while the children Catriona and Alisdair preferred to stay behind and join in the adventures of Sheena and Brian. Another set of annual visitors were the twenty or so student members of Heriot Watt University in Edinburgh who made their yearly pilgrimage to Barrisdale at the New Year. Tom would go down in the boat to collect their baggage, food and liquid refreshments at Kinloch Hourn while the students would walk up the five miles of the shoreline path to Barrisdale. On arrival they would all pack into the bothy and the Hogmanay parties were unforgettable. Some would have good intentions of doing some climbing the next day but this often did not materialise for many of them because of the onset of strange illnesses, especially around the first of January.

As the years pass and the gradual healing process following the traumatic loss of her Mum, Dad and brother Brian continues, Sheena can now cast her mind back to the great family happiness of the Barrisdale years. These are her memories which become more treasured as time goes on. Vital links with these early years which continue are those with the MacKenzie families of Iain and Jon, Willie, Christine, Shona and her brothers. These links were always very special and became even more treasured by Sheena as time goes on.

Now, Barrisdale is not so remote as it once was. In these days of fast powerful sea craft, Barrisdale can be reached very quickly from many locations on the shores of Loch Hourn. Likewise, those resident at Barrisdale can reach what were previously distant locations very quickly. For example, if folk at Barrisdale feel like going out for lunch and they have a good boat and sufficient finance, they can set off to have their lunch in Isleornsay on the Sound of Sleat in Skye, reach there within half an hour, have a leisurely lunch and be back in Barrisdale in the early afternoon to work or engage in whatever locally available leisure activity they fancy. Things have moved a long way from the days of rowing the boat from Camusban in Arnisdale across the often stormy Loch Hourn to the Barrisdale Landing Place - a journey which could take as long as three hours. The helicopter too - and the Tiger Moth - have made Barrisdale much more accessible if you have one or can cadge a lift from a friend who has!

**Top Left**.  View from the west end of Druim Fada on the northern side of Loch Hourn into the plain of Barrisdale with the Barrisdale river making its tortuous way to the sea.  The mighty Luinne Bheinn dominates from behind.
**Right**.  The view from the top of Luinne Bheinn looking north to the Barrisdale valley below and across the loch to Druim Fada.  To the left Beinn Sgritheall is clear and to its right the tops of Beinn na h-eaglaise and Beinn nan caorach are evident behind the mass of Druim Fada just across the loch..

**Middle Left**.  Looking down on Barrisdale from the path up Mam Barrisdale – the bealach between Barrisdale and Inverie.  The Barrisdale lodge buildings can just be seen to the right of the trees in the bottom right hand corner.
**Right**.  Barrisdale Bay at low tide and a view westwards down Loch Hourn.

**Bottom Left**.  The remains of the Barrisdale Chapel close to Eilean Choinnich – the tidal island just showing to the right.  The Barrisdale landing place is on the right hand side of this island with its ancient graveyard.  The three islands – the Corr Eileanan guard the entrance to Upper Loch Hourn which stretches eastwards (to the right) to Kinloch Hourn.  **Right**.  Children of the late 1930s – Mary and Angus Murchison from Corran play on the Barrisdale sands in the shadow of Coire Dhorrcail.

**Row 1. Left**. Barrisdale Lodge around 1920.   **Right.**   Among the party preparing for a stalk at Barisdale in the 1920s are L to R. Jimmag Stoddart (second from right) and Ewen MacMillan, Runival (far right).
**Row 2. Left.**  Stalkers, ghillies, shepherds and Barrisdale lodge staff in the 1920s.  L to R. Willie Stoddart, Jimmy Mackay, Leonard Kirby (Estate chauffeur) and two of the ladies who worked in the Lodge. **Right.**   A Barrisdale Estate group about to board the estate boat to set out on another day at the stalking. Ewen MacMillan, Runival is on the extreme left with Jimmag Stoddart second from the left.   **Row 3. Left.**   This group of Barrisdale estate staff include L to R. Ewen MacMillan (Runival), Willie Stoddart, Willie Douglas, ???? and Jimmy Mackay.  Another successful stalk.   **Right.**  Approaching the end of a successful day on the hill.   Willie Stoddart (far right) helps to load the stag on to the hill pony.
**Row 4. Left**. The Barrisdale Lodge boat  (The Eos) in the 1930s under the control of Angan MacTavish and Roddy Mackay.  The estate chauffeur helped with engine maintenance.   **Right**.  The end of a rare day out from Barrisdale to do some shopping.  Having anchored the big boat, Angan rows his passengers ashore – Willie Stoddart, his wife Mary and daughter Gwennie.

**Top Left**.  Willie Stoddart after he retired to his cottage in Camusban, Arnisdale following a lifetime's work as a stalker on Barrisdale estate (late 1940s).  **Right**.  Mary Ann MacCuaig from Camusban worked in Barrisdale Lodge for several seasons in her youth.  She relates to the author stories about her time in Barrisdale, walking over Mam Barrisdale in the late evening after work to the dances in Inverie on a Friday night and returning again over the 7 miles of hill track to be ready for work at 7 on the Saturday morning.  She asserted that although it was hard work, they had great fun together and it was all the fun that she remembered ---not the hard work!

**Middle Left.**  Donald Sheorais Campbell from Camusban (seated) who had worked at the stalking, shepherding and in building projects at Barrisdale in his young days.  His nephew George MacDougall (right) after a career in the police force in Glasgow 'retired' to Arnisdale but was shepherding in Barrisdale while well past his three score years and ten.   **Centre.**  George MacDougall while in his seventies crossing Loch Hourn to Barrisdale to start another week's work at the shepherding.  **Right**.  Iain MacKenzie (right) as a young man worked as an assistant ghillie/stalker at Barisdale along with Charlie MacTavish in the 1950s.

**Bottom Left**.  Bob MacRae (left) of Avernish near Balmacara with Mrs Chrissie MacRae (nee Morrison from Harris) and their children, Anne, Duncan and Joey, with Mary Kate Campbell (right) from Greepe, Skye and Charlie MacTavish, Arnisdale (second right).  Bob MacRae was the Barrisdale head stalker for many years. Mary Kate was the side school teacher and Charlie was stalker/ghillie/shepherd.  Charlie and Mary Kate were later to become man and wife.  **Right**.  Willie MacKenzie – Willie the Post I and II delivered the mail from Arnisdale to Barrisdale three times per week for a total of some 70 years between the early 1920s and the early 1990s.

**Top Left**. The Swanney family of Tom, Ivy and the children, Sheena and Brian, in Barrisdale. Tom was the Estate Handyman in the 1960-70 era while Ivy worked in the Lodge. **Right**. On the big days of the sheep gathering, clipping, dipping and stalking, Sheena Swanney remembers that many of the folk in this picture came down the loch from Kinloch Hourn to help. L to R. Peter MacRae, Duncan MacPhail, Jock MacAskill, Roddy MacRae, Alick Boyd, Andy Rogerson, George Stoddart, Stephen Potter, Lea MacNally, Farquhar Boyd, Sandy Lean, John Morgan and Donald Cameron.

**Middle**. Sheena and Brian Swanney first attended side school in Barrisdale but thereafter travelled daily to and from Glenelg, first in their Dad's boat across Loch Hourn and then in the 'School Bus' of Calum Iain Lamont (left). On returning from Glenelg, Sheena and Brian were well looked after by Maggie MacTavish (centre) or Mary MacIntyre (right) until their father arrived in his boat.

**Bottom Left**. Tom Swanney along with Iain MacKenzie (seen here servicing the equipment) were Arnisdale's TV engineers, locating the best place for a mast and attending to regular maintenance work. **Right**. The Corran MacKenzies at a family wedding – great friends of the Swanney family while at Barrisdale and continuing special friends with Sheena, so sadly deprived of her Mum, Dad and brother Brian.

## Chapter 27.

**LEA and Maggie's memories**

'Maggie Lea' (Mrs Margaret MacDonald, Caol) spent her early years at Lea (or Li) across Loch Hourn in Knoydart before coming to Arnisdale School at the age of ten years. Here are her memories:

"Oh dear, where does one start?

It has to be Lea as my first memories are of Lea. I think the children of today, including my own ten grandchildren, would find it hard or impossible to live life as we lived it in my childhood years in the 1920s and 1930s. Life was hard but there was no hunger or lack of fuel for heating and cooking involved - but there were no luxuries - one worked to live and lived to work. Despite having the only home in our corner of Knoydart, I never felt lonely in my early life as we had cows, calves, sheep (about 300), a pig, dogs and cats - so they were all my pals, shall I say. I talked to them all. We usually had pet lambs which were a great joy as were the calves, chickens etc. You would think in Lea at that time that you would never have visitors but Jimmy Stoddart, Chrissie Campbell and old Duncan MacPherson would row up from Crowlick to visit us. Willie Stoddart and different men working at Barrisdale also would often walk down by the lochside for a ceilidh.

My mother used to tell me that in her young days, herself and the rest of the family would row up the loch and go for a ceilidh across the water at Caolasmor. Halloween was a favourite time for such visits to the Paterson household there. There would be a feast of home baking, fresh butter and home made jam, and whipped cream. As they whipped up a big bowl of cream, when it started to thicken and 'fluff up', various articles would be popped into the bowl such as silver threepenny pieces, cheap little rings, thimbles and buttons. After further fluffing up of the cream and the other contents of the bowl, each one would be given a serving of the cream with keen anticipation of the treasures to be found within and of their relevance. If one of the ladies drew a thimble - she was destined to be an old maid, and likewise, predicted bachelor status was in store for the boys and men who found a button in their cream. For those who found a ring, of course, marriage was in the offing, while the finding of a silver threepenny piece indicated that they would never want for a penny or two or the other necessities of life.

Then the bag of hazel nuts from the recent autumn harvest from the surrounding woods would be brought out. A pair of nuts representing named people who were reported to be 'courting' in Arnisdale and the other Loch Hourn clachans would be placed very close to the peat fire. If one of the pair exploded with the heat, that indicated that the liaison was not going to last much longer. On the other hand, if the pair of nuts stood up to the heat together for a long time and eventually burned away together, that was all the proof that was needed that this couple were going to 'tie the knot' and have a long and happy life together.

They would continue to have great fun together recalling and replaying the old Halloween tales, of witches on broomsticks, reading cups and telling fortunes. It would be a fine long and most entertaining night together before the members of the Lea household would set off in the boat, rowing across the loch and then westwards up the shoreline to Lea.

There was no radio at that time and I remember the first gramophone that we got with 18 old records of melodeon music and Gaelic songs. No jazz!

The papers came once a week - the People's Journal and Oban Times. Old John MacGillivray (Iain Beag) used to have a paragraph in each with the Arnisdale news. He had news of deaths and the dances and once a year, in the springtime, he wrote a bit to report that the welcome notes of the first cuckoo had been heard.

We had our mails delivered twice weekly from Arnisdale by Willie the Post (Willie MacKenzie). Willie Senior was the first in the continuous line of Mackenzies delivering the mail in the area. Willie probably started as the local postman soon after he had finished his service in the Lovat Scouts in the first World War. Willie Senior was succeeded in the job by Willie Junior but the latter Willie has not long retired and has been succeeded by his son David.

Before Willie Senior, the postman was Duncan Campbell who was drowned tragically near Caolas Mor in the course of his duty delivering the mail to Lea, Barrisdale and Caolas Mor. Duncan stayed in Corran with his wife Kirsty, their house being at the rear of Mary Anne Cameron's just over the Corran Bridge and adjacent to the MacDonald's house. In fact, Rena's Post Office in Corran from the 1970s was in Duncan and Kirsty's old house.

In those early days before and during the Great War, the transport up the loch was by an open boat and sail. Nobody knows how the tragedy came about. Was the boat caught by a sudden squall as Duncan tried to hoist the sail or did he try to turn round and was caught by the fast current at that vulnerable spot? Duncan was in his 50s at the time and was an experienced and able boatman. His body was found only yards from the shore. He was a very fit man for his age and a powerful and able swimmer; on more than one occasion in his earlier years he had swum both ways across Loch Hourn from Arnisdale to Lea. Duncan sometimes had an attack of epilepsy so that may have been responsible for the tragedy.

Duncan was an excellent fiddler in the old style and it was he who taught my mother to play the fiddle. Although I say it myself, my mother was quite good on the fiddle, playing in the house in the old style taught her by Duncan. She did not play in public e.g. at the dances but only at our own ceilidhs in the house. Duncan also taught my Uncles Christopher and Neil MacPherson of Red Point to play the fiddle. He failed in his bid to teach Uncle Duncan MacPherson who was not musical. The MacPhersons were distantly related to the Glenelg MacPhersons and also to Charlie MacTavish and Archie MacLean in Arnisdale, whose Granny was a MacPherson.

We always looked forward to our visitors at Lea. Willie the Post, of course, was a regular twice weekly visitor with our mails. Sometimes in the autumn we would hear a knock on our door at Lea at 5 in the morning. We knew that this would be Willie starting his postal rounds very early - probably having been at Caolasmor and Barrisdale before he arrived at Lea at that unearthly hour. We would know that he had been on a special extra mission on such mornings. First he would come in for his tea, oatcakes and scones and then we would proceed with the further work to be done on such early morning calls. I would have to go down with Willie to the boat, which would contain a fine newly shot, grallached stag. Together we would get down to the skinning and further processing. We could now be sure of fine dinners of venison for several weeks ahead. On finishing the processing, the haunches would be hung up in seclusion and safety and Willie would clean himself up and return to Corran looking very clean and tidy in his postal uniform - with an empty boat. He would return to Lea in the evening darkness to take home his dinners for the next few weeks - and also those of many of his neighbours! Nothing was wasted in those tough days when people had very little and all nature's bounties were greatly appreciated by all.

Now let me back track to the earlier days at Lea. My great grandfather, Duncan McKay, came to Lea around the 1870s as a shepherd and our family remained there until we moved to Arnisdale in 1942.

Barrisdale and Lea were run as sheep stock farms in the 1870s and Donald MacKerlich was the manager at Barrisdale at that time. Donald's sister was married to Duncan MacKay and this is how our family arrived at Lea. I think Duncan and his wife had 5 of a family - 4 boys and 1 girl (my granny). Mother was born at Lea and the doctor lived at Glachoile at Inverie and rode on horseback to Barrisdale and then came by rowing boat to Lea. **Not bliss** for the mother to be waiting that long for a Doctor when her child was about to be born into this world!.

It was the middle of June when my mother was born and seemingly the snow was half way down the Knoydart Hills. Lea could be very wild in the winter time but so beautiful in summer when the loch was still and the sun shining.

In my grandparents' time, another family stayed in Lea up at the old fank. They were MacInnes, to name, I believe. The MacPhersons who were later at Crowlick were at Red Point (Rudha Ruadh) first. The house at Red Point was done up for the MacPhersons with a wooden floor and corrugated iron roof at a cost of £60! I'll just mention that a family Cameron were in Lea before the MacKay's came in the 1870s but I have no way of knowing who they were or where they went after leaving Lea.

There is a path called 'Dick's path' (Ceum Dick) from Lea to Red Point and on to Crowlick. In the aftermath of the '45, Mr Dick was one of Thomas Telford's surveyors who was surveying the area's potential as a major fishing and fish processing centre. In carrying out the survey while going along this path, the unfortunate Mr Dick lost his footing and toppled over a cliff to his death on the shore below. I cannot remember more about this story but I did see it mentioned in a book about Telford.

I remember in my earlier years, old Danny Stewart and his wife stayed at Barrisdale and they were connected with the Stewarts at Corran. Many of their grandchildren and great-grandchildren now live around the Fort William area. Later, there were MacMasters (a brother and sister) at Barrisdale in what was Willie Stoddart's house if I remember correctly. There was a chapel or church at Barrisdale. It will now be a ruin but it was roofed in my time. I think my cousin Johnnie MacKay's (late of Inverie) father and mother were married at Barrisdale at the little church there.

The first tenant or owner of Barrisdale estate that I remember was Smith-Ryland by name and then the Bell Irvines; in my early days it was Macmillans who were at Runival and the MacRaes at Caolasmor. A family Campbell came to Runival later on. Down from Barrisdale on the Lea side at "Inbhir Dhorcoil" there were the ruins of three houses and Uncle Farquhar remembered them being occupied. There were two families of MacGillivrays, 2 brothers married to 2 sisters, if I remember correctly. Only one of the couples had a family - a boy and a girl. The MacRaes at Kinlochourn (Roddy and Peter) will know more about the son than I ever did. He was known as Iain Ruadh - a well known character. The last time I saw Iain Ruadh at Lea he wandered into a place known as the "Carn Mor" but got rescued by old Willie Stoddart. The third family were Martin by name but I know nothing else about them.

There is an old graveyard in Barrisdale, Eilean Choinneach, which got covered by the sea during very high tides. There were also two or three isolated graves between Lea and Red Point just above sea level; I think the deceased would be men from a fishing boat, when the herring fishing was on the go. I heard that the men were supposed to belong to Mull.

There is a ruin at this place and it was a people's refuge for fugitives from the law at that time and they were held in an asylum or shelter in these places. I think it would be connected with the church at that time as this would go back a few centuries. They cultivated the hill face using the lazy bed system to grow their potatoes and oats. There was, also, up behind the house in Lea, a kiln - a stone kiln for drying the oats. It was covered in moss in my time but you could see where the fire was set under the kiln.

I went to Airor to school when I was seven years old and stayed with the teacher's family. The teacher (Mrs Joan MacDonald) was a sister of Peggy Ann of Arnisdale Post Office. Mrs MacDonald and her husband had one son (Hamish) and there was also another boy in the school, so we were well tutored - all three of us! I didn't have any English when I went to school but I quickly picked it up and spent a very happy three years in Airor. When the older boy left school, they were in the process of shutting down the Airor School so it was then that I went to Arnisdale School when I was ten years of age.

At the time I went to school in Airor, there were six families living there. They were all second or third generations of people who had come over from Camuscross and Ferindonald in Skye. There were three families of MacDonalds, two of MacInnes and one Campbell family. There is only one of these houses permanently occupied now - by an Englishman and he has been there for years.

There was a nice church there at that time - quite a big church for so small a village; it is now converted into a holiday home. There was a service held there at 3 o'clock in the afternoon every Sunday. The minister came over from Inverie on a motor bike. He also used to go over to Lea - he walked over the hill from Inverie about twice a year in the summer time. Latterly he got a motor launch, so maybe a little less effort was involved in getting to his parishioners. The MacKays - Johnny Mackay's (Inverie) mother and brothers were in Inverguseran at that time. There was nobody in Samadalan then but there is now. They are German or of German descent, I believe.

At the time I stayed there, the last of the MacBrayne paddle steamers on that route was plying between Mallaig and Kyle. It was called the "Glencoe". The steamer Lochness called at Mallaig in the morning on its run in from Stornoway and then went to Kyle for its return from there to Stornoway. The son of the family I stayed with in Airor, Hamish MacDonald, is married over in IsleOrnsay but, like myself, he is getting old and decrepit!

When I started in Arnisdale School it was a Miss Fletcher who was the teacher there at that time. She was from Breakish in Skye. Before Miss Fletcher, I think the teacher was Bessie Logan and before that I think it was Miss Cameron who was later teacher at Glenelg for many years. After Miss Fletcher we had Donald Finlayson from Portree - a very good teacher who taught me most of the reading and writing of Gaelic and also gave me my first experience of the belt for talking in class! Mrs Joan Kennedy came in after that and was there for a few years for some time after I left school. After Joan Kennedy, the teachers in turn were Miss Cruickshanks (later Mrs Norman Cameron, Glenelg), Miss Forsyth, Miss Ferguson and then Ann MacRae from Glenelg. Ann was the teacher for some of the war years until she married and became Mrs Bobby MacLean in 1946. When I went to Arnisdale School, Mabel and Roddy Fletcher had just left but Donald MacIntosh, Jessie Rarsaidh's son was there, Angus Stewart, Jimmy Campbell, Ian MacCuaig, Donald and Farquhar Fletcher (Alister Fletcher came later), the MacDonalds (Morag, Jessie, Mary and Rena), Chrissie MacCuaig, Effie and Betty MacLaren, Johan MacDonald came in later along with Charlie MacTavish and Ian Sinclair. The two MacCuaig boys from Glasgow (Donald and Iain) were in school for a short time and that would have been the maximum number in the school in its later years as far as my memory goes.

I stayed with Willie MacKenzie's family in Corran when Donald Finlayson was there, but the MacKenzie family was increasing from Willie to Nellie so I went to stay with Mrs Kennedy and family at the School. After our family came to stay in Arnisdale I remember that in the evening I often made my way up to visit my friends in Corran - Rena, Mary, Jessie, Morag and Johan MacDonald and Chrissie MacCuaig, as well as the Corran boys.

We used to have ceilidhs in many of the houses and particularly in Mary Ann Cameron's and Norman Morrison's. In Norman's house we used to sing the mouth music and dance to it. He was a fine old man. When I finished school at the age of fourteen, I then went to work in the Arnisdale Lodge for the season. Jessie MacDonald and I were there that season and Ian MacCuaig was in the garden - so it was great fun and an insight into another way of life that we could only dream about.

The Kitson family had the Lodge and estate at that time and they were nice people to work for. I worked with them over the years and never got carpeted for anything - though I was very guilty of laughing when I should have been serious! I worked in the kitchen for the first couple of years which meant being in the kitchen at 6.30 in the morning. Every other day you got two hours off in the afternoon, one half day a week and a half day every second Sunday. At night we had to be upstairs by 10 p.m. and lights had to be out at 10.30 p.m.!

Up to the finish of school days we were not allowed to dances, so my first memories of dances are mainly the same as Mabel Fletcher's (see Chapter 19). I remember Mabel's wedding dance in 1940. I was at Inverguseran with the MacKays at the time and Roddy took myself and Jimmy up in the estate's motor launch to Arnisdale. There was a big crowd of people there and Mabel was a lovely bride. The wedding was at New Year, I think, and I also think it would have been the last wedding in the church prior to my own in 1952. All this time my home was still at Lea and it was only in the early '40s that we went to the Mission House in Arnisdale after my uncle's death in Lea. I was working in Arnisdale Lodge the day war was declared in 1939 and we were all around the radio in the servants' hall. Even the toffs thought it would be over in weeks. Little did we know!

Food was rationed, of course, but we were perhaps more fortunate than others because we would get fish from neighbours - a good catch would always be shared. However, one fishing expedition was in vain. I will let my great friend Ann MacLean tell her story. Ann was the Arnisdale teacher at the time.

**A memorable escapade in Arnisdale (Ann MacLean)**

March 1942 - a clear, crisp, frosty morning - one of the gems that besparkle the West Highlands so frequently in spring and autumn. Whether we set out intentionally to look for scallops and misjudged the state of the tide I cannot remember, but mid-morning found Margaret and me miles from the village (where I was teacher!) with the waters of Loch Hourn lapping well above our knees as we hunted for scallops on a sandbank near Rarsaidh.

Soaked, chilled and ravenous, we were finally forced ashore by the rising tide and squelched and dribbled our way foodwards.

Rationing - and her mother had but one precious tin of "Spam" **but** she kept hens and ducks. Fried "Spam" and eggs eaten as we steamed by the fire!. No meal since - not even a memorable exotic dinner in London's Cafe Royal has compared with it.

A daft, youthful escapade but it culminated in the Meal of a Lifetime.

(Maggie Lea remembers this escapade very clearly and her mother, Jessie, having palpitations on the shore as the rising tide threatened to engulf the two marine explorers!).

Maggie continues: I remember a lovely Sunday in wartime when one of the hitherto not seen Lysander planes flew up Loch Hourn and the local Home Guard mobilised and followed it up the Loch by boat. I don't know why the plane was there but possibly it was just keeping an eye open for enemy activity. I remember one day in Lea when my mother and I saw a squad of soldiers walking down the lochside! Palpitations! But they were Free French soldiers based at Inverie. They had a British Liaison Officer with them and, being a hot summer's day, they thankfully drank all the milk my mother could provide. There was always plenty of milk and cream in those days.

The night war finally ended in 1945, we were in the Mission House in Arnisdale and dutifully went to bed with paraffin lights on after all the years of the blackout! We were not long in bed when there was a loud banging at the door, so we had to get up again and most of the neighbours had turned up to celebrate, some with a packet of tea, some sugar, biscuits and whatever they could muster, so we all had a sing song - Mrs Sinclair and Ian, Mary Ann and Nora, Mrs MacCuaig and one or two more. Old George MacDougall went home and got a shot gun and fired two shots into the night sky about 2 in the morning. On hearing the shots, Archie's mother and one or two of the older ones thought the war had started again!

We then started collecting money to give each of the returning servicemen and women a "Welcome Home" night and £10 to each to help get them started on ordinary life again. The musicians at the dances were usually Peter and Farquhar MacRae, Do MacKillop, Donald Fletcher plus the MacLaren family (Donald, his wife Jessie and daughters Betty and Effie) who were all very musical. The MacLaren family took the organ to the school and one of them played the organ, one the box and the father the fiddle. I remember on one occasion they took all that equipment to the coffee room in the old hotel at Glenelg. In the earlier days, Allan Murchison and Peter Fletcher played the fiddle, Angus Campbell the pipes, and I suppose the Kinlochourn boys (Peter, Farquhar and Do) were almost always there for the dances.

The favourite dances in my time were the Circassian Circle, Quadrilles, the Eightsome Reel, Military and Boston Two-step, Strip the Willow, Old Fashioned Waltz and the One Step - a modified quick step. We had the Petronella and the Flowers of Edinburgh for a change now and again. I am sure Roddie and Peter (MacRae) can improve on my memories of the players and singers.

The precentors in the churches were Sweyn MacIntosh (Free Church) and Angus Murchison in the school (Church of Scotland) followed later by Roddy Mor and Dannie MacDonald. I understood that the Free Church was built at the peak of the herring fishing. There was a book in the Library at Arnisdale Lodge (I forget the author) written about Arnisdale at the time King Edward VII came to Glenquoich. This person wrote of the people having the cows and hens in one end of the house and the humans in the other end. He wrote that when the Royal yacht (The Victoria and Albert?) was passing up Loch Hourn, the women took off their black stockings and pinned them on a white background to form the words - "God save the King"! The writer tended to ridicule the local folk as being backward and almost uncivilised, and Ewen Murchison was considering suing him for slander if he ever gained more authority in this world, as indeed he did as he progressed to high office in the medical and naval fields (as a Surgeon Captain). But I am sure that his threat to sue the author was forgotten over time.

I remember hearing about the story of Granny MacKenzie (Mairi Bhan), grandmother of Willie, Iain, Nellie and Flora, who are all resident in Arnisdale now (Nellie for part of the time). As a teenager soon after leaving school, Mairi Bhan was working in service in Glasgow when typhoid fever swept through Arnisdale, Glenelg not being affected. It probably came in via a fisherman on one of the herring drifters or possibly from an infected person coming into Arnisdale down the Glen from Kinlochourn. It took a terrible toll in Arnisdale with 16 deaths including Mairi Bhan's mother and father. No survivors dared go near affected houses or the sick and deceased therein. Mairi Bhan, immediately she heard the news, came home from Glasgow and, along with her sister Lexy Campbell, did all that was necessary to prepare the bodies of her mother and father and arrange the burial. All the deceased were buried in a specially marked area of the Arnisdale graveyard with the stipulation that none of the graves should be opened again for the burial of close relatives - because of the fear of re-infection. Mairi Bhan escaped the infection herself while her sister Lexy was affected to some extent and the fact that Lexy was very short-sighted thereafter was considered to be attributable to the disease.

Another sad angle to this story was that the local GP, Dr Graham in Glenelg, whose people had the Isleornsay Hotel in Skye, went to Arnisdale to give every help he could. Dr Graham contracted the disease himself and died soon afterwards. However, the noble Doctor continued to have an influence on the health care and well-being of the Arnisdale folk, for his daughter, Lisa, became the District Nurse for Arnisdale and Glenelg, was resident in Arnisdale and later married Donald MacKenzie, Lea. They settled in Lea, running the croft and raising their family of two daughters and a son ('Murdo the Ferry') there. Later they spent their retirement in Camusban.

As I indicated earlier, when I left Arnisdale School at 14, my first job was in Arnisdale Lodge for the Summer and Autumn season. I remember at the end of the season, three of the Lodge staff from Arnisdale (Mary Anne MacCuaig, Jessie MacDonald and myself) went to Glencoe House on Loch Leven to work for three weeks. Glencoe House was also owned by the Kitson family. We went on the Arnisdale Estate boat, the Morag, to Mallaig, got the train to Fort William and then a lift in a Ford V8 van from Fort William to Glencoe. It was a beautiful day and Loch Leven looked superb.

The history of Glencoe House, now a hospital, is interesting. It starts with Donald Smith from Northeast Scotland - from Forres, I think. He went out to Canada to work as a young and poor man. At the age of eighteen he signed on as a clerk with the Hudson's Bay Company and was sent to a trading post on the St Lawrence River. He spent five years there and fifteen more in Labrador, and rose from clerk to trader to chief trader to chief factor to chief executive officer of the Hudson's Bay Company in Canada, headquartered in Montreal. In time, he became High Commissioner for Canada and, as a member of the Canadian Parliament, author of the Smith Liquor Act, which prohibited the sale and use of alcoholic drinks in the Northwest Territories. To help enforce the act, he wrote the recommendation that resulted in the creation of the Northwest Mounted Police. He also became a founding director of the Canadian Pacific Railway Company and did pioneering work in finding a way for this great railway from the town of Banff through the Rocky Mountains to Craigellachie in British Columbia. Eventually he was awarded a Knighthood and chose as his title Lord Strathcona and Mount Royal, Strathcona being a name that he fancied while Mount Royal was one of the great peaks of the Rockies. He met and married a native Canadian and eventually took his wife home to Scotland - to Glen Coe. There they had built Glencoe House with 365 windows all facing away from Loch Leven and Ballachulish, because they had a disagreement with the Ballachulish folk. The roof was finished with Welsh slate - not Ballachulish slate - which was being produced in great quantity at that time! Later the family purchased the Island of Colonsay.

When Donald Smith (now Lord Strathcona and Mount Royal) died, his title went to his only child, a daughter. The daughter married Mr Howard, a Canadian physician and the son of this marriage inherited the title of Lord Strathcona and Mount Royal and also the Island of Colonsay. Glencoe House was bequeathed to their daughter, Frances Palmer Howard, who married Captain Kitson. They proceeded to knock down the servants' quarters in Glencoe House and install windows at the front with a great view across Loch Leven from the kitchen windows in which Jessie, Mary Anne and myself spent most of our time".

These are Maggie's memories - for the time being.

Maggie continued to work for the Kitsons both at Arnisdale Lodge and in their other homes. She also worked for Roddy Mor at the farm. She was adept at the full range of jobs which had to be done and always worked with a lightsome heart. She was a livewire in the Arnisdale community and was always at the forefront in organising and running the ceilidhs and the dances. She and her mother, Jessie, had one of the most popular ceilidh houses in the village.

Arnisdale was sad to lose Maggie and Jessie but overjoyed for them when Maggie got married in 1952. Maggie's wedding to John Angus MacDonald from the Island of Eigg on 4 April 1952 was the last wedding to take place in the Arnisdale Church. John Angus worked on the Eigg estate which was then owned by Lord Runciman. He was a first cousin of the MacDonald girls from Corran and Johan played a subtle part in suggesting to her cousin, John Angus, that he would not find a more suitable wife anywhere than Maggie Lea. John Angus took Johan's advice and sought out and 'captured' the charming, attractive and capable young lady from Arnisdale. John Angus' brother Hugh was best man at the wedding while Maggie's cousin, Morag MacPherson, was the bridesmaid. The Reverend Norman MacDonald from Glenelg was the officiating minister while Roddy Mor did the precenting. All the folk in Arnisdale and many others from Eigg, Glenelg, Kinlochourn and elsewhere were at the wedding so that required considerable preparations. Maggie and the MacDonald girls - Rena, Johan and Mary - and Maggie's mother, Jessie, had been making loads of egg and venison sandwiches and baking heaps of cakes and scones for days beforehand - to provide a sumptuous wedding feast for all. A barrel of beer also appeared on the scene to supplement the tea. With commodities such as sugar and bread still being subject to rationing, it was not easy in those times to obtain supplies in the quantities required for a big wedding. However, Maggie and the MacDonald girls were great planners and had influence in important places which made the great wedding feast possible. Maggie and John Angus were married on a Friday and the young couple took their leave of Arnisdale, along with Maggie's mother Jessie, on the following Tuesday. Almost the whole of Arnisdale turned out at the pier to give a great send-off to the young couple, Jessie and their many relations and friends from Eigg, as they sailed away in the Eigg Estate boat, skippered by John Angus' brother Archie and crewed by John Angus himself and his other brother Hugh. Arnisdale's great loss with the departure of the highly popular and respected Jessie and Maggie was Eigg's great gain.

John Angus' and Maggie's four boys - Donald, Duncan, Hugh and Christopher were all born in Eigg. There was great sadness in Arnisdale, Eigg and among their friends everywhere when John Angus lost his life by drowning when the children were between one and seven years of age.

Now Maggie, her four fine sons and their families, are resident around the Fort William and Glen Orchy areas. Maggie has been a key provider of information, a Gaelic language adviser and a source of great encouragement and stimulation in the production of this book. She was always a joyful, cheerful enthusiast and she always will be - that is the way Maggie was made.

She still keeps in close touch with all her friends in Arnisdale, Loch Hourn, Knoydart and Eigg. She has her own firm views about happenings in Eigg and in Knoydart. She thinks highly of the support provided by Sir Cameron MacKintosh in Knoydart in the purchase of the estate by the community. Maggie very much hopes that something of the great community spirit and industry of the Knoydart people of the past can be recaptured to start a healthy new beginning in the Knoydart Peninsula.

**Top Left**. It is believed that Li or Lea is derived from the Norse word HLIDH which means a cliff or slope. The folk resident at the lone house at Lea were a considerable distance by either land or sea from their neighbours eastwards and westwards and across Loch Hourn in Arnisdale. **Right**. Lea from behind the house and croft looking across to Arnisdale and L to R. Beinn Sgritheall, Beinn na h-eaglaise, Beinn Bhuidhe, Beinn nan Caorach, Beinn Chlachach and the western slope of Druim Fada.

**Middle Left**. The remains of the summer sheilings in the high ground beside Allt Li where the folk and their cattle went over the summer months to take advantage of the lush hill pastures and to allow haymaking and the growing of oats and potatoes on the arable croft land below. **Right**. The remains of the summer sheiling shelters for the people tending and milking their cattle and making cheese and butter for winter use – and for 'export' to Skye. The view looks eastwards to the Corr Eileanan and the entrance to upper Loch Hourn.

**Bottom Left**. The remains of the house at Rudha Ruadh, last occupied by Duncan and Kirsty MacPherson and their children in the 1930s. This was the birthplace of Ceitag an Stoirm. **Right**. A view of Rudha Ruadh from the west looking towards Eilean a' Phiobaire – the scene of the 'siege of Lea' (see Chapter 33). Luinne Bheinn shows its dominating presence in the east.

**Top Left**.  The big fank above Lea with Arnisdale, Beinn Sgritheall and its neighbouring tops to the right.  The fank was built when the Knoydart economy was based on large sheep farms (approximately 1800-1870 era).  Before that the emphasis was on cattle, mainly in smallholdings.  After 1870 the emphasis changed to deer forests.
**Right**.  One of the millstones of a horizontal mill above Lea.  Maggie 'Lea' remembers a stone kiln behind the Lea house for the drying of oats.  The very extensive lazy beds on the steep northern slopes of Knoydart indicate fairly intensive cultivation for growing potatoes and oats.

**Middle Left**.  Maggie 'Lea' as a toddler in the early 1920s with mother Jessie (right) and Christina Morrison who married Maggie's Uncle Duncan MacPherson of Red Point (Rudha Ruadh).   **Right**.  A group of family, friends and neighbours at Lea around 1930 with Jessie 'Lea' third from the right and little Maggie 'Lea' at the front.   L to R. Willie Campbell, Uncle Farquhar Mackay, Uncle Duncan 'Lea' MacPherson, Aunt Mary MacPherson, Uncle Christopher MacPherson and cousin Roddy Mackay.

**Bottom Left**.  Maggie Lea's mother Jessie (right) with L to R. Uncle Farquhar Mackay who was born in Samadalan near Airor, with his sons Duncan and Jimmy who were born in Lea (1910-1920 period).
**Centre.**     Old Mrs MacInnes (seated) whose home was at Falloch (Fholaich) beside the hill track between Inverie and Lea with Mrs Chrissie MacPherson, Red Point.      **Right**.  Angus MacInnes, the son of Mrs MacInnes, Falloch (centre) who worked as a ghillie/shepherd on the Arnisdale Estate and lived in the house in Achadh a' Ghlinne at a fancy dress ceilidh dance in Arnisdale around 1920 with Bella MacLeod (left), the sister of Roddy Mor, and Lizzie MacDonald, the Arnisdale schoolteacher (later Mrs Roddy Mor).

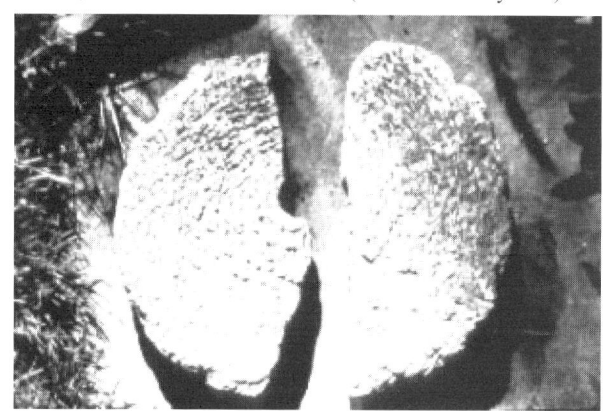

**Top Left**.   While there were tracks along the shoreline to neighbours at Barrisdale to the east and Rudha Ruadh, Coilledhubh and Crowlick to the west, the best way to travel was by boat.  About to make the two mile crossing to Arnisdale from Lea with Druim Fada providing the backdrop are Maggie Lea's uncles and aunt.  L to R. Farquhar Mackay, Chrissie MacPherson and Christopher MacPherson.
**Right**.  Two people who brightened up lives at Lea were Iain Beag MacGillivray from Arnisdale who had weekly reports about activities in the Loch Hourn area in both the Oban Times and The Peoples Journal and Willie MacKenzie (the first Willie the Post) who delivered the mails twice weekly and on occasions made very early morning calls when the stags were in their prime in the Autumn!

**Middle Left**.  The former school at Airor on the Knoydart shore opposite Skye which Maggie Lea attended in her early years.  The school is now converted into a dwelling house.  One of the 3 pupils in Airor School in Maggie Lea's time was Iain Hamish MacDonald.
**Right**.  Iain Hamish is a nephew of Peggy Ann MacLean in the Arnisdale Post Office and still runs his croft in Isleornsay, Skye with his wife Bella.

**Bottom Left**   The old church at Airor.    **Right**.  The MacBrayne Paddle Steamer 'The Glencoe' passed up the Sound of Sleat in front of Airor daily on the Mallaig to Kyle run during Maggie's early schooldays there..

**Top Left**. The Arnisdale School pupils and teacher just before Maggie transferred to the School in the early 1930s. Back row L to R. Ian MacCuaig, Jimmy Campbell, Roddy Fletcher, Morag MacDonald, Miss Fletcher (Teacher), Mabel Fletcher, Angus Stewart and Donald MacKintosh. Front row. Jessie MacDonald, Chrissie MacCuaig, Mary and Rena MacDonald, Farquhar and Donald Fletcher. **Right.** After leaving school, Maggie Lea's first job was in Arnisdale Lodge. L to R. Jessie MacDonald, Mrs Christina Thompson (wife of the Lodge gardener), Phyllis Cooke, Maggie 'Lea', Mary Ann MacCuaig, Beatrice Haines, Winnie Windsor and Connie Galloway (around 1938).

**Middle Left**. Arnisdale Lodge staff with some of the sailors from Commander Kitson's yacht, the Golden Hind in the 1936 season. Back L to R. Winnie Windsor (Tablemaid), Ginger Murdo MacKenzie, Gairloch, Mrs Christina Thomson (a wonderful cook), Captain Tait, Beatrice Haines (Head Housemaid), Phyllis Cooke (Cook), Connie Galloway (Lady's maid), Willie MacLean (Engineer). Front. ? Sweeney, Campbeltown, Calum Finlayson, Breakish, Skye, Jean Thomson, Maggie 'Lea', Mary Ann MacCuaig and Jessie MacDonald. **Right**. Maggie Lea (left) and Rena MacDonald, great friends, fine people, very competent in the great range of jobs which they tackled, full of fun and a great pair in organising the Arnisdale ceilidh dances.

**Bottom Left**. Maggie working at the hay in the lower Glen Arnisdale fields with Roddy Mor (left) and Aunt Lizzie (right). **Right**. Maggie Lea (right) with mother Jessie (centre) and Rena MacDonald at the entrance to their home in Camusban – a very popular ceilidh house where all would get a great welcome.

**Top Left**. Maggie Lea outside the Arnisdale Free Church after her marriage to John Angus MacDonald from Eigg in 1952. **Right**. The bridal group at the wedding.

**Middle Left**. John Angus, Maggie and mother Jessie leave Arnisdale Pier to join the Eigg Estate boat on their departure from Arnisdale for their new life in Eigg. **Right**. A large gathering of Arnisdale folk beside Roddy Mor's little converted Austin lorry at the pier to bid their farewells to a very popular family L to R. Allan MacAskill, Ludovic Fraser, John MacGillivray, Willie MacKenzie, Roddy Mor, Kenny Fletcher, Peter English, Jimmy Stoddart, Donald Fletcher, Roddy Fletcher and Iain Sinclair.

**Bottom Left**. A final group picture before departure L to R. Johnny Sinclair, Liza MacKenzie, Elizabeth Ann and Margaret Stevenson, Jessie 'Lea', Maggie MacAskill, Mrs Sinclair, Morag MacIntyre, Willie MacKenzie, Mary Ann MacCuaig, Maggie MacTavish, Mrs Thomson, Roddy Fletcher, Donald Fletcher, Kenny Fletcher, Ludovic Fraser, Peter English, Aonghas Dhaidh MacKintosh, John MacDonald, Maggie 'Lea', Norman Jamieson, Hugh MacDonald, Roddy Mor, Angus Beaton and Willie Stoddart. **Right**. Maggie in her home in Caol, Fort William in 1999 with two of her ten grandchildren, Iain Angus and Kayleigh.

**Top Left.** Donald 'Ban' MacKenzie (brother of the first Willie the Post) with Coinneach MacLeod of the Arnisdale Home Farm around 1910. Donald and his wife Lisa succeeded Maggie Lea's family as 'custodians' of Lea. **Right.** Lisa MacKenzie (nee Graham) was the district nurse in Arnisdale. Lisa is seen here with Granny MacKenzie (Mairi Bhan) and Granny Jane Campbell at Cosaig, Corran. Lisa's father, Dr Graham, died in the typhoid epidemic in Arnisdale around 1890. Mairi Bhan's mother and father died in the same epidemic.

**Middle Left.** Lisa MacKenzie (left) and Donald (right) with daughter Mary and their grandchildren at the landing place at Corran (mid 1950s). **Right.** A squad of Arnisdale and Glenelg folk prepare to board Colin Murchison's boat in the mid 1960s to cross Loch Hourn to Lea to clip Donald's sheep while he was in hospital. L to R. Dick MacDonald, Doch Chisholm, John 'Mor' MacDonald, Iain MacDonald, Allan Morrison, Iain Alastair MacRae, Archie MacLean, Allan MacAskill and Murdo MacKenzie.

**Bottom Left.** 'Many hands make the work light'. The Lea clipping has been completed and it is time for a dram. L to R. Allan Morrison, Angus Stewart, Iain MacKenzie, Tommy Moffat, Iain Macdonald, Willie MacKenzie, John Mor MacDonald, Archie MacLean, Uisdean MacLure, Allan MacDiarmid, Roddy Cameron, Murdo MacKenzie, Iain Alastair MacRae and Doch Chisholm (Photograph by Alan MacDiarmid).
**Right.** The Kylerhea Ferry between Skye and the mainland was operated by Donald and Lisa's son Murdo for many years in the 1960-1980 era.

**Top Left**.   Rick Rohde who succeeded Donald MacKenzie as tenant in Lea.  Rick and his wife Hillary took many initiatives in Lea, including generating hydro electricity from the nearby burn and also mussel farming.  Hillary established a network of expert knitters to produce high value knitted garments.   **Right**.  The Rohde children Zoe and Leif in 1979.

**Middle Left**.  Leif crosses Loch Hourn in 1989 with Lea in the background.   **Right**.  Harvesting and sorting the mussels (1988) are L to R. Zoe, Jon, Hillary, Mick Simpson and Romi Simpson.

**Bottom Left**.  Mick, Romi, Zoe, Amber and Rick work on the mussels close to the Lea shore (1988).   **Right**.  Lea, from its vantage point on the southern shore of Loch Hourn has seen great changes in the livelihoods of its people over the centuries – cattle and sheep, cropping oats and potatoes, the herring fishing, the deer forests and now the mussel farming.

# Chapter 28

**Crowlick, Willie Campbell, the Stoddarts and MacKays**

Croalig or Croalin or Crowlick is another hamlet on the Loch Hourn shore on Knoydart which was established by the Knoydart Estate to house the 'watchers', or custodians, one of whose jobs it was to control the poaching of deer by the fisherman working on the herring fishing on Loch Hourn. They often doubled up as shepherds/ghillies/stalkers working for the estate, which was owned by the Bowlby family for many decades. The 'watchers' also worked their crofts, growing as much of their own food as possible. Thus, they would have one or more cows, perhaps some goats for their milk, especially in the earlier days before the sheep, they had their hens, and they grew potatoes, oats, garden produce including cabbage and kale and made hay to winter the cattle. They would catch fresh fish for themselves and have their barrel of salt herring, and also salt venison, so that they were fairly independent in their isolated dwelling.

There were two dwellings on Crowlick and these remain today. There was the one at Coille Dhubh (the black forest) and half a mile away to the west was the other croft.

Maggie Lea remembers in her days at Li that Duncan MacPherson and his family from Red Point (Rudha Ruadh) later moved to Coille Dhubh. Duncan was married to Kirsty Morrison from Harris and they had three daughters and two sons. After Duncan's death, the family moved to Caol, near Fort William. In the other house at the time was Jimmag Stoddart and his niece Chrissie Campbell (sister of Willie, Jessie Ann and Angus) whose mother, Jimmag's sister, Mrs Jane Campbell, stayed at Corran.

Maggie Lea remembers Jimmag's mother, Mrs Christina (Kirsty) Stoddart at Crowlick. She was a Douglas before she married and came from Skiary, further up Loch Hourn. She was 98 years of age when she died. The Douglas family originally came from Skye.

The Stoddart home in Crowlick was much older than that at Coille Dubh and Maggie remembers in her time that the flooring in the living room was of rounded cobble stones from the shore.

Apart from Maggie Lea, the other person who had very clear memories of life at Crowlick in the old days was the late Willie Campbell, whose family now live at Letterfearn and other locations at home and overseas. Willie's mother, Jane Stoddart, married a Lewisman, John Campbell, who was a bonded storeman in Glasgow and he died at the early age of 44 years. Thus Jane was left with four young children - Chrissie, Jessie Ann, Willie and baby Angus - and without a bread winner. Just before he died, John Campbell and Jane had been planning to emigrate to Canada to start a new life there. With the help of her relations on Loch Hourn - at Barrisdale and Crowlick, Jane was given the tenancy of a vacant croft at Corran and - home she came to Corran with her four youngsters to work the croft and obtain a basic livelihood for her family by keeping a cow, hens and growing potatoes and garden produce. Crofting neighbours were always most supportive in these crises which befell families.

The children went to Arnisdale School where the teacher was David Mackintosh from Glenelg - a bit of a 'terror', according to Willie. Willie and the other children often went for school holidays to their relations at Crowlick. At Crowlick during these First World War years were their Uncle, Jimmag Stoddart (who had been invalided out of the Army during the War), and their Granny Stoddart (formerly Kirsty Douglas).

Willie thoroughly enjoyed his holidays in Crowlick and, with the MacPherson family as neighbours, they had plenty of company and there was always plenty to do - working on the croft, fishing and roaming the hills. The mails came in three times a week from Inverie, the postman walking over the hill from Inverguseran. Sometimes Willie would go over to Inverguseran himself to spend a few days with his Aunt Maggie (formerly Stoddart) who was married to Kenneth Mackay, manager at Inverguseran on Major Bowlby's Knoydart Estate. Willie greatly treasured these visits as the Mackays had four of a family - Duncan, Johnnie, Jimmy and Roddy (later the Customs and Excise Officer in Mallaig) who were the same age as Willie himself. Willie kept up this close contact with his cousins to the end of his days.

Back at Crowlick, Willie remembered his Granny, who could not speak English; nevertheless she would read the English newspapers and relate to them all (in Gaelic) every interesting piece of the news. While they grew or caught (by fishing) most of their food requirements - for other essential needs they crossed Loch Hourn in the sailing boat to get supplies from the MacLean's store in Arnisdale. Uncle Jimmag, Willie remembered, was an expert sailor. Jimmag was partial to a little dram now and again and would go across to Arnisdale on occasions and have a sociable time there. One very stormy day Willie remembered being at Crowlick when Jimmag set off for Arnisdale. Later in the evening the storm got much worse and when midnight arrived with no sign of Jimmag, his mother (Willie's Granny) was becoming extremely worried about the safety of Jimmag in trying to get across the raging loch in his little sailing boat. It was a clear bright night with a full moon so Granny and Willie set off (well wrapped up) towards the shore and sat on a rock on a knoll beside the shore with a full view of the route that Jimmag would take on his way home from Arnisdale. They scanned the loch in vain for hours. At about four o'clock in the morning - not far from the shore, there arose in front of them out of the water, a beast which Willie described as being 'like a sea serpent'. It had a big head and long neck and two humps were visible behind as it made its way up the loch in front of them. Willie, who was about 12 years old at the time, estimated that there was about four feet of neck above the water line. That sighting, of course, caused tremendous excitement to himself and his Granny while the beast remained visible and diverted their attention, at least momentarily, from their increasing concerns about Jimmag. However, it was not long afterwards that they spotted a sail - sure enough it was Jimmag and he made his way skilfully through the very rough seas to the safety of his usual landing point at Crowlick. Willie's Granny lived until she was 98 years of age. Willie remembered the rough floor of her living room at Crowlick - the rounded cobble stones described by Maggie Li and he wondered just how his old Granny managed to negotiate them without tripping over them and breaking her bones.

As well as his Uncle and Granny at Crowlick and his relations in Inverguseran, Willie also had an Uncle, Willie Stoddart, at Barrisdale. Willie married Mary Bridges, whose father (from Ayrshire) was a grieve on the Knoydart Estate. Willie and Mary had two daughters, Lina and Gwennie and when Willie finished his life's work as a gamekeeper/stalker/ghillie/shepherd in Barrisdale, he and his family retired to Arnisdale. One of the great tools of Willie's trade was his spying glass and in his retirement it was still his constant companion. As he sat outside his house in Camusban, he would always be scanning the loch, the Knoydart shore and focusing in on Barrisdale and all the well known haunts of his working life there.

The Stoddarts had come up as shepherds from the Scottish Border country with the Cheviot sheep. Their forebears first came to the head of Loch Nevis to tend their sheep and in Willie Campbell's young days, the following generations - now working and living in the Knoydart corners of Barrisdale, Crowlick and Inverguseran - were still not too far away from where their pioneering ancestors first settled on coming to the Western Highlands with the sheep.

On leaving school, Willie Campbell made for Knoydart to his Aunt, Uncle and Mackay cousins at Inverguseran. He liked working with the Estate joiner there and although he was not paid, he was picking up a lot of skills of the joinery trade. There was much building work going on at the Knoydart

Estate in those days and Milligans, a firm of joiners from Ayr, played a big part in it. Their seasoned joiners soon noticed the aptitude of young Willie and it was not long before he was 'signed on' and went to work for them in Ayr. Willie remembered that one of his great mentors in Ayr was a man called Bobby MacWhirter. After Willie served his time in Ayr, he worked with this firm on jobs in Edinburgh and Glasgow, but in 1928 he decided to cross the Atlantic. He worked in big building projects in New York for three to four years but was forced to come home during the severe recession associated with the Wall Street Crash. He came home to Arnisdale and started his joinery business there. Willie married Nettie (nee MacPherson) at Kylerhea in 1936 and they set up home at Letterfearn. Nettie, still hale and hearty at Letterfearn, is a native of Glenelg and, like her sister Isabella and brothers Donnie and Roddy, had many relations on Loch Hourn at one time or another - at Sandaig, Caolasmor, Runival and Kinlochourn. Willie and Nettie had five children, Ian, Donald, Eric, Jane and Fiona. Donald and Eric were schooled by their father in the building trade and they now carry on the business in Letterfearn, Arnisdale, Glenelg, Glenshiel and further afield.

Willie acquired a lorry before the Second War which was commandeered during the war towards the war effort. Willie required the lorry not only for his joinery business but he was also involved with John Donald MacLeod from Sandaig in the maintenance of the gravel main road from the top of Mam Ratagan to Arnisdale. Willie and his lorry were also in demand when the coal boat beached in Arnisdale and Glenelg to deliver the coal to the various households. In his joinery work at the start of the war, Willie had as his apprentice, his nephew, young Jimmy Campbell from Corran, until Jimmy joined the war effort and saw active service with the army in Tripoli.

After Willie retired and left Donald and Eric to get on with the business, he had more time to do the things that were near to his heart. Apart from crossing the Atlantic again with Nettie to visit daughters Jane and Fiona, and their families in Vancouver, Willie made an annual pilgrimage to his old haunts in Knoydart. He visited his cousin Johnnie Mackay in Inverie every year and his last visit was made just two months before he died. One of the boys would run him to Kyle, he would get the Kyle Steamer to Mallaig and then the Knoydart Estate boat to Inverie where he would get a great welcome from Johnnie. The two of them were very close - they were like brothers, Nettie asserts. When the two got together for Willie's sojourn of a fortnight or so, there was a great deal of reminiscing, some sadness too, but also much laughter, couthiness and joy in each other's company.

There is no doubt that on their later ceilidhs, one of Willie's experiences at Crowlick would be discussed and analysed at great length.

As indicated earlier, Willie had spent many of his Arnisdale school holidays at Crowlick helping his Uncle Jimmag (Stoddart) on the croft and in all the other chores which had to be done. Jimmag was a tireless worker and expected everybody else to be likewise - jobs could not be done quickly enough for Jimmag's liking. As they were working together at hay, at sheep, cutting peats or whatever, his most common 'encouragement' to Willie - no matter how hard young Willie was working - was 'Greas ort!' (Hurry up!).

In his later years, Willie made a little pilgrimage back to Crowlick along with an 'unofficial' hunting party of two others. By this time, Crowlick had been deserted and old Uncle Jimmag (Stoddart) had died years before. It was in the autumn when the stags were in fine condition and were fairly low down near the shore. The instruction from the man with the rifle to his two companions was to remain in the boat until they heard a shot and then they were to come to join him - hopefully with a fine stag lying at his feet. As they waited quietly and patiently on the shore, they eventually heard the shot and that was the signal to move in that direction. This was to take them up past Jimmag's former house, the byre, barn and croft lands where Willie had toiled so much as a youngster but never, apparently, was he doing the various jobs to his Uncle's satisfaction.   Willie recalled "As we were making our way past the old buildings and through the croft, I heard as clearly as anything a voice and the words 'Greas Ort!' and I heard it twice in quick succession 'Greas Ort, Greas Ort'"   Willie's step must still have not been quick enough yet to meet the approval of the spirit of old Jimmag who had spent most of his life at Crowlick. It was the only experience of the supernatural that Willie had had in his long and varied life.

**Top.** The little crofts of Coille Dhubh (left) and Crowlick (right) on the southern shore of Loch Hourn opposite the Mialairidh peninsula.

**Middle Left**. Willie Campbell (right) in Camusban with local characters, Johnny Sinclair (left) and Archie MacLean (1950s). **Right**. In Willie Campbell's young days, his Uncle Jimmag Stoddart, stalker/watcher on the Barrisdale Estate (centre) lived at Crowlick with his mother and Willie's Granny Kirsty (nee Douglas). Willie greatly enjoyed spending his school holidays there. **Below.** When Willie holidayed in Crowlick as a boy, the next door neighbours at Coille Dhubh were Duncan MacPherson, his wife Kirsty (nee Morrison) and their family who had moved earlier from their home at Rudha Ruadh.

**Bottom Left**. Willie Campbell's sister, Chrissie (right) seen here with Rena MacDonald (left) and Chrissie Morrison (nee MacCuaig) at a Clay Pigeon Shoot in Arnisdale in the 1960s, looked after her Uncle Jimmag at Crowlick after her grandmother died. **Right**. Willie Campbell (left) and his brother Angus in their latter years. Angus worked for many years on the Arnisdale estate. Angus was a fine piper and played for the Arnisdale shinty team in the battles with Glenelg in the 1930s.

**Top Left.** Willie Campbell (left) in his beloved Knoydart with cousins Johnny MacKay and Duncan MacKay.
**Right**. Willie with cousin Jimmy Mackay.

**Middle Left**. Jimmy Campbell from Corran, a nephew of Willie Campbell, worked for his uncle as an apprentice joiner before the outbreak of the second World War. **Right**. The marriage of Willie Campbell and Janet (Nettie) MacPherson from Glenelg at Kylerhea in 1935.

**Bottom Left**. Donald and Eric Campbell of Letterfearn who have continued the joinery and building business of their father in the Glenshiel, Glenelg and Loch Hourn areas. **Right**. The very large Loch Hourn fish farm now owned by Nutreco operates very close to Crowlick. Meanwhile the occupants of Crowlick and Coille Dhubh, Mick Simpson and Peter Carr continue their own fishing and shellfish initiatives in the area.

# Chapter 29

**Archie, his unique video record and his stories.**

When this book was first mooted in December 1996, one of the foremost thoughts of the author was to visit two old Arnsdale worthies - Archie MacLean in Camusban and Angus Campbell in Lairg. Both had reached, or were close to, their four score years and ten and while we 'knoweth not what an hour or a day may bring' to any of us, time was of the essence to visit Archie and Angus in particular. Both were in rapidly failing health at the time. Plans were made to visit both over the Christmas-New Year holiday period but - alas, alas, the flu bug struck the author at the planned time for the visits and both Archie and Angus were lost to this world - and all their wonderful Arnsdale and Loch Hourn memories with them in January 1997. It was another example of the regret felt by so many - 'It's a pity I didn't listen more carefully to the old folk and write down some of their stories' or 'if only I had gone to see them last year instead of leaving it until it was too late!'

However, in the case of both Archie and Angus, others have wonderful memories of both and these are recorded among these pages. Moreover, Archie's widow Betty is still with us, residing in the old family home in Camusban, so a visit was arranged to collect some photographs of Archie and his exploits through nine decades. Betty, still very hale, hearty and joyful, could not have been more helpful as she raided picture frames adorning her living room, boxes and drawers to find the sought after photographs. After obtaining some fine reminiscences of their own married life - Archie and Betty had married relatively late in life - Betty commented casually 'Oh, did you know about the thesis that was written about Archie?' And then an even more interesting question 'Have you seen the video of him when he was painting the boat?'

When such bait is dangled, the author is notorious for his lightning pouncing on such quarry, and soon both thesis and video were in his grasp with firm promises of their safe return after careful scrutiny. Both turned out to be wonderful treasures - great memory chests! First of all, let us have a look at the video through Archie's totally natural and free-flowing commentary - expletives and 'Archieisms' as well.

The video was produced by Bill Hurt from Penicuik in Midlothian. Bill, now retired from his post of Director of Medical Illustration at the University of Edinburgh had been Archie and Betty's next door neighbour over several summer holidays. The house next door to Archie had been leased by Bill's boss, Professor Donald Weir, and Donald provided Bill with the opportunity to take advantage of his lease and to enjoy Arnsdale, its people, places, the very interesting range of weather conditions - and all the stories! So Bill knew Archie very well, Archie liked Bill and had full confidence in him and the outcome of their empathy, in the form of the video, is a veritable gem to those interested in Arnsdale lore and the Arnsdale way of telling a story.

The video, accompanied initially by Hebridean music appropriate to the scenery and the subject matter, first spans Archie's favourite haunts and captures the aspects of the Loch Hourn environment which were dearest to his heart. There, on a beautiful late Spring-early Summer's day, towering above, are Beinn Sgritheall and Beinn na h-eaglaise, with Knoydart across the water, and Skye with the majestic Cuillins to the west. Then the camera focuses on the Mialairidh Forest where Archie's grandfather was employed and where his father was born, at Port Luinge. Then the camera scans back to the Rarsaidh Islands and Eilean Rarsaidh where the Camusban tups were 'incarcerated' when not required for their seasonal work and where Archie and Betty kept a wayward billy goat for a time! Then the camera focuses in turn on the little cottage and beautiful shoreline of Rarsaidh, on Eilean Tioram (the dry island) where the Camusban hoggs spent their winter nights, on the beautiful arc of the Camusban bay, the village and eastwards to the lodge, the farm and the Crudh Ard headland which hid Corran from the eye of the lens. And beyond - Barrisdale and upper Loch Hourn. Then there are fine shots of the flora and the fauna - the wild yellow iris and the mauve rhododendron, the seabirds, a hunting otter on the prowl - and then a focus on the village - moving from the base of the Arnisdale brae, passing each house in turn - past Allt an Beag and the Allt a' mhuilinn - where the camera catches up with a brace of Camusban cross-bred hoggs in fine fettle, as they walk together with some grace and purpose past the Camusban post-box and Archie's shed by the roadside. Then the camera, after a fine preamble, catches its real quarry - Archie - painting his upturned boat between the high water mark and the roadside.

The cameraman and interviewer (Bill Hurt) is cleverly unobtrusive, coaxing Archie's memory bank with brief questions on matters which are dear to Archie's memory and on which he can comment with clarity and authority. Archie, for his part, is his ever natural self, seemingly totally unconscious of the prying camera and recorder, and telling his stories with great fluency and flair in his typical Arnisdale dialect and the Arnisdale way of expressing himself - with his great lightheartedness and humour shining through as each story allows.

The 'interview' and Archie's responses run along the following lines, as Archie, resplendent in his breeches, hose and brogues, warm jumper and 'fore and aft', busily paints the hull of his boat.

"How many people were in the village in your young days, Archie?"

"Oh, there would be a hundred anyhow - oh yes - I would think so in the olden days". "There was how many when the fishing was on - five thousand - five thousand employed on the big herring fishing in Loch Hourn - it was around 1888, I think". "The herring were so plentiful they used to come ashore. My mother remembered it".

"Was the herring fishing finished when you were young, Archie?"
"Oh, yes - yes, I don't remember anything about it. A little herring came in after that but never like the early days. At the time of the big herring fishing it was the drift nets they used. There was no trawling or ring nets or anything of that sort. There were two pubs here then - and two policemen - two policemen in Arnisdale! (Great chortle from Archie). There used to be great fights with the people that used to be trawling the herring. The trawling was not on the go in these days so when the trawlers came in there were big fights between the other men and the men who were trawling".

(Mild expletive from Archie as he tried to catch a stray run of paint with his painting rag - Och - mo thogair!). And then he resumed -

"There was a pub there (pointing to the Fletcher's house beside Allt a' mhuilinn), and there was another at Corran - and there was another at Skiary - up the loch at Skiary. There was another pub there. There was another pub in Glenelg and one at the ferry in Glenelg - every place was full of people then - thousands of them!" And as more paint started to run astray - "Och, damn it, its running all over!" - but very quickly Archie continued his story -

"It's then that the church was built - when the big fishing was here".

"Where did you go to school, Archie - was it in Skye?"

"No, there were two schools here. There was a school room at Corran - the brae going down to it is still called the 'Schoolhouse Brae'. Then there was one along there at the back of the houses where they built the byres (Archie pointed to the other side of Alltan Beag and behind the house of Charlie and

Mary Kate MacTavish). That school was finished when I went to school - I went to that one" (pointing eastwards to the new school - now sadly closed).

"Were they good schools?"

"Well, I couldn't tell you - I'm sure it was just what was going then. There was a schoolmaster - it's not long since he died - well, I suppose its a few years ago now - he was a Skyeman - MacKenzie to name. My mother used to go to school with him. There was a man Fraser staying over there just across the burn (Allt a' mhuilinn) - Malcolm Fraser. He went abroad as a young boy when he left school. He came back on holiday when I suppose he would be thirty to forty years. He went to see my mother to talk about the olden days - he used to go to school with her. They were counting how many children went to school in their day. They counted 80. I don't know how many more were going to school in Corran at the time. Good gracious - 80 going to school - you'll be lucky to find eight people in the village now! (A hearty Archie laugh!). The few children left in Arnisdale go to the school in Glenelg now - they go there every morning. (Then the paint ran amok again) - Damn it, look at that stuff - och - I don't need to bother!"

"What about the Arnisdale postman who was drowned up the loch, Archie?"
"Yes, Duncan Campbell from Corran - he lived there with his wife. I don't think they had any family. I was in school at the time. It was his last day on the posting - he was retiring. He used to take big buckets of whisky, I think. He was delivering his last mails up the loch and was saying goodbye to them at Caolasmor. 'This is my last day' he said - it was his last day all right. It was a bad day with heavy showers of hailstones and snow. As he left Caolasmor, he said goodbye to them but added 'I'll be back to see you now and again - I'll be coming up to fish and I'll be calling to see you for a cup of tea'. It was a sail he had on his boat - there were no motors then. Just as he was leaving, there was a big shower of hailstones and a strong gust of wind. MacRae, the Caolasmor keeper was worried and said to his wife 'I hope he'll be all right' - he went out to the door. He looked for Duncan but - there was the boat upside down in the water and no sign of Duncan. MacRae made off down the path to Corran as quickly as he could and raised the alarm. The Corran men responded immediately and set off up the loch in their boats to Caolasmor. They searched at the spot where the boat overturned, coming ashore for safety between the showers and the worst gusts of the wind. But darkness came down and they had to abandon the search for Duncan for the day. Back up the loch they came the next day with big nets and lines with hooks on them - they would get bodies with them - but after two days of scraping and scratching the seabed they found no sign of Duncan's body. On the third day, MacRae the keeper said to his wife 'I think I'll have a look along the shore' - so off he set and he found him - he found Duncan's body - he was above the high water mark. He had swum ashore - he was a great swimmer - he had perished with the cold - he was old - over sixty or probably seventy - because that's when they were retiring then. I was a little boy going to school at the time - I barely remember it - I just faintly remember the hullabaloo".

(Note - Apparently Duncan suffered from diabetes and may have had a diabetic coma after succeeding in his superhuman efforts to swim to the shore in such cold, stormy conditions).

"Tell me about where you were born, Archie - down past Rarsaidh?"

"Where my father was born? - down at Port Luinge - did you see the ruins of the house there when you were down? My grandfather was watching the forest - the Mialairidh Forest - there was a big oak wood there at the time. They used to come in boats and were pinching the wood and selling it. That was my grandfather's job - he was watching the wood - he was the watcher.

One day some people came to cut the wood - legally.  My grandfather was out of tobacco and he was going mad for the want of tobacco - he couldn't get to Glenelg for his tobacco.  My Granny said to these people 'Its a good job you came - the old man in the house there is going daft for tobacco'.  'Well', they said 'we're very sorry - we don't smoke - none of us smoke'.  After supper every night these men would go along the shore for a walk and my granny twigged something.  A few days later - the day the men were going away, my granny was doing the beds when, under one of the pillows, she found a roll of Black Twist tobacco.  She gave it to the old man and never said a word.  These people weren't up to much, were they - and the poor man going daft for the want of a smoke!"

"I'll tell you another story about myself.  I was shooting seals and skinning them and selling the skins - you got a lot of money for them then.  One day I went down in the boat to Rarsaidh.  I had an outboard motor  - a Johnston motor, I think it was called - it was of American make.  Near Rarsaidh Island I saw a seal and I fired at him and I got him.  You had to get him into the boat quickly before all the air would go out of him and he would sink.  So I soon got close to him and got a rope round his neck - he was a big monster of a beast but I managed to get him into the boat.  That was that, so I went to the stern and started the engine.  Then I saw the seal moving, the tail of the seal was flapping.  By crumbs, I said, I'll have to do something about this.  So I  got one of the small rollers in the boat and went forward and gave the seal a good crack on the head with the roller.  Good gracious, what happened when I was busy at this but the engine swung round, jumped out of the water and lifted itself into the boat.  The Johnston engine had to be swung round for reversing the boat - it was a bad thing.  That's why it swung round when I was knocking the seal on the head and it came swinging round and right out of the water and into the boat.  Luckily the engine was tied to the boat - if not it was away - as it lifted itself out of the water.  However, now it was on the seat of the boat swinging from side to side with the propeller going like blazes.  What could I do?  How could I get to the engine as the propeller was blazing away in front of me and swinging from side to side across the seat of the boat between me and the controls?  There was a red knob on the controls for stopping it so I got one of the oars in desperation and I aimed the oar at the red button - and by good luck - I got it - and it stopped the engine.  Gosh, I got a terrible fright that day".

"Something similar happened to the MacAskill boys from Corran - Alan and Lachie - one day they were up the loch fishing and trying to get a seal for its skin.  They saw a seal, shot it, got it into the boat quickly before it would sink - and then carried on fishing.  They had the lines out for their fishing when Lachie saw the seal moving.  'That seal is living', said Lachie - 'put a shot in the bugger'.  'No' said Alan, 'that will put a hole in the boat - the shot will go through the boat' - it was a .22 they had.  'Well what do you want us to do' said Lachie, 'do you want it to eat the feet off us?  Put a shot in it!'  The seal was getting stronger and stronger - it was reviving and started flapping about in the boat, slapping against the side of the boat.  As the boat started to rock, Alan got frightened himself and he got so excited that he grabbed the .22 in desperation and shot - but missed the seal and the shot went through the boat!  Lachie was angry as he shouted at Alan 'I told you that, I told you that - we'll be drowned now!' as the water began to pour into the boat.  'Shut up, shut up', blazed Alan, 'put your finger in the hole!'  Lachie responded quickly to the desperate crisis by twisting his hankie and plugged the twisted cotton into the hole to stem the rushing inroad of seawater.  The hole was down the side of the boat so they further reduced the danger by rolling the seal to the other side of the boat after shooting it in the head, put their own weight on that side also and kept the boat on its side like this as they made for the shore as quickly and carefully as they could.  Having made it safely home, Alan soon plugged the hole in the boat.  He was good with his hands, was Alan.  He got a plank, cut it, and fixed a piece on the outside and another piece on the inside and it was fine.  There were a lot of seals in those days and you were allowed to shoot them but you're not allowed to shoot them now".

"What about the salmon, Archie?"

"Oh, the salmon - you are not allowed to get the salmon - but I used to get a few on the quiet. When I was in my trim, I remember Margaret's son (Neil MacDougall) coming home on holiday and we saw the salmon jumping close to the shore - just out there. We quickly put the boat out with the net and - oh boy! - the salmon that went into that net - we got 52 I think it was - in one haul. That's enough, I said. There were some monsters - about this size (stretching his arms almost as far as he could). There was a lot about two to three pounds - a nice lovely size. But I didn't care much for the salmon - I'm not a salmon man - but I liked going after them with the net. I would get them any time. Now its the police that take to do with that - in the olden days it was the keepers. In the old days it was the keeper who would be after you for the salmon. But now it's the law - which is terrible!

"And did you like the deer, Archie?"

"Oh yes - you can shoot deer if they come in on your croft. You can shoot them and sell them if you like. There will be very cold days yet - in June and July - with bad showers - I'll be on the lookout then. I shot one on the croft one morning in the second year after I came home. Oh, it was a monster, boy. I could hardly budge him - it went into a drain. I couldn't move it. I couldn't drag him out. I had to go for the tractor to drag it down to the back of the house. I left it lying there until I got my breakfast. Friends of Peter's (Peter Buneman) were staying in the schoolhouse and one of them was an American girl. When she heard about the stag, she came out with her camera to get photos of the beast. She took photos of it every way she could. A year or two afterwards she was up at Kinlochourn and she showed the Birkbecks the photos - the Birkbecks were the lairds! She told them that Archie next door had shot this fine stag. Iain MacKenzie was up at Loch Hourn, saw the photos at the Birkbecks and returned to report to Archie that he had seen photos of a fine stag lying dead behind Archie's house at the Birkbecks. Oh, bloody hell, I said, fancy showing the photos to the lairds - they would not be a bit pleased about that!

But you can now shoot the deer if they are on your own croft and you can sell them if you like. The Crofters' Commission have brought this about. Of course, the lairds don't like that - they tried to stop it and they would stop it yet if they could. You see, the lairds don't like the crofters - oh no - they see the crofters as a curse on the land! That's the way, boy - that's the way with Archie - with Archie and the stags".

With that Archie thought about his painting and enquired of the cameramen if he could see any spots not painted on the first side of the boat. With the first side appearing to have a complete coat, Archie concluded "That side will do" and proceeded to paint the other half. Then he continued his yarns.

"I couldn't see a rabbit last night. Well, there were hundreds of wee ones - well, not hundreds - but eight or ten of them. I think there were about ten roaming about, but nothing that you could shoot to eat". And then there was an invitation to the cameraman and his family, "will you come in with the camera tonight - all of you - and we'll have a wee nippy - what you call a dram!"

"Did you work for any of the lairds round about, Archie?"

"Just one season I went stalking for them - not this laird but one of the old lairds. Och, I didn't like working for them. It was difficult to get a job then. Most of my working life was spent away from Arnisdale. I used to go away to do shepherding and stalking in the season. Oh, I liked chasing the deer - oh, I liked chasing the deer - it was grand!"

Two cars had passed while Archie had been painting his boat. As each car approached, Archie would stop his painting, straighten himself up and give a hearty wave of apparently instant recognition to the passers-by. But just as it passed Archie would enquire "Who was that?"

As a few people approached from the west on foot, Archie remarked "Awful busy today. Fearful crowd there - fearful crowd altogether!" And then as the 'fearful crowd' passed the boat, Archie greeted them warmly "Good morning, its a grand day. Going out in the sun? Down the Glen? Well, you should take plenty coats with you. And then as they were out of earshot - "Oh hell - one, two, three, four, five, six, seven, eight, isn't it?" Archie then asked the cameraman if he was going up to Scourie (Sutherland) later in the week. This was confirmed and Archie was asked if he knew that area.

"No, I was never there but I was getting a job there once - but I didn't take it - heard it was too damn lonely - couldn't be much worse than Arnisdale!"

Then as the third car of the day passed, Archie had it identified immediately - "A Toyota, there is a Toyota".

The cameraman then coaxed Archie into his final story, enquiring about a ruined cottage - the last inhabitants of which had typhus.

Archie pointed westwards just beyond his garage at the bottom of his garden to the remnants of a wall into which the Camusban letter box is fitted. "That's where the letter box is - that's the one. Long, long, long ago - it was before my granny got married - my granny used to attend to them. They were sick and my granny was kind-hearted - they didn't know what was wrong with them. Then the Doctor came and after a while they discovered it was typhus. Nobody was allowed to go near them except those who were attending to them. Three or four of them died but some of them lived. Lexy, the mother of Mary Ann - the old woman who lives along there - she came through it and Granny came through it. But the rest of the family died and the Doctor died - yes - the doctor died too". The cameraman asked if that was the last of the old cottages of Arnisdale which were all close to the high tide mark and were all badly flooded by a very high tide in 1881. After that, all the houses, except two, were moved further back to their present line to avoid such flooding problems in the future. Archie confirmed the cameraman's suspicion - "Yes, that's it - that's one of the old cottages of Arnisdale. Nobody was allowed to go near it in case they would get the typhus. I remember when I was a little boy and I would be in the old ruins playing with the stones, Donald's father next door (Ali Fletcher) would come down and scold me 'Don't you dare touch any of these stones - do you want to be dead tomorrow? If you do any more of that, I'll go up and get your mother!' Ali was frightened to death of these stones. Och, I don't think you would get it out of these. I don't remember the old cottages close to the shore - I wasn't born at the time of the great high tide and the flood. I remember when that cottage had a roof on it but nobody stayed in it after the typhoid. The people in that other one along there beside the road (Johnny Sinclair's house) also had the typhoid and it was only rebuilt in the 1930s. The letter box landed on that wall on the suggestion of Donald Li. The postmaster came along looking for a place for the Camusban letter box and Donald said 'I'll tell you where you'll put it' and pointed to the wall of the last remnant of the old Camusban homes."

And then another passer-by appeared and, viewing the camera activity, enquired 'On the screen now, Archie?' "You'll see me on the telly tonight," responded Archie. 'We'll soon have to pay a pound to talk to you, Archie' joked his friend. 'Cheap at the price, cheap at the price' commented the cameraman (Bill Hurt).

Although the last comment of Bill was meant to be a flippant remark, Archie's video record is certainly 'cheap at the price' - a veritable treasure chest of old Arnisdale tales related with great flair, fluency and in inimitable fashion by one of Arnisdale's great characters - the one and only Archie.

As well as Bill Hurt's video being a valuable historical record, Archie was very proud of it himself and visitors to his and Betty's home would often be entertained by Archie showing them his video. Archie was also very proud of a thesis or dissertation which featured him. This was produced by Ann Eales as part of her Bachelor of Arts Degree Course at the University of Swansea in 1988. The thesis was entitled 'The dialect of Arnisdale, Wester Ross'. In lengthy conversations with Archie, Ann recorded aspects of his native Arnisdale dialect, with his unique words, phrases and his ways of expressing himself, which were influenced by his first language being Gaelic, with the transition to English only starting when he went to school.

Ann gleaned from Archie and others several other interesting pieces of historical interest. Mention is made of the 1772 Salt Tax Laws which made the salting and preservation of herring more difficult and more expensive. In these days of plenty in the Western world, it is difficult for us to conceive that a basic substance like salt was once very expensive and in short supply. The author, in discussing this aspect with his wife, Anne (daughter of Tony Mackay of Mialairidh Forest and Arnisdale ceilidh fame in the 1930s) was reminded of the fact that salt, because of its scarcity and value in these days, was often a part of the currency for both international and national trading, and its economic importance is commemorated in the names of such famous cities as Salzburg in Austria.

Ann Eales, in her thesis, refers to the decline in the population of Arnisdale from 600 in 1836 to around 40 in 1988 when she was carrying out her study. The potato blight of 1840 and the plague of typhus later (the typhus having been introduced by a sailor) were further causes of population decline. These disasters, and the fact that most of the population were living at or below subsistence level for most of the time, stimulated what Ann Eales terms as 'voluntary emigrations' between 1840 and 1850 and later periods, including those who joined in the American Civil War of 1861-65. The latter were able to send money back home to help their hard-pressed families in Arnisdale and other clachans on Loch Hourn. Ann further refers to the Great Storm of 1881 (the very high tide which flooded all the houses in Camusban and Corran - which hugged the shore line at that time) and the year of the Big Fishing in 1882. The fishing attracted the drift netters from all over Scotland and Ireland and also saw the sinister introduction of trawling by 'some southern boats', which culminated in a riot in Loch Hourn between the traditional fishermen, who were drift netting, and those new arrivals who were trawling. This riot culminated in the Riot Act being read in Loch Hourn at Runival Point in 1882.

Following the great high tide and the flooding of the houses in 1881, agreement was eventually reached with the laird to move the houses some 20 yards back from the shoreline to a higher and safer location. Ann reports that, in the late 19th century, Sir Michael Arthur Bass, head of the Bass Brewing Firm, on a visit to Arnisdale, watched a man thatching his roof. Discovering that this was a continuous task, owing to the inclement weather, he arranged for slates to be sent by boat (there being no road). This provided work for the Arnisdale tradesmen and labourers and ensured that the new houses were now capped by a permanent, rain and storm proof roof. Ann Eales comments further "Archie learned his English at school where his native Gaelic was forbidden. In the hearing of their schoolmistress, whether at school or outside, the speaking of English was compulsory".

Now, let us get back to some more details of the personal history of Archie and his family as provided by Betty, his widow.

Archie was born on 6 October 1907 and died in January 1997. His paternal grandfather (Duncan MacLean) was employed as a watcher in the Mialairidh oak forest, while his maternal grandmother (a MacPherson before her marriage) had married her husband, Archie MacTavish, at Barrisdale Church and they set up home in Archie's native Lochgilphead. But alas, Archie was drowned along with his fellow fisherman when their boat foundered a few years after their marriage and Archie's Granny MacTavish returned to Arnisdale with her young family (Duncan, Angan and Peggy - Archie's mother) to reside with her brother in Camusban. Archie's father Donald John and his mother had five of a family - Mary Anne (later Mrs Arthur), Margaret (later Mrs Colin MacDougall), Ina (later Mrs Semple), Johan and Archie, who was the youngest. Archie's father, Donald John was a crofter/stonemason/joiner/undertaker who got seasonal paid work from the neighbouring estates during the stalking season in particular. Just before Archie was born, his father was working in Barrisdale and was involved in building a bridge across the river on one of the major burns - almost certainly the bridge would be for the stalking to get the shooting party - including the ponies - across swollen streams without getting soaking feet and risking their lives on occasions. In the building of the bridge, heavy incessant rain had resulted in a swollen torrent and the men were wading waist deep in water at times as they built their bridge. Water in a Barrisdale October is not only wet, but also very cold, and Archie's father got pneumonia as a result. He came home to Arnisdale because of his condition and, as Archie was coming into the world in one room in their little Camusban cottage, his father was fighting for his life in the other room. Very sadly, the battle was lost and Archie's father died the day after Archie was born.

So Archie never knew his father. However, he had his loving mother and four equally doting sisters to bring him up and look after him. Did they spoil him? Some would say that they did! Others would say that, if they did spoil him, they made a very good job of it, for Archie was one of nature's gentlemen - courteous, humorous, ever helpful to his neighbours and others, he was great company, and a veritable delight to know.

Various references are made to Archie elsewhere in this book. These include his work in the Arnisdale Forestry Squad in the 1930s with Bill Stoddart, Tony Mackay, Jimmy MacLean and many Arnisdale, Sandaig and Glenelg cronies. He was also the semaphore expert in the Arnisdale 'Dad's Army' in the Home Guard during the war. And he always tried to be progressive in his crofting practices, such as his valiant attempts to mechanise his hay cutting and carting, by converting an old car into a little truck and pulling the mower with this vehicle. This inventiveness failed only because the 'truck' used to travel too fast for the mower, or because the mower, and its mechanisms failed to keep pace with the speed of the truck!

However, the latter memories of Archie in the author's boyhood days obviously followed Archie's first ownership of a vehicle with an internal combustion engine. This story was told to Betty, Archie's widow, who recently related it to the author. When the car was first delivered to the front of Archie's house, Archie had never started, driven or controlled such a vehicle before. He thought that the safest place to learn the rudiments of driving and steering would be in his hayfield at the back of the house - on the lower slopes of Beinn na h-eaglaise. So Archie persuaded a friend to drive the vehicle to the top of the field. After some brief instructions from his friend, Archie ensconced himself in the driver's seat and gripped the steering wheel with pride. With a few turns of the starting handle by his friend, the vehicle soon purred into life. His friend then went round to the proud occupant of the driving seat, told him to put his foot on the left hand pedal (the clutch) and put the gear lever in the required direction to engage first gear. Archie was then instructed to take his foot slowly off the left hand pedal. Archie obeyed the instructions to the letter and - off the vehicle sped with Archie full of boyish excitement, in control! Or was he? As the vehicle sped in first gear down Archie's little field, his friend thought that Archie was 'having him on' as was his wont, as the vehicle and Archie made a beeline for the wooden byre behind the house. It was just brinkmanship on Archie's part and he would swing the vehicle round at the very last moment, evade the byre and turn up the field again on his practice run! But no - his friend could only stand aghast as the byre loomed closer and closer to Archie and his machine - and then - bang! The gable end of the precious byre was breached but the vehicle was brought to a halt and stalled - at least the byre prevented Archie and the vehicle careering down across the road and down the shore into the sea!

But what of the wrecked byre?

Well, Archie was good with his hands and was well capable of carrying out the necessary major repairs - but it was not so straightforward as that!

This was because the introduction of the new vehicle to the croft, and Archie's ill fated baptism to driving, took place on a Sabbath morning. Archie's mother was still alive and she was a strict adherent to only the 'works of necessity and mercy' on the Sabbath Day. It was too risky to leave the repairs to the Monday, for Archie's mother might well have decided to come out for a stroll, to come round the back of the house of the croft to view the scene, including the towering hills above - and even to milk the cows in the evening.

Archie had to act immediately and as silently as he could. So he muffled the hammer by covering it with one of his old stockings and got to work on the repairs. He was as cute as ever as he went about restoring the byre to its former glories and he got the job done without his mother being in any way aware of his 'accident' and the desecration of the Sabbath day. As one of Archie's sisters told Betty after relating the story to her - "If mother had known about it - she would have killed him!"

Archie always had an eye for the ladies and he tried very hard from his teenage years to meet one that would meet his heart's desire for the rest of his days. But he had many failures - and perhaps by the time he finally met and married the love of his life (Betty) at the age of fifty-five, he was beginning to give up hope - or perhaps people like Archie are always hopeful and thoroughly optimistic.

Betty herself tells the story of their whirlwind romance. Betty, who belongs to Norfolk, was employed by British Road Services at the time and evaded the relative monotony of her work by escaping to the Highlands and West Coast for walking tours during her summer holidays. Betty had stayed at the Youth Hostel at Kylerhea Ferry at Glenelg on several occasions, and on a particular Saturday in 1962, found herself there but fancied spending the rest of the weekend somewhere else - but had little idea of where she might go. The Kylerhea Ferry at the time was being operated by Murdo MacKenzie (Li), son of Donald Ban and Lisa, who had by this time retired from crofting at Li to Camusban. Assisting Murdo at the Ferry was his cousin, Iain MacKenzie from Arnisdale. Betty had got to know Murdo and Iain from frequent chats between their ferry crossings to and from Skye. So off she set down to the pier to have a blether with the two ferrymen. In the course of conversation, the uncertainty over where Betty might go for the weekend arose, with various possibilities being mooted. Then Iain said to Betty "Why not come to Arnisdale with me and stay with my sister Nellie and her family?" Iain was persuasive, so the pair of them set off for Arnisdale after the last run of the ferry had been completed for the day.

Betty got a welcome from Nellie and they were soon discussing where they might go to ceilidh later in the evening. Nellie, perhaps with a bit of matchmaking at the back of her mind, suggested to Betty that they might go to visit Johan MacLean and her brother Archie in Camusban. Betty, being a guest, fell in with Nellie's suggestion. They arrived at Johan's house at about 9 p.m. but Nellie was disappointed that there was no sign of Archie. After a while, Nellie enquired of Johan as to Archie's whereabouts - "Oh, Archie's in his bed - he had a busy day at the hay and he was tired", responded Johan. Then Nellie encouraged Johan - "Go and tell him that I have a nice lady here to see him". Johan obviously agreed with Nellie's description of her visitor and duly transmitted the message to the bedded Archie. Archie's response was immediate - and totally unexpected in view of his constant life-long desire to find a nice woman! "I'm not getting up tonight for any woman", was his curt reply to Johan. Although Johan dutifully relayed his response to her visitors, they already knew of his response because it had come across to them loud and clear from Archie's bedroom.  So the night's ceilidh continued without Archie - probably to the disappointment of the scheming Nellie and Archie's devoted and loving sister Johan, while Betty's inquisitiveness as to who 'Archie' was, and what he looked like, was not satisfied as she had already heard quite a bit about the famous Archie - mainly from Nellie's teasing.   When Johan and Archie rose the next morning, Johan must have got the message across to Archie that he 'missed out' by not getting up to see the nice visitor on the previous evening and that he might have missed a good chance.

Archie obviously was listening carefully and Johan's description of the lady was exciting his curiosity and his interest.  Johan's persuasion was successful.  The bold Archie decided that he would set off on his motorbike and sidecar to Corran, to meet up with this woman whom he had 'spurned' on the previous evening.  He got to Corran, walked in Nellie's door, shouting as he went - "Where is this woman who was looking for me last night?".  When he got in, Archie and 'this woman' were duly introduced by Nellie and Nellie quickly had some tea and scones on the table, trying to buy time to give a possible liaison more of a chance to develop.  As Archie, Nellie and Betty blethered generally about this and that, Archie was obviously carefully weighing up 'the woman' and perhaps 'the woman' was examining Archie and trying to 'read' him.  The tea and the blethering had gone so far and things were all very pleasant when the brave Archie enquired of 'the woman' if she would like to go for a little run on his motor bike.  Betty took the chance - and off the two of them sped.  Archie stopped at Rarsaidh because he had some sheep to check on there.  After doing this, they walked through the Rarsaidh croftlands towards the little cottage.  When they reached the cottage, Archie commented quite coolly - "What do you think of that house - you and I could stay there when we get married!".  The bold Archie had weighed up 'the woman' and the situation and he was not going to miss another chance, as he had done by choosing to lie in his bed on the previous evening, rather than get up and meet 'the woman' as invited to do so by sister Johan.

Betty and Archie were married within three months of this momentous day for them both  on 19 October 1962.  Archie was 55 at the time but they enjoyed 34 years of married bliss together.  Their wedding took place in the Glenelg Church of Scotland Manse with the late Eddie MacRae, Lub an eorna (latterly Letterfearn), as best man and Betty's niece Frances Hurt, and Archie's great-niece, Fiona Douglas, as bridesmaids.   There is little doubt that Archie and Betty talked to each other a lot from time to time about the role of Iain MacKenzie and his sister Nellie in bringing them together for the very happy married life they shared joyfully.

**Top Left**.  The MacLean family cottage in Camusban with the croftland behind.  Archie reads his newspaper in the doorway to catch up with the happenings in the world.  **Right**.  Archie resplendent in Highland dress for a special occasion (1950s).

**Middle Left.**  At the door of Archie's shed by the roadside – a common place for a gathering of Arnisdale folk to exchange news, catch up with Archie's 'crack' and put the world to rights!  L to R.  Johnnie Murchison, Alistair Fletcher, Kenny Fletcher, Angus Stewart, Archie MacLean and Lachie Fletcher (mid 1930s).  **Right**.  Archie about to take off for a spin on his motorbike (mid 1930s).

**Bottom Left**.  Back to Archie's schooldays in 1919.  Archie is second left in the back row in this Arnisdale School group.  **Right**.  The remains of Archie's grandparents' house beside the shore at Port Luinge in Mialairidh.  Archie's grandfather, Duncan MacLean, was the Watcher of the Mialairidh Oak forest.  Archie's father, Donald John was born at Mialairidh.  Archie tells the story of his grandfather 'going mad for the want of tobacco'.

**Top Left**. Archie was the youngest in his family of five, having four older sisters. Archie's father, Donald John, died of pneumonia on the day that Archie was born. Despite, or perhaps because of, the sad loss of his father, Archie was very well cared for by his mother Peggy and his four older sisters. L to R. Margaret, Johan, Mary Anne and baby Ina. **Right**. Archie feeding the Eilanreach estate hoggs at Rarsaidh during winter. Archie for a time worked for the Eilanreach Estate as a stalker/shepherd. He knew the Rarsaidh – Mialairidh area very well and seemed to have a particular attachment to it.

**Middle Left**. Archie's sister Johan who remained with Archie in the old family home while her other sisters went away to work and eventually married. **Right**. Archie (right) with sister Ina and cousin Charlie MacTavish (around 1960).

**Bottom Left**. Archie (left) with next door neighbour Mabel Fletcher and friend Sandy Douglas (around 1935).
**Right**. The ruin beside the road between the Fletcher and MacLean houses had particular significance. This was the house in which Mairi Bhan MacKenzie's mother and father had died of Typhus around 1890. As a small boy, Archie was told never to touch the stones for fear of infection and the ruin has remained without interference ever since apart from the Camusban letter box being installed on its roadside wall.

**Top Left**. Archie having a spy to check the movements of the stags on the slopes of Beinn Sgritheall and Beinn na h-eaglaise above the croft land. (around 1990). **Right**. A deer fence surrounding the croft land at one time prevented access by the deer but now in need of repair, the stags raid the croft land in the early spring with Johan keeping an eye on them (around 1970). Archie was more interested in the stags when they put on a bit of condition on the late spring and summer grass.

**Middle Left** Archie and Willie MacKenzie exchange news in the Gaelic as 'Willie the Post' the second nears the end of his daily deliveries of mail (around 1990). **Right**. Archie and neighbour Donald Fletcher relax on a fine autumn day but from time to time will be checking on any movement of salmon along the shoreline below.

**Bottom**. Archie had a great way with the children (left), with the sheep and the dogs (centre), with the swans (right), with all the animals and also with all the folk - but despite his great popularity, Archie had difficulty finding a good wife.

**Top**. Fate and subtlety played their parts in Archie meeting his life's partner. Betty, holidaying at the time at the Kylerhea Youth Hostel, close to the Kylerhea Ferry (left) decided to go away for the weekend but was not sure where she might go. On chatting to the Kylerhea ferrymen, Iain and Murdo MacKenzie, Iain (right) suggested that Betty should go with him to Arnisdale and Corran and stay with his sister Nellie.
**Middle Left**. Nellie made her weekend guest very welcome at Corran and introduced Betty to several of her friends, including Archie.
**Right**. Archie invited Betty to accompany him on his motorbike to go to check the sheep at Rarsaidh, Betty consented and, after the sheep were attended to and as they approached the house at Rarsaidh, Archie announced that this would be a 'good house for them when they got married!'
**Bottom Left**. Archie did not wish to waste any more time and Betty was of the same mind! Archie, at the age of 55, and Betty were married three months later in Glenelg. They had 34 fine years together. **Right**. Betty's niece Frances Hurt and Archie's great niece, Fiona Douglas were bridesmaids and Eddie MacRae, Lub an Eorna (far right) was the best man.

372

**Top**. In addition to being a fine wife, Betty was very adept at helping with the hay (left) and with planting, weeding and lifting the potatoes as well as helping with the sheep on the croft which lies on the east side of Allt a' Mhuilinn (right).

**Middle**. They found time to talk and watch (left) and rest together (right).

**Bottom**. Archie found time to paint his boast in a leisurely way (left) and at the same time to relate some of his fine stories on video to Bill Hurt (right).

**Top**.  Archie told Bill Hurt about the fankle he once got in after shooting a seal and graphically described a similar experience of his friends at Corran, brothers Lachie MacAskill (left) and (right) Alan MacAskill (second from right).

**Middle**.  Archie related the story about the great fights among the herring fishermen – between those who were practising the traditional drift netting and those who started the trawling – and the reading of the Riot Act at Runival Point (left) in 1882.   He mentioned that there were once two pubs in Arnisdale and one at Skiary (right – the remains of the Skiary Pub).  In the great days of the herring fishing there were two policemen in Arnisdale!

**Bottom Left**.  Archie had many more stories to tell such as escapades in Arnisdale's 'Dads Army' in World War 2.  Archie seen here (left), accompanied at the clipping by Roddy Mor and young Callum Kennedy around 1936, was the semaphore expert in the Home Guard.
**Right**.  Archie would also have many yarns about working in the Mialairidh Forest when planting conifers in the 1930s –replacing the great oak wood in which his grandfather had been the 'Watcher'.  Archie is third from the left in the front row of this Mialairidh Forest Squad picture of around 1935.  However, despite Archie's stories which have been lost, we are very glad to have those he did record along with his unique way of telling them.

## Chapter 30

**The MacLeans - the Arnisdale 'Merchants'.   Peggy Ann and Mary**

As one enters Arnisdale after descending the steep brae, the first house is that of the MacLeans and in the author's boyhood the residents were Peggy Ann and Mary.   Their forebears had established the main 'Merchants' business last century, or even earlier, to supply the Arnisdale and Loch Hourn communities, and the herring fishermen, with their basic requirements.   In turn, the MacLean's 'goods' were delivered by boat from Mallaig in later years while in earlier times, weekly supplies were collected from the Glasgow boat when it stopped off at Isleornsay in Skye.

Peggy Ann's grandfather, Duncan MacLean, had married Peggy MacInnes from Skye and in Duncan MacTavish's memories of his youth at the end of last century, Duncan and Peggy were occupying House 23 in Camusban along with their five sons and two daughters.   One of these sons was John MacLean (Peggy Ann's father) while another son, Donald John, was Archie MacLean's father (See Chapter 29).   So that Peggy Ann and Archie were first cousins.

However, in addition to occupying House 23, running his little croft and fishing, grandfather Duncan MacLean was also employed by the Glenelg Estate as a watcher on the Mialairidh oak forest.   When undertaking this responsibility, Duncan and his family were resident in the house on the shore of Loch Hourn at Port Luinge.   This was a strategic position from which Duncan could keep an eye on boats coming in stealthily from other coastal areas, Skye and other islands to plunder some of the fine oaks to build their boats.

Not far along the shoreline from Port Luinge towards Arnisdale at that time were many other cottages and a shop.   This clachan was situated where the forestry hut was sited in the 1920s and 1930s when the Mialairidh Forest area was being planted with conifers by the likes of Bill Stoddart, Tony Mackay, Jimmy MacLean and many others from Arnisdale and Glenelg.

Whether or not the shop at this Mialairidh clachan was being run by the MacLean family is not known.   With the herring fishing at its height in the nineteenth century, undoubtedly the little shop got plenty of trade.   In the earlier part of the nineteenth century, the shop may have obtained its goods from as far away as Glasgow, the coastal puffers from the Clyde making regular deliveries of goods to the many villages and clachans up the coastline, including that on the Mialairidh shore.   Later in the century when the railhead was established at Mallaig, the goods to supply the merchants operating on the adjacent coastline would have been supplied from that port.

Whether or not the MacLeans were involved with the shop on the Mialairidh Forest clachan is not known but Peggy Ann's father, John MacLean (Johnnie Ruadh), ran the Arnisdale merchant's business from around the 1870s or perhaps from even earlier.

This was the main 'shopping centre' for the many clachans on the Loch Hourn shoreline including the folk at Loch Hournhead and Glen Quoich.   Representatives of the various households in a clachan would, in their boats powered by oars and sail, go for their 'messages' every fortnight or so, as sea conditions allowed, to the Arnisdale store.

John MacLean's first house and store was close to the Camusban shoreline so that goods could be transported to and from delivery and collecting boats very readily.   Later, however, after the disastrous high tide of 1881, another house was built further up the slope and hopefully out of reach of the highest possible tide.   Unlike the other 'new' houses built in Camusban after the great flood, which were single storey, Johnny Ruadh, who had the reputation of being a fine builder, erected a two-storey house with skylight windows upstairs.

Johnny Ruadh and his wife Ann (nee Fraser) had five daughters (Katie, Peggy Ann, Johan, Mary and Maggie ) and two sons, one of whom, Calum, died at three years of age while Duncan died in his late twenties.  This family probably had more contact with 'outsiders' than any other family in Arnisdale because the store was a mecca for all the Loch Hourn shoppers.

Perhaps it was such a meeting at the Arnisdale store with one of the members of a boatload of shoppers from Loch Hournhead that led to the marriage reported as follows in the Oban Times of Saturday, 29 June, 1901.

**"Arnisdale, Loch Hourn**

**Marriage Rejoicings.**  A very pretty wedding took place at Arnisdale on Tuesday, the 18th inst., when Miss Katie MacLean, eldest daughter of Mr John MacLean, merchant, Arnisdale, was married to Mr John Henderson, youngest son of Mr James Henderson, head gamekeeper, Glen Quoich.  The marriage ceremony took place in the Arnisdale Schoolhouse.  The officiating clergyman was Rev. Alex. MacTaggart, M.A., Glenelg.  The bride was stylishly and tastefully dressed in white and looked charming, and was attended by Miss Annie MacLean, Quarry, Glenelg, who acted as bridesmaid;  while the bridegroom was attended by Mr Alex Fletcher, as groomsman, who was dressed in the Highland garb.

Two boat loads of invited guests arrived from Glen Quoich and Loch Hournhead, and were enthusiastically received at the shore by the Arnisdale and Corran representatives.  Thereafter the bride and bridegroom with the invited company, headed by two pipers dressed in the Highland costume, marched to the Schoolhouse amid vociferous cheering.  Shortly after the marriage, a reception took place at the residence of the bride's father.  In the evening the company again marched in couples to the Schoolroom, where dancing took place to the strains of the piob'mhor till the small hours of the morning, each and all seeming to enjoy themselves to their heart's content.

The harmony and pleasantness that characterised the occasion was enjoyable throughout.  The presents to the bride were numerous.  On Thursday the happy couple left for their residence, Corry Buie, amid the hearty congratulations and good wishes of friends and acquaintances."

So ended the Oban Times report of what appeared to be a grand affair in Arnisdale almost 100 years ago.  One of the main suppliers of information and photographs for these pages on the MacLean family is Catherine Atkins, now resident in Stirling, who is a grand-daughter of Katie and John, the Arnisdale newly-weds of June 1901.

The main attendants on the young couple at the Arnisdale wedding were Alex Fletcher from Arnisdale and Annie MacLean, a cousin of the bride from Quarry, Glenelg.  Alex features along with the others of the Fletcher family in Chapter 18.  Annie was later to marry Donald Beaton, and their daughter Lolla (Mrs Calum Garde) was well known in Arnisdale and Glenelg while daughter Mimmie (Mrs Roddy MacPherson of Glenelg) is still hale and hearty at the time of writing.

While Katie MacLean made her home in Glen Quoich, her sister Johan became Mrs John MacDonald and was the teacher in Airor School for a long period.

The family members who remained at home to run the business, the house and the croft were Peggy Ann and Mary.  Peggy Ann assisted her father in the shop and the Post Office for many years, and from 1931 to 1958 she ran the business herself following her father's retirement;  Mary's role in the 'division of labour' was the working of the garden, the croft and keeping the house in good and tidy order .  Cooking and kitchen duties were shared.

The author remembers them as a fine, kindly pair.  There would be a welcome for everybody from

Mary as they went to do their shopping as she beavered away in her colourful garden with her well cared for and highly productive plots of vegetables and potatoes. She was a regular at the church services and, although in her 70s at the time, she was always at the dances as a spectator, smiling serenely as she watched the dancing - with her feet tapping in time with the music of the pipes, fiddle and accordion, and she relished the little chats with all her friends, giving and exchanging pieces of news and enjoying good humour.

Peggy Ann by this stage in the late 1940s would not venture too far away from her house, the adjacent shop and Post Office and the front garden. She too always had a great welcome for all who called and there was also plenty of time to catch up with the news. Probably Peggy Ann's was the main 'News Agency' in the Loch Hourn community, as members of all families would be calling there for their messages, pensions, stamps and postal orders - and to post their registered letters and parcels - at least once weekly. The Post Office also had the only telephone in the district for a very long time, so all incoming and outgoing emergency messages on illness and the well-being of dear ones in hospital came through Peggy Ann.

The postman at the time was 'Willie the Post' (Willie MacKenzie, Senior), later succeeded by his son Willie the Post the Second who himself has recently retired. All sorting of the Arnisdale mail was then carried out by Peggy Ann and Willie the Post. Johnnie Sinclair (and later in succession Ian MacCuaig, Calum Garde, Roddy Mor and Calum Lamont) would take the Arnisdale mail via the Glenelg Post Office (Donald MacPherson and later Donald and Charlotte Chisholm) in the morning and thereafter the mail would go on to Calum Garde's boat from Glenelg to Kyle for its onward journey. When Calum Garde and Donald John MacLeod returned from Kyle in the afternoon, the Arnisdale mail would be sifted off in the Glenelg Post Office and transported to Arnisdale in the Mail Car by Johnnie Sinclair or his successors. Peggy Ann and Willie the Post would be eagerly awaiting the sound of Johnnie's car coming down the steep gravel brae and would get stuck into the mail bag together, sorting out the letters and parcels in order for each house in Camusban and Corran. The mail for the other Loch Hourn coastline dwellings at Li, Barrisdale and Caolasmor would be kept separate, to be delivered by Willie on his thrice weekly runs to these locations in his little boat with his outboard motor. In the earlier days, the 'power drives' for Willie's boat were the oars and sail.

So Willie would deliver the mail and collect the money for the COD (Cash on Delivery) orders of clothes, shoes, hand tools such as graips or sheep shears, spare parts for outboard motors etc. He would also carry the news of the well-being of folk who were ill, about births, marriages and deaths - and of amusing stories and rumours. He would collect as many bits and pieces of news in return as Willie always made plenty of time to have a good chat at each port of call, particularly where there was illness and sadness in any household. Then as he and Peggy Ann were sorting out the morning and evening mail they could keep each other fully informed in the Gaelic about the well-being of folk and other items of interest and concern, while concentrating meticulously on the sorting of the letters and parcels.

The big 'business' day in Arnisdale was a Tuesday. That was the day when MacLennan's boat arrived from Mallaig around mid-day with all of the weekly 'goods'. First of all, the boat would come in to the jetty below the Lodge. There, materials ordered the previous week for the various crofts, the farm and the lodge would be unloaded. Then the boat would make its way round the Arnisdale bay and stop first in front of Johnnie MacGillivray's shop, offloading Johnnie's weekly order into a rowing boat which would then take the goods into the shore where several villagers would carry the boxes of bread, sugar, other groceries, sweets, household goods etc. up to Johnnie's shop. Thereafter the Mallaig boat would make its way round to Peggy Ann's where her weekly order would be transferred to another rowing boat and a few of the crofters would transport the materials from the shore to the shop. Peggy Ann, Mary and their helpers would then need an hour or so to open the boxes and stack the shelves and counter with the new food and other goods. Having allowed this time for getting things organised, there would then be a stream of people from Corran, Glenfield, the Farm, the Lodge and Camusban making their way on bikes or on foot to the two shops to purchase their weekly needs. Most would have run out of essential foodstuffs such as bread, tea and sugar by the Tuesday so hence the emphasis of all on making Tuesday the big shopping day.

While Peggy Ann was kind to everyone, she was particularly fond of the children and they would always get a special welcome when they went to collect 'messages' for their family. In the harsh rationing strictures of wartime and the post-war period when sweets were rationed and fruit was available only very rarely, no child would leave the shop without a 'handful' of sweets in his or her pocket. How Peggy Ann managed to balance her strictly rationed weekly allocation of sweets with the entitlement of each household, after having lavished such largesse on all the children, is a mystery and speaks volumes about the tidiness and control of her business operation. On the occasions when all her large 'sweetie' jars would be empty as she awaited her next weekly delivery on the Tuesday boat from Mallaig and after the items on the shopping list were ticked off, put into the shopping bag, hung on the handlebars of the old bike and paid for, Peggy Ann would scan the shelves to find some 'goodie' to give to the departing child. Sometimes she would find a tit-bit such as a cinnamon stick which was not rationed. The author remembers one such occasion when she had a slab of fine red cheese on the counter and a goodly slice of this was cut off and gifted to the departing cyclist - to be chewed as he made his way back up through the village with the bag of messages to the farm.

When Peggy Ann's and Mary's forebears first launched their 'merchants' business in Arnisdale is not certain. Peggy Ann retired as the Arnisdale Postmistress in 1958 and she closed the door of her lively, couthy little shop at the same time. Almost certainly the business had been carried on by the MacLean family for almost 100 years or perhaps even more. The family had provided a wonderful, unique service to Arnisdale and all the Loch Hourn households. The emphasis was very much on service rather than generating profits at the expense of all the folk who were dependent on them. For all of their customers were friends who lived close to subsistence level with very few luxuries. Margins on goods were kept to a minimum to enable people to buy the basics.

When Peggy Ann finally closed the doors of her little shop and Post Office, all her friends did not allow her to slip quietly into retirement without any fuss, as she almost certainly wished would be the case. They had a collection for her to allow herself and Mary to buy a few little extras for themselves that would increase their comforts in a very well earned retirement.

A very attractive presentation scroll was prepared which included a pencil drawing of the lifetime home of Peggy Ann and Mary with the wonderful little shop built on to its 'west end'. The list of the folk who donated to the presentation from Arnisdale, Glenelg, Loch Hourn and exiles from further afield was prepared very artistically and duly presented to Peggy Ann along with the considerable sum collected.

The scroll in somewhat faded form from its pristine original is reproduced later and Peggy Ann must have derived great pleasure in her retirement years taking it out from its safe keeping place and running through the names on the list, each of whom - along with their other family members -would bring back so many treasured memories of the 55 years she devoted, along with her father, mother and sisters, to looking after the needs of all her friends.

Catherine Atkins remembers stories about the sail driven boat (The Mary Balfour) owned by her great grandfather Johnny Ruadh on which he made trips as far away as Glasgow to collect goods. The remains of the boat can still be seen at low tide in its final resting place on the shore between Camusban and Eilean Tioram.

Maggie Lea recalls hearing stories about Johnny Ruadh having a tough time on occasions coping with the swell off Ardnamurchan Point on the sail home to Arnisdale with a cargo from Glasgow. Maggie also remembers Johnny Ruadh's boat which succeeded the 'Mary Balfour' - the 'Sgoth Caol' (long narrow boat) which was operating up to around the 1930s. This boat was 'powered' by sails and oars. Maggie recalls the Sgoth Caol being used as a barge towed by a little boat powered by an outboard motor taking a tonne cargo of goods (coal, oatmeal, flour and other essentials) from Camusban across to her home in Lea. She also remembers Johnny Ruadh in his old age as 'a trim wee man with his red hair and beard' and also his wife Ann still with 'her jet black hair when a very old lady'.

Johnny Ruadh's grandson, Ian Hamish MacDonald, now resident at Isle Ornsay, Skye, recalls that his grandfather used the Sgoth Caol to meet the Glasgow boat at Isle Ornsay once weekly to collect supplies for his Arnisdale Store to supply the Arnisdale and Loch Hourn communities. Ian Hamish also remembers that the Mary Balfour was used for curing the herring when berthed in the Arnisdale Bay.

Catherine Atkins has the following recollections of her family history. Following the marriage of her grandparents, Katie MacLean and John Henderson, in Arnisdale in 1901 they made their home at Coire Bhuidhe in Glen Quoich. When their children, Katie Ann, Amy and Jackie reached school age they went to school in Arnisdale, residing with their grandparents and aunts in Camusban. One of these children, Amy, is still with us and is now in her ninetieth year. Amy recalls a teacher she had in Arnisdale who was unable to exercise any control over the children. At playtime the children used to go up the hill and hide in the whins and the teacher would be blowing and blowing on her whistle and shouting to get them back while the children were all hiding and laughing.

Catherine continues: "One of Peggy Ann's passions was for painting things - she used small pots of enamel paint, especially gold. I still have the old shop clock. It has awful splashes of gold paint on it but I have never felt tempted to clean it up in any way. She used to paint handles and knobs and put splodges of gold paint on any ornament that came to hand.

When I was a child the house still had the same furniture that Johnnie Ruadh had bought in Glasgow when it was originally built. This meant that there were several quite nice antiques and occasionally a dealer would come to the door to see if there was anything for sale. Once, Peggy Ann told me, a man had come in and offered to buy the old leather chair at the side of the fire. She sent him packing with the words: 'And where would I sit my bum if I sold that to you?'

After Mary died in 1969 in her ninety-first year, Peggy Ann went on living alone. Maggie (Mrs MacTavish) next door was a very good soul and used to put the fire on for her every morning. One morning, the door was not open and the curtains still drawn so Maggie called the local men and they broke down the door. Peggy Ann was lying at the door of her bedroom, fully dressed and conscious, with a broken hip. Although she had been lying there all night, she was still as warm as toast and very sharp with the men. 'What kept you?' was her first remark. An ambulance came from Inverness to take her to Raigmore and she insisted that the ambulance men stay for a cup of tea and a bite to eat 'after driving all that way'. On the way out over the Carr Ruadh, she was most annoyed that they wouldn't let her sit up to look out the window as she 'hadn't been over the road for more than twenty years'.

Peggy Ann died in 1971 - also in her ninety-first year.

Catherine Atkins concludes: "My memories of both Peggy Ann and Mary are very happy ones. I loved Arnisdale and everyone there. I thought Mary was wonderful and followed her around like a puppy - she really was a gentle and kindly soul. She did all the heavy work, fetching the water, growing the vegetables and flowers - the garden was lovely when she was alive - and looking after the croft and the animals. The front of the house for years was covered with Virginia Creeper and Peggy Ann told me once that a man from Canada had come to stay when she and Mary were in their early twenties and made them a present each of a small pot of Virginia Creeper. So the Arnisdale environment and Mary's skilful husbandry obviously ensured that the small pots of Virginia Creeper flourished and multiplied in the Post Office garden and elsewhere in Arnisdale!"

Both Peggy Ann and Mary are remembered in Arnisdale and by many friends elsewhere with great respect and affection.

**Top**.  The other MacLean family in Arnisdale (cousins of Archie MacLean) lived in the first house in Camusban at the bottom of the Arnisdale brae.  The Post Office and general store was operated from the annex with a shed for storage of goods behind the annex.
**Middle Left**.  Peggy Ann and her older sister Mary in their beautiful garden overlooking the bay, along with a summer visitor.  **Right**.  Prior to the great high tide of 1881 the first house and store of the MacLean family were situated further west just below the base of the Arnisdale brae on the present track which leads to Eilean Tioram.   The ruins can still be seen.  The line of the road at that time was in front of that house and not behind it.  This situation made it easier to transport goods from the boats to the store.
**Bottom Left**.  The old house and store.  Peggy Ann's niece and nephew – Amy and Hamish Henderson return from a little sail.  **Centre**.  Peggy Ann's father and mother, Johnny Ruadh and Ann (nee Fraser).  Johnny Ruadh had his own boats – first the sail driven boat the 'Mary Balfour' and later the 'Sgoth Caol' with which he transported a full range of supplies for the district, including furniture from IsleOrnsay and from as far away as Glasgow.  **Right**.  In the 1870 to early 1900s period, Johnny Ruadh made a weekly trip to IsleOrnsay in Skye to meet the Glasgow boat for the Arnisdale and Loch Hourn supplies.  The IsleOrnsay hotel in 1888 – now the Hotel Eilean Iarmain.

381

**Top Left**. Eilean Tioram on the left which provided shelter from the west for Johnny Ruadh's boats anchored in front of his home and store. The old house and store is the second building from the left and the Arnisdale road then ran in front of the old house – not behind it. The new Arnisdale Lodge displays its splendour (around 1913).
**Right**. The new MacLean house and store built by Johnny Ruadh. This was the only two-storey house in Camusban at the time. Johnny Ruadh's daughter Mary was a splendid gardener and also did much of the work on the family croft.
**Middle Left**. There was a splendid wedding in Arnisdale in 1901 when Johnny Ruadh and Ann's daughter Katie married John Henderson (extreme right, middle row), son of James Henderson (second from right, front row). James was head gamekeeper on the Glen Quoich Estate. **Centre.** Ally Fletcher from Arnisdale was best man at this wedding while Annie MacLean from Quarry, Glenelg (later Mrs Donald Beaton) was bridesmaid. **Right**. Annie and Donald Beaton's daughters, Mimmie and Lolly were later to become Mrs Roddy MacPherson and Mrs Calum Garde respectively.
**Bottom Left**. The three children of the 1901 marriage of John and Katie, Katie Ann, Amy and Jackie later went to school in Arnisdale, 'boarding' with their grandparents. Amy is third from right, back row, in this Arnisdale School group of 1919. **Right**. The grandson of Johnny Ruadh and Ann, Hamish Henderson, at the doorway of the Arnisdale home with his wife Susan and daughter Catherine (now Mrs Atkins).

382

**Top Left**.  Iain Hamish MacDonald, grandson of Johnny Ruadh and Ann who attended Airor School (where his mother Johan was the teacher) along with Maggie 'Lea' in the late 1920s.  Iain Hamish, now living in retirement with his wife Bella in IsleOrnsay, remembers his grandfather's boat the 'Mary Balfour' being used for curing the herring while berthed in Arnisdale Bay.  No doubt the firkins (small barrels) of herrings would have been sold at the Arnisdale store and probably Johnny Ruadh would have transported them by sea to other locations to fulfil orders for the 'sgadan beag Loch Hourn'.  **Right.**  After Johnny Ruadh was no longer able to collect the Arnisdale supplies with his own boat, the goods came in weekly each Tuesday on MacLennan's boat from Mallaig, delivering first at the pier and then offloading the food and other supplies in front of the two stores in Camusban – Johnny MacGillivray's and Peggy Ann's.

**Middle**.  Some of the mail carriers between the Post Offices in Glenelg and Arnisdale over the years.  L to R. Johnnie Sinclair (left of photo), Iain MacCuaig (with his wife Lexy), and Roddy Mor.

**Bottom Left**.  Willie MacKenzie (Willie the Post II) and Calum Iain Lamont (right).  The boats of Calum Garde and Donald John MacLeod provided the daily mail links between Glenelg and Kyle.  **Centre.**  Donald John on his boat 'The Leading Lady'.  **Right**.  Calum Garde's boat the 'Chrisanne' about to leave the Glenelg pier on the morning run with Calum, Johnny MacLean and Donald John MacLeod at the controls (around 1950).

**Top.** The mail to and from Arnisdale was sorted in the Glenelg Post Office which was run over the years by Donald MacPherson (left) and later by Donald and Charlotte Chisholm seen here with their son Duncan (right). Later still, Alistair and Catriona Davidson did the needful.
**Row 2.** For many years it was Willie the Post I who sorted the mail in the Arnisdale PO along with Peggy Ann.
**Row 3.** The clock which was always at the correct time in the Arnisdale PO – adorned with blotches of gold paint by Peggy Ann.
**Row 4.** Maggie MacTavish, Peggy Ann's next door neighbour (photographed here with Kenny Fletcher) who looked after Peggy Ann and Mary in their latter years. Both Peggy Ann and Mary died in their 91st year.
**Row 5.** The top of the Presentation Scroll to Peggy Ann on her retirement after 55 years of devoted service to the Loch Hourn communities – a pencil drawing of the attractive house and adjoining shop/PO built by her father.
**Right.** The Presentation Scroll with the names of Peggy Ann's very many friends.

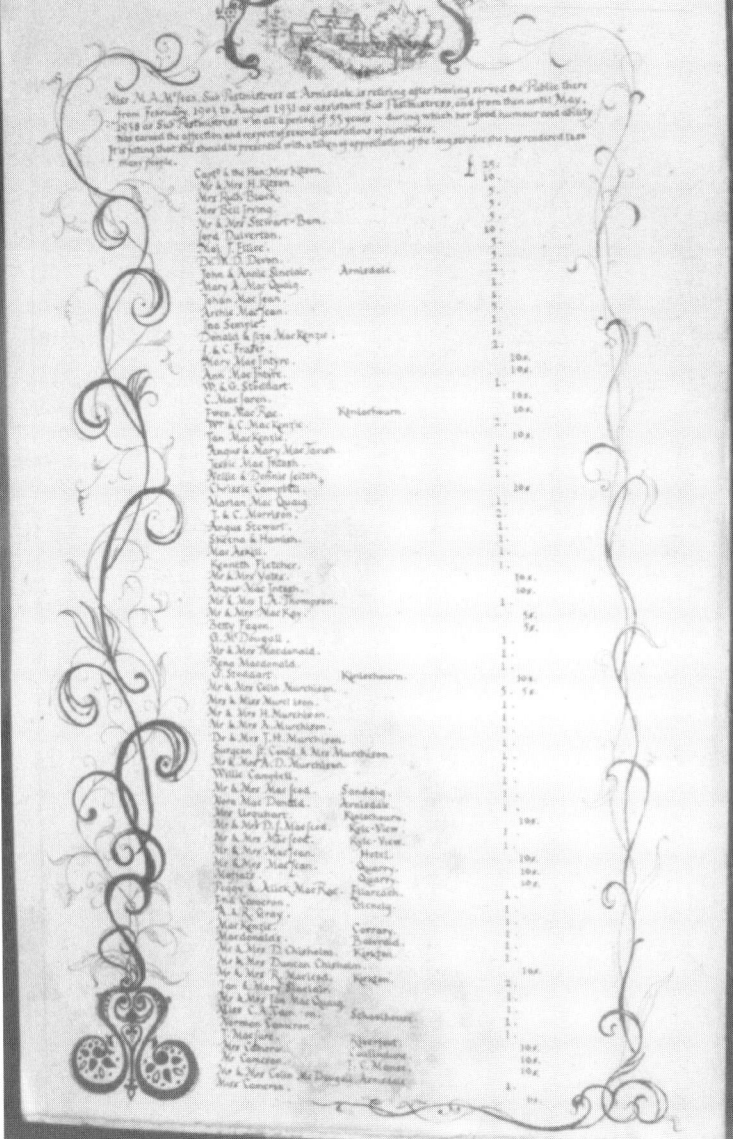

384

## Chapter 31

**Suil air ais: Looking Back - An Ulsterman's reflections on the West Highlands - Arnisdale and Glenelg in particular (by Victor Corbett)**

Following the end of World War 2 in 1945, the subsequent lifting of travel restrictions enabled itchy footed hill walkers in N. Ireland to set their sights further afield. For myself, and friends, Scotland was first choice - the Highlands had always attracted us, and perhaps due to historical fact, some of us, with tongue in cheek, considered West Scotland as a colony of our own! This dates back to the 6th Century when the three sons of Erc, King of a tribe called Scotti from Dalriada in N.E. Ulster, emigrated to Argyll and Islay. These three sons, Angus, Fergus and Lorne brought their tribal name and Gaelic language to the country of their adoption, and the foundation of Clan Donald was created.

So, for whatever reason, Scotland beckoned to us, and being active youth hostellers, the obvious course was to make use of the wonderful chain of Scottish Hostels. Over a period of three years, via Loch Lomond, the Trossachs, Glencoe and Fort William, Margaret and another friend Gerry Greer and I eventually made it north and west to Glenelg - a village that in the future always seemed to recall us in some mysterious fashion. Elg is an old poetic Gaelic name for Ireland. So perhaps there was some deeper significance in this place name - the only palindrome I know of in Scotland. Here we felt we were at home in the Highlands, among friendly Gaelic speaking country folk.

In August 1949, an old friend from Dublin, Brendan Hogan, expressed a wish to visit Scotland, and together with my young brother Harold we decided to plan a hostelling and camping trip - eventual destination Glenelg.

We arrived in Glasgow in early August and from then on the weather was atrocious. After a weekend in Glen Nevis, including a wet climb up the "Ben", we departed for Invergarry by bus. Our plan was to head west by Glengarry and Glen Quoich for Kinlochhourn, Arnisdale and eventually Glenelg.

After a dull, blustery, wet walk up Loch Garry side with little in the way of lifts, we spent the night in the ruins of the old Tomdoun Hotel - it was too wet to consider pitching a tent.

The following day after a stiff night on the floor boards we headed west once more, helped on our way by a lift with a German visitor to Glen Quoich lodge. We arrived eventually at Kinloch Hourn and on inquiry at the Lodge confirmed that we should head up the hill by the track to the north of Druim Fada, over the Bealach and then by Gleann Dubh Lochain and Arnisdale Glen to bring us back to Loch Hourn at Corran.

So far so good. Somewhere about the head of Gleann Dubh Lochain, everything closed in weatherwise, the skies opened and torrential rain persisted for half an hour. We had no option but to huddle under a peat bank with ex-army gas capes over our heads to protect us from the elements. Incidentally, no sophisticated wet weather gear in those days - mostly Army surplus material - jackets, boots etc.

I will never forget the scene and the sound when the rain eventually stopped - it eased off to a downpour! We were surrounded everywhere by the sound of rushing water. No distinction between mountains or sky - an eerie greyness laced with vertical streaks of whiteness which we soon realised were hill burns in spate, starting nowhere and ending nowhere - or so it appeared.

We proceeded, but the hill tack eventually disappeared under water and the ford was impassable. We had to keep to wild wet ground to the south of the Lochain which now appeared as a vast sea and eventually, after a knee deep walk for a few miles, arrived at the bridge over the burn at the head of Arnisdale Glen. From there on it was straightforward enough, down the zigzag path to the level track by the river ending at the bridge at Corran.

Here, on reflection, a period of my life, culminating in lifelong friendships, was to begin.

Two local men were leaning on the bridge rail watching the floodwater and debris flowing down. They greeted us, inquired where we had come from, sympathised with our condition and accompanied us on the road to Arnisdale, suggesting that it was no night to be putting up a tent and probably we could get bedded down in the barn of the farm which we were approaching. One of the men, I eventually discovered, was Iain MacCuaig who we got to know well during the subsequent years.

The friendly lady who appeared at the door coincidental with our arrival took one look at us and I'll always remember her first words "You poor dears, I'm sure you could do with a cup of tea". Our two companions bade us "Oidhche mheth", we were invited into the cosy lamplit living room, told to take our wet boots and socks off while tea was made, and to make ourselves comfortable. We made our introductions, and Mrs Macleod, our hostess introduced Betty and Peter, her niece and nephew from Glen Urquhart who were spending a holiday with her. Then her husband arrived home - Ruaridh Mor, Roddy Arnisdale, or Uncle Roddy as he was variously known and the introductions were completed.

Before agreeing to let us sleep in the hay barn for the night he asked the first of two questions - "Do any of you smoke?" A negative answer quickly obtained approval for a night in the hay. The second question - Do you know any Gaelic songs?" led to one of the most enjoyable ceilidh evenings I can remember.

Brendan spoke some Irish Gaelic, I had recently learned two Gaelic tunes on the tin whistle - "Fear a' Bhata" and "Chi mi na mor-bheannaibh", and that started things off. A great mixture of singing, Scots and Irish tunes, Mrs MacLeod playing the organ and myself helping out with the tin whistle. It was then I learned my first Gaelic phrase of more than two words: "Thoir dhuinn tuilleadh puirt air an fheadan" (Give us another tune on the whistle).

However, while this was going on I'll never forget the supper, sardine sandwiches and goodies galore washed down by cup after cup of tea. The sardines were suggested rather hesitatingly by Mrs Roddy, but we jumped at the offer of this delicacy. So to a flaked out sleep in the hay and in due course our thanks and farewell the following morning. "Bithidh mi air ais" I said trying out my growing Gaelic vocabulary, and I did return, many times.

We stopped at Peggy Ann MacLean's shop and Post Office, at the other end of the village, posted some cards and got some provisions, and then hit the high road to Glenelg and not much of a road in those days! The morning was sunny and warm for a change, fragrant steam arose from the spruce and fir woods beyond Rarsaidh and we eventually reached Sandaig, the only occupied house between Arnisdale and Eileanreach. We were offered a lift to Glenelg by two men in a landrover which we gladly accepted. The driver, we subsequently learned, was John Donald MacLeod of Sandaig, where he stayed with his wife Mary and their three sons. It was he to whom Gavin Maxwell dedicated his book "Ring of Bright Water" and who is referred to in the narrative as Calum Murdo MacKinnon.

John Donald the Road was responsible for local road maintenance and he also looked after the navigation light down at lower Sandaig. He entertained us to a learned political discussion en route, and it impressed us how well read he was. The remainder of our holiday was spent in the Glenelg Youth Hostel at Kylerhea - the weather deteriorated again but we enjoyed the company in the hostel, our trips to get evening milk from Mrs Campbell at Gallder and the cruises up to Kyle in Calum Garde's mail boat Chris Anne, even if only to pass a wet day.

On one trip some local humorists entertained us to "tall" stories about Johnny Sinclair's car. (Johnny ran the mail service between Arnisdale and Glenelg). In the post-war years spares were hard to obtain, improvisation was the name of the game, and Johnny had to resort, apparently, to fitting a boat's spoked wheel in replacement of a broken steering wheel. Road wheels were also of different sizes - "two great wheels on the one side and two small ones on the other: fine for going round the hills providing he kept going in one direction". Hard to believe, but well told.

Following that holiday, I wrote to Mrs Roddy (or Aunt Lizzie or Mrs Lizzie as she was variously called) and commenced a correspondence which we maintained for the duration of Lizzie's lifetime and within that period my brother Harold and Brendan both passed away leaving me the last of the pioneering trio.

The next year I returned with Margaret - we stayed with Peggy Ann and Mary and I introduced her to a growing number of friends in Arnisdale. Subsequently we visited many times in Arnisdale and Glenelg, travelling by foot, by mail boat and mail car and once by the Tuesday boat from Mallaig operated by Alexander MacLennan. After our marriage, Margaret and I came by car over Mam Ratagan with our young son Garry to stay with Roddy and Lizzie in their new home at Kirkton in Glenelg.

My friendship with their nephew Peter English developed and matured over all these years, and we observed with interest as his University and future career developed. Roddy was so pleased that he had pursued an agricultural career, specialising in animal science - stimulated by the milking and caring of the Arnisdale cows and calves, the shepherding of the sheep, the feeding of the hens and the lone pig, and the handling and care of Dick the working horse, the collie dogs - and of the farm cats. Perhaps it was this experience in his childhood which inspired Peter to attain his present position of Professor of Animal Science and Husbandry at the University of Aberdeen.

During these years lasting friendships were established with many of the local people. The stalker at Arnisdale, the late Angus Beaton and his wife Margaret and their family with which we still have contact. Iain MacCuaig who drove the mail car for a while and his wife Lexie, the school teacher at Arnisdale when we first arrived there, Duncan MacTavish, whose boat we borrowed to row over to Li. Donnie MacPherson and his mother in the croft at Riverfoot, Glenelg, where Donnie entertained us to piping recitals in the evenings. Ewen Campbell and his wife and family at Gallder from whom the hostellers obtained their milk. Donald John MacLeod of Quarry and the MacKenzies of Corrary in Glen Beag where we helped with the hay making down below the Broch. And many more.

Although living outside the Arnisdale/Glenelg area in Loch Carron, I must not forget Roddy Mor's sister Flo and her husband Alisdair MacKenzie - better known in West Ross as "Jeck" - a great character. Also Roddy's brother Murdo, who stayed up in Moyle in Glen More - a fine Gaelic singer too.

My collection of Gaelic songs vastly increased from the initial two, thanks to Roddy's tuition, and a basic working knowledge of colloquial Gaelic developed, although I always do remember Roddy's reply when Margaret once asked him if I was any good at it. "Aye, he's not too bad - he's got plenty words but at times he's putting them in the wrong places".

My two treasured mementoes of Roddy, presented to me by Lizzie after his death on 8 August 1975, are his Gaelic Bible dated 1936, and his favourite cromag which is still put to good use on my outings to the hills. Our son, Garry, is also the proud possessor of Roddy's 'Dad's Army' bonnet worn during World War 2 when Roddy commanded the local Home Guard in Arnisdale. He gifted this memento to

Garry during one of our Glenelg holidays.

Lizzie went to stay in Glenurquhart and Inverness with her sister Babs where we visited her frequently, and then transferred to the Elmgrove Nursing Home where she made her reputation as the "crossword queen". She passed away on 30 August 1994, aged 97.

Although my great friends, Roddie and Lizzie, and many others, are no longer with us, the many wonderful memories are still very much to the fore and help to keep all those worthy, kindly folk alive in our minds as we recall so many happy days and experiences. The following are some of the tales I was told and other experiences we treasured.

**Salted Water.** One evening in the Arnisdale farm kitchen, I recollect a learned discussion, with some visitors, on lesser used Gaelic words. "Burn" an alternative for water to the usual more common "uisge" was quoted, and Roddy related an incident from his early days on the farm when he first heard the word. Custom then was for folks inland to visit Arnisdale with a train of Highland ponies or garrons loaded with supplies of potatoes, oatmeal etc. for trading for Loch Hourn salt herring. One hot September day a party from Glen Moriston way came down the Arnisdale glen, and halfway between Corran and Arnisdale lodge discovered that a high autumn tide resulted in the water being almost at the road edge. A youth in the party, sunburned and streaming with sweat, as Roddy described him, upon seeing the water sparkling in the sunshine, but never having been on the sea coast before in his life, jumped off his garron, knelt at the tides edge, took a great mouthful of water, immediately spat it out again, and declared in Gaelic: "Tha an t-salainn anns an burn airson an lite cheana". (The water's salted for the porridge already).

**Great War Reminiscences - Roddy.** Roddy never talked much about his experiences in Mesopotamia during World War I, but two anecdotes have always stayed in my mind.

**Rifle Practice.** After joining the Lovat Scouts, together with his own horse called Sam, the recruits were instructed in rifle drill, and then lined up for their first attempt at target practice with live ammunition. They had accepted all the instruction quietly, without comment, as good recruits should, and when given the order to fire in turn at the targets, every shot was declared: 'Bullseye - Bullseye - Bullseye etc' - much to the Sergeant Instructor's amazement. "Little did he know", said Roddy, "that the squad were all sons of keepers, farmers, shepherds etc, used to handling rifles since we could walk".

**Russians.** Roddy reminded me of a rumour that I had heard as a boy, that the Russians had landed in the North of England to help in the conflict - they were identified as Russians, so the imaginative story went, because they had "snow on their boots".!!! "A lot of nonsense", said Roddy, "it was our company just landed at Newcastle from training camp, all speaking Gaelic - they didn't know any better and thought we were speaking Russian!!

**Clach Chuilinn.** I first read about "Clach Chuilinn", or holly stone, in A A MacGregor's book "Somewhere in Scotland". On visits to Arnisdale I located the burn which flows down between Beinn Bhuidhe and Beinn Chlachach through Achadh a'Ghlinne and joins the Arnisdale river upstream from Corran, and collected some samples. It's a soft, soapy, greenish stone and local tradition has it that it is calcified holly wood - hence its name. The woodlike grain can certainly be identified. (See Note below).

The stone is easily carved and shaped and the resulting stone dust is similar in texture to talcum powder. According to MacGregor, stone pots and cruises used to be fashioned out of this stone, and it was also used for whitening hearth stones, door steps and windowsills.

**Additional Note.** In N. Ireland the water of Lough Neagh has the ability to calcify wood. Traditionally, in days gone bye, sharpening stones for scythes were obtained following the immersion of timber in the Lough's waters. An old doggerel goes –

"Lough Neagh hones, Lough Neath hones,
Throw them in sticks, pull them out stones".

(Hone - sharpening stone for a scythe (colloquial Ulster)

**Uisge Bheatha - The Water of Life.** Once when discussing whisky - the home made variety from Ireland called poteen, Roddy confirmed that the Highlands also had a reputation for good quality illicit spirit. He quoted two anecdotes:-

A man and his two sons operated a profitable still not too far away on the hill. In due course items of equipment wore out and at that time the Authorities were offering a reward of £5 for information leading "to the seizure of a still, or parts thereof!" The manufacturers removed the defective gear to a remote cave in another area, a son reported to the local Excise Authority that he had been out on the hill after lost sheep and discovered these bits of copper and wondered if they would be of interest. The broken gear was duly collected, the £5 reward handed over, and £3 bought the replacement equipment, leaving the family £2 in profit.

A cask of illicit spirit had been seized and stored in a ground floor room in Bogroy Inn, near Beauly, with a gauger keeping guard for the night. A hotel maid admitted the manufacturers quietly to a basement room directly underneath - they drilled a hole with an auger through the floorboards, into the base of the barrel and drained off the contents into containers below, which were then carefully removed. The following morning a pony and cart arrived to collect a, by then, very light barrel!

**Roddy's favourite Gaelic songs.** Roddy's favourites which he often sang were:
'A Ghruagach og an fhuilt bhain' (Lassie with the Golden Hair or The fair maid of Barra)
'Failte Rudha Bhatairnis' (Salute to Waternish) and
'Caisteal a'Ghlinne' (Castle in the Glen).
I think his real favourite was 'A Ghruagach Og'.

**The Eggs.** During one stay in Arnisdale we met Donald MacKenzie from Li and his wife, Lisa. Li, on the opposite shore of Loch Hourn from Arnisdale, must be one of the shortest place names in Scotland. Mrs MacKenzie was preparing to go off on a visiting holiday and some days later we met her in the station at Mallaig, where we were all heading off in the Fort William direction. It was a hot day - I got some ice cream at the Station shop, brought it back to the carriage and it was much appreciated all round. The train departed and Mrs MacKenzie bade us farewell at Loch Eil side where she was visiting relatives.

Several weeks later Margaret and I received a parcel with a letter of thanks for the ice cream and the company on the train journey. The parcel contained a dozen eggs, none the worse for their journey, and the most far travelled eggs we've ever received - by rowboat across Loch Hourn to Arnisdale, mail car to Glenelg, mail boat to Kyle, train to Glasgow, night boat to Belfast and final delivery to home. A simple gift, much appreciated, especially for the thoughtfulness involved.

**The Beatons.** We first met Angus Beaton and family at Arnisdale. He stayed in the stalker's house

(Glenside), with his wife Margaret, daughters Mary and Anne, son Iain and his nephew Jimmy Dickie. Margaret's sister Ina also stayed there at that time - around 1951. Angus was a fine piper and many the grand recital we enjoyed. The family then moved to Dorus Duan in Kintail, where I visited a couple of times. Angus was head stalker on the Inverinate estate and with him and Jimmy I made my first trek to the Falls of Glomach.

For a few years then we lost contact. The family moved to Invercharnon at the head of Loch Etive, and then to Attadale, Loch Carron, where Angus was head stalker until his retirement. By this time his son Iain had taken over his responsibilities. Iain was killed in a tragic road accident a few years later, and Frances, his widow still lives in Loch Carron. She, incidentally, was a MacKinnon, and her father had been born in the old house at Sandaig, later acquired by Gavin Maxwell, and called Camusfearna in his book "The Ring of Bright Water". Mary married Douglas Cameron and lives at Treslaig, Loch Linnhe side, Anne married Ewen Borman and lives at Duisky on Loch Eil. The last I heard of Jimmy Dickie was that he was living in the Loch Carron area. Margaret Beaton died in 1976, and Angus died in 1983.

**The MacLellans - Morar.** Other old friends in the West Highland area are Archie and Barbara MacLellan, who still live at Silver Sands, Morar. We first met Barbara Gillies in Glencoe Youth Hostel during our earlier hostelling holidays. Margaret and Barbara kept up a correspondence, and Barbara eventually married Archie MacLellan, the eldest son of the proprietors of the West Highland hotel in Mallaig. They first lived in the house at Silver Sands, and, upon his father's retirement, took up residence in the Hotel which Archie and Barbara continued to run as a family business. The parents at this time had moved to Silver Sands.

After the death of his parents, Archie and Barbara eventually returned to their original home, sold the Hotel and are both enjoying a well earned retirement. They have a family of twelve - six boys and six girls, all married now with families of their own. We still visit Silver Sands - Archie is a mine of local and historical information, and still maintains close contact with the RNLI, of which he was Secretary at Mallaig for many years. Incidentally, Archie's late father (Archie Senior) also served with the Lovat Scouts in Mesopotamia during the first World War and was acquainted with Willie MacKenzie (Willie the Post), Willie's brother Donald MacKenzie, Li, as well as with Roddy Mor.

**Amazing Grace.** During one holiday in Glenelg we attended the evening service at the Free Church with Lizzie and Roddy, who acted as precentor. It was the week for the English service, and in advance we were advised that we would stand to pray and sit during the singing of psalms - the opposite to our own convention, and were well provided with peppermints to sustain us during the sermon. The lasting memory was of a haunting tune to which Psalm 40 was sung - led by Roddy as precentor. The following year Margaret told me of a new hit tune she had heard on the radio that day, and which she found vaguely familiar. Eventually it was broadcast again - I was called to listen to it, and we both identified it as so similar to the Psalm tune remembered from Glenelg - Judy Collins singing the new hit "Amazing Grace".

**The Curtain Track Killer Lure.** After leaving Arnisdale on their retirement from farming, Roddy and Lizzie took up residence in Kirkton, Glenelg, where we spent several holidays with them. Roddy had developed a passion for sea fishing and invited me to accompany him to Kylerhea one evening. I had fishing gear with me, mostly the fresh water variety but none of my lures appealed to Roddy. "I'll make you a killer", said he, and taking me up to his workbench in his garage he produced a length of brass curtain valance tracking, cut off about 4 inches, drilled holes at either end to take a treble hook and a swivel, and then, holding it up against the light he carefully put a small bend in it, "That will do the job", said he. So, off to Kylerhea where he had an arrangement with the ferryman to use his row boat to get aboard the anchored ferry, services having finished for the evening. Roddy produced a large bucket saying "We'll quit when its full!" I secretly admired his optimism, but after the first cast I realised it was for real. The fish even took the lure as it sank and it didn't take long to fill the basket with a mixture of saithe, lythe and cuddies.

We repeated the operation several other evenings and to vary the routine we rowed up and down off the rocks below the old Hostel, trailing our curtain tracks, and myself at the oars keeping time to Roddy's singing of "Morag of Dunvegan" and "Eilidh". Happy evenings of nostalgic and atmospheric memories.

But the story doesn't end here - there's an intriguing sequel. The remainder of that holiday was spent with our friends the MacLellans, then in residence in the West Highland Hotel in Mallaig. In the bar after dinner on our first evening I recounted my fishing experiences at Kylerhea, produced Roddy's lure as evidence but none of the fishing community there would believe it - another fishy yarn!

Archie said the only way to prove it was by a trial down at the harbour - so as soon as duty permitted a party of us set off, all respectably dressed and myself armed with rod, line and lure. The back of the pier was lined with woolly clad fishermen, mostly from Yorkshire, spaced out at intervals, hunched up on stools, and according to my inquiries - just watching floats and catching nothing. I selected a suitable gap, and on the third cast surprised everyone, including myself, by catching a mackerel, and shortly after that a saithe. Needless to say, there was a buzz of interest from the nearby anglers, my lure was examined, and as it had proved its worth and honour satisfied, we packed up and returned to the Hotel.

A couple of nights later my son Garry and I took a walk down the pier, more informally dressed and not fishing this time - just interested spectators because there was something vaguely familiar about the flashing bits of copper being cast into the sea and the numerous fish lying on the quay. Upon casual inquiry I was told about the fellow who had been fishing a few nights before and had caught over 30 fish in ten minutes using a home made curtain track lure!! He had not been seen fishing since, but I learned that the local hardware shop was practically sold out of curtain valance tracking!!
I never said a thing, and still possess Roddy's lure to the present day - it even caught pike for me!

Memories are such wonderful treasures!

**Top Left**.  Victor Corbett (right) now retired from his position as Chief Architect in the Department of the Environment for Northern Ireland, with son Garry and Roddy Mor and Lizzie after their retirement to Glenelg (around 1965).  Garry is sporting Roddy Mor's Home Guard 'Dad's Army' bonnet.  **Right**.  Victor's wife Margaret with son Garry and Roddy Mor in Glenelg.

**Middle Left**.  On Victor's first visit to Arnisdale along with his brother Harold and friend Brendan Hogan they sheltered en route for a night from the 'monsoon' in the ruins of the old Tomdoun Hotel which lies just west of the present hotel at the junction of the old road which branches off to Cluanie via Loch Loyne.  **Right**.  Glen Quoich Lodge was still there in all its splendour as they passed on their way to Kinloch Hourn.

**Bottom Left**.  After climbing the face above Kinloch Hourn and getting on the hill track to Arnisdale, they were thwarted by the raging torrent at the ford east of the Gleann Dubh Lochain.  The violent spate was far removed from the gentle trickle as in this picture.  **Right**.  They had no option other than to keep to the wild wet ground to the south of the Lochain – knee deep in water and peat bogs for several miles!

**Top Left**.  "Confronted with the saturated trio, the friendly lady who answered the door at Arnisdale Farmhouse exclaimed:  'Oh, you poor dears, I'm sure you could do with a cup of tea'.  Mrs MacLeod then introduced us to her niece and nephew from GlenUrquhart – Betty and Peter English".   **Right**.  When Mrs MacLeod's husband Ruaraidh Mor arrived and knew we were seeking refuge in the haybarn for the night he asked us two questions:  'Do any of you smoke?' and 'Do you know any Gaelic songs?'

**Middle Left**.  A wonderful supper and ceilidh followed in the evening.  L to R.  Victor Corbett, Angus Beaton, Aunt Lizzie and Roddy Mor.  **Right**.  On the walk to Glenelg the next day the trio met up with John Donald MacLeod at Sandaig – Calum Murdo MacKinnon in Gavin Maxwell's classic 'Ring of Bright Water'.

**Bottom Left**.  The house at Kylerhea – then a Youth Hostel.  **Right**.  Evening trips to the Campbell family at Gallder, Glenelg to buy milk and sometimes to help with the hay.   (L to R. Margaret, Garry, Donnie Campbell and Mrs Campbell).

393

**Top Left**. On return visits to Glenelg there were enjoyable trips to Kyle on Calum Garde's boat the 'Chrisanne'. L to R. on the Glenelg Pier. Mrs Roddy, little Dolan MacLean, Mrs MacLean, Roddy Mor, Margaret, and Donald MacLean. **Right**. Margaret with Roddy Mor on his Glenelg to Arnisdale mail run after his retirement from the farm in Arnisdale. A stop on the Eilanreach brae to admire the view across Glenelg Bay to the Narrows of Kylerhea.

**Middle Left**. Duncan MacTavish from Arnisdale who lent us his boat to row across to Li. **Right**. Donnie MacPherson (right) and his cousin Neil MacPherson at Riverfoot, Glenelg. Donnie gave us fine piping recitals in the evenings during visits to himself and his mother Isabella (nee MacRae)

**Bottom**. The Beaton family whom we followed on their travels from Arnisdale to Dorus Duan in Kintail, Invercharnon at the head of Glen Etive, Attadale, Loch Carron and beyond. Left – Angus, Jimmy Dickie, Garry, Margaret Beaton, Margaret Corbett and the Beaton grandchildren. **Centre**. Another fine welcome on the pipes from Angus. **Right**. Victor and Margaret catching up with Mrs Roddy in Aberdeen at the home of Anne and Peter English. L to R. Garry, Anne, Margaret, Mrs Roddy and Victor.

**Top Left**. Allt Utha, the burn which tumbles down the steep slope between Beinn Bhuidhe and Beinn Chlachach before meandering through Achadh a' Ghlinne to join the Arnisdale River. Clach Chuillinn or holly stone can be found in the bed of this burn. This is a soft, soapy, greenish stone which some folk think is calcified holly wood. It has a woodlike grain. **Middle.** The clach chuillinn or holly stone. **Right**. A seal carved from the clach chuillinn.

**Middle Left**. The carved seal sits on a ledge of the clach chuillinn. **Middle**. Roddy Mor fishing off the anchored ferry boat at Kylerhea in the evening – a favourite and productive pastime with the help of his home made lure from a four inch piece of brass curtain valance tracking. **Right**. The lure which proved so attractive to the saithe, lythe and cod at Kylerhea Ferry, Mallaig Pier and many other locations.

**Bottom Left**. Another favourite pastime for Roddy Mor and Lizzie in their retirement – an afternoon picnic, sitting in the sun and enjoying the sea breezes at Kylerhea. **Middle**. Donald 'Ban' MacKenzie, Lea (right), his wife Lisa (left), their daughter Mary and grandchildren. A gift of a dozen eggs was sent by post from Lea to the Corbett home in Belfast – and not one was broken! **Right**. Victor with Roddy Mor and Aunt Lizzie in Glenelg in 1974 – 25 years after that first memorable ceilidh in Arnisdale.

# Chapter 32

**Duncan MacTavish's memories of the 1880s and 1890s**

Duncan MacTavish was born on the 13th September 1881 and died on the 29th May 1966. Duncan's mother, Mary MacPherson was born and reared in Camusban and in her young days, which coincided with the great herring fishing in Loch Hourn, she met and married a young fisherman from Lochgilphead on Loch Fyne, Archie MacTavish. They were married in the little church in Barrisdale and made their home in Glassary in Argyll. Archie and Mary had five children but tragedy struck the family when father Archie was drowned while away at the fishing. The youngest member of the family, Angus (Angan), was only a few days old when his father was drowned while Duncan, the subject of this chapter, was 2 years old at the time. Having lost the breadwinner for the young family, relatives in Arnisdale came to the rescue and Mary went back to Camusban with her five young children to reside with her brother Angus and her father John MacPherson and her mother Ann (nee MacCuaig).

Baby Angan was later to become the father of Charlie MacTavish (see Chapter 7) while Duncan remained a bachelor throughout his life. It would have been 1883 when Angan and Duncan returned to Camusban with their bereaved mother and their older brothers and sisters. This was the boom time for the Loch Hourn herring fishing so at least the large extended family packed together in their little thatched cottage would not want for food - there would be plenty of fresh herring when the herring shoals came into the loch and salt herring for the rest of the year.

However, a mini disaster had struck Arnisdale in 1881. This was the year of the great high tide. At that time the little thatched cottages in Camusban and Corran were sited along the shoreline - just above the normal high tide mark. With the great high tide of 1881 all the little cottages were flooded. In addition, with the prevailing high winds and very heavy rainfall, repairing the thatch on the roof was a constant job and with good thatching material being in short supply locally, undoubtedly considerable dampness prevailed in the little cottages. The rain seeping through the thatch was bad enough but the great flood of 1881 was a further calamity that they all had to address as best they could.

The owner of all the cottages, the croftlands and the neighbouring estate at the time was Mr Baillie of Dochfour near Inverness. Following the great high tide of 1881, negotiations started with Mr Baillie and his factors to plan to avoid a repeat of the 1881 flooding disaster. The discussion focused on the possibility of rebuilding the houses further up the slope towards the sentinel mountains of Beinn Sgritheall and Beinn na h-eaglaise behind, and away from the shore so that no matter how unusual the high tides in the future, at least flooding of the cottages would be avoided.

This was the background situation that Duncan MacTavish found himself in as a little boy in the 1880s and as a growing lad in the 1890s. From the age of two years, Duncan's home was in Camusban. He worked at the fishing and as a ghillie/stalker/shepherd on various local estates, perhaps mainly on the Glen Quoich Estate. He knew Loch Hourn and the adjacent hill ranges extremely well, and he knew all the folk even better. He was a couthy, kindly, mild mannered and thoroughly gentlemanly character. In the evening of his years he liked nothing better than the fireside ceilidhs with his good friends. Because of his great interest in the area and its people, his very long experience, his excellent memory and his couthy, clear way of telling a story, both in the Gaelic and in English, cronies round the fireside would encourage him to relate experiences, clarify contradictory tales, and comment on great characters long since gone in a physical, worldly sense but still very much alive in the memories of local folk. Duncan's graceful and humble nature would not see him willingly take the initiative at the fireside ceilidhs but clever cronies would inveigle him into 'taking the floor'. Duncan was a man of great integrity, always interesting and at the end of a ceilidh evening with him, all would have felt the benefit of being in his company as they returned to their respective homes.

When Duncan was in his eighty-first year, in 1962, some wise, persuasive local crony managed to coax Duncan to put some of his memories of his boyhood days in Camusban down in print. Who this friend with foresight was is not known but the author has his own thoughts on who it might have been.

The following then are Duncan's memories of each of the thirty thatched tiny cottages hugging the Camusban shore in the 1880s along with the details of all their occupants. Duncan provides his 'census' starting at the west end and he carefully describes the location by specifying the demarcation lines of the three burns which channel the copious rainfall from the slopes of Beinn Sgritheall and Beinn na h-eaglaise to the sea. These three burns are Alltan Beag (the little burn), Allt a' mhuillinn (The Mill burn) and Allt an t-Siucair (The Sugar burn).

The location of the thirty homes which Duncan describes in relation to these burns and the curvature of the bay are as follows:

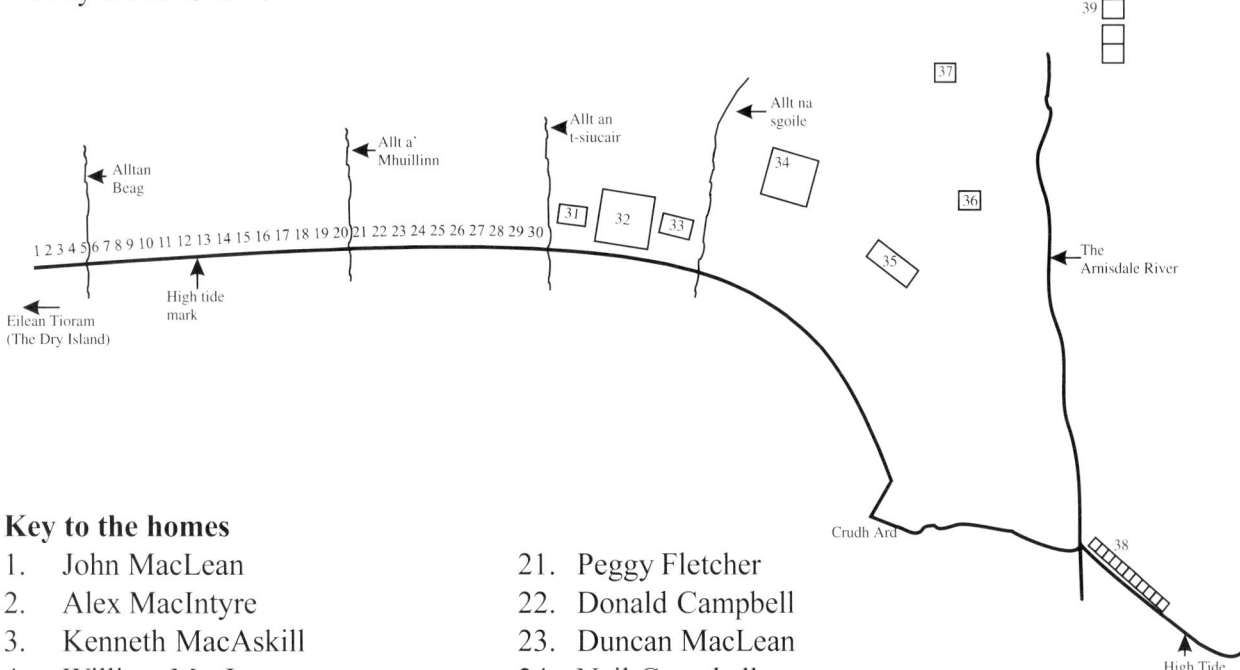

**Key to the homes**

1. John MacLean
2. Alex MacIntyre
3. Kenneth MacAskill
4. William MacInnes
5. Archie MacCuaig
6. Norman MacGillivray
7. Alexander MacLeod
8. Kenneth Fraser
9. John MacGillvray
10. Archie Fraser
11. John MacInnes
12. Seonaid
13. Jihn MacGillivray (Iain Ban)
14. Duncan MacCuaig
15. John MacPherson
16. George Campbell
17. Effie Campbell
18. Norman MacKintosh
19. William Fraser
20. Lachlan Fletcher
21. Peggy Fletcher
22. Donald Campbell
23. Duncan MacLean
24. Neil Campbell
25. Donald MacKintosh
26. Farquhar Campbell
27. Archie MacKintosh
28. Neil MacKintosh
29. David MacKintosh
30. John Sinclair
31. The Mission House
32. The Free Church and Graveyard
33. The School and Schoolhouse
34. Arnisdale Lodge
35. The Farmhouse
36. Glenfield
37. The cottage in Achadh a'Ghlinne
38. The small thatched cottages at Corran packed along the river estuary and shore just above the high tide mark.
39. The ruins at Blar nan Each

Here then, in his own words, are Duncan's memories of the Camusban homes of his youth.

"I think I shall give you an idea of how the thatched cottages were at Camusban when I was a young lad.   Starting at the West End:

<u>First</u> - John MacLean, his wife Ann Fraser, five daughters and two sons.  They had a shop.
<u>Second</u> - Alex MacIntyre, a carpenter, his wife was Kate Campbell - five sons and one daughter.
<u>Third</u> - Kenneth MacAskill - retired shepherd - wife Mary MacLeod - four  daughters, a son and grandson.
<u>Fourth</u> - William MacInnes, his wife Janet MacIntosh, one son and one daughter who married Donald Sinclair - they had two sons and one daughter.
<u>Fifth</u> - Archie MacCuaig and his wife Christina MacMillan from Kintail.  They had three sons and one daughter. One son, Angus, went to Africa as a teacher.  After his retiral he came to visit his old friends but died soon after in a friend's house in Glasgow.

Now there is a burn running down called Alltan Beag (Little Burn);  on this side of it is a house occupied by Norman McGillivray and his wife Mary MacIntosh - family consisted of three sons and two daughters and a grand-daughter.   Next was Alexander MacLeod who was a widower when he came from Lochalsh as a Gaelic teacher.  He had two sons and three daughters.  One daughter married a man from Tobermory, Ewan MacPhail.   They had two daughters.

Kenneth Fraser's house came next.  His wife was Flora MacIntosh and they had one daughter.  In the ninth house stayed John MacGillivray.  His wife was Lexy MacIntosh and they had four sons and five daughters.

Next came Archie Fraser and his wife Mary MacAskill.   They had six sons.   Then came the home of John MacInnes and his wife Mary MacKenzie.  They had a family of three sons and one daughter.  In the twelfth house lived Seonaid.  Seonaid means Jessie.  Seonaid was blind and lived alone.  When she became ill she was removed to Corran where she died along with friends.

Next to Seonaid lived John MacGillivray or Iain Ban - Fair John - his wife - I am sorry I cannot remember her name - she was always known as Bean Iain Ban (Iain Ban's wife).   They had three daughters and one son, two grandchildren.  Later came two grandchildren from Glasgow whose parents died young.  They were Thomsons.   Then in the fourteenth cottage lived Duncan MacCuaig and his wife Christina Campbell.   They had no children.

John MacPherson and his wife Ann MacCuaig stayed in the fifteenth cottage with two sons and a daughter.  Their daughter married a man from Lochgilphead who was lost at sea when their five children were young.  Her brother Angus, a bachelor, brought mother and children home to stay with him.  (Author's Note:  Duncan himself was one of the children).

Next lived George Campbell and his wife Flora - surname Campbell but not related.  They had two sons and a daughter and a grandson called George MacDougall.

In the seventeenth house lived two sisters - also Campbells.  They were Effie and Christine and a brother Farquhar, later married, stayed there too.

At number eighteen were Norman MacIntosh with his wife Sarah Fraser and two sons and two daughters.

Next door were William Fraser, his wife Ann MacGillivray and three sons and two daughters.  In the twentieth cottage stayed Lachlan Fletcher, his wife Janet MacLeod with a family of three sons and a daughter. For a time they kept a small inn. Their son married and had a family of seven sons and two daughters. Some of the sons are still around.

Now I am at the burn Allt a'mhuillinn - the burn of the Mill, where the inhabitants drew their supply of water as it was never dry whether it was a long dry season or not. Allt a'mhuillinn was never dry.

Across the burn, in the twenty-first house lived Peggie Bhan - Peggie Fletcher. Her son and grandson, Peter Livingstone, were staying with her.

At the twenty-second house was Donald Campbell and his wife Flora Mackay who was from Skye. They had a family of four daughters and one son and one grand-daughter.

Twenty-three. Duncan MacLean stayed with his wife Peggy MacInnes from Skye and his five sons and two daughters. Before setting up home here he was living down at Port Luinge on this side of Sandaig opposite Sgeir Mhor which is in the middle of the loch.

In the twenty-fourth was a bachelor Neil Campbell. He was a great fox hunter and named Niall Brocair (Neil the Hunter).

Next was Donald MacIntosh with his wife Sheila Campbell and three sons.
Then there lived Jane Mae MacGillivray, she married Farquhar Campbell. Mrs Campbell, as she was known, had a shop. Her one daughter married Duncan Fletcher and they had one son who died after the first World War as a result of his Army Service. He was not wounded.

Next was the home of Archie MacIntosh a bachelor known as Leasbuig (Gilleasbuig) Ban (Fair Archie). His sister and nephew were with him.

In the twenty-eighth house lived Neil MacIntosh who was postman between Arnisdale and Glenelg for a long period. After his retirement his son Donald took the job. He also was on the route for a long time walking twice daily but now a mail car is on the run. Neil's wife, I am sorry I don't know her Christian name but I think her surname was MacNeil. There were four daughters and two sons. Neil died at the ripe age of 107.

Next to them lived David MacIntosh, Leasbuig's brother - wife was Kirsty Sinclair. They had two daughters. Next came John Sinclair. He came as a farm manager. His wife was Kirsty MacPhee. They had a family of six sons and two daughters."

So ended Duncan's memories of the thirty homes packed along the shore between John MacLean's house at the west end and John Sinclair's at the west side of Allt an t-siucair. Duncan, his mother, brothers, sisters, uncle and grandparents resided at Cottage Number 15. Duncan proceeded to jot down his memories of the Arnisdale Estate and its proprietors and these will be related later.

However, for the present it is useful to take stock of his memories to date. As far as is known, not more than four of the families mentioned by Duncan are not related to current Arnisdale families (i.e. those resident at Numbers 7, 11, 12 and 24). However, some may dispute this and be able to demonstrate that the family of Norman MacLeod (No. 7), John MacInnes (No. 11), Seonaid (No. 12) and Neil Campbell (No. 24) are in fact connected to current Arnisdale families. The occupations of folk at the time are interesting - two shops, one pub, a teacher, carpenter, mail carrier, fox hunter, shepherd and farm manager being mentioned. Duncan would have found it superfluous, of course, to mention crofting and fishing activities as almost all the homes would have family members engaged in these activities, and, in addition, many of the young men would have served in the armed forces for part of their lives.

What is most surprising when the concentration of cottages is considered, is the very large number between Alltan Beag and Allt a'mhuillinn. There are fifteen cottages packed into this relatively short distance whereas currently there are only seven homes occupying this space.

Duncan's description of the homes does not go beyond those east of Allt an t-siucair. He does not mention the Mission House which is the next house eastwards of Allt an t-siucair which had almost certainly already been built in his young days. Neither does he proceed to the Free Church, the School, the Lodge, the Farmhouse, or to Glenfield and Corran.

In view of the relatively small part of the Arnisdale Community which Duncan covers in his memories, it is interesting to check the population of this part in Duncan's youth around the year 1890. These details are summarised below.

**A summary of the boyhood memories of Duncan MacTavish (Born 1881) of the thatched houses in Camusban and their occupants (houses numbered from the west end)**

| | Tenant | Wife | Daughters | Sons | Others | |
|---|---|---|---|---|---|---|
| 1. | John MacLean | Ann Fraser | 5 | 2 | | Had a Shop |
| 2. | Alex MacIntyre | Kate Campbell | 1 | 5 | | Carpenter |
| 3. | Kenneth MacAskill | Mary MacLeod | 4 | 1 | 1 Grandson | Retired Shepherd |
| 4. | William MacInnes x Donald Sinclair | Janet MacIntosh / Daughter | 1 / 1 | 1 / 2 | | Daughter married Donald Sinclair |
| 5. | Archie MacCuaig (from Kintail) | Christina MacMillan | 1 | 3 | | Son Angus went to Africa as a teacher. Came home to retire |
| 6. | Norman MacGillivray | Mary MacIntosh | 2 | 3 | 1 Grand-daughter | |
| | Burn Alltan Beag (Little burn) | | | | | |
| 7. | Alexander MacLeod | | 3 | 2 | | Widower. Came from Lochalsh as a Gaelic teacher. One daughter married a man from Tobermory, Ewan MacPhail |
| 8. | Kenneth Fraser | Flora MacIntosh | 1 | | | |
| 9. | John MacGillivray | Lexy MacIntosh | 5 | 4 | | |
| 10. | Archie Fraser | Mary MacAskill | | 6 | | |
| 11. | John MacInnes | Mary MacKenzie | 1 | 3 | | |
| 12. | Seonaid (Jessie) | | | | | Blind & lived alone. Became ill - went to Corran - Died with friends |
| 13. | John MacGillivray or Ian Ban (Fair John) | Bean Ian Ban | 3 | 1 | 2 Grandchildren. 2 other '' | came later from Glasgow. Parents died young - they were Thomson to name. |
| 14. | Duncan MacCuaig | Christina Campbell | | | | No children |

|   | Tenant | Wife | Daughters | Sons | Others |  |
|---|---|---|---|---|---|---|
| 15. | John MacPherson | Ann MacCuaig | 1 | 2 | | Daughter married a man from Lochgilphead - lost at sea when 5 children were young. Brother Angus (bachelor) brought mother & children home to stay with him. |
| 16. | George Campbell | Flora Campbell | 1 | 2 | 1 Grandson →(George MacDougall) | |
| 17. | 2 sisters + 1 brother Effie, Christine and Farquhar Campbell + Farquhar's wife. Farquhar's wife stayed there too | | | | | |
| 18. | Norman MacIntosh | Sarah Fraser | 2 | 2 | | |
| 19. | William Fraser | Ann MacGillivray | 2 | 3 | | |
| 20. | Lachlan Fletcher | Janet MacLeod | 1 | 3 | | Kept a small inn for a time. Son married & had family of 7 sons & 2 daughters |
| | Allt a' mhuilinn | | | | Drew water. Never went dry | |
| 21. | Peggie Fletcher Peggie Bhan | | 1 | 1 Grandson (Peter Livingstone) | | |
| 22. | Donald Campbell | Flora MacKay | 4 | 1 | 1 Grand-daughter | Flora came from Skye |
| 23. | Duncan MacLean | Peggy Mac Innes | 2 | 5 | | Peggy came from Skye. Before he lived in Port Luing oppositeSgeir Mhor in middle of loch |
| 24. | Neil Campbell | | | | | Bachelor. Great fox hunter. Niall Brocair- Neil the Hunter |
| 25. | Donald MacIntosh | Sheila Campbell | | 3 | | |
| 26. | Farquhar Campbell | Jane MacGillivray | 1 | | | Mrs Campbell had a shop. 1 daughter married Duncan Fletcher - had one son –died after first War - army service - not wounded. |
| 27. | Archie MacIntosh, Sister + Nephew (Leasbaig Ban) | | | | | Bachelor |
| 28. | Neil MacIntosh | ? MacPhail | 4 | 2 | | Postman between Glenelg and Skye Arnisdale. After he retired, son Donald took on the job. Walked route twice / day. Neil died at 107 years of age |
| 29. | David MacIntosh (Leasbaig's brother) | Kirsty Sinclair | 2 | | | |
| 30. | John Sinclair | Kirsty MacPhee | 2 | 6 | | Came as farm manager |
| | Totals 36 adults | 25 | 50 | 63 | 9 | Overall total = 183 |

The grand count of folk occupying the thirty cottages described by Duncan comes to a total of 61 adults and 122 children or a grand total of 183.

When the occupants of the houses east of Allt an t-siucair, the Lodge, farm, Glenfield, Achadh a'Ghlinne and the village of Corran are considered it seems likely that the overall Arnisdale population was close to 400 at this time.

Duncan proceeds as follows with further memories of his boyhood:

"Now then I think I will start with the Arnisdale Estate.

Mr Milligan was tenant when I remember. He owned sheep and cattle on all the ground from the river at Kinlochhourn down to Allt a' mhuilinn which runs down about to Camusban. He had nothing to do with the crofts. They were paying rents to Mr Baillie, Dochfour. So also were the Corran Crofters at that time until the late Mr Birkbeck bought the Estate. He gave the crofters at Camusban Beinn na h-eaglaise and the park in which the Free Church is built. The rent was given for the upkeep of the Church. Mr Birkbeck did repair all the houses at Corran and also built new byres and small sheds where they had their boats and stored their fishing gear.

I think it was in 1892 that Mr Birkbeck bought the estate from Mr Baillie. Mr Milligan had only a lease of the Estate. Two years of the lease did not expire so Mr Birkbeck gave him a lump sum to let it go - except for a few hundred sheep which Mr MacMorran was allowed to keep. Mr MacMorran came as Mr Milligan's Farm Manager. He then rented the hill ground that the Corran crofters have this day. He also was in possession of all the low ground up to Glenfield. But he left some years later as he took a big farm in Mull.

Mr Birkbeck was letting part of the estate to tenants who were allowed to shoot so many stags each year and also to fish the Corran river. One year, a Mr Phipps was tenant so before returning to London he was buying about half of the Estate from Coire Mhalagain down to the Schoolhouse burn (Allt na sgoile) and part of Druim Fada. The march of Druim Fada goes up between the two lochs up the glen, and comes down on the loch side a little distance from the Caolasmor houses. A little burn runs down which is the border march. Mr Phipps was coming for a number of years.

He died at Arnisdale and was buried here. Mr Phipps was coming for a number of years and after his death his trustees were letting it now and again for a while. A little before the War (1914-1918 War) started, one Major Fleming bought the place and it was he who built the present lodge. It was not completed when war broke out so I am sorry to say that he did not pass many nights in his new lodge. He was killed in France. Again the Estate was up for sale. So one Sir John Harmood Banner bought it. He was well on in years and was unable to go shooting but his son and relations were quite able. However, the grand old man died but he was coming for many years although in failing health. Again the Estate was sold to Captain Kitson who is at this time still living. He sold it after being in possession for thirty years, to one Mr Watson in May 1960. Mr Watson also bought Camusban in 1961. Camusban had belonged to the Baillies of Dochfour for generations.

I have told you about the thatched cottages which were at the roadside. There was a high tide in 1881 which came into almost all the houses doing much damage but no lives were lost. They then started to build new houses in the late 19th Century and completed in the early twentieth Century. These houses are good, and many yards from where the old ones stood and have slated roofs. So every crofter got his house on his croft but I am sorry to say that most of those who did inhabit these houses are now at their rest. But their sons and daughters are in possession and maybe their grandchildren in a few of them.

It was said at that time that the houses were paid for by the late Lord Burton and that they were in lieu of the old ones so severely damaged by the high tide of 1881. It was also said that when Lord Burton's only daughter, Miss Nellie, married Mr Baillie, he, Lord Burton, did not want thatched cottages to be seen on his son-in-law's estate.

I am afraid that cannot be proven but it can be said of the Lord Burton, of that time, that he was the poor man's friend.

I am not going to write any more but I am sure it is all correct what I have written. Maybe some of the dates are not accurate but they are not very far wrong. But I am sure my English and spelling may be wrong. Please excuse.

Duncan MacTavish
14th February 1962.

I am nearing 81 years of age."

And so Duncan concluded jotting down his comprehensive and detailed memories of the Arnisdale of his boyhood, ending on a typically modest note with self doubt about the quality of his English and his spelling.

Duncan had no reason whatsoever to question his own abilities. Although he had spoken much more Gaelic than English throughout his life, had very limited schooling and worked locally on the sea, the rivers, the glens and the mountains all his days, his hand writing and expression were immaculate. He, like many others of his era, was a scholar but never had the opportunity for further education and to enter the professions.

However, he had a long, satisfying life, he was a great friend to many and those who knew him had nothing but great admiration for all that he was and all that he stood for.

And he has left us a unique record of Camusban and its folk, and their varied challenges and activities in the latter part of the nineteenth century. Tapaidh leibh, Donnchadh.

Several additional observations are relevant on Duncan's memories on the owners of Arnisdale Estate and the shooting/fishing tenants over the years. Duncan gives due credit to Mr Baillie of Dochfour who had the cottages of the Camusban folk relocated and rebuilt with slated roofs after the great flood of 1881. Duncan also spoke highly of Mr Birkbeck who purchased the Arnisdale Estate from Mr Baillie. Mr Birkbeck gave the Camusban crofters extended rough grazing for their sheep and cattle on Beinn na h-eaglaise and also the park in which the Free Church is situated. Mr Birkbeck asked that the fairly nominal rents due by the crofters for the latter area should be paid to the Free Church to help with the upkeep and maintenance of the church. Mr Birkbeck also attended to the rebuilding of the Corran cottages after the 1881 flood and these were also located further back and at higher elevation from the high tide mark to avoid a repeat of the 1881 disaster. Mr Birkbeck also had byres built for all the Corran crofters and also small sheds down close to the shore where they could store their boats and their fishing gear.

The estate owners of that era often had two other types of tenants, in addition to the crofters. The hill and lowland grazings were let out to sheep farmers such as Mr Milligan who probably ran several thousand sheep, both breeding ewes and mature wethers (castrated male sheep) on the Arnisdale grazings. In turn, these sheep farming tenants often employed a farm manager and Mr MacMorran was one of Mr Milligan's managers. It appeared from Duncan MacTavish's comments that Mr MacMorran had a few hundred of his own sheep on Mr Milligan's grazings. This 'perk' to the farm manager was almost certainly in lieu of wages due to Mr MacMorran by Mr Milligan. It appears that when Mr MacMorran gave up his manager's job in Arnisdale he himself took on the tenancy of a large sheep farm in Mull - around the turn of the century. However, in a subsequent generation, the MacMorran family returned to these parts when the late Jimmy MacMorran and his wife Margaret, who is still with us at the time of writing, decided to spend their retirement in the village of Quarry in Glenelg.

The family who assumed the tenancy of the Home Farm and the hill grazing after Mr Milligan were the MacLeods from Reraig near Loch Carron. This was Kenny MacLeod and his family of four daughters and three sons, one of whom, Roddy Mor, was eventually to take over the tenancy from his father when he returned safe and sound from his service at the front throughout the Great War.

One of the shooting and fishing tenants of Mr Birkbeck was a Mr Phipps who, Duncan tells us, died in Arnisdale and was buried in the churchyard there. In his memories (Chapter 15), Donald MacCuaig relates the stories he heard around fireside ceilidhs about Mr Phipps' request for a Highland funeral which was duly granted and an interesting time was had by one and all as they laid Mr Phipps to his rest in Arnisdale.

The final comment on Duncan MacTavish's memories of the lairds and tenants will be reserved for Major Valentine Fleming who had the present lodge built just before the start of the 1914-18 war. There was great sadness in Arnisdale when the news came through that Major Fleming had been killed in France. Major and Mrs Fleming were the parents of Ian Fleming, the famous author from whose writings the character James Bond was conceived. The portraying of James Bond by actors such as Sean Connery and others in desperate crises and daring escapes is well known to all.

**Top Left**. Duncan MacTavish (1881-1966) who left a very detailed record of the Camusban of his boyhood in the 1880s and 1890s and also of the Arnisdale estate owners along with their farm and shooting tenants. Duncan worked as a ghillie/stalker/shepherd on the local estates as well as being involved in fishing and crofting activities. **Right**. The old thatched cottages in Camusban which were situated very close to the shore just above the normal high tide mark. These were badly flooded by the great high tide of 1881. Duncan lived in House Number 15 in this row as a very young boy. His grandfather, grandmother, two uncles, his widowed mother and four brothers and sisters along with Duncan were packed into their tiny house.

**Middle.** The estate proprietor of the time, Lord Burton of Dochfour, financed the building of new houses with slated roofs on slightly higher ground in the 1890 – early 1900s era. The photograph shows the transition between the line of the new houses and the old, since some of the old thatched houses still remain much closer to the shore. The four burns which reach the sea at Camusban are L to R. Alltan Beag, Allt a' Mhuillinn, Allt an t-siucair and Allt na sgoile. Duncan used these as his markers to describe the location of the 30 thatched cottages close to the shore.

**Bottom Left**. The arable crofting area behind the Free Church which was leased to the crofters by the estate proprietors, Mr and Mrs Birkbeck, the rent being payable to the church to assist with its upkeep. **Right**. The population of Arnisdale in Duncan MacTavish's early childhood, including the occupied house in Achadh a' Ghlinne was probably close to 400.

**Top Left**. The thatched houses in Corran in Duncan MacTavish's early childhood. They were situated very close to the tidal mouth of the River Arnisdale and were also flooded by the great high tide of 1881. **Right**. A different view of the same thatched houses from above the bridge. The house on the left is still in existence and was last occupied by Mary Ann Cameron.

**Middle Left.** An artist's record of the thatched houses at Corran (Artist: J Farquharson). **Right.** Corran following the rebuilding of the houses on higher ground to prevent a repeat of the 1881 flooding. The row of 14 new byres are in the bottom right hand corner. The new sheds for the boats and fishing gear do not appear in this picture. These are to the left, closer to the tidal river mouth.

**Bottom Left.** The row of sheds for the boats and fishing gear of the crofters close to the tidal river mouth. The new houses, byres and fishing gear sheds were financed by the Arnisdale Estate owners in the 1890s, Mr and Mrs Birkbeck. **Centre and Right**. Mr and Mrs Birkbeck, who had rented the Arnisdale and Kinloch Hourn estates from 1873 to 1990, purchased the 15,000 acres for £24,000 in 1890. Robert Birkbeck (1836-1920) and Mary Harriet Birkbeck (nee Lubbock) (1935-1910). Mary learned to speak Gaelic.

**Top Left**. The old Arnisdale Lodge which would have been occupied by owners and tenants of the Arnisdale Estate since its erection (around 1870?). These would have included Lord Burton, the Birkbeck family, Mr Phipps and Major Valentine Fleming. **Right**. The new lodge built by Major Fleming just before World War 1 was completed in the early years of the War. Duncan MacTavish commented: 'I am sorry to say that Major Fleming did not pass many nights in his new lodge. He was killed in France.' Major and Mrs Fleming were the parents of Ian Fleming, the famous author from whose writings the character James Bond was conceived.

**Middle Left**. Niall 'Brocair' Campbell, a great fox hunter – occupant of House 24 in the Camusban of Duncan MacTavish's boyhood around 1890. **Right**. Tenants of Arnisdale Home Farm in the later part of the 19th century and up to 1901 were the MacMorran family, forebears of Jimmy and Margaret MacMorran who were resident in Glenelg during their retirement in more recent times. Jimmy's relations, Mr and Mrs MacMorran are in the middle of the back row at the wedding of Jimmy MacDonald and Lily Rosier around 1930.

**Bottom Left**. The tenants of the Arnisdale home farm who succeeded the MacMorrans in 1901 were Coinneach MacLeod and his family from Reraig near Loch Carron. With Coinneach (seated) are his two sons, Donald (left) and Roddy (Roddy Mor). **Right**. Duncan MacTavish in his later years with friends in Quarry, Glenelg. L to R. Duncan, Calum MacLeod, retired Free Church Missionary and a native of Bernera, Harris; Kenneth MacKenzie, Church of Scotland Missionary and a native of Lewis; Calum's brother John MacLeod, a retired lobster fisherman from Bernera, Harris.

# Chapter 33

**The herring fishing and the 'Sgadan Beag Loch Hourn'**

The clachans round Loch Hourn were established originally because of the quality of fishing in the loch, and particularly the herring fishing. Folk such as Peter MacRae, Maggie Lea and Chrissie MacCuaig relate the memories of their parents and grandparents regarding the great days of the herring fishing in the nineteenth century. In the upper reaches of the loch near Runival and Skiary one could walk from shore to shore by stepping across the mass of herring drifters. In the Arnisdale bay you could walk from the Crudh Ard to Eilean Tioram across the larger and smaller boats packed together there as they all chased the herring. The herring catch provided income, while salted herring was a vital component of the daily diet, along with potatoes, for a large part of the year. The herring fishing provided the basis of the subsistence economy for centuries.

But Loch Hourn herring also helped to feed the outside world as the fishermen from all along the west coast, from the inner and outer Hebrides, from the East Coast and also from Ireland came to harvest the herring.

(In 'Antiquarian Notes', II, Pages 152-153, Charles Fraser Mackintosh states that Coll MacDonell of Barrisdale held from 1788 a commission to regulate the fisheries - there had been disputes between the fishermen on thieving. He quotes from a letter by Coll in 1809. "We have now 60 to 70 boats on the coast this season from the south that did not used to frequent our lochs and they are very much suspected by all the fishermen for stealing and destroying of nets". In August of 'another year', Coll writes "We had no less than one thousand coasting boats there last week and every vessel on the fishing").

In the latter part of the 18th century, Thomas Telford's engineers and planners were 'surveying' Loch Hourn with a view to establishing a port for landing and processing the herring and then exporting the cured products to help feed the nation. Arnisdale was considered as such a major centre while locations on the southern shore of the loch were also under review. Maggie Lea in Chapter 27 provides the origin of the track 'Ceum Dick' or Dick's path between Lea and Crowlick where Telford's unfortunate surveyor, Dick, slipped and fell over the adjacent cliff to his doom on the shore below. After intensive surveys to find the best location for a major herring port in the area, it would seem that it was Mallaig - at the mouth of adjacent Loch Nevis which was selected for such development rather than any location on Loch Hourn.

The herring is a migratory fish which basically follows its food source which is almost entirely plankton. The shoals move from place to place according to the movements of plankton. Some of the main wintering locations of the herring are areas of the North Sea, the Atlantic and the sea lochs of the Outer Hebrides. Some herring are spring spawners while others are autumn spawners, the timing of spawning being governed by the balance of darkness and daylight hours through the influence of the hormone melatonin which is produced during the hours of darkness. As spawning time approached, the herring shoals would make for the spawning grounds where they themselves hatched. The herring spawn in gravel beds or on coarse shell sand and among the traditional spawning grounds were areas west of the Outer Hebrides near St Kilda, Ballantrae off the Ayrshire coast (the Clyde herring), the south end of Arran (which was a spring spawning area), locations close to Coll and Canna, Kilmaluig off the north coast of Skye, Melvaig near Gairloch, Whiten Head near Cape Wrath, areas around Fair Isle, east of Start's Point in Orkney and off the Buchan Coast. Some of these areas such as Coll, Canna and Melvaig are now used considerably less as spawning grounds as they were formerly. Willie MacKenzie of Arnisdale is certain that some herring spawned in Loch Hourn on gravel beds opposite Lea and also up at Skiary, and his memory is that they were spring spawners.

The arrival of the herring at the traditional spawning grounds each season is fairly predictable (within one to two weeks) because the timing of spawning is dependent on daily light to dark cycles. However, the arrival of the herring in sea lochs such as Loch Hourn was much less predictable - it might vary from season to season by a month or more.

Since the herring shoals followed their food source - the plankton - it is interesting to know of the forces which carried the plankton around on their migratory journeys over the seasons. These journeys appear to be influenced by the currents and by water temperature - which in turn is influenced by air temperature and the effects of storms in mixing the water from different parts of the ocean. When the adult herring reached mainland sea lochs, such as Loch Hourn, they were mixed with the juvenile herring which used the sea lochs as nursery areas.

In days gone by, when the herring fishing started in the season, with the sound conservation measures practised at that time, only the largest herrings were netted, the smaller herrings and fry passing through the mesh of the drift nets to allow them to grow and mature and to provide the basis of the harvest for subsequent years. Having sampled a sea loch such as Loch Hourn in their earlier years it is possible that, having escaped the harvest, the same herring may have returned in subsequent seasons. Thus, a pattern of migration back to the territory of their young lives may have been established in the same way as applies to the migratory habits of other fish such as salmon although there is no real evidence for this in the case of herring. However, it is more likely that herring returned in successive seasons to the areas in which they first spawned.

If there was a tendency to migrate back in successive seasons to the spawning grounds in Loch Hourn, this might explain the characteristics claimed for Loch Hourn herring as the 'Sgadan Beag Loch Hourn' (the small Loch Hourn herring). These herring as well as being smaller were also reputed to be fatter, sweeter, tastier and altogether a much more delectable dish than the large coarse herring characteristic of, for example, the herring fishings around Barra. Of course, it is also possible that Loch Hourn herring may have been smaller because they were younger at harvesting and they may have been fatter because they enjoyed better feeding. In his 'Tales of Barra - told by the Coddy' (Johnston and Bacon, Publishers, Edinburgh), John MacPherson ('The Coddy') reports that: 'At the beginning of November it was customary for the Barra fishermen to go to the lochs, Loch Hourn and Loch Nevis, to fish herrings'. They went to Loch Hourn in early November perhaps simply because the remaining herrings had by then deserted the traditional fishing grounds closer to Barra but possibly also because the Loch Hourn herring were in greater demand by the Barra folk and others because they were of better eating quality.

Certainly, Donald John MacLeod of Glenelg who sailed the seven seas, knows the western seaboard like the back of his hand, and who is well acquainted with sailors and fishermen who know it equally well, confirms that Loch Hourn herring were reputed to have a unique quality.

Among these worthy characters who knew Loch Hourn herring and who are still with us at the time of writing are Ali Finlayson from Kyle of Lochalsh and Roddy MacRae, Milton, Applecross. Roddy MacRae tells the story of the special pilgrimage he was sent on in his younger days to buy barrels of Loch Hourn salt herring for many neighbours in the Applecross district. From the north coast of Applecross at Ardheaslaig he would set off walking over the Applecross hill to Kishorn and would then take a short cut via Reraig across the hill to Stromeferry. He would cross on the ferry boat, catch the train for Kyle on the other side and at Kyle he would catch Calum Garde's mail boat to Glenelg. There, after Donald Sinclair loaded the Arnisdale and Loch Hourn mail on to the horse and trap, he would set off with Donald for Arnisdale. On arrival there he would purchase the required number of barrels of

Loch Hourn herring for the Applecross folk. Roddy described the Loch Hourn herring as 'small, fat, very tasty herring'. He commented further: 'The fishermen knew the best herring. They could tell the difference between the Loch Hourn, the Loch Torridon, the Loch Kishorn herring and the sgadan from other fishing grounds. They knew by the size, the shape, the fatness and by the eating quality'.

Another character who was very familiar with the quality of the Loch Hourn herring was Sandy Mor (MacLean) from Mallaig. Sandy would come into Loch Hourn with his little white launch and buy boxes of fresh herring from the drifters and the ring net boats. He would then set off and call at the piers at Arnisdale, Glenelg, Loch Duich, Dornie and Ardelve in turn. When Sandy arrived 'in port' at that time of the year, the folk would know the reason of his 'errand'. They would flock to the pier with their containers and do a deal with Sandy to get their supplies of 'sgadan beag Loch Hourn' to take home and prepare a delicious fresh fry in oatmeal for the family.

The great resilience of the folk who fished Loch Hourn for herring in the old days is typified by the story told by John MacLeod of Daviot, Inverness whose ancestral home was in Kilmuir, Skye. John's grandfather, John MacKenzie was fishing out of Uig with the Stewarts – Calum 'Lottie' and Calum Beag – and with William and Angus Campbell. They shared two herring skiffs and while fishing in Loch Hourn one October in the late 1920s and setting their nets at dusk, John MacKenzie fell overboard in fairly rough weather. With the darkness coming down they quickly lost sight of John. They searched the area very thoroughly for a long time – but in vain. They were devastated and in the intense darkness had desperate feelings of hopelessness. They decided that it was futile to search any longer so they made for Mallaig to unload their morning's catch. Having done this, Calum 'Lottie' Stewart asserted that their great friend John MacKenzie was a fine swimmer and he might have made it to the shore, despite the rough seas and the low water temperature. All willing themselves to believe in such a miracle, they set off through the night for Loch Hourn and their fishing location of the previous night, aiming to arrive before dawn so that they could search thoroughly again at first light. They reached the area while still very dark and as dawn broke one of them noticed movement next to a float which was supporting a herring net. They moved in as quickly as they could and their spirits overflowed as one, for there was John holding fast to the float. They hauled him aboard, dried him off as quickly as they could, rubbed him down to stimulate his circulation and got him into some of the warm dry clothes they themselves were wearing. Sitting as close as he could to benefit from the heat of the engine John gradually began to lose his blue colour and his external temperature started to change from extreme coldness to some semblance of warmth. John recovered without further treatment and resumed his fishing with his friends immediately. Grandson John MacLeod commented that few fishermen could swim at that time but luckily his grandfather was an exception to the rule. Now in his forties, John MacKenzie had been in the Merchant Navy as a young man and had become an accomplished swimmer. This was to stand John in good stead during that stormy cold night on Loch Hourn. However, John MacLeod remembered his grandmother telling him that Grandfather had never been the same again after that long night in the very cold waters of Loch Hourn and he died of heart trouble a few years later at the age of fifty.

For decades and centuries, Loch Hourn yielded a bountiful harvest of herring. No records are available now on the precise extent of this harvest. However, it is reported that in 1882 the herring catch in Loch Hourn was 90,000 crans. A cran was four standard willow baskets full of fresh herring. Each full basket weighed approximately 8 stones (112 lb. or 50kg). So that four baskets weighed 448 lb. or 200 kg. Thus there were approximately five crans to the tonne and 90,000 crans weighed approximately 18,000 tonnes. Since the total annual herring harvest around the British Isles at the time was about one million tonnes, Loch Hourn made a sizeable contribution to this total harvest. Regarding the number of herrings per cran, for normal sized herring there were, on average, some 650 herrings per cran but probably closer to 700 per cran for Loch Hourn herring because they were smaller. Thus there were about 3,500 Loch Hourn herring per tonne and therefore over sixty million herring in the 1882 catch. This would be enough to give every member of the current population in Britain one dinner of Loch Hourn herring each year with several million surplus for people to fight over for another dinner the next day!

The latter part of last century was a great boom time for Arnisdale and the other clachans around Loch Hourn. The population numbered around 600 folk, they were sure of a major quality component of their total annual diet and the herring fishing provided a reasonable income for the fishermen, the boat builders, the curers, the shops and stores supplying the fishermen with food and their other requirements, the pubs and also the crofts in supplying the fishermen with any surplus potatoes and dairy produce, as well as perhaps some mutton and venison.

Arnisdale and Loch Hourn have gone from 'boom to bust' in the intervening period. Why has the very basis of the local economy been destroyed in the interim?

The answer to this vital question almost certainly lies in the desecration of the careful fish stock conservation policies practised by local Loch Hourn people and the fishermen from neighbouring parts of the western seaboard over many centuries. The beginning of the end occurred when the 'sea raiders' came in from other parts of Britain and Europe and, with utter selfishness, based their fishing policies on short term gains rather than long term conservation methods. However, fishery experts speculate that changes in sea currents, the associated movement of plankton and therefore the basic diet of the herring, may also have contributed to the decline in the herring fishing in the western seaboard.

Some background on the fish stock conservation practices of old is desirable to explain the effects of the latter day plunderers. Traditional herring fishing was based on drift netting from steam or motor driven herring drifters. Drift nets were selective in the size of fish caught, smaller fish escaping through the mesh to ensure a harvest for later years. In addition, the drift nets were set only at night and lifted in the early morning. The plankton are nearer the surface of the water at night and the herring rise from the seabed to feed. Ian Campbell from Glenelg spent a year at the herring fishing on the ring net boat the 'Misty Isle' (which belonged to the MacRae brothers from Kyleakin in Skye) in the 1950s. They operated from Loch Hourn to the Outer Hebrides and he recalls that in the summer fishing (May to September) they could not set their drift nets before 5 p.m. each day and the net had to be hauled in and the catch made before 4 a.m. the next morning. In addition, they could not set nets between 4 p.m. on a Saturday and Monday morning. The selective nature of the drift nets and the specified non-fishing times gave a goodly proportion of the fish a chance to avoid capture and to provide the basis of good harvests in subsequent years.

However, the drift netters were first replaced by ring netters, then by pair trawlers and finally by purse seiners. These techniques were very non-selective in the fish caught, with the result that many smaller younger fish were needlessly caught and wasted. In addition, trawlers and purse seine net boats can operate throughout the day and deep trawls can capture everything from the sea bed during the day when the fish are operating in deeper water.

In addition, with echo sounding and sonars, detection of the herring shoals is much more accurate - on either side of the boat and in deeper water. Previous to echo sounding, the fisherman had to use much simpler techniques to detect the location of the shoals. When the shoals first appeared in an area, perhaps the first indication that the sgadan had arrived was when they were seen playing on the surface of the water. If they were below the surface, their density and rapid movements could create phosphorescence which experienced fishermen could spot. In addition, Ian Campbell was told by some old fishermen that they could actually smell the herring when they arrived in their large shoals.

The activity of the seagulls and gannets were always tell-tale signs that the herring had arrived. Seagulls can only catch the herring when they are close to the surface of the water. However, if the fish were well below the surface, the gannets dive for their quarry. If the gannets dive from only a short height above the sea, the herring are not too far below the surface. However, when gannets dive from a great height, this allows them to achieve a much deeper dive and this behaviour indicates to the fishermen the depth at which the shoals are to be found. Another indicator of the herring being in the vicinity, according to Ian Campbell, is when the fishermen see a particular variety of whale around. This type of whale goes for the herring and the fishermen call it the 'herring hog'. It appears that most types of whale and porpoises will use the herring as a food source when available. Donald John MacLeod mentioned another technique used in the past to detect the shoals. As the boat moved along, one of the fishermen would trail a fine wire, weighted down at its end, from the stern of the boat. When sensitive experienced fingers felt the herring hitting the wire they had detected a shoal and could get to work at their harvesting.

Another reason for the serious decline in the herring fishing is because of the harvesting which now goes on as the shoals arrive at their traditional spawning grounds. The timing of this arrival can be predicted within a week or so each year. Two of the best known spawning grounds close to Loch Hourn are at Kilmaluaig at the north end of Skye and at Melvaig near Gairloch. Obviously catching the herring when heavy with roe before they spawn is not the most sensible practice in terms of conservation of stocks for the future! Herring caught at this stage or 'roe herring' once commanded a much higher than average price to supply the Japanese market.

Ian Campbell recalls that while they spent their summer (May to September) fishing closer to home, for their winter fishing they would go to the Outer Hebrides and operate in the lochs around the Uists, in the sound of Harris, around Lewis and off Barra Head. They stopped their winter fishing in February which gave them time to repair their boats and their nets before the summer herring fishing started again in May.

The serious decline in the annual herring harvest around the British Isles is indicated by the facts that the UK herring catch in 1882 was reported to be one million tonnes, whereas the current UK herring quota is for 90,000 tonnes per year - less that one tenth of the 1882 catch in British waters and only five times more than the Loch Hourn catch in that year.

It is not surprising in view of the crucial importance of the herring to the folk in Arnisdale and the other Loch Hourn clachans that so many of the contributors to this book have mentioned the 'sgadan beag Loch Hourn' in their own memories and in stories about their forebears. However, the herring fishing did not please all sectors in the communities. While the landowners no doubt enjoyed their salt and fresh herring like everybody else, they knew from experience that many of the fishermen enjoyed a bit of roast venison; these same people were also very knowledgeable about the habits of the deer, they were good with the 'glass' as they scoured the steep hillsides rising above both shores of the loch, they were adept at stalking and were excellent marksmen with the rifle. So the landowners invested in employing and housing resident 'watchers' at locations such as Caolasmor, Torr a' choit, Skiary, Runival, Lea and Crowlick. The watchers kept an eye on the fishing boats and their occupants and, of course, they doubled up as ghillies/stalkers/shepherds working for their respective estates.

There were many confrontations between the estates and the herring fishers and one of the best known of these is still known as 'The Siege of Lea'. This occurred in the mid 1920s and Maggie Lea remembers the incident very well as she and her relatives watched the drama unfold close to their home in Lea. 'There was great tension in the air, throughout the day in question', she recalls. The month was early October, the herring were in Loch Hourn and the stags were in prime condition before the start of the breeding season or the rut. A Lochcarron boat was purportedly drift netting for herring close to Eilean a'Phiobaire (The Piper's Island) which is fairly close to the shore to the north-west of Lea. However, the Arnisdale gamekeeper of the time was on the move at first light in the morning and, as he scanned the face of Mam Li on the other side of the loch, he picked out two figures furtively making their way up the face of the hill just opposite Eilean a'Phiobaire. He cycled with all speed to Peggy Ann's Post Office at the far side of Camusban and arranged for Peggy Ann to send a telegram to the Knoydart Estate Office at Inverie on the other side of the Knoydart Peninsula from Lea. The message was duly received, the powerful estate launch was boarded with all speed by a formidable force of Knoydart Estate employees - the factor, head game-keeper and several robust and agile under-keepers. They were rounding Rudha Raonuill in double quick time and they made great speed as they passed the shores of Sandaig, Doune, Airor and Samadalan in turn. When they rounded Rudh Ard Slisneach they were already into Loch Hourn and soon Crowlick, Creag an t-Sagairt and Rudha Ruadh were behind them. They were now within sight of Eilean a'Phiobaire and the herring drifter. Undoubtedly the fishermen still aboard the drifter were taken by surprise but these Carrannachs were seasoned campaigners and knew all the tricks about keeping cool in the crisis which had just begun. They hoped, of course, that the launch was on its way on estate business further up the loch to Barrisdale but reality soon dawned as it slowed down, came alongside and they were subjected to intense interrogation as to why they were so apparently understaffed. The Carrannachs still on board bluffed as best they could as they busied themselves sorting their nets and boxing their fish after their night's fishing. The two hunters on the hill, who had not long before shot a fine stag, had a grandstand view of proceedings as they peered through the rank autumn grass as they lay on their bellies on their vantage point near the summit of Meall Gruamach.

They hoped, of course, that their mates still on board their drifter would manage to convince the Estate officials that nothing of an unsavoury nature was afoot. However, the Knoydart Estate band knew they were on to something and decided to mount a siege so as to cut off the suspected Carrannach poachers from their boat. The launch was duly anchored between the herring drifter and the shore and six or seven 'glasses' were trained almost constantly to try to pick out any unusual human movements on the hill face.

As the day progressed, the two Carrannachs marooned on the hill dared not move, the day became colder, wetter and breezier by the minute. They were becoming hungrier and colder as each hour progressed and they hoped against hope that soon after dusk the siege would be lifted and they could make their escape to the drifter and their friends. However, the Knoydart Estate boys were equally determined to teach the Carrannachs and their fellow fishermen a hard lesson on this occasion and the siege continued into the darkness. However, the two Carrannachs could now at least get up and try to warm themselves up a bit. When they got the blood pursing through their veins a bit more they dragged the stag to a hideaway and covered it, along with their rifle, with sphagnum moss. Although it was a very dark night, their eyes were well attuned to the darkness and as they made their way stealthily down to the shore, they could see very clearly the outline of the launch and the drifter beyond. They decided to swim for it and ploughed as quietly as they could through the cold sea of an October night. Eventually the drifter was reached, their mates heard a quiet gurgle of water beside the boat and found the two worthies alongside. As some of their mates hauled them aboard, another pulled up the anchor. The engine was started and off the drifter sailed into the darkness to the mouth of Loch Hourn and northwards towards the Kylerhea narrows. The two Carrannachs not only survived their severe hypothermia but, the story goes, the drifter wheeled round when they thought the Knoydart Estate boys would have left for Inverie. Sure enough, at around midnight the Knoydart launch had gone, the stag and rifle were duly retrieved from their hiding place on the hill face and no doubt there would have been some fine feasts of roast venison in several homes in Lochcarron in the days and weeks ahead. And, no doubt, the story of the great 'Siege of Lea' was retold in the right company many times over.

As stated earlier in this chapter, although the arrival of the herring at their main spawning grounds each summer was predictable within about a week or so, when the herring would arrive in inland sea lochs such as Loch Hourn was anybody's guess. On the only year which the author spent in Arnisdale as a boy (1946), he was mesmerised early one morning in mid-October as he went outside to start the milking when the gulls were making an unearthly noise and were involved in feverish activity out in the bay. On glancing round with quizzical surprise at Roddy Mor who was following, the latter commented excitedly, 'Oh, the sgadan boy, the sgadan'. That was the first arrival of the herring in Loch Hourn that year.

Another young lad was equally excited in 1963 when he experienced the arrival of the herring one August evening. This was Peter Fletcher, son of Lachie and Chrissie Fletcher, who lived at Glenfield, Lachie being estate manager at the time. Here Peter records his clear memories of that exciting evening.

**The Last Great Herring Fishing in Loch Hourn (by Peter Fletcher)**

It was August 1963, and I was ten years of age. It was a mild, still overcast Friday evening and I was on my way from Corran by boat up Loch Hourn heading for Barrisdale. In the boat with me was the local postman Willie Mackenzie who, in those days, delivered the mail to Barrisdale on Friday evenings. This was convenient for my grandfather (George MacDougall) to get a sail back down to Arnisdale for the weekend. My grandfather worked as a ghillie on Barrisdale Estate and looked forward to coming home to stay with us in Arnisdale for the weekend. After sailing for ten minutes or so, having just passed the Rudha Camas na Cailinn, Willie suddenly stopped the Seagull outboard motor, stood up in the boat and said: 'I think there is herring in the loch, you know'. After studying the surface of the water for a few minutes, he pointed to what looked like froth on the surface and said: 'I'm pretty sure that's herring'. He started the engine again and once more headed in the direction of Barrisdale. When we arrived at the Fraoch Eilean, which is just beside Barrisdale, my grandfather was waiting patiently on the shore for the pick up. As soon as we hit the shore, Willie told him very excitedly the good news of the herring shoal. After dumping the mail in a collection box, we once more headed back down the loch towards Arnisdale. After passing the Corr Eileanan, Willie cut the engine once more to look again for the herring. After seeing the froth on the surface of the water - and by this time accompanied by seagulls, my grandfather confirmed it was herring - and in abundance - as the froth stretched all the way back down the loch to Rudha Camus na Cailinn. On arrival back at Willie's boat shed, which is situated at the east end of the enclosed croftlands at the back of Corran, we sorted out the herring nets before going home to the house for something to eat. After tea and home-made scones, and managing to persuade my mother and father to allow me to go, my grandfather and I threw on our jackets and headed back to Corran to Willie's boat shed. When we arrived at the boat shed Willie was waiting for us, anxious to get away up the loch to where we had spotted the herring earlier. By this time it was dark - just right for setting the net. We pushed the boat out and steered back up the loch towards Barrisdale. It took us about ten minutes to round the Rudha Camus na Cailinn and at that point Willie stopped the engine to listen for the sound of herring playing. A few seconds after the boat had come to rest, the sound of herring playing could clearly be heard all around the boat. You could also see the fish breaking the surface of the water in the moonlight.

For me, there was great excitement as my grandfather took the oars and Willie started to feed the net out the back of the boat. When the net was set it was time then to move fifty yards or so away and wait for the net to do its job. By this time it was around one o'clock in the morning and I was feeling very cold - not having long trousers on. After waiting for an hour or so, it was time to move back in to lift the net. The excitement was building up as my grandfather took the oars and moved back in towards the net. The first thing we noticed was some of the corks were below the water, indicating that the net was heavy with fish. Willie grabbed the buoy at the end of the net and started to haul the rope - and then the net - into the boat. The net was a mass of silver darlings glinting in the moonlight. It seemed to take ages to remove the fish from the net and by the time we were finished, the floor of the boat was about a foot deep in herring - in fact, I had to hold my feet off the bottom of the boat to keep the herring from going down inside my wellie boots! Before heading home, the net was set again for Willie and my grandfather to check in the morning on their way across the loch to a sheep clipping in Li.

When we arrived back at Willie's boat shed, we beached the boat and carried the herring in buckets up the shore and emptied them into fish boxes in the boat shed. When the job was complete, we made our way home - cold, hungry and stinking of fish. The following morning I had a long lie in bed while my grandfather and Willie were out again checking the net before going on to the clipping in Li. When they lifted the net, there was nothing left in it but herring heads - the dogfish had eaten them through the night. On the Saturday, one or two of the locals phoned over to Kyle for coarse salt - for salting the herring. It was a big mistake! Word was now out of the herring bonanza in Loch Hourn and on Monday night there were three or four boats (ring netters) in the loch from Kyle. The following day it was eight or nine boats and by the end of the week it was forty or fifty boats from all down the west coast and from as far away as Ayr. And at night the loch was lit up like a small town. The bonanza lasted around three weeks, and by that time everybody in the village and beyond had their firkins (small barrels) of herring salted for the winter. Over the next few years there were small shoals of herring in the loch but nothing on the scale of the bonanza of 1963. Hopefully, one day, if given a chance - they will return and the local folk will once more talk of the 'Sgadan beag Loch Hourn'.

Many will echo these last sentiments of Peter Fletcher. Tapaidh leat, a Phadraig.

**Top Left**. In the great days of the herring fishing in the nineteenth century it was said that the fishing boats were so concentrated in Arnisdale Bay that one could walk from boat to boat from the Crudh Ard to Eilean Tioram. **Right**. It was also said that up the loch at Runival, Skiary and Torr a' Choit, one could walk from shore to shore across the massed boats. The picture shows Aileen Cameron from Kinloch Hourn high up on the slope of Druim Fada almost directly across from Skiary on the southern shore. The headlands upper left are those at Runival while the headland opposite and just below Aileen's position is the croftland at Torr a Choit. The width of the loch at this point is approximately one mile.

**Middle Left**. A welcome catch of 'sgadan beag Loch Hourn' in more recent times in Arnisdale (November 1985). L to R. Willie MacKenzie, Andy MacLaren, Charlie MacTavish, Bob Crombie, Doug Jacobs, Archie MacLean, Alan MacKenzie and the local Coast Guard. **Middle**. Donald John MacLeod from Glenelg who heard from the old folk about the special qualities and popularity of the Loch Hourn herring. Donald John also commented on the trailing weighted fine wire techniques used to detect the herring shoals in the old days before the days of echo sounding equipment. **Right**. Iain Campbell from Gallder, Glenelg who in his young days had a few seasons at the herring fishing with the MacRae brothers from Kyleakin.

**Bottom**. The MacRae boat from Kyleakin, 'The Misty Isle' (left) with skipper Alistair MacRae at the helm (centre) and some of the crew of the pair trawlers, the Misty Isle and the Acorn (right).

**Top Left**. When the herring came into Loch Hourn each season, the MacKenzie brothers from Ardneaskan on Loch Carron with their herring drifter the 'Caberfeidh' would be among the first to arrive for the fishing (around 1930). L to R. Alick MacRae, Kenny, Ewan and Donald MacKenzie and their father, Murdo. **Right**. Kenny MacKenzie, co-owner of the 'Caberfeidh'.

**Middle**. The herring drifter, the 'Caberfeidh'.

**Bottom Left**. The family of Kenny MacKenzie of the 'Caberfeidh' - Murdo (left) and Janet. On the right is Janet's husband-to-be Roddy 'Jeck' MacKenzie (1950s). **Right**. John MacKenzie from Uig, Skye who survived overnight for almost 10 hours in the cold October waters of Loch Hourn (around 1930) after falling overboard in the darkness of the previous night. John was a good swimmer and when morning light came in, John was found hanging on to the float of a herring net.

**Top Left** Mesmerised by the feverish activity of the gulls in the bay one mid October morning while setting off towards the byre to start the milking, brought the excited response from Roddy Mor 'Oh, the sgadan boy, the sgadan'. The herring had arrived on their annual call to Loch Hourn.  **Right**.  Willie MacKenzie (left) and young Peter Fletcher. 'Willie suddenly stopped the Seagull outboard motor, stood up in the boat, looked, listened and then said "I think there is herring in the loch".'
**Middle Left**.  Peter Fletcher's grandfather, George MacDougall (left).  'After seeing the froth on the surface of the water – and by this time accompanied by seagulls – my grandfather confirmed that it was herring – and in abundance!'  **Right**.  Eilean a' Phiobaire, just offshore between Lea and Rudha Ruadh – the scene of 'The Siege of Lea'.
**Bottom Left**.  The estate boat was anchored between the herring drifter and the shore – and six or seven 'glasses' were trained on the face of the hill to try to spot the suspected poachers.  **Right**.  When darkness fell, the two Carranachs swam out to the drifter, the anchor was raised and off they set for home, to return later when the 'coast was clear' to collect their rifle and the fine stag.

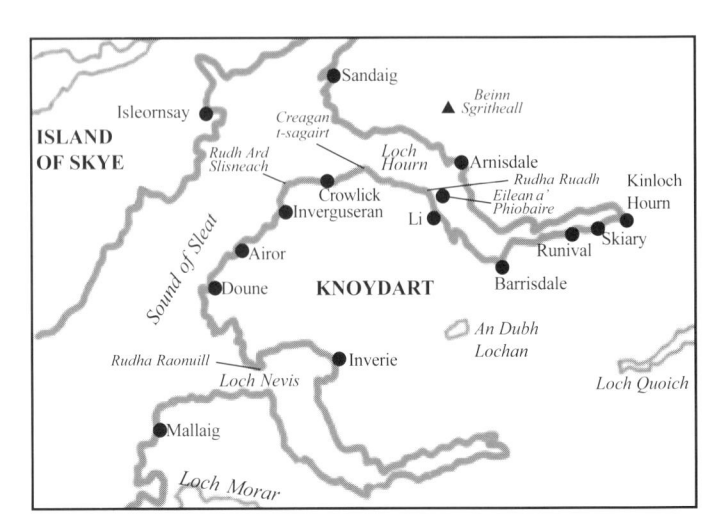

418

## Chapter 34

**Sightings of 'sea monsters' of uncertain origin in Loch Hourn**

There are several accounts in previous chapters of sightings of strange 'sea creatures' in Loch Hourn over the past century or so.

In her letter of 19 December 1933, Mrs Mary MacTaggart, the wife of the Glenelg Church of Scotland Minister wrote to Daniel MacDonald of Corran about the strange sea creature he had seen in Loch Hourn some ten years previously (see Chapter 13). In her letter, Mrs. MacTaggart jotted down her memories of what Daniel had described to her what he had seen:

"I have a vague idea that you saw a long neck rise out of the water, turn its head from side to side as if looking round about, then sinking into the water again. The other day I got the enclosed article from an old gentleman in Glasgow. He wanted to know if I had heard of the Rev. John Macrae of Glenelg seeing the sea serpent in Loch Hourn in 1872. I got the story of that event a good many years ago, from an old man, who, as a boy was along with Mr Macrae, helping to sail the little yacht when they saw a very big animal, black and round like a herring barrel. When it rose quite close to them, it sent a wave aboard the yacht, causing them great alarm. It wriggled through the water like a huge eel, and they counted 8 or 9 humps showing above the water. You will see a sketch of it in the cutting I enclose.

It seems to me that the sketch of the creature seen in Loch Ness at Fort Augustus by Mr Russell, is very like what you saw in Loch Hourn. It looks as if it is a sea-serpent that is in Loch Ness.

Will you be so kind as to write and describe to me what you actually saw, and about what year. And will you please return this article, as I want to send it back to the old gentleman. Mr MacTaggart is in Edinburgh just now but will be home on Saturday.

With kindest regards, and wishing you all a very Happy Christmas.

                    Yours very sincerely
                    Mary MacTaggart.

Unfortunately, there is no record of Daniel MacDonald's reply to Mrs MacTaggart, nor of the article to which Mrs MacTaggart refers.

**Mrs Mary MacTaggart's drawing (1933) of her interpretation of the sightings of Donald MacDonald (around 1920) and the Rev. John MacRae (1872) of a 'sea monster' in Loch Hourn and of Russell's sightings of a strange creature in Loch Ness (1933)**

419

In addition to Daniel MacDonald, several other Loch Hourn folk had reported seeing a strange creature in the loch. These included the present Willie MacKenzie (Willie the Post) from Corran, Willie's grandmother (Mairi Bhan) and Robert Foster, also from Corran (Chapter 8), Willie Campbell and his grandmother, Mrs Christina Stoddart (Chapter 28), the three MacDiarmid brothers - Tom, Sandy and Alan (Chapter 20), and Roddy MacPherson along with two friends (Chapter 20) and Hugh MacMillan, Runival (Chapter 25).

Another sighting of a strange 'beast' was made by Donald Stewart, Fish Merchant at Kyle of Lochalsh, who died in the mid 1950s. Donald had reported his sighting to the late Calum Garde from Glenelg who in turn passed the story on to Donald John MacLeod of Glenelg. Donald John's memory of the story was that Donald Stewart was fishing at the mouth of Loch Hourn opposite Port Luinge, 'which was a great place for catching dogfish'. As Donald was fishing, a 'big thing' came up out of the water fairly close to the boat. He did not know what it was. It submerged soon after it surfaced and he saw no further sign of the strange beast. Donald knew all members of the whale and shark families very well but the creature he saw did not resemble any sea creature that was known to him. Donald John commented that the location where Donald Stewart made his sighting is very deep - around 90 fathoms or approximately 540 feet.

The creature sighted by Roddy MacPherson and his two friends in the 1930s very near the small island of Eilean a' Chlamhain is very close to Donald Stewart's fishing location. Roddy MacPherson considers that he and Donald may have seen the same type of creature.

Another who spotted a sea monster in the same area was Willie MacLeod of Sandaig (see Chapter 20). Willie recalls a frightening experience as a small boy as he was returning to the shore in the rowing boat with his father and two brothers after servicing the light in the Sandaig Island Lighthouse. However, the characteristic huge dorsal fin of the beast as it approached their little boat at speed, left little doubt in father John Donald's mind that this was a very large bull killer whale. On describing their experience to their friend and neighbour Gavin Maxwell after they reached the safety of the shore, the identity of their sighting as a killer whale was confirmed.

Further along the shore towards Glenelg from Sandaig in the early 1940s, the young MacDiarmid brothers had a terrifying experience as they fished for cod in a productive location just offshore which was well known to them. When they spotted a great commotion in the sea between themselves and the shore and heard a great roar from the beast, their fishing was promptly abandoned as they rowed frantically to the safety of the shore. From Gavin Maxwell's description of the various well known 'monsters of the deep', this creature would again appear to be a killer whale, the roar which terrified the young boys probably being the exhalation of air as the whale surfaced combined with the inhalation of a new supply of fresh air.

However, the identity of the sea serpent - like creatures seen in Loch Hourn by the Rev. John MacRae and his companion in 1872, by Mairi Bhan (Mrs MacKenzie) in the 1890s, by Willie Campbell and his grandmother and also Robert Foster in the early 1900s, by Daniel MacDonald around 1920, by Roddy MacPherson and his two friends in the early 1930s and by young Willie MacKenzie around 1940 remains a mystery. As far as is now known, these folk, although living on the shores of Loch Hourn and sailing its waters throughout their lives, made their sighting only once in each of their lifetimes. The spotting of strange sea creatures is not unique to Loch Hourn. Many islanders, mainland seaboard dwellers and seafarers have reported over the centuries making 'once in a lifetime' sightings of strange marine beings.

In 'Tales of Barra - told by The Coddy', the narrator (John MacPherson of Barra - alias 'The Coddy') relates experiences of Barra and other Hebridean fishermen as follows:

**THE SEA MONSTER**
This story is from my father and from the people who were with him in the boat at the time. One day my father was on the west side of Barra fishing lobsters and it was in the herring fishing season, and lo and behold, they saw what they thought was a fleet of herring nets that were lost by a boat — it was that big. On going nearer to it, they discovered it was moving, and what they were thinking were buoys on the nets were not buoys at all, and they came to a decision that it must have been a tremendous beast. And some of the lumps were going down, and others coming up, and that led them to understand it was a monster, and an unusual monster, and they tried to get past it — which they managed — and they rowed to the shore as quickly as they could. Well, they were so terrified that they could not even look behind them, but the last look they gave, there were only two bits of the monster showing and then it went down, and never after or before were any of the fishermen working in that place or in that direction seeing it again. And after hearing so much about monsters nowadays it is very probable it was a sea monster - of what nature nobody can say.

The Coddy proceeds:

**ANOTHER SEA MONSTER**
Now the crew of the fishing-boat 'Fly-by-Night' was herring fishing and that evening I am going to talk about particularly they were about thirty-three and a quarter miles off Barra Head, on the famous ground called Stanton Bank. There was not a breath of wind and they began to shoot the nets with the assistance of the oars. There was no motor of any description, with the result they had to shoot the nets with their oars. When the nets were shot and everything was still and calm they were on top almost of Stanton Bank and they heard a fearful moaning from a sou'westerly direction and they all looked at each other with astonishment, wondering what was this moaning. Then shortly afterwards they saw at the stern of the boat a tremendous beast breaking the water, and this beast, which was horrible to look at with the size of it, put its paws on the very deck of the stern of the fishing-boat. They all looked at each other and did not know what to say and one of them cried out " Get a bucket of fire from the stove." And they took the bucket of fire and they gave it to the beast right in the head and in the eyes and the moment the beast felt the heat he went down to the very bottom and fortunately he did not make another attempt to put in an appearance.

Had not these men acted so quickly and thrown the bucket of fire on, more than probably the whole boat would have been sunk. Now they set about hauling the gear. They started to haul their nets -they had about forty or fifty out - and when it was finished there was nothing else for them to do. There was no wind - they had to lie there and still the beast had every opportunity to come to the surface again and attempt to board them, but she did not. And when the wind broke out, they put all the sails they had up, three sails - the fore-sail. the mizzen and the jibsail - and they made for Castlebay as fast as the wind would drive them. That is the story of the monster that was seen thirty-three and a quarter miles off Barra.

(For a description of various sea monsters which have been seen at different times, see Willy Ley, The Lungfish, the Dodo and the Unicorn, Chapter 7, " The Great Unknown of the Seas").

Thus The Coddy completed his reference to mystery creatures of the sea by directing interested folk to read 'The Great Unknown of the Seas'.

Another who wrote about sightings of strange sea creatures was Gavin Maxwell in his book 'Harpoon at a Venture' (Four Square Publications). This was based on his experiences of hunting Basking Shark in the western seas in the late 1940s to supply his 'Island of Soay Shark Fisheries Ltd' where the sharks were processed.

In the Appendix to 'Harpoon at a Venture' Gavin Maxwell has a section entitled 'Here be Dragons' and he writes as follows:

**"HERE BE DRAGONS**
I should preface this appendix by saying at once that during the few years I was at sea I saw no living object that I was not able, perhaps after a moment's doubt, to identify as belonging to a known species, sometimes in an unfamiliar aspect. Although my own experience - and that of my crew was separated from that of the great bulk of inshore seamen by the fact that
as a matter of routine we examined carefully every object appearing at the sea's surface, that we saw nothing inexplicable is quite inconclusive. I have met men of very much longer qualification than myself who have seen phenomena outside their very considerable experience, and it is with the greatest hesitation, and only after the minutest examination, that such records should be dismissed as beyond the boundaries of practical science.

I do not want to trespass upon Commander Gould's preserves; the existence or non-existence of the sea-serpent was his preoccupation for many years. If one or more very large marine species does remain unknown to science, it is quite certain that its appearances, like those of the much-exploited Loch Ness monster, are rare, and the fact that we saw nothing during four summers is negative evidence. The belief, factual and unsuperstitious, in the existence of at least one giant sea species at present unrecognised by science is widespread in the Hebrides, and is as strong among some of the educated people as it was among their less-informed ancestors.

To appreciate the basis for this belief, one must understand just how familiar an islander, constantly either in sight of the sea or actually on it, becomes with all its apparent life. His names for the creatures he sees, whether bird, fish, whale, or seal, would be unintelligible to modern taxonomy, but they are constant names, the result of repeated identification, and when he sees for the first time some species unknown to him, he is generally able to give an accurate enough description of it, often resulting in its identification beyond reasonable doubt as a rare visitor to the seas he knows.

As very few people who spend much time at sea in the Hebrides have any particular interest in accurate identification, it is perhaps not surprising that I should find the commonest of all creatures other than the Basking Shark described in a well-known and reputable text-book as a rare visitor to British waters. Because of these popular misconceptions I shall describe the species with which I became familiar before producing any secondhand evidence of creatures unknown to science."

So that before Gavin Maxwell produced his 'secondhand evidence of marine creatures unknown to science', he described the Cetacea or whale order from the giant Blue Whale to the Common Porpoise. Of the members of this order, Gavin Maxwell had identified the following in the western seas in the course of his shark fishing: the Blue Whale, Common Rorqual, Killer Whale, Risso's Grampus, White-sided Dolphin, Common Dolphin and Common Porpoise. Maxwell then proceeded to describe other sea creatures which are common in West coast waters such as the Basking Shark, the Great Atlantic Seal and the Common or Brown Seal as well as rare visitors to these areas such as the White Whale or Beluga and the Ocean Sun-Fish. Maxwell emphasized the importance of having accurate observation and then providing a good description of a sea creature as a basis of identifying it. He then proceeded to write about sea creatures which have been observed and described but cannot be identified in terms of known species. He wrote:

"Hebridean stories of the 'Sea-serpent,' or of some unknown giant of the sea, are common enough to make it pointless for me to quote experiences unconnected with my own island and its vicinity. The stories which follow are of creatures seen by Soay men, of creatures whose description fits no animal known to science, and whose appearance has been exceedingly frightening to these men who know the familiar life of the sea so well.

I am not entirely clear whether there were in fact two or three such incidents at Soay. I have heard Sandy Campbell, eye- witness of the first, tell the story many times, but I found it difficult to remember the details when I came to write it down and asked him to send me an account by letter. The story is arid by comparison with his spoken word, and beyond it I have drawn upon certain details that I well remember but which are not included in his letter. The second incident which he mentions may well refer to the story told to Ronald Macdonald and his brother Harry, by their father, who is now dead. The discrepancy between implied dates has inclined me to treat them as separate experiences; Sandy is alive, and I hope will remain so for many years, so that anyone sufficiently interested may check the details."

Sandy's own experience took place when he was a boy. It made a very strong impression upon him; his letter to me ends with the words: 'I was only young at the time, but I have never forgotten that night.'

It was during the early years of the present century, and Loch Scavaig, in common with all the West Coast sea lochs, teemed with herring. It was the custom then for crofters to cure herring for their own use, and scores of boats would congregate where there was a big shoal. One early autumn night Sandy was fishing from a skiff in Loch Scavaig with two men. One, I think, was his uncle, the other was a man called John Stewart; both were elderly, and had had a lifetime of experience. They shot their net well up towards the head of Loch Scavaig, close to the small island. There were a large number of other boats in the Loch, but none very close to them. It was dusk; the sky was still light, but the land was dark - a fine night with a light northerly breeze and a ripple on the water. Sandy and the two old men began to haul their net. He was only a young boy, and his arms tired easily; he rested for a moment, and as he did so he noticed an object rising out of the water about fifty yards to seaward of them. It was about a yard high when he first saw it, but, as he watched, it rose slowly from the surface to a height of twenty or more feet - a tapering column that moved to and fro in the air.

Sandy called excitedly to the old men, but at first got only an angry retort to keep on hauling the net and not be wasting time. At last Stewart looked up in exasperation, and then sprang to his feet in bewildered astonishment, as he too saw what Sandy was looking at. While this 'tail' was still waving in the air they could see the water rippling against a dark mass below it which was just breaking the surface, and which they presumed to be the animal's body. The high column descended slowly into the sea as it had risen; and as the last of it submerged, the boat began to rock on a commotion of water like the wake of a passing steamer. Stewart was terrified; they dropped the net and rowed as fast as they could for the shore.

Sandy's letter ends with a paragraph that may or may not refer to Macdonald's story, but Ronald and his brother Harry date the latter as 1917, long after Sandy's experience, and while he himself was at sea during the First World War.

The following summer two old men were fishing lobsters from a coble and rowing towards Rhu when they saw an object about thirty feet in height waving to and fro out of the sea. The day was fine and hot, and they thought they could see the body in the water moving at speed towards them. They got such a scare that they made for the shore at once.

Macdonald was in a boat at the mouth of Loch Brittle on a bright summer's day, when the phenomenon passed, travelling north at about five knots, a mile to seaward of him. It appeared as a high column, said to be a great deal higher than the object Sandy had seen in Loch Scavaig, and light flashed at the top of the column as though a small head was being turned from side to side. There was a considerable commotion of water astern of it, but no other portion of the body was visible above the surface. It submerged slowly until nothing was left showing above the sea, and it seemed to descend vertically and without flexion.

I do not think that the finer details of these stories are important. The points of dissimilarity are fewer than those of similarity, and whereas they correspond to the description of no animal known to science, they do resemble closely a great number of descriptions given by honest and experienced seamen from all corners of the ocean. Sandy and Macdonald describe an object broadly speaking corresponding to those recorded by Dr Matheson at Kyle of Lochalsh in 1893; by Captain Cringle of the Umfuli, sailing for Cape of Good Hope in the same year; by the Valhalla in 1905; by H.M.S. Kellett in 1923; to the description of the Hoy animal in 1919, and to that given by the Third Officer of the Tyne in 1920. This is to mention but a few of Commander Gould's generally ignored records*.
(*The Case for the Sea-serpent, R. T. Gould, 1930).

We have seen how living and unfamiliar objects in the sea are described by people of experience. We have seen that there are often certain inaccuracies and discrepancies, but we have seen, too, that the word-picture is usually complete enough and accurate enough to identify the creature when it is a known species. We may theorise as to the impossibility of the existence of these creatures unknown to us, but we must recognise both the general resemblance between many of the descriptions, and that a number of experienced men of great integrity have believed that they saw very large animals with which they were entirely unfamiliar.

The feelings of men who offer such testimony to find it rejected are summed up in a letter from Captain Cringle (Umfuli, 1893), quoted by Commander Gould.

Dear Sir,
Re the matter of the Sea-serpent. I have suffered so much ridicule on this that I must decline to have anything more to do with it. Whatever unbelief there is in such a monster's existence, I am certainly convinced that what I saw was a living creature capable of moving at the rate of ten knots. I chased it for ten minutes at that speed and had got no nearer to it. I had at that time 23 years' experience in Sail and Steam and was not likely to mistake what I saw.
                    Yours faithfully,
                    R. J. Cringle.

He believed with absolute certainty that he had seen some entirely strange animal, and the explanations which were forced down his throat seemed to him puerile. If Sandy's story is not believed, I hope it will be of some comfort to him to know that seventy-five years ago Charles Gould wrote: 'The West Coast of the Isle of Skye is another locality from which several reports of it have been received during this century.'

During the centuries when science had not progressed far in the identification and classification of marine species, the world had an open ear for stories of strange sea monsters. The general view of natural historians was that anything might exist in the sea, and their efforts were directed more to the correlation of descriptions that might build up more or less complete pictures of animals unknown to them. As more and more species were named and classified (often incorrectly), the tendency by the nineteenth century was to try to relate 'travellers tales' to creatures already listed. The rapid growth of science gave it the intolerance of an adolescent, and the empiricism which had been one of the most praiseworthy features of the early writers went temporarily out of fashion.

The positive identification of an entirely new giant sea- creature during the latter half of the century was a heavy blow to many dogmatists. From earliest times a number of 'monster' stories had referred to a dragon with many arms of enormous length, which could reach into a boat and drag men into the sea to be eaten at leisure. This creature, almost universally derided by scientists at the time, had become a *fait accompli* by 1875; it was only then that the Giant Squid (*Loligo architeuthis*), a ten-armed relative of the octopus, its longest tentacles having a length of more than thirty feet, was finally recognised by science.

'One might have thought,' writes Commander Gould, 'that, since naturalists had been brought to see that a so-called myth had a real foundation, and that the sea held at least one large creature of which they had no knowledge, they might have gone a step further, and admitted that there might be others also.

The Giant Squid was not the last practical joke that the sea had in store for scientists. During the winter of 1938 a fish about five feet long was caught in a trawl-net at a depth of forty fathoms off the coast of South Africa. It was not recognised by its captors, and was preserved for identification. It was, however, immediately recognised by scientists as Latimeria, one of the Coelacanths that were well known from fossils of the Cretaceous Period, which lasted from a hundred and forty million to seventy million years ago. It was believed to have become extinct by the end of that period, which was dominated on land by the great dinosaurs. In other words, it was presumed to have been already extinct for about sixty million years before man appeared upon the earth. How would the scientific world have received an unsupported claim to have seen it in 1938? The species is now recognised by the name of *Latimeria chalumnae*.

Many stories of the 'sea-serpent' would be treated as barely distorted descriptions of a *Plesiosaur* were this not a pre- historic animal. The plesiosaurs, however - giant lizards of the shallow seas, with a long neck and tail and four paddle-like flippers - are presumed to have become extinct with or before *Latimeria*.

The Mososaurs, too, were contemporaries of this Rip van Winkle of the sea, and they were veritable sea-serpents; huge rapacious reptiles almost as slender as a snake. So let us 'never never doubt what nobody is sure about'."

So ends Gavin Maxwell's account of the stories he gleaned on sightings of strange sea creatures which could not be identified in terms of any 'animal known to science'. He treated these reported sightings with great respect. He was impressed by "the general resemblance between many of the descriptions" of these creatures in different sightings and he fully acknowledged that the sightings were made by 'a number of experienced men of great integrity who saw very large animals with which they were entirely unfamiliar".

It is interesting that the sighting of a strange sea creature near Sandaig by Roddy MacPherson and his companions from Glenelg (Chapter 20) appears to tally very closely with the descriptions given by those quoted by Gavin Maxwell of sightings by Soay and Skye men in Loch Scavaig and Loch Brittle in Skye. When Roddy read these latter descriptions he commented: 'That is exactly what I saw close to Sandaig in the early 1930s'.

(In a recent issue of the 'Herald' (10 May 1999) quoting snippets from past issues, one such from 10

May 1895 reports a big creature seen in Kilmory Bay on the Ardnamurchan coast by Mr Duncan MacPherson, Merchant, Branault).

For those interested in delving more deeply into this intriguing area of 'mysteries of the deep', Gavin Maxwell cited the following publications.

**Bibliography**
*Sea Dragons,* Hawkins, 1840.
*Sea Monsters Unmasked,* H. Lee, 1883.
*The Great Sea-serpent,* Oudemans.
*Mythical Monsters,* Charles Gould, 1886.
*The Case of the Sea-serpent,* R T Gould, 1930.

So much for mysterious creatures observed in Loch Hourn, the western seas and in the wider oceans. What about the Loch Ness mystery which Gavin Maxwell referred to?

The author, having been reared on Loch Ness-side in Glenurquhart, and intrigued by the sightings of strange sea creatures in Loch Hourn by many people well known to him, cannot let the Loch Ness phenomenon pass without further mention.

The story about old Sandy MacRaild and his experiences when diving in Loch Ness near Fort Augustus around 1920 in an attempt to find the body of a man following a drowning tragedy is told in Chapter 25. This chapter focuses on Runival on Loch Hourn, and Sandy MacRaild was related through marriage to the MacMillans of Runival. Sandy was an able diver with long experience in his job for the Caledonian Canal Company and something which he either saw, heard, felt or some very unusual swirling of water round about him, or other sensation which he experienced on that occasion, made him decide that he would never dive again. After decades of diving in the area in his work for the Canal Company he decided to retire there and then. This was a momentous decision on Sandy's part. He did not explain the details of that last diving experience to his relatives because he could not adequately analyse or understand fully his sensations on that final dive. Sandy's relative Bill MacRaild told the author in Australia in 1984, 'the MacRailds would never try to explain any experience they had unless they could fully understand it themselves'. They were not given to speculation. Only one thing was certain - the sensations were such that old Sandy did not want to experience them ever again. (Sandy's experience may have been similar to those of the divers brought in to try to recover the body of a Mrs Hambro who was drowned in Loch Ness near Glendoe in the 1930s. After making one exploratory dive, these divers also refused to go down a second time. There is a monument to the memory of Mrs Hambro on the shore of Loch Ness close to the location of the tragedy).

The author has spoken to many natives of Loch Ness-side who, once in their lifetime, had seen some 'object' or apparent creature in Loch Ness which they could not explain. Many of these sightings went to the grave with them without being reported to the media or any official of a relevant monitoring organisation, but were told in a 'matter of fact way' in fireside chats with good friends. These folk who made such sightings had good vision, they were good observers of nature, like Maxwell's observers of strange sea creatures - 'they were folk of great integrity' and - far from seeking publicity - they positively shunned it. It is possible that such sightings were made on Loch Ness by such folk back through the centuries to St Columba's time and earlier.

Of course, there have also been many official reports on sightings of 'The Loch Ness Monster' and there has been global interest and much speculation about the 'phenomenon'. Some reported sightings and photographs in more recent times have been contrived but many genuine sightings of a 'phenomenon' have been unexplained.

More recent speculation in television documentaries focuses on the connection between Loch Ness and the sea via the River Ness and the experts suggest that the Loch Ness creatures are not permanent residents of the Loch but flit between the sea via the Moray Firth and the River Ness and Loch Ness. The suggestion that the monster is a sturgeon which behaves in this way has been made.

From the author's earliest years there has always been some local speculation of a connection between Loch Ness and the western seaboard via the 'caverns of the deep'. However, with any knowledge of the laws of physics, such speculation is difficult to sustain because the level of Loch Ness is some 50 feet higher than the level of the sea. If there was a connection, Loch Ness would be at the same level as the sea and a higher salt content would be detected in the waters of Loch Ness.

The only possibility of a connection between Loch Ness and the western seas, in the circumstances, is that the connection by a series of underwater caverns at some point forms a 'trap' which is above the surface level of Loch Ness.

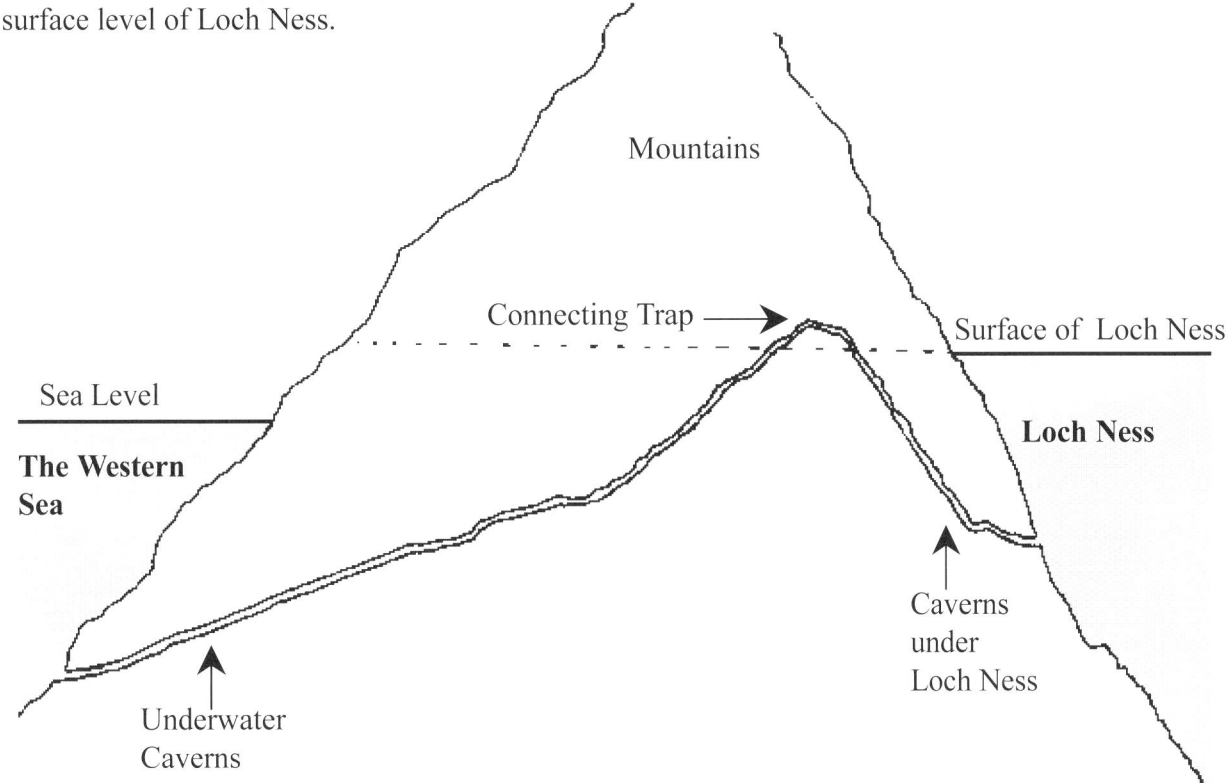

It must be emphasised that this speculation of connections between Loch Ness and the western sea via a series of underwater caverns is not the author's - this possibility has been cited by old local speculators and it has probably been handed down through the generations from time immemorial. The author's sole contribution to the speculation is that if there is such a connection, then there must exist a trap which is higher than the surface level of Loch Ness. This being so, one would expect that only amphibious creatures could move between Loch Ness and the sea.

The possibility of underwater caverns in the Great Glen area might be suggested because of knowledge of great earth movements in this area in past ages. An information booklet entitled 'The Great Glen' produced by the Nature Conservancy Council for Scotland makes reference to the cataclysmic fracture of the earth's crust which formed the Great Glen many millions of years ago. This area is also the most active earthquake zone in the country. The Great Glen fault constitutes 'a fracture more extensive than any other in Britain'. The indications are that one side of the Great Glen moved considerably sideways and downwards from the other side as a result of the cataclysmic fracture of the earth's crust. The last

Ice Age also had an influence on the land masses in this area - 'The fracture through the schists, granites and sandstones of the Great Glen has resulted in a zone of weakened shattered rocks, two to four kilometres in width which has guided the forces of erosion ever since'. These cataclysmic movements of the earth's crust in the Great Glen area and the effects of the Ice Age almost certainly caused severe reverberations of the land areas on either side and, as the crow flies, the distance from Loch Ness to the western seaboard is little more than forty miles.

Authorities in geology consider that it is very unlikely but not outwith the bounds of possibility that Loch Ness and perhaps also Loch Lochy could have connections with western sea lochs via sub-marine caverns.

While the existence of such caverns connecting Loch Ness and the sea may one day be confirmed, this possibility may forever remain open to speculation - just another mystery like those of the Loch Ness Monster and the as yet unidentified creatures of Loch Hourn and the western seas.

**Top**. Some of the folk who have seen a strange sea creature in Loch Hourn. L to R. Granny MacKenzie (Mairi Bhan) in the 1890s, Robert Foster (early 1900s), Willie Campbell (left) (early 1900s).

**Middle.** L to R. Ewen MacMillan, Runival (early 1900s), Daniel MacDonald (around 1920), Roddy McPherson (right) (early 1930s).

**Bottom Left.** Willie MacKenzie (around 1940). **Right**. Gavin Maxwell (centre), who knew these waters very well during shark fishing days from his base on the Island of Saoy, never observed any sea creature which he could not identify. However, he obtained eyewitness accounts of strange sea creatures spotted in the waters around Skye and had great respect for these reports.

**Top**.  Loch Ness and the Great Glen as it makes its way south-westwards visa Loch Oich and Loch Lochy to the Western seas. Borlum Bay, Glen Urqhuhart is to the right in the middle of the picture while, top left, Ben Nevis displays it aerial dominance (© Donald M. Fisher, F.B.I.P.P.).

With regards to the geological history of this area the following extracts from 'The Great Glen' (Nature Conservancy Council for Scotland Publication) are interesting.  '...cataclysmic fracture of the earth's crust which formed the Great Glen many millions of years ago'.  The Great Glen fault constitutes 'a fracture more extensive than any other in Britain'.  'The fracture through the schists, granites and sandstones of the Great Glen has resulted in a zone of weakened shattered rocks, two to four kilometers in width which has guided the forces of erosion ever since!

In view of the different surface levels of Loch Ness and the sea, the only possibility of a connection between Loch Ness and the sea is via a connecting 'trap' above the level of Loch Ness.  (See Page 427).

# Chapter 35

**Knoydart - a brief potted history**

It is probably true to say that the northern boundary of Knoydart - the southern shore of Loch Hourn - was more closely linked with Arnisdale and the other Loch Hourn clachans than it was with the southern part of the Knoydart peninsula bordering Loch Nevis. There were always very close ties between the Knoydart Loch Hournside communities at Skiary, Runival, Barrisdale, Lea, Rudha Ruadh and Crowlick - and Arnisdale across the water. The herring fishing gave those on the northern and southern shores of Loch Hourn common objectives while those folk on the Knoydart shore depended on Arnisdale for many essential services.

The main access to Knoydart from time immemorial was by sea. The only alternative access was on foot or on horseback, while in these modern times the helicopter helps a few folk to get in and out of the 'Rough Bounds' (na Garbh Chriochan).

In more ancient times, Knoydart was part of the territory of the descendants of Somerled, Lord of the Isles. Following periods of possession by the MacDonalds of Clanranald and the Camerons of Lochiel, the peninsula eventually came into the hands of the MacDonells of Glengarry.

The Knoydart folk were mainly of the Catholic faith and following their support of the Jacobite cause in the Rising of 1745-46, the Glengarry lands were forfeited to the Crown following the aftermath of Culloden. The forfeited lands were not restored to the MacDonells of Glengarry until 1784.

However, the Glengarry MacDonells were to find themselves back in trouble in the middle of the next century when they became bankrupt, mainly through the extravagant lifestyle of Alasdair MacDonell, the fifteenth Chief. The MacDonells had been forced to sell part of their once vast estates in 1838 when Mr Edward Ellice purchased the Glen Quoich part of their estate.

Knoydart was the last of the Glengarry possessions and it was decided by the family that the sale price could be enhanced by clearing many of the tenant crofters and small farmers from their lands so that the lands could then be sold on the basis of vacant possession. This was the objective of the notorious Knoydart evictions of 1851-1853 when four hundred of the Knoydart residents were evicted from their holdings and dwellings. Three hundred and thirty of these were sent to Canada in 1853 on the sailing ship, the 'Sillery', The seventy who refused to go were hounded mercilessly by the agents of the owners as they tried in vain to gain a renewed basic foothold in their ancestral lands. The Knoydart Estate was then sold to Mr Baird, a Lowland Ironmaster. With so much of the area now cleared of the previous tenants, the land was now re-let to larger sheep farmers, undoubtedly at higher rents.

On the Loch Hourn side of Knoydart, the farming system changed following the clearing of the previous tenants from a mixed farming system to one based on sheep farming. The old system was based on black cattle with some sheep and goats. There was also extensive cultivation even on the Loch Hourn side of the peninsula, with potatoes, oats and barley being grown in rotation with a grass break in between. Soil fertility was maintained by using cattle dung, ferns and seaweed on the cultivated areas. Although the soil on the steep north facing slopes was thin, the spade - generated cultivation system involved heaping the thin soil into parallel ridges with the resulting channels assisting drainage in what was, and still is, a very high rainfall area. Precautions were also taken in planning these cultivations to prevent erosion or 'hillwash' so that as the copious surplus water drained out of the system, it carried as little as possible of the precious soil with it. These so called 'lazy beds' are still evident on the steep slopes on the Loch Hourn side of Knoydart today. In some areas, a terraced system of cultivations was deployed, again to achieve a greater depth of soil on the terraces and to minimise erosion. Close to Lea, the ruins of a drying kiln for the oats and of a water driven horizontal mill are still evident today as relics from this era of mixed farming. While the crops were growing in the late spring and high summer, the cattle, sheep and goats were taken up to the summer sheilings on the higher mountain areas and the remains of the basic shelters for the folk tending their livestock are still in evidence on the Knoydart hills and inner glens.

Compared to the current Knoydart population of around fifty folk, the population around 1770 was estimated to be around one thousand eight hundred. A total of eight hundred of the Knoydart inhabitants voluntarily emigrated to the colonies in the 25 year period after 1770, leaving behind a resident population of one thousand folk in 1795. The population was further reduced to around five hundred following the notorious evictions of the 1851-54 years.

The small basic dwellings of the people in the 1750 to 1850 period were constructed with walls of stone or turf. The roofs were made of woven wattle supporting a lining of turf, with thatch of rushes or bracken above.

The basic diet of the people consisted of the fish (especially herring) harvested from the sea along with their home produced potatoes, oatmeal, and the produce of their cattle. It is reported that some oatmeal was brought in by boat from the Sleat area of Skye in exchange for the Knoydart home produce of butter and cheese. The fuel source was, of course, peat harvested from the plentiful reserves in the area.

As in all areas of the Highlands, the population of Knoydart has continued to decline in the past century but the decline in Knoydart has been considerably more severe than in other areas. These statistics are clear from national census data.

An interesting set of unofficial census statistics from Knoydart is provided by those households making contributions to the Morar and Knoydart District Nursing Association in 1913 to pay for the services of a District Nurse in a very extensive area. The details of Districts 9 and 10 of this Association are as follows:

**District No. 9 - From Li by Lochournside, Inverguseran, Airor, Doune, Sandaig, Glaschoile, Scottas, to the School House.**

Collector - Mr Alex MacDonald, Missionary, Knoydart.

| Mr Alex. Campbell | £0 | 2 | 0 |
| Mr Donald Macdonald | £0 | 2 | 6 |
| Mr John C Macdonald | £0 | 2 | 6 |
| Mr Jonathan MacInnes | £0 | 2 | 0 |
| Mr John MacInnes | £0 | 2 | 6 |
| Mr John MacDougall | £0 | 2 | 6 |
| Mr John S MacDonald | £0 | 2 | 6 |
| Mr Jno. MacPherson | £0 | 2 | 6 |
| Mr Ewen MacDougall | £0 | 2 | 6 |
|  | £1 | 1 | 6 |

**District No 10 - From Barrisdale to Mr Macarthur's, Inverie, including Glenguseran; also from Kilchoan to Lochnevishead on north side.**

Collector - Miss M MacKinnon, Schoolhouse, Knoydart.

| | | | |
|---|---|---|---|
| Mr Aneas Macdonald | £0 | 3 | 0 |
| Mrs D Stewart | £0 | 1 | 0 |
| Miss Macmaster | £0 | 1 | 0 |
| Mr J Macmaster | £0 | 2 | 0 |
| Mr D Stewart | £0 | 2 | 0 |
| Mr E Macmaster | £0 | 2 | 0 |
| Miss P Macpherson | £0 | 2 | 0 |
| Mr Harry Stuart | £0 | 5 | 0 |
| Mr W Maclennan | £0 | 2 | 0 |
| Mrs Don Maclennan | £0 | 3 | 0 |
| Mrs Duncan Macdonald | £0 | 1 | 0 |
| Mrs Ronald Stewart | £0 | 1 | 0 |
| Mrs J MacEachen | £0 | 2 | 0 |
| Mrs J Macphee | £0 | 1 | 0 |
| Mrs A Macarthur | £0 | 2 | 6 |
| Mrs Jas Macrae | £0 | 2 | 6 |
| Mrs M McHardy | £0 | 2 | 0 |
| Mrs K Kennedy | £0 | 2 | 0 |
| Mr D Macdougall | £0 | 2 | 0 |
| Mr Angus Macdonald, Toree | £0 | 2 | 0 |
| Rev W Gettins | £0 | 3 | 0 |
| Mr Jas Macrae | £0 | 2 | 6 |
| Mrs Jas Macdonald | £0 | 1 | 0 |
| Mr J S Macmaster | £0 | 2 | 0 |
| Mr J Macphail | £0 | 1 | 0 |
| Miss J Grieve | £0 | 2 | 0 |
| Mrs Macdougall, Sandaig | £0 | 2 | 6 |
| Miss Katie Macdonald | £0 | 1 | 0 |
| Mrs Macleod | £0 | 1 | 0 |
| Mrs Arch. Macdonald | £0 | 3 | 0 |
| Mrs Macdonald, Toree | £0 | 2 | 0 |
| Mrs Campbell, Manse | £0 | 4 | 0 |
| Mr Alex Fleming | £0 | 2 | 0 |
| Miss Jane Macdonald | £0 | 2 | 0 |
| Miss M Mackinnon | £0 | 2 | 0 |
| Mrs W Stoddart | £0 | 2 | 0 |
| Mrs K Mackay | £0 | 2 | 0 |
| Mr C MacEachen | £0 | 0 | 6 |
| Mr John Maclennan | £0 | 2 | 0 |
| Mr William Purcell | £0 | 1 | 0 |
| Mr Peter Sheridan | £0 | 1 | 0 |
| | £4 | 0 | 6 |

These details provide a useful record of the areas of Knoydart which were inhabited at that time and of the fifty families resident in the two collection districts.

The 1913 Report of this Nursing Association from which these records were extracted was kept in immaculate order by the Collector in District Number 10. This was Miss Mary MacKinnon, the teacher in Inverie School at the time. Mary was a native of Tiree. Earlier (from about 1907 to 1910) Mary had been the teacher in Arnisdale School when she met up with young Donald MacLeod from Arnisdale Farm (the older brother of Roddy Mor). Donald and Mary were married a few years after Mary had completed her teaching period in Knoydart. This Nursing Association Report of 1913 was loaned to the author, still in immaculate condition, by Mary and Donald's daughter, Anne, who resides in Norfolk.

In the interim period, Knoydart's interesting and often troubled story has continued. Following the end of the Second World War, the 'Seven Men of Knoydart' (Duncan MacPhail, big Archie MacDonald, Jock MacHardy, Sandy MacPhee, Donald MacPhee, Willie Quinn and Archie MacDougall) made a vain attempt at a 'Land Grab' to express their grievances against Lord Brockett, the Knoydart proprietor of the time. Also named on the plaque which commemorates this incident is the Rev. Father Colin MacPherson who acted as advocate for the raiders. Today, at the end of the Millennium, the few remaining residents in the Knoydart Peninsula have campaigned successfully for more control over their own destiny.

For these and other reasons Knoydart has been very much 'in the news' in recent times. It is often said that 'any publicity is good publicity'. This publicity has made folk throughout the country very curious about Knoydart - one of 'our last great wildernesses'. People usually want to satisfy their curiosity once aroused and this should stimulate tourist trade. Knoydart is already a mecca for hill climbers, nature lovers and wilderness seekers and there is potential to provide for an expanding tourist business. The wise folk in Knoydart, are, without doubt, thinking along these lines.

The author was brought up-to-date with some of the current activities and crystal ball gazing in Knoydart by one of his former shinty playing team-mates, Iain Wilson. Iain, a Lochaber native, first went to Knoydart for seasonal work as a stalker in 1985. There he met his future wife, Joanna Wolseley, who was working in Inverie House for the summer and autumn period when the proprietors and guests were resident for the river fishing and deer stalking. Jo is a native of West Gloucestershire.

Iain returned to Knoydart to work in the following year and was offered a limited partnership for ten years to farm the Inverguseran area. Iain's main input to the partnership was to be the year-round management of the farm and the shepherding of the large flock of over one thousand Blackface ewes. He was also to have continued responsibilities for deer management and stalking and for managing the sea trout and salmon fishing on the river. Iain accepted the offer, married Jo soon afterwards and now their two children Calum (9) and Anna (7) form a significant component of five pupils attending the Inverie Primary School. In 1996, Iain and Jo bought the shares of their previous partner and are now the sole owners of Inverguseran Farm.

On the shinty field, Iain was a centre field man who was always 'as fit as a fiddle'. When he would pick up a clearance from his own defence, he would control the ball, keep his eye on it and then drive forward at speed and with great determination. He was difficult to catch and hard to stop. Sometimes, head down, he was not quite sure where he was going but now and again he would glance up, assess the situation and create scoring opportunities for his forward colleagues which often led to goals and victories for his team.

The impression one now gets from talking to Iain is that he is as energetic and enthusiastic as ever, he is grafting at his sheep farming but he is looking at a wide range of opportunities in Knoydart and is already exploiting some of these.

One of the great problems of sheep farming in Knoydart is in the marketing of the stock - the lambs and older 'cast' ewes. But Iain has worked out a way. In calm weather a few days before the sale at the Fort William market, Iain loads some of his stock on to his own 33 foot launch and borrows a barge from a neighbour at Doune to take the rest of them. They then set off northwards to Loch Hourn, making for the pier in Arnisdale. There the sheep and lambs are unloaded and, by prior arrangement with the Richmond-Watson family and the farm manager (Iain MacKenzie, until his recent retirement), they are herded into the lodge park. There they settle down and graze for the next few days until the Friday Sale Day, when they are loaded into the livestock transporter of Ruaridh Campbell of Shiel and are soon en route for the two hour journey to Fort William.

The lambing percentage of the ewe flock is about eighty in a good dry early spring and slightly lower in wet cold springs. Iain is constantly striving through consistent care and attention to detail to improve the output of his flock. However, even before the very low market prices of 1998, Iain knew that he had to have more 'irons in the fire' to win a decent living for his family in the challenging Knoydart environment. "I've got about six other jobs at the moment as well as being a farmer", he asserts and then proceeds to reel them off. He is still the river manager for the sea trout and salmon fishing but, as in many other parts, the catches have been poor in recent years. However, they have restocked the river with 10,000 sea trout smoults this year so hopefully that will liven up the fishing in years to come.

He still works as a stalker during the stag shooting season and his knowledge of the deer and of their behaviour has opened up a further enterprise. He provides a service of conducted tours to those tourists, nature lovers and photographers who want to 'hunt with the camera' to observe red deer in their native environment, to study their behaviour and, with the unobtrusive aim of the telephoto lens, to capture their natural behaviour and antics on print, slide and video tape.

Such conducted tours on the Knoydart shoreline, glens and mountains will not be confined to the red deer. Knoydart has its foxes, badgers, pine martens and otters and a great variety of bird life, including sea eagles. The series of islands just offshore are very popular nesting areas for a great variety of birds. Iain is a keen student of the behaviour of the rich variety of wildlife in Knoydart and is building up his expertise to cope with the conducted tours for tourists for which he anticipates increasing demand.

As well as exploiting the Knoydart land resources, Iain also has to be a good sailor. He was brought up from his earliest years and taught about the moods of the sea and on the handling of boats and good seamanship in general. His launch is the family's link with Mallaig and Arnisdale and many other coastal locations. However, the boat has to pay its way in other ways in addition to the transporting of the family, family and farm provisions and in the marketing of the sheep. The coastal area off the western shoreline of the Knoydart Peninsula is a favourite playground for porpoises and whales in summer. So sails in the launch to observe these intriguing marine creatures passing up or down the Sound of Sleat constitute another conducted tours option. Iain also takes tour parties for sails to many interesting nearby islands and coastal locations including the islands of Canna, Rhum, Eigg and Skye, to Gavin Maxwell's Camusfearna to Arnisdale, up intriguing Loch Hourn to view its many coastal clachans all of which have a proud history and also down Loch Nevis to admire the picturesque coastlines and the wildlife. Sea fishing too comes into Iain's long list of opportunities for the tourists.

As if not busy enough with all his Knoydart activities and initiatives, Iain also runs the family croft in the Roy Bridge area of Lochaber. There in his absence he is well supported by former shinty playing team-mates Ronnie MacKintosh and Billy MacLachlan. There has always been a fine spirit of mutual support in crofting communities and Billy and Ronnie will make sure that they get their 'pound of flesh' from Ian when he arrives back in his old family home at the busiest times in the sheep and cattle handling calendar.

So much for Iain Wilson's personal activities and initiatives in Knoydart. What about the Knoydart Foundation, that conglomerate of Knoydart residents, organisations with interests in Knoydart and private benefactors who recently assumed ownership and control over the destiny of the Peninsula?

Among the projects being discussed towards increasing the viability of the Knoydart community and for developing the resources are woodland regeneration, forestry and the processing of timber, restoring the old walking highways through the Knoydart hills and glens, creating new woodland and moorland walkways, sea fishing, outward bound and adventure activities. Deer stalking will continue to have an important role and the Knoydart folk had the benefit in recent years of the short sojourn with them of expert stalker Louis MacRae who has had a lifetime's experience of observing and managing the red deer population on the Island of Rhum with the Nature Conservancy. The Knoydart Foundation owns both Inverie House and the Walkers' Hostel and there are plans for developing both of these existing facilities to cater for the needs of a wide spectrum of tourists with interests in the increasing range of opportunities on offer throughout the year, but particularly in the spring, summer and autumn months.

To cater for the anticipated increase in tourist activity, the provision of basic services such as electricity must be considered. Electricity to the Inverie area is supplied by the local Hydro-Electric scheme which has been in existence for a considerable time. Clachans outwith the Inverie area have to make their own provisions and electricity generation using diesel fuel is most common in locations such as Iain Wilson's Inverguseran.

Inverie, as well as being blessed with the provision of hydro electric power, also has the school, the village hall, the church, it has a shop, a pub and a Tearoom/Restaurant which is kept fairly busy, particularly in the summer months.

Regarding activities to provide residents with an acceptable standard of living, in addition to those mentioned, there are developments in a range of craft activities where expansion and 'pay-off' can only come from attracting greater numbers of tourists.

What about farming? Apart from Iain Wilson's large sheep farming enterprise, the only other resident involved in conventional agriculture is Dave Smith and his sheep enterprise on his croft at Airor. There is scope for increasing farming activities but this potential is very dependent on the general economy of agriculture and on finding easier ways to market products.

In the past, a large Knoydart population survived on a mixed farming system with the combination of cattle, goats and sheep on the livestock side and the growing of potatoes, oats and barley when the livestock were taken to their summer shielings in the hills. It would be unrealistic to expect that the full range of these activities will be resuscitated in Knoydart. However, perhaps at least an element of mixed grazing of cattle and sheep with red deer might be re-established, to be managed in harmony with the recovery of native woodland remnants so as to meet a wide range of land use objectives. If increasing cattle numbers proves to be unmanageable or uneconomic, even with environmental support funding, then the mixed grazing of sheep and red deer is a 'second best' alternative.

It is to be hoped that blanket plantations of pine species will be avoided in the interests of preserving the unique Knoydart landscape as well as the native flora and fauna. While some current regeneration of native tree species in Knoydart has many supporters it would be undesirable for many would-be explorers of Knoydart to be impeded by the proliferation of deer fences from their 'freedom to roam' and admire all corners of the Knoydart environment.

What must be kept in mind is Knoydart's rich history, and the restoration and preservation of historical relics are likely to constitute an attraction to a considerable number of prospective visitors to the peninsula. The extensive lazy beds, the drying kilns for oats and barley, the mills for grinding the grains and the summer shielings are but a few components of a balanced system of agriculture which sustained a very large Knoydart population in past centuries. It is hoped that these relics will be preserved for the interest of Knoydart residents and tourists alike and not be incarcerated within the confines of deer fences protecting new plantations of trees.

Dick Balharry who has had 40 years experience of managing national nature reserves in the Highlands has suggested that the flora and fauna of Knoydart could be protected more effectively by controlling the deer numbers through the employment of local stalkers rather than by deer fencing large tracts of the territory. That proposal has the added advantage of creating regular employment in deer management, stalking and processing of the venison as well as providing a basis for the development of crafts using by-products of the deer such as antlers, tusks and hides.

One area of thinking which Iain Wilson would like to see developed is the establishment of a Heritage/Study Centre in Knoydart. This would focus on the wide ranging flora and fauna of the peninsula and also its intriguing history. It would also constitute a very welcome alternative activity for tourists on wet days in Knoydart and residents will tell you that the area only very rarely suffers from a drought!

It seems that the folk in Knoydart are unanimous on at least one point and that is that the future development of their home base and their livelihood must place a major focus on developing their tourism potential. They also know that they have a wonderful resource but it needs sound thinking, togetherness and considerable input of capital and hard graft to develop it and make it more attractive. One problem in the past for those wanting to explore and enjoy this intriguing peninsula was the great difficulty of access. It is fortunate that a facility which has never been better than at present in the entire history of Knoydart is that of ease of access. The availability of a range of suitable seagoing craft - and the helicopter - makes access to Knoydart to take advantage of all that it has to offer easier than ever before.

Selected Publications on Knoydart

Knoydart: An archaeological survey (1991). Royal Commission on the Ancient and Historical Monuments of Scotland, 54 Melville Street, Edinburgh EH3 7HF

Morrison, W (1771). Forfeited Estates Plans. Li : SRO RHP 3460 Muineil: SRO 3465.

Morrison, W (1805). Plans of the Annexed Estate of Barrisdale, a copy from the original lodged by the exchequer by William Morrison 1805. SRO RHP 112.

Morrison, W (1825). Plan of the estate of Barrisdale, the property of Duncan MacDonell of Glengarry 1825. SRO RHP 111.

Munro, R W (1984). Taming the Rough Bounds, Knoydart 1745-1784. Inverness.

Wills V (Ed.) (1973). Reports on the Annexed Estates 1755-1769. (Barrisdale Reports by Mungo Campbell 1755 (Pages 49-52) and by Archibald Menzies 1768 (Pages 99-101). Edinburgh.

Morar and Knoydart District Nursing Association Annual Report 1913. Printed by Wm. Culross & Son Ltd, Coupar Angus.

Rixson D & M (1982). The Rough Bounds. An historical guide to Mallaig, Morar and Arisaig.

Rixson D (1999). Knoydart. A History. Birlinn Ltd., Edinburgh.

**Top Left**. Knoydart's main centres of human habitation in the past (1891) were along its coastline (Rixson, 1999).  **Right**.  The remains of the rough shelters for the people in the summer shieling on the high slopes above Lea with a view westwards along the coast of Knoydart to Barrisdale and inner Loch Hourn.   **Middle Left**.  Remains of some of the very extensive lazy beds on the steep slopes of Knoydart above Loch Hourn.  In the days before the sheep era in the early 1800s, the economy was based on one of mixed farming with potatoes, oats and barley being grown on the lazy beds in late spring and summer while the cattle were taken to the sheilings on the high tops and inner mountain areas to produce milk and preserve cheese and butter for winter use and for export to Skye.  **Middle Right**.  Part of Knoydart's northern coastline from Barrisdale and Luinne Bheinn on the left.  Rarsaidh Island is on the right.  **Bottom Left**.   The remains of the grinding wheel of the water driven mill at Lea for grinding the oats and the barley.  **Right**.  The big fank near Lea.  A reminder of the era of the large sheep flocks from the early 1800s to around 1870.  It was at this stage that the emphasis began to change towards deer forests.

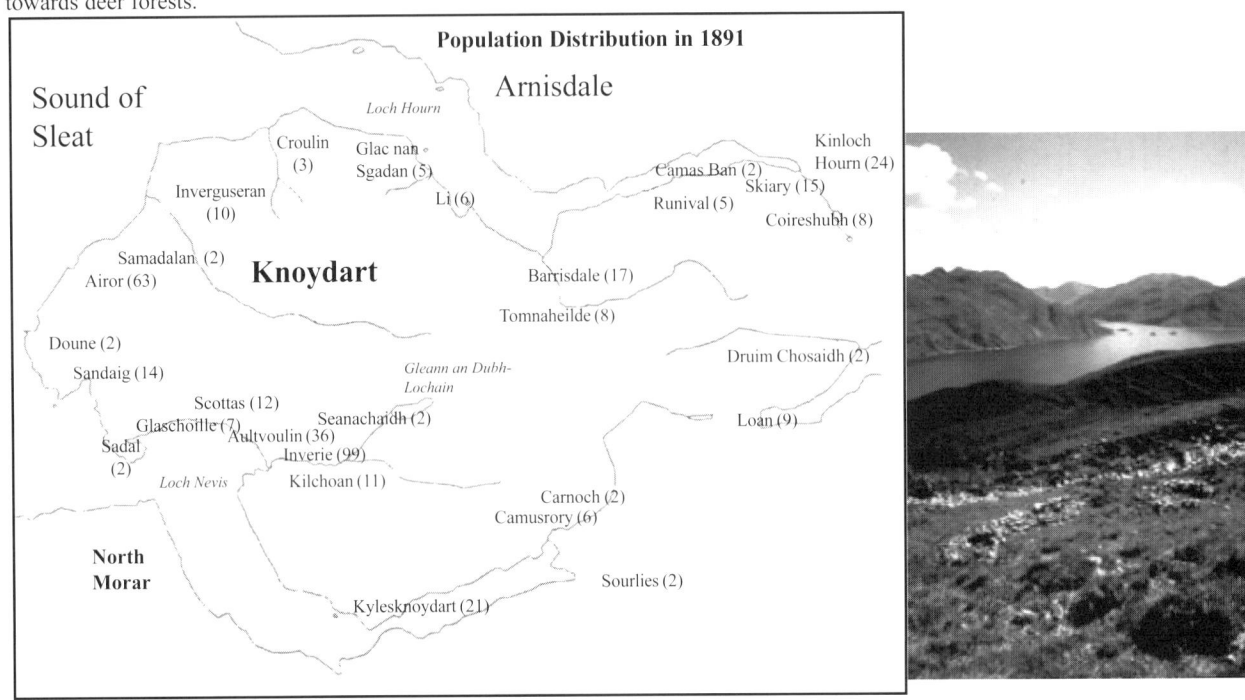

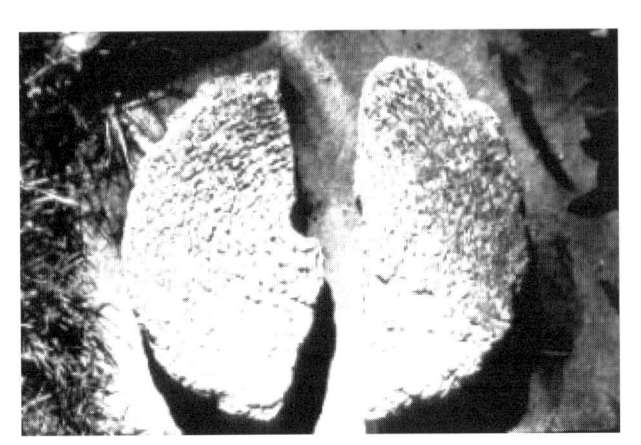

**Top Left**. Mary MacKinnon (a native of Tiree) at her marriage to Donald MacLeod of Arnisdale home farm in the early 1920s. Mary was the teacher in Arnisdale School from approximately 1907 to 1910 and then was the teacher at Inverie for several years. She was the collector in District Number 10 in 1913 of funds for the Morar and Knoydart District Nursing Association. **Right**. The monument at Inverie to commemorate the 'land grab' attempt after the Second World War by the 'Seven Men of Knoydart'.

**Middle Left**. Iain and Jo Wilson with children Calum and Anna with friend Gay Jose (second from right). Iain and Jo currently run Knoydart's largest farming enterprise. **Right**. Iain, along with young assistants, Calum, Anna and the dogs, shepherd the sheep into the fank at Inverguseran.

**Bottom Left**. One of the main farming challenges in Knoydart is getting produce to the market. Iain, with his boat and a borrowed barge in tow, fully loaded with his main crop of lambs, in en route here for market with a stop on the way in Arnisdale. The direction finder has Beinn Sgritheall in its sights. **Right**. Anna and Calum on their pedestals overlooking the fine sheep grazing area in Glenguseran.

439

**Top Left**. A 'royal' examining the Wilson washing line at Inverguseran. Iain is involved both in the stalking during the stag shooting season in Knoydart and also in guiding interested tourists to 'hunt with their cameras' the red deer, otters, foxes, badgers, the rich bird life, including sea eagles, in their natural habitats. **Right**. Joanna at the Arisaig Agricultural Show where she was a major prizewinner in the home baking section.

**Middle Left**. Iain is not to be 'outdone' and wins a prize for his cromags (shepherd's crooks).
**Right**. On the way home from the Show to Inverguseran with their sheep exhibits at the Show and the lady in the elevated position, the Show Champion, appears to be fully aware of her superiority!

**Bottom**. Iain runs a wide range of attractions for the tourists, including sails to Eigg and Rhum, up Loch Nevis and Loch Hourn, to Gavin Maxwell's Camusfearna (left), to upper Loch Hourn (right) and on trips to spot the porpoises, whales and rich bird life in the area. The range of tourist attractions being developed by Iain, Jo and their fellow Knoydart residents is increasing, and such initiatives are likely to become increasingly important in developing the Knoydart economy.

# Chapter 36

**The Future of the Arnisdale and Loch Hourn Community - hopes and possibilities**

On the basis of superficial analysis of the Arnisdale situation, future prospects would appear to be bleak. The population has declined from a reported 600 in the Arnisdale and Loch Hourn communities in the heydays of the herring fishing to around 40 at the present time. Most of the current population are retired folk. Apart from the Free Church, Arnisdale has no community facilities. There is little local employment apart from the fish farm and one man is employed on the Arnisdale Estate. Only five families are active in crofting activities and almost all active crofters are now over 60 years of age. Private enterprise activities are on a modest scale with Charlie MacTavish and Len Morrison operating sailing trips in their little boats from Camus Ban, Sheena Nash running her tea-hut facility at Corran while Mick Simpson and Peter Carr at Crowlick have their small scale mussel farming and prawn fishing enterprises respectively.

One young man who was born and reared in Arnisdale commented: 'Arnisdale is becoming just like a museum - if things go on as they are it will soon be another St. Kilda'. He was referring, among other constraints, to the conservation orders which have been imposed on the area for several years now. Official classifications range from an 'Area of Great Landscape Value' to a 'European Scenic Reserve', while Corran is classified as a 'Conservation Village'. These conservation orders impose severe restrictions on development. 'Everything is being conserved except for the local people', my young friend added in obvious frustration.

Many also claim that the Crofting Acts of the 1880s, which were so essential in providing security of tenure and a basis for a subsistence living for crofting families at the time, have now outlived their usefulness. Uncertainties over boundaries between crofts and inheritance details tend to impede the 'freeing up' of now virtually unused crofting land for development of appropriate projects which would provide homes for local folk, tourist facilities, employment possibilities, help to maintain the community and reinvigorate the economy.

The possibility of Arnisdale becoming a museum piece like the old village street in St Kilda and be relegated to the realms of history is not idle speculation, given the current trends in population, employment and restrictions on development imposed by conservation bodies and the current Crofting Acts.

For any community such as Arnisdale to have a future, at least three things are necessary. The first is that the area has good resources to develop, the second is that there are enough young people around with an interest in the area who have good ideas for development and also the enthusiasm and energy to take them through to fruition, and the third is that the landowners are equally interested in, and supportive of, good development ideas. On the basis of these criteria, there would appear to be no reasons why the Arnisdale and Loch Hourn communities should not have a bright future.

The attraction and value of the resources of the area to people in general have already been officially recognised with the definitions of 'An Area of Great Landscape Value', a 'European Scenic Reserve' and with Corran's classification as a 'Conservation Village'. Many of the photographs in this book provide some indication why the Arnisdale and Loch Hourn areas have been accorded these accolades which makes the area so attractive to tourists. Moreover, in addition to its scenic splendour and the local flora and fauna, the area has its intriguing history and its rich culture of language, music, traditions and stories. These are assets which are becoming increasingly valuable and attractive to native folk and visiting tourists alike. The main stimulus to the redevelopment of the Arnisdale and Loch Hourn communities must lie in the tourist industry because of the quality and great range of the marketable assets.

However, the traditional industries of crofting, farming sheep and cattle, of red deer management and stalking, of forestry and woodland management, and of fishing and sailing must not be forgotten. They will all have a role to play, since the future of localities such as Arnisdale and Loch Hourn must lie in making balanced use of the full range of resources, including, of course, the human resource, which is the most valuable of all. The greater the range of commercial activities, the more viable the community will be and the greater will be the range of attractions and activities to interest the tourists.

Typical of the young Arnisdale folk who are deeply interested in the future of Arnisdale and in reinvigorating the local economy and community activities is Billy MacKenzie, oldest son of the second 'Willie the Post' and grandson of the first 'Willie the Post'. Billy served his apprenticeship during his schooldays with his father, working the croft, shepherding the sheep and becoming well versed in seamanship skills in the challenging and very variable conditions of Loch Hourn. On leaving school, he served a second apprenticeship as a stalker on Knoydart Estate, being based at Inverie. He became thoroughly well versed with the Knoydart mountains and corries and with the wiles and behaviour of the red deer, as well as becoming familiar with the wide range of other wildlife on both the land and surrounding waters of the peninsula.

Billy then spent several years as a deer stalker on the famous Mar Lodge Estate on Upper Deeside and got to know the great Grampian mountains, the valleys and the wildlife, not only in his deer stalking activities but as a member of the Braemar Mountain Rescue Team. After several years as a full time stalker at Mar Lodge, he then started to work there seasonally during the main stag shooting months after which he moved slightly further south to Glen Shee and worked over the winter season at the Skiing Centre there. His next move took him even further south - to New Zealand's North and South Islands, working on the large sheep farms, where he not only fine-tuned his shepherding and sheep handling skills, but also his horsemanship, since the sheep gathering on the extensive high mountain ranges of the South Island was greatly facilitated if you could strike up a good relationship with a fit horse!

While the New Zealand experience was most interesting and enjoyable, the homing instinct was also strong and when the first fish farming venture started on Loch Hourn with a partnership between Strathaird Fish Farms and the local Arnisdale Estate proprietor, Mr Richmond-Watson, Billy came back home to work on the Fish Farm. There he gained his Boatmaster's Certificate with Marine Harvest MacConnell. In the intervening years Billy has taken an SVQ in Landscapes and Ecosystems where he developed competence in dry stone dyking and in building footpaths to improve access for local people and visitors alike to attractive and interesting places along the shoreline and mountain valleys of the west coast. He now works as an estate worker/stalker on the neighbouring Eilanreach Estate and his temporary home is a caravan on his Arnisdale croft.

Billy and his young friends in Arnisdale are very aware of the potential for sensible and environmentally sensitive development in the area but initiatives which they have taken in the past to develop commercial activities which had the potential to create employment and reinvigorate the community have so far failed to get through the initial planning stages. While understandably very frustrated by much rebuffs, Billy is conscious of the difficulties Planning Officers find themselves in with the constraints to development imposed by 'higher authority'. These are the frustrations, with their good development ideas being rebuffed by planners and their enthusiasm consequently deflated, which make Billy and his younger friends conclude that Arnisdale will become a museum - a latter day St Kilda.

This discouragement and the sapping of the enthusiasm of young folk with good ideas and abilities in places such as Arnisdale is a matter of great concern which must be addressed - certainly sooner rather than later - before the St Kilda scenario becomes reality.

The sadness about these situations is that localities such as the Arnisdale and Loch Hourn areas are looked upon as 'Advantageous Areas' for some (visitors and tourists) but, in reality, they are 'Disadvantageous Areas' for local enterprising folk.

Another great frustration is that many of the young people from these areas have a great range of skills but, despite their own good ideas and sustained efforts to develop local business initiatives, they are denied the opportunity to use their skills for the benefit of themselves and of the community in which they have been born and reared, and in which they aspire to earn their living.

Billy's list of personal skills and competencies is typical of those of many young folk in these localities. Youngsters in crofting townships in coastal areas have undergone a long apprenticeship in a wide range of skills just by following the example of their elders and by being involved in the full range of on-going activities. Billy's list of skills runs as follows: Crofting activities, seamanship, fishing, stalking, wildlife behaviour and appreciation (land and water), skiing, kayaking, shepherding, horsemanship, dry stone dyking, fencing, building, carpentry, footpath construction, fish farming, landscaping, mountaineering and mountain rescue. One could probably add to that long list skills such as oral communication, storytelling, conducted tours - countryside ranger skills and environmental appreciation.

Such young people very often take their skills for granted and are self-effacing when these abilities are highlighted. Billy MacKenzie would be very pleased if one of his skills was Gaelic speaking but this is not yet the case. However, he is taking evening classes in Glenelg on winter evenings and he practices his developing ability in Gaelic conversation with folk such as Mary Kate MacTavish in Arnisdale.

In the case of folk like Billy MacKenzie, who is very conscious of Arnisdale's needs and opportunities, it is most important to find ways of channelling their enthusiasm and skills into areas which will help them to make a living in Arnisdale and which will at the same time help to strengthen the local community.

The main employer of Arnisdale and Glenelg folk in the area currently is the fish farm on Loch Hourn. This large salmon producing farm is currently owned by the Netherlands Company, Nutreco and it employs a basic staff of 15 folk with additional staff employed seasonally at the busiest times. Alex Harvey, a Glaswegian with extensive experience of fish farming in Skye and Lewis, is the recently appointed Manager and he is now settled in Glenelg with his wife and young family. The sea cages are situated on the Knoydart side of the loch and therefore are well protected from the prevailing south west winds. The farm has an average stock of over one million salmon and aims to sell one thousand tonnes of fish each year. The harvested fish are collected and delivered by boat to Kyle and the feed supplies also come in by boat. The salmon grow very well on this site and Alex Harvey attributes this to good management and fine water quality in terms of purity and oxygenation. Despite the current low prices, Alex is confident about the future of the industry and of at least maintaining the current level of employment.

In order to reinvigorate communities such as Arnisdale and Loch Hourn, as stated earlier, the three main requirements are to have good resources to develop, sufficient able, enthusiastic young people with good ideas and determination to succeed, and thirdly interested landowners who are supportive of good development ideas.

The Richmond-Watson family have been the owners of Arnisdale Estate since 1958. The family have become very attached to Arnisdale and Loch Hourn over these years, they are concerned about the current low employment opportunities, the lack of community facilities and are interested in doing their best to foster future developments.

The head of the household at the time of purchase of the estate in 1958 from the Kitson family, Mr R N Richmond-Watson, is still hale and hearty at the age of 91 but he and his wife Jean have now delegated the running of the estate to their family of Julian, Adel, Stewart and Colin, with eldest son Julian being the chairman of the family company.

When Mr 'R N' purchased the estate, he had firm ideas on how to develop the farming and sporting enterprises so as to create employment and at the same time to make the business economically viable and sustainable. He was shrewd in his recruitment of workers to operate the cattle and hill sheep enterprises and the staff also had to be competent in stalking as well as in maintaining buildings, footpaths, dykes and fences on the estate. 'R N' knew that the best employees would be not only those of proven ability but also those with an interest in and firm commitment to the Arnisdale community. Thus, Lachie Fletcher was brought back home to Arnisdale as Manager, Peter Fletcher as Estate Handyman, Iain MacKenzie and George MacDougall as Shepherds/Stalkers with Danny Mackay and Bob MacRobbie being cattleman in turn. The breeding ewe flock was pushed up to 3000, the suckler cow herd to around 60 and silage making was initiated to provide winter keep for the cattle. Large areas of ground were reclaimed for growing more grass for silage both on the moor adjacent to Corran and in Achadh a' Ghlinne.

Julian recalls that while the cattle enterprise was profitable, sheep prices in the 1960s and 1970s were poor and tough decisions had to be made. Sensitivity to Lachie's love for his sheep delayed the closing down of the sheep enterprise until Lachie had retired. Among Julian's memories of the stalking was that Lachie, when on the hill, was always much more interested in the sheep than in the deer. So when others such as Kenny Fletcher, Peter, Iain and George were trying to spot the location of the deer with the glass, Lachie would have his glass focused on the sheep to check their behaviour and well-being.

In retrospect, perhaps the sheep flock should have been retained for a year or two more. The new European Union Sheepmeat Scheme was instituted in the early 1980s and this resulted in an unprecedented increase in the profitability of sheep production from hill farms. But it is always easy to be wise after the event!

The second Arnisdale generation of the Richmond-Watson family were youngsters when the Arnisdale Estate was purchased by their parents and they have all become very attached to the entire Arnisdale and Loch Hourn environment over the years. The third generation are equally bonded to all that the area has to offer around the lodge, along the shoreline, on boat trips up Loch Hourn and in the magnificent hills. Not even all the rain and the midges dampen their enthusiasm!

Julian recalls the excitement of the annual visit of the Royal Yacht Britannia to Loch Hourn on the Royal Family's annual holiday around the Hebrides in the 1970s through to the early 1980s. While the Royal Family would picnic in 'Horseshoe Bay' adjacent to Lea in the privacy and security of the Knoydart shore, many of the crew would come ashore in Arnisdale looking for the shops! Alas, by that time, the once thriving little shops of Peggy Ann and Johnnie MacGillivary were no more!

The Richmond-Watson family, well schooled by Lachie, Peter, Iain and George on all the Arnisdale hills, bealachs and corries, are now very familiar with all the features and landmarks around the estate, as well as with the history of these parts. Thus, Julian asserts that the old clachan at Crionaich situated at the meeting of the hill tracks from Arnisdale on the one hand, and from Kylerhea, Glenelg and Glen

Beag on the other, had a smiddy to provide for the needs of the pack and riding horses passing on this main route and also for the huge droves of cattle from the Outer Hebrides and Skye which passed Crionaich on their long journey to southern markets at Crieff, Falkirk and places beyond. The cattle were shod as well as the horses to help them on their long journey over rough terrain. Julian also refers to the gravestones on the main drove route at Bealach a' Chasain - not far from Crionaich - where two cattle rustlers were caught in the act and shot by the drovers. The latter then gave them a decent burial and took the trouble to erect gravestones to mark the location of their mortal remains.

While Julian and his wife Sarah are interested in the history of the locality, they are also forward thinkers and are conscious of opportunities to attend to important conservation issues, to maintain the economic viability of the estate and to improve the vibrancy of the Arnisdale Community.

Fairly recently the main area of natural woodland on the estate on the southern slopes of Beinn Clachach beyond Achadh a' Ghlinne has been fenced to exclude the deer and allow regeneration of the varied mix of natural species - oak, birch, holly, rowan, hazel, alder and willow.

In addition to preventing access of deer to this area of woodland, the other 'control' which Julian would appreciate, is reduced activity of hill walkers and Munro baggers aspiring to climb hills such as The Saddle or Beinn Sgritheall in the main stalking months of September and October. He considers that the best way to influence the activities of the hill walkers is by education about their impact on the movements of the deer. He stresses the need for mutual respect, for the interests of the hill walking fraternity on the one hand, and of those of the stalkers on the other. He feels that both sets of interests can be met and conflict avoided with better mutual understanding.

In the mushrooming of general interest in wildlife, Julian suggests that the educational process should focus on developing more respect for wildlife. Wildlife such as deer, eagles and otters naturally seek privacy and security and this basic need should be respected more, he asserts. With appropriate training, good binoculars and telephoto lenses, those interested in viewing and photographing wildlife should be able to do so from a distance without disturbing them.

The Richmond-Watson family have a range of ideas on how to create more employment opportunities in Arnisdale in acceptable ways, how best to reinvigorate the community and at the same time how to create more interest and attractions for tourists.

Julian considers that Loch Hourn, as in the era of the great herring fishing, has a key role to play in providing employment and in stimulating the local economy. The family had shares in the earliest salmon farming activities on the loch in conjunction with Strathaird Fish Farms. Returns were good in these early days with prices of £3 to £4 per pound for salmon compared to the current paltry figure of £1.40 per pound. Julian is concerned about the future of conventional intensive salmon farming with the current low prices for the end product. However, he foresees a good future for fish farming activities on Loch Hourn because of the purity of its water and the tidal water movements which help in both the oxygenation of the water and the control of pollution. He considers that while salmon farming may become relatively less important over time, the farming of species such as halibut and shellfish could well increase greatly in importance. He has visions of fish farming becoming more extensive and less intensive in Loch Hourn - a form of ranching - and stresses the need for greater security for the investments of local folk. He cites the case of one local man who was diving for scallops and conserving immature scallops in what he considered was a secure area of the sea near his home only to find one day that they had all disappeared. Some marauders had come in and scooped up his future harvests. He deprecates the activity of the trawlers which trail their nets along the mud and sand banks, scooping up everything in a totally unselective way, with no thought of conserving the immature forms which should constitute the harvest of future months and years. Such totally destructive trawling by 'pirates' should be banned in sea lochs such as Loch Hourn, he asserts. They are the latter day desecrators who are equivalent to the ruthless Colla Bàn and his followers who destroyed the old widow Mairi's living off the shellfish from the Barrisdale shore in the aftermath of Culloden. Loch Hourn could be managed as a sort of marine 'wildlife park' similar to the management of the wild deer on the hill, with the mature animals being selectively harvested in order to control the stocking density, while conserving the nursery and young stock to enable them to grow and mature. Julian considers that with greater security and improved conservation measures, Loch Hourn could provide a living from the fishing for many enterprising local folk in years to come.

The land - shoreline, moor, corries and mountains also have many attractions but Julian stresses the need always to respect nature and the rather fragile environment in many areas. Fine walkways inherited from the industry and skills of past generations such as the 'Stone of Meal Road' up the shoreline from Corran towards Caolas Mor is in a serious state of disrepair in parts. Repair of this footpath and several others in the area could provide employment for local folk and be a considerable tourist attraction.

Creating a range of attractions for tourists must be a priority in these areas and Julian sees such activities as providing a firm basis for development, employment and sustaining a viable community in the Arnisdale and Loch Hourn areas. 'People are retiring earlier, living longer and looking for interesting pursuits and attractive places, and are willing to invest in the local economies if appropriate provisions are made for them' Julian claims. His view almost echoes the statement of Lord Gordon of Strathblane, Chairman of the Scottish Tourist Board. In a letter to 'The Scotsman' of 12 July 1999, Lord Gordon asserts: 'Tourism helps to support 177,000 jobs across Scotland, and contributes in excess of £2.4 billion to the economy every year. The industry helps sustain and develop local amenities, underpins local and national transport services, reinvigorates local culture and remedies depopulation to a degree unmatched by any other.' Apart from its natural splendour, Arnisdale provides very few facilities for tourists. Some local folk are doing their best with their modest facilities such as Sheena Nash with her 'Tea hut' and Len Morrison and Charlie MacTavish with their boat trip services. However, despite the current modest provisions, there is great scope for increasing the attraction of Arnisdale to tourists and for re-invigorating the economy and the community. Arnisdale needs a public facility such as a hall with toilet facilities which could serve the local folk and tourists alike - community social activities, a tea-room, a place for ecumenical worship, a 'welcoming home' haven for returning exiles, a heritage centre and for many other purposes. There is scope for restoring and 'labelling' the many places of historical interest in the Arnisdale and Loch Hourn areas both to preserve the history and interest the tourists. Many of the hill paths, moorland and shoreline walkways are in need of restoration to allow those who are not so fit to have easy access to the interesting and beautiful places in the locality and to appreciate peacefully and unobtrusively the rich flora and fauna. Julian shares this vision of scope for development. However, like others, he worries about the impediments to progress imposed by the various planning authorities and also by the Crofting Acts. These Acts which over 100 years ago provided such a boost to native folk in improving their security and the basis of their survival have now outlived their usefulness. From being the salvation of the crofters when passed in the 1880s, their existence now imposes a serious threat to the survival of the communities they once did so much to sustain and preserve.

The restrictions to economic development in sensible acceptable ways imposed currently by conservation bodies and the Crofting Acts in places such as Arnisdale is depressing. This is especially so to young local folk with good ideas, a wide range of skills, plenty of vigour and enthusiasm and with an intense interest in preserving and reinvigorating their community, with all its culture and traditions, its flora and fauna. They know that any development must tone in with the natural environment - they would not have it any other way - they are as much conservationists as the planning authorities - as their forebears have been for generations before them. Yet they are powerless as they strive to progress and preserve their community and all it is, and all it means to them. The Planning Authorities have all the power - the right of veto - to dampen the fervent spirits, destroy enthusiasm, create depression and diffidence and visions of the St Kilda scenario not too many decades distant. It is a sombre, gloomy picture.

What of the conservation bodies and Planning Authorities which are the butt of so much criticism in these areas? The officers of these organisations are people too, doing their best to carry out the will of their masters - the stipulations in the cold, insensitive 'White Papers' and 'Planning Protocols'. Finding a balanced and acceptable way forward demands a coming together of the able enthusiastic young local folk, trying their best to preserve their
community of people, their culture and all the other inherent community 'treasures' on the one hand, and on the other hand, of the conservation bodies and the Planning Authorities whose brief is to protect the 'Environment'. The term 'Environment' needs to be defined and if it is found that the present definition does not include the local folk with their rich history, culture and traditions, then the term must be redefined to include this most important component of all of any 'environment'. Very interesting as St Kilda currently is with its 'rickles' of stones, its famous grassy street, its great cliffs, sea bird colonies and history, how much more interesting it would be if it still had its native folk?

While the current scenario in Arnisdale is a sombre one to many, particularly for its able young folk who have strong ambitions to reinvigorate the economy and the community, there is light and brightness on the horizon. One basic reason for this is that the local folk and the owners of Arnisdale estate share many good ideas and sound objectives and have a steely determination to bring them to fruition. The other factor which helps greatly to lift the spirits when thinking about the future of Arnisdale and the Loch Hourn area is the splendour of the landscape of mountain, moor, shoreline and sea and the richness of the resources. With such like-minded people and the quality of the available resources, the prospects are considerable.

The way ahead must lie in all the folk putting their heads and ideas together and drawing up a comprehensive development plan to exploit the considerable potential of both the local people and the rich natural resources. Such a plan would encompass in a balanced way the objectives of developing business initiatives, creating employment, preserving the history and culture, reinvigorating the community and preserving the 'environment'. Such a carefully formulated balanced plan could then be submitted to the conservation bodies and Planning Authorities for consideration and subsequent full discussion with the Community Group and potential support agencies to work out the best balanced ways ahead for the benefit of all.

The hopeful outcome from such a process would be a start, after decades of decline, to laying a firm foundation for the gradual reinvigoration of the local economy and of the Arnisdale and Loch Hourn community.

**Top**. An 'Area of Great Landscape Value' a 'European Scenic Reserve'. **Middle**. Corran – 'A Conservation Village'. Camusban – 'a rich culture of language, music, history, traditions and folklore of an industrious and proud people'. **Bottom**. No community centre since the school closed in 1958 and was sold for private use. No public toilets. No public provision for tourists who come to admire the great landscape value, the scenic splendour, the conservation village etc. No public toilets! Not so much scenic splendour behind the whin bushes! 'Everything is being conserved apart from the people with their rich history and culture' – the most important environmental component of all! Unless balanced planning is undertaken soon and carefully formulated plans implemented, the St Kilda scenario will become reality.

'People are retiring earlier, living longer and looking for interesting pursuits and attractive places, and are willing to invest in the local economies if appropriate provisions are made for them'. (Julian Richmond Watson).

The Richmond-Watson family, owners of the Arnisdale Estate, have a range of ideas on how to create more employment opportunities in Arnisdale in acceptable ways, on how best to re-invigorate the community and at the same time how to create more interest and attractions for tourists.

**Top Left**. Antony Sheppard, Julian Richmond-Watson and Will Garfit in front of the south (Knoydart facing) wing of Arnisdale Lodge. **Right**. Another successful stalk on Beinn na h-eaglaise for Julian Richmond-Watson and his friend Charles Dent. In the background, the Rarsaidh Islands and the Mialairidh Peninsula lead the way into the Sound of Sleat.

**Middle Left**. On the high tops of Beinn nan Caorach hunting the ptarmigan are (L to R.) Dan Richmond-Watson, Charles Dent, Sarah Richmond-Watson, Mark Jackson Stops, Julian Richmond-Watson and Sue Jackson Stops. The Royal Yacht Britannia anchored close to Rudha Ruadh (Red Point) on Knoydart makes a fine picture by day and illuminates Loch Hourn by night. **Right**. Iain MacKenzie sets out on a stalking venture up Loch Hourn with Antony Sheppard and Chrissie.

**Bottom Left**. Young Dan Richmond-Watson (left) with his first stag shot on Beinn na h-eaglaise (with Knoydart in the background). Dan is the first of the third generation of Richmond-Watsons to receive his stalking guidance from Iain MacKenzie. **Right**. When the rain and the midges didn't stop the play on the Arnisdale Lodge Green! Perhaps the solution to England's Test match problems lies in the Arnisdale 'cricket academy'.

449

**Top Left**.  Some of the Fish Farm staff on the foreshore just below the old Arnisdale boatshed.   L to R.  John Park (Kyleakin), Thomas Watson (Dornie), Peter Lane and Alex Harvey (Glenelg).  Alex is the Fish Farm Manager.  **Right**.  Looking towards the old boatshed, now extended as the Fish Farm HQ.

**Middle Left**.  Beinn Sgritheall has watched fishing activity in Loch Hourn over very many millennia.  **Right**.  The Fish Farm tucked in on the Knoydart shore between Rudha Ruadh and Crowlick.

**Bottom**.   Some of Arnisdale's young people.   Billy (left) and David MacKenzie.   Right.  Alan and Carol MacKenzie.

More of Arnisdale's young folk.

**Top Left**.   Helen MacLeod and her brother Stuart.   **Right**.   Gordon and Yvonne Crombie (with dog Blue).

**Middle Left**.   Ewan Ballantyne and Catriona with little Beth.   **Right**.   Eliot Jones and Jo Tatum with children Rowan and Arthur.

**Bottom Left**.   Peter and Shirley Fletcher now resident in Inverness.   Arnisdale folk such as Peter and Shirley would readily return to Arnisdale if there was a better balanced attitude by planning authorities to carefully formulated tourism related commercial initiatives. 'There is a way back for Arnisdale and Loch Hourn' asserts Peter.  "As well as the scenic splendour and rich flora and fauna, Arnisdale and Loch Hourn have an intriguing history and a rich culture of language, music, traditions and folklore.   These are assets which are becoming increasingly valuable and attractive".

"The future of localities such as Arnisdale and Loch Hourn must lie in making balanced use of the full range of resources, including, of course, the human resource, which is the most valuable of all".

A panoramic view of Arnisdale from the top of Beinn Sgritheall. Directly below, the village and croftlands of Camusban hug the crescent shaped bay round to Arnisdale Lodge with the little jetty below. From the lodge, the roadway runs past the farm towards the village of Corran with a branch to the left going up Glen Arnisdale. To the right before the river estuary is the headland – the Crudh Ard. The village and croftlands of Corran nestle at the side of the river mouth with the mass of Druim Fada behind. The small island adjacent to Corran – the Sgeir Leathann is followed by the island trio – the Corr Eileanan – sentinels to the entrance to Upper Loch Hourn to their left. At the top is Knoydart, the Barrisdale plain and river estuary. The lines of the four burns which deliver their contents to the sea in Camusban are evident (L to R.) Allt na sgoile, Allt an t-siucair, Allt a'mhuillinn and Alltan Beag.

A more detailed focus on Arnisdale with Eilean Tioram – the 'Dry Island' coming into view on the extreme right. In the great days of the herring fishing and the massing of boats in the bay it was said that one could walk from the Crudh Ard to Eilean Tioram by stepping from boat to boat

From Eilean Tioram – a view of the village of Camusban from 'Peggy Ann's' on the left to the farm on the right.   The mountains from the left are Beinn na h-eaglaise, Beinn Bhuidhe and Beinn Chlachach.   On the extreme right is the pass up the Arnisdale Glen to Kinloch Hourn.

Part of Camusban adjacent to the Free Church (centre) with the now closed graveyard separating it from the former school and schoolhouse on the right.   The gorge of Allt na Sgoile descending Beinn na h-eaglaise is directly behind the school.   The enclosed croftlands in this area were the 'church lands', each croft having an equal share of this area for their cropping.

Approaching the Arnisdale pier from the mouth of Loch Hourn with the school on the left and to the right the lodge and farm. From left to right behind are Beinn Bhuidhe, Beinn Chlachach, the Arnisdale Glen and the mass of Druim Fada to the right.

The view from the Crudh Ard along the shoreline fields to the farm and to Camusban beyond. The magnificient Beinn Sgritheall has Beinn na h-eaglaise to its right.

A view from Beinn Bhuidhe towards Corran with Knoydart's magnificent mountains across Loch Hourn. The Arnisdale river separates the farm glenside fields from the croftlands on the southern bank. The communal fank is on the extreme right. The Corran crofters' sheep grazing was on Beinn Bhuidhe while their cattle grazing was above the enclosed croftlands on the lower slopes of Druim Fada on the left hand side of the picture.

A closer view of Corran with the house at Glenfield in the bottom right hand corner. Some of the crofters' haybarns on the riverside fields can be seen. In the bottom right hand corner is the peat moss which was used by the farm, Glenfield and Lodge folk. The peat moss above the Glenfield road was used by some of the Corran crofters.

9. The village of Corran with one house to the north of the river. The little clachan of Cosaig which was occupied by three families is on the left. The main Corran 'street' is in the centre of the picture. The row of 14 byres can be seen at right angles to the 'street' towards the hill ground while the line of sheds built for storing the fishing gear are on the right. Before the great high tide in 1881 the houses were situated very close to the river bank. Following the severe flooding, the houses were moved to the higher ground they occupy at present. The subdivision of the croftlands between the original crofts are obvious.

The Arnisdale river is tidal to above the bridge at Corran. The view also shows the line of the shoreline track to Caolasmor – the 'Stone of Meal' road. The clachan of Coalasmor is some three miles from Corran towards Kinloch Hourn.

The pattern of subdivision of the enclosed croftlands for growing hay, potatoes and oats is very clear in this view from the top of Beinn Bhuidhe. The line of the wall and deer fence to exclude the deer from the arable and cattle grazing areas can be seen on the lower slopes of Druim Fada above the arable areas.

A tranquil scene from the river mouth looking towards the village of Corran with the mass of Druim Fada behind.

A wintry scene from above the Corran bridge with Knoydart's magnificent Ladhar Bheinn across Loch Hourn.

The view eastwards from the Crudh Ard across the Corran road and the peat flats to the Glenside farm fields on the left and the Corran croftlands on the right of the tree lined river.   Below the mass of Beinn Chlachach in the middle is Achadh a'ghlinne and from there the hill track winds its way past Blar nan each, the Dubh Lochain and Crionaich to Kinloch Hourn.

The red deer stags in the Arnisdale Glen fields in early June toss their antlers for the camera. The view looks eastwards up Glen Arnisdale with Druim Fada on the right.

An early summer scene from behind Arnisdale Lodge to the mouth of Loch Hourn, Skye and the Cuillins. Knoydart is on the left with the village of Camusban on the right. The 'bridge' to Eilean Tioram (the Dry Island) in the middle of the picture is obvious at low tide.

Skye returns the compliment with a view eastwards to Loch Hourn from Isleornsay with its lighthouse on the right and Knoydart beyond. Beinn Mhialairidh and the towering Beinn Sgritheall are on the left. (© Martin Guppy)

The view from the lower slopes of Beinn Sgritheall to the croft at Rarsaidh and eastwards to Barrisdale with, left to right from centre, Luinne Bheinn, Sgurr na Ciste, Coire Dhorcoil and the east shoulder of Ladhar Bheinn.

From the top of Arnisdale brae a wintry view westwards to the single home at Rarsaidh and its adjacent islands, Eilean a' Chuilinn and Eilean Rarsaidh. Beyond is the Mialairidh peninsula and forest with Beinn Mhialairidh above. In the far distance is Skye and the snow shrouded Cuillin.

Sunset at Mialairidh, Eilean Rarsaidh and Eilean a' Chuilinn.

Lower Sandaig or Gavin Maxwell's 'Camusfearna', with the Sandaig Islands, Lighthouse and Skye beyond.

'Camusfearna' in more recent times from one of the Sandaig Island meadows across the tidal strand to the former croftlands, the conifer plantation and the peak of Beinn a' Chapuill in the distance.

Knoydart's boundary on the southern shore of Loch Hourn taken from the heights of Beinn Sgritheall.
From right to left are Rudha Ruadh (Red Point), Eilean a' Phiobaire, the croft at Li, Horseshoe Bay (Poll-a-Mhuineilal) and Barrisdale with Ladhar Bheinn (right) and Knoydart's other high tops showing themselves to advantage.

Another view from Beinn Sgritheall across Loch Hourn to the point of the Knoydart Peninsula, with the holdings at Coille Dhubh and Crowlick tucked into the bay before the point. Beyond from left to right are the islands of Eigg and Rhum, and the south end of Skye across the Sound of Sleat

A closer glimpse of the croft at Li from Eilean a' Phiobaire with Ladhar Bheinn providing its protection from the south but also depriving it of winter sunshine.

The house and croft at Li and a view of Arnisdale and the mass of Druim Fada from Loch Hourn's southern shore.

From Ladhar Bheinn's top, Charles Mackay admires a magnificent vista across to Arnisdale, from Beinn Sgritheall on the left, Beinn na h-eaglaise, Beinn Bhuidhe, Beinn nan caorach, Beinn Chlachach and Druim Fada with Horseshoe Bay (Poll-a-Mhuineilal) directly below.

An eastwards look from the same vantage point captures Barrisdale Bay with Eilean Choinneach at the entrance to upper Loch Hourn, the 'narrows' at Caolasmor, Eilean Mhogh -sgeir opposite Runival, and Kinloch Hourn's Beinn Bhuidhe imposing a formidable barrier at the end of the loch. Druim Fada (the 'long ridge') forms the northern boundary of the loch, while across the southern ridge, Glen Barrisdale makes its way into Glen Chosaidh to the east.

A view to the south from Glenmore in Glenelg to Arnisdale's mountain tops (L to R.) Beinn nan Caorach, Beinn na h-eaglaise, Beinn Sgritheall and the eastern shoulder of Beinn Chapuill. The hill track from Glenmore makes its way by Swordland, Bealach a' Chasain, Bealach Aoidhdailean and joins the old drove road from Kylerhea and Glen Beag on the northern side of Beinn nan Caorach on its way via Crionaich to the east and south.

Travellers from Glen More to Arnisdale would turn westwards at the junction of the Glenmore and Glenbeag hill tracks before making their way over Bealach Arnasdail (centre) between Beinn na h-eaglaise and Beinn Sgritheall.

Blar nan each – the site of an old clachan which had a smiddy and almost certainly an inn in the Arnisdale Glen on the hill track to Kinloch Hourn. The ancient oakwood (left and centre) on the southern slope of Beinn Chlachach is the Coille Mhor. The northern slope of Druim Fada is on the right.

A view from the top of the Arnisdale Glen looking westwards. The slope of Druim Fada is on the left with Blar nan each at its base nestling beside the ancient 'highway'. The Arnisdale river snakes its way to Corran and Loch Hourn with Achadh a' ghlinne on its right. From right to left of the picture are the slopes of Beinn Chlachach, Beinn Bhuidhe, Beinn Sgritheall and Beinn Mhialairidh.

The view from the west end of Druim Fada across Loch Hourn into the plain of Barrisdale with the Barrisdale River making its tortuous way to the sea. The mighty Luinne Bheinn dominates from behind. (©Ruurd and Mieke Groot)

The reciprocal view from the top of Luinne Bheinn looking northwards to the Barrisdale valley below and across the loch to Druim Fada. To the left, Beinn Sgritheall, Beinn na h-eaglaise and Beinn nan Caorach make their presence felt once again. (©Ruurd and Mieke Groot)

The remains of the Chapel at Barrisdale close to the ancient burial ground on Eilean Choinnich.
The three islands - the Corr Eileanan act as sentinels to Upper Loch Hourn which runs eastwards to the right of the photograph.
The westward view ahead captures the corner of Beinn Sgritheall and the Mialairidh peninsula. (©Ruurd and Mieke Groot)

A glimpse of the dwellings and croftlands at Caolasmor on the south side of Druim Fada as the sailor makes his way from the Corr Eileanan into upper Loch Hourn.

Now a westward look from Kinloch Hourn or Loch Hournhead. The view is from above the ledge of Sgurr a'Mhaoraich Beag. Despite the haze, Ladhar Bheinn on the southern side and Beinn Sgritheall on the northern shore still raise their heads above the crowd. (©Ruurd and Mieke Groot)

The entrance to Kinloch Hourn with the road to the left making for the farm, the landing place and the lochside track to Skiary, Runival, Barrisdale and thence across Knoydart to Inverie. The road across the bridge to the right makes for Kinloch Hourn Lodge, the splendid wooded policies around the lodge and the hill track to Arnisdale.

A wintry scene from Kinloch Hourn Lodge looking on to the head of Loch Hourn –Loch Beag.

'If winter comes, can spring be far behind?'   The stalker at Kinloch Hourn, Donald Angus Cameron and his wife Aileen.

An autumn scene looking across Loch Beag to the varied shrubs and woodland surrounding Kinloch Hourn Lodge. The hill track to Arnisdale follows the line of pylons above the wooded policies.

Donald Angus Cameron and Stephen Russell (ghillie) make their way home with the pony after a successful stalk.

Another autumn scene close to Kinloch Hourn looking westwards down the loch. Just beyond the wooded area in the foreground is the single dwelling house of Torr a' choit. Directly across the loch are the ancient clachans of Skiary and Runival.

On Carn nan Caorach (1500 feet) on the east end of Druim Fada looking down on Lochan Charn nan Caorach just below and a further 1300 feet down on Loch Hourn as it makes its way eastwards to Kinloch Hourn. Directly across the loch on the Knoydart side is Skiary which housed five families within living memory. This clachan also had a thriving pub in the great days of the herring fishing.

Skiary in the present day looking westwards down Loch Hourn to Caolasmor. (© John Everett)

The view from behind Runival looking out to the island Eilean Mhogh-sgeir and the northern shore.

Back to the Kinloch Hourn hill track – the Cadha Mor – at the junction of the paths to Glenshiel to the right and Crionaich, Arnisdale and Glenelg to the left. The view westwards down the loch picks out the 'narrows' at Caolasmor, Coire Dhorrcail and Ladhar Bheinn. (©Ruurd and Mieke Groot)

The Cadha Mor winds its way towards the river and Crionaich beyond.

The ford eastwards of Crionaich – often impassable following the frequent 'monsoons' – demonstrates its more 'user friendly' face.

Crionaich – the meeting of the hill track from Arnisdale and Loch Hourn on the one hand and that from Kylerhea, Glenelg, Glenbeag and Glenmore on the other. The house was the home of generations of shepherds in the 1800s. To the west of Crionaich en route to Arnisdale, the traveller passes An Dubh Lochain (the black lochs) (© JohnTarlton and Stuart Richmond-Watson)

From the top of Mullach Gorm, the stalkers scan the hill face for their quarry. Below, the Arnisdale river makes its way into An Dubh Lochain. The 'long ridge' of Druim Fada is on the left with Ladhar Bheinn's mighty top in Knoydart across Loch Hourn reminding the viewer of its imposing presence.

(© JohnTarlton and Stuart Richmond-Watson)

The stalker / shepherd in the glen between Beinn Chlachach to the left and Beinn nan Caorach to the right. The burn snakes its way to the ridge where it joins up with its fellow flowing down between Beinn nan Caorach and Beinn Bhuidhe. Together, as Allt Utha, then they tumble down a series of waterfalls into Achadh a'ghlinne. The mountain beyond is Beinn Cailleach in Knoydart.

The scene from the northern slope of Druim Fada to the Arnisdale river below with Blar nan each in the bottom right-hand corner. Beyond the river is Achach a'ghlinne – subdivided by the waters of Allt Utha as they follow their tortuous course to the river. The old dwelling house can be seen just below the hill face to the right of the burn. The bridle path makes its way uphill to the right of the burn with Beinn Chlachach on its right and Beinn Bhuidhe on its left. Dominating the scene in the centre is Beinn nan Caorach. Deposits of Clach Chuilinn (holly stone) are to be found in Allt Utha.

The view from the western face of Druim Fada to the village of Corran below at the mouth of the Arnisdale river, with the houses of Camusban hugging the crescent shaped bay beyond. The two villages are separated by the territory occupied by the headland (to the left) – the Crudh Ard, the house at Glenfield, the farm and the lodge. Beinn Sgritheall and Beinn na h-eaglaise (right) make their presence felt, as always.

The village of Camus Ban in the 1890s. Following the great high tide of 1881 which flooded the thatched houses close to the shoreline, the proprietor financed the rebuilding of the houses further up the shore so as to avoid the possibility of further flooding. The village is in transition with some new houses already built but with many of the villagers still resident in the old homes close to the roadway. At the end of the row of buildings is the Mission House beside the Free Church. The schoolhouse and school is partly hidden by the trees just beyond the church while the farm is on the extreme right. The farm steading, then close to the shore and also a victim of the 1881 high tide, was later re-erected to the right of the farmhouse – its present position. (© RCAHMS)

The bridge over the Arnisdale river and the village of Corran around 1890, with the houses built very close to the shoreline of the tidal river estuary. The houses also suffered serious flooding in the great high tide of 1881 and all were later rebuilt on the higher ground of their present position except for the house on the extreme left of the picture. Knoydart's Coire Dhorrcail (left) and Ladhar Bheinn impose themselves on the scene from the other side of Loch Hourn. (© Aberdeen University Library. George Washington Wilson Collection)

The Arnisdale farmhouse – a very happy home through the ages. In the background, Beinn Chlachach rises beyond the lower slopes of Beinn Bhuidhe on the left and Cnor an Oir on the right.

An idyllic evening view from the farm down to the mouth of Loch Hourn, across the Sound of Sleat to Skye and the Cuillins beyond.

The estuary of the Arnisdale river (around 1970) with a view across the Corran shoreline croftlands to the imposing splendour of Ladhar Bheinn on Loch Hourn's southern shore